## AMERICA ON WHEELS

# Florida

MACMILLAN • USA

Frommer's America on Wheels: Florida

Regional Editor: Ian Keown
Assistant Regional Editor: Georgiana Kingsbury
Inspections Coordinator: Laura Van Zee
Contributors: Judy Alexandra DiEdwardo, Helene Epstein, Kathy Horak, Herbert Bailey Livesey,
Donna McClary, Daphne J Nikolopoulos, Dale Northrup, Mike Radigan, Robin Rowan,
Chelle Koster Walton, Fred W Wright Jr

Frommer's America on Wheels Staff
Project Director: Gretchen Henderson
Senior Editor: Christopher Hollander
Database Editor: Melissa Klurman
Assistant Editor: Marian Cole
Editorial Assistant: Tracy McNamara

Design by Michele Laseau

**Macmillan Travel**
A Simon & Schuster Macmillan Company
1633 Broadway
New York, NY 10019-6785

Find us online at **http://www.mcp.com/mgr/travel** or on America Online at keyword SuperLibrary.

MACMILLAN is a registered trademark of Macmillan, Inc.

Manufactured in the United States of America

ISSN: 1079-3593
ISBN: 0-02-861111-X

**SPECIAL SALES**
Bulk purchases (10+ copies) of Frommer's and selected Macmillan travel guides are available to corporations,
organizations, mail-order catalogs, institutions, and charities at special discounts, and can be customized to suit
individual needs. For more information write to Special Sales, Macmillan General Reference, 1633 Broadway,
New York, NY 10019.

# Contents

# Introduction

*America on Wheels* introduces a brand-new lodgings rating system—one that factors in the latest trends in travel preferences, technologies, and amenities and is based on thorough inspections by experienced travel professionals. We rate establishments from one to five flags, plus a unique rating we call Ultra, a special award reserved for only a handful of outstanding properties in each category. Our restaurant selections represent the ethnic diversity of today's dining scene and are categorized with symbols according to their special features, ambience, and services available. In addition, the series provides in-depth sightseeing information, including driving tours and best-of-the-state highlights.

## State Introductions

Coverage of each state in the *America on Wheels* series begins with background information that will help familiarize you with your destination. Included is a summary of the state's history and an overview of its geography, followed by practical tips that we hope you will find useful in planning your trip—what kind of weather to expect, what to pack, sources of information within the state, driving rules and regulations, and other essentials.

The "Best of the State" section provides you with a rundown of the top sights and attractions and the most popular festivals and special events around the state. It also includes information on spectator sports and an A-to-Z list of recreational activities available to you.

## Driving Tours

The scenic driving tours included guide you along some of the most popular sightseeing routes. Every tour is keyed to a map and includes mileage information and precise directions, refreshment stops, and, for longer tours, recommended places to stay.

## The Listings

The city-by-city listings of lodgings, dining establishments, and attractions together make up the bulk of the book. Cities are organized alphabetically within each state. You will find a brief description or "profile" for most cities, including a source to contact for additional information. Any listings will follow.

### TYPES OF LODGINGS

Here's how we define the lodging categories used in *America on Wheels*.

#### Hotel

A hotel usually has three or more floors with elevators. It may or may not have parking, but if it does, entry to the guest rooms is likely to be through the lobby rather than directly from the parking lot. A range of lodgings is available (such as standard rooms, deluxe rooms, and suites), and a range of services is available (such as bellhops, room service, and a concierge). Many hotels have a restaurant or coffee shop open for breakfast, lunch, and dinner; they may have a cocktail lounge/bar. Recreational facilities may be available (such as a swimming pool, fitness center, and tennis courts).

#### Motel

A motel usually has one to three floors, and many of the guest rooms have doors facing the parking lot or outdoor corridors. A motel may only have a small, serviceable lobby and usually offers only limited services; the nearest restaurant may be down the street. A motel is most likely to be located alongside a highway or in a resort area.

#### Inn

An inn is a small-scale hotel or lodge, usually in an older building that may or may not have been designed for lodgings, and it is often located in scenic surroundings. An inn should have a warm, welcoming atmosphere, with a more homelike quality to its furnishings and facilities. The guest rooms may be individually decorated in a style appropriate to the inn's age and location, and the rooms may or may not have telephones, televisions, or private bathrooms. An inn usually has a lounge or sitting room for guests (with parlor games and perhaps a television) and a small dining room that may or may not be open to the public. Breakfast, however, is almost always served.

## Lodge

A lodge is essentially a small hotel in a rural, remote, or mountainous location. The atmosphere, service, and furniture may be more casual than you'd find in a regular hotel, and there may not be televisions or telephones in every guest room. The facilities usually include a coffee shop or restaurant, bar or cocktail lounge, games room, and indoor or outdoor swimming pool or hot tub. In ski areas, the lounge usually has a fireplace and facilities for storing ski gear.

## Resort

A resort usually has more extensive facilities and recreational activities than a hotel, and offers three meals a day. The atmosphere is generally more informal than at comparable hotels.

## HOW THE LODGINGS ARE RATED

Every hotel, motel, resort, inn, and lodge rated in this series has been subjected to a thorough hands-on inspection by our team of accomplished travel professionals. We ask the kinds of questions that readers would ask if they could inspect the rooms in advance for themselves (How good is the sound-proofing? How firm is the bed? What condition are the room furnishings in?). Then all of the inspection reports are reviewed by regional editors who are experts on their territories. The top-rated properties are then rechecked by a special consultant who has been reviewing and critiquing luxury hotels around the world for almost 25 years. *Establishments are not charged to be included in our series.*

Our ratings are based on *average* guest rooms— not lavish suites or concierge floors—so they're not artificially high. Therefore, in some cases a hotel rated four flags may indeed have individual rooms or suites that might fall into the five-flag category; conversely, a four-flag hotel may have a few rooms in its lowest price range that might otherwise warrant three flags.

The detailed ratings vary by category of lodgings —for example, the criteria imposed on a hotel are more rigorous than those for a motel—and some features that are considered essential in, for example, a four-flag city hotel are relaxed for a resort that offers alternative attractions, sporting facilities, and/or beautiful and spacious grounds. Likewise, amenities such as telephones and televisions—essential in hotels and motels—are not required in inns, whose guests are often seeking peace and quiet. Instead, the criteria take into account such features as individually decorated rooms and complimentary afternoon tea.

There are, of course, several basic attributes that apply to all lodgings across the board: the cleanliness and maintenance of the building as a whole; the housekeeping in individual rooms; safety, both indoors and out; the quality and practicality of the furnishings; the quality and availability of the amenities; the caliber of the facilities; the extent and/or condition of the grounds; the ambience and cleanliness in the dining rooms; and the caliber and professionalism of the service in relation to the rates and types of lodging. Since the *America on Wheels* rating system is highly rigorous, just because a property has garnered only one flag does not mean it is inadequate or substandard.

### WHAT THE INDIVIDUAL RATINGS MEAN

### ▤  One Flag

These properties have met or surpassed the minimum requirements of cleanliness, safety, convenience, and amenities. The staff may be limited, but guests can generally expect a friendly, hospitable greeting. Rooms will have basic amenities, such as air conditioning or heating where appropriate, telephones, and televisions. The bathrooms may have only showers rather than tubs, and just one towel for each guest, but showers and towels must be clean. The one-flag properties are by no means places to avoid, since they can represent exceptional value.

### ▤ ▤  Two Flags

In addition to having all of the basic attributes of one-flag lodgings, these properties will have some extra amenities, such as bellhops to help with the luggage, ice buckets in each room, and better-quality furnishings. Some extra services may include availability of cribs and irons, and wake-up service.

### ▤ ▤ ▤  Three Flags

These properties have all the basics noted above but also offer a more generous complement of amenities, such as firmer beds, larger desks, more drawer space, extra blankets and pillows, cable or satellite TV, alarm clock/radios, room service (although hours may be limited), and dry cleaning and/or laundry services.

### ☰☰☰ Four Flags

This is the realm of luxury, with refinements in amenities, furnishings, and service—such as larger rooms, more dependable soundproofing, two telephones per room, in-room movies, in-room safes, thick towels, hair dryers, twice-daily maid service, turndown service, concierge service, and 24-hour room service.

### ☰☰☰☰ Five Flags

These properties have everything the four-flag properties have, plus a more personal level of service and more sumptuous amenities, among them bathrobes, superior linens, and blackout drapes for lightproofing. Facilities normally include a business center and fitness center. Generally speaking, guests pay handsomely to stay in these properties.

### ☙ Ultra

This crème-de-la-crème rating is reserved for those rare hotels and resorts, possibly also motels and inns, that are truly outstanding in every or almost every department—places with a "grand hotel" presence, an almost flawless level of service, and a standard of dining equal to that of the finest restaurants.

#### UNRATED

In the few cases where an inspector was not able to make a detailed inspection, the property is listed as unrated. Also, in some cases where a property was in the process of changing owners or managers, or if the property was undergoing the kind of major renovations that made formal evaluation impossible, then, again, it is listed as unrated.

## TYPES OF DINING

### Restaurant

A restaurant serves complete meals and almost always offers seating.

### Refreshment Stop

A refreshment stop serves drinks and/or snacks only (such as an ice cream parlor, bakery, or coffee bar) and may or may not have seating available.

## HOW THE RESTAURANTS WERE EVALUATED

All of the restaurants reviewed in this series have been through the kind of thorough inspection described above for lodgings. Our inspectors have evaluated everything from freshness of ingredients to noise level and spacing of tables.

Unique to the *America on Wheels* series are the easy-to-read symbols that identify a restaurant's special features, its ambience, and special services. (See the inside front cover for the key to all symbols.) With them you can determine at a glance whether a place is a local favorite, offers exceptional value, or is "worth a splurge."

## HOW TO READ THE LISTINGS

#### LODGINGS

### Introductory Information

The rating is followed by the establishment's name, address, neighborhood (if applicable), telephone number(s), and fax number (if there is one). Where appropriate, location information is provided. In the resort listings, the acreage of the property is indicated. Also included are our inspector's comments, which provide some description and discuss any outstanding features or special information about the establishment. You can also find out whether an inn is unsuitable for children, and if so, up to what age.

### Rooms

Specifies the number and type of accommodations available. If a hotel has an "executive level," this will be noted here. (This level, sometimes called a "concierge floor," is a special area of a hotel. Usually priced higher than standard rooms, accommodations at this level are often larger and have additional amenities and services such as daily newspaper delivery and nightly turndown service. Guests staying in these rooms often have access to a private lounge where complimentary breakfasts or snacks may be served.) Check-in/check-out times will also appear in this section, followed by information on the establishment's smoking policy ("No smoking" for properties that are entirely nonsmoking, and "Nonsmoking rms avail" for those that permit smoking in some areas but have rooms available for nonsmokers). This information may be followed by comments, if the inspector noted anything in particular about the guest rooms, such as their size, decor, furnishings, or window views.

### Amenities

If the following amenities are available in the majority of the guest rooms, they are indicated by symbols (see inside front cover for key) or included in a list: telephone, alarm clock, coffeemaker, hair dryer, air conditioning, TV (including cable or satellite hookup, free or pay movies), refrigerator, dataport (for fax/modem communication), VCR, CD/tape player, voice mail, in-room safe, and bathrobes. If some or all rooms have minibars, terraces, fireplaces, or whirlpools, that will be indicated here. Because travelers usually expect air conditioning, telephones, and televisions in their guest rooms, we specifically note when those amenities are not available. If any additional amenities are available in the majority of the guest rooms, or if amenities are outstanding in any way, the inspector's comments will provide some elaboration at the end of this section.

## Services

If the following services are available, they are indicated by symbols (see inside front cover for key) or included in a list: room service (24-hour or limited), concierge, valet parking, airport transportation, dry cleaning/laundry, cribs available, pets allowed (call ahead before bringing your pet; an establishment that accepts pets may nevertheless place restrictions on the types or size of pets allowed, or may require a deposit and/or charge a fee), twice-daily maid service, car-rental desk, social director, masseur, children's program, babysitting (that is, the establishment can put you in touch with local babysitters and/or agencies), and afternoon tea and/or wine or sherry served. If the establishment offers any special services, or if the inspector has commented on the quality of services offered, that information will appear at the end of this section. Please note that there may be a fee for some services.

## Facilities

If the following facilities are on the premises, they are indicated by symbols (see inside front cover for key) or included in a list: pool(s), bike rentals, boat rentals (may include canoes, kayaks, sailboats, powerboats, jet-skis, paddleboats), fishing, golf course (with number of holes), horseback riding, jogging path/parcourse (fitness trail), unlighted tennis courts (number available), lighted tennis courts (number available), waterskiing, windsurfing, fitness center, meeting facilities (and number of people this space can accommodate), business center, restaurant(s), bar(s), beach(es), lifeguard (for beach, not pool), basketball, volleyball, board surfing, games room, lawn games, racquetball, snorkeling, squash, spa, sauna, steam room, whirlpool, beauty salon, day-care center, playground, washer/dryer, and guest lounge (for inns only). If cross-country and downhill skiing facilities are located within 10 miles of the property, then that is indicated by symbols here as well. Our "Accessible for People With Disabilities" symbol appears where establishments claim to have guest rooms with such accessibility. If an establishment has additional facilities that are worth noting, or if the inspector has commented about the facilities, that information appears at the end of this section.

## Rates

If the establishment's rates vary throughout the year, then the rates given are for the peak season. The rates listed are EP (no meals included), unless otherwise noted. We'll tell you if there is a charge for an extra person to stay in a room; if children stay free, and if so, up to what age; if there are minimum stay requirements; and if AP (three meals) and/or MAP (breakfast and dinner) rates are also available. The parking rates (if the establishment has parking) are followed by any comments the inspector has provided about rates.

If the establishment has a seasonal closing, this information will be stated. A list of credit cards accepted ends the listing.

### DINING

## Introductory Information

If a restaurant is a local favorite, an exceptional value (one with a high quality-to-price ratio for the area), or "worth a splurge" (more expensive by area standards, but well worth it), the appropriate symbol will appear at the beginning of the listing (see inside front cover for key to symbols). Then the establishment's name, address, neighborhood (if applicable), and telephone number are listed, followed by location information when appropriate. The type of cuisine appears in boldface type and is followed by our inspectors' comments on everything from decor and ambience to menu highlights.

## The "FYI" Heading

"For your information," this section tells you the reservations policy ("recommended," "accepted," or "not accepted"), and whether there is live entertainment, a children's menu, or a dress code (jacket required or other policy). If the restaurant does not have a full bar, you can find out what the liquor policy is ("beer and wine only," "beer only," "wine only," "BYO," or "no liquor license"). This is also where you can check to see if there's a no-smoking policy for the entire restaurant (please note that smoking policies are in flux throughout the country; if smoking—or avoiding smokers—is important to you, it's a good idea to call ahead to verify the policy). If the restaurant is part of a group or chain, address and phone information will be provided for additional locations in the area. This section does not appear in Refreshment Stop listings.

### Hours of Operation

Under the "Open" heading, "Peak" indicates that the hours listed are for high season only (dates in parentheses); otherwise, the hours listed apply year-round. If an establishment has a seasonal closing, that information will follow. It's a good idea to call ahead to confirm the hours of operation, especially in the off-season.

### Prices

Prices given are for dinner main courses (unless otherwise noted). If a prix-fixe dinner is offered throughout dinner hours, that price is listed here, too. This section ends with a list of credit cards accepted. Refreshment Stop listings do not include prices.

### Symbols

The symbols that fall at the end of many restaurant listings can help you find restaurants with the features that are important to you. If a restaurant has romantic ambience, historic ambience, outdoor dining, a fireplace, a view, delivery service, early-bird specials, valet parking, or is family-oriented, open 24 hours, or accessible to people with disabilities (meaning it has a level entrance or an access ramp, a doorway at least 36 inches wide, and restrooms that are on the same floor as the dining room, with doorways at least 36 inches wide and properly outfitted stalls), then these symbols will appear (see inside front cover for key to symbols).

### ATTRACTIONS

### Introductory Information

The name, street address, neighborhood (if located in a major city), and telephone number are followed by a brief rundown of the attraction's high points and key attributes so you can quickly determine if it's worth a full day of exploration or just a brief detour.

### Hours of Operation & Admission

Service information includes hours of operation ("Peak" indicates that the hours listed are for high season only) and the cost of admission. The cost is

| ABBREVIATIONS | |
|---|---|
| A/C | air conditioning |
| AE | American Express (charge card) |
| AP | American Plan (rates include breakfast, lunch, and dinner) |
| avail | available |
| BB | Bed-and-Breakfast Plan (rates include full breakfast) |
| bkfst | breakfast |
| BYO | bring your own (beer or wine) |
| CC | credit cards |
| CI | check-in time |
| CO | check-out time |
| CP | Continental Plan (rates include continental breakfast) |
| ctr | center |
| D | double (indicates room rate for two people in one room (one or two beds)) |
| DC | Diners Club (credit card) |
| DISC | Discover (credit card) |
| EC | EuroCard (credit card) |
| effic | efficiency (unit with cooking facilities) |
| ER | En Route (credit card) |
| info | information |
| int'l | international |
| JCB | Japanese Credit Bureau (credit card) |
| ltd | limited |
| MAP | Modified American Plan (rates include breakfast and dinner) |
| MC | MasterCard (credit card) |
| Mem Day | Memorial Day |
| mi | mile(s) |
| min | minimum |
| MM | mile marker |
| refrig | refrigerator |
| rms | rooms |
| S | single (indicates room rate for one person) |
| satel | satellite |
| stes | suites (rooms with separate living and sleeping areas) |
| svce | service |
| tel | telephone |
| V | Visa (credit card) |
| w/ | with |
| wknds | weekends |

indicated by one to four dollar signs (see inside front cover for key to symbols). It's a good idea to call ahead to confirm the hours.

## SPECIAL INFORMATION

### DISABLED TRAVELER INFORMATION

The Americans with Disabilities Act (ADA) of 1990 required that all public facilities and commercial establishments be made accessible to disabled persons by January 26, 1992. Any property opened after that date must be built in accordance with the ADA Accessible Guidelines. Note, however, that not all establishments have completed their renovations to conform with the law; be sure to call ahead to determine if your specific needs can be met.

### TAXES

State and city taxes vary widely and are not included in the prices in this book. Always ask about the taxes when you are making your reservations. State sales tax is given under "Essentials" in the introduction to each state.

### A DISCLAIMER

Readers are advised that prices fluctuate in the course of time, and travel information changes under the impact of the varied and volatile factors that affect the travel industry. The publisher cannot be held responsible for the experiences of readers while traveling. Readers are invited to send ideas, comments, and suggestions for future editions to: *America on Wheels*, Macmillan Travel, 1633 Broadway, New York, NY 10019-6785.

---

## TOLL-FREE NUMBERS/WORLD WIDE WEB SITES

The following toll-free telephone numbers and URLs for World Wide Web sites were accurate at press time; *America on Wheels* cannot be held responsible for any number or address that has changed. The "TDD" numbers are answered by a telecommunications service for the deaf and hard-of-hearing. Be sure to dial "1" before each number.

## LODGINGS

**Best Western International, Inc**
800/528-1234 North America
800/528-2222 TDD

**Budgetel Inns**
800/4-BUDGET Continental USA and Canada

**Budget Host**
800/BUD-HOST Continental USA

**Clarion Hotels**
800/CLARION Continental USA and Canada
800/228-3323 TDD
http://www.hotelchoice.com/cgi-bin/res/webres?clarion.html

**Comfort Inns**
800/228-5150 Continental USA and Canada
800/228-3323 TDD
http://www.hotelchoice.com/cgi-bin/res/webres?comfort.html

**Courtyard by Marriott**
800/321-2211 Continental USA and Canada
800/228-7014 TDD
http://www.marriott.com/lodging/courtyar.html

**Days Inn**
800/325-2525 Continental USA and Canada
800/325-3297 TDD
http://www.daysinn.com/daysinn.html

**DoubleTree Hotels**
800/222-TREE Continental USA and Canada
800/528-9898 TDD

**Drury Inn**
800/325-8300 Continental USA and Canada
800/325-0583 TDD

**Econo Lodges**
800/55-ECONO Continental USA and Canada
800/228-3323 TDD
http://www.hotelchoice.com/cgi-bin/res/webres?econo.html

**Embassy Suites**
800/362-2779 Continental USA and Canada
800/458-4708 TDD
http://www.embassy-suites.com

**Exel Inns of America**
800/356-8013 Continental USA and Canada

**Fairfield Inn by Marriott**
800/228-2800 Continental USA and Canada
800/228-7014 TDD
http://www.marriott.com/lodging/fairf.html

**Fairmont Hotels**
800/527-4727 Continental USA

**Forte Hotels**
800/225-5843 Continental USA and Canada

**Four Seasons Hotels**
800/332-3442 Continental USA
800/268-6282 Canada

**Friendship Inns**
800/453-4511 Continental USA
800/228-3323 TDD
http://www.hotelchoice.com/cgi-bin/res/
webres?friendship.html

**Guest Quarters Suites**
800/424-2900 Continental USA

**Hampton Inn**
800/HAMPTON Continental USA and Canada
800/451-HTDD TDD
http://www.hampton-inn.com

**Hilton Hotels Corporation**
800/HILTONS Continental USA and Canada
800/368-1133 TDD
http://www.hilton.com

**Holiday Inn**
800/HOLIDAY Continental USA and Canada
800/238-5544 TDD
http://www.holiday-inn.com

**Howard Johnson**
800/654-2000 Continental USA and Canada
800/654-8442 TDD
http://www.hojo.com/hojo.html

**Hyatt Hotels and Resorts**
800/228-9000 Continental USA and Canada
800/228-9548 TDD
http://www.hyatt.com

**Inns of America**
800/826-0778 Continental USA and Canada

**Intercontinental Hotels**
800/327-0200 Continental USA and Canada

**ITT Sheraton**
800/325-3535 Continental USA and Canada
800/325-1717 TDD

**La Quinta Motor Inns, Inc**
800/531-5900 Continental USA and Canada
800/426-3101 TDD

**Loews Hotels**
800/223-0888 Continental USA and Canada
http://www.loewshotels.com

**Marriott Hotels**
800/228-9290 Continental USA and Canada
800/228-7014 TDD
http://www.marriott.com/MainPage.html

**Master Hosts Inns**
800/251-1962 Continental USA and Canada

**Meridien**
800/543-4300 Continental USA and Canada

**Omni Hotels**
800/843-6664 Continental USA and Canada

**Park Inns International**
800/437-PARK Continental USA and Canada
http://www.p-inns.com/parkinn.html

**Quality Inns**
800/228-5151 Continental USA and Canada
800/228-3323 TDD
http://www.hotelchoice.com/cgi-bin/res/
webres?quality.html

**Radisson Hotels International**
800/333-3333 Continental USA and Canada

**Ramada**
800/2-RAMADA Continental USA and Canada
http://www.ramada.com/ramada.html

**Red Carpet Inns**
800/251-1962 Continental USA and Canada

**Red Lion Hotels and Inns**
800/547-8010 Continental USA and Canada

**Red Roof Inns**
800/843-7663 Continental USA and Canada
800/843-9999 TDD
http://www.redroof.com

**Renaissance Hotels International**
800/HOTELS-1 Continental USA and Canada
800/833-4747 TDD

**Residence Inn by Marriott**
800/331-3131 Continental USA and Canada
800/228-7014 TDD
http://www.marriott.com/lodging/resinn.html

**Resinter**
800/221-4542 Continental USA and Canada

**Ritz-Carlton**
800/241-3333 Continental USA and Canada

**Rodeway Inns**
800/228-2000 Continental USA and Canada
800/228-3323 TDD
http://www.hotelchoice.com/cgi-bin/res/
webres?rodeway.html

**Scottish Inns**
800/251-1962 Continental USA and Canada

**Shilo Inns**
800/222-2244 Continental USA and Canada

**Signature Inns**
800/822-5252 Continental USA and Canada

**Super 8 Motels**
800/800-8000 Continental USA and Canada
800/533-6634 TDD
http://www.super8motels.com/super8.html

**Susse Chalet Motor Lodges & Inns**
800/258-1980 Continental USA and Canada

**Travelodge**
800/255-3050 Continental USA and Canada

**Vagabond Hotels Inc**
800/522-1555 Continental USA and Canada

**Westin Hotels and Resorts**
800/228-3000 Continental USA and Canada
800/254-5440 TDD
http://www.westin.com

**Wyndham Hotels and Resorts**
800/822-4200 Continental USA and Canada

## CAR RENTAL AGENCIES

**Advantage Rent-A-Car**
800/777-5500 Continental USA and Canada

**Airways Rent A Car**
800/952-9200 Continental USA

**Alamo Rent A Car**
800/327-9633 Continental USA and Canada
http://www.goalamo.com

**Allstate Car Rental**
800/634-6186 Continental USA and Canada

**Avis**
800/331-1212 Continental USA
800/TRY-AVIS Canada
800/331-2323 TDD
http://www.avis.com

**Budget Rent A Car**
800/527-0700 Continental USA and Canada
800/826-5510 TDD

**Dollar Rent A Car**
800/800-4000 Continental USA and Canada

**Enterprise Rent-A-Car**
800/325-8007 Continental USA and Canada

**Hertz**
800/654-3131 Continental USA and Canada
800/654-2280 TDD

**National Car Rental**
800/CAR-RENT Continental USA and Canada
800/328-6323 TDD
http://www.nationalcar.com

**Payless Car Rental**
800/PAYLESS Continental USA and Canada

**Rent-A-Wreck**
800/535-1391 Continental USA

**Sears Rent A Car**
800/527-0770 Continental USA and Canada

**Thrifty Rent-A-Car**
800/367-2277 Continental USA and Canada
800/358-5856 TDD

**U-Save Auto Rental of America**
800/272-USAV Continental USA and Canada

**Value Rent-A-Car**
800/327-2501 Continental USA and Canada
http://www.go-value.com

## AIRLINES

**American Airlines**
800/433-7300 Continental USA and Western Canada
800/543-1586 TDD
http://www.americanair.com/aahome/aahome.html

**Canadian Airlines International**
800/426-7000 Continental USA and Canada
http://www.cdair.ca

**Continental Airlines**
800/525-0280 Continental USA
800/343-9195 TDD
http://www.flycontinental.com

**Delta Air Lines**
800/221-1212 Continental USA
800/831-4488 TDD
http://www.delta-air.com

**Northwest Airlines**
800/225-2525 Continental USA and Canada
http://www.nwa.com

**Southwest Airlines**
800/435-9792 Continental USA and Canada
http://iflyswa.com

**Trans World Airlines**
800/221-2000 Continental USA
http://www2.twa.com/TWA/Airlines/home/
home.html

**United Airlines**
800/241-6522 Continental USA and Canada
http://www.ual.com

**USAir**
800/428-4322 Continental USA and Canada
http://www.usair.com

## TRAIN

**Amtrak**
800/USA-RAIL Continental USA
http://amtrak.com

## BUS

**Greyhound**
800/231-2222 Continental USA
http://greyhound.com

# The Top-Rated Lodgings

## FIVE FLAGS

Four Seasons Ocean Grand, Palm Beach
The Ritz-Carlton Amelia Island
The Ritz-Carlton Naples
The Ritz-Carlton Palm Beach, Manalapan

## FOUR FLAGS

Amelia Island Plantation, Amelia Island
Bellevue Mido Resort Hotel, Clearwater
The Biltmore Hotel, Coral Gables
The Breakers, Palm Beach
Boca Raton Resort & Club, Boca Raton
Buena Vista Palace—WDW Village,
Lake Buena Vista
Disney's Grand Floridian Beach Resort,
Lake Buena Vista
Disney's Wilderness Lodge, Lake Buena Vista
The Don CeSar Beach Resort & Spa,
St Pete Beach
Edgewater Beach Hotel, Naples
The Fisher Island Club, Fisher Island
Grand Bay Hotel, Miami
Hotel Astor, Miami Beach
Hyatt Regency Grand Cypress, Orlando
Hyatt Regency Miami
Hyatt Regency Pier 66, Fort Lauderdale
Hyatt Regency Westshore, Tampa
Innisbrook Hilton Resort, Palm Harbor
Josephine's French Country Inn,
Fort Walton Beach
Little Palm Island, Little Torch Key

Marco Island Hilton Beach Resort
The Marquesa Hotel, Key West
Marriott at Sawgrass Resort, Ponte Vedra Beach
Marriott's Bay Point Resort, Panama City Beach
Marriott's Orlando World Center
Ocean Reef Club, Key Largo
Omni Colonnade Hotel, Coral Gables
The Peabody Orlando
Ponte Vedra Inn & Club, Ponte Vedra Beach
The Registry Resort, Naples
Renaissance Vinoy Resort, St Petersburg
Renaissance Orlando Resort, Orlando
Saddlebrook, Wesley Chapel
Sandestin Beach Resort, Destin
Sanibel Harbour Resort & Spa, Fort Myers
Seaside Cottage Rental Agency,
Fort Walton Beach
Sheraton Bal Harbour Resort, Bal Harbour
Sheraton Fort Lauderdale Airport Hotel, Dania
Sonesta Beach Resort, Key Biscayne
Turnberry Isle Resort & Club, North Miami
Walt Disney World Dolphin, Lake Buena Vista
Walt Disney World Swan, Lake Buena Vista
Wyndham Harbour Island Hotel, Tampa

# FLORIDA

# Summons to Paradise

## STATE STATS

### CAPITAL
Tallahassee

### AREA
54,153 square miles

### BORDERS
Georgia, Alabama,
the Atlantic Ocean,
and the Gulf of Mexico

### POPULATION
13,400,000 (1992)

### ENTERED UNION
March 3, 1845 (27th state)

### NICKNAMES
Sunshine State

### STATE FLOWER
Orange blossom

### STATE BIRD
Mockingbird

### FAMOUS NATIVES
Mary Bethune,
Zora Neale Hurston,
Sidney Poitier,
Faye Dunaway

It's short on ski runs, but Florida revels in most of the other ingredients of a happy vacation, and in all seasons. Every year, millions of frostbitten Americans and Europeans from northerly climes funnel themselves into this subtropical state. Tens of thousands of them dig their heels into sugary sand and refuse to leave, having discovered a place where no task seems so urgent it can't be put off until tomorrow.

Even sloth has its rewards, however, in afternoons lazed away in open-sided tiki bars or watching sportfishing boats return from their days on the high sea. Boredom is rare. Lovers of wildlife catch glimpses of dozens of native birds and mammals, which turn up in the most implausible places. Atop telephone poles are nests of osprey, as big as eagles. In the Keys are deer that stand no higher than a man's knees. Dolphins make graceful leaps out in the bays, and lovably homely manatees lumber in channels. Roseate spoonbills, great blue herons, pink flamingoes, and snowy egrets stalk mud flats and marshlands. Pelicans squat on dock pilings. Alligators and armadillos are reminders that Florida's genealogy dates back to the days of the dinosaurs.

More active visitors can exhaust themselves on any of more than 1,000 golf courses and on the tennis courts that adjoin every other hotel. Even on short excursions, novice snorkelers and scuba divers can spot scores of the 600 species of marine creatures that inhabit these waters. Anglers with the wherewithal can troll the edges of the Gulf Stream for such prey as the pinwheeling sailfish and the awesome marlin. Those with thinner wallets can replicate those big-time thrills from dinghies or from shore, seeking out the "Big Three" of tarpon, snook, and permit. More passive pursuits include shelling on the islands off the southwest edge of the peninsula and birding, especially in the vast Everglades basin.

Disney's sprawling kingdom dominates central Florida, but it is ringed by ever-increasing concentric circles of competing

Frommer'

#1

theme parks and amusement centers. Attractions include 16th-century forts built by Spanish conquistadores and a space center that may eventually establish colonies among the stars. Mansions built by fabulously wealthy northerners in the last century and in the early years of this one dot both coastlines. Some of them can be visited, for a look at life before the dire fact of the federal income tax.

Those who crave a brisk urban beat find it in abundance beside the hip southern strand of Miami Beach and along Calle Ocho, the effervescent Latino enclave of its sister city across the bay. Visitors seeking nonstop nightly parties bump into kindred spirits just about everywhere, but especially in the earthy resorts of the Panhandle, on the lively downtown streets of Key West, beside the busy canals of Fort Lauderdale, and, during the famed spring break for college students, at Daytona Beach. Florida is invitingly sensual, and delightfully diverse, and it beckons even the most satiated of travelers.

## A Brief History

**The Flowery Land** Middle-aged Ponce de León, conqueror of Puerto Rico, sailed north in 1513 in quest of an alleged fountain of youth, and in April, he sighted the glistening sands of an unknown land. Given the time of year, he dubbed it "Pascua Florida"—Easter—and claimed it for the Spanish crown. As it happens, "florida" also means "flowery," a happy coincidence given the profusion of blossoms he surely found. His continued search proved fruitless and the native peoples he encountered were not friendly. On a return visit in 1521, he was felled in battle and died soon after.

Subsequent expeditions ran afoul of hurricanes and assorted other hardships and barely left a trace, their leaders more interested in booty than in permanence. The first determined Spanish settlers didn't arrive until 1565, when Pedro Menéndez de Avilés put ashore with a force of 1,500 soldiers and settlers. They swept aside a French trading post called Fort Caroline and established their own St

Augustine, 25 miles south of the present Jacksonville. It was to become the oldest continually occupied European settlement in the future United States, established 42 years before the English first put down roots in Virginia. The moated castle they built still stands.

**The British are Coming** The people of St Augustine endured yellow fever, malaria, vicious tropical storms, and brigands. (Sir Francis Drake, for one, sacked the town in 1586.) No matter the calamity, they always rebuilt. But mere survival wasn't enough to attract other colonists and no gold was discovered in Florida.

There had been an earlier Spanish outpost at Pensacola, on the Gulf Coast, but it was abandoned after only two years, and the Spanish didn't return there until 1698. Pensacola took on a measure of strategic importance four years later, when France and Spain were allied against England and Austria in what was called Queen Anne's War. Such coalitions were short-lived. Six years after the treaty ending the war was signed, France launched repeated attacks against Pensacola from Louisiana, taking the colony in 1719 only to hand it back to Spain in 1723.

Imperial maneuvering between Spain, France, and Britain, their New World battles an extension of Old World struggles, continued through mid-century. By 1763, the end of the Seven Years War (known on this side of the Atlantic as the French and Indian War), England had taken charge of the territory. All this churning and bloodshed was curious, however, since, except for St Augustine, Pensacola, and a few small outlying ports, most of Florida was a backwater, and not many people other than the native Creeks and Seminoles wished to live there. A 1771 census tallied only 1,200 whites and slaves east of the Apalachicola River.

**The Americans Take Over** The British didn't stay long. At the end of the American Revolution, the Treaty of Paris ceded Florida back to Spain. When the expansionist young republic to the north pur-

---

### Fun Facts

- The oldest city of European origin in the United States is St Augustine. It was founded as a Spanish colony on September 8, 1565.
- More than 55 million rounds of golf are played annually on the state's 1,032 courses.
- No location in Florida is more than 60 miles from saltwater.
- The first integrated professional baseball game was played on March 17, 1946, at City Island Ball Park in Daytona Beach. Future Hall-of-Famer Jackie Robinson represented the minor league Montreal Royals in the game.
- Three-quarters of the oranges consumed in the United States are grown in Florida.
- Walt Disney World covers 43 square miles, making the theme park approximately the same size as San Francisco!

chased the Louisiana Territory from the French in 1803, it insisted that west Florida was part of the package. Various groups nibbled at the region, and Andrew Jackson marched on Pensacola in 1813, returning in 1818 to make war against the Seminoles. Three years later, Spain gave Florida to the United States in return for clear title to Texas. That bargain wasn't to hold for long, but Jackson was on hand again to preside at the Spanish concession.

A site midway between St Augustine and Pensacola—Tallahassee—was declared the capital of the new territory. (Three log cabins served as legislative buildings.) Another bitter war with the Seminoles erupted in 1835. In a hardly unique act of perfidy, the army arrested Chief Osceola when he came to them under a flag of truce. In 1842, nearly 4,000 Seminoles and runaway slaves who lived among them were deported to Arkansas.

## Statehood & Conflict

A new brick capitol was completed in Tallahassee in 1845, just in time for statehood. Florida signed on with the Confederacy during the Civil War, although it wasn't destined to play a major role, because of its small population. Its troops held forts in the northeastern and northwestern parts of the state, while Union forces dominated in strategically more important Key West and the Dry Tortugas. The war over, a new state constitution in 1868 granted suffrage to all male citizens, regardless of race. Suddenly, enfranchised blacks actually outnumbered whites, some of whom flocked to the Ku Klux Klan. In 1871 alone, the KKK lynched 163 black people in a single Florida county.

## Railways to the Sun

After the withdrawal of Federal troops in 1877, investors finally began to see the enormous agricultural and tourism potential of the undeveloped peninsula. Industrialist Henry B Plant financed a new rail line running diagonally across the state between Jacksonville and Tampa on

---

### DRIVING DISTANCES

**Jacksonville**

90 mi NW of Daytona Beach
202 mi NE of Tampa
358 mi E of Pensacola
463 mi SE of Birmingham, AL
503 mi N of Key West

**Miami**

164 mi NE of Key West
229 mi SE of Orlando
268 mi SE of Daytona Beach
348 mi SE of Jacksonville
663 mi SE of Atlanta, GA

**Orlando**

84 mi NE of Tampa
166 mi NW of West Palm Beach
232 mi NW of Miami
258 mi SE of Tallahassee
648 mi SE of New Orleans, LA

**Tampa**

78 mi SW of Orlando
201 mi SW of Jacksonville
238 mi SE of Tallahassee
269 mi NW of Miami
440 mi SW of Charleston, SC

---

the Gulf Coast (1884), and oil magnate Henry M Flagler commenced construction of his East Coast Railway from St Augustine south to Miami. Linking the luxury hotels he built along the way, his "Railroad That Went to Sea" eventually reached Key West.

A post–World War I land boom poured millions of speculative dollars into the economy. Immigration and tourism grew apace. Criminals flourished, too, for this was the Prohibition era and Florida, with its 1,800 miles of coastline, was a magnet for rumrunners. The bubble burst in 1926, when investors began to discover that much of the acreage they had purchased unseen didn't exist or was underwater. The final blow was a devastating hurricane the same year that all but leveled Miami, leaving almost 200 dead.

**Bust to Battleships** Seven years later, yet another hurricane destroyed much of Flagler's railroad between Miami and Key West. The state acquired the right-of-way and constructed a road, which opened for traffic in 1938, aiding in the economic revival of the Keys. The Great Depression was beginning to ease by then, due to New Deal social programs and the industrial and military buildup prior to World War II. Florida was deemed crucial to the defense of Gulf shipping and the Panama Canal.

**Blast-off** With the recovery following Japan's surrender, Americans sought sun and frolic as never before. Resorts, hotels, and condominium complexes sprang up along the two coasts. Rapacious developers and municipalities sucked so much water from interior lakes and aquifers that the great Everglades began to shrink, an alarming process and one that has yet to be resolved.

When NASA set up shop on Cape Canaveral in 1958, launching the Apollo missions that landed the first men on the moon, the state received a shot of scientific prestige as well as a further boost to tourism. Theme parks contributed to the increasing tides of visitors. Cypress Gardens and Busch Gardens led the way and they still thrive, but it took the phenomenon named Disney to transform central Florida into the world's most popular tourist destination. Disney's Magic Kingdom opened in 1971.

**Mickey, Minnie, Margarita** Monumental demographic and economic change was prompted by the Cuban Revolution, which caused waves of refugees to flee to south Florida. Many of them were prosperous and educated, with the drive and vision to invigorate the society they found waiting for them. Miami soon became the de facto capital of the Caribbean.

Another revolution took place with the arrival of contemporary versions of Prohibition's rumrunners. America's escalating taste for illicit drugs was—and is—a bonanza for drug traffickers and the pilots and boat captains they hired to dump tons of cocaine and marijuana on these shores every week.

| AVG MONTHLY TEMPS (°F) & RAINFALL (IN) | | |
|---|---|---|
| | **Miami** | **Jacksonville** |
| Jan | 67/2.1 | 53/3.1 |
| Feb | 68/2.1 | 55/3.5 |
| Mar | 72/1.9 | 61/3.7 |
| Apr | 75/3.1 | 68/3.3 |
| May | 79/6.5 | 74/4.9 |
| June | 81/9.2 | 79/5.4 |
| July | 83/6.0 | 81/6.5 |
| Aug | 83/7.0 | 81/7.2 |
| Sept | 82/8.1 | 78/7.3 |
| Oct | 78/7.1 | 70/3.4 |
| Nov | 73/2.7 | 61/1.9 |
| Dec | 69/1.9 | 55/2.6 |

That challenge, and those of rapid growth and the depleted environment, will dog the state for decades. Now the fourth-largest state in population—it was only tenth in 1960—it is destined to move up to third place, after California and Texas and ahead of New York, by the end of this century.

# A Closer Look

## GEOGRAPHY

The elongated thumb of land pointing at the tropics is the youngest part of the United States, geologically speaking. For the most part, it is as flat as a billiard table, with any elevation higher than a three-story building qualifying as a hill. Its highest "peak" is 345 feet, 2 miles from the Georgia border. Otherwise, the state offers a remarkably diverse landscape, with dense forests of live oak and cypress, hundreds of rivers and streams, barrier reefs and islands protecting long stretches of both coasts, the primordial wilderness known as the Everglades, and over 10,000 lakes, including Okeechobee, second-largest in the United States. And yes, beaches—over 1,000

miles of them.

The **Florida Keys** trail off the south tip of the peninsula like a broken necklace drifting in the current. These hundreds of coral and mangrove islands are largely uninhabited, apart from those linked by US 1, the "Overseas Highway." Off Key Largo, at the northern end, is John Pennekamp Coral Reef State Park. From there down, only Islamorada and Marathon have significant populations until the southernmost terminus of US 1, Key West. That island city is closer to Havana than to Miami.

Moving north to the mainland, Homestead is a modest introduction to the glittery **Miami** region, which includes cosmopolitan Miami itself, an ethnic and cultural mosaic. Continuing north, Fort Lauderdale signals the beginning of the **Gold Coast,** whose busy canals prompt chamber of commerce comparisons to Venice. Strung along the shore, with resort hotels and luxurious homes at every turn, are the wealthy communities of Boca Raton, Delray Beach, Boynton Beach, and Palm Beach, the last established by Henry Flagler for his monied chums. West of Miami and the Gold Coast, the Everglades stretch all the way to the Gulf Coast, nearly empty of human habitation apart from the Miccosukee Seminoles who were there thousands of years before Europeans arrived. The expanse is crossed by I-75, known as Alligator Alley.

On this side of the state, the less urban and more sedate Lee County coast incorporates upscale **Naples** and engagingly frowsy **Fort Myers,** winter home to Thomas Edison. Offshore are Sanibel, Captiva, Estero, and Marco resort islands, bearing a relatively tranquil family identity and incorporating notable wildlife refuges.

Farther north, the **Central Gulf Coast** centers on the cities and resorts that ring **Tampa Bay** and constitute the largest concentration of population on the Florida Gulf Coast. St Petersburg, nearly as large, has the beaches and marinas Tampa lacks.

**Orlando** and **Central Florida** spell one thing to most people anticipating a visit with a carful of youngsters: Disney. New attractions, restaurants, and hotels are added by the month, but that picture is incomplete. There are many quiet corners too, as in the gracious municipality of Winter Park and in peaceful Bok Tower Gardens.

The **Central Atlantic Coast,** often called the Space or Treasure Coast, is a short drive east of Orlando. Its shore is protected by a rarely broken string of barrier islands from Fort Pierce to Daytona Beach. Cape Canaveral and the Kennedy Space Center contrast space-age technology with the surrounding nature refuge and with the rural character of nearby Indian River, famed for its citrus groves.

In the **Northeast,** sometimes referred to as the Crown of Florida, is historic St Augustine, the oldest continuously occupied town in the United States and a prize that has thrived under five flags—Spanish, French, British, Old Glory, and the Stars and Bars of the Confederacy. Jacksonville is a thriving metropolis straddling the broad St Johns River. Beyond the city, in the last corner of the state before Georgia, is Amelia Island, with a trove of several hundred Victorian dwellings behind its impressive sand dunes.

The northwest arm of the state, which reaches under Alabama toward Mississippi, is commonly known as the **Panhandle.** At its eastern edge is the capital, Tallahassee, its antebellum plantation houses and venerable trees lending a distinctive Old South flavor. Pensacola, at the western border, is older, with a village of restored houses harking back to the 18th century. From there, the "Emerald Coast" curves southeast through the bustling Gulf-side resorts of Fort Walton Beach, Destin, and Panama City. This strip has its honky-tonk aspects, but it also has segments protected by state and national recreation areas. Soon, both give way to secluded cottage colonies and drowsy old-time fishing villages.

## CLIMATE

Warm breezes and blue skies rule throughout the state. There is ample room for variations, however, since it is over 500 miles from the Georgia border to the tip of Key West.

While January in Jacksonville won't remind anyone of New Year's Day in Minneapolis, it is usually cool during the day and chilly at night. Freezing temperatures, albeit short in duration, are an almost yearly threat to citrus crops as far down the coast as Palm Beach. From Miami on south, though, frosts are virtually unknown, even in deepest winter. Residents of South Florida and the Keys, who fear the onset of chilbains if the temperature falls below 65°F, pay a price in heavier rainfall during the off-season (May through October), when thunderstorms and lightning are frequent. That period is also hot and can be stiflingly humid, but not much worse than in northern cities in summer. Interior sections of the state, notably around Orlando, tend to be less comfortable in summer than the coastal cities.

June through October is also hurricane season, which usually peaks in July and August. While past storms have brought great tragedy and even altered the course of the state's history, the National Hurricane Center in Miami gives ample warning of possible danger, and routes of escape.

## WHAT TO PACK

In winter months, a sweater is necessary even in South Florida, where there can be unexpected cold snaps with temperatures occasionally dropping into the 50s. A light, water-repellent windbreaker is useful, especially from June to October, when short showers are an almost daily occurrence. Take it along, too, when spending time on a boat.

With the exception of a handful of restaurants, most of them in Miami or Palm Beach, men won't need ties unless on a business trip. A blazer and trousers will do for almost all social situations, with a cocktail dress or two for women. Leave splashy jewelry at home, especially when traveling in the larger cities. The rest of the time, shorts or jeans or light cotton dresses should do. And no one needs to be told to take a swimsuit or two to Florida.

Tuck in a bottle of sunscreen lotion with an SPF of 15 or higher, or buy some immediately upon arrival, as well as insect repellent for comfort in forested areas, marshes, swamps, and even on beaches. Other necessities are a sunhat, and sandals or flip-flops to protect feet on hot sand.

## TOURIST INFORMATION

Contact the Florida Division of Tourism at 126 W Van Buren St, Tallahassee, FL 32399 or call 904/ 487-1462 to obtain the free *Florida Vacation Guide* and road maps, as well as answers to general questions. For information about Walt Disney World, contact the Walt Disney World Company, PO Box 10000, Lake Buena Vista, FL 32830-1000 (tel 407/ 824-4321). General information about accommodations can be obtained from the Florida Hotel and

Motel Association, Box 1529, Tallahassee, FL 32302-1529 (tel 904/488-1133). The Tour Florida home page on the World Wide Web (http://www.florida.com) features links to over 90 attractions throughout the state, while the *I'm Going to Disney World Vacation Planner* (http://www.travelweb.com/thisco/wdwhome/wdw.html) provides the latest information on Disney parks and resorts.

To find out how to obtain information for individual cities and parks in Florida, look under separate cities in the listings section of thic book.

## DRIVING RULES AND REGULATIONS

Seat belts are mandatory for all front-seat passengers, and for children four or five years old anywhere in the vehicle. Every child under three must use an approved safety seat. Speed limits are 55 mph on state roads unless otherwise posted, and 55 or 65 mph on interstate highways. Liability insurance is required.

## RENTING A CAR

Visitors wanting to rent a car on arrival in Florida are faced with a bewildering profusion of offers. To save time, it is preferable to ask a travel agent to sort through the possibilities and make advance reservations. An agent can also suggest packages that include not only airfare and rental car but lodging, sightseeing tours, and other features.

All major rental companies are represented, including:

- **Alamo** (800/327-9633)
- **Avis** (800/331-1212)
- **Budget** (800/527-0700)
- **Dollar** (800/365-5276)
- **Hertz** (800/654-3131)
- **National** (800/227-7368)
- **Thrifty** (800/367-2277)

## ESSENTIALS

**Area Codes:** The number of area codes in Florida has doubled in the last few years. The area code for northern Florida, including Jacksonville, Tallahassee, Daytona Beach, and Panama City, is still **904.** The central Gulf Coast (including Clearwater, St Petersburg, and Tampa) is still **813,** but the Gulf Coast south of Bradenton (including Fort Myers, Naples, and Sarasota) is now **941.** Orlando and the Space Coast are **407,** while the area north of Orlando (including Gainesville and some of the northern Gulf Coast like Homosassa and Crystal River) is now **352.** Miami and the Keys are still **305,** but the Fort Lauderdale area (including Hollywood, and up to Pompano Beach) is now **954,** and Boca Raton, the Palm Beaches, and other southeastern cities (up to Vero Beach) are now **561.**

**Emergencies:** To summon the police, the fire department, or an ambulance from anywhere in the state, call 911.

**Liquor Laws:** The minimum legal age to buy or consume alcoholic beverages in Florida is 21, although the law is observed with varying degrees of rigor. Bars are open at least until midnight, and often as late (or early) as 4 or even 6am. They are closed Sunday mornings.

**Smoking:** Florida law prohibits smoking in public buildings. Most restaurants have nonsmoking areas, many hotels have smoke-free rooms, and the major airports forbid smoking except in designated areas.

**Taxes:** Florida's sales tax is 6%. Many municipalities and counties impose additional taxes, especially on hotel and restaurant bills.

**Time Zone:** Most of the state observes Eastern Standard Time, but the section of the Panhandle west of the Apalachicola River, including Pensacola and Panama City, is on Central Standard Time, an hour behind the rest of Florida. Daylight saving time is observed.

# Best of the State
## WHAT TO SEE AND DO

Below is a general overview of some of the top sights and attractions in Florida. To find out more detailed information, look under "Attractions" under individual cities in the listings portion of this book.

**Theme Parks** Almost everyone who crosses the border journeys into the heart of the state, where the Disney organization has spawned its own clutch of theme parks and inspired a dozen or so commendable competitors. **Walt Disney World** is really three theme parks in one, beginning with **the Magic Kingdom,** a repository of nostalgia, Americana, and fantasy, with electrifying rides through a faux mountain, a sanitized jungle, and over water. Next came **Epcot Center,** a semi-educational paean to technology and the future. Most popular of its entertainments is Spaceship Earth, a 15-minute sojurn through the entire history of the planet. Youngest of the three complexes is **Disney–MGM Studios,** where rides and multimedia theaters revel in Hollywood lore, and visitors plunge into replications of famous film scenes as well as a couple of imaginative water parks.

Also in Orlando is **Sea World,** with its performing dolphins, killer whales, and flock of penguins. One of the most popular exhibits is an underwater glass tunnel that allows spectators to look out at sharks and barracudas on the prowl. Shamu the killer whale is the headliner, with his own stadium. **Universal Studios Florida,** easily the equal of the Disney-MGM collaboration, is also in the neighborhood, making the most of its associations with hit films and Hollywood lore. Besides movie sets, stunt shows, and state-of-the-art films, it includes impressive sound stages actually used in film production. Out of the Orlando orbit, but deserving of consideration, is **Busch Gardens,** near Tampa Bay. A full day is barely enough to take in its extensive animal exhibits, which include apes, lions, zebras, and giraffes.

**Beaches** They are never far away, but some are better known than others, for a variety of reasons. **Daytona Beach,** famed for its automobile races and as the destination of choice for college students on spring break, is a wide avenue of sand so hard-packed that sun-worshipers can drive right up to the spot they choose to pitch their blankets. Odds-on favorite for the "most glamorous" are the miles of reconstituted sands alongside Miami's fashionable **South Beach.** Manmade **Smathers Beach** in Key West draws crowds as diverse as the residents of the island itself. In the Tampa Bay area, avoid swimming in bays, which may look fine but are subject to pollution. Instead, head south to the barrier islands off Sarasota—**South Lido Beach** is long and well equipped—or Bradenton, where the top choice for families is **Manatee County Beach.** Farther south,

the gulf beaches of **Captiva** and **Sanibel Islands** are famous for shelling. In the Panhandle, superb strands are among the several accessible portions of **Gulf Island National Seashore,** opposite Pensacola, and they have none of the commercial clutter associated with beaches farther east along the Panhandle.

**Historical Buildings** The wealthy men and women responsible for developing Florida around the turn of the century left eye-popping hotels and mansions all along the east coast, especially in St Augustine, Palm Beach, and Miami.

James Deering's Italianate seaside **Villa Vizcaya** and its extensive gardens are fabulously theatrical. Despite its Spanish name, the 70-room mansion and its outbuildings are Venetian in style; interiors are lavishly appointed with imported tiles, coffered ceilings, and collections of European decorative and fine arts. The estate, a decided must-see, is on the outskirts of Miami.

Also make time for the 1902 **Whitehall** mansion, built in Palm Beach by the oil and railroad tycoon who was responsible in great measure for Florida's development. Now officially named the Henry M Flagler Museum, it has scores of rooms replete with paintings, carpets, sculptures, and furnishings of the period, many of them original to Flagler. His private railroad car is also on display.

Many of the distinctive designs of the flamboyant architect **Addison Mizner** survive as restaurants, hotels, and private homes in the Boca Raton–Fort Lauderdale area. Noted for his use of Mediterranean styles and materials in combinations entirely his own, he created structures that are enjoyed more for their exuberance than for their contributions to the art of architecture. Two Mizner creations accessible to the public are La Vieille Maison restaurant and portions of the Boca Raton Hotel and Club.

In Pensacola's **Seville District,** preserved blocks of dozens of houses dating from the colonial period cluster around Seville Square and along streets named after Spanish cities—Tarragona, Zaragoza, Alcañiz. Eleven of the buildings constitute **Historic Pensacola Village,** and function as museums illustrating the heritage, commerce, and industries of the city or as examples of colonial and antebellum architecture. Earnest guides in period garb conduct tours.

The Spanish founded **St Augustine** and occupied it for over 250 years, apart from a 20-year interim of British control. While little remains from the 16th and 17th centuries, the **Spanish Quarter** does contain a large number of buildings surviving from the early 1700s and 1800s and most are intriguing. The majority are Spanish in origin, with British and French overlays, and have been much restored. Many are used as shops and cafes, while some serve as mini-museums.

The youngest preservation district in the state is the **Miami Beach Art Deco District** of south Miami Beach (also known as SoBe). Its buildings, dating from the 1930s and early 1940s, are reminiscent of old radios and between-the-wars passenger liners. Neon, bands of pastel colors, eyebrow windows, mock portholes, and stylized representations of palm trees and sunsets inform block after block of restored structures. Many are now boutique hotels, clubs, and restaurants, a scene that has attracted the attention of model agencies and big-time Hollywood stars and investors.

**State & National Parks** Quite apart from the artificial naturalism of commercial safari parks and aviaries, wildlife and a profusion of luxuriant subtropical vegetation can be viewed up close and personal in the waters and fields outside every town, as well as in parks that are never far away from any urban center.

In **Everglades National Park,** easily the best environment for viewing native fauna, the ecosystem's birds of prey, lizards, giant turtles, wading birds, and alligators can be seen in abundance from escorted trams and elevated walkways. The profoundly endangered Florida panther also makes the swamp its home, but not even the resident park rangers are likely to spot one. Hurricane Andrew caused considerable damage to visitor facilities and the grasslands, and both are still recovering.

**John Pennekamp Coral Reef State Park,** the first underwater state park in the continental United States, embraces almost 80 square miles of ocean floor east of Key Largo, northernmost of the hundreds of Florida Keys. Snorkeling party boats make the short trip to the park's central feature, a long coral reef, almost every day. The reef provides shelter and sustenance to fish so brilliantly hued they look like fragments spilled from a broken kaleidoscope. Farther north, just outside the Miami city limits, another section of the same reef system was the motivation for the creation of **Biscayne National Park.**

North of the bustling Orlando area lies **Ocala National Forest,** a large preserve virtually surrounded by lakes and rivers inviting to campers, hikers, canoeists, and anglers. With 13 major campgrounds, there are ample bases from which to engage in these activities as well as exploration of the large springs that dot the region. Surrounding farms and estates are known for horse breeding, with wranglers tending to their charges under trees draped in Spanish moss.

**Canaveral National Seashore,** a protected marine environment adjoining the grounds of the Kennedy Space Center, has opportunities for sightings that are legend among bird-watchers. Over 300 types of waterfowl and other species have been identified. Pristine beaches attract swimmers and sunbathers, and the preserve also contains Mosquito Lagoon, where alligators and egg-laying sea turtles are often observed.

Take binoculars for the circuit of the small but engaging **J N "Ding" Darling National Wildlife Refuge.** Along the park's five-mile Wildlife Drive visitors can spot roseate spoonbills, egrets, herons, pelicans, and alligators, among others, most of them accommodating enough to roost and wade beside signs that announce their presence.

**Cuisine** Once characterized as a gastronomic wasteland of chicken shacks and barbecue joints, Florida now boasts a burgeoning cadre of three-star chefs, many of them immigrants from New York and Europe. They are fashioning a distinctive "sunshine cuisine," giving inventive twists to the produce and ideas of Caribbean and Latin American kitchens. The best of this innovative breed are in Palm Beach, Fort Lauderdale, Miami, and Key West, but other areas are catching up. Whether in evolving forms of cookery that are yet to be given labels or in more traditional domestic or imported cuisines, the growing American taste for spicy, even fiery, dishes is abundantly served.

**Creole/Cajun** cooking has successfully made the short journey from its birthplace, Louisiana, especially in the northwestern part of the state. The lowly crawfish and vegetable greens have been raised to epicurean status, and the vogue for blackened redfish threatened the very existence of that species until the technique was applied to other types of fish.

The **Cuban** culinary repertoire, by contrast, is more limited in scope but well worth seeking out, if only for the tasty toasted sandwiches of layered ham, pork, Swiss cheese, pickles, and tangy sauce. Many Cuban recipes have their origins in Spain, naturally, as with paella and arroz con pollo. Others take advantage of Caribbean fruits and produce, as in *lechon al trozo*—roast pork with rice, black beans, and yucca, often with fried plantains on the side. **Jamaican** food is increasingly popular, using similar ingredients, but usually with a hotter kick. Jerked pork is typical. Look for these and related Caribbean cuisines in South Florida, especially in Miami.

**Seafood** figures prominently on all restaurant menus. Some of it rarely travels north, so visitors inevitably encounter fish and crustaceans with which they are unfamiliar. Mahimahi is a Hawaiian name often applied to the delectable *fish* properly called dolphin. This is not—repeat, *not*—the lovable mammal we know as Flipper. Ground or diced conch (pronounced "conk") is a rubbery shellfish served in chowder and fritters, each of which merits a taste. Stone crabs are a happily renewable resource. Properly harvested, they are made to surrender only one claw and are then returned to the sea, where they obligingly grow another. A restaurant in Miami Beach is so devoted to the stone crab that it closes its doors when the delectable creature is out of season.

## EVENTS AND FESTIVALS

### THE KEYS

- **Old Island Days,** Key West. Various events and celebrations, including house and garden tours, parades, boat races, arts and craft shows. Mid-January to April. Call 305/294-9501 for information.
- **Seven-Mile Bridge Run,** Marathon. Foot race across the namesake bridge, with international participants. April. Call 305/743-8513.
- **Hemingway Days,** Key West. Story competition, Hemingway look-alike contest, arm wrestling. Mid-July. Call 305/294-4440.
- **Fantasy Fest,** Key West. Bizarre, often ribald costume parties and Halloween parades. October. Call 305/296-1817.

### MIAMI & THE GOLD COAST

- **Orange Bowl,** Miami. One of the five major post-season college football games, preceded by the King Orange parade. New Year's Day. Call 305/642-1515 for information.
- **Taste of the Grove,** Coconut Grove, Miami. Two days of food and music. Mid-January. Call 305/624-3714.
- **Art Deco Festival,** Miami Beach. Street fair, dances, music in South Beach's restored Deco district. Mid-January. Call 305/672-2014.
- **Arts Festival,** Coconut Grove, Miami. Hundreds

of local artists display their work; food and music. Mid-February. Call 305/447-0401.
- **Sistrunk Historical Festival,** Fort Lauderdale. Street fair celebrates the African-American experience with food, music, and crafts displays. February. Call 954/357-7514.
- **International Boat and Sailboat Show,** Miami. Mid- to late February. Call 305/531-8410.
- **Seminole Tribal Fair,** Hollywood. Traditional Native American music, dance, crafts. Late February. Call 954/321-1000.
- **Grand Prix,** Miami. Formula One cars race on Biscayne Boulevard. Late February to early March. Call 305/379-7223.
- **Calle Ocho/Carnavale,** Miami. Festivities include parades and dancing in Little Havana. Early March. Call 305/324-7349.
- **Broward County Fair,** Hallandale. A week of rides, games, concerts, and food. November. Call 954/923-3247.
- **Winterfest Boat Parade,** Fort Lauderdale. Scores of gaily decorated craft sail and chug along the Intracoastal Waterway. Many other events fill the month. December. Call 954/767-0686.

### THE GULF COAST

- **Hall of Fame Bowl,** Tampa. New Year's Day college football extravaganza, with road race and concerts. Call 800/448-2672 for information.
- **Gasparilla Festival,** Tampa. Buccaneers sail into the bay and "invade" the city. Torchlight parade, road races, golf tournaments, and parties fill out the month-long celebration. Late January to early February. Call 800/448-2672.
- **Florida State Fair,** Tampa. Dozens of rides and a midway packed with games and food booths. Country music stars, agricultural exhibits, and prize-winning livestock. February. Call 800/345-3247.
- **Edison Festival of Light,** Fort Myers. The inventor of the electric light is honored by two weeks of festivities, including foot races, regatta, dancing, shell show, and parade. February. Call 941/334-2550.
- **Medieval Fair,** Sarasota. Knights and ladies besport themselves at jousts and games at the Ringling Museum of Art. Theatrical performances. Early March. Call 941/355-5101.
- **Jazz Festival,** Sarasota. Blues shouters, combos, and big bands rejoice. Week in early April. Call 941/366-1552.

- **Tropicool Fest,** Naples. Canoe races, concerts, and art shows stretch the winter season by two weeks. Mid-May. Call 941/262-6141.
- **Music Festival,** Sarasota. Concerts by chamber and symphony orchestras with prominent guest artists. June. Call 941/953-4252.
- **Jazz on the Green,** Sanibel. Annual jazz festival with food prepared by noted area chefs. October. Call 941/481-2011.

### ORLANDO & CENTRAL FLORIDA

- **Citrus Bowl,** Orlando. One of Florida's several post-season college football matchups. New Year's Day. Call 407/423-2476 for information.
- **Scottish Highland Games,** Orlando. Highland games, dancing, and athletic events, all to the skirl of bagpipes. Last weekend in January. Call 407/672-1682.
- **Silver Spurs Rodeo,** Kissimmee. One of the most important rodeos in the country, featuring many top-rated cowboys. February and July. Call 407/677-6336.
- **Bluegrass Festival,** Kissimmee. Gospel and blue-grass singers, with crafts shows and down-home cookery. March. Call 800/472-7773.
- **Sun 'n' Fun Fly-In,** Lakeland. Week-long meeting of the Experimental Aircraft Association, featuring unusual planes and aerobatics. Second week of April. Call 941/644-2431.
- **Florida State Air Fair,** Kissimmee. Nostalgic throwback to barnstorming air shows of the past. Vintage planes. Late October or early November. Call 407/933-7998.
- **Light Up Orlando.** Parade and street festival with food and live entertainment kicking off the winter season. November. Call 407/648-4010.

### CENTRAL ATLANTIC COAST

- **Speed Weeks,** Daytona Beach. Three weeks of NASCAR races at the Daytona Speedway. February. Call 904/253-7223 (RACE) for information.
- **Bike Week,** Daytona Beach. Championship motorcycle races. February. Call 904/255-0981.
- **Daytona 500,** Daytona Beach. The number one stock car race in the United States. At Daytona Speedway. February. Call 904/253-7223 (RACE).
- **Air Show,** Titusville. Mock dogfights and precision flying by World War II fighter planes and antique aircraft. March. Call 407/268-1944.
- **Space Week,** Brevard County. Commemoration of the *Apollo 11* moon landing. Concerts, hot-air balloons, other events. July. Call 407/452-2121.

### THE NORTHEAST

- **Gator Bowl,** Jacksonville. Fireworks and other entertainments spark the hours leading to a post-season college football game. New Year's Day. Call 904/353-1188 for information.
- **Blessing of the Fleet,** Jacksonville. An excuse for lavish food festival, live music, and boat show. Palm Sunday. Call 904/396-4900.
- **Easter Parade,** St Augustine. Floats, bands, and horse-drawn carriages circle through downtown. Late March or early April. Call 904/692-1032.
- **Flagler County Bluegrass Jamboree,** Bunnell. Accomplished bluegrass musicians play throughout the day; games and pony rides for kids, and a Civil War reenactment. May. Call 904/437-0106.
- **Heritage Days,** Jacksonville. Actors in period costumes stage vignettes from Florida's past. May. Call 904/356-6307.
- **Mug Race,** Palatka. Sailboats race 40 miles downriver to Jacksonville. Entertainment. First Friday in May (usually). Call 904/264-4094.
- **Cross and Sword,** St Augustine. Popular musical drama depicts establishment of the colony by the Spanish. Mid-June to late August. Call 904/471-1965 or 829-6476.
- **Jazz Festival,** Jacksonville. Major event with many stars and up-and-comers of the jazz world. Second weekend in October. Call 904/353-7770.
- **Grand Illumination,** St Augustine. Torchlight parade winds through the historic district. Mid-December. Call 904/824-9550 or 829-6476.

### THE PANHANDLE

- **Natural Bridge Battlefield Reenactment,** Tallahassee. Staged Civil War battle. Early March. Call 800/628-2866 or 904/681-9200 for information.
- **Springtime Tallahassee.** Arts and crafts exhibits, processions, house and garden tours, and a hot-air balloon race, among many events. Mid-March to early April. Call 800/628-2866 or 904/681-9200.
- **Eglin Air Show,** Fort Walton Beach. Mock dogfights and breathtaking aerobatics by the illustrious Navy Thunderbirds. April. Call 800/322-3319 or 904/651-7131.
- **Hog's Breath Hobie Regatta,** Fort Walton Beach. Some 200 boats dance all day across the Gulf past party boats loaded with spectators. All-night pig roast. May. Call 800/322-3319 or 904/651-7131.
- **Fiesta of Five Flags,** Pensacola. Parades on water and land, waterskiing competitions, and other events commemorate the first Spanish explorers. Mid-June. Call 800/874-1234.

- **Volleyball Tournament,** Destin/Fort Walton Beach. One of the country's premier beach volleyball tourneys. September. Call 800/322-3319 or 904/651-7131.
- **Fishing Rodeo,** Destin/Fort Walton Beach. A month-long fishing tournament, open to all. Prizes. October. Call 904/837-6241.
- **Florida Seafood Festival,** Apalachicola. The drowsy fishing port comes alive in celebration of its meal ticket—the succulent Apalachicola oyster. Parades, eating contests. First Saturday in November. Call 904/653-8051.
- **Blue Angels Homecoming Airshow,** Pensacola. The renowned Navy aerobatics team performs free of charge from its home base. November. Call 800/874-1234.

## SPECTATOR SPORTS

**Auto Racing** Daytona Beach is one of the country's prime venues for stock car and hot rod racing. Events are held throughout the year at **Daytona International Speedway,** site of the famous Daytona 500. Call 904/254-2700 for schedule information. Miami attracts cars and drivers from around the world for its annual Formula One **Toyota Grand Prix,** held on a course plotted along downtown streets, usually in February or March. Call 305/379-5660 for dates, 305/379-7223 for tickets.

Hot rodders and drag racing enthusiasts flock to the **Gatornationals,** held in Gainesville in March (tel 352/377-0046), and there are weekly events during the winter at **Hialeah Speedway** (tel 305/821-6644). The thrilling **Twelve Hours of Sebring** thunders around Sebring International Raceway in March (tel 941/655-1442).

**Baseball** Until 1991, Floridians hungering for big-league baseball had to settle for its short spring "Grapefruit League," when professional teams from other states arrived for a few weeks of training. Now, they have a home team to root for, the **Florida Marlins.** The National Leaguers play at Pro Player Stadium (tel 954/779-7070), a short drive north of Miami.

Twenty rival clubs spend the late winter and early spring in Florida conducting their training camps, including the **Philadelphia Phillies** (tel 813/442-8496) in Clearwater, the **Pittsburgh Pirates** (tel 941/747-3031) in Bradenton, the **Toronto Blue Jays** (tel 813/733-9302) in Dunedin, the **Cincinnati Reds** (tel 941/752-7337) at Plant City, the **Chicago White Sox** (tel 941/954-7699) in Sarasota, the **New York Yankees** (tel 954/776-1921) in Fort Lauderdale, the **Texas Rangers** (tel 941/625-9500) at Port Charlotte, the **New York Mets** (tel 561/871-2115) at Port St Lucie, the **St Louis Cardinals** (tel 813/822-3384) in St Petersburg, the **Minnesota Twins** (tel 941/768-4278) and **Boston Red Sox** (tel 941/334-4700) in Fort Myers, the **Atlanta Braves** (tel 561/683-6100) and the **Montreal Expos** (tel 561/689-9121) at West Palm Beach, and the **Los Angeles Dodgers** (tel 561/569-4900) at Vero Beach. Almost all exhibition games sell out weeks in advance, so it's wise to plan ahead.

**Basketball** Florida has joined the National Basketball Association with a vengeance, with two basketball teams that have recently begun to make an impact on the standings. The **Miami Heat** play at the downtown Miami Arena (tel 305/577-4328). Central Florida has its own **Orlando Magic,** with star center Shaquille O'Neal, playing in the gleaming new Orlando Arena (tel 407/896-2442).

**Football** Teams from 3 universities in the state are routinely ranked among the top 20 in national polls. Hailed as a cradle of superstar quarterbacks, the **Hurricanes** of the **University of Miami** harass their opponents at the Orange Bowl (tel 305/643-7100). At Gainesville, 34,000 students and uncounted supporters cheer on the **Gators** of the **University of Florida,** who appear at Doak Campbell Stadium (tel 904/644-1830). And the **Seminoles** of **Florida State University,** who play their tough home schedule in Tallahassee, do their work at Ben Griffin Stadium (tel 352/375-4683).

Florida's first professional club was the **Miami Dolphins,** the only NFL team ever to post an unbeaten season. They perform at Pro Player Stadium (tel 305/620-5000). The **Tampa Bay Buccaneers** were the second expansion team. While they haven't enjoyed the same level of success as their cross-state rivals, their followers are no less loyal. Buccaneer games are played at Tampa Stadium (tel 813/879-2827). In 1995, the new **Jacksonville Jaguars** joined the roster, clawing their way to contention at the Gator Bowl (tel 904/633-2000).

**Greyhound Racing** Controversial though it may be, the dog racing industry thrives, with many venues throughout the state. Pari-mutuel betting is the lure, and tracks are open on a staggered basis throughout the year.

In the Northeast, Jacksonville has **Orange Park**

Kennel Club, St John's Greyhound Park, and the **Jacksonville Kennel Club.** They have alternating schedules, so at least one is open at almost any time of the year. Call 904/646-0001 for information about all three. Over in the Panhandle is the **Pensacola Greyhound Track** (tel 904/455-8598), with an air-conditioned grandstand.

In the Tampa Bay area, the active tracks are **Derby Lane** in St Petersburg (tel 813/576-1361), **Sarasota Kennel Club** (tel 941/355-7744), and **Tampa Greyhound Track** (tel 813/932-4313). To the south of Tampa, races are held all year at the **Naples–Fort Myers Greyhound Track** (tel 941/992-2411).

Central Florida has **Seminole Greyhound Park** (tel 407/699-4510) in Casselberry and **Sanford Orlando Kennel Club** (tel 407/831-1600) in Longwood. Gold Coast venues are the venerable **Palm Beach Kennel Club** (tel 561/683-2222), the **Hollywood Greyhound Track** (tel 954/454-9400) and, in the Miami area, the **Biscayne Kennel Club** (tel 305/754-3484) and the **Flagler Dog Track** (tel 305/649-3000).

**Hockey** As unlikely a locale as it might seem, Florida now has two major league professional hockey teams. The **Tampa Bay Lightning** of the NHL can be followed at the Exposition Hall (tel 813/229-8800). Miami has its own **Florida Panthers,** sharing Miami Arena (tel 305/577-4328) with the Miami Heat basketballers. Minor-league clubs represent Jacksonville, Daytona Beach, West Palm Beach, and Lakeland.

**Horse Racing** **Hialeah Park** (tel 305/885-8000), with its extravagant clubhouse and resident flock of hundreds of flamingoes, is a virtual synonym for the sport of kings. In Miami, **Calder Race Course** (tel 305/625-1311) has an air-conditioned grandstand, which makes it possible to hold races throughout the year. The periods of activity vary annually, however, so call ahead. For harness racing, the only possibility is **Pompano Track** (tel 954/972-2000) in Pompano Beach. Its future is uncertain, so, again, call ahead. In nearby Fort Lauderdale, thoroughbreds run at **Gulfstream Park** (tel 954/454-7000), site of the famous Breeders Cup. It observes a winter season. On the Gulf Coast, **Tampa Bay Downs** (tel 813/855-4401) hosts thoroughbreds from late December to early May.

**Jai Alai** The ancient Basque sport provokes furious and complicated betting. Players catch the ball *pelota*) in a long curved wicker basket (*cesta*) strapped to the arm, then fling it against a wall of the three-sided court (*fronton*) in the same fluid action. Ball speeds have been recorded at nearly 190 mph. Jai alai was introduced to the United States here, where the betting is legal and the game is played all year at various venues.

Frontons are found in Dania (tel 954/428-7766), Fort Pierce (tel 561/464-7500), Miami (tel 305/633-6400), Ocala (tel 904/591-2345), Orlando (tel 407/699-4510), Palm Beach (tel 561/844-2444), and Tampa (tel 813/831-1411).

## ACTIVITIES A TO Z

**Bicycling** Hills are low and the flatlands vast, so pleasant excursions of an hour or two or demanding tours covering 100 miles and more are equally possible and easy to plot. All cities and most of the larger towns have shops with bicycles for rent and advice about local trails and precautions. Many resort hotels make bikes available to guests, as well. For a free guide to cycling trails write the Florida Department of Transportation, Mail Station 82, 605 Suwanee St, Tallahassee, FL 32399 or call 904/487-1200.

**Camping** There are private campgrounds throughout the state, but the most desirable facilities and settings are usually found in state-owned recreation areas. About half of the 3 dozen preserves have campsites. Usage fees are rarely more than $20 a night. Stays are limited and there are restrictions on pets. Additional fees are charged for features and services such as waterfront locations, use of boat ramps, nature tours, and electrical hookups.

For a copy of the *Florida State Parks Guide*, write the Bureau of Parks Planning, Department of Natural Resources, Mail Station 535, 3900 Commonwealth Blvd, Tallahassee, FL 32399 or call 904/488-9872. For information about private campgrounds, write the Florida Campground Association, 1638 N Plaza Dr, Tallahassee, FL 32308, or call 904/656-8878.

**Canoeing** Enthusiasts find stretches of inviting water throughout the state, often with marked trails, as between Everglades City and Flamingo, along the Santa Fe River in the northeast, and on Little Manatee River, north of Tampa Bay. For information, write the Florida Association of Canoe Liveries and Outfitters, PO Box 1764, Arcadia, FL 33821 or call 941/494-1215.

**Diving/Snorkeling**  It is estimated that Florida's offshore waters hold over 4,000 shipwrecks, from Spanish galleons to German U-Boats. High underwater visibility and ideal temperatures contribute mightily to the diving and snorkeling experience, especially on expeditions to the only living coral reef in the continental United States, which lies a short distance east of the Keys, part of it contained by John Pennekamp State Park. Snorkelers can visit by party boat, and only average swimming ability is required.

Special certification is required for scuba diving. Most coastal localities have dive shops that provide lessons, and some resort hotels have intensive programs that can qualify students in a matter of days.

For a brochure about diving in the state, write the Florida Sports Foundation, 107 W Gaines St, Tallahassee, FL 32399 or call 904/488-8347.

**Fishing**  With thousands of miles of coastline, hundreds of miles of rivers and streams, and over 7,700 lakes of 10 acres or more, Florida can be likened to a 500-mile pier down the middle of a giant tank packed with fish. Anglers can wet their lines from a chartered sportfishing yacht, a thronged party boat, a dinghy, or a bridge or beach; every inclination and wallet can be accommodated. **Licenses** are required for both saltwater and freshwater fishing. Nonresidents can obtain licenses good for as few as seven days. They are sold in the bait-and-tackle shops found near every promising body of water. Rods, reels, and bait are provided by guides and chartered boats, with the client expected to provide food and drink, as a rule. Tackle can usually be rented at waterside hotels and tackle shops.

For a brochure, write the Florida Sports Foundation, 107 W Gaines St, Tallahassee, FL 32399 or call 904/488-8347. Questions about **freshwater fishing** can be addressed to the Florida Game and Fresh Water Fish Commission, Ferris Bryant Building, 620 S Meridian St, Tallahassee, FL 32399 or call 904/488-1960. Send questions about **saltwater fishing** to the Florida Department of Natural Resources, Mail Station 30, 3900 Commonwealth Blvd, Tallahassee, FL 32399 or call 904/488-7326.

**Golf**  Apart from the short but sudden downpours often experienced during the hottest months, Florida is a nearly ideal place to challenge the world's most prominent designers of golf courses. The presence of 20 PGA and LPGA tournaments every year is testimony to that happy fact, as are the more than

---

## SELECTED PARKS & RECREATION AREAS

- **Biscayne National Park,** PO Box 1369, Homestead, FL 33090 (tel 305/247-7275)
- **Dry Tortugas National Park,** c/o Everglades National Park, PO Box 279, Homestead, FL 33030 (tel 305/242-7700)
- **Everglades National Park,** PO Box 279, Homestead, FL 33030 (tel 305/242-7700)
- **Canaveral National Seashore,** 308 Julia St, Titusville, FL 32796-3521 (tel 407/267-1110)
- **Gulf Islands National Seashore,** 1801 Gulf Breeze Pkwy, Gulf Breeze, FL 32561 (tel 904/934-2600)
- **Big Cypress National Preserve,** HCR61, Box 110, Ochopee, FL 33943 (tel 941/695-4111)
- **Castillo de San Marcos National Monument,** One S Castillo Dr, St Augustine, FL 32084 (tel 904/829-6506)
- **Bahia Honda State Park,** US 1, MM 37, Big Pine Key, FL 33043 (tel 305/872-2353)
- **Big Lagoon State Recreation Area,** 12301 Gulf Beach Hwy, Pensacola, FL 32507 (tel 904/492-1595)
- **Falling Waters State Recreation Area,** Rte 5, Box 660, Chipley, FL 32428 (tel 904/638-6130)
- **Florida Caverns State Park,** 3345 Caverns Rd, Marianna, FL 32446 (tel 904/482-9598)
- **John Pennekamp Coral Reef State Park,** PO Box 487, Key Largo, FL 33037 (tel 305/451-1202)
- **John D MacArthur Beach State Park,** 10900 FL 703 (US A1A), North Palm Beach, FL 33408 (tel 561/624-6950)
- **Lake Griffin State Recreation Area,** 103 US 441/27, Fruitland Park, FL 34731 (tel 904/787-7402)
- **Lake Kissimmee State Park,** 14248 Camp Mack Rd, Lake Wales, FL 33853 (tel 813/696-1112)
- **Lake Manatee State Recreation Area,** 20007 FL 64, Bradenton, FL 34202 (tel 941/741-3028)
- **Manatee Springs State Park,** FL 320, Chiefland, FL (tel 352/493-6072)
- **Oscar Scherer State Park,** 1843 S Tamiami Trail, Osprey, FL 34229 (tel 941/483-5956)
- **Tomoka State Park,** 2099 N Beach St, Ormond Beach, FL 32174 (tel 904/676-4050)

---

1,000 courses—more than in any other state. The PGA itself is headquartered in Palm Beach. While knowing a member or being the guest of a participating hotel is necessary for entrance to some courses, many others are open to all, and many of the best courses are owned by resort hotels rather than country clubs. Consult a travel agent about current golf packages.

To obtain a guide listing important details about

all the state's courses, write the Florida Sports Foundation, 107 W Gaines St, Tallahassee, FL 32399 or call 904/488-8347.

**Guided Tours**   There is no end to the opportunities for informative and entertaining escorted tours, from the Conch Train that circulates through colorful Key West to the walks led by costumed lecturers through the historic district of Pensacola. The Everglades inspire many companies to offer a variety of excursions: riveting airboat rides from bases along the Tamiami Trail to Miccosukee "villages" deep in the swamp; two-hour and daylong cruises from Fort Lauderdale, Flamingo, and Everglades; tram tours from Shark Valley and Flamingo; even customized ecology-minded tours out of Miami of several days' duration.

Sightseeing boats steam around the Port of Miami and along the New River from Fort Lauderdale, while trolley tours take in the major sights on land in the same cities. Orientation tours of theme parks in the Orlando region are a virtual necessity and most of the major attractions provide them.

For information about the organizations affording these services, contact the chamber of commerce in the appropriate locality.

**Tennis**   Resort hotels with their own golf courses typically have tennis courts, too—something to keep in mind when making travel arrangements. Visitors staying in less expensive lodgings have access to over 7,700 courts throughout the state, many of them run by municipalities and open to all. Year-round playing conditions make Florida highly attractive; grass, clay, and hard courts are all available and many of them are lighted for night play.

For a brochure, write the Florida Tennis Association, 801 NE 167th St, Ste 301, North Miami Beach, FL 33162 or call 305/652-2866.

**Windsurfing**   Also known as sailboarding, this increasingly popular aquatic sport is pursued both on the ocean and on thousands of inland lakes. Most waterside resorts have sailboards for rent and provide instruction.

## ST AUGUSTINE, DAYTONA BEACH, AND CAPE CANAVERAL

| Start | Jacksonville |
|---|---|
| Finish | Kennedy Space Center |
| Distance | About 325 miles round-trip |
| Time | 3 days |
| Highlights | Historic sites, a marine life park, sugar mill ruins, pristine beaches, NASA facilities and exhibits |

This trip along the coast south of Jacksonville takes you to a number of historic places: St Augustine, with restored 18th-century buildings and homes; Fort Matanzas, an 18th-century Spanish defense outpost; and Bulow Plantation Ruins, with the remains of a sugar mill. You also stop at several small seaside towns and the world-renowned Daytona Beach, where the Daytona 500 auto race is held each year. After driving through an undeveloped natural seashore area, you will end your trip on a high note at the John F Kennedy Space Center at Cape Canaveral.

For additional information on accommodations, restaurants, and attractions in the region covered by the tour, look under specific cities in the listings portion of this book.

From downtown Jacksonville, take I-95 southbound to exit 98 and pick up US 1 south. Continue about 30 miles to:

1. **St Augustine.** Although this charming city has palm-fringed beaches, St Augustine is primarily known for its sense of history, with a 17th-century fort, horse-drawn carriages, cobblestone streets, old city gates, and the restored 18th-century Spanish Quarter. On Easter in 1513, Spanish explorer Juan Ponce de León claimed the land that was to become St Augustine for Spain, but the city wasn't founded until 1565 by Pedro Menéndez de Avilés, a Spanish admiral who arrived that year with some thousand settlers and a priest. St Augustine became America's first city, established 55 years before the Pilgrims landed at Plymouth Rock.

The city was owned by both the Spanish and the British over the years until Spain sold it to the United States in 1821. Union forces occupied St Augustine from 1862 until the end of the Civil War. In 1883, Standard Oil magnate Henry Flagler arrived to develop the area as a fashionable resort for the wealthy. By the turn of the century, Flagler had expanded tourism throughout Florida, building posh hotels and developing rail lines along the

eastern coastline. In 1887 and again in the early 1900s, fires destroyed several of St Augustine's original buildings. Then in the 1950s, a plan was devised to preserve and restore the remaining historic buildings, which may be visited today. You'll probably want to spend a day exploring Florida's past on foot.

Centrally located at St George St and Cathedral Place is the **Visitor Information Center** (tel 904/825-1064) situated at the beginning of a pedestrian walkway lined with shops, restaurants, and historic buildings. On sale at the center is a walking tour brochure (95¢) covering two main areas of the city. One tour begins and ends at the **Oldest House,** at 14 St Francis St. From here, the tour covers 33 stops; it turns up Marine St and wanders through the neighborhood, passing a number of 18th- and 19th-century homes and Marin House, Countess de Montjoye House, St Francis Barracks, the King's Bakery, St Francis Inn, and St Francis Park. The second tour begins at the **Plaza de la Constitucion,** south of the information center. It covers 31 stops, including the Basilica Cathedral of St Augustine, Government House, Flagler College, St Augustine City Hall, St John's County Court House, Palm Row, St Joseph's Convent, and Trinity Episcopal Church, as well as Victorian homes and bed-and-breakfast inns. These walking tours take about three or four hours total and provide a good overview of the city.

If you would like to visit a few sights rather than take a prescribed walking tour, here are a few highlights:

**Authentic Old Jail,** 167 San Marco Ave, at Williams St (tel 904/829-3800). This 1890 Victorian brick prison was built with the financial assistance of Henry Flagler and served the area until 1953. During the day, tours are conducted by costumed guides; visitors are shown the sheriff's living quarters, the kitchen, and prison cells, as well as exhibits relating to the jail's history.

**Castillo de San Marcos National Monument,** 1 Castillo Dr, between Orange and Charlotte Sts (tel 904/829-6506). This fort, designed to protect the city against British attacks, took the Spanish 23 years (1672–1695) to complete; it was made of massive coquina (shell rock) walls, with a double drawbridge entrance over a 40-foot moat. The Castillo was so well built that it was never captured in battle, nor did its walls ever crumble. Today you

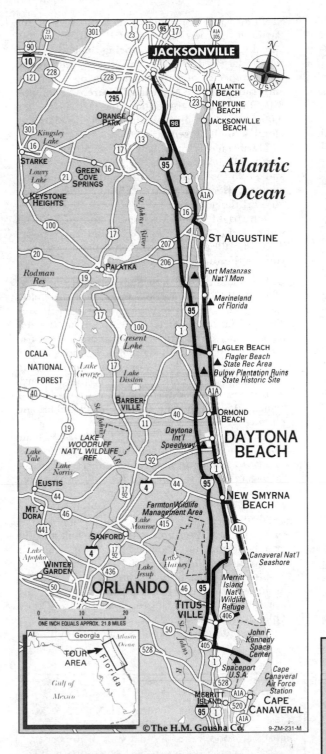

ry. You can also walk the upper-level gundeck; many of the copper and cast-iron cannons still present are at least 200 years old.

**Lightner Museum,** 75 King St, at Granada St (tel 904/824-2874). Henry Flagler's lavish Spanish Renaissance–style Alcazar Hotel, constructed in 1889, was bought in 1948 by publishing magnate Otto Lightner to house his collection of Victoriana. The first floor is devoted to a Victorian village with shopfront windows filled with period wares. Among the various displays are Victorian furnishings, porcelain and glass, automated musical instruments, artifacts, stuffed birds, train models, toys, and even an Egyptian mummy from 500 BC.

**The Oldest House,** 14 St Francis St, at Charlotte St (tel 904/824-2972). The Gonzales-Alvarez House, named after two of its past prominent owners, evolved from a two-room coquina dwelling built between 1702 and 1727. Rooms are furnished to simulate various historical times. Abandoned wells are on the site, and Native American, Spanish, and British artifacts (some of them found in the wells) are displayed.

**St Augustine Alligator Farm,** 999 Anastasia Blvd (FL A1A), at Old Quarry Rd (tel 904/824-3337). First opened in 1893, this attraction houses the world's largest collection of crocodilians, including alligators, crocodiles, caymans, and gavials.

**St Augustine's Restored Spanish Quarter,** entrance on St George St, between Cuna and Orange Sts (tel 904/825-6830). This two-block area south of the City Gate is St Augustine's most comprehensive historical neighborhood, re-creating Spanish colonial period architecture and landscape. Although about 90% of the area's buildings are reconstructions, several structures date back to the mid-18th century, including a few homes, such as the **Triay, Gómez, Gallegos, Gonzáles,** and **José Peso de Burgo and Francisco Pellicer houses.** Guides and craftspeople dressed in 18th-century attire are on site to provide information, and at the blacksmith shop hardware is manufactured using 18th-century methods.

## Take a Break

Finding a place to eat won't be hard in the restored Spanish Quarter. One pleasant, casual establishment in the area is the **Florida Cracker Cafe,** 81 St. George St (tel 904/829-0397), a lively eatery with hearty food and seating indoors and out.

can tour the vaulted powder-magazine room, a dank prison cell, a chapel, and guard rooms. Old storerooms now house exhibits on the fort's histo-

If you got a late start from Jacksonville, you may want to spend a night in St Augustine, which has a variety of lodging choices. Some bed-and-breakfasts are housed in historic inns, such as the **Kenwood Inn,** 38 Marine St (tel 904/824-2116). Also consider **Ponce de León Golf & Conference Resort,** 4000 US 1 N (tel 904/824-2821), a 350-acre complex with all the facilities of a traditional hotel. Many of the chain hotels have properties in town; look along FL A1A for family-oriented motels.

Next, from St Augustine, cross the Intracoastal Waterway to FL A1A and head south 14 miles until you reach:

2. **Fort Matanzas.** At this 298-acre national park, you can take a ferry (operating daily 9am–4:30pm except Tuesday) from the visitors center on the Anastasia River across the Matanzas River to an 18th-century fort on Rattlesnake Island. Completed in 1742, Fort Matanzas prevented enemy vessels from passing through the inlet south of the fort, thus protecting St Augustine.

As you enter the building's main stairway, imagine the approach by wooden ladder 200 years ago. The two original cast-iron cannons, left behind by the Spanish when they departed in 1821, can still be seen guarding the fortress. The lower level once housed 7 to 10 enlisted men who brought supplies in longboats. A low wall kept the powder magazine away from open flames used for heat and light in the officers' quarters. Up a narrow ladder, the observation deck provides a good view of the inlet to the south. The fort is open Wednesday–Monday 8:30am–5:30pm. Admission free.

While the island doesn't offer picnicking areas, you may wish to take a dip in the ocean across FL A1A, opposite the visitors center entrance, and enjoy your picnic there. A $4 parking fee is charged for the beach.

From Fort Matanzas, continue on FL A1A a little over 3½ miles south to:

3. **Marineland,** 9507 Ocean Shore Blvd (FL A1A) (tel 904/471-1111). First opened in 1938 as an underwater motion picture studio and tourist attraction, this marine park on the Atlantic Ocean and the Intracoastal Waterway has long been known for its dolphin shows held in the Dolphin Stadium tank. The performing dolphins leap as high as 16 feet in the air to take food from a jumpmaster's hand. The 20-minute shows are held 5 times a day.

You can also observe the circular **Oceanarium,** home of a permanent colony of Atlantic bottlenose dolphins. This underwater setting is created with 400,000 gallons of filtered sea water. In another, rectangular Oceanarium are 1,000 specimens representing 124 different species of game and predator fish and other marine life. Fish are hand-fed four times a day by scuba divers.

Other attractions include colorful fish of the Pacific in the new **"Secrets of the Reef"** exhibit, and the **"Wonders of the Spring"** aquarium, the world's largest freshwater fish display, with native Florida species of gar, largemouth bass, sunfish, and crappie. At the **Aquarius Theatre,** a 22-minute, 3-D film is shown throughout the day. More than 6,000 rare shells may be admired at the **Margaret Herrick Shell Museum.**

Marineland is open daily 9am–5:30pm. Admission is $14.95 for adults, $9.95 for teens 13–18, and $7.95 for children 3–12; children under 3 are admitted free, and visitors 65 and older receive 20% off the adult price.

Turn right out of Marineland and go 14 miles south on FL A1A to FL 100 and the Bulow loop. Take FL 100 a little more than 3 miles west until you see the turnoff, left or south, to:

4. **Bulow Plantation Ruins State Historic Site** (tel 904/439-2219). Continue 3 miles, past the Bulow Campground, to the entrance of the historic site. The plantation site has a dirt road on the left leading into a wooded area. About one mile ahead is a walking path known as the Bulow Woods Hiking Trail, a four-mile loop for those interested in communing with nature. A bit further onward, visitors are required to pay a $2 entrance fee per vehicle. Beyond the entrance are picnic tables and parking.

Established in 1821 by Maj Charles William Bulow, the plantation once contained 2,200 acres of sugar cane, cotton, rice, and indigo. Under the management of Bulow's son, John, it thrived until the outbreak of the Second Seminole War when John abandoned it and moved northward. Around 1836, the Seminoles burned "Bulowville," and all that is left are the ruins of the sugar mill and the crumbling mansion foundation. Visitors can walk the grounds or drive along a 2.7-mile scenic loop.

Stop at the interpretive center near the ruins for an informative history of the plantation, and have lunch at the picnic area overlooking Bulow Creek. Open 9am–5pm.

Just south of the cutoff to Bulow Plantation is:

---

## Take a Break

**Pier Restaurant on Flagler Beach,** 215 S FL A1A, Flagler Beach (tel 904/439-3891), serving mostly seafood, offers a great view of the ocean and the pier. Another good local spot for the freshest fish is **High Tides at Shack Jack's,** 2805 S FL A1A (tel 904/439-3344).

**5. Flagler Beach.** This stretch of sand's most visible landmark is the 898-foot pier extending out into the Atlantic. To walk onto the pier costs 75¢. If you bring your own rod and reel, you can fish for $2.75. There's also a shack at the pier entrance that rents fishing equipment.

Continue 3 miles south on FL A1A from the pier area to:

**6. Gamble Rogers Memorial State Recreation Area,** at Flagler Beach, 3100 S FL A1A (tel 904/439-2474). This fine family camping area is a 145-acre park bordering the Atlantic Ocean on the east and the Intracoastal Waterway on the west. From the campgrounds, cross the dune walkovers for swimming and surf fishing along the beach; pompano, whiting, and bluefish are frequently caught here. Stroll the shell-strewn beaches and observe pelicans and sandpipers.

From May to September sea turtles return to the beach here to lay their eggs. You can also catch sight of various songbirds as they migrate along the Atlantic Flyway in the spring and fall.

The park has a boat ramp on the Intracoastal Waterway, a picnic area with shelters, and hiking trails.

As you continue the drive south on FL A1A, you'll notice the sea oats and scrub oak that protect the dunes. Leaving Flagler Beach city limits, you will enter the North Peninsula State Recreation Area. After driving 14 miles, you'll pass Ormond Beach, where hotels, condominiums, and shopping centers vie for tourists' attention. Then, 3 miles south of Ormond Beach, is:

**7. Daytona Beach.** This world-renowned beach is 23 miles long and 500 feet wide at low tide, and you can still drive and park on the sand (maximum speed is 10 mph). Opportunities for boating, tennis, golf, and water sports abound. The area, however, becomes much less relaxed when the Daytona 500 comes to town; the event is the culmination of Speedweeks, held from late January to mid-February at the Daytona International Speedway (see below). Also in February, during Bike Week, thousands of leather-clad motorcyclists congregate here. Finally, the area plays host to thousands of college students from around the country during their spring break. (You'll especially want to avoid Daytona Beach at this time if you're looking for a peaceful holiday.)

Daytona is filled with hotels, though few can be considered standouts. One of the nicer large hotels is the **Adam's Mark Daytona Beach Resort,** 100 N Atlantic Ave (tel 904/254-8200). If you're seeking something cozier, you might want to try **Captain's Quarters Inn,** 3711 S Atlantic Ave (tel 904/767-

3199). For the budget-minded, there's the **Days Inn Daytona Central,** 1909 S Atlantic Ave (tel 904/255-4492).

If the beach doesn't have enough to keep you busy, you can visit the **Birthplace of Speed Museum,** 160 E Granada Blvd (tel 904/672-5657), a small showcase of exhibits on racing history; the **Daytona International Speedway,** 1801 W International Speedway Blvd (US 92) (tel 904/253-RACE), with a visitors center that has tours of the racing facility; the **Museum of Arts and Sciences,** 1040 Museum Blvd (tel 904/255-0285), with a notable collection of Cuban art; and **Ponce de Leon Inlet Lighthouse,** 4931 S Peninsula Dr (tel 904/761-1821), the second-tallest US lighthouse, with 203 steel steps for you to climb to the top.

From Daytona Beach, continue south along the US 1 about 12 miles into New Smyrna Beach. Turn left, or east, at FL 44 and follow that road, which becomes FL A1A and leads to:

**8. Canaveral National Seashore.** Continue on FL A1A for about 9 miles, when you'll see a sign welcoming visitors to this undeveloped, gorgeous natural seashore; about a mile further is the visitors center (tel 904/428-3384), open daily 8am–4:30pm. You're now in the north district of the seashore.

Retrace your steps to US 1 and drive south 29 miles into **Titusville** and turn left on FL 406. Follow this road 7 miles to **Merritt Island** and the south district of Canaveral National Seashore. Merritt Island, which has its own visitors center (tel 904/861-0667), encompasses a refuge for endangered waterfowl, birds, alligators, and other wildlife. The pristine beaches here are lovely to stroll along. Both the north and south districts of the Seashore are administered by the National Park Service. Continue to the ocean for a view of the uninhabited, pristine beach.

Follow signs from Merritt Island to:

**9. Cape Canaveral** and the **John F Kennedy Space Center.** Cape Canaveral, practically synonymous with NASA, is where all US manned space missions are launched. From the early 1960s and America's first manned space flight to today's manned and unmanned shuttle launches, the events at Cape Canaveral have captured the world's attention. The Kennedy Space Center comprises the Air Force Museum, the main space center, the Astronauts Memorial, US Space Camp, and Spaceport USA.

**Spaceport USA** (tel 407/452-2121), the center's main exhibition hall, features two 5½-story screens in the IMAX Theater, which shows three space-exploration films: *Destiny in Space, Blue Planet,* and *The Dream Is Alive,* which features footage filmed by

NASA astronauts. Admission to the theater is $4 for adults and $2 for children 3–11. Other parts of Spaceport USA are free, including a full-size replica of a space shuttle dubbed *Explorer*. Here you can see a cockpit, a payload bay cargo area, and flight crew living quarters. The best time to visit Spaceport USA is before 11am, when lines are shortest.

Guided tours originate at Spaceport USA. Don't miss the tour that includes the *Apollo 11* and space shuttle launch sites, the Flight Crew Training Build-ing, and the Vehicle Assembly Building. Another tour takes you to the Air Force Museum, which has military rockets that have been modified for NASA use. Other points of interest include the mission control station for the *Gemini* and *Mercury* projects and a memorial to the original seven astronauts.

Exit Spaceport USA on FL 405 and drive west to US 1, or cross US 1 and continue on FL 405 to I-95 N, which is the faster route back to Jacksonville, a distance of about 165 miles.

## MIAMI TO THE EVERGLADES

| | |
|---|---|
| Start | Miami |
| Finish | Everglades National Park |
| Distance | About 160 miles round-trip |
| Time | 1 day |
| Highlights | Art deco district, scenic drive, nature trails, cruises, outdoor recreation |

For those seeking to escape the hectic pace of Miami and the neon glitter of Miami Beach, this fairly short tour takes you to Everglades National Park, a majestically beautiful subtropical wildlife sanctuary that allows you to observe delicate plant and animal life up close in their natural state. First, however, you may opt for a quick refreshment stop in either the art deco district of South Miami Beach or the trend-setting community of Coconut Grove before setting off on the longer drive to the wildlife refuge. At the park, you can drive a scenic 38-mile road, walk on nature trails, take a sightseeing cruise, have a picnic lunch, or, if you're feeling more adventurous, rent a canoe for an afternoon. If you're looking to escape crowds, you may wish to drive to the park either during midweek or on an overcast day.

You should also keep in mind that mosquitoes and other biting insects can make your visit particularly unpleasant from May through the summer months. However, if you do visit the park during this time, *be sure to bring insect repellent.* Otherwise, winter is a better time to explore the park, when the mosquitoes are on vacation as well. All park activities are in full operation during the winter months, and the best viewing of wildlife is from December through March.

For additional information on accommodations, restaurants, and attractions in the region covered by the tour, look under specific cities in the listings portion of this book.

1. **Miami and Miami Beach.** Any first-time visitor to South Florida usually spends at least two nights in Miami, Florida's largest city, known around the world for its white sand beaches, glistening waters, sun-filled days, and vibrant multicultural population. Miami Beach is clearly the main draw for visitors. Although tourism declined here in the 1960s and 1970s, the area has witnessed a resurgence in visitors since the late 1980s. Its huge self-contained resort hotels, with restaurants, activities, and entertainment, appeal to international tourists and large convention crowds.

2. **South Beach.** Located at the southern end of Miami Beach, this neighborhood contains the largest concentration of **art deco architecture** in the world. The district culminates in the chic 15-block beachfront stretch known as **Ocean Drive;** most of the glamorous old and not-so-old hotels with flowing designs and pastel exteriors on this strip were built in the late 1930s and early 1940s. South Beach, or SoBe, as it is also called, is a thrilling renaissance community populated by poor artists, up-and-coming young investors, pensioners, and the usual mixture of Miami's ethnic groups. The trendy clubs and cafes along Ocean Drive attract working models and photographers, celebrities, musicians, writers, artists, and vacationers.

From Miami Beach, take Washington St or Collins Ave south to reach 5th St W, which becomes the MacArthur Causeway (US 41) and turns into I-395. First you'll pass Star Island on your right. Stay in the left lanes so you don't end up taking a wrong exit, but take a quick look at the cruise ships docked in the Port of Miami. You'll likely see a dozen or so of these vessels on weekends.

From I-395 enter I-95, heading south while the downtown area whizzes by on your left. Stay in the middle lanes and shortly you'll see the Key Biscayne exit. That's your cue that I-95 will end in half a mile to become US 1, a three-lane highway hemmed in on one side by concrete overpasses and strip shopping centers.

From here you can choose to continue immediately on to the Everglades or to make the next stop on this tour. Off US 1, also known as Dixie Hwy at this point, go left on Lejeune Rd and left again on Poinciana Ave into the center of:

3. **Coconut Grove,** a colorful upscale community of pedestrian walkways, boutiques, nightspots, restaurants, and cafes, which lend themselves to great people-watching, especially at night. Sidewalks are often packed with business types, college students, and a multitude of foreign tourists. The heart of Coconut Grove lies at the intersection of Grand Ave, Main Hwy, and McFarlane Rd. At the turn of the century, workers came here from the Bahamas for employment at a new hotel called the Peacock Inn; today Bahamian-style wooden homes, built by these early transplants, still stand on Charles St.

Take US 1 south from Coconut Grove. About 9 miles south of downtown is FL 878, also known as the Snapper Creek Expressway. Take the right here under the overpass and head west: You'll avoid

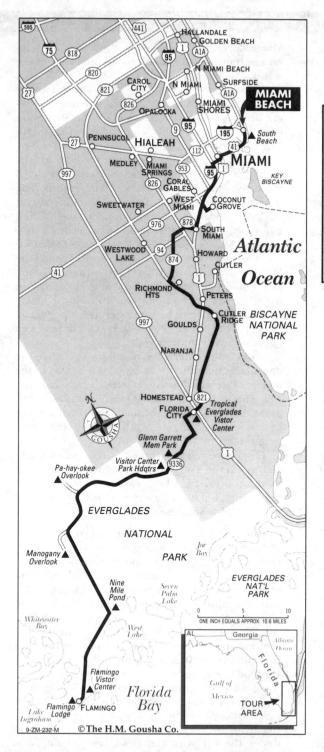

several miles of stop-and-go traffic. Continue on FL 878 until it enters the Don Shula Expwy and a tollgate (25¢).

After you exit the tollgate, you're now driving on what is known as Florida's Turnpike. Continue for 8 miles to the next toll (50¢). Along this route is mostly flat farmland. In another 10 miles, the turnpike ends at US 1 in Florida City.

---

## Take a Break

If you are leaving Miami early in the day, make a stop at one of Coconut Grove's many sidewalk cafes. **Joffrey's Coffee & Tea Co,** 3434 Main Hwy (tel 305/448-0848), will provide you with a caffeine fix to keep you perky until noon. If you stop in the area later in the day, **Green Street Cafe,** 3468 Commodore Plaza (tel 305/444-0244), will serve you more substantial fare like rack of lamb and various pastas, as well as satisfying coffee and dessert.

---

At US 1, you'll see a sign for **Everglades National Park.** About 1,000 feet past the turnoff, on the right next to the Burger King, is the:

4. **Tropical Everglades Visitor Association,** 160 US 1, in Florida City (tel 305/245-9180 or toll free 800/388-9669), operated by the Greater Miami Convention and Visitors Bureau. The office provides brochures and information about the area and is open daily 8am–5pm.

From the turnoff to the Everglades National Park Main Visitors Center, proceed 14 miles on FL 9336. At the 4-way stop sign near the Robert Is Here farm stand, make a left onto 192nd Ave SW; after driving 1½ miles you'll come to another stop sign, where you turn right onto 376th St SW. The area around here is mostly farmland, and from fall to early spring several trucks are parked at this intersection selling fresh vegetables and fruits.

Just before the entrance to Everglades National Park is a small picnic area called **Glenn Garrett Memorial Park,** with a handful of picnic tables and palm trees on hand but little more. You may prefer to wait until you get into the park to choose a picnic site.

At the tollgate to the park, visitors pay $5 per carload; hikers and cyclists pay $3 per person. The gatehouse is open 24 hours. On the right is the:

5. **Main Visitors Center** (tel 305/242-7700), which is open daily 8am–5pm. The center has orientation brochures and maps of the park, as well as rest rooms and refreshments in vending machines.

Everglades National Park covers the entire southern tip of the Florida peninsula and encompasses more than 2,000 square miles and 1.5 million acres. The term "everglades" came into use more than a century ago as a corruption of "river glades," which was used on an 18th-century map. The term refers to the sheets of slow-moving water clogged with tall sawgrass that characterize the Everglades. This unique, marshy tropical area, dotted by hammocks of hardwood trees and clumps of coastal mangroves, contains a treasure trove of plant and animal life.

Originally, water flowed unimpeded from **Lake Okeechobee,** the main source of water nourishing the land. But beginning in the late 1800s, large tracts were drained through a system of canals in the hopes of using the swampland for agriculture. In the late 1920s, two hurricanes caused extensive flooding and loss of life in South Florida, and the southern end of Lake Okeechobee was diked. The retaining walls built in the 1960s at this end of the lake, together with land development in Big Cypress Swamp (another major source of water), have partially choked off the natural flow of water to the Everglades, threatening its many fragile ecosystems. Today, nesting and wading birds are only a small fraction of their former number. The federal government is currently working with the state as part of a water- and land-management agreement to preserve the Everglades and reverse its decline.

Meanwhile, visitors come here to experience what the Everglades still has to offer: beautiful and unusual vegetation; tens of thousands of birds, including beautiful white egrets, blue herons, and eagles; and otters, tiny tree frogs, alligators, racoons, bobcats, deer, and many other creatures, all trying to survive in a shrinking homeland.

For your one day in the park, take the single road that winds its way for about 38 miles from the Main Visitors Center to the **Flamingo Visitors Center** (open daily 7:30am–5pm) in the southwest corner of the state. This scenic drive provides a lovely introduction to the area; along the road, you'll drive through a half-dozen distinct ecosystems, including a dwarf cypress forest, endless saw grass, and thick mangroves. You'll also discover well-marked walking trails, elevated boardwalks, and informative signs.

Just beyond the main entrance, at the Royal Palm Visitors Center, are two of the park's most well-trodden paths. All year, you can usually be assured of seeing wildlife on the **Anhingo Trail,** a ½-mile loop on a boardwalk popular for photographing birds and alligators. The **Gumbo Limbo Trail** took a beating from Hurricane Andrew in 1992, but it's still open for a walk through tropical hardwood hammock. Experienced hikers can get advice at the Main Visitors Center for more challenging hikes around the park. The staff can direct you to pineland, marsh, and hammock trails. Those

looking for less demanding routes will appreciate the boardwalk trails, ranging from ¼- to ½-mile in length, along the main park road; these trails include Pa-hay-okee Overlook, West Lake Trail, Pinelands Trail, and Mahogany Hammock.

At the end of the 38 miles on the park's main road lies the tiny "town" of Flamingo, and the:

6. **Flamingo Lodge Marina and Outpost Resort,** 1 Flamingo Lodge Hwy (tel 305/253-2241 or 941/ 813/695-3101). The starting point for several sightseeing excursions, it is the only lodging inside the park. The clean, simple rooms overlook Florida Bay, and the hotel has a swimming pool and gift shop. It is most busy in February.

> ## Take a Break
> The Flamingo Lodge complex includes the second-floor **Flamingo Lodge Restaurant** (tel 941/ 695-3101), which serves a mostly traditional American menu and a few regional dishes at moderate prices. You have a fine view here of Florida Bay.

The day-tripper might plan his or her day by arriving in the park before noon and lunching at the Flamingo Restaurant or taking a picnic lunch in a canoe. This could be followed by an afternoon tour or hike to complete your introduction to the park.

Just steps away from the Flamingo Lodge is the:

7. **Flamingo Visitor Center,** which provides information on park activities such as canoe rentals. For advance information on sightseeing tours and times, contact the Flamingo Lodge Marina (see above).

The marina is the starting point for two cruises which travel around nearby estuaries and sandbars for a look at local plant and animal life. The 90-minute **Florida Bay Cruise,** held daily, gives you a chance to observe egrets, herons, ibis, ospreys, bald eagles, and pelicans (cost: $8.50 adults, $4.50 children 6–12; children under 6 free). On the 2-hour **White Water Bay Cruise,** you see the same wildlife species as on the other tour, but you'll also sight alligators and crocodiles; this trip also runs daily (cost: $12 adults, $6 children 6–12, children under 6 free).

A two-hour tour on the **Wilderness Tram** takes visitors through tropical hardwood hammock and mangrove forests, where you're likely to encounter turtles, alligators, snakes, and other wildlife and plant species. A naturalist guide narrates each tour.

The tram departs from Flamingo Lodge from November to April only (cost: $7.50 adults, $4 children 6–12, children under 6 free).

To do sightseeing on your own, you may elect to rent a skiff with a 15-horsepower motor for $65 for an entire day or $47 for a half day. Canoes rent for $7 an hour, $20 for a half day, $25 for a full day. A full-day rental begins at 7am and runs to 5pm. Half-day rentals are good for up 5 hours. Bicycles rent for $2.50 per hour, $7 for half days, or $12 for full days. A small office at the marina provides rental equipment.

Hardcore nature lovers may come to the Everglades to do some backcountry exploring by canoe to remote campsites dotting the shoreline, from the Flamingo Visitor Center in the south to the Gulf Coast Visitor Center in Everglades City in the north. Everglades City is accessed from Miami via US 41 and FL 29, which should not be confused with the Florida City route into the Everglades.

The **Wilderness Waterway,** between the two visitor centers, is open to both canoes and powerboats and meanders for 99 miles through the largest mangrove forest in the United States. A considerably more modest canoe route goes from Flamingo around Cape Sable, providing a good opportunity to see majestic sunsets on an overnight round trip of 10 miles. In addition, the nine-mile **Canoe Trail** offers viewing of wading birds and other wildlife such as alligators, as well as a freshwater marsh. Canoeists can do some hiking on this trip to a ground site or backcountry chickee (a wooden platform with partial roof) for staying overnight.

Visitors who would rather camp out than stay overnight at the Flamingo Lodge can use park **campsites** when they bring their own equipment. The Flamingo camping area on the Florida Bay has 300 sites and provides free (cold) outdoor showers. At Long Pine Key, a pine forest that wraps partly around a lake, 100 sites for camping and RVs are available, with a dumping station but no hookups. Campers can arrange for space on a first-come, first-served basis by calling the Main Visitor Center (tel 941/695-3941) for reservations. The busiest time for camping is February.

Exiting the park at about 5pm allows you to return to Miami in daylight. Retrace your steps, following the road to the park entrance and continuing to the 4-way intersection, where you turn right on FL 9336, which leads to Florida City and US 1 N. A nonstop drive to downtown Miami takes about 75 minutes in normal traffic. And if you haven't yet made it to Coconut Grove, now is a good time on your way back.

# Driving the State

| | |
|---|---|
| Start | Orlando |
| Finish | Lakeland |
| Distance | About 130 miles round-trip |
| Time | 1–3 days |
| Highlights | Rural countryside, baseball stadiums, lavish gardens, the lake district, horticultural amusement park, Frank Lloyd Wright–designed college buildings |

Everything is at your fingertips when you vacation in central Florida. Orlando is less than 1 hour from Cape Canaveral and the John F Kennedy Space Center, 90 minutes from Tampa and exciting Busch Gardens, 1 hour from the famous Daytona Beach, and of course, in the middle of a magical kingdom called Walt Disney World. On this tour, the varied route takes you to amusement parks, historic sights, and quiet countryside. Realistically, you can't do all these activities in one day, especially with children in tow, so plan your itinerary selectively.

For additional information on accommodations, restaurants, and attractions in the region covered by the tour, look under specific cities in the listings portion of this book.

From almost anywhere in the Orlando area, you can hop on I-10 to begin this trip. Heading west on I-10 through Kissimmee, you'll cross under the overpass of US 192, also known as Irlo Bronson Memorial Hwy, which runs north-south. Following this road south would bring you to Florida's Turnpike, but instead keep heading west on I-10 for 9 miles to exit 23 and US 27, and:

1. **Baseball City.** It's mainly an area of chain restaurants and hotels, but if you look left or east from the highway you'll immediately spot **Baseball City Stadium,** a sports complex that is the spring training camp site for the Kansas City Royals.

    Five miles south from the exit, on US 27 past citrus groves, is **Webb's Candy Factory.** If it's not too early, you may wish to sample the candy factory's goat-milk fudge or ice cream.

    Continue south an additional 2 miles on US 27 and you'll reach the:

2. **Haines City Tourist Information Center** (tel 941/422-3751), located on the southwest corner of US 27 and Commerce Ave. Operated by the Chamber of Commerce, the center, which is open Monday–Friday 8:30am–4:30pm, can provide helpful information on golf and freshwater fishing in Haines City. For the more adventurous, the center will provide names of companies who offer airboat rides and hang-gliding instruction.

If you're in the Haines City area in the evening, you can take the whole family to:

3. **Southern Country Danceland,** 117 N 7th St, just north of US 92 and east of US 27 (tel 941/422-1642). This dance hall sponsors evening line dancing Monday–Thursday 7:30–10pm for beginners, and children are welcome. Friday and Saturday is open dance night (8pm–midnight) with a DJ and band. Smoking and alcohol are not permitted. Admission is $5.30 for adults, $2.65 for children 6–12.

    Next continue 1 mile from the tourist information center along US 27 to US 17 and US 92 west to Winter Haven (see below). Cypress Gardens is a 13-mile drive from here, and Lake Wales is a 16-mile drive. If you wish to spend the day playing golf, you can take FL 544 east from Winter Haven through Dundee to the **Grenelefe Golf and Tennis Resort,** 3200 FL 546, Haines City (tel 941/422-7511), about 7 miles away.

    Nine miles south of Haines City on US 27 is the Cypress Gardens turnoff, also known as FL 540. You can take this road west to the gardens if you want a nonstop route. But to get to the next stop on this tour continue on US 27 another 6 miles into Lake Wales. Turn left on County Rd 17A and go 1½ miles to Alternate US 27. (It may seem as though you're going south on 17A, but the sign says north.) Take a right on Alternate US 27 and continue to the entrance of:

4. **Bok Tower Gardens** (tel 941/676-9412). This sanctuary was envisioned by the editor and publisher Edward William Bok (1863–1930). The 128-acre estate comprises the lovely Pinewood House and Gardens, a cafe and gift shop, picnic areas, and a visitor center where lecture films are presented. The grounds include walking paths and landscaped grounds bursting with azalea and camellia. More than 125 species of birds live within the gardens.

    A central attraction is a 205-foot pink marble and coquina stone structure known as the **Bok Singing Tower,** dedicated by President Calvin Coolidge in 1929. Atop the tower is a carillon where recitals are held each day at 3pm; clock music is heard every half hour beginning at 10am. The

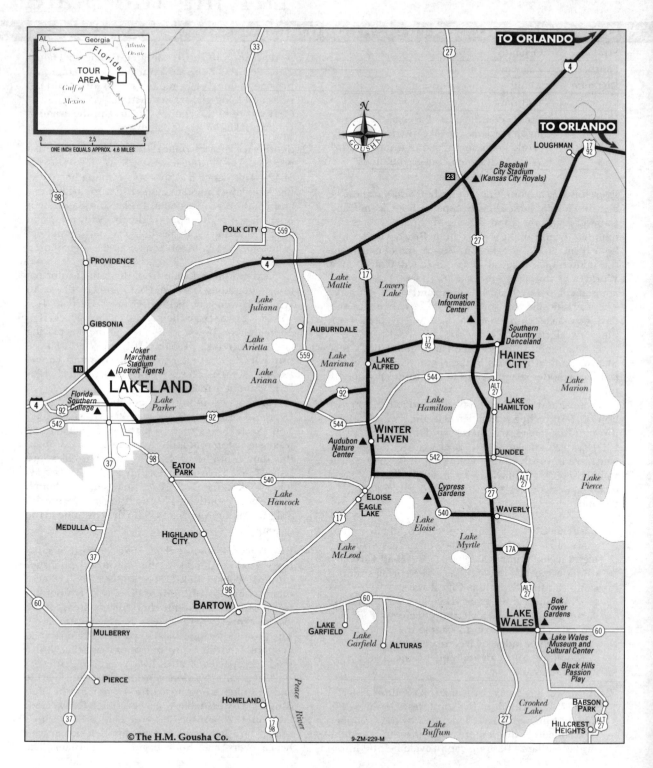

ONE INCH EQUALS APPROX. 4.6 MILES

TO ORLANDO

TO ORLANDO

LOUGHMAN

Baseball
City Stadium
(Kansas City Royals)

POLK CITY

PROVIDENCE

GIBSONIA

Lake
Mattie

Lake
Juliana

Lowery
Lake

Tourist
Information
Center

Southern
Country
Danceland

HAINES
CITY

Lake
Marion

AUBURNDALE

Lake
Arietta

Lake
Mariana

LAKE
ALFRED

Joker
Marchant
Stadium
(Detroit Tigers)

LAKELAND

Lake
Ariana

Lake
Hamilton

LAKE
HAMILTON

Florida
Southern
College

Lake
Parker

Lake
Hamilton

DUNDEE

Lake
Pierce

WINTER
HAVEN

Audubon
Nature
Center

EATON
PARK

Cypress
Gardens

WAVERLY

MEDULLA

Lake
Hancock

ELOISE

Lake
Eloise

Lake
Myrtle

HIGHLAND
CITY

EAGLE
LAKE

Lake
McLeod

Bok
Tower
Gardens

LAKE
WALES

BARTOW

Lake Wales
Museum and
Cultural Center

MULBERRY

LAKE
GARFIELD

Lake
Garfield

ALTURAS

Black Hills
Passion
Play

PIERCE

HOMELAND

Peace
River

Crooked
Lake

BABSON
PARK

HILLCREST
HEIGHTS

Lake
Buffum

©The H.M. Gousha Co.

9-ZM-229-M

## Take a Break

Shaded by lovely trees, the **Garden Cafe and Gift Shop** inside Bok Tower Gardens makes an excellent stop for a late morning bite or a full lunch, with hot and cold entrees and a daily special. The cafe operates daily from 9am–5pm, although the menu is on the lighter side from 3pm till closing.

57-bell carillon houses bronze bells that weigh from 17 pounds to nearly 12 tons. Bok Tower Gardens is open daily all year from 8am to 6pm.

As you exit the gardens, continue on Tower Blvd, which leads to:

5. **Lake Wales.** Here you can relax by the small, serene lake or stroll through the charming downtown **historic district,** listed on the National Register of Historic Places and featuring an arcade of shops and restaurants.

If you exit the gardens and turn right on Burns Ave, you'll head back toward Alternate US 27. Tower Blvd ends at the water, where the road comes to a T; turn right here on N Lakeshore Blvd and then right again at Central Ave and follow signs to US 27. Stop by the:

6. **Lake Wales Museum and Cultural Center,** 325 S Scenic Hwy (Alternate US 27) (tel 941/676-5443), housed in a restored 1928 railroad station that was once a stop on the Atlantic Coast Line. You can see a 1916 Pullman train car, a locomotive from 1944, a 1926 caboose, and more railroad memorabilia.

Lake Wales is also the winter home of the **Black Hills Passion Play** (tel 941/676-1495), whose season runs from mid-February through mid-April and Easter Sunday. The very popular two-hour matinee and evening performances illustrate the last days of Christ. Reserve tickets well in advance.

Follow US 27 north, then FL 540 west, and 4 miles later you'll reach:

7. **Cypress Gardens,** Cypress Gardens Blvd, Winter Haven (tel 941/324-2111, or toll free 800/237-4826, 800/282-2123 in FL). Opened in 1936 as Florida's first theme park with 16 acres of public gardens, Cypress Gardens now extends over 200 lush acres and features more than 8,000 varieties of flowers and plants from more than 75 countries. The gardens are combined with park rides and shows for the young and young-at-heart. Among the many offerings here are a lake cruise on a pontoon boat; a revolving platform rising 153 feet above the gardens for a bird's-eye view; an entertaining bird show starring macaws, cockatoos, and Amazon parrots; boat rides on inner canals; and exhibits ranging from hundreds of antique radios to a fine sculpture garden.

Each season has its own floral splendor. In late winter and early spring, you can see more than 40 varieties of bougainvillea, 60 kinds of azalea, and 500 types of roses in bloom. Late spring brings the scent of crape myrtles, magnolias, and gardenias. During the summer, visitors are dazzled by jasmine, hibiscus, and birds of paradise. Autumn is notable for the floss silk trees, camellias, and golden rain trees, while winter brings displays of thousands of red, white, and pink poinsettias, as well as chrysanthemums, and trees decorated for the holiday season.

You can easily spend several hours here viewing the gardens and watching the shows, which include the famous year-round **waterskiing show.** There are a variety of indoor and outdoor dining spots in the park for both snacks and full meals, at reasonable prices.

Cypress Gardens is open daily 9:30am–5:30pm, except on Christmas Eve (shorter hours), and November 25 through January 8 (when the park closes at 10pm). Admission (excluding tax) is $24.95 for adults, $21.20 for senior citizens over 55, and $16.45 for children 3–9; children under 3 are admitted free.

From Cypress Gardens, bird-watchers and other nature enthusiasts will want to turn right onto FL 540 E, and go 2 miles to visit the:

8. **Audubon Nature Center,** 115 Lameraux Rd, Winter Haven (tel 941/324-7304), a 40-acre refuge partly embracing Lake Ned. Here you can stroll along two nature trails or stop for a picnic. Bring binoculars for up-close views of eagles, blue herons, and ospreys.

If instead you turn *left* on FL 540 from Cypress Gardens and drive 5 miles west, you will come to:

9. **Winter Haven.** This area, with 14 lakes, is a mecca for freshwater fishing, particularly for large-mouth bass, bream, black crappie, and sunshine bass.

Meanwhile, baseball's **Cleveland Indians** call Winter Haven their home in winter. The **Holiday Inn Winter Haven/Cypress Gardens,** 1150 3rd St SW (tel 941/294-4451), becomes headquarters for the American League team during spring training.

If at this point you wish to head on to Orlando, you have a choice of taking US 17 north about 12 miles to I-4 and heading east to Orlando proper, 53 miles away; or staying on US 17 as it joins US 92 northward, and proceeding east to Orlando via the backroads of Orange and Osceola Counties. The backroads are a bit more adventuresome as you drive through Haines City, Davenport, Loughman, and Kissimmee back to the familiar territory of the

Beeline Expressway, International Dr, and everything else at Walt Disney World's doorstep.

From Winter Haven, head north on US 17, then west on US 92 for about 20 miles, at which point you will reach:

**10. Lakeland.** From US 92, turn left on Florida Ave and proceed 1 mile to Pine St, and turn left again for some antique shopping in this small city's **antiques district,** which begins a block from Florida Ave. Lakeland is the winter home of the **Detroit Tigers** baseball team, who play about 30 "Grapefruit League" exhibition games from early March to early April, half of them at Joker Marchant Stadium, 2305 Lakeland Hills Blvd (tel 941/682-1401).

An exciting spectacle takes place here each April, when as many as 300,000 visitors gather to watch and participate in Lakeland's weeklong **Sun 'n' Fun EAA Fly-In and Annual Aviation Convention,** held in back of Linder Regional Airport, 4175 Medulla Rd. See air shows, lectures, and aircraft displays. Adjacent to the airport is a 40-acre campus housing the **Sun 'n' Fun Air Museum and Aviation Center** (tel 941/644-0741), with its many informative displays on the history of flight. The museum hours are Monday–Friday 9am–5pm, Saturday 10am–4pm, Sunday noon–4pm.

From the Pine St turnoff that took you into the antiques district, continue 3 miles to McDonald St and turn left. Proceed 6 blocks to Johnson St (which dead-ends at Lake Hollingsworth) and take a right. You are now on the west side of the campus of:

**11. Florida Southern College,** Johnson and McDonald Sts (tel 941/680-4110), a liberal arts institution affiliated with the United Methodist Church. Concentrated on the west side of the campus are 12 buildings designed by Frank Lloyd Wright, which are usually open to the public throughout the day, except during holiday recess and weekends.

The **Thad Buckner Building,** completed in 1945, was originally a library but today houses the **Frank Lloyd Wright Visitors Center.** Among the classic Wright touches here are the use of geometric shapes and design, fireplaces, and clerestory windows. There are exhibits of furniture pieces as well as drawings and photographs. The center is open Tuesday–Friday 11am–4pm, Saturday 10am–2pm, and Sunday 2pm–4pm. For a monthly calendar of events, call 941/860-4597 or 941/680-4110.

The **Annie Pheiffer Chapel,** also designed by Wright, was constructed with student labor between 1939 and 1941. Its tower is fondly referred to as a "bicycle rack in the sky." Wright used leaded glass to complete the **William Danforth Chapel,** with a frame constructed of native Florida tidewater red cypress wood. He also designed the pews and cushions that were constructed by industrial arts and home economics students. The last Wright building erected on campus was the 1958 **Polk County Science Building,** which contains the only planetarium Wright designed that was actually built. Among the other Wright buildings on campus are the **Industrial Arts Center,** featuring a series of 30°, 60°, and 90° triangles, each lying on its hypotenuse; the **Water Dome,** completed in 1948; the skylighted **Hawkins Seminar Building;** and the **Benjamin Fine Administrative Building,** with a copper-lined ceiling.

From the campus, return to Florida Ave and turn right for about 6 miles, crossing US 92. Florida Ave becomes US 98 N and runs into I-4. The Disney World exits off I-4 begin about 35 miles from Lakeland; downtown Orlando is 55 miles away.

# Driving the State

## THE SUNCOAST AND THE SEASHELL COAST

| | |
|---|---|
| Start | Tampa |
| Finish | Don CeSar Beach Resort |
| Distance | About 400 miles round-trip |
| Time | 3 days |
| Highlights | Gulf Coast beaches, Florida's cultural center, quaint beach towns, beautiful islands, shopping, and glamorous resorts |

This tour concentrates on the heart of Florida's central west coast as you explore the Tampa Bay area, often known as the Suncoast, and the Seashell Coast, which encompasses Fort Myers and Naples. You'll stop at pleasant beach villages, serene islands, and lively resort cities with plenty of opportunities for shopping, watersports, and fine dining. Culture fans will especially enjoy Sarasota, with its arts and music festivals and the Ringling Museum Complex. The trip allows you to be comfortable in sandals and shorts, but you can also dress up, if you wish, for a night on the town.

For additional information on accommodations, restaurants, and attractions in the region covered by the tour, look under specific cities in the listings portion of this book.

1. **Tampa.** Sitting on the Hillsborough River and rimmed by Hillsborough Bay and Tampa Bay, the city of Tampa has numerous waterfront views and activities that attract vacationers year-round. This metropolis of nearly 300,000 inhabitants is a major business hub on Florida's west coast and the seventh-largest US port. From Tampa's city center, get on the South Crosstown Expressway (FL 618) heading east and continue 12 miles to I-75. Take I-75 southbound toward Naples.

   After continuing 28 miles to where I-75 meets I-275 (exit 44), you're given the opportunity to make your way toward St Petersburg and St Petersburg Beach. Continue another 3 miles to exit 43 and the:

2. **Tourist Information Office,** where you can pick up information on the area and Anna Maria Island, the next stop. The office (tel 941/729-7040) is open daily 7:30am–5:30pm and has vending machines and rest rooms. Return to I-75 south and go to exit 42. At this point, you've driven about 38 miles from where you first got on I-75.

   At exit 42, take FL 64 west about 17 miles, crossing part of Sarasota Bay to:

3. **Anna Maria Island.** Spanish explorers made their way to Anna Maria Island in the early 1500s. Legend has it that early settlers were so taken with the island's beauty that they named it "Ana-Maria Cay," in honor of Mary, the mother of Jesus, and her mother, Anne. Except for the presence of low-rise buildings, much of the 7½-mile island, with its long stretches of white sand beaches studded with sea oats, remains the same as in the past. The island's narrow streets are a favorite of cyclists and walkers who come to the town of Anna Maria to explore its old buildings and quaint boutiques and crafts shops. The town shares the island with two other communities, Holmes Beach and Bradenton Beach.

   You'll enter Anna Maria Island via FL 64 and the Manatee Avenue Bridge at about mid-island. The **Chamber of Commerce,** located south of Manatee Ave on East Bay Dr (tel 941/778-1541), has a tourist information center open Monday–Friday 9am–5pm. Here you're just south of Holmes Beach.

> ## Take a Break
>
> The **Sandbar,** 100 Spring Ave, Anna Maria Island (tel 941/778-0444), overlooking the Gulf of Mexico, has a menu of seafood combo plates, steaks, pastas, and chicken. Another local choice, **Rotten Ralph's,** 902 S Bay Blvd, Anna Maria Island (tel 941/778-3953), offers crab cakes, deep-fried oysters, and other fish platters, as well as British favorites like fish-and-chips and steak-and-kidney pie.

For the next part of the tour, follow Gulf of Mexico Dr (also known just as Gulf Dr) on Anna Maria Island, via FL 789 south, through Longboat Key up to St Armands Key and Lido Beach. The drive is about 21 miles from Anna Maria to St Armands Key, depending upon the nooks and crannies you explore. First, take FL 789 south from Anna Maria Island for about 8 miles to:

4. **Longboat Key.** One of Florida's wealthiest areas, this island contains private homes and condominiums in gated communities between the Gulf of Mexico and Sarasota Bay. A number of hotels lined along the Gulf shore provide fine accommodations

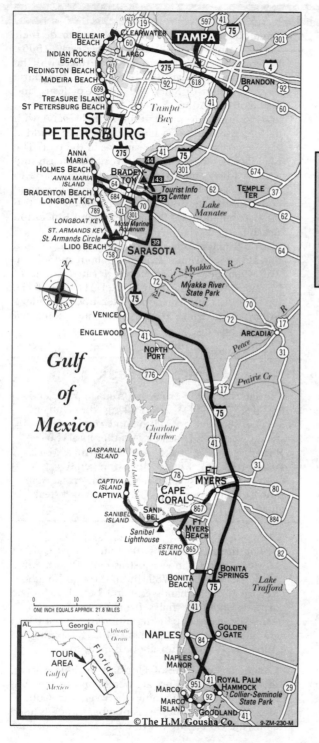

expensive hotels to consider, starting on the north end with the **Holiday Inn Longboat Key,** 4949 Gulf of Mexico Dr (tel 941/383-3771), and followed by **Longboat Key Hilton Beach Resort,** 4711 Gulf of Mexico Dr (tel 941/383-2451), the **Colony Beach & Tennis Resort,** 1620 Gulf of Mexico Dr (tel 941/383-6464), and the **Resort at Longboat Key Club,** 301 Gulf of Mexico Dr (tel 941/383-8821).

---

## Take a Break

The **Chart House,** 210 Gulf of Mexico Dr, Longboat Key (tel 941/383-5593), cooks steaks and prime rib to order and also has an extensive seafood menu, with lobster, swordfish, mahi-mahi, shrimp, and scallops. It features panoramic views of the water and a large bar, if you're simply looking for a cool drink.

---

On the southern side of Longboat Key, about a mile from the resorts on Gulf Dr, is:

5. **St Armands Key,** a delightful enclave named after Charles St Amand (early spelling), a 19th-century French homesteader. The community has a traffic rotary, known as **St Armands Circle,** lined with flower beds and filled with trendy shops, boutiques, sidewalk cafes, and restaurants. Plan to spend a couple of hours here looking at shops and relaxing at a sidewalk cafe as you people-watch.

Little more than 100 yards south of St Armands Circle is:

6. **Lido Beach.** This fine stretch of public beach on a lively, well-developed island has ample parking, concession stands, changing rooms, and rest rooms. You can bring lunch in a cooler here and sit at one of the picnic tables.

From Lido Beach, take the John Ringling Causeway (FL 789) south to downtown:

7. **Sarasota.** This tourist mecca is known as the cultural center of Florida and serves as the home of the Florida West Coast Symphony, which performs at **Van Wezel Performing Hall,** 777 N Tamiami Trail (tel 941/953-3366); and the Asolo Center for the Performing Arts (see below). Annual events include the Sarasota French Film Festival, which screens premieres that often draw French celebrities; the Sarasota Jazz Festival; the Sarasota Music Festival; and the Sarasota Festival of New Plays.

Although the early European settlers of Florida's west coast never achieved their dream of finding gold and silver treasure, today's visitors will find Sarasota one of the richest and most beautiful parts of the state. With about 50,000 people, this

in a variety of settings, though this is not an area for economy lodging.

The area has a number of moderately priced and

vibrant city has an average of 361 days of sunshine per year and encompasses 150 miles of waterfront, 11 beaches, 6 barrier islands, and a number of distinct communities, including Longboat Key, Lido Beach, and St Armands Key (see above); Siesta Key, an island resort and arts center; and Venice, Englewood, and Northport, all quiet beach havens.

The area was originally established by the region's early Native American inhabitants, the Calusas, whose ancient mounds and middens can be seen along the coastline and the keys. As in much of Florida, Hernando de Soto is noted as being the first European to explore the area in the 16th century. According to legend, the city was named after de Soto's daughter, Sara. Later arrivals included adventurous Scots, who, after hewing out a bustling city from the palmetto and pine forests, introduced the game of golf to the region in their spare time.

By the early 1900s, northern socialites arrived to begin building palatial winter retreats on Sarasota Bay. The region soon attracted a large following among the wealthy and influential, who continue to come to Sarasota today. Among the early magnates was circus entrepreneur **John Ringling,** who arrived in Sarasota in the 1920s and left his imprint (see below).

US 41 is the major north-south traffic artery in Sarasota. For a look at the city's most renowned attraction, take US 41 north from downtown to DeSoto Rd and turn left onto Ringling Plaza and soon you'll approach the:

8. **Ringling Museum Complex,** 5401 Bayshore Rd (tel 941/359-5700). This impressive, larger-than-life 60-acre site, the former estate of John Ringling, has four primary attractions. Ringling, a real estate mogul, was a partner in the world-famous Ringling Bros and Barnum & Bailey Circus. He spent his winters in Sarasota and eventually moved the circus here for its winter home. Ringling also spent much time in Europe searching for fine works of art and became enamored of Italian and Spanish art and architecture.

Eventually he needed a museum to house the world-class paintings and other priceless art works he had acquired. The result was the **John and Mable Ringling Museum of Art,** which was constructed in the 1920s in the style of a fabulous pink Italian Renaissance villa. Today the building is Florida's official state art museum, with 22 galleries featuring exquisite works by Rubens, Van Dyck, Velázquez, Hals, Poussin, and others. It also displays decorative arts and antiques as well as traveling exhibits.

Outside the museum are elaborate grounds with beautiful rose gardens, the Dwarf Garden, and fountained courtyards, including one with a 17-foot bronze replica of Michelangelo's David. Also on the complex grounds is the 30-room **Ca'd'Zan** (House of John), the Ringling winter residence modeled after a Venetian palace, and the **Circus Museum,** with a vast collection of circus memorabilia that encompasses parade wagons, calliopes, costumes, posters, and the Barlow Animated Miniature Circus, a scale replica of a famous circus from the 1930s.

Finally, the grounds include the **Asolo Center for the Performing Arts,** 5555 N Tamiami Trail (tel 941/351-8000), which has a year-round program of plays, concerts, lectures, and art films. The center incorporates an Italian-style court playhouse with interior friezes, carved box fronts, and cornice work from the Dunfermline Opera House in Scotland.

The complex is open daily 10am–5:30pm, except Thanksgiving, Christmas, and New Year's Day. Admission is $8.50 adults, $7.50 seniors; free for children under 12. Admission to the art galleries only is free on Saturdays.

To reach another Sarasota attraction take the causeway to St Armands Circle, and head north on FL 789 toward the bridge at Longboat Key. Just to the right, at the foot of the bridge, is:

9. **Mote Marine Aquarium,** 1600 Ken Thompson Pkwy, City Island Park (tel 800/691-MOTE). Part of the Mote Marine Laboratory complex, a world-renowned research center, the aquarium concentrates on marine life in the Sarasota area. You can see more than 200 varieties of sea life, and even touch some of them in the 30-foot touch tank. Displays include a living mangrove swamp and seagrass environment, a shark tank, loggerhead turtles, dolphins, manatees, and an extensive shell collection. Well-informed guides are on hand to tell you about the creatures and the work of the laboratory. Open daily 10am–5pm; closed Easter, Thanksgiving, and Christmas.

On your second day, plan to get an early start. St Armands Circle is a good place to stop for a coffee and danish to go. Leaving the circle, take the John Ringling Causeway to the traffic light at the intersection of US 41 and pick up FL 780; take FL 780 west to exit 39 and head south on I-75 for a speedy 75-minute trip to:

10. **Fort Myers.** Fort Myers is home to a great many "snowbirds," who come south to escape the cold northern winters. This dignified city, with palm-tree-covered boulevards, began as a humble US Army outpost named Fort Harvie in 1844. Today Fort Myers is an easy-going place where you can stroll or ride a bike, stay in a comfortable hotel, dine in good restaurants, play golf, and participate in water sports.

Fort Myers is also home base to baseball's Minnesota Twins and Boston Red Sox, who both play in Florida's Grapefruit League during spring training. Both teams play at the Lee County Sports Complex. For schedules, call 941/768-4210. Tickets must be purchased well in advance.

To visit the former residence of one of Fort Myers's most famous citizens, take US 41 north to Colonial Blvd and go west to McGregor Blvd (FL 867), where you'll find the:

11. **Thomas Alva Edison Winter Home,** 2350 McGregor Blvd (tel 941/334-3614). Situated on the riverfront, this lovely 14-acre estate contains inventor Thomas Alva Edison's former winter retreat, Seminole Lodge, as well as his laboratory and botanical gardens (with the world's largest banyan tree). Edison created thousands of inventions at his laboratory here. Inside the museum on the grounds are some of his inventions, such as early motion picture equipment and talking machines. Open Monday–Saturday 9am–5:30pm, Sunday noon–5:30pm.

Right next door is the **Henry Ford Winter Home** (same address and telephone number as the Edison home). This restored former winter dwelling of billionaire industrialist Henry Ford is modestly decorated and furnished in 1920s style, and features tropical landscaping.

From the Edison Winter Home, go east past US 41 to:

12. **Fort Myers Historical Museum,** 2300 Peck St (tel 941/332-5955). Contained in a former Spanish Mediterranean–style Atlantic Coast line railroad depot, this museum devoted to Fort Myers's and southwest Florida's history has rare artifacts, photographs, and exhibits dealing with the area's past settlers. You can see a replica fort, the exceptional Cooper Glass Collection of carnival and Depression glass, and "Esperanza," the longest and last of the fancy Pullman private railroad cars. Open Monday–Friday 9am–4:30pm, Sunday 1–5pm.

Make your way back to McGregor Blvd and head west for about 17 miles, following the well-marked signs to:

13. **Sanibel and Captiva Islands.** These two islands are accessed via Sanibel Bridge with a $3 round-trip toll. As soon as you enter Sanibel Island, stop at the Visitors Information Center at Causeway Rd (tel 941/472-1080), on your right, to pick up brochures on the island, local restaurants, and island accommodations. From the center, you can make reservations at local hotels. Sanibel and Captiva Islands make for a wonderful weekend. Pirates treasured these islands 200 years ago, and they are still held in high regard.

Sanibel is the larger island, about 12 miles long and 3 miles wide. Connected to Sanibel by a bridge, Captiva is about six miles long and even narrower than Sanibel. The islands have wide, white sand beaches touched by clear, iridescent gulf waters, colorful tropical flora, and wooded areas of pine and banyan trees. Much of the land area of the islands consists of wildlife sanctuaries. It's easy to get around Sanibel and Captiva, as there are only a couple of major roads.

One of the main attractions here is the 1842 **lighthouse** on the eastern end of Sanibel, which is surrounded by refuge lands that attract as many as 50 species of birds each winter. This is one of Florida's few operational lighthouses, marking the entrance from the Gulf of Mexico into San Carlos Bay. The peaceful nature of both islands encourages shelling, bird-watching, and cycling. The more adventurous might try a canoe trip, an organized walking tour, or a visit to the small **Island Historical Museum,** 850 Dunlop Rd (tel 941/472-4648), housed in a Florida pine home. Its displays cover the islands' early history, and you can see old photographs and clothing and other fascinating memorabilia. Open Wednesday–Saturday 10am–4pm.

Those with an interest in environment and ecology will want to visit **CROW** (Care and Rehabilitation of Wildlife), Sanibel-Captiva Rd (tel 941/472-3644), a sanctuary for recuperating local hawks, owls, pelicans, otters, and other wildlife; **Ding Darling National Wildlife Refuge** (tel 941/472-1100), encompassing approximately 5,000 acres and serving as a home to hundreds of species of birds and migrating waterfowl, as well as alligators, raccoons, and otters; and the **Sanibel/Captiva Conservation Foundation,** 333 Sanibel-Captiva Rd (tel 941/472-2329), which offers information about the islands' ecosystem. Call ahead for hours or consult the Visitors Information Center (see above).

You can reach Captiva from Sanibel on the appropriately named Sanibel-Captiva Rd. The road from the causeway to the northern end of Captiva is only about 10 miles long. Along this stretch, you'll find many beaches fronting the hotels and resorts.

---

## Take a Break

Captiva has a number of good restaurants. Try **Sunshine Cafe,** Captiva Village Sq (tel 941/472-6200), offering continental cuisine in a friendly cafe atmosphere, and **Bellini's of Captiva,** Andy Rosse Lane (tel 941/472-6866), serving northern Italian entrees in a romantic setting.

When you depart Sanibel Island and cross the causeway back to McGregor Blvd, stay to the right and continue on Summerlin Rd until you reach San Carlos Blvd, where you'll take a right. Continue south and drive through:

14. **Fort Myers Beach.** Located on Estero Island off the coast at the city of Fort Myers, Fort Myers Beach is a casual, laid-back community, with quaint cottages, garden apartments, and high-rise hotels available for tourists. Estero Island has all the amenities of a city, yet with small-town friendliness. The area's least endearing aspect is the traffic which continuously clogs the bridge to the island and Estero Blvd. Usually the traffic is northbound in the afternoon as beachgoers head back to Fort Myers.

**World-class fishing** is the attraction for many who visit this beach locale. More than 30 species of fish inhabit the waters, and professional charters are available to take you deep-sea fishing (no individual license is required). Rental boats are also available from the marina for exploring the back bays on your own. Other options include fishing from the beach and from the 500-foot pier.

Fort Myers Beach has additional opportunities for windsurfing, waterskiing, sailing, and jet skiing. If you're interested in shelling, the beach has plenty of pretty shells to spare, especially at low tide during the winter. Bird-watchers will find many species of wading birds, shorebirds, and waterfowl native to the area. For more information, contact the **Fort Myers Beach Chamber of Commerce,** 394 Estero Blvd (tel 941/454-7500), open Monday–Friday 9am–5pm.

From Fort Myers Beach, continue 19 miles south on Estero Blvd (FL 865) toward:

15. **Bonita Springs.** A former fishing village, this area has white sand beaches and acres of wildlife habitats and parks. The gulf and back bays are popular spots for saltwater and freshwater fishing.

From Bonita Springs, cross east to the mainland on Bonita Beach Rd until you reach US 41 (about 4 miles); head south on US 41 for 8 miles to:

16. **Naples.** One of Florida's most glamorous communities, Naples exudes charm, elegance, and sophistication without being snobbish. This highly regarded beach resort has its fair share of cultural diversions, art galleries, high-fashion shops, and fine dining spots, as well as golf courses and tennis courts. Although Naples has a strong appeal for the affluent who live and holiday here, the city also caters to families and travelers on more modest budgets.

It isn't surprising that Naples is home to some of Florida's finest lodgings, including the **Ritz-Carlton Naples,** 280 Vanderbilt Beach Rd (tel 941/598-3300 or toll free 800/241-3333). Some good moderately priced lodgings include **Cove Inn Resort and Marina,** 1191 8th St S (tel 941/262-7161 or toll free 800/255-4365) or **La Playa Beach and Racquet Inn,** 9891 Gulf Shore Dr (tel 941/597-3123 or toll free 800/237-6883). For those looking to spend even less, try **Red Roof Inn,** 1925 Davis Blvd (tel 941/774-3117 or toll free 800/272-0106), or **Hampton Inn,** 3210 Tamiami Trail N (tel 941/261-8000 or toll free 800/732-4667).

Naples has several impressive nature reserves, such as **Big Cypress National Preserve,** accessible by 1-75 and US 41 (tel 941/695-4111), a 2,000-square-mile sanctuary for alligators, deer, and numerous birds; the **Conservancy Nature Center,** Goodlette Rd on 14th Ave N (tel 941/262-0304), with a science museum, nature trails, butterfly atrium, and aviary; and **Corkscrew Swamp Sanctuary,** Sanctuary Rd (tel 941/657-3771), an 11,000-acre wilderness, maintained by the National Audubon Society, that features alligators as well as migratory and wading birds.

To come to Naples and not visit the fine boutiques and galleries is like missing a mouse named Mickey in the Magic Kingdom. The **Fifth Avenue South** district has more than 100 shops, galleries, and restaurants, and for many it is Naples's finest shopping area. **Old Naples,** along 3rd St S and the avenues, is a nine-square-block historic area in the southern part of the city between the Gulf and Naples Bay. It has handsomely restored old balconied buildings, trend-setting shops, art galleries, and top restaurants. Additional shopping centers include **Coastland Center,** 1900 Tamiami Trail N; **Coral Isle Factory Shops,** on FL 951; **Tin City,** at US 41 and Goodlette Rd; the **Village on Venetian Bay,** 4200 Gulf Shore Blvd N; and the **Waterside Shops at Pelican Bay,** Seagate Dr and Tamiami Trail N.

From Naples, drive 8 miles south on US 41 to Isle of Capri Rd (FL 951); proceed another 7 miles and go over the bridge to:

17. **Marco Island,** about a half-hour drive from Naples. Ordinarily, Marco Island requires its own overnight stay, at least if you're a beachgoer. The pace here is slow and you can easily slip from your bed to a hammock without skipping a page from your best-seller.

Like Sanibel Island but a bit more commercialized, Marco Island has a number of boutiques, art galleries, and casual restaurants. **Tiger Tail Beach State Park** has a nice beach that offers opportunities for swimming and watersports, as well as changing rooms and showers.

At Isle of Capri Rd turn right, away from Marco Island, and continue 7 miles to I-75 N. From here, the drive is approximately 125 miles north to the

## Take a Break

**Stan's Idle Hour Seafood Restaurant** (tel 941/ 394-3041) is located in Goodland, less than a 10-minute drive east from Marco Island's center, just off to the right before the bridge on FL 92. Stan Gober owns this rustic seafood eatery on the dock, where locals like to gather for good food, drinks, and sometimes live entertainment. Besides the fresh fish and seafood entrees, try the frogs' legs (seasonal), the large fried onion rings, and the buffalo chicken wings. The outdoor patio with thatched huts is fun for lunch or dinner.

interchange of I-75 and I-275. To proceed to St Petersburg Beach, take exit 44 from I-75 and drive toward St Petersburg until you see signs for the beach. Follow these signs to Gulf Blvd, where you'll see the:

18. **Don CeSar Beach Resort,** 3400 Gulf Blvd (tel 813/360-1881), a big pink National Landmark hotel sitting magnificently on 7½ miles of beachfront. This 1928 palace, combining Moorish and Mediterranean architecture, was renovated in the 1980s. You'll enjoy looking at its elegant interior, with classic high windows and archways, crystal chandeliers, marble floors, and artworks on display. Enjoy drinks on the terrace, a romantic dinner in the fine dining room, or stroll the grounds and slip off your shoes for a walk on the beach.

Turn right out of the Don CeSar and drive north on Gulf Blvd from St Petersburg Beach. Take this drive at a leisurely pace as you continue past a handful of little beach towns, including Treasure Island, Madeira Beach, Redington Beach, Indian Rocks Beach, Belleair, and Clearwater. At Clearwater Beach, proceed east on FL 60 to the Courtney Campbell Causeway (FL 60). It's about 30 minutes from Clearwater back to downtown Tampa.

# Florida Listings

## Altamonte Springs

This fast-growing city in the densely developed region north-west of Orlando is the state's de facto softball capital. Its Seminole County Softball Complex hosts several national tournaments.

### HOTELS 🏢

#### ▆▆ Best Western Altamonte Springs

150 Douglas Ave, 32714; tel 407/862-8200 or toll free 800/327-5560; fax 407/862-5750. Exit 48 off I-4. This recent arrival on the Altamonte hotel scene is centrally located, yet surprisingly quiet and restful. **Rooms:** 144 rms. CI 3pm/CO 11am. Nonsmoking rms avail. Rooms are tastefully decorated with upgraded furnishings. **Amenities:** 🛁 🏃 📺 A/C, cable TV w/movies, refrig, dataport. Microwave. **Services:** 🖼 ⊙ **Facilities:** 🏋 ⛳ 🏊 Washer/dryer. **Rates (CP):** $99 S or D. Extra person $8. Children under age 16 stay free. Min stay peak. Lower rates off-season. Parking: Outdoor, free. AE, CB, DC, DISC, MC, V.

#### ▆▆▆ Embassy Suites Orlando North

225 E Altamonte Dr, 32701; tel 407/834-2400 or toll free 800/EMBASSY; fax 407/834-2117. Exit 48 off I-4. A modern all-suites hotel within walking distance of the local mall. **Rooms:** 210 stes. CI 3pm/CO noon. Nonsmoking rms avail. All rooms overlook the soaring atrium. **Amenities:** 🛁 🏃 📺 A/C, cable TV w/movies, refrig, dataport, voice mail. Some units w/terraces. Wet bars, microwaves. **Services:** ✕ 🖼 ⊙ 🔔 Babysitting. Evening social hour. **Facilities:** 🏋 🎿 ⛳ 🏊 🖥 🏊 1 restaurant, 1 bar, games rm, spa, sauna, steam rm, whirlpool, washer/dryer. **Rates (BB):** Peak (Dec 15–Mar) $129–$189 ste. Children under age 18 stay free. Min stay special events. Lower rates off-season. Parking: Outdoor, free. AE, CB, DC, DISC, ER, JCB, MC, V.

#### ▆▆ Hampton Inn Altamonte Springs

151 N Douglas Ave, 32714; tel 407/869-9000 or toll free 800/HAMPTON; fax 407/788-6746. Exit 48 off I-4. Offers pleasant surroundings and good value. Recently remodeled. **Rooms:** 210 rms. CI 3pm/CO noon. Nonsmoking rms avail. **Amenities:** 🛁 🏃 📺 A/C, cable TV w/movies, refrig, dataport. **Services:** 🚐 🖼 ⊙ 🔔 Babysitting. **Facilities:** 🏋 ⛳ 🏊 🖥

⛳ Whirlpool, washer/dryer. **Rates (CP):** $69–$79 S; $79–$89 D. Children under age 18 stay free. Parking: Outdoor, free. AE, CB, DC, DISC, MC, V.

#### ▆▆ Holiday Inn Orlando–Altamonte Springs

230 W FL 236, 32714; tel 407/862-4455 or toll free 800/226-4544; fax 407/682-5982. Exit 48 off I-4. A four-story building with a pretty driveway leading to a well-maintained lobby and public area. The building wraps around a central courtyard, which contains the pool and deck. Caters largely to a corporate clientele. **Rooms:** 202 rms and stes. CI 2pm/CO noon. Nonsmoking rms avail. **Amenities:** 🛁 🏃 A/C, dataport. **Services:** ✕ 🚐 🖼 ⊙ Masseur, babysitting. **Facilities:** 🏋 ⛳ 🖥 🏊 1 restaurant, 1 bar (w/entertainment), games rm, playground, washer/dryer. **Rates:** Peak (Jan 15–March) $99 S; $109 D; $125–$225 ste. Extra person $10. Children under age 17 stay free. Min stay special events. Lower rates off-season. Parking: Outdoor, free. AE, CB, DC, DISC, JCB, MC, V.

#### ▆▆ La Quinta Motor Inn

150 S Westmonte Dr, 32741; tel 407/788-1411 or toll free 800/531-5900; fax 407/788-6472. Exit 48 off I-4. Clean, pleasant hotel with Spanish-style architecture and decor. **Rooms:** 115 rms and stes. CI noon/CO noon. Nonsmoking rms avail. All rooms overlook the pool and courtyard. **Amenities:** 🛁 🏃 A/C, cable TV w/movies, dataport. **Services:** 🖼 ⊙ 🔔 **Facilities:** 🏋 ⛳ 🏊 **Rates (CP):** Peak (Jan–March) $69–$79 S or D; $89–$109 ste. Extra person $10. Children under age 18 stay free. Min stay special events. Lower rates off-season. Parking: Outdoor, free. AE, CB, DC, DISC, MC, V.

#### ▆▆▆ Orlando North Hilton

350 S North Lake Blvd, 32715; tel 407/830-1985 or toll free 800/HILTONS; fax 407/331-2911. Exit 48 off I-4. More a corporate address than one for tourists. Sleek and appealing, and well maintained. **Rooms:** 322 rms and stes. Executive level. CI 3pm/CO noon. Nonsmoking rms avail. Rooms were renovated several years ago. **Amenities:** 🛁 🏃 📺 A/C, cable TV w/movies, voice mail. All units w/minibars. **Services:** ✕ 🚐 🖼 ⊙ Car-rental desk. **Facilities:** 🏋 ⛳ 🖥 🏊 1 restaurant, 1 bar, whirlpool. Guests receive free membership in Bally's Fitness Center across the highway. **Rates:** Peak (Jan

15–Mar) $120–$130 S or D; $275–$375 ste. Extra person $10. Children under age 18 stay free. Min stay special events. Lower rates off-season. Parking: Outdoor, free. AE, CB, DC, DISC, ER, MC, V.

### ≣≣ Residence Inn by Marriott
270 Douglas Ave, 32714; tel 407/788-7991 or toll free 800/331-3131; fax 407/869-5468. Exit 48 off I-4. A condo-like community featuring units ranging from studios with full kitchens to large units with separate bedrooms and living rooms with fireplaces. **Rooms:** 128 stes. CI 3pm/CO noon. Nonsmoking rms avail. **Amenities:** 🛁 ⚙ 🖥 A/C, cable TV w/movies, refrig, dataport, voice mail. Some units w/terraces, some w/fireplaces. Units outfitted with microwaves, icemakers, dishwashers, utensils, and ample cupboard space. **Services:** 🖥 ⟲ ⟳ Car-rental desk, babysitting. Guests have free use of Bally's Fitness Center. Discount at nearby golf course. **Facilities:** ⛱ 🟦25 ⛓ Basketball, whirlpool, washer/dryer. **Rates (CP):** Peak (Jan–May) $129–$179 ste. Children under age 18 stay free. Lower rates off-season. Parking: Outdoor, free. Extended-stay discounts avail. AE, DC, DISC, JCB, MC, V.

### ≣ Travelodge
450 Douglas Ave, 32714; tel 407/862-7111 or toll free 800/327-2221; fax 407/862-6663. Exit 48 off I-4. A low-rise complex that is a bit run-down. **Rooms:** 229 rms and stes. CI 3pm/CO 11:30. Nonsmoking rms avail. **Amenities:** 🛁 A/C, cable TV w/movies. Some units w/terraces. **Services:** 🖥 ⟳ Babysitting. **Facilities:** ⛱ 🟦15 ⛓ 1 restaurant, playground, washer/dryer. **Rates:** Peak (Feb–Apr/June–Aug) $69 S or D; $79 ste. Extra person $6. Children under age 18 stay free. Min stay special events. Lower rates off-season. Parking: Outdoor, free. AE, CB, DC, DISC, JCB, MC, V.

## ATTRACTION 📷

### Wekiwa Springs State Park
Wekiwa Circle, Apopka; tel 407/884-2009. The varied topography of this 7,000-acre park includes everything from pine flatwoods and sand hills to hammock and swampland; 13 miles of trails survey much of it. Swimming, fishing, boating, canoe rentals, camping, hiking, nature trails. **Open:** Daily 8am–sunset. $$

# Amelia Island

European settlers, Africans, pirates, and Native Americans have each dominated this marshy, oceanside island at one time or another. Today, visitors can enjoy boating, fishing, and golfing. Civil War re-enactments take place at nearby Fort Clinch. **Information:** Amelia Island-Fernandina Beach-Yulee Chamber of Commerce, 102 Centre St, PO Box 472, Fernandina Beach, 32035 (tel 904/261-3248).

## RESORTS 🏨

### ≣≣≣≣ Amelia Island Plantation
FL A1A S, PO Box 3000, 32035-1307; tel 904/261-6161 or toll free 800/874-6878; fax 904/277-5159. Exit 129 off I-95. 1,250 acres. One of Florida's most extensive resorts, sprawled along pristine ocean shoreline and encompassing an unusual array of accommodations and dining and recreational facilities. Sure to please the tennis and golf enthusiast, as well as those seeking simple relaxation. **Rooms:** 570 rms, stes, and effic. CI 4pm/CO noon. Nonsmoking rms avail. **Amenities:** 🛁 ⚙ 🖥 🍽 A/C, cable TV w/movies, refrig, dataport, voice mail, in-rm safe. All units w/terraces, some w/fireplaces, some w/whirlpools. **Services:** ✕ ☎ 🚐 🖥 ⟳ Car-rental desk, social director, masseur, children's program, babysitting. Cordial, smiling staff. **Facilities:** ⛱ 🚲 ⛰ ⛳ ▶54 🏕 🏌 🎣15 ⛳6 🏓 💻 ⛓ 6 restaurants, 6 bars (1 w/entertainment), 1 beach (ocean), lifeguard, basketball, volleyball, board surfing, games rm, lawn games, racquetball, squash, spa, sauna, steam rm, whirlpool, beauty salon, playground. **Rates:** Peak (Mar 17–Apr 27) $181–$214 S; $186–$219 D; $224–$408 ste; $224–$408 effic. Extra person $5. Children under age 12 stay free. Lower rates off-season. AP rates avail. MAP rates avail. Parking: Outdoor, free. Golf and tennis packages avail. AE, DC, DISC, MC, V.

### ≣≣≣≣ The Ritz-Carlton Amelia Island
4750 Amelia Island Pkwy, 32034; tel 904/277-1100 or toll free 800/241-3333; fax 904/261-9063. 26 mi N of Jacksonville, exit 129 off I-95. 26 acres. A deluxe establishment located alongside a superb stretch of barrier island beach. Designed with the care and attention to detail familiar in other Florida Ritz-Carlton properties: plush interior styling, superior recreational facilities, superior service. **Rooms:** 449 rms and stes. Executive level. CI 3pm/CO noon. Nonsmoking rms avail. All rooms have rich appointments and ocean views. **Amenities:** 🛁 ⚙ 🍽 A/C, cable TV w/movies, dataport, voice mail, in-rm safe, bathrobes. All units w/minibars, all w/terraces, some w/fireplaces, some w/whirlpools. **Services:** 🍽 ☎ 📼 🚐 🖥 ⟳ Twice-daily maid svce, car-rental desk, masseur, babysitting. **Facilities:** ⛱ 🚲 ⛰ ▶18 🏊 🎣4 🏌5 🏓 🟦1500 💻 ⛓ 3 restaurants (see "Restaurants" below), 3 bars (w/entertainment), 1 beach (ocean), volleyball, lawn games, spa, sauna, steam rm, whirlpool, beauty salon, day-care ctr, playground. One of the pools is indoor. **Rates:** Peak (Mar–May/Sept 29–Nov 16) $250–$355 S or D; $480–$2,000 ste. Extra person $15. Children under age 18 stay free. Lower rates off-season. Parking: Indoor/outdoor, $9/day. Tennis and golf packages avail. AE, CB, DC, DISC, ER, MC, V.

## RESTAURANTS 🍴

### ★ Brett's Waterway Cafe
In Fernadina Harbour Marina, 1 S Front St (Downtown); tel 904/261-2660. At Centre St. **American/Continental.** Intrusive piped-in pop music adds nothing to the nautical setting,

although the panoramic ocean views tend to calm the nerves. The menu offers especially good value at lunchtime (salads, burgers, seafood); dinner menus include swank items like grilled brie and veal chardonnay. The lure at either meal is fresh shrimp direct from the adjoining dock, grilled or deep fried in 100% peanut oil. **FYI:** Reservations recommended. Dress code. **Open:** Lunch Mon–Sat 11:30am–2:30pm; dinner daily 5:30pm–close. **Prices:** Main courses $15–$23. AE, MC, V. 🖼️ 🖼️ ⛬

### ⚘ The Grill
In The Ritz-Carlton Amelia Island, 4750 Amelia Island Pkwy; tel 904/277-1100. Exit 129 off I-95, 26 mi N of Jacksonville. **Regional American.** An elegant bar with Italian marble fireplace leads to this grand dining room with refined table settings and an arc of floor-to-ceiling windows. Award-winning chef Matthew Medure offers three categories of prix-fixe meals, which might range from English pea soup with Mayport shrimp tempura to charred foie gras with Vidalia onion marmalade to dorade filet with white asparagus and lemon potatoes. Special "Adventurous Gourmet" dinners include tableside consultation with the chefs followed by nine specially prepared tasting courses (for $175 per person). **FYI:** Reservations recommended. Piano. Children's menu. Jacket required. No smoking. **Open:** Dinner Mon–Sat 6–10pm. **Prices:** Prix fixe $49–$65. AE, CB, DC, DISC, ER, MC, V. ♥ 🖼️ VP ⛬

### ★ The Southern Tip
In Palmetto Walk Shopping Mall, 4802 First Coast Hwy; tel 904/261-6184. Off A1A 5 mins S of The Ritz-Carlton. **Eclectic.** Charming eatery located in a two-story plantation-style house with yellow shutters. The country-inn decor makes a bright and cheerful background for chef/owner Richard Schmidt's innovative yet simple cuisine: turkey and asparagus melt, margarita chicken, black-eyed-pea cakes, and pork chops grilled with jalapeño and Dijon are all big favorites. **FYI:** Reservations recommended. Children's menu. Dress code. No smoking. **Open:** Lunch daily 11:30am–2pm; dinner daily 5:30–9:30pm. **Prices:** Main courses $12–$19. AE, DC, DISC, ER, MC, V. 🖼️ ⛬

## ATTRACTIONS 🖼️

### Centre Street Historic District
Fernandina Beach; tel 904/261-3248. This 50-block historic area of downtown Fernandina Beach boasts many restored 19th-century buildings housing shops, restaurants, and many homes in a carefully preserved Victorian setting that recalls the city's "golden age."

### Amelia Island Museum of History
233 S 3rd St, Fernandina Beach; tel 904/261-7378. On display are artifacts from an excavation of a nearby 17th-century Spanish mission, many documents, and several greatly enlarged photographs of 19th-century Fernandina. A research library is here as well. A walking tour of the 50-block Centre Street Historic District includes interiors of a church

and a Victorian home, and complimentary tea at a 19th-century inn. Tour begins at the Depot, Thurs and Fri at 3pm. Museum tours given Mon–Sat 11am and 2pm. **Open:** Mon–Fri 10am–5pm. **$$**

### Fort Clinch State Park
2601 Atlantic Ave, Fernandina Beach; tel 904/277-7274. Two-thirds of this 1,100-acre park consist of hardwood hammock, the remainder of sandy dunes. The masonry fort built here in 1847 could garrison more than 500 men and had 74 gun emplacements. Rangers in period uniform stage a reenactment of life at the fort at the beginning of each month. Swimming, fishing, boating, hiking, camping, nature trail. **Open:** Daily 8am–sunset. **$$**

# Anna Maria Island

See Bradenton

# Apalachicola

St George Island and Apalachicola Bay separate this town of 2,700 from the Gulf of Mexico. Home of the John Gorrie State Museum (named after the inventor whose 19th-century ice machine presaged air conditioning). **Information:** Apalachicola Bay Chamber of Commerce, 57 Market St, Apalachicola, 32320 (tel 904/653-9419).

## LODGE 🖼️

### ≡ The Pelican Inn
Dog Island, Carrabelle, PO Box 123, Apalachicola, 32329; tel 904/697-4710 or toll free 800/451-5294. Take US 98 about 30 mi E of Apalachicola. The only lodging available on this island of 14 year-round residents, the Pelican Inn is appealing for what it lacks—phones, TVs, radios, and clocks are conspicuously absent. Guests must bring all provisions with them, since there are no stores, restaurants, or gas stations on the island. From Carrabelle, take the ferry to Dog Island ($19 round trip). Boats leave once or twice a day, depending on the season. **Rooms:** 8 effic. CI open/CO open. **Amenities:** 🖼️ A/C, refrig. No phone or TV. All units w/terraces. **Facilities:** 1 beach (ocean), washer/dryer. **Rates:** Peak (Mar–Oct) $150 effic. Children under age 18 stay free. Lower rates off-season. MC, V.

## ATTRACTIONS 🖼️

### John Gorrie State Museum
6th St at D Street; tel 904/653-9347. Seeking a way to cool the hospital rooms of malaria and yellow fever patients, Dr John Gorrie developed the first artificial cooling device, a forerunner of modern ice-makers and air conditioners. A model of the machine is on display, with a diagram of how it worked; there is also a diorama of the sick room first cooled

by the machine. This small museum also houses exhibits on early Apalachicola history. **Open:** Thurs–Mon 9am–noon and 1–5pm. **$**

**St George Island State Park**
St George Island; tel 904/927-2111. On St George Island, via the causeway from Eastpoint, this park offers miles of undeveloped, near-primitive beaches, plus dunes, forests, and marshes. Gulf swimming, fishing, boating, hiking, nature trails, camping. **Open:** Daily 8am–sunset. **$$**

**St Vincent National Wildlife Refuge**
Tel 904/653-8808. Most of the refuge's 12,000-plus acres are on St Vincent Island, an undeveloped barrier island in Apalachicola Bay. Originally established as a waterfowl preserve, the refuge has broadened its scope to include such endangered species as bald eagles and loggerhead sea turtles. The visitor center houses exhibits on the wetlands and wildlife of the refuge and on Apalachicola Bay. Recreational activities include fishing, boating, and hiking along old logging roads. **Open:** Daily dawn–dusk. **Free**

# Atlantic Beach

One of three beach municipalities located just east of Jacksonville, Atlantic Beach's 12,500 residents range from artists to retired executives.

## HOTEL 🏨

### ≣≣ Sea Turtle Inn
1 Ocean Blvd, 32233; tel 904/249-7402 or toll free 800/874-6000; fax 904/247-1517. 1 block E of FL A1A. Modest eight-story oceanfront hotel. **Rooms:** 194 rms and stes. CI 3pm/CO noon. Nonsmoking rms avail. Rooms on the north end of the building provide a most unappealing view of the parking lot/Dumpster area. **Amenities:** 🛏 🔥 A/C, cable TV w/movies. Some units w/terraces. **Services:** ✕ 🖼 🛎 Social director, babysitting. Complimentary coffee and newspaper daily. Happy hour held afternoons in lounge. **Facilities:** 🔥 🏊 1 restaurant, 2 bars (1 w/entertainment), 1 beach (ocean), volleyball, washer/dryer. **Rates:** Peak (Mar–Oct) $109–$159 S or D; $199 ste. Children under age 19 stay free. Min stay special events. Lower rates off-season. Parking: Outdoor, free. AE, CB, DC, DISC, MC, V.

## RESTAURANT 🍴

### ★ Ragtime Tavern Seafood & Grill
207 Atlantic Blvd; tel 904/241-7877. **Creole/Seafood.** A home-style eatery with exposed brick and a country atmosphere. The bar, known as the Tap Room Brewery, serves beer made on the premises. Try the skewered seafood or sesame tuna on a bed of fresh spinach, with ginger-mustard remoulade. The owner's mother makes award-winning key lime cheesecake. Come early to avoid the noisy crowds. Live jazz at Sunday brunch. **FYI:** Reservations not accepted. Jazz.

Children's menu. **Open:** Sun–Thurs 11am–10:30pm, Fri–Sat 11am–11pm. **Prices:** Main courses $11–$18. AE, DC, DISC, MC, V. 🔥

# Bal Harbour

See Miami Beach

# Big Pine Key

Two-thirds of the way down the Florida Keys, this island is a major haven for nature lovers, who can kayak, snorkel, fish, or view the key deer and the great white heron. **Information:** Lower Keys Chamber of Commerce, Overseas Hwy, MM 31, PO Box 430511, Big Pine Key, 33043 (tel 305/872-2411 or toll free 800/872-3722).

## RESTAURANTS 🍴

### ★ Dip 'n Deli
Overseas Hwy MM 31; tel 305/872-3030. **American.** Known for its large menu of reasonably priced items. Extensive dessert menu lists over 100 tasty items, many of them made with reduced-fat ingredients. **FYI:** Reservations accepted. Children's menu. Beer and wine only. **Open:** Mon–Sat 6:30am–9pm, Sun 6:30am–3pm. **Prices:** Main courses $7–$11. No CC. 🖼 🔥

### ★ Island Reef
Overseas Hwy MM 31.3; tel 305/872-2170. **Regional American.** Overhead fans keep the breeze swirling in this nautically inspired cafe serving a wide variety of seafood dishes. Island-style daily specials are available for both lunch and dinner. **FYI:** Reservations not accepted. Children's menu. Beer and wine only. **Open:** Lunch Mon–Sat 11am–2:30pm; dinner Mon–Sat 5–9:30pm. **Prices:** Main courses $9–$17. MC, V. 🖼

### ⑤ K.D.'s Steak & Seafood House
Overseas Hwy MM 30.5; tel 305/872-2314. **Seafood/Steak.** Sea shells and fish netting adorn this casual restaurant, where two TVs play constantly in the bar. Sauteed reef snapper, deep-sea scallops, and shrimp dishes are among the menu highlights. **FYI:** Reservations accepted. Children's menu. Beer and wine only. **Open:** Daily 6am–10pm. **Prices:** Main courses $9–$25. AE, MC, V.

### ★ Montego Bay
Overseas Hwy MM 30.2; tel 305/872-3009. **Seafood/Steak.** "Relax & enjoy" is the motto at this super-casual Jamaican-inspired spot. Steak, seafood, and spicy jerk chicken are the most popular entree options. **FYI:** Reservations accepted. Children's menu. **Open:** Daily 11am–10pm. **Prices:** Main courses $8–$18. DISC, MC, V. 🔥

## ATTRACTIONS

### National Key Deer Refuge
Overseas Hwy MM 30; tel 305/872-2239. A preservation area for the endangered key deer, which can most likely be observed in early morning or early evening. There is a nature walk 1½ miles north of Watson Blvd on Key Deer Blvd. Nearby is Blue Hole, a depleted rock quarry inhabited by alligators. Refuge headquarters are located north of US 1 between Key Deer Blvd and Wilder Ave. **Open:** Daily sunrise–sunset. **Free**

### Bahia Honda State Park
Overseas Hwy MM 37; tel 305/872-2353. The best park in the Lower Keys is spread out across 635 acres and offers large stretches of white sandy beach, the only natural sand beach in the Keys (most are coral). Deep waters close to shore are perfect for snorkeling and diving, and there are miles of trails packed with unusual plants and animals. Docking and camping facilities; beachside picnic areas with tables and grills. **Open:** Daily 8am–sunset. **$$**

# Boca Grande

Panfilo de Narvaez landed near this southwest Florida paradise in 1528, beating the town's founding duPonts by about 350 years. Still an exclusive resort, the city is known worldwide for its tarpon fishing. **Information:** Boca Grande Area Chamber of Commerce, PO Box 704, Boca Grande, 33921 (tel 941/964-0568).

## MOTEL

### UNRATED The Innlet
11th St and East Ave, PO Box 248, 33921; tel 941/964-2294; fax 941/964-0382. Just north of downtown. Fronting the Intracoastal Waterway with boat docks and ramps, this pretty motel pleases water recreationists. The nearby Gasparilla Inn, which has redecorated it in its trademark yellow-and-lattice guise, operates the property. **Rooms:** 32 rms and effic. CI 2pm/CO 11am. **Amenities:** A/C, cable TV, refrig. All units w/terraces. **Services:** Babysitting. **Facilities:** Playground, washer/dryer. Nice, private pool with wood deck. **Rates:** Peak (Feb–July 15) $100 S or D; $125 effic. Extra person $10. Children under age 12 stay free. Lower rates off-season. Parking: Outdoor, free. MC, V.

## INN

### Gasparilla Inn
5th St at Palm Ave, 33921; tel 941/964-2201; fax 941/964-2733. Exit 35 off I-75 to the shores of Placida. 500 acres. This turn-of-the-century grande dame is a fine example of traditional innkeeping. A welcoming veranda fronts the three-story main structure, while individual cottages and inn facilities are scattered around downtown. **Rooms:** 145 rms and stes; 19 cottages/villas. CI 2pm/CO 11am. No smoking.

**Amenities:** A/C. No TV. Some units w/terraces. TVs are rented for $5. **Services:** Twice-daily maid svce, car-rental desk, social director, masseur, children's program, babysitting, afternoon tea served. **Facilities:** 4 restaurants, 3 bars (1 w/entertainment), 1 beach (ocean), lawn games, spa, sauna, beauty salon, playground, washer/dryer, guest lounge w/TV. Nearby beach club provides manmade beach, deluxe pool, and fitness area. **Rates (AP):** Peak (Feb–Apr) $200–$450 D; $280–$500 ste; $280–$500 cottage/villa. Extra person $87. Lower rates off-season. MAP rates avail. Parking: Outdoor, free. Closed June 15–Dec 15. No CC.

## RESTAURANT

### Theater Restaurant
In Old Theatre Mall, 321 Park Ave; tel 941/964-0806. **Seafood/Steak/Pasta.** This two-story restaurant with an outdoor dining room uses unpainted wood and candlelight to create a natural, intimate atmosphere. Daily specials regularly include five kinds of fresh fish. The key lime chicken is a specialty. Extensive wine selection. **FYI:** Reservations recommended. Guitar. Children's menu. **Open:** Lunch Mon–Sat 11:30am–2:30pm; dinner Mon–Sat 5:30–10pm. Closed Aug–Sept. **Prices:** Main courses $15–$21. AE, MC, V.

## ATTRACTIONS

### Cayo Costa Island State Park
Tel 941/964-0375. The park encompasses most of the Cayo Costa, an unspoiled island paradise of deserted white sand beaches, pine forest, mangrove swamp, and oak palm hammocks. Shelling is especially good on the northern portion of the island, and the swimming is excellent. Fishing, boating, picnicking, and primitive camping are allowed. Access by boat only. For cabin rentals and information contact Barrier Islands GEO Park, PO Box 1150, Boca Grande, FL 33921. **Open:** Daily 8am–sunset. **$**

### Gasparilla Island State Recreation Area
Tel 941/964-0375. Located on the southern end of Gasparilla Island, the park features year-round swimming, picnic areas, and excellent saltwater fishing in the Gulf of Mexico. The beautifully restored Boca Grande Lighthouse (built circa 1890) is located at the southern tip of the park. **Open:** Daily 8am–sunset. **$**

# Boca Raton

See also Deerfield Beach

An upscale and business-minded community of 64,000 residents. Visitors can enjoy the Caldwell Theater Company, Florida Symphonic Pops, Royal Palm Polo Club, and Singing

Pines Museum. **Information:** Greater Boca Raton Chamber of Commerce, 1800 N Dixie Hwy, PO Box 1390, Boca Raton, 33432 (tel 561/395-4433).

## HOTELS 🛏

### ≡≡≡ Boca Raton Marriott Crocker Center

5150 Town Center Circle, 33486; tel 561/392-4600 or toll free 800/228-9290; fax 561/369-9223. Exit 39 off I-95. This leading business hotel features a handsome marble lobby that makes a nice first impression. **Rooms:** 256 rms and stes. CI 3pm/CO noon. Nonsmoking rms avail. **Amenities:** 🛏 🅰 🍸 A/C, cable TV w/movies, refrig, voice mail, in-rm safe, bathrobes. All units w/minibars, all w/terraces. **Services:** 🍽 🖼 🔁 Babysitting. **Facilities:** 🏋 🎿 🔥 1 restaurant, 1 bar, steam rm, whirlpool. **Rates:** Peak (Dec–Apr) $159 S or D; $209 ste. Extra person $15. Children under age 18 stay free. Lower rates off-season. MAP rates avail. Parking: Outdoor, $7/day. AE, DISC, MC, V.

### ≡≡≡ The Bridge Hotel

999 E Camino Real, 33432; tel 561/368-9500 or toll free 800/327-0130; fax 561/362-0492. Palmetto Rd exit off I-95. Located on a waterway next to a small bridge, from which the hotel takes its name. This commendable hotel has a cozy lobby and attractive guest rooms. **Rooms:** 121 rms and stes. CI 3pm/CO noon. Nonsmoking rms avail. **Amenities:** 🛏 🅰 🍸 A/C, cable TV w/movies. All units w/terraces. **Services:** ✕ 🆅🅿 🖼 🔁 Babysitting. **Facilities:** 🏋 🚲 ⚠ 300 2 restaurants, 2 bars (1 w/entertainment), sauna. Rooftop restaurant. **Rates:** Peak (Dec–Apr) $140–$180 S; $150–$185 D; $280 ste. Extra person $10. Children under age 18 stay free. Lower rates off-season. Parking: Indoor/outdoor, free. AE, MC, V.

### ≡≡ Courtyard by Marriott

2000 NW Executive Court, 33431; tel 561/241-7070 or toll free 800/321-2211; fax 561/241-7080. Exit 39 off I-95. A pretty and well-kept facility offering pleasing accommodations and better-than-average decor. **Rooms:** 152 rms and stes. CI 3pm/CO noon. Nonsmoking rms avail. **Amenities:** 🛏 🅰 🔁 A/C, cable TV w/movies, voice mail. Some units w/terraces. **Services:** 🖼 🔁 **Facilities:** 🏋 🔥 40 🔥 1 restaurant (bkfst only), 1 bar (w/entertainment), whirlpool, washer/dryer. **Rates:** Peak (Dec–Apr) $115 S; $125 D; $130–$140 ste. Children under age 18 stay free. Lower rates off-season. Parking: Outdoor, free. AE, DC, DISC, MC, V.

### ≡≡≡ DoubleTree Suites

701 NW 53rd St, 33487; tel 561/997-9500 or toll free 800/222-8733; fax 561/994-3565. Exit 40 off I-95. A Southwest-accented hotel marked by a handsome courtyard. **Rooms:** 182 stes. CI 3pm/CO 1pm. Nonsmoking rms avail. **Amenities:** 🛏 🅰 🔁 🍸 A/C, cable TV w/movies, refrig, voice mail, in-rm safe, bathrobes. Some units w/terraces. Microwaves. **Services:** 🍽 🚐 🖼 🔁 Babysitting. **Facilities:** 🏋 🚲 🔥 50 🔥 1 restaurant, whirlpool, washer/dryer. **Rates:** Peak

(Dec–Apr) $149–$159 ste. Extra person $10. Children under age 12 stay free. Lower rates off-season. MAP rates avail. Parking: Indoor/outdoor, free. AE, DISC, MC, V.

### ≡≡≡ Embassy Suites Boca Raton

661 NW 53rd St, 33487; tel 561/994-8200 or toll free 800/521-9183; fax 561/994-9518. Exit 40 off I-95. An appealing, midrise, all-suites hotel. **Rooms:** 263 stes. CI 3pm/CO noon. Nonsmoking rms avail. **Amenities:** 🛏 🅰 🔁 🍸 A/C, cable TV w/movies, refrig, dataport, voice mail, in-rm safe, bathrobes. All units w/terraces. **Services:** 🍽 🖼 🆅🅿 🚐 🖼 🔁 Car-rental desk, masseur, babysitting. **Facilities:** 🏋 🚲 🔥 600 🔥 1 restaurant, 1 bar, sauna, whirlpool, washer/dryer. **Rates:** Peak (Dec–Apr) $159 ste. Extra person $10. Children under age 12 stay free. Lower rates off-season. MAP rates avail. Parking: Indoor/outdoor, free. AE, DISC, MC, V.

### ≡≡≡ Holiday Inn Glades Road

1950 W Glades Rd, 33431; tel 561/368-5200 or toll free 800/HOLIDAY; fax 561/395-4783. Exit 39 off I-95. Featuring a lobby set in Mexican tile adjoining a sunny courtyard. **Rooms:** 181 rms and stes. CI 3pm/CO noon. Nonsmoking rms avail. Upholstered reading chairs in each room. **Amenities:** 🛏 🅰 A/C, cable TV w/movies. Some units w/minibars, all w/terraces. **Services:** ✕ 🖼 🔁 Babysitting. **Facilities:** 🏋 200 🔥 2 restaurants (bkfst and dinner only), 1 bar (w/entertainment), games rm, whirlpool, beauty salon. **Rates (CP):** Peak (Dec–April) $125–$150 S; $135–$160 D; $199 ste. Extra person $10. Children under age 18 stay free. Lower rates off-season. Parking: Indoor/outdoor, free. AE, DC, DISC, JCB, MC, V.

### ≡≡ Holiday Inn West

8144 Glades Rd, 33434; tel 561/482-7070 or toll free 800/HOLIDAY; fax 561/482-6076. Off FL Tpk. Satisfactory lodging, although the bar is probably more popular than the hotel. **Rooms:** 100 rms. CI 2pm/CO noon. Nonsmoking rms avail. A few units open to the pool area. **Amenities:** 🛏 🅰 A/C, cable TV w/movies. Some units w/terraces. **Services:** ✕ 🔁 Babysitting. **Facilities:** 🏋 1 restaurant, 2 bars (1 w/entertainment). Extremely busy restaurant and sports bar has memorabilia of former baseball great Pete Rose, who is a part-owner. **Rates:** Peak (Dec–April) $99–$105 S or D. Extra person $6. Children under age 18 stay free. Lower rates off-season. Parking: Outdoor, free. AE, DISC, MC, V.

### ≡≡≡ Radisson Suites Hotel

7920 Glades Rd, 33434; tel 561/483-3600 or toll free 800/333-3333; fax 561/479-2280. Glades Rd exit off I-95. Very appealing hotel earns high marks for its good blend of business and leisure facilities. Public areas are noteworthy for their eye-catching look. Hardworking housekeeping staff keeps everything spotless. **Rooms:** 200 stes. Executive level. CI 3pm/CO noon. Nonsmoking rms avail. **Amenities:** 🛏 🅰 🔁 🍸 A/C, cable TV w/movies, dataport, VCR, CD/tape player, voice mail. All units w/minibars, some w/terraces. **Services:** ✕ 🖼 🖼 🔁 🍽 Babysitting. **Facilities:** 🏋 🎿 200 🔥 1 restaurant (bkfst only), 1 bar, whirlpool, washer/dryer. **Rates (BB):** Peak (Jan–Apr) $179 ste. Extra person $10. Children under age 18 stay free. Lower rates off-season. Parking: Outdoor, free. AE, DC, DISC, JCB, MC, V.

### ▤▤ Ramada Hotel of Boca Raton

2901 N Federal Hwy, 33431; tel 561/395-6850 or toll free 800/228-2828; fax 561/368-7964. Between Glades Rd and Spanish River Rd on US 1. A tropical-themed, four-story hotel with a rather glitzy lobby with a fountain and lots of jungle foliage. **Rooms:** 95 rms. CI 3pm/CO noon. Nonsmoking rms avail. **Amenities:** 🛏 A/C, cable TV. Some units w/terraces. **Services:** ✕ ▨ ↵ **Facilities:** 🖎 🛁 ⅙ 1 restaurant (dinner only), 1 bar, spa, whirlpool. **Rates:** Peak (Dec–Apr) $85–$115 S or D. Children under age 18 stay free. Lower rates off-season. Parking: Outdoor, free. AE, CB, DC, DISC, MC, V.

### ▤▤▤ Residence Inn by Marriott

525 NW 77th St, 33487; tel 561/994-3222 or toll free 800/331-3131; fax 561/994-3339. Congress Ave exit off I-95. Located on a manmade lake, this all-suites hotel in a pastoral setting features a sports court with tennis, volleyball, and basketball. **Rooms:** 120 stes. CI 3pm/CO noon. Nonsmoking rms avail. **Amenities:** 🛏 🕭 📺 A/C, cable TV w/movies, refrig. Some units w/terraces, all w/fireplaces. VCRs available on request. **Services:** ▨ ↵ 🐾 Babysitting. Social hour held Mon–Thurs 5–7pm. **Facilities:** 🖎 ▣ 🛁 ⅙ Whirlpool, washer/dryer. Breakfast served in clubhouse with fireplace. Gold's Gym is free to guests. **Rates (CP):** Peak (Dec–Apr) $179–$199 ste. Children under age 18 stay free. Lower rates off-season. Parking: Outdoor, free. AE, DC, DISC, MC, V.

### ▤▤▤ Sheraton Boca Raton Hotel & Towers

2000 NW 19th St, 33431; tel 561/368-5252 or toll free 800/394-7829; fax 561/750-5437. 2½ mi off FL Tpk; Glades Rd W exit off I-95. Close to a mall. **Rooms:** 193 rms and stes. Executive level. CI 3pm/CO noon. Nonsmoking rms avail. **Amenities:** 🛏 🕭 A/C, cable TV w/movies. Some units w/terraces. **Services:** ✕ ▨ ↵ Twice-daily maid svce, car-rental desk, babysitting. **Facilities:** 🖎 ●² 🛁 🛏 ⅙ 1 restaurant, 1 bar (w/entertainment), washer/dryer. **Rates (CP):** Peak (Dec–Apr) $139–$149 S or D; $159–$199 ste. Extra person $10. Children under age 12 stay free. Lower rates off-season. Parking: Outdoor, free. AE, CB, DC, DISC, MC, V.

## MOTEL

### ▤ Shore Edge Motel

425 N Ocean Blvd, 33432; tel 561/395-4491 or toll free 800/BOCA SUN. Palmetto Pk Rd exit off I-95. A mom-and-pop motel. **Rooms:** 16 rms and effic. CI 1pm/CO 11am. Nonsmoking rms avail. Efficiencies with full baths, standard rooms with showers only. **Amenities:** 🛏 🕭 A/C, cable TV w/movies, refrig. **Services:** ↵ Babysitting. **Facilities:** 🖎 Washer/dryer. **Rates:** Peak (Jan–March) $75 S or D; $95 effic. Lower rates off-season. Parking: Outdoor, free. MC, V.

## RESORT

### ▤▤▤▤ Boca Raton Resort & Club

501 E Camino Real, PO Box 5025, 33431; tel 561/395-3000 or toll free 800/327-0101; fax 561/391-3183. Exit 38 or 37 off I-95. 356 acres. Back in the 1920s, the Cloisters, as it was then known, was one of the pace-setting pamperers to winter-weary northerners, and a pioneer of the Spanish-Moorish style of Florida's grand hotels. The original Cloister wing still retains its placid courtyards and tiled fountains, but the Boca Raton now incorporates a 27-story tower and a midrise beach resort across the Intracoastal Waterway. And the nabobs have been replaced by conventioneers (three guests in every four are there for a business meeting); some vacationers may think twice about checking into a resort with signs saying "Shhhh! You're friends are sleeping. . ." However, if resorts were judged solely on their sports facilities, the Boca Raton would rate six out of five—everything here is offered in duplicate or better. **Rooms:** 963 rms and stes; 60 cottages/villas. Executive level. CI 3pm/CO noon. Nonsmoking rms avail. Lodgings vary from cramped and makeshift to spacious and sunny, with the most stylish in the Beach Club, although many guests prefer the traditional styling of the Cloister, especially those rooms facing the inner courtyard. **Amenities:** 🛏 🕭 🍴 A/C, cable TV w/movies, dataport, voice mail, in-rm safe, bathrobes. All units w/minibars, some w/terraces. **Services:** |◎| ▭ VP 🚐 ▨ ↵ Twice-daily maid svce, car-rental desk, social director, masseur, children's program, babysitting. Concierge International Program; Shuttle service 7am–3am to Beach Club and Country Club. **Facilities:** 🖎 ▶₃₆ ●²¹ ▣ 🛏 ▢ ⅙ 11 restaurants, 8 bars (2 w/entertainment), 1 beach (ocean), lifeguard, games rm, lawn games, racquetball, snorkeling, squash, sauna, steam rm, whirlpool, beauty salon, day-care ctr, playground. 1 croquet court, 4 indoor racquetball courts, 3 fitness centers, 111 beach cabanas, 24-slip marina (offering sailing, fishing, power craft, and boogie boards). The original El Patio Restaurant has now been relegated to a breakfast room. **Rates:** Peak (Jan 2–Apr 13) $230–$495 S or D; $470–$5,500 ste; $240–$425 cottage/villa. Extra person $30. Children under age 16 stay free. Lower rates off-season. MAP rates avail. Parking: Outdoor, $7/day. Rates determined by location rather than size or amenities, the least expensive being in the original wing, the most expensive by the beach. AE, DC, JCB, MC, V.

## RESTAURANTS 🍽

### ★ Baci

In Mizner Park, 344 Plaza Real; tel 561/362-8500. **Italian.** A casual, upscale eatery with a festive atmosphere. You can sit indoors in wrought-iron chairs at black-topped tables and watch your meal being prepared in the spotless open kitchen. Or, if you prefer, dine on the outdoor patio as you watch the crowds go by. Poached pear and pecan risotto, and angel-hair pasta with shrimp, scallops, and mussels are specialties. **FYI:**

Reservations accepted. Dress code. **Open:** Lunch daily 11:30am–2:30pm; dinner daily 5–11pm; brunch Sun 11am–3pm. **Prices:** Main courses $10–$15. AE, MC, V. ⬕ VP &

**♣ Bistro l'Europe**
In Mizner Park, 346 Plaza Real; tel 561/368-4488. **Continental/French.** Rich walnut furnishings and flooring, French artwork, and an attractively displayed selection of wines set the scene at this relaxed, civilized bistro. The menu includes rack of lamb, couscous-stuffed Cornish game hen, veal medallions, and Black Angus steak au poivre. **FYI:** Reservations accepted. Dress code. **Open:** Lunch Mon–Sat 11:30am–5pm; dinner daily 6–11pm. **Prices:** Main courses $20–$26. AE, DC, MC, V. ⦿ ⬕ VP &

**✹ Cafe Ole**
In Arvida Parkway Center, 7860 Glades Rd; tel 561/852-8063. Exit 75 off FL Tpk. **Mexican.** Spanish tile and *nuevo* Mexican decor help to create a comfortable, festive atmosphere. The cantina's covered patio overlooks a manmade lake. Chili relleno is a house specialty, and three fresh fish entrees are offered daily. **FYI:** Reservations accepted. Children's menu. Beer and wine only. No smoking. **Open:** Lunch Mon–Fri 11:30am–2pm; dinner daily 5–10pm. **Prices:** Main courses $7–$14. AE, CB, DC, DISC, MC, V. ▦ VP &

**♣ The Gazebo Cafe**
4199 N Federal Hwy; tel 561/395-6033. **French.** An excellent dining experience on all counts. Decorated in antiques, crisp linen, and French art, with a marble-topped bar overlooking the spotless open kitchen. A grand chandelier dominates the room. The menu regularly includes rack of lamb, chateaubriand for two, fresh salmon and scallops, and veal medallion. **FYI:** Reservations accepted. Piano/singer. **Open:** Lunch Mon–Fri 11:30am–3pm; dinner daily 5:30–10pm. **Prices:** Main courses $17–$30. AE, CB, DC, DISC, MC, V. ⦿ &

**La Finestra**
171 E Palmetto Park Rd; tel 561/392-1838. **Italian.** A petite, romantic cafe adorned with pink linen and fresh roses. Fare includes antipasti as well as pasta, chicken, fish, and beef tenderloin dishes. The pasta with crabmeat, clams, and shrimp in a light tomato sauce is a house specialty. **FYI:** Reservations accepted. Beer and wine only. **Open:** Daily 6–10pm. **Prices:** Main courses $15–$29. AE, MC, V. ⦿ &

**✹ La Truc**
299 E Palmetto Park Rd; tel 561/392-4568. **Vietnamese.** Authentic Vietnamese dishes served in simple but attractive surroundings. French pastries for dessert. **FYI:** Reservations accepted. Beer and wine only. **Open:** Lunch Mon–Sat 11am–2:30pm; dinner Mon–Sat 5–10pm, Sun 5–9pm. **Prices:** Main courses $12–$17. AE, DC, MC, V.

**L'Auberge le Grillon**
6900 N Federal Hwy; tel 561/997-6888. **Continental.** A tiny, antique-filled, vine-covered cottage with an intimate atmosphere. The traditional French menu typically includes veal and beef tenderloin medallions, the chef's fresh seafood specialty, and a particularly good vegetable platter. There is a fine selection of wines. Banquet facilities are available for small or large parties. **FYI:** Reservations recommended. Dress code. Beer and wine only. No smoking. **Open:** Tues–Sun 6–9:30pm. **Prices:** Main courses $20–$36. AE, DC, MC, V. VP &

**♣ La Vieille Maison**
770 E Palmetto Park Rd; tel 561/391-6701. 1½ blocks W of FL A1A. **French.** A Mediterranean-style manor house filled with antiques, handsome dark carpets, and loads of country-French charm. Dine in one of several intimate rooms, each of which holds only two or three cozy linen-covered tables. Appetizers include bell-pepper soup and open-faced ravioli with duck confit and sage butter. For dinner, options include roast rack of lamb with thyme and goat cheese, and salmon wrapped in rice paper. Service is laudable. **FYI:** Reservations accepted. Dress code. **Open:** Dinner daily 6–9:30pm. **Prices:** Main courses $18–$35. AE, DC, DISC, MC, V. ⦿ VP &

**✹ Maxaluna Tuscan Grill**
In the Crocker Center, 5050 Town Center Circle #245; tel 561/391-7177. **Italian.** Trendy, stylish restaurant serving innovative contemporary northern Italian cuisine, with many dishes prepared on the Tuscan oak-fired grill. Wide selection of wines by the glass. **FYI:** Reservations accepted. Children's menu. Beer and wine only. **Open:** Lunch Mon–Fri 11:30am–2:30pm; dinner Sun–Fri 5:30–10:30pm, Sat 6–10:30pm. **Prices:** Main courses $16–$35. AE, DC, MC, V. ⬕ ▦ &

**✹ Max's Grille**
In Mizner Park, 404 Plaza Real; tel 561/368-0080. **New American.** A casually elegant art-deco bistro and bar with an innovative menu that includes New York strip steak or yellowfin tuna prepared on the oak wood grill, as well as a variety of creative salads. **FYI:** Reservations accepted. Dress code. **Open:** Dinner Mon–Thurs 5:30–10:30pm, Fri–Sat 5–11pm, Sun 5–10pm; brunch Sat 11:30am–2:30pm, Sun 11:30am–3pm. **Prices:** Main courses $11–$20. AE, DISC, MC, V. VP &

**✹ Nick's Italian Fishery**
In One Boca Place, 2255 Glades Rd; tel 561/994-2201. **Seafood/Pasta.** Enjoy seafood dishes prepared Italian-style in an attractive, upbeat dining room with a wall of windows and a thousand-gallon aquarium. The popular eatery is known for its huge portions. **FYI:** Reservations accepted. Band. Dress code. **Open:** Lunch Mon–Fri 11:30am–2:30pm; dinner daily 5–11pm; brunch Sun 11:30am–2:30pm. **Prices:** Main courses $15–$50. AE, DC, DISC, MC, V. ⦿ ▦ ▢ &

**Outback Steakhouse**
In the Shoppes at Village Pointe, 6030 18th St SW; tel 561/338-6283. **Seafood/Steak.** This rustic steakhouse, housed in a vibrant pink edifice, keeps its patrons happy with enormous portions and a rollicking atmosphere. **FYI:** Reservations not

accepted. Children's menu. **Open:** Mon–Thurs 4:30–10:30pm, Fri–Sat 4–11:30pm, Sun 4–10:30pm. **Prices:** Main courses $10–$20. AE, DC, DISC, MC, V. &

**Peking**
2300 N Federal Hwy; tel 561/392-0666. **Chinese.** Standard Chinese menu offered in a casual setting. **FYI:** Reservations accepted. Dress code. **Open:** Daily 11:30am–10pm. **Prices:** Main courses $7–$18. AE, CB, DC, MC, V. 🚗 ☑ &

**★ Prezzo**
In Arvida Parkway Center, 7820 Glades Rd; tel 561/451-2800. Glades Rd exit off FL Tpk. **Italian/Pizza.** A stylish, upbeat place with a menu designed to make the most of the kitchen's wood-fired brick oven. A young and friendly staff serves brick-oven pizzas and other house specialties. If you have to wait for a table, you can enjoy a drink at one of the attractive bar area's granite-topped tables. **FYI:** Reservations not accepted. Children's menu. **Open:** Lunch Mon–Fri 11:30am–2:30pm; dinner Mon–Thurs 5:30–11pm, Fri–Sat 5pm–midnight, Sun 5–10pm. **Prices:** Main courses $7–$19. AE, CB, DC, DISC, MC, V. 🖼 &

**Tom's Place**
7251 N Federal Hwy; tel 561/997-0920. **Soul/Southern.** A casual eatery with vinyl tablecloths and customers' pictures on the walls. Known for its food, not its decor. The specialties here are Tom's meaty baby-back ribs, his St Louis–style barbecue, and chicken prepared to order, either barbecued or fried. **FYI:** Reservations not accepted. Children's menu. Beer and wine only. **Open:** Mon 4–10pm, Tues–Fri 11:30am–10pm, Sat noon–10pm. **Prices:** Main courses $6–$17; prix fixe $9–$15. MC, V. &

**★ Uncle Tai's**
In Crocker Center, 5250 Town Center Circle; tel 561/368-8806. **Chinese.** The menu is as sophisticated as the decor in this handsome, refined Chinese restaurant, done in linen and polished woods. Specialties include Hunan-style sliced lamb. **FYI:** Reservations accepted. Beer and wine only. **Open:** Lunch Mon–Sat 11:30am–2:30pm; dinner Sun–Thurs 5–10pm, Fri–Sat 5–10:30pm. **Prices:** Main courses $9–$18. AE, DC, DISC, MC, V. ♥ ⚑ ☑ VP &

**⑤ Wilt Chamberlain's**
In Somerset Shoppes, 8903 W Glades Rd; tel 561/488-8881. **American.** Sports memorabilia, TV monitors, and video games fill this sports bar and restaurant. Both the food and the atmosphere make this a great family eatery. However, the same features that make this place festive and fun can also make it a madhouse at times. **FYI:** Reservations not accepted. Children's menu. No smoking. **Open:** Daily 11:30am–1:30am. **Prices:** Main courses $6–$15. AE, DC, DISC, MC, V. 🖼 🚗 &

## ATTRACTIONS 🏛

### Boca Raton Museum of Art
801 W Palmetto Park Rd; tel 561/392-2500. In addition to a small permanent collection that is strongest in 19th-century European oils, the museum holds temporary exhibitions by local and international artists. **Open:** Mon–Fri 10am–4pm, Sun noon–4pm. $

### Children's Science Exploratorium
131 SE Mizner Blvd, Ste 15; tel 561/395-8401. Located in the Royal Palm Plaza shopping center. Interactive exhibits teach children how things work. Displays on magnetic fields, bridge construction, gravitational forces, and computer technology. **Open:** Tues–Sat 10am–5pm, Sun noon–5pm. $

# Bokeelia

See Pine Island

# Bonita Springs

Capitalizing on its location at the northwestern edge of Big Cypress Swamp, this tiny Collier County town offers visitors the Everglades Wonder Garden tour and boat tours of Estero Bay. **Information:** Bonita Springs Area Chamber of Commerce, 25071 Chamber of Commerce Dr, PO Box 1240, Bonita Springs, 33959 (tel 941/992-2943).

## MOTEL 🏨

### ≣≣ Comfort Inn Motel
9800 Bonita Beach Rd, 33923; tel 941/992-5001 or toll free 800/892-3605; fax 941/992-9283. Exit 18 off I-75. A three-story motel featuring a handsome courtyard with oversized pool. **Rooms:** 69 rms. CI 3pm/CO 11am. Nonsmoking rms avail. **Amenities:** 🛏 ♨ A/C, cable TV w/movies, refrig, in-rm safe. All units w/terraces. All units with wet bars. **Services:** ⇦ **Facilities:** 🏠 & 1 restaurant, whirlpool, washer/dryer. **Rates:** Peak (Jan 15–Apr 15) $88 S; $93 D. Extra person $5. Children under age 18 stay free. Lower rates off-season. Parking: Outdoor, free. AE, CB, DC, DISC, MC, V.

## RESTAURANTS 🍴

### McCully's Rooftop
In Rooftop Plaza, 25999 Hickory Blvd; tel 941/992-0033. **Regional American/Continental.** Views of the back bay and Gulf give guests the chance to watch the sun set and the porpoises play as they dine. Grouper maison, seafood strudel, prime rib, and catch of the day are all good bets for dinner. **FYI:** Reservations not accepted. Piano. Children's menu. **Open:** Lunch Mon–Fri 11:30am–2:30pm; dinner daily 5–10pm; brunch Sun 10:30am–2pm. **Prices:** Main courses $16–$18. AE, CB, DC, DISC, MC, V. 🏔 &

### The Ship Restaurant & Tavern
24080 N Tamiani Trail; tel 941/947-3333. N of Bonita Springs. **Seafood/Steak.** The nautical theme is unrelenting at this replica of a double-masted pirate schooner: the kids' menu can be made into a pirate mask, servers dress like "wenches" and "swashbucklers." The menu emphasizes seafood, but salads, sandwiches, and steaks are also available. **FYI:** Reservations not accepted. Rock. Children's menu. **Open:** Lunch daily 11:30am–3pm; dinner daily 4–11pm. **Prices:** Main courses $12–$17. AE, DISC, MC, V. 🖼

## ATTRACTION 🏛

### Koreshan State Historic Site
Estero; tel 941/992-0311. Located off US 41 along the Estero River, this historic landmark was the site inhabited by a now-extinct religious sect, the Koreshan Unity Movement, which believed that man lived inside the Earth. Several buildings and gardens have been restored, and a museum explains the sect's story. Nature trails and canoe trails run through the settlement. Boating, canoe rentals, hiking, camping. **Open:** Daily 8am–sunset. **$$**

# Boynton Beach

Railroad magnate Henry Flagler turned this sleepy settlement into a vacation boomtown when he opened a hotel here in the 1890s. A century later, retirees are fueling another boom, as population has tripled in the last 25 years. **Information:** Greater Boynton Beach Chamber of Commerce, 639 E Ocean Ave #108, Boynton Beach, 33435 (tel 561/732-9501).

## HOTELS 🏨

### 🏨🏨 Holiday Inn Catalina
1601 N Congress Ave, 33436; tel 561/737-4600 or toll free 800/23-HOTEL; fax 561/734-6523. 1 mi N of Boynton Beach Blvd. A fine choice off the beach, good for families and business clientele alike. Spanish-style courtyard with pool and palms is popular among guests. Boynton Beach Mall is next door. **Rooms:** 152 rms and effic. CI 2pm/CO noon. Nonsmoking rms avail. **Amenities:** 🛗 ⚙ A/C, cable TV w/movies. All units w/terraces. **Services:** ✕ 🚐 ⛱ ♫ Car-rental desk, babysitting. Housekeeping can be a little slow. **Facilities:** 🛗 📶 ♿ 1 restaurant, 1 bar, whirlpool. Popular dance club. **Rates:** Peak (Dec–Apr) $105–$120 S or D; $130 effic. Extra person $20. Children under age 18 stay free. Lower rates off-season. Parking: Outdoor, free. AE, DISC, MC, V.

### 🏨🏨 Holiday Inn Express
480 W Boynton Beach Blvd, 33435; tel 561/734-9100 or toll free 800/HOLIDAY; fax 561/734-9100 ext 252. Exit 44 off I-95. A slimmed-down version of the bigger Holiday Inns, only one mile from the beach. **Rooms:** 102 rms. CI 2pm/CO noon. Nonsmoking rms avail. **Amenities:** 🛗 ⚙ A/C, cable TV w/movies. **Services:** ♫ Babysitting. Cocktail party offered Mon–Sat 5–7pm. **Facilities:** 🛗 📶 ♿ **Rates:** Peak (Dec–Apr)

$59 S; $69 D. Extra person $15. Children under age 19 stay free. Lower rates off-season. Parking: Outdoor, free. AARP discounts avail. AE, DISC, MC, V.

## RESTAURANTS 🍽

### ★ Banana Boat Restaurant
739 E Ocean Ave; tel 561/732-9400. **American/Seafood.** This popular waterside eatery features two indoor bars and one outdoors. A great place to mingle with beautiful people enjoying après-sun delights. The menu features a catch of the day; the Oreo cheesecake is the special dessert. **FYI:** Reservations not accepted. Band. Children's menu. **Open:** Mon–Sat 11am–12:30am, Sun 9am–1pm. **Prices:** Main courses $8–$25. AE, DC, DISC, MC, V. 🚢 ♿

### ★ Benvenuto
1730 N Federal Hwy; tel 561/364-0600. 1 mi N of Boynton Beach Blvd. **Continental/Italian.** Housed in a restored 1929 abode designed by Addison Mizner, this restaurant consists of three upbeat, stylized rooms, all with lovely appointments. The cuisine is well-known for both its quality and presentation. Menu highlights include lamb chops, snapper, and salmon dishes. **FYI:** Reservations recommended. Beer and wine only. **Open:** Mon–Fri 5–10pm. **Prices:** Main courses $14–$23; prix fixe $46. AE, DC, MC, V. ♥ 🖼 ♿

## ATTRACTION 🏛

### Arthur R Marshall Loxahatchee National Wildlife Refuge
Tel 561/734-8303. This 145,000-acre refuge protects such endangered species as the snail kite and wood stork, and threatened species like the American alligator. Migrating waterfowl flock here in the winter. Observation tower, visitor center with exhibits and introductory slide show; also nature trails and a 5.5-mile canoe trail. The refuge also offers fishing, boating, and birdwatching opportunities at its three recreation area entrances. **Open:** Daily 6am–sunset. **$$**

# Bradenton

In 1539, conquistador Hernando de Soto landed nearby at the Manatee River's entrance to Tampa Bay. Today, this Gulf Coast town remembers its heritage with a weeklong festival (held every April) and a 25-acre living history park. Nearby, quaint Anna Maria Island has prohibited high rises; its beaches are superb for shelling. **Information:** Manatee Chamber of Commerce, 222 10th St W, PO Box 321, Bradenton, 34206 (tel 941/748-3411).

## HOTELS 🏨

### 🏨🏨 Bradenton Inn
2303 1st St E, 34208; tel 941/747-6465 or toll free 800/447-6465. At 23rd Ave. Nicely kept property convenient to local attractions and close to town. **Rooms:** 150 rms and effic.

CI 1pm/CO 11am. Nonsmoking rms avail. Recently renovated rooms are clean and comfortable. **Amenities:** 🔒 A/C, cable TV. **Services:** ⛵ ↺ **Facilities:** 🎣 📶 1 bar (w/entertainment), playground, washer/dryer. **Rates (CP):** Peak (Jan–Apr) $60–$65 S or D; $75 effic. Extra person $6. Children under age 12 stay free. Lower rates off-season. Parking: Outdoor, free. AE, CB, DC, DISC, MC, V.

### ≣ ≣ Days Inn
3506 1st St W, 34208; tel 941/746-1141 or toll free 800/329-7466; fax 941/745-2382. On US 41 S at 35th Ave. Within seven miles of Gulf coast beaches and centrally located to area attractions. The friendly staff caters to families. **Rooms:** 134 rms. CI 3pm/CO noon. Nonsmoking rms avail. **Amenities:** 🔒 A/C, satel TV, in-rm safe. **Services:** ⛵ ↺ ↢ **Facilities:** 🎣 📶 ⅄ 1 restaurant, playground. **Rates:** Peak (Jan–Apr) $70–$99 S; $83–$88 D. Extra person $5. Children under age 12 stay free. Lower rates off-season. Parking: Outdoor, free. AE, DC, DISC, MC, V.

### ≣ ≣ ≣ Holiday Inn Riverfront
100 Riverfront Blvd, 34205; tel 941/747-3727 or toll free 800/23-HOTEL; fax 941/746-4289. At intersection of US 41 and Manatee. A quiet hotel with mission-style architecture. Attractive river view from a courtyard pool nestled among gardens and waterfalls. **Rooms:** 153 rms and stes. CI 2pm/CO noon. Nonsmoking rms avail. **Amenities:** 🔒 🌀 📶 A/C, cable TV w/movies, dataport. All units w/terraces. **Services:** ✗ ⛵ ↺ Twice-daily maid svce. **Facilities:** 🎣 ♨ 📶 ⅄ 1 restaurant, 1 bar, whirlpool. Poolside bar has a covered outside terrace overlooking the courtyard. **Rates (MAP):** Peak (Jan–Apr) $99–$109 S or D; $129 ste. Extra person $10. Children under age 18 stay free. Lower rates off-season. Parking: Outdoor, free. AE, CB, DC, DISC, EC, MC, V.

## MOTELS

### ≣ ≣ Catalina Beach Resort
1325 Gulf Dr N, Bradenton Beach, 34217; tel 941/778-6611; fax 941/778-6748. Take Cortez Road over the bridge to Bradenton Beach. Small family-owned hostelry directly across from the beach. A good value for family vacations. **Rooms:** 35 rms and effic. CI 2pm/CO 11am. **Amenities:** 🔒 A/C, TV, refrig. **Services:** ✗ ↺ **Facilities:** 🎣 △ 📶 1 restaurant (dinner only), 1 beach (ocean), washer/dryer. Gas grills available. **Rates:** Peak (Feb–Apr) $77 S or D; $107 ste; $92 effic. Extra person $6. Children under age 3 stay free. Min stay special events. Lower rates off-season. Parking: Outdoor, free. AE, DC, DISC, MC, V.

### ≣ Knights Inn
668 67th St Circle E, 34208; tel 941/745-1876 or toll free 800/843-5644; fax 941/745-1876 ext 615. Exit 42 off I-75. Situated off the highway, it's fine for a night's rest. Fast food restaurants are a few yards away. **Rooms:** 105 rms and effic. CI 3pm/CO 11am. Nonsmoking rms avail. **Amenities:** 🔒 A/C, satel TV. **Services:** ↺ ↢ **Facilities:** 🎣 Washer/dryer.

**Rates:** Peak (Jan–May) $50 S; $55 D; $60 effic. Extra person $5. Children under age 18 stay free. Lower rates off-season. Parking: Outdoor, free. AE, CB, DC, DISC, MC, V.

### ≣ ≣ Park Inn Club and Breakfast
4450 47th St W, 34210; tel 941/795-4633 or toll free 800/437-PARK; fax 941/795-0808. Off Cortez Rd. Spacious motel with relaxing, comfortable atmosphere. **Rooms:** 128 rms and stes. CI 3pm/CO noon. Nonsmoking rms avail. **Amenities:** 🔒 🌀 ⅄ A/C, cable TV. Some units w/whirlpools. TV speaker in bathroom. **Services:** ⛵ ↺ ↢ Car-rental desk, babysitting. Complimentary coffee and evening cocktails. **Facilities:** 🎣 📶 ⅄ 1 bar, whirlpool. **Rates (CP):** Peak (Nov–Apr) $111 S; $106 D; $115 ste. Extra person $8. Children under age 18 stay free. Lower rates off-season. Parking: Outdoor, free. AE, CB, DC, DISC, MC, V.

### ≣ Sand & Sea Motel
2412 Gulf Dr, Bradenton Beach, 34217; tel 941/778-2231. Between Cortez Rd and Manatee Ave (FL 64). Simple but pleasant three-story building with spectacular Gulf views. **Rooms:** 28 rms and effic. CI 2pm/CO 11am. **Amenities:** 🔒 📶 A/C, cable TV, refrig. Some units w/terraces. Units equipped with dishes, utensils, and other items for multiple-night stays. **Services:** ↺ ↢ Pets allowed (October–May) with $25 fee. **Facilities:** 🎣 ⅄ 1 beach (ocean), washer/dryer. Gas grill on premises. **Rates:** Peak (Feb–Apr 15) $90 S or D; $95 effic. Extra person $5. Children under age 5 stay free. Min stay special events. Lower rates off-season. Parking: Outdoor, free. MC, V.

## RESTAURANTS 🍴

### Asia Restaurant and Lounge
6844 14th St W; tel 941/758-7133. S of airport. **Chinese.** Unusually tasty Chinese fare served in large portions by attentive wait staff in spiffy uniforms. Take-out also available. **FYI:** Reservations recommended. Children's menu. **Open:** Daily 11am–11pm. **Prices:** Main courses $7–$18. AE, DISC, MC, V. 🚗 ✉ ⅄

### Beachhouse Restaurant
200 Gulf Dr N, Bradenton Beach; tel 941/779-2222. **Seafood/Steak.** A casual eatery with an outdoor deck overlooking the Gulf. Sample one of the nightly specials or the fresh catch of the day and follow your choice with the pound cake and vanilla ice cream topped with a raspberry. **FYI:** Reservations not accepted. Singer. Children's menu. Dress code. **Open:** Daily 11:30am–10pm. **Prices:** Main courses $10–$16. AE, CB, DC, DISC, ER, MC, V. ✉ ⅄

### Leverock's Seafood House
12320 Manatee Ave W; tel 941/794-8900. Exit 42 off I-75. **Seafood.** A spectacular waterfront dining room with a great bar. Dine on fresh local catch as you watch a bevy of boats enter and leave the nearby marina. **FYI:** Reservations not

accepted. Children's menu. **Open:** Daily 11:30am–10pm. **Prices:** Main courses $7–$20. AE, DC, DISC, MC, V. ▰ ▽ ♿

### ★ Miller's Dutch Kitchen

3401 14th St W; tel 941/746-8253. 15 mi S of Bradenton; exit 42 off I-75. **American.** An oasis of home-style Amish food, nestled along a busy road known more for fast food. The menu includes Dutch casserole (noodles, peas, cheese, potatoes, beef, mushrooms, and chicken soup with croutons), pan-fried chicken, and cabbage rolls. To top it off, there are more than 20 varieties of freshly baked pies. Gift shop and bakery also on premises. **FYI:** Reservations not accepted. Children's menu. No liquor license. No smoking. **Open:** Mon–Sat 11am–8pm. **Prices:** Main courses $6–$13. MC, V. ♿

### ★ Old Hamburg Restaurant

In Island Centre Shopping Center, 3246 East Bay Dr, Anna Maria Island; tel 941/778-1370. Off Cortez Blvd. **German/Polish.** Old-world eatery offering an unexpected array of ethnic food: meat pierogi, red borscht, potato pancakes, sauerbrauten, and potato soup. Snapshots of smiling customers plaster the walls. **FYI:** Reservations recommended. Beer and wine only. **Open:** Daily 11:30am–10pm. **Prices:** Main courses $9–$13. No CC. ▽

### The Oyster Bar

100 Bay Blvd, Anna Maria Island; tel 941/778-0475. At Pine Blvd. **Seafood.** Seafood from Florida and Maine is the focus of this down-to-earth eatery. The dining room itself sits just 700 feet from shore at the end of a rough, rail-less wooden pier, while paper towels suspended over each table invite diners to dig right in and get messy. **FYI:** Reservations not accepted. Beer and wine only. **Open:** Sun–Thurs 11:30am–9pm, Fri–Sat 11:30am–10pm. **Prices:** Main courses $8–$18. AE, DISC, MC, V. ▰ ♿

### The Pier

1200 1st Ave W; tel 941/748-8087. **Seafood/Steak.** Panoramic harbor views, a saltwater aquarium, and mounted fish set a very nautical tone. The menu offers such local favorites as red snapper meunière, crab-stuffed shrimp, baked oysters imperial, and Florida crab cakes. Outside service and dockside moorings also available. **FYI:** Reservations recommended. Singer. Children's menu. **Open:** Mon–Thurs 11:30am–9pm, Fri–Sat 11:30am–10pm, Sun 11:30am–9pm. **Prices:** Main courses $9–$20. AE, CB, DC, DISC, MC, V. ⛴ ▰ VP ♿

### Rotten Ralph's

902 S Bay Blvd, Anna Maria, Anna Maria Island; tel 941/778-3953. **American/Seafood.** Relax in a casual setting overlooking the bay as you dine on the fisherman's platter, crab cakes, deep-fried oysters, or chicken pot pie. A good value. **FYI:** Reservations not accepted. Children's menu. **Open:** Daily 11am–9pm. **Prices:** Main courses $7–$15. CB, DC, DISC, MC, V. ♿

### Sandbar

100 Spring Ave, Anna Maria, Anna Maria Island; tel 941/778-0444. Take Gulf Dr to Spring Ave. **Seafood.** Menu changes daily, depending on the local catch, but often includes shrimp sautéed with mushrooms and white wine, scallops in garlic butter, and stuffed grouper or flounder. Seafood combination platters, surf and turf, pasta, and chicken round out the menu. **FYI:** Reservations not accepted. Children's menu. **Open:** Daily 11:30am–10pm. **Prices:** Main courses $9–$22. AE, DC, MC, V. ▽ ♿

### Seafood Shack

4110 127th St W, Cortez; tel 941/794-1235. At Cortez Rd. **Seafood/Steak.** Overlooking the Intracoastal Waterway. You can take the showboat from the restaurant and receive $7 off dinner. Pay a visit to the Marina Grill lounge, located downstairs. **FYI:** Reservations not accepted. Children's menu. **Open:** Sun–Thurs 11:30am–9pm, Fri–Sat 11:30am–10pm. **Prices:** Main courses $10–$26. AE, MC, V. ♿

### ★ Shells in the Island Centre

3200 E Bay Blvd, Holmes Beach, Anna Maria Island; tel 941/778-5997. **Seafood/Steak.** This brightly colored seafood restaurant, with mounted fish on the walls, is known for its large portions. A good value. **FYI:** Reservations not accepted. Children's menu. Additional locations: 7253 S Tamiami Trail, Sarasota (tel 924-2568); 17855 Gulf Blvd, Redington Beach (tel 813/393-8990). **Open:** Sun–Thurs 4–10pm, Fri–Sat 4–11pm. **Prices:** Main courses $5–$15. AE, DISC, MC, V. ♿

## ATTRACTIONS 📷

### South Florida Museum and Bishop Planetarium

201 10th St W; tel 941/746-4131. Florida's history, from prehistory to the modern age, is told in exhibits that include a Native American collection with life-size dioramas; a replica of a 16th-century Spanish courtyard; and an indoor aquarium. The adjacent Bishop Planetarium features a 50-foot hemispherical dome for laser light shows and star-gazing activities. Star show is offered at 1:30pm and 3pm. **Open:** Tues–Sat 10am–5pm, Sun noon–6pm. **$$$**

### Manatee Village Historical Park

6th Ave E and 15th St E; tel 941/749-7165. This national historic site, located in a tree-shaded park, showcases restored buildings from the Bradenton area. Among the structures are the Manatee County Courthouse, dating to 1860; a Methodist church built in 1887; and the Wiggins General Store, dating to 1912 and full of local memorabilia and antique furnishings. **Open:** Mon–Fri 9am–4:30pm, Sun 1:30–4:30pm. **Free**

### De Soto National Memorial Park

75th St NW; tel 941/792-0458. Commemorates Spanish explorer Hernando de Soto's 1539 landing in Florida. The park features a restoration of de Soto's original camp site, as well as a scenic nature trail through a mangrove swamp that leads to the ruins of one of the first settlements in the area.

From December through March, park employees dress in 16th-century costumes and portray the lifestyle of the early settlers, including demonstrations of musket-firing and cooking. The visitor center displays weapons and armor from the era. **Open:** Daily 9am–5pm. **Free**

### Gamble Plantation
3708 Patten Ave, Ellenton; tel 941/723-4536. The oldest structure on the southwest coast of Florida, and a fine example of an antebellum plantation home. Built in the late 1840s by Maj Robert Gamble, it is maintained as a state historic site and includes an excellent collection of 19th-century furnishings. The only opportunity to view the interior is through guided tours given Thurs–Mon at 9:30 and 10:30am, and at 1, 2, 3, and 4pm. Visitor center open 8am–sunset. Closed some hols. **Open:** Park grounds, daily 8am–sunset. **$**

# Cape Coral

A city of 82,000 on a southwestern Florida peninsula, rivers separate it from Fort Myers (to the east) and popular Sanibel Island (to the south). Largely residential, it's also popular for fishing, golf, and boating. **Information:** Chamber of Commerce of Cape Coral, 2051 Cape Coral Pkwy E, PO Box 747, Cape Coral, 33910 (tel 941/549-6900).

## HOTEL 🏨

### 🛏🛏 Quality Inn–Fort Myers/Cape Coral
1538 Cape Coral Pkwy, 33904; tel 941/542-2121 or toll free 800/221-2222; fax 941/542-6319. Exit 21 off I-75. A good value. Roomy lobby done in a casual Florida style. **Rooms:** 142 rms. CI 1pm/CO 11am. Nonsmoking rms avail. **Amenities:** 🔒 ⚬ A/C, cable TV. Some units w/terraces. **Services:** 🛎 🍽 🐕 Babysitting. **Facilities:** 🏋 🏊₆₀ 🚹 1 bar (w/entertainment), washer/dryer. **Rates (CP):** Peak (Jan–Apr) $50–$55 S or D. Extra person $10. Children under age 18 stay free. Lower rates off-season. Parking: Outdoor, free. AE, CB, DC, DISC, MC, V.

## RESORT

### 🛏🛏🛏 Cape Coral Golf and Tennis Resort
4003 Palm Tree Blvd, 33904; tel 941/542-3191 or toll free 800/648-1475; fax 941/542-4694. Exit 21 off I-75. 205 acres. A heavenly haven for the golf enthusiast, with newly renovated course and facilities. **Rooms:** 100 rms. CI 3pm/CO noon. Nonsmoking rms avail. **Amenities:** 🔒 A/C, cable TV w/movies, voice mail. Some units w/terraces. **Services:** ✗ 🛎 🍽 Twice-daily maid svce, car-rental desk. **Facilities:** 🏋▶₁₈ 🏊₈ 🏊₂₀₀ 🚹 3 restaurants, 2 bars (1 w/entertainment), volleyball, lawn games. Restaurants range from the upscale Tee Cafe to the casual poolside bar and grill. **Rates:** Peak (Jan–

Mar) $99–$130 S or D. Extra person $15. Children under age 17 stay free. Lower rates off-season. MAP rates avail. Parking: Outdoor, free. AE, CB, DC, DISC, MC, V.

## RESTAURANTS 🍴

### ★ Dario's Restaurant and Lounge
In Coral Pointe Shopping Center, 1805 Del Prado Blvd; tel 941/574-7798. **Continental/Northern Italian.** The extensive menu includes veal prepared several ways. **FYI:** Reservations recommended. Children's menu. Dress code. **Open:** Lunch Mon–Fri 11:30am–2pm; dinner Mon–Sat 4–10pm, Sun 5–9pm. **Prices:** Main courses $9–$24. AE, CB, DC, DISC, MC, V. 📧 🚹

### Iguana Mia
1027 Cape Coral Pkwy; tel 941/945-7755. 2 mi W of the Cape Coral toll bridge. **Mexican.** All the familiar choices are offered, including fajitas, burritos, and taco salads. **FYI:** Reservations not accepted. Children's menu. Additional location: 4329 Cleveland Ave, Fort Myers (tel 939-5247). **Open:** Sun–Thurs 11am–10pm, Fri–Sat 11am–11pm. **Prices:** Main courses $4–$9. AE, DISC, MC, V. 🚹

# Cape Haze

## RESORT 🏨

### 🛏🛏🛏 Palm Island Resort
7002 Placida Rd, 33946; tel 941/697-4800 or toll free 800/824-5412, 800/282-6142 in FL; fax 941/697-0696. exit 34 off I-75 N; exit 32 off I-75 S. 200 acres. Spread between the mainland and an island lies this complex of privately owned condominiums, most of which are housed in three-story Victorian-style buildings. Mainland efficiences are at a marina (where registration and boat docking are). A private retreat for those who want to drop anchor and stay put. **Rooms:** 160 effic. CI 2:30pm/CO 11:30pm. **Amenities:** 🔒 ⚬ 📺 A/C, cable TV, refrig. All units w/terraces. **Services:** 🚐 🍽 Social director, children's program. Daily maid service on request. **Facilities:** 🏋₅ 🚴 ⛰ 📍 🎿 🏊 🏊₁₁ 🛶 🏊₁₂₀ 1 restaurant (lunch and dinner only), 1 bar, 1 beach (ocean), volleyball, lawn games, whirlpool, playground, washer/dryer. Golf-cart rentals available for traveling around the island. Barbecue grills poolside. **Rates:** Peak (Dec 15–Apr 15) $110–$425 effic. Extra person $15–$20. Min stay. Lower rates off-season. Parking: Outdoor, free. Rates (based on 2 people per bedroom) do not include one-time ferry fee of $15–$20. AE, DC, DISC, MC, V.

# Captiva Island

See also Pine Island, Sanibel Island

South Seas Plantation Resort—with 22 tennis courts, 17 pools, 9 holes of golf, and 700 employees—epitomizes the nature of this southwestern Gulf Coast destination. Guests can charter a cruise among other Lee Islands, or visit the Collier County Museum in nearby Naples. Wine fair held every June. **Information:** Sanibel–Captiva Islands Chamber of Commerce, 1159 Causeway Rd, Sanibel, 33957 (tel 941/472-1080).

## HOTEL 🏨

### ≣≣ 'Tween Waters Inn

15951 Captiva Dr, PO Box 249, 33924; tel 941/472-5161 or toll free 800/223-5865, 800/282-7560 in FL; fax 941/472-0249. 1.5 miles N of Captiva Bridge. 14 acres. Separated from its own beach by a road, this low-key lodging on the northern end of the island attracts both couples and families. The friendly staff partakes in the weekly activities, which include the long-standing tradition of crab races. **Rooms:** 84 rms, stes, and effic; 51 cottages/villas. CI 4pm/CO noon. Nonsmoking rms avail. Complex of 10 new rooms added in 1996. **Amenities:** 🛎 🕹 🖥 🎣 A/C, satel TV w/movies, refrig, in-rm safe. All units w/terraces, some w/fireplaces. **Services:** 🛎 ⟲ Full-service marina on property with charters, fuel, ships store, and rentals. **Facilities:** 🐟 🚴 ⚠ 🛶 📷3 📍150 2 restaurants (*see* "Restaurants" below), 3 bars (1 w/entertainment), 1 beach (ocean), volleyball, games rm, washer/dryer. **Rates:** Peak (Dec 22–Apr) $140–$215 S or D; $155–$255 effic; $215–$275 cottage/villa. Extra person $15. Children under age 12 stay free. Lower rates off-season. Parking: Indoor/outdoor, free. AE, DISC, MC, V.

## RESORT

### ≣≣≣ South Seas Plantation Resort

5400 Captiva Road, PO Box 194, 33924; tel 941/472-5111 or toll free 800/237-3162; fax 941/472-7541. Exit 21 off I-75, W to FL 869; S to Sanibel Causeway. 300 acres. One of the largest resorts in this region, occupying the southern end of Captiva Island. It could take days to explore the entire complex. The entirely self-sufficient facility provides all the resort amenities as well as maximum privacy. Security gate ensures safety. **Rooms:** 601 rms, stes, and effic; 11 cottages/villas. CI 4pm/CO noon. Nonsmoking rms avail. Some efficiencies are situated in duplex cottages. **Amenities:** 🛎 🕹 A/C, cable TV, refrig, VCR, voice mail, in-rm safe. Some units w/minibars, all w/terraces, some w/fireplaces, some w/whirlpools. Irons and ironing boards in each room. **Services:** ✕ 🗝 🚗 🖼 ⟲ Car-rental desk, social director, masseur, children's program, babysitting. **Facilities:** 🐟 🚴 ⚠ 🛶 ▶9 🎾 ⚓11 🛶 🦆 ⛳ 🛥 📍500 🎱 🔥 6 restaurants, 5 bars (2 w/entertainment), 1 beach (ocean), volleyball, games rm, whirlpool, beauty salon, day-care ctr, playground, washer/dryer. Great lunch and theme dinner buffets at Chadwick's Restaurant. **Rates:** Peak (Feb–Apr) $165–$280 S or D; $290 ste; $265–$670 effic; $400–$620 cottage/villa. Extra person

$25. Children under age 12 stay free. Min stay special events. Lower rates off-season. Parking: Outdoor, free. AE, CB, DC, DISC, MC, V.

## RESTAURANTS 🍽

### Bellini's of Captiva

11521 Andy Rosse Lane; tel 941/472-6866. **Seafood/Northern Italian.** An attractive enclosed patio and wood furnishings create an informal atmosphere at this large, airy bistro. Kitchen specialties include filet of salmon Capriccio, fettuccine Alfredo, and a variety of veal and chicken entrees. **FYI:** Reservations recommended. Piano. Children's menu. **Open:** Daily 5:30–10pm. **Prices:** Main courses $11–$25. AE, MC, V. ♿

### The Bubble Room

15001 Captiva Dr; tel 941/472-5558. **New American.** A fun-filled cottage restaurant with bubbles painted on the facade, white wrought-iron furniture, and whimsical memorabilia from the 1930s and 1940s. Prime Ribs Weismuller, Eddie Fisherman filet of fresh grouper, and Henny Young-One boneless breast of chicken are among the cinematically inspired entrees. **FYI:** Reservations not accepted. Children's menu. **Open:** Lunch daily 11:30am–2:30pm; dinner daily 5–10pm. **Prices:** Main courses $16–$27. AE, CB, DC, DISC, MC, V. 🏞 ♿

### Captiva Inn

11509 Andy Rosse Lane; tel 941/472-9129. **New American/Caribbean.** Recently redone in cool tropic tones, this intimate dining room sets a relaxing mood. The kitchen specializes in fine cuisine prepared from fresh ingredients. Even the worcestershire sauce—which accompanies the three-peppercorn filet mignon—is made on the premises. **FYI:** Reservations recommended. Dress code. Beer and wine only. No smoking. **Open:** Tues–Sun 5:30–9:30pm. Closed Sept. **Prices:** Main courses $17–$23. AE, MC, V. ♥

### The Moonlight

In Captiva Village Square, 14970 Captiva Dr; tel 941/472-1956. **Southwestern.** An immaculate eatery with an upbeat atmosphere and Southwestern decor. The menu includes wood-grilled fillet of beef, herb-crusted rack of lamb, and a nightly selection of fish entrees. **FYI:** Reservations recommended. Beer and wine only. No smoking. **Open:** Mon–Sat 5:30–9:30pm. Closed Sept. **Prices:** Main courses $16–$23. AE, DC, DISC, MC, V. ♿

### ★ The Mucky Duck

11546 Andy Rosse Lane; tel 941/472-3434. End of Andy Rosse Lane on the Gulf. **Pub/Seafood.** This good-natured parody of a typical British pub treats guests to a fun atmosphere, terrific Gulf views, and fresh seafood specialties. Barbecue shrimp wrapped with bacon is a trademark, and there's a variety of burgers, sandwiches, and seafood for lunch. Extensive selection of imported beers. **FYI:** Reservations not accepted. Children's menu. Beer and wine only. No smoking. Additional location: 2500 Estero Blvd, Fort Myers Beach (tel 463-5519). **Open:** Peak (Jan–Apr) lunch Mon–Sat 11am–2:30pm; dinner Mon–Sat 5–9:30pm. **Prices:** Main courses $12–$19. AE, DC, DISC, MC, V. 🖼 🖼 ⛵

### Old Captiva House
In 'Tween Waters Inn, 15951 Captiva Dr; tel 941/472-5161. **Seafood/Steak.** An elegant inn, with a beautiful dining room and an informal piano bar. A variety of seafood, chicken, and pork dishes are available, and there's a great selection of desserts fresh from the bakery. **FYI:** Reservations recommended. Piano. Children's menu. Dress code. No smoking. **Open:** Peak (Dec 15–Apr) breakfast daily 7:30–10:30am; lunch daily noon–3pm; dinner daily 5:30–10pm. **Prices:** Main courses $16–$22. AE, DISC, MC, V. ⛵

### Sunshine Cafe
In Captiva Village Square, 14900 Captiva Dr; tel 941/472-6200. **New American.** An upbeat, little cafe with crisp white linen (topped with paper) and an open kitchen. Fresh fish selections are served nightly; sandwiches and salads are available for lunch. **FYI:** Reservations recommended. Beer and wine only. **Open:** Peak (Dec–Apr) daily 11:30am–9:30pm. **Prices:** Main courses $6–$22. AE, DC, DISC, MC, V. ⛵

# Chattahoochee

## ATTRACTION 🖼

### Torreya State Park
Bristol; tel 904/643-2674. Located off County Rd 1641 north of Bristol, this park along the Apalachicola River was named for the Torreya tree, an endangered species that grows naturally only in this area. There is a 15-mile double-loop trail that is unusually hilly for Florida; wildflowers bloom profusely along the trailside in the spring. Two small primitive campsites are accessible only by a 1¼-mile hike. The Gregory House, an 1840s plantation home furnished in period style, is open for guided tours. **Open:** Daily 8am–sunset. $

# Chipley

Nearby Falling Waters State Recreation Area draws visitors to this town of 4,000, seat of Washington County in the mid-Panhandle. **Information:** Washington County Chamber of Commerce, 685 7th St, PO Box 457, Chipley, 32428 (tel 904/638-4157).

## ATTRACTIONS 🖼

### Ponce de León Springs State Recreation Area
US 90; tel 904/836-4281. The centerpiece of this 440-acre park is its natural spring, which produces 16 million gallons of clear water each day. Swimming, fishing, nature trails. **Open:** Daily 8am–sunset. $

### Falling Waters State Recreation Area
1130 State Park Rd; tel 904/638-6130. A 67-foot waterfall drops into a 100-foot-deep, 20-foot-wide sinkhole with moss-and-fern-covered walls; an overlook platform provides an excellent vantage point. The park offers swimming, hiking, picnicking, and overnight camping. **Open:** Daily 8am–sunset. $$

# Clearwater

### See also Clearwater Beach

Established as Fort Harrison in 1841, today's city of 100,000 is a retirement mecca. Ruth Eckerd Hall is home to the Clearwater Symphony; Jack Russell Stadium is the spring training ground of the Philadelphia Phillies. **Information:** Greater Clearwater Chamber of Commerce, 128 N Osceola Ave, PO Box 2457, Clearwater, 34615 (tel 813/461-0011).

## HOTELS 🖼

### 🚃🚃 Best Western Clearwater Central
21338 US 19 N, 34625; tel 813/799-1565 or toll free 800/528-1234; fax 813/797-6801. Modest low-rise hotel recommended for short stays and its convenient highway location. **Rooms:** 148 rms. CI 1pm/CO noon. Nonsmoking rms avail. **Amenities:** 🛁 ♨ A/C, cable TV. Some units w/minibars, some w/terraces. **Services:** 🖐 **Facilities:** 🏊 ⛵ Washer/dryer. **Rates:** Peak (Feb–Apr) $80–$90 S or D. Extra person $5. Children under age 12 stay free. Lower rates off-season. Parking: Outdoor, free. AE, CB, DC, DISC, MC, V.

### 🚃🚃 Comfort Inn
3580 Ulmerton Rd, 34622; tel 813/573-1171 or toll free 800/221-2222; fax 813/572-8736. Exit 18 off I-275. Comfortable lodgings located across from popular dinner theater and nine miles from Gulf beaches. **Rooms:** 120 rms. CI 3pm/CO noon. Nonsmoking rms avail. **Amenities:** 🛁 ♨ A/C, cable TV w/movies. Some units w/terraces. **Services:** ✕ 🖐 🖐 🖐 **Facilities:** 🏊 🍴 50 ⛵ Whirlpool. **Rates (CP):** Peak (Jan–Apr) $75–$85 S or D. Extra person $6. Children under age 18 stay free. Lower rates off-season. Parking: Outdoor, free. AE, DISC, MC, V.

### 🚃🚃 Courtyard by Marriott
3131 Executive Dr, 34622; tel 813/572-8484 or toll free 800/321-2211; fax 813/572-6991. Exit 6 from I-275 N; exit 18 from I-275 S. Conveniently located, yet in a tranquil, pastoral setting. **Rooms:** 149 rms and stes. CI 4pm/CO noon. Nonsmoking rms avail. **Amenities:** 🛁 ♨ 🖐 A/C, dataport. All

units w/terraces. Instant hot water for coffee or tea. **Services:** ✕ 🚐 🖼 🔌 **Facilities:** 🏋 ⓹⓪ ♿ 1 restaurant, 1 bar (w/entertainment), whirlpool, washer/dryer. **Rates:** Peak (Jan–Apr) $89 S; $99 D; $105 ste. Children under age 12 stay free. Lower rates off-season. Parking: Outdoor, free. AE, CB, DC, DISC, EC, ER, JCB, MC, V.

### ≡≡ Days Inn
3910 Ulmerton Rd, 34622; tel 813/572-8540 or toll free 800/638-2343; fax 813/573-3334. Exit 18 off I-275. Adequate accommodations, for business or leisure. **Rooms:** 118 rms. CI 3pm/CO noon. Nonsmoking rms avail. **Amenities:** 🏋 🖼 A/C, cable TV w/movies, in-rm safe. **Services:** 🚐 🖼 🔌 Car-rental desk. **Facilities:** 🏋 ⓸⓹ ♿ Washer/dryer. Complimentary admission to nearby Bally's Health Spa. **Rates (CP):** Peak (Jan–Apr) $72 S; $79 D. Extra person $6. Children under age 16 stay free. Lower rates off-season. Parking: Outdoor, free. AE, CB, DC, DISC, MC, V.

### ≡≡ Hampton Inn
3655 Hospitality Lane, 34622; tel 813/577-9200 or toll free 800/HAMPTON; fax 813/572-8931. I-275 N to exit 16. Designed for the value-conscious traveler. **Rooms:** 118 rms and effic. CI 3pm/CO noon. Nonsmoking rms avail. **Amenities:** 🏋 🅰 A/C, cable TV w/movies. Complimentary evening cocktails. **Services:** 🚐 🖼 🔌 Babysitting. **Facilities:** 🏋 🖼 ♿ Sauna, whirlpool, day-care ctr. Golf and tennis courts are within walking distance. **Rates (CP):** Peak (Jan–Apr) $66–$76 S or D; $86 effic. Extra person $5. Children under age 18 stay free. Lower rates off-season. Parking: Outdoor, free. AE, CB, DC, DISC, ER, MC, V.

### ≡≡ Holiday Inn Express
13625 Icot Blvd, 34620; tel 813/536-7275 or toll free 800/HOLIDAY; fax 813/530-3053. Exit 18 off I-275. A mid-range hotel with many conveniences for families or corporate guests. **Rooms:** 128 rms and stes. CI 2pm/CO noon. Nonsmoking rms avail. **Amenities:** 🏋 🅰 🍽 A/C, cable TV w/movies. Some units w/whirlpools. Television speaker and phone extension in bathroom. **Services:** 🖼 🔌 🍴 Babysitting. **Facilities:** 🏋 🖼 ⓷⓪ ♿ Whirlpool. **Rates (CP):** Peak (Feb–Apr) $85–$95 S or D; $95 ste. Extra person $5. Children under age 18 stay free. Lower rates off-season. Parking: Outdoor, free. AE, CB, DC, DISC, MC, V.

### ≡≡ Holiday Inn Hotel & Suites
20967 US 19 N, 34625; tel 813/799-1181 or toll free 800/741-1181; fax 813/797-8504. At Gulf-to-Bay Blvd. Recently renovated establishment, where the rooms are unimaginative but clean and new. **Rooms:** 148 rms, stes, and effic. CI 3pm/CO noon. Nonsmoking rms avail. **Amenities:** 🏋 🅰 🖼 A/C, cable TV w/movies, dataport, voice mail. Some units w/terraces. **Services:** ✕ 🖼 🔌 Car-rental desk, babysitting. **Facilities:** 🏋 🖼 ②⑤⓪ 🖥 ♿ 1 restaurant, 1 bar (w/entertainment), games rm, spa, steam rm, whirlpool, playground, washer/dryer. **Rates:** Peak (Feb–Apr) $95 S; $93 D; $108 ste;

$98–$100 effic. Extra person $6. Children under age 18 stay free. Min stay special events. Lower rates off-season. Parking: Outdoor, free. AE, CB, DC, DISC, JCB, MC, V.

### ≡≡≡ Holiday Inn Select
3535 Ulmerton Rd, 34622; tel 813/577-9100 or toll free 800/HOLIDAY; fax 813/573-5022. Exit 18 off I-275. This five-story property, outfitted with all the essentials, attracts a largely business clientele. **Rooms:** 174 rms and stes. Executive level. CI 3pm/CO noon. Nonsmoking rms avail. **Amenities:** 🏋 🅰 🖼 🍽 A/C, cable TV w/movies, dataport, voice mail. **Services:** ✕ 🔑 🚐 🖼 🔌 **Facilities:** 🏋 🖼 🖼 ⑥⓪⓪ ♿ 1 restaurant, 1 bar, washer/dryer. **Rates (MAP):** Peak (Jan–Apr) $90–$108 S or D; $125 ste. Extra person $10. Lower rates off-season. MAP rates avail. Parking: Outdoor, free. AE, CB, DC, DISC, EC, ER, JCB, MC, V.

### ≡≡≡ Howard Johnson Clearwater Central
21030 US 19 N, 34625; tel 813/797-8173 or toll free 800/647-8944; fax 813/791-7759. Well-liked by the shop-till-you-drop crowd for its location opposite the Clearwater Mall. Families that don't require an on-beach hotel will find this a suitable locale as well. **Rooms:** 195 rms and stes. CI 3pm/CO noon. Nonsmoking rms avail. **Amenities:** 🏋 A/C, cable TV w/movies. **Services:** 🚐 🖼 🍴 **Facilities:** 🏋 ①⑤⓪ ♿ 1 restaurant, 1 bar (w/entertainment), games rm, washer/dryer. **Rates:** Peak (Feb–June) $75–$85 S; $80 D; $150 ste. Extra person $10. Children under age 18 stay free. Lower rates off-season. Parking: Outdoor, free. AE, CB, DC, DISC, MC, V.

### ≡≡ La Quinta Inn
3301 Ulmerton Rd, 34622; tel 813/572-7222 or toll free 800/531-5900; fax 813/572-0076. Exit 18 off I-275. This modern hotel is set back from the highway in a quiet area. **Rooms:** 115 rms. CI 2pm/CO noon. Nonsmoking rms avail. **Amenities:** 🏋 🅰 A/C. **Services:** 🚐 🖼 🔌 🍴 **Facilities:** 🏋 🖼 ⓷⓹ ♿ Whirlpool, washer/dryer. **Rates (CP):** Peak (Jan–Apr) $73–$80 S or D. Extra person $7. Children under age 18 stay free. Lower rates off-season. Parking: Outdoor, free. AE, DISC, MC, V.

### ≡≡ Ramada Inn Countryside
26508 US 19 N, 34621; tel 813/796-1234 or toll free 800/2-RAMADA; fax 813/796-0452. At Countryside Blvd. Tries to impart a rural setting, but difficult highway access and surly staff may make effort not worth it. **Rooms:** 128 rms and stes. CI 3pm/CO noon. Nonsmoking rms avail. **Amenities:** 🏋 🅰 🖼 A/C, cable TV. Some units w/terraces, all w/whirlpools. **Services:** 🖼 🍴 **Facilities:** 🏋 ①⑤ ♿ 1 restaurant (lunch and dinner only), 1 bar (w/entertainment), washer/dryer. **Rates:** Peak (Feb–Apr) $69–$99 S; $79–$109 D; $99 ste. Extra person $10. Children under age 18 stay free. Lower rates off-season. Parking: Outdoor, free. AE, DISC, MC, V.

## MOTELS

### ☰☰ Belleair Beach Resort Motel

2040 Gulf Blvd, Belleair Beach, 34634; tel 813/595-1696 or toll free 800/780-1696; fax 813/593-5433. 3 mi S of Clearwater Beach. Directly on the beach and handy to shopping and restaurants. **Rooms:** 43 rms and effic. CI 2pm/CO 11am. Nonsmoking rms avail. **Amenities:** 🔒 ⚙ A/C, cable TV, refrig. Some units w/terraces. **Services:** 🛏 🛎 Babysitting. **Facilities:** 🏖 1 beach (ocean), washer/dryer. Sailing and boating available nearby. **Rates:** Peak (Jan–Apr) $68–$73 S or D; $77 effic. Children under age 5 stay free. Min stay special events. Lower rates off-season. Parking: Outdoor, free. AE, CB, DC, DISC, ER, MC, V.

### ☰☰☰ Residence Inn by Marriott

5050 Ulmerton Rd, 34620; tel 813/573-4444 or toll free 800/331-3131; fax 813/572-4446. Exit 18 off I-275. Condominium-style living in a professional environment; popular with repeat business and leisure travelers. **Rooms:** 88 stes and effic. CI 3pm/CO noon. No smoking. Nonsmoking rms avail. Each unit has kitchen facilities. **Amenities:** 🔒 ⚙ 🖥 A/C, cable TV w/movies, refrig, dataport, voice mail. Some units w/terraces, all w/fireplaces. Free fire log upon check-in. **Services:** 🛏 🛎 🛍 Babysitting. Happy hour in the lobby Monday–Thursday, when beer and wine is complimentary. **Facilities:** 🏖 ▣ 🏊25 ⚙ Basketball, volleyball, whirlpool, playground, washer/dryer. **Rates (CP):** Peak (Jan–Apr) $109–$175 effic. Min stay special events. Lower rates off-season. Parking: Outdoor, free. AE, CB, DC, DISC, JCB, MC, V.

## RESORT

### ☰☰☰☰ Belleview Mido Resort Hotel

25 Belleview Blvd, PO Box 2317, 34617; tel 813/442-6171 or toll free 800/237-8947; fax 813/441-4173. 21 acres. A turn-of-the-century architectural tour de force that is sure to appeal to couples and other romantics. **Rooms:** 292 rms and stes. CI 3pm/CO noon. Nonsmoking rms avail. Delightfully decorated in period style. **Amenities:** 🔒 ⚙ A/C, cable TV w/movies, bathrobes. Some units w/terraces. **Services:** ✗ VP 🛏 🛎 Masseur, babysitting. **Facilities:** 🏖 ⛳ ▶18 ⚓4 🎾 🏊1000 🖥 ⚙ 2 restaurants, 3 bars (1 w/entertainment), volleyball, games rm, lawn games, spa, sauna, whirlpool. Cabana beach club requires a ride from the hotel but food service is provided there. **Rates:** Peak (Jan–Apr) $190–$210 S or D; $260 ste. Extra person $20. Children under age 18 stay free. Lower rates off-season. Parking: Outdoor, free. AE, CB, DC, DISC, MC, V.

## RESTAURANTS 🍴

### Panache Cabaret

415 Cleveland St; tel 813/441-8522. **French.** Nouvelle French food served in a rather spartan location. Cabaret and other entertainment provides a nice atmosphere. **FYI:** Reservations recommended. Cabaret. Dress code. **Open:** Peak (Feb–July) Sun–Thurs 4pm–midnight, Fri–Sat 4pm–2am. **Prices:** Main courses $13–$20. AE, MC, V. VP ⚙

### ★ Tio Pepe's

2930 Gulf-to-Bay Blvd; tel 813/799-3082. **Spanish.** An Old Spanish restaurant with rustic decor, a festive atmosphere, a celebrated menu, and an award-winning wine list. **FYI:** Reservations recommended. Children's menu. **Open:** Lunch Tues–Fri 11am–2:30pm; dinner Tues–Thurs 5–11pm, Fri–Sat 5–11:30pm, Sun 4–10pm. **Prices:** Main courses $11–$55. AE, MC, V. 💙 🛍 ⚙

## ATTRACTIONS 🏛

### Florida Military Aviation Museum

16055 Fairchild Dr; tel 813/535-9007. This outdoor museum is devoted to aircraft from all branches of military aviation, from World War II patrol bombers to supersonic jet fighters. **Open:** Tues, Thurs, and Sat 10am–4pm, Sun 1–5pm. $

### Clearwater Marine Science Center

249 Windward Passage; tel 813/447-0980. Located on an island in Clearwater Harbor, this facility is dedicated to the rescue and rehabilitation of marine mammals and sea turtles. A turtle hatchery releases more than 3,000 hatchlings each year in local waters. Visitors can view a 400-pound sea turtle and baby turtles, a bottle-nosed dolphin, and a coral reef tank. **Open:** Mon–Fri 9am–5pm, Sat 9am–4pm, Sun 11am–4pm. $$

### Moccasin Lake Nature Park

2750 Park Trail Lane; tel 813/462-6024. A 51-acre wildlife preserve with a 5-acre lake, nature trails, and an aviary, plus exhibits on animals, birds of prey, reptiles, plants, and energy sources. **Open:** Tues–Fri 9am–5pm, Sat–Sun 10am–6pm. $

### Jack Russell Stadium

800 Phillies Dr; tel 813/442-8496. The Philadelphia Phillies conduct their spring training activities at this stadium. Exhibition season mid-Feb–Mar. $$$

### Heritage Village

11909 125th St N, Largo; tel 813/582-2123. This 21-acre, turn-of-the-century historical park features more than 20 of Pinellas County's oldest existing historic homes and structures, which have been moved here from their original sites. There are periodic demonstrations of crafts such as rug-hooking, wool-spinning, flax-making, and weaving on a loom. Guided tours available. **Open:** Tues–Sat 10am–4pm, Sun 1–4pm. **Free**

### Safety Harbor Museum of Regional History

329 S Bayshore Blvd, Safety Harbor; tel 813/726-1668. This small museum focuses on local history, with particular emphasis on the 16th century, when Hernando De Soto discovered five mineral springs here. Also displayed are local Native American artifacts and photographs of Safety Harbor around

the turn of the century, when visitors flocked to the mineral springs. **Open:** Tues–Fri 10am–4pm, Sat–Sun 1–4pm. Closed last 2 weeks of August. $

# Clearwater Beach

Memorial Causeway connects this central Gulf Coast community with downtown Clearwater. Thick with condos and hotels, it also offers charter and dinner-cruise boats, a substantive Marine Science Center, and arty shopping at 1890s-style Boatyard Village. **Information:** Greater Clearwater Chamber of Commerce, 128 N Osceola Ave, PO Box 2457, Clearwater, 34615 (tel 813/461-0011).

## HOTELS 🛏

### ≡≡≡ Adam's Mark Caribbean Gulf Resort

430 S Gulfview Blvd, 33515; tel 813/443-5714 or toll free 800/444-2326; fax 813/442-8389. FL 60 to Gulfview Blvd. Right on the beach, it's a local favorite and popular with younger folks for its many bars. **Rooms:** 216 rms and stes. CI 4pm/CO 11am. Nonsmoking rms avail. Generally good-quality accommodations. **Amenities:** 🛏 ⚭ A/C, satel TV w/movies, dataport. All units w/terraces. **Services:** ✕ VP ⌧ ⌑ Children's program, babysitting. **Facilities:** 🛠 1000 🖥 ㋡ 2 restaurants, 4 bars (2 w/entertainment), 1 beach (ocean), lifeguard, volleyball, games rm, whirlpool, washer/dryer. Coconut Comedy Club every Friday and Saturday night. Guests have use of nearby health club for a fee. **Rates:** Peak (Feb–Apr) $129–$189 S or D; $195 ste. Extra person $10. Children under age 18 stay free. Lower rates off-season. Parking: Indoor, free. AE, CB, DC, DISC, EC, ER, JCB, MC, V.

### ≡≡ Best Western Sea Stone Resort

445 Hamden Dr, 34630; tel 813/441-1722 or toll free 800/444-1919; fax 813/461-1680. At Gulfview Blvd. Although not on the beach, this better-than-average establishment has its own marina. **Rooms:** 109 rms and stes. CI 4pm/CO noon. Nonsmoking rms avail. Guests staying in suites section will be pleased with the new upbeat decor and the extra space for relaxing. **Amenities:** 🛏 ⚭ A/C, cable TV, refrig, in-rm safe. Some units w/terraces. **Services:** ⌧ ⌑ ⌱ Car-rental desk, children's program. **Facilities:** 🛠 125 ㋡ 1 restaurant (bkfst only), 2 bars, whirlpool, beauty salon, washer/dryer. **Rates:** Peak (Feb–Apr) $90–$111 S or D; $184 ste. Extra person $10. Children under age 18 stay free. Lower rates off-season. Parking: Outdoor, free. AE, CB, DC, DISC, MC, V.

### ≡≡ Best Western Sea Wake Inn

691 S Gulfview Blvd, 34630; tel 813/443-7652 or toll free 800/444-1919; fax 813/461-2836. Families make up a large part of the guests at this sun-drenched lodging. **Rooms:** 110 rms and effic. CI 4pm/CO noon. Nonsmoking rms avail. Rooms are tastefully decorated with updated furnishings. Beachfront rooms are usually well-booked because of their

balconies and sunset views. **Amenities:** 🛏 ⚭ A/C, cable TV, in-rm safe. Some units w/terraces. **Services:** ✕ ⌧ ⌑ Children's program. Free pass provided for Clearwater Beach Trolley. **Facilities:** 🛠 50 ㋡ 1 restaurant, 1 bar (w/entertainment), 1 beach (ocean), volleyball, playground. Children's program is available during summer months (no fee). **Rates:** Peak (Feb 11–Apr) $120–$146 S or D; $130–$156 effic. Extra person $10. Children under age 18 stay free. Lower rates off-season. Parking: Outdoor, free. AE, CB, DC, DISC, JCB, MC, V.

### ≡≡≡ Clearwater Beach Hotel

500 Mandalay Ave, 34630; tel 813/441-2425 or toll free 800/292-2295; fax 813/449-2083. This holdover from a bygone era still retains much of its splendor. The well-appointed lobby features high-backed chairs and artwork. **Rooms:** 156 rms, stes, and effic. Executive level. CI 3pm/CO noon. Nonsmoking rms avail. **Amenities:** 🛏 A/C, cable TV. Some units w/terraces. **Services:** ✕ VP ⌧ ⌑ ⌱ Babysitting. **Facilities:** 🛠 75 ㋡ 1 restaurant (see "Restaurants" below), 1 bar (w/entertainment), 1 beach (ocean). Library with fireplace. Beachside bar adjacent to the pool. **Rates:** Peak (Feb–Apr) $98–$160 S or D; $160–$210 ste; $98–$160 effic. Extra person $8. Lower rates off-season. Parking: Indoor/outdoor, free. AE, DC, MC, V.

### ≡≡≡ DoubleTree Resorts Surfside

400 Mandalay Ave, 34630; tel 813/461-3222 or toll free 800/753-3954; fax 813/461-0610. Near FL 60. This large beachfront staple has long been favored by families. Rooms throughout offer Gulf and harbor views. Lively public areas always seem to have something going on. **Rooms:** 428 rms and stes. CI 4pm/CO 11am. Nonsmoking rms avail. Rooms throughout offer Gulf views. Appointments are of high quality. **Amenities:** 🛏 ⚭ A/C, cable TV w/movies, dataport, in-rm safe. Some units w/minibars, some w/terraces. **Services:** ✕ ⌥ VP 🚐 ⌧ ⌑ Social director, masseur, children's program, babysitting. Complimentary cookies upon check-in. **Facilities:** 🛠 ⚿ ⛴ 1500 🖥 ㋡ 3 restaurants, 3 bars (1 w/entertainment), 1 beach (ocean), volleyball, games rm, washer/dryer. **Rates (AP):** Peak (Feb–Apr) $120–$215 S or D; $225 ste. Extra person $10. Children under age 18 stay free. Lower rates off-season. MAP rates avail. Parking: Indoor/outdoor, free. AE, CB, DC, DISC, EC, ER, JCB, MC, V.

### ≡≡≡ Holiday Inn SunSpree Resort

715 S Gulfview Blvd, Clearwater, 34630; tel 813/447-9566 or toll free 800/HOLIDAY, 800/282-3566 in FL; fax 813/446-4978. Off Sandkey Bridge. This sprawling complex on the Gulf offers a variety of rooms from high-rise to beachside low-rise units for both couples and families. **Rooms:** 210 rms and stes. CI 4pm/CO 11am. Nonsmoking rms avail. **Amenities:** 🛏 ⚭ 🍽 A/C, cable TV w/movies, refrig, in-rm safe. Some units w/terraces. Some rooms have coffeemakers. **Services:** ✕ ⌧ ⌑ Social director, children's program, babysitting. Scarce front-desk staff sometimes leaves guests stranded. **Facilities:** 🛠 ⚿ ⛴ 350 🖥 ㋡ 2 restaurants, 2 bars

(1 w/entertainment), 1 beach (ocean), volleyball, games rm, whirlpool, playground, washer/dryer. **Rates:** Peak (Feb–Apr) $109–$159 S or D; $205–$255 ste. Extra person $10. Children under age 18 stay free. Min stay peak. Lower rates off-season. Parking: Outdoor, free. AE, DC, DISC, JCB, MC, V.

### ▤▤ Palm Pavilion Inn
18 Bay Esplanade, 34630; tel 813/446-6777 or toll free 800/ 433-PALM; fax 813/446-4255. Three-story art deco–style hotel with beach access. **Rooms:** 29 rms and effic. CI 2pm/ CO noon. Furnishings are sparse but acceptable. **Amenities:** 🛄 ⬠ A/C, cable TV w/movies. **Services:** ⬠ **Facilities:** 🔓 ⬠ 1 beach (ocean). Rooftop sundeck. Gift shop and burger stand next door. **Rates:** Peak (Feb–Apr) $80–$115 S or D; $100–$110 effic. Extra person $8. Children under age 16 stay free. Lower rates off-season. Parking: Outdoor, free. AE, DISC, MC, V.

### ▤▤ Quality Inn Beach Resort
655 S Gulfview Blvd, 34630; tel 813/442-7171 or toll free 800/228-5151; fax 813/446-7177. A recently renovated, mid-rise beachfront property that commands great sunset views. **Rooms:** 90 rms, stes, and effic. CI 3pm/CO noon. Nonsmoking rms avail. Bright colors with many private balconies and floral print spreads. Rooms are attractively decorated in bright colors and well-insulated from neighbors. **Amenities:** 🛄 ⬠ A/C, TV, in-rm safe. Some units w/terraces. **Services:** ✗ ⬠ ⬠ Babysitting. **Facilities:** 🔓 ⬠ 1 restaurant, 1 bar, 1 beach (ocean), playground, washer/dryer. Marina nearby. The restaurant is a chain pancake house with inexpensive fare. **Rates:** Peak (Feb–Apr) $120–$150 S or D; $160 ste; $130–$150 effic. Extra person $20. Children under age 18 stay free. Lower rates off-season. Parking: Outdoor, free. AE, CB, DC, DISC, MC, V.

### ▤▤▤ Radisson Suite Resort
1201 Gulf Blvd, 34630; tel 813/596-1100 or toll free 800/ 333-3333; fax 813/595-4292. On Sand Key. Fresh and appealing, this waterfront operation is one of the top hotels in the area. The spacious lobby is only an introduction to the other smart-looking public areas. **Rooms:** 220 stes. CI 4pm/ CO noon. Nonsmoking rms avail. **Amenities:** 🛄 ⬠ ⬠ A/C, satel TV w/movies, refrig, dataport, CD/tape player. All units w/minibars, all w/terraces. All w/microwaves. **Services:** ✗ ⬠ VP ⬠ ⬠ ⬠ Car-rental desk, social director, masseur, children's program, babysitting. Shuttle to beach operates every half hour; also takes guests to town for nightlife. **Facilities:** 🔓 ⬠ ⬠ 300 ⬠ ⬠ 2 restaurants, 2 bars (w/entertainment), 1 beach (ocean), volleyball, games rm, spa, sauna, steam rm, whirlpool, beauty salon, playground, washer/dryer. **Rates:** Peak (Dec–Apr) $160 ste. Extra person $10. Children under age 18 stay free. Lower rates off-season. Parking: Outdoor, free. AE, CB, DC, DISC, ER, MC, V.

### ▤▤ Ramada Inn Gulfview
521 S Gulfview Blvd, 34630; tel 813/447-6461 or toll free 800/2-RAMADA; fax 813/443-5888. S of Memorial Causeway. Located in the midst of the beach district, though its own frontage is not ideal for swimming. **Rooms:** 288 rms. CI 4pm/CO 11am. Nonsmoking rms avail. Badly needed room renovations should have been completed by press time. **Amenities:** 🛄 A/C, cable TV w/movies, in-rm safe. All units w/terraces. **Services:** ⬠ ⬠ ⬠ ⬠ Car-rental desk. **Facilities:** 🔓 150 ⬠ 1 restaurant, 2 bars (w/entertainment), games rm, beauty salon. Public beach is close by. **Rates:** Peak (Feb–Apr) $100–$125 S; $110–$135 D. Extra person $10. Children under age 18 stay free. Min stay special events. Lower rates off-season. Parking: Outdoor, free. AE, CB, DC, DISC, MC, V.

## MOTELS

### ▤▤ Aegean Sands Resort Motel
421 S Gulfview Blvd, 34630; tel 813/447-3464 or toll free 800/942-3432; fax 813/446-7169. Opposite a public beach, this hotel prides itself on its family comforts and ambience. Popular among European vacationers. **Rooms:** 68 rms, stes, and effic. CI 3pm/CO noon. Rooms vary from motel-style units to efficiencies and two-bedroom apartments. **Amenities:** 🛄 ⬠ A/C, TV. Some units w/terraces. **Services:** ⬠ ⬠ Babysitting. **Facilities:** 🔓 1 beach (ocean), washer/ dryer. **Rates:** Peak (Feb–Apr) $40–$100 S or D; $80–$135 ste; $80–$135 effic. Extra person $5. Children under age 18 stay free. Lower rates off-season. Parking: Outdoor, free. AE, DC, DISC, MC, V.

### ▤ Flamingo Motel Apartments and Suites
450 N Gulfview Blvd, 34630; tel 813/441-8019 or toll free 800/821-8019; fax 813/446-6599. Off Mandalay Ave from FL 60. A mainstay for families on a budget. **Rooms:** 35 stes and effic. CI 3pm/CO 10am. Lodgings vary in size from apartments with separate bedrooms to studios with sofabeds. Some beachfront rooms. **Amenities:** 🛄 ⬠ A/C, cable TV. Some units w/terraces. **Services:** ⬠ **Facilities:** 🔓 ⬠ 1 beach (ocean), whirlpool, washer/dryer. A quiet street separates units from the large pool. **Rates:** Peak (Feb–Apr) $70–$110 ste; $65–$98 effic. Extra person $6. Lower rates off-season. Parking: Outdoor, free. DISC, MC, V.

### ▤ Sun West Beach Motel
409 Hamden Dr S, 34630; tel 813/442-5008. A small family-run harborside motel with a private dock; only a short walk from the beach. **Rooms:** 14 rms, stes, and effic. CI 1pm/CO 10am. Poolside rooms are the favorites, although they may be a little more noisy. **Amenities:** 🛄 ⬠ ⬠ A/C, cable TV, refrig. **Facilities:** 🔓 ⬠ Washer/dryer. The pool deck leads directly to the dock, where guests can fish or just relax. **Rates:** Peak (Feb–Apr) $59 S or D; $79–$93 ste; $67 effic. Extra person $5. Lower rates off-season. Parking: Outdoor, free. MC, V.

## RESORT

### ≣≣≣ Sheraton Sand Key Resort

1160 Gulf Blvd, 34630; tel 813/595-1611 or toll free 800/325-3535; fax 813/596-8488. Off FL 60. 20 acres. A major resort in the area. Set on spacious grounds with views all around. **Rooms:** 390 rms and stes. Executive level. CI 3pm/CO 11am. Nonsmoking rms avail. Some rooms are due for a renovation, but they are in generally decent repair. **Amenities:** 🛏 🕸 📺 🍴 A/C, cable TV w/movies, dataport, voice mail. All units w/terraces. **Services:** ✕ VP 🖼 🔔 Masseur, children's program, babysitting. **Facilities:** 🏢 🚴 ⚠ 🏊3 🛶 🍴🍴 1000 ⅙ 3 restaurants, 2 bars (1 w/entertainment), 1 beach (ocean), games rm, snorkeling, sauna, whirlpool, playground, washer/dryer. **Rates:** Peak (Feb–Apr) $120–$170 S; $130–$180 D; $240 ste. Extra person $10. Children under age 18 stay free. Min stay special events. Lower rates off-season. Parking: Outdoor, free. AE, CB, DC, DISC, EC, JCB, MC, V.

## RESTAURANTS 🍴

### Bob Heilman's Beachcomber

447 Mandalay Ave; tel 813/442-4144. 1 block N of FL 60. **New American/Continental.** A simple, casual restaurant with a jumbo bar area. Menu highlights include seafood, steaks, and prime rib. **FYI:** Reservations recommended. Piano. Children's menu. **Open:** Mon–Sat 11am–midnight, Sun noon–midnight. **Prices:** Main courses $9–$24. AE, CB, DC, DISC, MC, V. 🔽 VP

### ★ Capri Restaurant

411 Mandalay Ave; tel 813/441-1111. ¼ mi N off Memorial Causeway. **Italian.** Exceptionally friendly, quiet service and delightful, health-conscious pasta, veal, fish, and steak dishes. The garlic chicken is outstanding. **FYI:** Reservations recommended. Children's menu. Beer and wine only. **Open:** Peak (Mar–Aug) daily 5–10:30pm. **Prices:** Main courses $10–$19. AE, CB, DC, DISC, MC, V. ⅙

### Cha Cha Coconuts

In the Shops of Sand Key, 1241 Gulf Blvd; tel 813/596-6040. **Burgers.** Neon lights and tropical colors illuminate this festive bar, which caters to the younger set. The menu offers burgers, salads, Jamaican jerk chicken, sandwiches, and other munchies. **FYI:** Reservations not accepted. Big band. Children's menu. **Open:** Mon–Thurs 11am–11pm, Fri–Sat 11am–1am, Sun 11am–10pm. **Prices:** Main courses $4–$7. AE, CB, DC, DISC, ER, MC, V. 🍽 ⅙

### Clearwater Beach Hotel Dining Room

In Clearwater Beach Hotel, 500 Mandalay Ave; tel 813/441-2425. **New American/Continental.** This attractive, men's club–style room is casual for lunch and upscale for dinner. Traditional menu. **FYI:** Reservations recommended. Piano. Children's menu. **Open:** Breakfast Mon–Sat 7:30– 10:30am, Sun 7:30–11am; lunch daily 11:30am–2:30pm; dinner Sun–Thurs 4:45–10pm, Fri–Sat 4:45–10:30pm. **Prices:** Main courses $10–$24. AE, DC, MC, V. ♥ 🔽 VP ⅙

### The Columbia

In the Shops of Sand Key, 1241 Gulf Blvd; tel 813/596-8400. Just across Sand Key Bridge. **New American/Cuban/Spanish.** Beautiful, colorful Mediterranean tile sets the mood in this relaxed waterside restaurant. Menu items such as filet mignon, bean soup, and the catch of the day are served Spanish style. **FYI:** Reservations accepted. Children's menu. Dress code. **Open:** Sun–Thurs 5–10pm, Fri–Sat 5–11pm. **Prices:** Main courses $9–$17. AE, CB, DC, DISC, ER, MC, V. 🔽 ⅙

### Frenchy's Cafe

41 Baymount St; tel 813/446-3607. **Cafe.** The cafe and its adjacent bar share a relaxed, casual atmosphere. Specialties include grouper burger, buffalo shrimp, and Greek salad. **FYI:** Reservations not accepted. **Open:** Mon–Thurs 11:30am–11pm, Fri–Sat 11:30am–midnight, Sun noon–11pm. **Prices:** Main courses $3–$6. AE, MC, V.

### Frenchy's Rockaway Grill and Beach Club

7 Rockaway St; tel 813/446-4844. **Seafood/Grill.** A tavern-style establishment very popular with the college crowd. Walk in right off the beach for a beer and a burger. **FYI:** Reservations not accepted. **Open:** Sun–Thurs 11am–midnight, Fri–Sat 11am–1am. **Prices:** Main courses $3–$13. AE, MC, V. 🍽 ⅙

### ★ Jesse's Seafood House of Clearwater

20 Island Way; tel 813/443-6210. **Seafood.** This casual restaurant with several rooms is a fun spot for both families and the older generation. There's even a dockside mooring for boats. Great view and gardens. **FYI:** Reservations not accepted. Children's menu. Additional locations: 10400 Park Blvd, Seminole (tel 393-0896); 345 Causeway Blvd, Dunedin (tel 736-2611). **Open:** Daily 11:30am–10pm. **Prices:** Main courses $5–$16. AE, CB, DC, DISC, MC, V. 🔺 🔽 ⅙

### Leverock's Seafood House

551 Gulf Blvd; tel 813/446-5884. **American/Middle Eastern.** Seafood specials, early bird bargains, and affordable prices make this cheerful waterside restaurant a popular stop. **FYI:** Reservations not accepted. Children's menu. Additional locations: 4927 US 19 S, New Port Richey (tel 849-8000); 7000 US 19 N, Pinellas Park (tel 526-9188). **Open:** Daily 11:30am–10pm. **Prices:** Main courses $7–$20. AE, DC, DISC, MC, V. 🍽 🔺 🎴 🔽 ⅙

### ★ Seafood and Sunsets at Julie's

351 S Gulfview Blvd; tel 813/441-2548. **Cafe.** Great beach location facing the Gulf, with semi-wild birds wandering about. The menu includes steaks, chicken, and fresh salads in addition to Florida lobster, stone crabs, conch, grouper, and other fish. **FYI:** Reservations accepted. Children's menu. Beer and wine only. **Open:** Daily 11am–10pm. **Prices:** Main courses $8–$21. AE, MC, V. 🍽 🔺 🔽 ⅙

### ★ Waterfront Restaurant
490 Mandalay Ave; tel 813/442-3684. **American/Greek.** A busy, neon-lit eatery that offers good food at low prices. The diverse menu includes Italian and Greek dishes. **FYI:** Reservations recommended. Children's menu. **Open:** Daily 7am–11pm. **Prices:** Main courses $5–$20. AE, CB, DC, DISC, MC, V. 🏖️💟♿

## ATTRACTION 🧳

*Starlite Majesty*
Cruise Boat, 25 Causeway Blvd; tel 813/462-2628 or toll free 800/444-4814. This air-conditioned, 400-passenger, triple-decker craft tours Clearwater Bay in both the afternoon and evening. Afternoon sightseeing cruises, offered with an optional luncheon, depart at 12:30pm and last 2 hours. Evening dinner/dance cruises with live band and sit-down dinner depart at 7pm and run 3 hours (3½ hours on Sat). Cruises operate Tues–Sun. Boarding is half-hour before departure time; reservations required for meal cruises. $$$

# Cocoa

See also Cocoa Beach, Kennedy Space Center

A hub of eastern Florida's Space Coast. Its Astronaut Memorial features one of the nation's 10 largest planetariums. The circa-1916 Porcher House is the starting point for tours of Cocoa's historic district. **Information:** Cocoa Beach Area Chamber of Commerce, 400 Fortenberry Rd, Merritt Island, 32952 (tel 407/459-2200).

## HOTEL 🏨

### ≡≡ Best Western Cocoa Inn
4225 W King St, 32926; tel 407/632-1065 or toll free 800/528-1234; fax 407/631-3302. Exit 75 off I-95. An economical two-story property embracing a pool and courtyard area. **Rooms:** 120 rms. CI noon/CO 11:30am. Nonsmoking rms avail. **Amenities:** 🛏️♨️A/C, cable TV. **Services:** 🚐🧺🛎️🤵 Car-rental desk, babysitting. **Facilities:** 🛗🏊♿ 1 bar, games rm, washer/dryer. Barbecue grills and picnic area. Covered wooden deck. **Rates:** Peak (Jan–Apr) $49–$59 S or D. Children under age 18 stay free. Lower rates off-season. Parking: Outdoor, free. AE, CB, DC, DISC, MC, V.

## MOTELS

### ≡≡ Econo Lodge Space Center
3220 N Cocoa Blvd, 32926; tel 407/632-4561 or toll free 800/446-6900; fax 407/632-3756. A three-story budget motel near several highways. **Rooms:** 150 rms. CI 3pm/CO 11am. Nonsmoking rms avail. **Amenities:** 🛏️ A/C, cable TV w/movies. **Services:** 🚐🛎️🤵 Car-rental desk. **Facilities:** 🛗🏊 1 restaurant, 1 bar, lawn games, washer/dryer. **Rates:**

Peak (Jan–Apr) $80 S or D. Children under age 18 stay free. Lower rates off-season. Parking: Outdoor, free. AE, DC, DISC, MC, V.

### ≡≡ Ramada Inn Kennedy Space Center
900 Friday Rd, 32926; tel 407/631-1210 or toll free 800/2-RAMADA; fax 407/636-8661. Exit 76 off I-95. A pleasant place for families to stay. Guests can feed the ducks in the pond nearby. **Rooms:** 150 rms. CI 2pm/CO noon. Nonsmoking rms avail. **Amenities:** 🛏️♨️A/C, cable TV. **Services:** ✗🚐🛎️🤵 Car-rental desk. **Facilities:** 🛗🏊♿ 1 restaurant, 1 bar (w/entertainment), games rm, lawn games, washer/dryer. **Rates:** Peak (Jan–Apr) $50–$80 S or D. Children under age 18 stay free. Lower rates off-season. Parking: Outdoor, free. AE, CB, DC, DISC, ER, JCB, MC, V.

## ATTRACTION 🧳

**Brevard Museum**
2201 Michigan Ave; tel 407/632-1830. This history and science museum chronicles Florida's history from the Ice Age to the Space Age. The Discovery Room has games, computers, and toys for children and features an aquarium and active beehive. Traveling exhibits. **Open:** Peak (Nov–Apr) Tues–Sat 10am–4pm, Sun 1–4pm. Reduced hours off-season. $

# Cocoa Beach

Travelers on I-95 can't miss the billboards for Ron Jon Surf Shop, a self-made landmark in this oceanfront town of 12,000. Cocoa Beach Pier offers restaurants, shops, and periodic festivals. **Information:** Cocoa Beach Area Chamber of Commerce, 400 Fortenberry Rd, Merritt Island, 32952 (tel 407/459-2200).

## HOTELS 🏨

### ≡≡≡ Cocoa Beach Hilton
1550 N Atlantic Ave, 32931; tel 407/799-0003 or toll free 800/526-2609; fax 407/799-0344. Exit 77 off I-95. The tropical motif creates a fun yet still professional look. Guests can stroll across the boardwalk over the dunes to the beach. **Rooms:** 297 rms and stes. CI 3pm/CO 11am. Nonsmoking rms avail. Most rooms have ocean views. **Amenities:** 🛏️♨️ A/C, cable TV. **Services:** ✗🔑🚐🧺🛎️ Car-rental desk, babysitting. **Facilities:** 🛗⚠️🏊♿ 1 restaurant, 2 bars, 1 beach (ocean), board surfing, games rm, whirlpool, washer/dryer. **Rates:** Peak (Feb–Apr/July–Aug) $119–$169 S; $129–$179 D; $150–$180 ste. Extra person $15. Children under age 18 stay free. Lower rates off-season. Parking: Outdoor, free. AE, CB, DC, DISC, ER, MC, V.

### ≡≡ Comfort Inn & Suite Resort
3901 N Atlantic Ave, 32931; tel 407/783-2221 or toll free 800/247-2221; fax 407/783-0461. Exit 77 off I-95. Mid-rise hotel featuring a courtyard with a waterfall and fish pond.

**Rooms:** 144 rms, stes, and effic. CI 2pm/CO 11am. Non-smoking rms avail. **Amenities:** 🛜 ⚱ 🖃 🕭 A/C, cable TV w/movies, refrig, in-rm safe. Some units w/terraces. **Services:** � 🖼 🍹 Car-rental desk. Complimentary cocktail hour. **Facilities:** 🏊 ⌊350⌋ ⟨ 2 bars, games rm, lawn games, whirlpool, playground, washer/dryer. Poolside snackbar. **Rates:** Peak (Feb–Apr/June–Aug) $53–$76 S or D; $105–$123 ste; $60–$83 effic. Extra person $8. Children under age 12 stay free. Lower rates off-season. Parking: Outdoor, free. AE, CB, JCB, MC, V.

### ≣≣≣ Holiday Inn Cocoa Beach

1300 N Atlantic Ave, 32931; tel 407/783-2271 or toll free 800/226-6587; fax 407/784-8878. On FL A1A. Sprawling beachfront complex with nice ocean views. **Rooms:** 500 rms, stes, and effic; 15 cottages/villas. CI 4pm/CO 11am. Non-smoking rms avail. Cheerful, inviting room decor throughout. Rooms in the three-story beachfront building are the most up-to-date. **Amenities:** 🛜 ⚱ 🖃 A/C, cable TV w/movies, voice mail. Some units w/terraces. **Services:** ✕ 🖼 🍹 Car-rental desk, children's program. **Facilities:** 🏊 🚲 ⚠ 🖥 🍴 ⌊1000⌋ 🖵 ⟨ 3 restaurants, 2 bars (1 w/entertainment), 1 beach (ocean), volleyball, board surfing, games rm, whirlpool, beauty salon, playground, washer/dryer. Reggae band plays weekends at the luau. **Rates:** Peak (Feb 15–Apr 15) $85 S or D; $249 ste; $184 cottage/villa. Children under age 19 stay free. Lower rates off-season. Parking: Outdoor, free. AE, CB, DC, DISC, MC, V.

### ≣≣≣ Howard Johnson Plaza Hotel

2080 N Atlantic Ave, 32931; tel 407/783-9222 or toll free 800/55-BEACH; fax 407/799-3234. Exit 77 off I-95. A six-story, oceanfront facility that draws a leisure-business mix. **Rooms:** 210 rms, stes, and effic. Executive level. CI 3pm/CO 11am. Nonsmoking rms avail. **Amenities:** 🛜 ⚱ A/C, satel TV w/movies. Some units w/terraces. **Services:** ✕ 🖛 VP 🖼 🍹 Babysitting. **Facilities:** 🏊 🍴 ⌊500⌋ ⟨ 2 restaurants, 2 bars (1 w/entertainment), 1 beach (ocean), games rm, spa, washer/dryer. Special observation deck allows guests to watch space shuttle launches. **Rates:** Peak (Feb 17–Apr) $85–$115 S; $95–$135 D; $135–$145 ste; $105–$115 effic. Extra person $10. Children under age 18 stay free. Lower rates off-season. Parking: Outdoor, free. AE, CB, DC, DISC, ER, JCB, MC, V.

### ≣≣ Ocean Landings Resort & Racquet Club

900 N Atlantic Ave, 32931; tel 407/783-9430 or toll free 800/323-8413; fax 407/783-1339. FL 528 E to A1A S 8 mi or US 192 E to A1A N 16 mi. 13 acres. This oceanfront property offers many activities to keep vacationing guests busy. **Rooms:** 228 rms, stes, and effic. CI 5pm/CO 11am. Florida-inspired furnishings. **Amenities:** 🛜 ⚱ 🖃 A/C, cable TV w/movies, refrig. Some units w/terraces, some w/whirlpools. **Services:** � 🍹 Car-rental desk, children's program, babysitting. **Facilities:** 🏊 🔲4 🖥 ⌊50⌋ ⟨ 1 restaurant (dinner only), 2 bars (1 w/entertainment), 1 beach (ocean), basketball, volleyball, board surfing, lawn games, racquetball, spa, sauna, steam rm, whirlpool, playground, washer/dryer. **Rates:** Peak (May 29–Sept 7) $70–$106 S or D; $106–$142 ste; $106–$202 effic. Children under age 18 stay free. Lower rates off-season. Parking: Indoor/outdoor, free. AE, DC, DISC, MC, V.

## MOTEL

### ≣ Econo Lodge

1275 N Atlantic Ave, 32931; tel 407/783-2252 or toll free 800/795-2252; fax 407/783-4485. Exit 77 off I-95. A commendable tourist-class hotel situated away from beach but near Kennedy Space Center. **Rooms:** 128 rms and effic. CI 3pm/CO 11am. Nonsmoking rms avail. **Amenities:** 🛜 ⚱ A/C, cable TV, in-rm safe. Some units w/terraces. **Services:** ✕ � 🖼 🍹 🕭 **Facilities:** 🏊 ⟨ 1 restaurant, 2 bars, games rm, beauty salon, washer/dryer. **Rates:** Peak (Feb–Apr/July–Sept 7) $80–$100 S or D; $90 effic. Children under age 18 stay free. Lower rates off-season. Parking: Outdoor, free. AE, CB, DC, MC, V.

## RESTAURANTS 🍴

### Alma's

306 N Orlando Ave; tel 407/783-1981. **Italian.** A comfortable, old-fashioned restaurant of several rooms, all ornamented with artwork, tile flooring, and potted plants. The menu offers a variety of seafood and beef entrees, as well as traditional Italian dishes. **FYI:** Reservations accepted. Children's menu. **Open:** Daily 4–10pm. **Prices:** Main courses $7–$32. AE, CB, DC, DISC, MC, V. 🖃⟨

### Bernard's Surf

2 S Atlantic Ave; tel 407/783-2401. At FL A1A and Minute Man Causeway. **Seafood.** A dimly lit, casual restaurant with an extensive menu offering sandwiches and burgers as well as pasta, seafood, and beef entrees. **FYI:** Reservations recommended. **Open:** Daily 11am–11pm. **Prices:** Main courses $12–$25. AE, CB, DC, DISC, MC, V. 🖃⟨

### 🍷 Mango Tree

118 N Atlantic Ave; tel 407/799-0513. Corner of 1st St N and N Atlantic Ave. **American/Continental.** Probably the best restaurant in the area, with an elaborate menu and an attentive staff. The conscientious owner oversees all aspects of the daily operation. The dining room sports a saltwater fish tank, and the beautifully landscaped garden features a lovely gazebo. **FYI:** Reservations recommended. Piano. Children's menu. **Open:** Tues–Thurs 6–10pm, Fri–Sat 6–10:30pm, Sun 6–8:30pm. **Prices:** Main courses $13–$27. AE, MC, V. 🖤

## ATTRACTION 🏛

### Cocoa Beach Pier

401 Meade Ave; tel 407/783-7549. This pier, extending 800 feet into the Atlantic Ocean, has restaurants, nightclubs, shops, and a bait and tackle store that rents fishing equipment. **Open:** Daily 11am–11pm. **Free**

# Coconut Grove

See Miami

# Coral Gables

Broad streets and Mediterranean architecture are hallmarks of this gracious community founded by George Merrick in the 1920s. Now a south Miami suburb of 40,000, Coral Gables hosts the University of Miami, Lowe Art Museum, and the elegant Biltmore Hotel. **Information:** Coral Gables Chamber of Commerce, 50 Aragon Ave, Coral Gables, 33134 (tel 305/446-1657).

## HOTELS

### Holiday Inn

2051 LeJeune Rd, 33134; tel 305/443-2301 or toll free 800/HOLIDAY; fax 305/446-6827. Well-equipped hotel catering to business travelers. **Rooms:** 168 rms and stes. Executive level. CI 3pm/CO noon. Nonsmoking rms avail. Pastel decor, with wicker headboards and dark furnishings. Redecorated in 1995. **Amenities:** A/C, cable TV, voice mail. **Services:** Car-rental desk, babysitting. **Facilities:** 1 restaurant, 1 bar (w/entertainment), washer/dryer. **Rates:** Peak (Dec 15–Apr 15) $129–$139 S or D; $155 ste. Extra person $10. Children under age 19 stay free. Lower rates off-season. Parking: Outdoor, free. AE, CB, DC, DISC, MC, V.

### UNRATED Hotel Place St Michel

162 Alcazar Ave, 33134; tel 305/444-1666; fax 305/529-0074. At Ponce de Leon Blvd. This romantic hotel in a three-story corner building is something of a charmer, a look back to a time when elevators had operators and guest rooms were individually decorated. **Rooms:** 27 rms and stes. CI 2pm/CO noon. Rooms may have an antique or two; some have original marble floors and original fixtures. **Amenities:** A/C, cable TV w/movies, dataport. 1 unit w/terrace. **Services:** Twice-daily maid svce, car-rental desk, babysitting. **Facilities:** 1 restaurant, 1 bar (w/entertainment). **Rates (CP):** Peak (Nov–Apr) $150 S or D; $185 ste. Extra person $10. Children under age 12 stay free. Min stay special events. Lower rates off-season. Parking: Outdoor, $7/day. AE, CB, DC, DISC, MC, V.

### Omni Colonnade Hotel

180 Aragon Ave, 33134; tel 305/441-2600 or toll free 800/533-1337; fax 305/445-3929. At Ponce de Leon Blvd. A wonderful hotel housed in a historic building containing many striking architectural features. Grand rotunda entrance, luxurious public areas, lovely appointments. Dedicated staff. **Rooms:** 157 rms and stes. Executive level. CI 3pm/CO noon. Nonsmoking rms avail. **Amenities:** A/C, cable TV w/movies, dataport, voice mail, in-rm safe, bathrobes. All units w/minibars, some w/terraces. **Services:** Twice-daily maid svce, car-rental desk, social director, masseur, babysitting. **Facilities:** 1 restaurant, 1 bar (w/entertainment), sauna, steam rm, whirlpool, beauty salon. Sophisticated, very popular bar. **Rates:** Peak (Oct–Apr) $215–$255 S or D; $295 ste. Extra person $30. Children under age 18 stay free. Min stay special events. Lower rates off-season. Parking: Indoor, $9/day. AE, CB, DC, DISC, MC, V.

## RESORT

### The Biltmore Hotel

1200 Anastasia Ave, 33134; tel 305/445-1926 or toll free 800/456-1926; fax 305/442-9496. I-95 to US 1, off Grenada St. 20 acres. Opulent furnishings and Mediterranean elegance are the hallmarks of this historic landmark. The focal point of the majestic lobby is a 12-foot wooden birdcage which many colorful finches call home. High arches, marble floors, and fireplace give the lobby a palatial appearance. **Rooms:** 275 rms and stes. Executive level. CI 3pm/CO noon. Nonsmoking rms avail. Guest rooms are spacious and luxurious. **Amenities:** A/C, cable TV w/movies, dataport, voice mail, in-rm safe, bathrobes. Some units w/terraces, some w/fireplaces. **Services:** Twice-daily maid svce, car-rental desk, social director, masseur, babysitting. **Facilities:** 2 restaurants, 2 bars (1 w/entertainment), spa, sauna, steam rm, whirlpool, beauty salon. The legendary 17,000-ft pool surrounds half the hotel. **Rates:** Peak (Oct–Apr) $269 S or D; $389 ste. Children under age 18 stay free. Lower rates off-season. AP and MAP rates avail. Parking: Outdoor, free. AE, CB, DC, DISC, MC, V.

## RESTAURANTS

### The Bistro

2611 Ponce de Leon Blvd; tel 305/442-9671. **Continental/French.** A charming and unpretentious French eatery favored by couples. The menu includes a selection of fine seafood dishes as well as rack of lamb, veal steak in lemon sauce, and veal Theresa. **FYI:** Reservations recommended. Beer and wine only. **Open:** Lunch Tues–Fri 11:30am–2pm; dinner Tues–Sat 6–11pm. **Prices:** Main courses $14–$23. AE, CB, DC, DISC, MC.

### Caffe Abbracci

318 Aragon Ave; tel 305/441-0700. **Italian.** The dark, finely furnished bar and stylish dining rooms create an aura of affluence. The menu features such specialties as risotto al Porcini, grilled Norwegian salmon, and a swordfish, shrimp, and salmon combination. **FYI:** Reservations recommended. Dress code. No smoking. **Open:** Lunch Mon–Fri 11:30am–3pm; dinner Sun–Thurs 6–11:30pm, Fri–Sat 6pm–midnight. **Prices:** Main courses $16–$23. AE, CB, DC, DISC, MC, V.

## Caffe Baci
2522 Ponce de Leon Blvd; tel 305/442-0600. **Italian/Mediterranean.** A bright, cozy cafe. Romantic pink pastel interior is adorned with Roman prints and fresh floral displays. **FYI:** Reservations recommended. Beer and wine only. **Open:** Lunch Mon–Fri noon–3pm; dinner Mon–Thurs 6:30–11pm, Fri–Sat 6:30–11:30pm. **Prices:** Main courses $14–$24. AE, CB, DC, DISC, MC, V. ❂ ♿

## Casa Rolandi
1930 Ponce de Leon Blvd; tel 305/444-2187. At Navarre St. **Italian.** An attractive eatery renowned for its creative northern Italian cooking. **FYI:** Reservations recommended. Beer and wine only. **Open:** Lunch Mon–Fri noon–3pm; dinner daily 6–11pm. **Prices:** Main courses $13–$25. AE, CB, DC, DISC, MC, V. ❂

## ★ Christy's
3101 Ponce de Leon Blvd; tel 305/446-1400. **Continental/Steak.** A landmark steak house, styled like a gentleman's club, where you can rub elbows with longtime area residents. Cozy atmosphere. **FYI:** Reservations recommended. Piano music. Dress code. **Open:** Mon–Thurs 11:30am–11pm, Fri 11:30am–midnight, Sat 5pm–midnight, Sun 5–11pm. **Prices:** Main courses $18–$33. AE, CB, DC, MC, V. ♿

## House of India
22 Merrick Way; tel 305/444-2348. 1 block N of Miracle Mile. **Indian.** This dark restaurant, with its soft Indian music, is a real treat. The very reasonably priced lunch and dinner buffets include chicken, lamb, shrimp, fish, and bread prepared authentically in a tandoor, the clay oven of India. **FYI:** Reservations accepted. **Open:** Lunch daily noon–3pm; dinner daily 5–10pm. **Prices:** Main courses $5–$18. AE, DISC, MC, V. ♿

## Le Festival
2120 Salzedo St; tel 305/442-8545. 5 blocks N of Miracle Mile. **French.** Elegant French dining in a refined, flower-filled setting. Seafood, steak, chicken, and wild game dishes are served, followed by splendid desserts. **FYI:** Reservations recommended. **Open:** Lunch Mon–Fri 11:45am–2:30pm; dinner Mon–Thurs 6–10:30pm, Fri–Sat 6–11pm. **Prices:** Main courses $16–$25. AE, CB, DC, DISC, ER, MC, V. ♿

## ★ L'Osteria
2271 Ponce de Leon Blvd; tel 305/442-2033. I-95 S to US 1 to Bird Rd. **Northern Italian.** A small and comfortable dining room decorated with an attractive blend of blond woods. Menu specialties include veal-stuffed ravioli, and fresh fettuccine topped with veal, marscapone, and wild mushrooms. **FYI:** Reservations recommended. Dress code. Beer and wine only. **Open:** Lunch daily 11–2:30am; dinner daily 6:30–11pm. **Prices:** Main courses $13–$23. AE, MC, V. ❂ VP

## Peppy's in the Gables
216 Palermo Ave; tel 305/448-1240. **Northern Italian.** Northern Italian cuisine served by a friendly staff in a cozy, Euro-style dining room. **FYI:** Reservations accepted. Beer and wine only. **Open:** Lunch Mon–Fri 11am–3pm; dinner Sun–Thurs 5–11pm, Fri–Sat 5pm–midnight. **Prices:** Main courses $12–$21. AE, DC, DISC, MC, V. ❂ ♿

## Restaurant St Michel
In Hotel Place St Michel, 162 Alcazar Ave; tel 305/446-6572. **New American/French.** A very elegant, rather formal dinner spot (slightly more casual for lunch) with chandeliers, antiques, hardwood floors, and beautiful flowers. A wide variety of entrees is available, including grilled veal with pink peppercorn and mustard cream sauce, roast Long Island duckling, yellowtail snapper, and fresh Maine lobster. The changing wine list is extensive. **FYI:** Reservations recommended. Children's menu. Jacket required. **Open:** Breakfast Mon–Fri 7–9:30am; lunch Mon–Sat 11am–3pm; dinner Sun–Thurs 5–10:30pm, Fri–Sat 5–11:30pm; brunch Sun 11am–3pm. **Prices:** Main courses $14–$27. AE, CB, DC, DISC, MC, V. ❂ ♿

## Ristorante Tanino
2312 Ponce de Leon Blvd; tel 305/446-1666. **Italian.** A cozy bistro particularly popular with families. House specialties include veal scaloppine marsala, and a variety of pastas. **FYI:** Reservations recommended. Dress code. Beer and wine only. **Open:** Lunch Mon–Fri 11:30am–2:30pm; dinner Mon–Thurs 6–10:30pm, Fri–Sat 6–11pm. **Prices:** Main courses $18–$29. AE, CB, DC, DISC, MC, V. 🎦

## Two Sisters
In the Hyatt Regency Coral Gables, 50 Alhambra Plaza; tel 305/445-1234. **Caribbean/Spanish.** A spacious, stylish, and romantic setting for the Spanish-influenced dishes. The tapas are popular. **FYI:** Reservations accepted. Children's menu. Dress code. **Open:** Breakfast Mon–Sat 7–11am; lunch Mon–Sat 11am–3pm; dinner daily 6–11pm; brunch Sun 11am–3pm. **Prices:** Main courses $12–$24. AE, CB, DC, DISC, MC, V. ❂ VP ♿

## Yuca
177 Giralda; tel 305/444-4448. **Cuban/Latin.** An immaculate, upscale new Cuban restaurant where smartly dressed chefs prepare inspired gourmet entrees. Inventive specialties include grilled veal chops with black beans, rice, and chayote slaw seasoned with onion essence, as well as citrus-planked salmon with mango-mustard glaze. **FYI:** Reservations recommended. Big band. **Open:** Mon–Thurs noon–11pm, Fri–Sat noon–midnight. **Prices:** Main courses $18–$28. AE, CB, DC, MC, V. VP ♿

# ATTRACTIONS 🏛

## Fairchild Tropical Gardens
10901 Old Cutler Rd; tel 305/667-1651. These large botanical gardens feature a veritable rain forest of both rare and exotic plants. Narrated tram tours are available; phone ahead for the schedule. **Open:** Daily 9:30am–4:30pm. **$$$**

## Venetian Pool

2701 De Soto Blvd; tel 305/460-5356. Miami's most unusual swimming pool, dating from 1924, is hidden behind pastel stucco walls and is honored with a listing in the National Register of Historic Places. The pool is ornamented with palm-studded paths, Venetian-style bridges, and coral rock caves. Visitors are free to swim and sunbathe here year-round. **Open:** Call for hours. **$$**

# Crystal River

One of two large towns in Citrus County along the northern Gulf Coast, Crystal River attracts manatee lovers who swim with the sea cows at natural springs. There's also a pre-Columbian archaeological site here; a museum displays selected artifacts. **Information:** Crystal River–Nature Coast Chamber of Commerce, 28 NW US 19, Crystal River, 34428 (tel 352/795-3149).

## HOTEL 🏨

### ⊫⊫ Days Inn Resort

2380 US 19 N, PO Box 785, 32629; tel 352/795-2111 or toll free 800/343-4230; fax 352/795-4126. Exit 40 off I-75. ½ mile N of Crystal River Mall. Family-oriented, with manicured grounds and a landscaped courtyard. **Rooms:** 106 rms and effic. CI 3pm/CO noon. Nonsmoking rms avail. **Amenities:** 🛏 A/C, cable TV. 1 unit w/terrace. **Services:** ✕ 🍴 🏃 Free shuttle to mall. **Facilities:** ⚖ 🔲 1 restaurant, 1 bar (w/entertainment), lawn games, washer/dryer. **Rates:** Peak (Feb–Mar) $70 S or D; $80 effic. Extra person $6. Children under age 18 stay free. Lower rates off-season. Parking: Outdoor, free. AE, DC, DISC, MC, V.

## RESORT

### ⊫⊫⊫ Plantation Inn & Golf Resort

9301 W Fort Island Trail, PO Box 1116, 34423; tel 352/795-4211 or toll free 800/632-6262; fax 352/795-1368. 420 acres. Columned, white-brick "estate" with a classic interior and some antiques. **Rooms:** 155 rms, stes, and effic. CI 2pm/CO noon. Nonsmoking rms avail. **Amenities:** 🛏 A/C, cable TV w/movies. Some units w/terraces. **Services:** ✕ 🚗 🍴 **Facilities:** ⚖ ⛳27 🏊4 🔲 2 restaurants, 3 bars, games rm, lawn games, snorkeling, sauna, washer/dryer. Marina. **Rates:** Peak (Jan–Mar) $79–$89 S or D; $175–$185 ste; $115–$125 effic. Extra person $15. Children under age 12 stay free. Lower rates off-season. AP rates avail. Parking: Outdoor, free. AE, DISC, MC, V.

## ATTRACTION 🏛

### Crystal River State Archeological Site

3400 N Museum Pointe; tel 352/795-3817. Archeologists have recovered numerous artifacts from this site, mainly from about 200 BC to AD 1400, when a community of pre-Columbian mound-builders resided here. Six mounds, used for various purposes, remain in the park, and there are two large limestone boulders thought to have been used as part of a solar calendar system. An on-site museum focuses on the mound-builders, but also has pieces recovered from even earlier settlements. A half-mile loop trail is marked with plaques explaining many features of the mounds. Gift shop, picnic area. **Open:** Park, daily 8am–dusk; museum, daily 9am–5pm. **$**

# Dania

Home of two jai alai frontons and John U Lloyd Beach State Recreation Area, with its 244 acres of sand dunes and mangrove swamps. **Information:** Dania Chamber of Commerce, 102 W Dania Beach Blvd, PO Box 838, Dania, 33004 (tel 954/927-3377)

## HOTELS 🏨

### ⊫⊫⊫ Fort Lauderdale Airport Hilton

1870 Griffin Rd, 33004; tel 954/920-3300 or toll free 800/445-8667, 800/426-8578, 800/654-8266 in FL; fax 954/920-3348. A spiffy hotel with good security. Tropical motif, airy three-story lobby. **Rooms:** 388 rms and stes; 16 cottages/villas. Executive level. CI 3pm/CO noon. Nonsmoking rms avail. High-quality furnishings. **Amenities:** 🛏 A/C, cable TV w/movies, dataport, voice mail. Some units w/terraces, 1 w/whirlpool. **Services:** ✕ 🛎 VP 🚗 🍴 Twice-daily maid svce, masseur, babysitting. **Facilities:** ⚖ 🏊 🎾50 🔲 ⚖ 1 restaurant (bkfst only), 3 bars (2 w/entertainment), spa, sauna, steam rm, whirlpool. Rooftop terrace. **Rates:** Peak (Jan–Apr 15) $139–$179 S or D; $395–$495 ste; $169 cottage/villa. Lower rates off-season. Parking: Indoor/outdoor, free. AE, CB, DC, DISC, EC, MC, V.

### ⊫⊫⊫⊫ Sheraton Fort Lauderdale Airport Hotel

1825 Griffin Rd, 33004; tel 954/920-3500 or toll free 800/325-3535; fax 954/920-3571. 5 minutes from Fort Lauderdale Int'l Airport. A stylish, first-rate commercial hotel. **Rooms:** 250 rms and stes. Executive level. CI 3pm/CO noon. Nonsmoking rms avail. **Amenities:** 🛏 A/C, cable TV w/movies, dataport, voice mail. Some units w/minibars, 1 w/whirlpool. **Services:** ✕ 🛎 🚗 🍴 Twice-daily maid svce, babysitting. **Facilities:** ⚖ 🎾 🏊2 🎾 130 🔲 ⚖ 1 restaurant, 2 bars (w/entertainment), basketball, racquetball, spa, sauna, whirlpool. **Rates:** Peak (Nov–Apr) $155 S or D; $275–$425 ste. Children under age 21 stay free. Lower rates off-season. AP and MAP rates avail. Parking: Outdoor, free. AE, DC, DISC, EC, MC, V.

# Davenport

See also Haines City

## HOTEL

### ≡≡ Ramada Limited
4825 US 27, PO Box 1536, 33837; tel 941/424-2211 or toll free 800/422-2414; fax 941/424-3312. At I-4 jct. This popular hotel is often understaffed, so queues are not uncommon. **Rooms:** 200 rms. CI 3pm/CO noon. Nonsmoking rms avail. **Amenities:** 🛏 ⚅ A/C, cable TV, in-rm safe. **Services:** ⬜ ⤴ ⬗ Babysitting. Complimentary shuttle to Walt Disney World. Staff can suggest day trips to local attractions. **Facilities:** 🏋 🔲₅₀ ⅙ 1 bar, games rm, whirlpool, playground, washer/dryer. **Rates:** Peak (Feb–Apr/June–Aug) $49–$89 S or D. Children under age 18 stay free. Lower rates off-season. Parking: Outdoor, free. AE, CB, DC, DISC, MC, V.

# Daytona Beach

See also New Smyrna Beach, Ormond Beach, Ponce Inlet

Speed is the creed in this oceanside city of 62,500. (You can tour the famed Speedway between races.) Alternatives include wide beaches (yes, you can drive on them), the $16 million Halifax Harbor Marina, and several museums (including one outfitted by deposed Cuban President Fulgencio Batista). **Information:** Destination Daytona Convention & Visitors Bureau, 126 E Orange Ave, PO Box 910, Daytona Beach, 32115 (tel 904/255-0415).

## HOTELS

### ≡≡ Acapulco Inn
2505 S Atlantic Ave, 32110; tel 904/761-2210 or toll free 800/874-7420; fax 904/761-2216. Exit 87 off I-95. This eight-story property is popular with students during spring break and with couples and others off-peak. **Rooms:** 133 rms and effic. CI 3pm/CO 11am. Nonsmoking rms avail. Sturdy rooms in tropical colors, furnished with adequate appointments for this grade of hotel. Units are categorized oceanview or oceanfront. **Amenities:** 🛏 ⚅ 🖫 A/C, cable TV w/movies, refrig, in-rm safe. All units w/terraces. Some have microwaves. **Services:** 🚐 ⬜ ⤴ Car-rental desk. **Facilities:** 🏋 🔲 ⅙ 1 restaurant (bkfst and lunch only), 1 bar, 1 beach (ocean), games rm, lawn games, whirlpool, washer/dryer. Restaurant provides ocean vistas. **Rates:** Peak (Feb–Aug) $159–$173 S or D; $167 effic. Extra person $10. Children under age 18 stay free. Lower rates off-season. Parking: Outdoor, free. AE, DC, MC, V.

### ≡≡≡ Adam's Mark Daytona Beach Resort
100 N Atlantic Ave, 32118; tel 904/254-8200 or toll free 800/872-9269; fax 904/253-8841. ½ mi N of US 92. One of Daytona's most luxurious—and most central—beachfront hotels, located right at the clock tower and bandshell. It makes a striking architectural statement in a resort city where blasé is the norm. The three-story marble lobby is shiny and impressive. The style and craftsmanship in this hotel really shows. **Rooms:** 402 rms and stes. Executive level. CI 4pm/CO 11am. Nonsmoking rms avail. Every room offers a beautiful ocean view. **Amenities:** 🛏 ⚅ A/C, cable TV w/movies. All units w/minibars, some w/terraces, 1 w/whirlpool. **Services:** ✕ 🖬 VP ⬜ ⤴ Twice-daily maid svce, masseur, children's program, babysitting. Reduced fees at local golf courses. **Facilities:** 🏋 🚴 🔲 🏓 🔲₁₅₀₀ 🖥 ⅙ 3 restaurants, 4 bars (3 w/entertainment), 1 beach (ocean), lifeguard, volleyball, board surfing, spa, sauna, steam rm, whirlpool, beauty salon, playground, washer/dryer. **Rates:** Peak (Feb–Oct) $119–$194 S or D; $265–$1,000 ste. Extra person $10. Children under age 19 stay free. Min stay special events. Lower rates off-season. Parking: Indoor/outdoor, $10/day. AE, CB, DC, DISC, MC, V.

### ≡≡ The Aladdin Inn
2323 S Atlantic Ave, 32110; tel 904/255-0476 or toll free 800/874-7517; fax 904/255-3376. Exit 87 off I-95. A six-story oceanfront hotel flanked on one side by a pool and furnished with a routine mix of accommodations. **Rooms:** 120 rms, stes, and effic. CI 3pm/CO 11am. Nonsmoking rms avail. **Amenities:** 🛏 A/C, cable TV, refrig, in-rm safe. All units w/terraces. **Services:** 🚐 ⬜ ⤴ Car-rental desk, children's program, babysitting. **Facilities:** 🏋 1 beach (ocean), games rm, lawn games, washer/dryer. **Rates:** Peak (June–Aug) $125 S or D; $240 ste; $240 effic. Children under age 18 stay free. Lower rates off-season. Parking: Outdoor, free. AE, DC, DISC, MC, V.

### ≡≡≡ Beachcomer Oceanfront Inn
2000 N Atlantic Ave, 32118; tel 904/252-8513 or toll free 800/245-3575; fax 904/252-7400. Exit 87A off I-95. Away from the fray of beach action, this modest but attractive seven-story hotel has accommodations facing the ocean or street. Couples and others hoping to avoid boom boxes and corridor parties will be happy here. **Rooms:** 174 rms and effic. CI 3pm/CO 11am. Nonsmoking rms avail. **Amenities:** 🛏 ⚅ A/C, cable TV w/movies, refrig, dataport, voice mail, in-rm safe. All units w/terraces. Some have coffeemakers. **Services:** ✕ ⬜ ⤴ Children's program. **Facilities:** 🏋 1 restaurant, 1 bar, 1 beach (ocean), lifeguard, games rm, whirlpool, washer/dryer. **Rates:** Peak (June 10–Aug 15) $68–$80 S or D; $74–$86 effic. Extra person $8. Children under age 17 stay free. Min stay special events. Lower rates off-season. Parking: Outdoor, free. AE, CB, DC, DISC, MC, V.

### ≡≡≡ Best Western La Playa Resort
2500 N Atlantic Ave, 32118; tel 904/672-0990 or toll free 800/874-6996; fax 904/677-0982. 3¼ mi N of US 92. High-rise hotel on the north end of the beach, opposite a shopping plaza. **Rooms:** 239 rms, stes, and effic. CI 3pm/CO 11am. Nonsmoking rms avail. Rooms are more than adequately

furnished and outfitted. Each offers an ocean view; some have oceanfront balconies. **Amenities:** ▣ ▣ ▣ A/C, cable TV w/movies, refrig, in-rm safe. All units w/terraces, some w/whirlpools. Microwaves. **Services:** ✕ ▣ ⟿ Children's program. **Facilities:** ▣ ▣ ▣ ▣ ▣ 1 restaurant, 2 bars (1 w/entertainment), 1 beach (ocean), lifeguard, volleyball, board surfing, games rm, sauna, steam rm, whirlpool, washer/dryer. Indoor heated pool; shuffleboard courts. **Rates:** Peak (June 8–Aug 17) $101–$129 D; $130–$180 ste; $111–$139 effic. Extra person $6. Children under age 18 stay free. Min stay special events. Lower rates off-season. Parking: Indoor/outdoor, free. AE, CB, DC, DISC, MC, V.

### ▣▣ Captain's Quarters Inn

3711 S Atlantic Ave, 32127; tel 904/767-3119 or toll free 800/332-3119; fax 904/767-0883. Exit 8S off I-95. This all-suites hotel has fine accommodations and quality appointments. Limited public areas. **Rooms:** 26 stes. CI 3pm/CO 11am. Nonsmoking rms avail. **Amenities:** ▣ ▣ ▣ A/C, cable TV, refrig, VCR. All units w/terraces, 1 w/fireplace, 1 w/whirlpool. **Services:** ✕ ▣ ▣ ⟿ **Facilities:** ▣ ▣ 1 restaurant (bkfst and lunch only), 1 beach (ocean), washer/dryer. **Rates:** Peak (June–Aug) $85–$125 ste. Extra person $5. Children under age 18 stay free. Lower rates off-season. Parking: Outdoor, free. AE, DISC, MC, V.

### ▣▣ Days Inn Daytona Central

1909 S Atlantic Ave, 32118; tel 904/255-4492 or toll free 800/224-5056; fax 904/238-0632. Exit 87 off I-95. A nine-story, beachfront tourist hotel. **Rooms:** 191 rms and effic. CI 4pm/CO noon. Nonsmoking rms avail. Rooms with partial or full ocean views. Oceanfront efficiencies. **Amenities:** ▣ ▣ A/C, cable TV w/movies. All units w/terraces. **Services:** ▣ ▣ ⟿ ⟿ **Facilities:** ▣ ▣ 1 restaurant (bkfst and dinner only), 1 bar, 1 beach (ocean), games rm, washer/dryer. **Rates:** Peak (Feb–Apr) $75–$95 S; $85–$125 D; $95–$145 effic. Extra person $6. Children under age 18 stay free. Lower rates off-season. Parking: Outdoor, free. AE, CB, DC, DISC, MC, V.

### ▣▣▣ Daytona Beach Hotel

2637 S Atlantic Ave, 32118; tel 904/767-7350 or toll free 800/525-7350; fax 904/760-3651. Volusia Ave exit off I-95. An attractive high-rise hotel located on the beach. Spacious lobby. **Rooms:** 214 rms, stes, and effic. CI 3pm/CO 11am. Nonsmoking rms avail. First-class accommodations are neat and stylish, with excellent ocean and beach views. **Amenities:** ▣ ▣ ▣ A/C, cable TV w/movies, refrig, in-rm safe. Some units w/minibars, some w/terraces. Some rooms have coffeemakers. **Services:** ✕ ▣ ▣ ▣ ▣ ⟿ Car-rental desk, babysitting. **Facilities:** ▣ ▣ ▣ ▣ ▣ ▣ ▣ 2 restaurants, 2 bars (1 w/entertainment), 1 beach (ocean), games rm, lawn games, whirlpool, beauty salon, washer/dryer. Drive-up entrance is joined by a skywalk to additional parking across the street. **Rates:** Peak (Feb–Apr/July) $140–$179 S or D; $235–

$560 ste; $170 effic. Extra person $15. Children under age 18 stay free. Lower rates off-season. Parking: Indoor/outdoor, free. AE, CB, DC, DISC, ER, JCB, MC, V.

### ▣ Hawaiian Inn

2301 S Atlantic Ave, Daytona Beach Shores, 32118; tel 904/255-5411 or toll free 800/922-3023, 800/922-3023 in the US, 800/635-3502 in Canada; fax 904/253-1209. On FL A1A, 2 mi S of US 92. A popular spot for college students on spring break and others in search of unpretentious accommodations and a large, sunny pool deck. **Rooms:** 202 rms, stes, and effic. CI 3pm/CO 11am. Nonsmoking rms avail. Room decor and age of furnishings varies. **Amenities:** ▣ ▣ A/C, cable TV w/movies, refrig. All units w/terraces. **Services:** ✕ ▣ ⟿ **Facilities:** ▣ ▣ 2 restaurants, 2 bars (1 w/entertainment), 1 beach (ocean), lifeguard, games rm, whirlpool, washer/dryer. **Rates:** Peak (Mar–Aug) $60–$75 S or D; $80–$95 ste; $70–$85 effic. Extra person $10. Children under age 17 stay free. Min stay special events. Lower rates off-season. Parking: Outdoor, free. AE, CB, DC, DISC, MC, V.

### ▣▣ Holiday Inn Daytona Beach Oceanfront

2560 N Atlantic Ave, 32118; tel 904/672-1440 or toll free 800/874-6996; fax 904/677-8811. 3¼ mi N of US 92. Far enough away from the action to provide guests with a relaxing atmosphere, yet close to restaurants and shopping. **Rooms:** 143 rms and effic. CI 3pm/CO 11am. Nonsmoking rms avail. All rooms have mini- or full kitchens. **Amenities:** ▣ ▣ ▣ A/C, cable TV w/movies, refrig, in-rm safe. All units w/terraces. **Services:** ✕ ▣ ⟿ Children's program. **Facilities:** ▣ ▣ ▣ ▣ 1 restaurant, 1 beach (ocean), lifeguard, board surfing, whirlpool, washer/dryer. Guests receive complimentary use of fitness and recreational facilities at adjacent Best Western La Playa Resort. **Rates:** Peak (June 8–Aug 17) $93–$125 S or D; $99–$131 effic. Extra person $6. Children under age 18 stay free. Min stay special events. Lower rates off-season. Parking: Outdoor, free. AE, DC, DISC, JCB, MC, V.

### ▣▣ Holiday Inn Oceanside

905 S Atlantic Ave, 32118; tel 904/255-5432 or toll free 800/334-4484; fax 904/254-0885. Exit 87 off I-95. A clean, stable, and attractive choice, it does a commendable job under the pressure of the annual spring break influx and an even better one off-season. Alert staff. **Rooms:** 107 rms and effic. CI 3pm/CO 11am. Nonsmoking rms avail. **Amenities:** ▣ ▣ A/C, cable TV w/movies, in-rm safe. Some units w/minibars, all w/terraces. **Services:** ✕ ▣ ⟿ Car-rental desk, babysitting. **Facilities:** ▣ ▣ 1 restaurant, 1 bar, 1 beach (ocean), lawn games, washer/dryer. Reserved and intimate restaurant is a surprise for a beach city. Fireplace in lounge. **Rates:** Peak (Feb–Mar/June–July) $199–$229 S or D; $199–$299 effic. Extra person $10. Children under age 18 stay free. Lower rates off-season. Parking: Outdoor, free. AE, DC, DISC, MC, V.

### Holiday Inn SunSpree Resort

600 N Atlantic Ave, 32118; tel 904/255-4471 or toll free 800/767-4471; fax 904/253-7543. 1¼ mi N of US 92. Public spaces bustle with activity during spring break, Bike Week, and Race Week. **Rooms:** 322 rms. CI 4pm/CO 11am. Nonsmoking rms avail. Rooms are cheerfully decorated. **Amenities:** 📷 🍸 📺 🍴 A/C, cable TV w/movies, in-rm safe. Some units w/terraces, some w/whirlpools. Guests may request a refrigerator if room is not equipped with one. **Services:** ✕ 🖼 🛎 🦮 Car-rental desk, social director, children's program, babysitting. **Facilities:** 🏊 🎾 🚤 📳 🖥 🚾 1 restaurant, 4 bars (1 w/entertainment), 1 beach (ocean), basketball, volleyball, games rm, playground, washer/dryer. Shuffleboard. **Rates:** Peak (Feb–Mar) $109–$139 S or D. Children under age 19 stay free. Min stay special events. Lower rates off-season. Parking: Indoor/outdoor, free. AE, CB, DC, DISC, ER, JCB, MC, V.

### Ocean Sands Hotel

1024 N Atlantic Ave, 32118; tel 904/255-1131 or toll free 800/543-2923; fax 904/255-5670. 1¾ mi N of US 92. A veritable spring break mecca, this eight-story lodging has a sunny pool deck and ocean-facing accommodations. **Rooms:** 94 rms, stes, and effic. CI 3pm/CO 11am. Nonsmoking rms avail. Some rooms with ocean view, others with street view. **Amenities:** 📷 A/C, cable TV, in-rm safe. All units w/terraces. **Services:** ✕ 🖼 🛎 Babysitting. **Facilities:** 🏊 🚾 1 restaurant, 1 beach (ocean), lifeguard, games rm, washer/dryer. Indoor heated pool. Across the street from city shuffleboard and basketball courts. **Rates:** Peak (Mar–Apr 15/June 7–Aug 14) $65–$75 S or D; $90 ste; $85 effic. Extra person $5. Children under age 12 stay free. Min stay special events. Lower rates off-season. Parking: Outdoor, free. AE, DISC, MC, V.

### Palm Plaza

3301 S Atlantic Ave, 32118; tel 904/767-1711 or toll free 800/DAYTONA; fax 904/756-8394. Exit 85 off I-95. A cheerful high-rise on the south side of town, it presents a fresh, tropical face. Its pleasant, well-kept lobby provides an ocean view. **Rooms:** 98 effic. CI 3pm/CO 11am. Nonsmoking rms avail. **Amenities:** 📷 📺 A/C, cable TV w/movies, refrig, in-rm safe. All units w/terraces. **Services:** 🚐 🖼 🛎 Car-rental desk, children's program, babysitting. **Facilities:** 🏊 🚾 1 beach (ocean), games rm, whirlpool, washer/dryer. **Rates:** Peak (June–Sept) $50–$270 effic. Children under age 18 stay free. Lower rates off-season. Parking: Outdoor, free. AE, DC, DISC, MC, V.

### Perry's Ocean Edge Resort

2209 S Atlantic Ave, 32118; tel 904/255-0581 or toll free 800/447-0002; fax 904/258-7315. A modest family operation offering quite extensive facilities. **Rooms:** 204 rms and stes. CI 4pm/CO 11am. Standard motel appointments. **Amenities:** 📷 🍸 A/C, cable TV. Some units w/terraces. **Services:** 🚐 🖼 🛎 Car-rental desk, children's program, babysitting. **Facilities:** 🏊 🚾 🚾 1 restaurant (bkfst and lunch only), 1 beach (ocean), games rm, lawn games, whirlpool, washer/dryer. **Rates (CP):** Peak (June–Aug) $60–$120 S or D; $85 ste; $70–$130 effic. Lower rates off-season. AP and MAP rates avail. Parking: Outdoor, free. AE, CB, DC, DISC, MC, V.

### Seagarden Inn

3161 S Atlantic Ave, Daytona Beach Shores, 32118; tel 904/761-2335 or toll free 800/245-0575; fax 904/756-6676. A neat, friendly hotel with smart appointments. **Rooms:** 144 rms and effic. CI 3pm/CO 11am. Nonsmoking rms avail. **Amenities:** 📷 A/C, cable TV w/movies, in-rm safe. All units w/terraces. **Services:** 🚐 🖼 🛎 Car-rental desk, children's program, babysitting. **Facilities:** 🏊 🚾 🚾 1 restaurant (bkfst and lunch only), 2 bars (1 w/entertainment), 1 beach (ocean), whirlpool, washer/dryer. Restaurant offers pool views. **Rates:** Peak (Feb–Mar) $40–$135 S or D; $40–$140 effic. Extra person $6. Children under age 18 stay free. Lower rates off-season. Parking: Outdoor, free. AE, CB, DC, DISC, ER, MC, V.

### Treasure Island Inn

2025 S Atlantic Ave, Daytona Beach Shores, 32118; tel 904/255-8371 or toll free 800/543-5070; fax 904/255-4984. 1¾ mi S of US 92. This beachfront property does a substantial group-tour business, yet has a more "at-home" atmosphere than most hotels of its size. Personable staff. **Rooms:** 241 rms, stes, and effic. CI 4pm/CO 11am. Nonsmoking rms avail. Most rooms have ocean views. **Amenities:** 📷 🍸 📺 A/C, cable TV w/movies, refrig, dataport, voice mail, in-rm safe. Some units w/terraces. **Services:** ✕ 🔑 📋 🖼 🛎 Children's program, babysitting. **Facilities:** 🏊 🎾 🚾 2 restaurants, 2 bars (1 w/entertainment), 1 beach (ocean), lifeguard, volleyball, board surfing, games rm, whirlpool, washer/dryer. **Rates:** Peak (Jun 15–Aug 15) $66–$85 D; $162–$179 ste; $84–$119 effic. Extra person $10. Children under age 18 stay free. Min stay special events. Lower rates off-season. Parking: Outdoor, free. AE, CB, DC, DISC, ER, MC, V.

### Turtle Inn Beach Club

3233 S Atlantic Ave, Daytona Beach Shores, 32118; tel 904/761-0426; fax 904/788-0195. Exit 85 off I-95. Pleasant four-story oceanfront complex offering studios and one- and two-bedroom units. The small room count ensures that guests won't get lost in the shuffle. **Rooms:** 39 effic. CI 3pm/CO 10am. Nonsmoking rms avail. **Amenities:** 📷 🍸 📺 A/C, cable TV, refrig. Some units w/terraces, some w/whirlpools. **Services:** 🛎 **Facilities:** 🏊 🚾 1 beach (ocean), whirlpool, washer/dryer. **Rates:** Peak (June–Sept) $70–$120 effic. Children under age 18 stay free. Lower rates off-season. Parking: Outdoor, free. MC, V.

## MOTELS

### Bahama House

2001 S Atlantic Ave, Daytona Beach Shores, 32118; tel 904/248-2001 or toll free 800/571-2001; fax 904/248-0991. 1¾ mi S of US 92. Offers a more refined atmosphere than is generally found at most beachfront motels. **Rooms:** 87 effic. CI 3pm/CO 11am. Nonsmoking rms avail. Large, attractively furnished rooms, each with ocean views. **Amenities:** ☎ ▣ ▣ A/C, cable TV w/movies, refrig, dataport, in-rm safe. All units w/terraces, some w/whirlpools. Complimentary local newspaper delivered to room. **Services:** ▣ ▱ Children's program, babysitting. Manager's reception daily 5:30–6:30 pm. **Facilities:** ▣ ⅙ 1 beach (ocean), lifeguard, whirlpool, washer/dryer. **Rates (CP):** Peak (Feb–Aug) $89–$115 effic. Extra person $10. Children under age 18 stay free. Min stay special events. Lower rates off-season. Parking: Indoor/outdoor, free. AE, DC, DISC, MC, V.

### ≣≣ Best Western Mayan Inn

103 S Ocean Ave, 32118; tel 904/252-0584 or toll free 800/443-5323; fax 904/252-8670. From US 92, 1 block N on A1A. An unpretentious (but clean and well-maintained) beachfront motel. **Rooms:** 112 rms and effic. CI 3pm/CO 11am. Nonsmoking rms avail. **Amenities:** ☎ A/C, cable TV w/movies, dataport, voice mail, in-rm safe. Some units w/terraces. **Services:** ▱ Children's program, babysitting. **Facilities:** ▣ ▣ 1 bar, 1 beach (ocean), lifeguard, board surfing, games rm, washer/dryer. **Rates (CP):** Peak (Apr–Sept 15) $92 D; $98 effic. Extra person $10. Children under age 18 stay free. Min stay special events. Lower rates off-season. Parking: Outdoor, free. AE, CB, DC, DISC, MC, V.

### ≣≣ La Quinta Motor Inn

2725 Volusia Ave, 32114; tel 904/255-7412 or toll free 800/531-5900; fax 904/255-5350. Exit 87 off I-95. Located immediately off the exit ramp. Handy to the Speedway and the dog track, this superior budget hotel focuses on good housekeeping and routine maintenance. **Rooms:** 143 rms and stes. CI 1pm/CO noon. Nonsmoking rms avail. **Amenities:** ☎ ▣ A/C, cable TV. All units w/terraces. **Services:** ▣ ▱ ▱ **Facilities:** ▣ ▣ ⅙ Washer/dryer. **Rates:** Peak (Jan–Apr) $119–$179 S or D; $265–$310 ste. Extra person $8. Children under age 18 stay free. Lower rates off-season. Parking: Outdoor, free. AE, DC, DISC, MC, V.

## RESORT

### ≣≣≣ Indigo Lakes Resort Limited

2620 W International Speedway Blvd (US 92), 32120; tel 904/258-6333 or toll free 800/874-9918, 800/223-4161 in FL; fax 904/254-3615. Exit 87 off I-95. 7 acres. Large-scale resort close to the Speedway and a five-minute drive to the beach. The handsome accommodations are housed in two-story tan stucco buildings set on beautifully landscaped grounds that contain duck-filled lakes and lagoons spanned by arched bridges. **Rooms:** 211 rms, stes, and effic. CI 3pm/CO 11am. Nonsmoking rms avail. Rooms attractively decorated in earth tones, with dark oak furnishings. **Amenities:** ☎ ▣ ▣ ▱ A/C, cable TV w/movies, refrig. All units w/terraces. **Services:** ✗ ▣ ▣ ▱ Masseur, babysitting. **Facilities:** ▣ ▸₁₈ ▣₁₀ ▱ ▣₅₀₀ ▣ ⅙ 2 restaurants, 2 bars, lawn games, washer/

dryer. Championship golf course with putting green and pro shop. **Rates:** Peak (Feb–Apr/June–July) $90–$115 S or D; $125 ste; $95 effic. Extra person $10. Children under age 18 stay free. Min stay special events. Lower rates off-season. Parking: Outdoor, free. AE, CB, DC, DISC, MC, V.

## RESTAURANTS ▥

### Anna's Italian Trattoria

304 Seabreeze Blvd; tel 904/239-9624. At Peninsula Dr. **Italian.** Diners at this attractive pasta house may choose from a wide selection of appetizing pasta dishes. Veal and chicken entrees are also served. **FYI:** Reservations recommended. Children's menu. Beer and wine only. **Open:** Mon–Sat 5–10pm. Closed Aug 14–28. **Prices:** Main courses $9–$17. AE, DISC, MC, V. ♥

### Live Oak Inn

448 S Beach St; tel 904/252-4667. **New American/Continental.** These two intimate, Victorian-style dining rooms have lace curtains and French doors which open onto an enclosed porch. The menu changes frequently, but might include grilled filet mignon with mushrooms, and many fresh fish selections. **FYI:** Reservations recommended. No smoking. **Open:** Lunch Mon–Fri 11:30am–2pm; dinner Tues–Sat 5:30–9:30pm. **Prices:** Main courses $9–$15. AE, MC, V. ♥ ▣

### Riccardo's

610 Glenview Blvd; tel 904/253-3035. **Italian.** Candlelight and stained-glass panels set an intimate mood. The menu offers a selection of pasta entrees, including the house specialty, shrimp Riccardo (shrimp sautéed in garlic butter and served over fettuccine). **FYI:** Reservations recommended. Children's menu. **Open:** Daily 5–10pm. **Prices:** Main courses $8–$17. AE, DC, MC, V.

### St Regis Restaurant

8970 FL 84; tel 904/252-8743. Between Wild Olive and Grandview Aves. **Continental.** This old Victorian home with hardwood floors provides a nice backdrop for a dinner that might include the St Regis lasagna, caesar salad with shrimp, or one of the daily specials. **FYI:** Reservations accepted. Guitar. No smoking. **Open:** Mon–Thurs 5:30–10pm, Fri–Sat 5:30–11pm. **Prices:** Main courses $7–$22. AE, DC, DISC, MC, V. ▣ ⅙

### Top of Daytona

2625 S Atlantic Ave; tel 904/767-5791. **Seafood/Steak.** Enjoy the views from the 29th floor as you dine. Menu highlights include the queen-cut roast prime rib, lobster filet, and chicken parmigiana. **FYI:** Reservations accepted. Piano/singer. Children's menu. **Open:** Daily 4–10pm. **Prices:** Main courses $13–$24. AE, CB, DC, DISC, MC, V. ▣ ▣ ⅙

## ATTRACTIONS 📷

### Daytona International Speedway
1801 W International Speedway Blvd (US 92); tel 904/253-RACE. Opened in 1959 with the inaugural Daytona 500, the "World Center of Racing" presents about 8 weekends of major racing events annually, featuring stock cars, sports cars, motorcycles, and go-karts, and is also used for automobile testing. Its grandstand seats nearly 98,000 and is a mile long. Major annual races include the Daytona 500 by STP, the world's most prestigious stock car racing event; the Rolex 24, a major event for sports cars; and the Daytona 200 by Arai, which features motorcycles.

The **Visitors' Center** at the west end of the Speedway is the departure point for 30-minute guided van tours of the facility, given every half-hour from 9am to 4:30pm, except during races, special events, or car testing. Also here are a gift shop; the Gallery of Legends, with photographs and memorabilia documenting the history of motor racing in the Daytona Beach area; and the Budweiser Video Wall. **$$**

### Museum of Arts and Sciences and Gamble Place
1040 Museum Blvd; tel 904/255-0285. An eclectic museum featuring both art and natural science exhibits. Displayed are fine and folk art from Cuba; American fine and decorative art; African art and objects; graphic art; and the Pre-History of Florida collection, which features Pleistocene-era fossils and a 130,000-year-old, 13-foot-tall skeleton of a giant ground sloth. Contemporary sculpture garden and planetarium.

The museum also runs **Gamble Place,** the hunting and fishing retreat built by James Gamble (of Proctor & Gamble fame) in 1907. Items of interest include a citrus packing house, azalea garden, and tours of the house itself. Also on the grounds is Snow White House, which was modeled after the classic Disney film. Pontoon-boat tours of Spruce Creek available on the second and fourth Fridays of the month; call for hours and prices. **Open:** Tues–Fri 9am–4pm, Sat–Sun noon–5pm. **$$**

### Halifax Historical Museum
252 S Beach St; tel 904/255-6976. This small museum contains pieces of local history that date from early Native American settlements. Also items from Spanish colonial period, antiques, and memorabilia from the War of 1812 through World War II. Library and gift shop. **Open:** Tues–Sat 10am–4pm. **$**

### Daytona Beach Kennel Club
2201 W International Speedway Blvd (US 92); tel 904/252-6484. Greyhound racing and pari-mutuel betting. Pavilion Clubhouse Restaurant overlooks racetrack. Night races Mon–Sat at 7:45pm; matinees Mon, Wed, and Sat at 1pm. **$**

# Deerfield Beach

Fifteen miles north of Fort Lauderdale on the Atlantic Coast, this is a heavily residential and retirement city. Surf off North Beach; walk the South Beach boardwalks; boat to nature walks at Deerfield Island Park; imagine local life circa 1920 at Butler House. **Information:** Greater Deerfield Beach Chamber of Commerce, 1601 E Hillsboro Blvd, Deerfield Beach, 33441 (tel 954/427-1050).

## HOTELS 🏨

### 🔲🔲 Comfort Suites
1040 E Newport Center Dr, 33442; tel 954/570-8887 or toll free 800/228-5150; fax 954/570-5346. Exit 36C off I-95. Set amid pleasant surroundings, this hotel shares its dining facilities with the Quality Suites next door. The young staff is chipper and outgoing. **Rooms:** 100 stes. CI 3pm/CO noon. Nonsmoking rms avail. Suites are on the small side. **Amenities:** 🛁 🔥 📷 🍴 A/C, cable TV w/movies, refrig, dataport, voice mail. All units w/terraces. **Services:** 🔺 🍴 🛎 **Facilities:** 🔲 🔯 🔲 🔲 1 restaurant, 1 bar, games rm, washer/dryer. **Rates (CP):** Peak (Dec–Apr) $100 ste. Extra person $10. Children under age 18 stay free. Lower rates off-season. Parking: Outdoor, free. AE, CB, DC, DISC, MC, V.

### 🔲🔲🔲 Crown Sterling Deerfield Beach Resort
950 SE 20th Ave, 33441; tel 954/426-0478 or toll free 800/433-4600; fax 954/360-0539. Off FL AIA S. Breezy decor and style at this beachfront location. Attentive staff bolts to assist arriving guests. **Rooms:** 244 stes. CI 3pm/CO noon. Nonsmoking rms avail. Few suite hotels offer two bathrooms per unit like this one does. **Amenities:** 🛁 🔥 📷 🍴 A/C, cable TV w/movies, dataport, VCR, CD/tape player, voice mail. All units w/minibars, all w/terraces. All units have 2 TVs, wet bar, microwave. **Services:** ✗ 🔑 📼 🔺 🍴 🛎 Twice-daily maid svce, car-rental desk, masseur, children's program, babysitting. **Facilities:** 🔲 🔺 🔯 🔲 🔲 🔲 1 restaurant, 1 bar (w/entertainment), 1 beach (ocean), volleyball, board surfing, games rm, lawn games, snorkeling, sauna, steam rm, whirlpool, washer/dryer. **Rates (BB):** Peak (Dec–Apr) $205 ste. Extra person $10. Children under age 12 stay free. Min stay special events. Lower rates off-season. Parking: Indoor/outdoor, $3–$7/day. AE, CB, DC, DISC, MC, V.

### 🔲🔲🔲 Deerfield Beach–Boca Raton Hilton
100 Fairway Dr, 33441; tel 954/427-7700 or toll free 800/624-3606; fax 954/427-2308. Exit 37 off I-95. A sophisticated operation that incorporates an interesting array of architectural styles. It will likely enthrall guests with its fine public areas, more stylish than those usually found in a beach town. **Rooms:** 220 rms and stes. CI 3pm/CO noon. Nonsmoking rms avail. **Amenities:** 🛁 🔥 A/C, cable TV w/movies. Some units w/terraces. **Services:** ✗ 🔺 🍴 Babysitting. **Facilities:** 🔲 🔲 🔲 2 restaurants, 1 bar (w/entertainment), whirlpool. **Rates:** Peak (Dec–Apr) $119–$179 S or D; $265–$310 ste.

Extra person $10. Children under age 18 stay free. Lower rates off-season. Parking: Outdoor, free. AE, DC, DISC, MC, V.

### ⊟⊟ Howard Johnson Ocean Resort Hotel
2096 NE 2nd St, 33441; tel 954/428-2850 or toll free 800/426-0084; fax 954/480-9639. Exit 37 off I-95. A great location for an otherwise ordinary offering. Opposite the beachfront and pier. **Rooms:** 177 rms and stes. CI 3pm/CO noon. Nonsmoking rms avail. **Amenities:** 📺 ♨ A/C, cable TV w/movies, in-rm safe. Some units w/terraces. **Services:** ✕ ⊠ ⌑ **Facilities:** 350 ₺ 1 restaurant, 1 bar, games rm. **Rates:** Peak (Dec–Apr) $139–$159 S; $149–$169 D; $289 ste. Extra person $10. Children under age 18 stay free. Min stay special events. Lower rates off-season. Parking: Outdoor, free. AE, CB, DC, DISC, ER, JCB, MC, V.

### ⊟⊟ Oceanside Inn
50 SE 20th Ave, 33441; tel 954/428-0650 or toll free 800/827-4735; fax 954/427-2666. At Hillsboro Blvd and FL A1A. Superior budget property. **Rooms:** 69 rms and effic. CI 2pm/CO 11am. Nonsmoking rms avail. **Amenities:** 📺 ♨ A/C, cable TV w/movies. Some units w/terraces. **Services:** 🍽 **Facilities:** 📶 110 ₺ 1 restaurant, 1 bar, 1 beach (ocean), games rm, washer/dryer. **Rates:** Peak (Dec–Apr) $109–$139 S or D; $119 effic. Children under age 18 stay free. Min stay wknds and special events. Lower rates off-season. Parking: Outdoor, free. AE, CB, DC, DISC, MC, V.

### ⊟⊟⊟ Quality Suites
1050 E Newport Center Dr, 33442; tel 954/570-8888 or toll free 800/221-2222; fax 954/570-5346. Exit 36C off I-95. Rooms have a bit more flair than most in this price category. **Rooms:** 107 stes. CI 3pm/CO noon. Nonsmoking rms avail. **Amenities:** 📺 ♨ 📠 ℉ A/C, cable TV w/movies, refrig, dataport, VCR, voice mail. All units w/terraces. **Services:** ⊠ ⌑ ⌑ Car-rental desk. **Facilities:** 📶 🏋 75 ₺ 1 restaurant, 1 bar, games rm, washer/dryer. **Rates (BB):** Peak (Dec–Apr) $124–$139 ste. Extra person $10. Children under age 18 stay free. Lower rates off-season. Parking: Outdoor, free. AE, CB, DC, DISC, MC, V.

### ⊟⊟ Ramada Inn
1401 S Federal Hwy, 33431; tel 954/421-5000 or toll free 800/283-9946; fax 954/426-2811. 1 mi S of Hillsboro Blvd. Low-rise, pink-toned highway hotel. Peaceful courtyard. **Rooms:** 107 rms, stes, and effic. CI noon/CO noon. Nonsmoking rms avail. **Amenities:** 📺 A/C, cable TV w/movies. Some units w/terraces. **Services:** ✕ ⊠ ⌑ **Facilities:** 📶 25 1 restaurant, 1 bar, beauty salon, washer/dryer. **Rates:** Peak (Dec–Apr) $55–$99 S; $60–$125 D; $105–$155 ste; $65–$135 effic. Extra person $10. Children under age 18 stay free. Lower rates off-season. Parking: Outdoor, free. AE, CB, DC, DISC, EC, MC, V.

### ⊟⊟ Wellesley Inn
100 SW 12th Ave, 33442; tel 954/428-0661 or toll free 800/444-8888; fax 954/427-6701. Exit 37 off I-95. With newly renovated guest rooms. Well-liked for its affordability. **Rooms:** 79 rms and stes. CI 2pm/CO 11am. Nonsmoking rms avail. **Amenities:** 📺 ♨ A/C, cable TV. **Services:** ⊠ ⌑ ⌑ **Facilities:** 📶 ₺ Washer/dryer. **Rates (CP):** Peak (Dec–Apr) $100–$110 S; $110–$120 D; $120–$130 ste. Children under age 18 stay free. Lower rates off-season. Parking: Outdoor, free. AE, CB, DC, DISC, MC, V.

## MOTEL

### ⊟⊟ La Quinta Motor Inn
351 W Hillsboro Blvd, 33441; tel 954/421-1004 or toll free 800/531-5900; fax 954/427-8069. Exit 37 off I-95. Popular, basic, budget motel. **Rooms:** 130 rms. CI 2pm/CO noon. Nonsmoking rms avail. **Amenities:** 📺 ♨ A/C, cable TV. **Services:** ⊠ ⌑ ⌑ **Facilities:** 📶 35 ₺ Washer/dryer. **Rates (CP):** Peak (Dec–Apr) $89–$95 S; $99–$106 D. Extra person $7. Children under age 18 stay free. Lower rates off-season. Parking: Outdoor, free. AE, CB, DC, DISC, MC, V.

# De Funiak Springs

The seat of Walton County in the western Panhandle, De Funiak Springs retains an old-Florida feel. **Information:** Walton County Chamber of Commerce, Circle Dr, PO Box 29, De Funiak Springs, 32433 (tel 904/892-3191).

## ATTRACTIONS 🏛

### Circle Drive
Along Circle Drive, a one-mile road encircling the perfectly round natural lake that lies in the center of town, are magnificent Victorian homes with ornate turrets and fancy "gingerbread" trimmings. All are as elegantly furnished as when these prestigious residences were built in the 1880s. At certain times of the year, the historic homes are open for touring.

### Chautauqua Vineyards
1330 Freeport Rd; tel 904/892-5887. Located at the intersection of I-10 and US 331, this is Florida's largest winery. Tastings are offered during the free daily tours. A wine festival is held during the harvest in early September. **Open:** Mon–Sat 9am–5pm, Sunday noon–5pm. **Free**

# De Land

This landlocked town of 17,500 (northeast of Orlando) enjoys a charming and historic Main Street. September brings the "Anything That Floats" raft race on the St Johns River. **Information:** De Land Area Chamber of Commerce, 336 N Woodland Blvd, PO Box 629, De Land, 32721 (tel 904/734-4331).

## ATTRACTIONS 🏛

### De Land Museum of Art

600 N Woodland Blvd; tel 904/734-4371. The small permanent collection consists mostly of works by Florida artists in various media, and a collection of Native American craftwork. Traveling exhibitions are presented each year; guided tours are available upon request. Every other year the Florida Watercolor Exhibition, a juried show open to artists from the southeastern states, is held here. **Open:** Tues–Sat 10am–4pm, Sun 1–4pm. **$**

### Hontoon Island State Park

2039 River Ridge Rd; tel 904/736-5309. Located on an island in the St Johns River, this 1,600-acre park is accessible only by passenger ferry. The island was once home to members of the Timucuan tribe, who left behind a mound 300 feet long and 20 feet high. A reflection of their diet, it is composed mainly of shells, including those of snails, various shellfish, and turtles. The park also has an 80-foot observation tower. Fishing, boating, hiking, camping, nature trails. **Open:** Daily 8am–sunset. **$**

### Blue Spring State Park

2100 W French Ave, Orange City; tel 904/775-3663. This 1,500-acre park is very popular between October and April; about 80 manatees winter here every year, enjoying the relatively warm waters of the spring. Swimming in the spring and fishing in St Johns River are allowed. Canoe rentals, camping, nature trails. **Open:** Daily 8am–sunset. **$$**

# Delray Beach

Southeastern coastal city of 49,000, midway between Palm Beach and Fort Lauderdale. The 155-acre Morikami Museum and Gardens commemorate a turn-of-the-century Japanese colony. **Information:** Greater Delray Beach Chamber of Commerce, 64 SE 5th Ave, Delray Beach, 33483 (tel 561/278-0424).

## HOTELS 🏨

### 🎗🎗 The Colony

525 E Atlantic Ave, PO Box 970, 33447; tel 561/276-4123 or toll free 800/552-2363; fax 561/274-0035. Off I-95 between 5th and 6th Aves. This west-of-the-shore oldie offers very basic accommodations considered dowdy by some but adored by others, who keep coming back year after year. And the New England hospitality is genuine—these folks work half the year in Kennebunkport, Maine. All that's missing from the working 1920s switchboard is Ernestine. **Rooms:** 66 rms and stes. CI 3pm/CO noon. Nonsmoking rms avail. **Amenities:** 🔒 ⚱ A/C, cable TV w/movies, bathrobes. **Services:** ✗ 🚐 🛆 🗘 🐾 Children's program, babysitting. **Facilities:** 🔥 🏊 ⚲ 1 restaurant, 2 bars (1 w/entertainment), 1 beach (ocean), beauty salon. The dining room is a real look back in time. **Rates:** Peak (Jan–Mar 15) $50–$90 S; $70–

$130 D; $110–$150 ste. Extra person $20. Lower rates off-season. MAP rates avail. Parking: Outdoor, free. Closed Apr–Dec. AE, MC, V.

### 🎗🎗 Holiday Inn Camino Real

1229 E Atlantic Ave, 33483; tel 561/278-0882 or toll free 800/23-HOTEL; fax 561/278-1845. Off I-95. Adorned with Spanish and Mediterranean touches, this standard-bearer opposite the beach does a brisk winter business. **Rooms:** 150 rms and stes. CI 3pm/CO noon. Nonsmoking rms avail. **Amenities:** 🔒 ⚱ 🖥 ⚲ A/C, cable TV w/movies. All units w/terraces. **Services:** 🍽 💵 🚐 🛆 🗘 Babysitting. **Facilities:** 🔥 🟦250🟦 ⚲ 1 restaurant, 2 bars (1 w/entertainment), whirlpool. Rooftop restaurant provides ocean views. **Rates:** Peak (Dec–Apr) $170–$215 S or D; $189 ste. Extra person $15. Children under age 16 stay free. Lower rates off-season. MAP rates avail. Parking: Indoor/outdoor, free. AE, MC, V.

### 🎗🎗🎗 Holiday Inn Oceanside

2809 S Ocean Blvd, Highland Beach, 33487; tel 561/278-6241 or toll free 800/234-6835; fax 561/278-6241. 1 mi S of Linton Blvd. Housed in three-story and six-story buildings on the water. **Rooms:** 119 rms. CI 3pm/CO noon. Nonsmoking rms avail. **Amenities:** 🔒 ⚱ ⚲ A/C, cable TV w/movies. Some units w/terraces. **Services:** ✗ 🚐 🛆 🗘 Babysitting. **Facilities:** 🔥 🟦125🟦 ⚲ 1 restaurant, 2 bars (1 w/entertainment), 1 beach (ocean), games rm. Cabanas operate on beach Dec–Sept. **Rates:** Peak (Dec–Mar) $119–$169 S; $129–$169 D. Extra person $10. Children under age 18 stay free. Lower rates off-season. MAP rates avail. Parking: Outdoor, free. AE, DISC, MC, V.

### 🎗🎗🎗 Seagate Hotel & Beach Club

400 S Ocean Blvd, 33483; tel 561/276-2421 or toll free 800/233-3581; fax 561/243-4714. A pleasant facility located across the road from the beach, with its own beach property. **Rooms:** 70 stes and effic. CI 3pm/CO noon. **Amenities:** 🔒 ⚱ 🖥 A/C, cable TV, refrig, in-rm safe. All units w/terraces, 1 w/whirlpool. **Services:** ✗ 💵 🛆 🗘 Car-rental desk, social director, children's program, babysitting. Coffee and muffins are set out every morning in the lobby. **Facilities:** 🔥 🚲 ⚠ 🟦50🟦 1 restaurant (lunch and dinner only), 1 bar (w/entertainment), 1 beach (ocean), board surfing, washer/dryer. Lending library in lobby. Freshwater and saltwater pools. Vendor operates watersports. **Rates:** Peak (Jan–Mar) $223 ste; $96 effic. Extra person $15. Children under age 18 stay free. Min stay special events. Lower rates off-season. Parking: Outdoor, free. AE, DC, DISC, MC, V.

## MOTEL

### 🎗 Riviera Palms Motel

3960 N Ocean Blvd, 33438; tel 561/276-3032. This family-owned outfit is fine for the budget-minded traveler who doesn't require many amenities. Just a short walk to the beach. **Rooms:** 17 rms, stes, and effic. CI 2pm/CO 11am. Decor is 1960s and 1970s, with baths out of the 1950s. **Amenities:** 🔒 A/C, cable TV, refrig. Phone supplied on request. **Services:** 🛏 **Facilities:** 🔥 **Rates:** Peak (Dec–Apr) $60 S or D; $75 ste; $67 effic. Extra person $6. Min stay. Lower rates off-season. Parking: Outdoor, free. No CC.

## RESTAURANTS 🍽

### ★ Boston's on the Beach
40 S FL A1A; tel 561/278-3364. **American.** This oceanfront restaurant, popular with beachgoers, is a great spot for people-watching. The menu includes a selection of seafood entrees as well as sandwiches and burgers. **FYI:** Reservations not accepted. Jazz/reggae/rock. **Open:** Mon–Fri 11am–2am, Sat 6:30pm–2am, Sun 6:30pm–1am. **Prices:** Main courses $5–$25. AE, DC, MC, V. 🍽 🖼 &

### ★ Busch's Seafood
840 E Atlantic Blvd; tel 561/278-7600. **Seafood.** A rather sophisticated fish house with a sizeable bar area and great water views. The menu includes sautéed grouper and a clambake special. **FYI:** Reservations accepted. **Open:** Sun–Thurs 11:30am–10pm, Fri–Sat 11:30am–11pm. **Prices:** Main courses $14–$24. AE, DC, MC, V. 🖼 🖼 🖼 VP &

## REFRESHMENT STOP 🍵

### Doc's All-American Grill and Dairy
10 N Swinton Ave; tel 561/278-DOCS. **Diner.** The simplest of diners, offering up American fast-food favorites, including hamburgers, hot dogs, hot and cold sandwiches, and omelettes, as well as ice cream, milk shakes, and pies. **Open:** Sun–Thurs 10am–midnight, Fri–Sat 10am–2am. No CC. 🖼 &

## ATTRACTION 🏛

### Morikami Museum and Japanese Gardens
4000 Morikami Park Rd; tel 561/495-0233. This museum in Morikami Park showcases traveling exhibitions of Japanese arts, crafts, history, and culture. The main building houses expansive galleries, a teahouse with a viewing gallery, a 225-seat theater, and an electronic multimedia resource center.

Located a short distance away, the original museum building (called the Yamato-kan), modeled after a Japanese residence, contains a permanent exhibit chronicling the history of the Yamato Colony. The colony was founded by a group of Japanese farmers who settled in this area around the turn of the century. Although the colonists eventually dispersed, the park and museum were created as a memorial to these settlers, on property bequeathed to the state by one of the members who remained. The 200-acre park also has nature trails, lakes and ponds, Japanese-style gardens, picnic areas, and a rare bonsai tree collection. **Open:** Museum, Tues–Sun 10am–5pm; garden, daily dawn–dusk. $$

# Destin

See also Fort Walton Beach, Niceville

Nestled on US 98 between the Gulf of Mexico and Choctawhatchee Bay, the self-styled "world's luckiest fishing village" offers a Museum of Fishing and the luxurious Sandestin Resort. **Information:** Destin Chamber of Commerce, 1021 US 98, PO Box 8, Destin, 32541 (tel 904/837-6241).

## HOTEL 🏨

### UNRATED Holiday Inn of Destin
1020 US 98 E, PO Box 577, 32541; tel 904/837-6181 or toll free 800/HOLIDAY; fax 904/837-1537. On Destin's eastern end along US 98, 4 mi W of the Mid-Bay Bridge. The three-story Holidome is the hotel's centerpiece with a restaurant and indoor pool; the nine-story rotunda is in need of some updating. **Rooms:** 233 rms. CI 3pm/CO 11am. Nonsmoking rms avail. Rooms have undergone recent renovation. **Amenities:** 🛏 🔥 A/C, cable TV, in-rm safe. All units w/terraces. **Services:** ✗ 🚐 🖼 🛏 Children's program. **Facilities:** 🔥 🖼 🖼 & 1 restaurant, 2 bars, 1 beach (ocean), volleyball, games rm, sauna, whirlpool. **Rates:** Peak (May–Sept) $110–$155 S or D. Extra person $10. Children under age 18 stay free. Min stay special events. Lower rates off-season. Parking: Outdoor, free. AE, CB, DC, DISC, JCB, MC, V.

## MOTEL

### ≣ ≣ Frangista Beach Inn
1860 US 98, 32541; tel 904/654-5501 or toll free 800/382-2612; fax 904/654-5876. Off US 98 on old US 98 (follow signs to beaches). This older Gulf-front inn began as a guest house in the 1940s, and now has a beautiful pool area surrounded by columns and a nice restaurant. Rooms are spacious, but certainly not fancy. One possible drawback is that the inn is right on the highway; guests have to cross it to get to the pool or the restaurant. **Rooms:** 37 rms and stes. CI 3pm/CO 11am. Nonsmoking rms avail. The whitewashed rooms have wicker furnishings and hardwood floors. **Amenities:** 🛏 🖼 🖼 A/C, cable TV, dataport, voice mail, bathrobes. Some units w/terraces. Complimentary newspapers delivered to room. **Services:** ✗ 🖼 🛏 Babysitting. Beach service in season. Free local calls. **Facilities:** 🔥 🖼 1 restaurant, 1 beach (ocean), washer/dryer. Guests receive 10% discount at Frangista Seafood & Spirits. **Rates (CP):** Peak (May 16–Labor Day) $125 S or D; $180–$375 ste. Extra person $10. Children under age 18 stay free. Min stay special events. Lower rates off-season. Parking: Outdoor, free. AE, DISC, MC, V.

## INN

### ≣≣≣ Henderson Park Inn

2700 US 98 E, 32541; tel 904/654-0400 or toll free 800/336-4853; fax 904/654-0405. On the eastern edge of Henderson Beach State Recreation Area, where the road dead-ends. Reminiscent of a turn-of-the-century lifesaving station or island beach cottage, the Henderson Park Inn shows few signs of the extensive damage it suffered from Hurricane Opal in the fall of 1995. Unsuitable for children under 12. **Rooms:** 39 rms. CI 3pm/CO 11am. Nonsmoking rms avail. Antique reproductions mix with contemporary pieces in large, airy rooms with wooden blinds and lovely Gulf views. All rooms have private baths and bathrobes. **Amenities:** 🛗 🕎 🖭 A/C, cable TV, refrig, in-rm safe, bathrobes. All units w/terraces, some w/fireplaces, some w/whirlpools. **Services:** ✕ 🖂 Wine/sherry served. Beach service in season. Complimentary happy hour daily. **Facilities:** 🏠 ⅙ 1 restaurant, 1 beach (ocean). **Rates (BB):** Peak (May 17–Sept 2) $169–$239 D. Extra person $10. Children under age 12 stay free. Lower rates off-season. Parking: Outdoor, free. $50 advance deposit. AE, DISC, MC, V.

## RESORTS

### ≣≣≣≣ Sandestin Beach Resort

9300 US 98 W, 32541 (Beaches of South Walton); tel 904/267-8150 or toll free 800/277-0800; fax 904/267-8222. 8 mi E of Destin. 2,400 acres. Expansive resort property offering everything from one-bedroom condos in a Gulf-front high-rise to cozy villas on the golf course to a sprawling beach cottage with a bedroom loft and a screened-in front porch. **Rooms:** 175 rms and stes; 425 cottages/villas. CI 4pm/CO 11am. Nonsmoking rms avail. Units are individually owned, and most go above and beyond in providing creature comforts. **Amenities:** 🛗 🕎 🖭 A/C, cable TV, refrig, VCR, CD/tape player. All units w/terraces, some w/fireplaces, some w/whirlpools. **Services:** ✕ 🖛 🚗 🖂 🗒 Car-rental desk, social director, masseur, children's program, babysitting. **Facilities:** 🏠 🚴 ⚠ 🛝 ▶63 🖾 🖭14 🚤 🖢 🗊1100 ⅙ 2 restaurants (see "Restaurants" below), 2 beaches (ocean, bay), volleyball, spa, sauna, steam rm, whirlpool. Total of 22 swimming pools, and 7½ miles of beach. Baytowne Marina offers a wilderness boat trip through swamps and waterways off Choctawhatchee Bay (in season). The Market at Sandestin offers 30 outstanding shops. **Rates:** Peak (May–Aug) $125–$135 S or D; $175–$190 ste; $180–$490 cottage/villa. Children under age 18 stay free. Min stay wknds. Lower rates off-season. Parking: Outdoor, free. AE, CB, DC, DISC, MC, V.

### UNRATED Tops'l Beach & Racquet Club

9011 US 98 W, 32541 (Beaches of South Walton); tel 904/267-9222 or toll free 800/476-9222; fax 904/267-2955. 8 mi E of Destin next to Sandestin Resort. 55 acres. Beautifully landscaped with native plantings and natural vegetation. Tops'l spreads in a thin line all the way to the Gulf of Mexico.

Although high-rise condos and villas are comfortable, new construction (and especially pile-drivers) make the stay here a bit too noisy for most tastes. **Rooms:** 35 rms; 40 cottages/villas. CI 3pm/CO 10am. Nonsmoking rms avail. **Amenities:** 🛗 🕎 🖭 A/C, cable TV, refrig, VCR. All units w/terraces, some w/fireplaces, some w/whirlpools. **Services:** 🖛 🖂 🗒 Social director, masseur, children's program. Beach service in season. Tram/shuttle service for guests. **Facilities:** 🏠 🚴 🖾 🖭12 🖢 🗊100 ⅙ 1 restaurant, 1 bar, 1 beach (ocean), racquetball, sauna, steam rm, whirlpool. **Rates:** Peak (May–Sept) $138–$209 S or D; $198–$470 cottage/villa. Min stay special events. Lower rates off-season. Parking: Indoor/outdoor, free. AE, DC, DISC, MC, V.

## RESTAURANTS 🍽

### Buster's Oyster Bar and Seafood Restaurant

In Delchamps Plaza, 5013 US 98 E; tel 904/837-4399. **Seafood.** Buster claims that more than five million oysters have been shucked here, and with good reason, since they go for 99¢ a dozen during the daily 5–6pm happy hour. The menu changes every three months or so, but the emphasis is always on fish and seafood dinners prepared to order. **FYI:** Reservations not accepted. Children's menu. Additional location: 410 Government Ave, Valparaiso (tel 729-1919). **Open:** Peak (Mar–Oct) daily 11am–10pm. **Prices:** Main courses $7–$16. AE, DC, DISC, MC, V. ⅙

### Destin Diner

1038 US 98 E; tel 904/654-5843. **Diner.** A fun, diner-style eatery with the popular hits of yesterday continuously playing in the background. The menu consists of standard diner fare: omelettes, burgers, malts, and thick milkshakes. **FYI:** Reservations not accepted. Children's menu. No liquor license. No smoking. **Open:** Peak (Apr–Nov 15) Mon–Sun 5am–11pm. **Prices:** Main courses $29; prix fixe $75. AE, CB, DC, DISC, MC, V. 🖂

### ♟ The Elephant Walk

In Sandestin Beach Resort, 9300 US 98 W; tel 904/267-4800. 8 mi E of Destin. **European.** Everything about The Elephant Walk says "class," from the architecture inspired by a movie of the same name to the cozy conversation groupings in the upstairs lounge to the four-servers-per-table service. Typical dinner menu might include sautéed grouper, or seasoned lump crabmeat with almonds and white-wine sauce. Expect to feel totally pampered. **FYI:** Reservations recommended. Children's menu. **Open:** Daily 5–11pm. Closed Jan. **Prices:** Main courses $17–$27. AE, DC, DISC, MC, V. 🖂 ⅙

### ★ Harbor Docks

538 US 98 E; tel 904/837-2506. **Steak.** Seafood, Thai dishes, and great views make this restaurant overlooking Destin Harbor a local favorite. Sushi bar. **FYI:** Reservations not accepted. Blues/reggae/rock. Children's menu. **Open:** Breakfast daily 6–10am; lunch daily 11am–11pm; dinner daily 11am–11pm. **Prices:** Main courses $10–$20. AE, DC, DISC, MC, V. 🏔 🆅🅿 ⅙

## Marina Cafe
404 US 98 E; tel 904/837-7960. US 98 E next to Yacht Club. **Continental.** Unbelievable views of Destin Harbor, subdued music, formally attired waiters, and elegant high ceilings make Marina Cafe a perfect place for a romantic meal. The creative chef prepares pizza and pastas with a special flair; other menu highlights include a fettuccine combined with andouille sausage, shrimp, crayfish tails, and tomato-cream sauce. **FYI:** Reservations recommended. Piano. Children's menu. **Open:** Daily 5–11pm. Closed 2–3 weeks in Jan. **Prices:** Main courses $6–$25. AE, DC, DISC, MC, V.

## ATTRACTIONS
### Destin Fishing Museum
2009 Emerald Coast Pkwy; tel 904/654-1011. World- and state-record catches, from blue marlin to red snapper, are displayed along with thousands of photos and various maritime memorabilia. Hands-on tidal pool and dry walk-through aquarium. **Open:** Tues–Sat noon–4pm, Sun 1–4pm. Call ahead to confirm hours. **$**

### Henderson Beach State Recreation Area
17000 Emerald Coast Pkwy; tel 904/837-7550. Located just east of Destin, this is one of the 18 beaches of South Walton. A natural environment for magnolias, scrub oaks, sand pines, and a variety of wildflowers, the park has miles of white sand, towering dunes, and clear emerald waters. **Open:** Daily 8am–sunset. **$**

# Dunedin

This Gulf Coast town was founded by Scots, who called it Dunedin ("peaceful rest" in Gaelic). Today, Dunedin is sister city of Stirling, Scotland, and it hosts Highland festivals and boat excursions to Caladesi Island State Park. **Information:** Dunedin Chamber of Commerce, 301 Main St, Dunedin, 34698 (tel 813/733-3197).

## HOTEL
### Best Western Jamaica Inn
150 Marina Plaza, 34698; tel 813/733-4121 or toll free 800/447-4728; fax 813/736-4365. Perched at the water's edge—so close, in fact, that you can hear water lapping outside your door. **Rooms:** 55 rms and effic. CI 3pm/CO 11am. Nonsmoking rms avail. Second-floor units have cathedral ceilings. **Amenities:** A/C, cable TV. All units w/terraces. Large chairs on balconies. **Services:** **Facilities:** 1 restaurant (see "Restaurants" below), 1 bar, lawn games. **Rates:** Peak (Dec–Apr) $99 S or D; $109 effic. Extra person $7. Children under age 12 stay free. Lower rates off-season. Parking: Outdoor, free. AE, DC, DISC, MC, V.

## RESORT
### Innisbrook Hilton Resort
36750 US 19 N, Palm Harbor, 34684; tel 813/942-2000 or toll free 800/456-2000; fax 813/942-5576. S of Klosterman Rd on US 19. 1,100 acres. An expansive and lush complex located in a gated community, with several restaurants and lounges. Golfers and others are drawn to its manicured greens and its lakes, pools, and lovely natural setting. **Rooms:** 1,185 effic. CI 3pm/CO noon. Nonsmoking rms avail. **Amenities:** A/C, cable TV w/movies, refrig. All units w/minibars, some w/terraces. **Services:** Car-rental desk, social director, masseur, children's program, babysitting. Free laundry facilities on every floor. Shuttle takes guests around huge property and to area beaches (for free) or to shopping and special events (for a fee). **Facilities:** 4 restaurants, 4 bars (1 w/entertainment), basketball, volleyball, games rm, lawn games, racquetball, spa, sauna, whirlpool, beauty salon, daycare ctr, playground, washer/dryer. Home of Nick Bolletieri Tennis Academy. Peak (Dec–Apr) $187 effic. Children under age 18 stay free. Min stay peak and special events. Lower rates off-season. Parking: Outdoor, free. AE, CB, DC, DISC, EC, ER, MC, V.

## RESTAURANTS
### ★ Bon Appetit
In Best Western Yacht Harbor Inn & Suites, 148 Marina Plaza; tel 813/733-2151. **Continental.** A bistro popular with elderly area residents for its quiet, relaxing atmosphere and pretty locale on the water. Serves rack of lamb, crab cakes, fresh local fish, and French bistro classics like onion soup, steak frites, and pot au feu. **FYI:** Reservations recommended. Children's menu. Dress code. **Open:** Daily 7am–10pm. **Prices:** Main courses $8–$19; prix fixe $8. AE, DC, DISC, MC, V.

### Sabal's
315 Main St; tel 813/734-3463. **New American.** This moderately priced, informal, contemporary American cafe is noted for its inventive dishes, such as linguine primavera, filet mignon served in a Roquefort sauce, and garlic shrimp. Lamb chops and chicken dishes are also offered. **FYI:** Reservations recommended. Dress code. Beer and wine only. **Open:** Lunch Tues–Fri noon–3pm; dinner Tues–Thurs 6–9pm, Fri–Sat 6–10pm. **Prices:** Main courses $12–$22. DISC, MC, V.

## ATTRACTIONS
### Grant Field
311 Douglas Ave; tel 813/733-0429. The spring training site for the Toronto Blue Jays. Exhibition games are played here throughout March. **$$$**

### Caladesi Island State Park
Causeway Blvd; tel 813/469-5918. Three miles long and a half-mile wide, this is one of Florida's few remaining undis-

turbed barrier islands. No cars are allowed, and access is only by private boat or by ferry boat from Honeymoon Island. Ideal for swimming, shelling, and scuba diving, the island's beaches front the Gulf of Mexico. Facilities include palm-shaded picnic pavilions, snack bar, boardwalks, and shower houses. **Open:** Daily 8am–sunset. **$**

# Everglades National Park

See also Homestead, Islamorada, Key Largo, Marco Island

Encompassing over 2,000 square miles and 1.5 million acres, Everglades National Park covers the entire southern tip of Florida. Established as a national park in 1947, it comprises one of America's most unique regions. Unlike Yosemite or Grand Canyon National Parks, the Everglades' awesome beauty is more subtle. The park is a wildlife sanctuary, set aside for the protection of its delicate plant and animal life. Species making their home here include deer, otters, great white egrets, hawks, herons, and—of course—alligators.

The **Main Visitor Center** (tel 305/247-7700) is located on the east side of the park, just outside of Homestead. FL 9336 runs to the park entrance (follow signs). This is the park's official headquarters, housing audiovisual exhibits on the park's fragile ecosystems. A single road winds its way for 38 miles from the Main Visitor Center to the **Flamingo Visitor Center,** in the southwest corner of the park. The scenic drive provides a beautiful introduction as it passes through several distinct ecosystems, including a dwarf cypress forest, endless saw grass, and dense mangroves. Well-marked trails and elevated boardwalks are plentiful along the entire stretch; all contain informative signs.

In addition to a small visitor center and bookstore, **Shark Valley** (tel 305/221-8455) offers an elevated boardwalk, hiking trails, bike rentals, and an excellent tram tour that delves 7.5 miles into the wilderness to a 50-foot observation tower. Built on the site of an old oil well, the tower gives sweeping views of the park. Tours run regularly, year-round (phone for details).

At the **Miccosukee Indian Village,** (tel 305/223-8380), visitors can take a half-hour, high-speed airboat "safari" through the rushes. Birds scatter as the boats approach, and when they slow down, alligators and other animals appear. Rides offered daily (phone for details).

**Big Cypress National Preserve**, Ochopee; tel 941/695-4111 or 695-2000. This 728,000-acre chunk of protected land encompasses Big Cypress Swamp and helps to provide water to the Everglades. The preserve is a sanctuary for alligator, deer, panther, and many types of birds. During the 19th-century Seminole Wars, many Seminoles escaped to the swamp to avoid forced emigration to Oklahoma; their descendants live in Big Cypress Seminole Indian Reservation

and Miccosukee Indian Village. Ranger-led programs Jan–Mar. Visitor center located on US 41 about 60 miles east of Naples. **Open:** Visitors center, daily 8:30am–4:30pm. **Free**

## MOTEL 🏨

**≣≣ Flamingo Lodge Marina & Outpost Resort**
1 Flamingo Lodge Hwy, Flamingo, 33034; tel 941/695-3101 or toll free 800/600-3813; fax 941/695-3921. 38 mi S of Everglades National Park Visitors Center. The only game in town, this motel has clean cottages with fully equipped kitchens. Nothing fancy, but popular in season. **Rooms:** 103 rms and stes; 24 cottages/villas. CI 3pm/CO 11am. Non-smoking rms avail. **Amenities:** 🛁 A/C, TV. **Services:** 🍴 🧹 Breakfast is not offered during summer at restaurant, so continental breakfast is served in registration area. **Facilities:** 🛖 🚲 ⛰ 🛝 🛟 🏧 & 1 restaurant (see "Restaurants" below), 1 bar, washer/dryer. **Rates:** Peak (Dec–Apr) $81–$95 S or D; $120–$142 ste; $95–$111 effic. Extra person $10. Children under age 12 stay free. Lower rates off-season. Parking: Outdoor, free. AE, DC, DISC, MC, V.

## RESTAURANTS 🍴

★ **Captain's Table Restaurant**
125 Collier Blvd, Everglades City; tel 941/695-2727. **Seafood/Steak.** One of only a handful of full-service restaurants in the area, with a cool and pleasant interior. The menu includes alligator piccata, snapper, catfish, and fisherman's plate. **FYI:** Reservations accepted. Children's menu. **Open:** Daily 11am–10pm. **Prices:** Main courses $10–$23. AE, DC, DISC, MC, V. 🏔

**Flamingo Lodge Restaurant**
In the Flamingo Lodge, 1 Flamingo Lodge Hwy, Flamingo; tel 941/695-3101. 38 mi S of Everglades National Park Visitors Center. **American/Caribbean.** This well-regarded multilevel restaurant provides a stunning view of Florida Bay. Fresh fish prepared a variety of ways is offered along with several meat and poultry selections. **FYI:** Reservations accepted. Children's menu. No smoking. **Open:** Peak (Dec–Apr) breakfast daily 7–10am; lunch daily 11:30am–3pm; dinner daily 5:30–9pm. **Prices:** Main courses $8–$17. AE, DC, DISC, MC, V. 🏔

# Fernandina Beach

See Amelia Island

# Fisher Island

See Miami

# Flagler Beach

Named for oil mogul and entrepreneur Henry Morrison Flagler, who was largely responsible for turning the east coast of Florida into a tourist mecca. Today's 4,000 residents enjoy fishing off a city pier, nature and sports at Gamble Rogers State Park, and the historic ruins of Bulow Plantation. **Information:** Flagler Beach Chamber of Commerce, 400D S FL AIA, PO Box 5, Flagler Beach, 32136 (tel 904/439-0995).

## RESTAURANTS 🍴

### ★ High Tides at Shack Jack's
2805 S Ocean Shore Blvd; tel 904/439-3344. 2 miles S of the pier. **American/Seafood.** A casual, screened-in eatery with picnic tables, peachy, rustic decor, and great ocean views. House specialties include steak sandwiches and New England clam chowder. **FYI:** Reservations not accepted. Big band. Beer and wine only. No smoking. **Open:** Daily 11am–11pm. **Prices:** Main courses $5–$15. No CC. 🍽️ 🏔️

### Pier Restaurant on Flagler Beach
215 S FL A1A; tel 904/439-3891. **American/Seafood.** A seafood eatery with maritime decor and large windows offering lovely ocean and pier views. The daily menu usually includes lemon flounder, salmon, and homemade crab cakes. **FYI:** Reservations not accepted. Children's menu. **Open:** Daily 6:30–9pm. **Prices:** Main courses $9–$14. AE, MC, V. 🏔️ 🥤

# Fort Lauderdale

See also Dania, Deerfield Beach, Hollywood, Hollywood Beach, Lighthouse Point, Pompano Beach

Named for an 1848 fort, the "Venice of America" has matured considerably since the 1960 movie *Where The Boys Are*. Today, Jamaicans add spice to its population of 150,000 and the city offers plentiful museums and shopping. Activities range from day sails to Grand Bahama Island to the International Swimming Hall of Fame to Seminole Reservation tours. An autumn film festival is one of the largest on the East Coast. **Information:** Greater Fort Lauderdale Convention & Visitors Bureau, 200 E Las Olas Blvd #1500, Fort Lauderdale, 33301 (tel 954/765-4466).

## HOTELS 🏨

### 🔳🔳🔳 Best Western Oceanside Inn
1180 Seabreeze Blvd, 33316; tel 954/525-8115 or toll free 800/367-1007; fax 954/527-0957. A small hotel nestled among the high-rises. **Rooms:** 100 rms and stes. CI 3pm/CO 11:30am. Nonsmoking rms avail. **Amenities:** 📺 🍷 A/C, cable TV w/movies, refrig, in-rm safe. Some units w/terraces. **Services:** ✕ 🛎️ Car-rental desk. **Facilities:** 🚴 ⛰️ 🏊 ⛱️ 1 restaurant (bkfst and lunch only), 1 bar, 1 beach (ocean), snorkeling, washer/dryer. Access to public beach's

widest section, with its picnic tables, volleyball nets, barbecues, and showers. **Rates (BB):** Peak (Dec–Apr) $74–$119 S; $84–$129 D; $129–$159 ste. Extra person $10. Children under age 12 stay free. Lower rates off-season. Parking: Indoor, free. AE, CB, DC, DISC, EC, JCB, MC, V.

### 🔳🔳🔳 Embassy Suites Hotel
1100 SE 17th St, 33316; tel 954/527-2700 or toll free 800/362-2779; fax 954/760-7202. A Mediterranean-accented hotel that stands comfortably away from the beach. Convenient for those heading to Port Everglades. **Rooms:** 358 stes. CI 3pm/CO noon. Nonsmoking rms avail. Suites have a pleasing mix of Florida style and Mediterranean flair. All have microwaves. **Amenities:** 📺 A/C, cable TV, refrig, voice mail. All units w/terraces. **Services:** ✕ 🛎️ Car-rental desk, babysitting. **Facilities:** 🏊 ⛱️ 1 restaurant (lunch and dinner only), 1 bar (w/entertainment), sauna, steam rm, whirlpool, washer/dryer. **Rates (BB):** Peak (Oct–Apr 15) $199–$214 ste. Extra person $10. Children under age 12 stay free. Lower rates off-season. Parking: Outdoor, free. AE, DC, DISC, MC, V.

### 🔳🔳🔳 Fort Lauderdale Beach Resort
909 Breakers Ave, 33304; tel 954/566-8800 or toll free 800/741-7869; fax 954/566-8802. At NW 19th Ave. A commendable offering located in the fray of beach activity but set off from the strip. **Rooms:** 210 rms, stes, and effic. CI 4pm/CO 11am. Pastel interiors. Some Murphy beds or sofa beds in larger units. **Amenities:** 📺 A/C, cable TV, refrig. Some units w/terraces. **Services:** 🛎️ Car-rental desk, children's program, babysitting. **Facilities:** 🏊 Sauna, steam rm, whirlpool, washer/dryer. **Rates:** Peak (Feb–Apr 7) $130–$190 S or D; $168–$322 ste; $133 effic. Children under age 16 stay free. Lower rates off-season. Parking: Outdoor, free. AE, CB, DISC, MC, V.

### 🔳🔳🔳 Fort Lauderdale Marriott North
6650 N Andrews Ave, 33309; tel 954/771-0440 or toll free 800/343-2459; fax 954/772-9834. A smart address appropriately tuned to the needs of business travelers. **Rooms:** 321 rms and stes. CI 3pm/CO noon. Nonsmoking rms avail. Stylish look is presented in rooms with dark woods and light fabrics. Executive floor offers a few more perks. **Amenities:** 📺 A/C, cable TV w/movies. Some units w/minibars, some w/terraces. **Services:** ✕ 🛎️ Car-rental desk. **Facilities:** 🏊 💻 1 restaurant, 1 bar, sauna, whirlpool, washer/dryer. Free admission to nearby Gold's Gym. **Rates:** Peak (Jan–Mar) $179 S; $189 D; $250–$350 ste. Extra person $10. Children under age 17 stay free. Lower rates off-season. AP rates avail. Parking: Indoor/outdoor, free. AE, DC, DISC, MC, V.

### 🔳🔳🔳 Fort Lauderdale Sunrise Hilton
3003 N University Dr, Sunrise, 33322; tel 954/748-7000 or toll free 800/533-9555; fax 954/572-0799. Spiffy interior adds to this first-class hotel of glass and concrete. Lavender and seafoam-green blend nicely in public areas. **Rooms:** 297

rms and stes. CI 3pm/CO noon. **Amenities:** 🛏 A/C, cable TV w/movies, voice mail. Some units w/minibars, some w/terraces. **Services:** ✕ 🚐 🖾 ⌐ Car-rental desk. **Facilities:** 🔂 🖬 400 ⅙ 1 restaurant, 1 bar (w/entertainment), sauna, whirlpool. **Rates (CP):** Peak (Dec 20–Apr) $109–$149 S or D; $129 ste. Extra person $10. Lower rates off-season. AP rates avail. Parking: Outdoor, free. AE, MC, V.

### UNRATED Holiday Inn Fort Lauderdale Beach

999 N Atlantic Blvd, 33304; tel 954/563-5961 or toll free 800/HOLIDAY; fax 954/564-5261. At Jct 838 (East Sunrise Blvd). A high-rise facility close to shopping and beach action. A popular rendezvous for the beach crowd. **Rooms:** 240 rms and stes. CI 3pm/CO 11am. Nonsmoking rms avail. **Amenities:** 🛏 A/C, cable TV w/movies, dataport, in-rm safe. **Services:** ✕ 🖛 🚐 🖾 ⌐ Twice-daily maid svce, car-rental desk, masseur, children's program, babysitting. **Facilities:** 🔂 280 ⅙ 1 restaurant, 1 bar, 1 beach (ocean), lifeguard. **Rates:** Peak (Dec 15–Apr 24) $125–$155 S or D; $250–$300 ste. Extra person $10. Children under age 19 stay free. Min stay special events. Lower rates off-season. AP and MAP rates avail. Parking: Outdoor, $5/day. AE, CB, DC, DISC, MC, V.

### 🎗🎗 Ocean Manor Resort

4040 Galt Ocean Dr, 33308; tel 954/566-7500 or toll free 800/955-0444; fax 954/564-3075. Lobby replete with a chandelier and marble coffee tables makes a smart impression. **Rooms:** 84 rms, stes, and effic. CI 3pm/CO noon. Nonsmoking rms avail. **Amenities:** 🛏 A/C, cable TV, refrig. Some units w/terraces. **Services:** ✕ 🖛 VP ⌐ Car-rental desk, babysitting. **Facilities:** 🔂 ⚠ 200 ⅙ 2 restaurants, 2 bars (1 w/entertainment), 1 beach (ocean), volleyball, board surfing, games rm, snorkeling, beauty salon, washer/dryer. **Rates (CP):** Peak (Dec–Apr) $139–$189 S or D; $229–$389 ste; $153–$173 effic. Extra person $15. Children under age 17 stay free. Min stay special events. Lower rates off-season. AP rates avail. Parking: Outdoor, free. AE, CB, DC, DISC, EC, ER, JCB, MC, V.

### 🎗🎗 Pelican Beach Resort

2000 N Atlantic Blvd, 33305; tel 954/568-9431 or toll free 800/525-6232; fax 954/565-2622. A comfortable place, where the owners are on hand to keep everything running smoothly. **Rooms:** 85 rms, stes, and effic. CI 3pm/CO 11am. Handsome sunlit rooms in pastel tones with white appointments. Some have ocean views. **Amenities:** 🛏 🖬 A/C, cable TV, refrig. Some units w/terraces, 1 w/whirlpool. **Services:** ⌐ Babysitting. **Facilities:** 🔂 1 beach (ocean), washer/dryer. **Rates (CP):** Peak (Jan–Apr 15) $125–$145 S or D; $175–$195 ste; $145–$165 effic. Extra person $10. Children under age 12 stay free. Min stay special events. Lower rates off-season. Parking: Outdoor, free. AE, CB, DC, DISC, MC, V.

### 🎗🎗🎗 Ramada Plaza Beach Resort

4060 Galt Ocean Dr, 33308; tel 954/565-6611 or toll free 800/678-9022; fax 954/564-7730. Tropically flavored throughout. **Rooms:** 223 rms and stes. CI 4pm/CO 11am.

Nonsmoking rms avail. **Amenities:** 🛏 A/C, cable TV, refrig, in-rm safe. All units w/minibars, some w/terraces, some w/whirlpools. **Services:** ✕ 🖛 VP 🖾 ⌐ Car-rental desk, babysitting. **Facilities:** 🔂 ⚠ ⚓ 🖬 250 ⅙ 2 restaurants, 2 bars (1 w/entertainment), 1 beach (ocean), board surfing, games rm. Watersports rentals available from vendor on beach. **Rates:** Peak (Dec–Apr) $109–$189 S or D; $295–$315 ste. Extra person $10. Children under age 17 stay free. Min stay peak. Lower rates off-season. MAP rates avail. Parking: Outdoor, $3/day. AE, CB, DC, DISC, MC, V.

### 🎗🎗🎗 Riverside Hotel

620 E Las Olas Blvd, 33301; tel 954/467-0671 or toll free 800/325-3280; fax 954/462-2148. I-95 to Broward Blvd. Enchanting 1936 building with muraled facade. Lobby with Mexican tile, and a coral-rock fireplace creates a romantic atmosphere. **Rooms:** 109 rms and stes. CI 3pm/CO 11am. Upgraded superior rooms feature canopied king beds and fresh tropical prints on the bedspreads and drapes. **Amenities:** 🛏 🕹 A/C, cable TV, refrig, dataport, voice mail. Some units w/terraces. **Services:** ✕ 🖛 VP 🚐 🖾 ⌐ Twice-daily maid svce, car-rental desk, babysitting. **Facilities:** 🔂 100 ⅙ 2 restaurants (see "Restaurants" below), 2 bars (1 w/entertainment). Lighted walkways. 560 feet of dockage on New River. **Rates:** Peak (Dec 16–Apr 15) $109 S; $149–$169 D; $199 ste. Extra person $10. Children under age 16 stay free. Lower rates off-season. Parking: Outdoor, $3/day. AE, CB, DC, DISC, MC, V.

### 🎗🎗🎗 Sheraton Yankee Clipper Beach Resort

1140 Seabreeze Blvd, 33316; tel 954/524-5551 or toll free 800/325-3535; fax 954/523-5376. A longtime favorite stop on the beach scene, this multi-building complex caters to beachgoers and some spring-breakers. Hotel can be a hectic place in mid-winter. **Rooms:** 502 rms and stes. CI 3pm/CO noon. Nonsmoking rms avail. **Amenities:** 🛏 🕹 🖬 🍴 A/C, cable TV w/movies, in-rm safe. Some units w/terraces. **Services:** ✕ VP 🖾 ⌐ Car-rental desk, babysitting. **Facilities:** 🔂3 🖬 100 ⅙ 1 restaurant, 3 bars (w/entertainment), 1 beach (ocean), games rm, snorkeling, washer/dryer. Guests also have use of facilities at the nearby sibling hotel, the Sheraton Yankee Trader (see below). **Rates:** Peak (Dec–Apr) $150–$190 S or D; $295 ste. Extra person $20. Children under age 15 stay free. Lower rates off-season. Parking: Outdoor, $5/day. AE, CB, DC, DISC, MC, V.

### 🎗🎗🎗 Sheraton Yankee Trader Resort

321 N Atlantic Blvd, 33304; tel 954/467-1111 or toll free 800/325-3535; fax 954/462-2342. Between Sunrise Blvd and Las Olas Blvd. Two high-rise towers opposite the beach. It's a favorite stomping ground for beachgoers and has exchange privileges with its sister hotel, the Sheraton Yankee Clipper. **Rooms:** 465 rms and stes. CI 3pm/CO noon. Nonsmoking rms avail. Standardized rooms are outfitted in tropical motif. **Amenities:** 🛏 🕹 🖬 🍴 A/C, cable TV w/movies, in-rm safe. **Services:** ✕ 🚐 🖾 ⌐ Car-rental desk, social director, babysitting. **Facilities:** 🔂 ⚓3 🖬 350 ⅙ 2 restaurants, 4 bars (2

w/entertainment), 1 beach (ocean), lifeguard, games rm, washer/dryer. Restaurants and lounges are often social meccas for the bikini and Speedo set. **Rates:** Peak (Dec–Apr) $150–$190 S or D; $295 ste. Extra person $15. Children under age 18 stay free. Lower rates off-season. Parking: Outdoor, $5/day. AE, CB, DC, MC, V.

### ≣≣≣ The Westin Hotel Cypress Creek

400 Corporate Dr, 33334; tel 954/772-1331 or toll free 800/228-3000; fax 954/491-9087. 1 block east of I-95 and Cypress Creek Rd. A deluxe business-class hotel that is set on a lagoon and easily accessible from the interstate. Receives high marks from many business guests who come to use its smart and attractive facilities. **Rooms:** 293 rms and stes. CI 3pm/CO 1pm. Nonsmoking rms avail. **Amenities:** 🛏 🕭 🔲 📺 A/C, cable TV w/movies, refrig, voice mail, bathrobes. All units w/minibars, some w/terraces. Fax machines in all executive rooms. **Services:** 🍽 VP 🚗 🖾 🛏 🍴 Car-rental desk, masseur, babysitting. **Facilities:** 🔊 �️ 🏋 🖭 🖵 400 🖥 🕭 1 restaurant, 2 bars, sauna, whirlpool. **Rates:** Peak (Jan–mid-Apr) $164–$234 S; $184–$254 D; $354–$504 ste. Extra person $15. Children under age 18 stay free. Lower rates off-season. Parking: Outdoor, free. AE, CB, DC, DISC, ER, JCB, MC, V.

## MOTELS

### ≣≣ Banyan Marina Apartments

111 Isle of Venice, 33301; tel 954/524-4430; fax 954/764-5629. A charming apartment complex situated on one of the intracoastal islands. **Rooms:** 10 rms, stes, and effic. CI 3pm/CO 11am. Black and white leather pieces and light-colored decor. **Amenities:** 🛏 🕭 🔲 A/C, cable TV, refrig. Limited groceries supplied upon check-in. **Services:** 🛏 **Facilities:** 🔊 Washer/dryer. Dock for boats. **Rates:** Peak (Dec–Apr) $69–$80 S or D; $120–$175 ste; $100–$120 effic. Extra person $15. Children under age 6 stay free. Lower rates off-season. Parking: Outdoor, free. MC, V.

### ≣≣ Holiday Inn Lauderdale-by-the-Sea

4116 N Ocean Blvd, Lauderdale-by-the-Sea, 33308; tel 954/776-1212 or toll free 800/465-4329; fax 954/776-1212 ext 600. ¼ mi S of Commercial Blvd. Two five-story buildings with private beach access across the street. **Rooms:** 187 rms and effic. CI 3pm/CO noon. Nonsmoking rms avail. **Amenities:** 🛏 🕭 A/C, cable TV w/movies. Some units w/terraces. **Services:** ✕ 🖾 🛏 Babysitting. **Facilities:** 🔊 🚲 100 🖥 🕭 1 restaurant, 1 bar, 1 beach (ocean), lawn games, snorkeling, washer/dryer. **Rates:** Peak (Dec 16–Apr 24) $123 S or D; $139 effic. Extra person $10. Children under age 18 stay free. Lower rates off-season. Parking: Outdoor, free. AE, DC, DISC, MC, V.

### ≣ Oakland East Motor Lodge

3001 N Federal Hwy, 33306; tel 954/565-4601 or toll free 800/633-6279; fax 954/565-0384. **Rooms:** 110 rms, stes, and effic. CI 2pm/CO 11am. Nonsmoking rms avail. **Amenities:** 🛏 🕭 A/C, cable TV, VCR, CD/tape player, voice mail, in-rm safe. Some units w/whirlpools. **Services:** 🛏 **Facilities:** 🔊 �️ 1 bar (w/entertainment), washer/dryer. **Rates (CP):** Peak (Dec 31–Easter) $80–$150 S or D; $150 ste; $150 effic. Extra person $10. Children under age 12 stay free. Lower rates off-season. Parking: Outdoor, free. AE, DC, DISC, MC, V.

### ≣ Santa Barbara Motel

4301 El Mar Dr, 33308; tel 954/491-5211; fax 954/489-0386. An owner-managed motel that tries hard to offer contemporary styling at competitive rates. **Rooms:** 13 rms, stes, and effic. CI 2pm/CO 11am. Full kitchens with microwaves and stoves. **Amenities:** 🛏 🔲 A/C, cable TV, refrig. Some units w/terraces. **Services:** 🛏 Babysitting. **Facilities:** 🔊 **Rates:** Peak (Jan–Apr) $45 S or D; $90 ste. Extra person $8. Lower rates off-season. Parking: Outdoor, free. AE, MC, V.

### ≣ Surf and Sun Hotel and Apartments

521 N Atlantic Blvd, 33304; tel 954/564-4341 or toll free 800/248-0463; fax 954/522-5174. Off SE 17th St. Well-situated budget property. **Rooms:** 22 rms, stes, and effic. CI open/CO 11am. Basic rooms offered without frills. **Amenities:** 🛏 🕭 A/C, cable TV, refrig. Some units w/terraces. Coffeemakers, microwaves, and utensils available free from office. **Facilities:** 1 beach (ocean), lifeguard, washer/dryer. Barbecue area. **Rates:** Peak (Dec 20–Apr 14) $59 S or D; $94–$150 ste; $75 effic. Extra person $4. Children under age 16 stay free. Lower rates off-season. Parking: Outdoor, free. AE, DC, DISC, MC, V.

### ≣≣ Villas-by-the-Sea

4456 El Mar Dr, Lauderdale-by-the-Sea, 33308; tel 954/772-3550 or toll free 800/247-8963; fax 954/772-3835. Affords good privacy and features a delightful pool area; close to beach and shopping. **Rooms:** 144 cottages/villas. CI 3pm/CO 11am. Upbeat decor with designer appointments. Large units may have three TVs. **Amenities:** 🛏 🔲 A/C, cable TV, refrig. Some units w/terraces. **Services:** 🔑 🚗 🛏 Babysitting. **Facilities:** 🔊 🚲 🖾 🏋 🖭 🖭 60 1 restaurant, 1 beach (ocean), lawn games, whirlpool, washer/dryer. **Rates (CP):** Peak (Feb–Apr) $125–$310 cottage/villa. Extra person $8. Children under age 12 stay free. Lower rates off-season. Parking: Outdoor, free. AE, DC, DISC, MC, V.

## RESORTS

### ≣≣≣ Bahia Mar Resort & Yachting Center

801 Seabreeze Blvd, 33316; tel 954/764-2233 or toll free 800/327-8154; fax 954/523-5424. 40 acres. Located on a marina in a complex of buildings connected by a skywalk to the oceanside. **Rooms:** 295 rms. CI 3pm/CO noon. Nonsmoking rms avail. Cheerful rooms, some with ocean views. **Amenities:** 🛏 🕭 🕭 A/C, cable TV w/movies. Some units w/terraces. **Services:** ✕ VP 🚗 🖾 🛏 Twice-daily maid svce, masseur, babysitting. **Facilities:** 🔊 🚲 🔼 🖭 🖾 1200 🖥 2 restaurants, 1 bar, 1 beach (ocean), games rm, snorkeling, beauty salon, washer/dryer. Children under seven eat free in

restaurants. **Rates:** Peak (Dec–Apr) $149–$189 S; $159–$199 D. Extra person $20. Lower rates off-season. MAP rates avail. Parking: Outdoor, $5/day. AE, CB, DC, DISC, MC, V.

### ≣≣≣ Bonaventure Resort & Spa
250 Racquet Club Rd, 33326; tel 954/389-3300 or toll free 800/327-8090; fax 954/384-6157. Exit 1 off I-595. 1,250 acres. A glamourous resort operation with beautiful grounds, catering to affluent golfers and spa-goers. **Rooms:** 504 rms and stes. CI 3pm/CO noon. Nonsmoking rms avail. Rich appointments and attention to detail in rooms. **Amenities:** A/C, cable TV w/movies, refrig. Some units w/minibars, some w/terraces. **Services:** ✕ ☞ VP 🚐 ☒ ↺ Twice-daily maid svce, car-rental desk, social director, masseur, children's program. **Facilities:** 🛋 🚲 ▶36 ⛵ 🎾 ⛱24 🏋 1000 💻 ⚒ 4 restaurants, 2 bars (w/entertainment), racquetball, squash, spa, sauna, steam rm, whirlpool, beauty salon, playground. **Rates:** Peak (Jan–May) $185 S or D; $210–$255 ste. Extra person $15. Children under age 17 stay free. Lower rates off-season. Parking: Outdoor, free. AE, DC, DISC, MC, V.

### ≣≣≣≣ Hyatt Regency Pier 66
2301 SE 17th St Causeway, 33316; tel 954/525-6666 or toll free 800/327-3796; fax 954/728-3595. Off I-95 to 595 E. 22 acres. Arguably the top dog in town, this deluxe choice caters to the yachting crowd (who dock their boats in the marina), and those who appreciate the civilized service and surroundings but can survive without a beachfront position. Its lovely grounds all but compensate for the lack of beach. **Rooms:** 142 rms and stes; 238 cottages/villas. CI 4pm/CO noon. Nonsmoking rms avail. Units are in top shape, with pastel tones, bed ruffles, and fancy window dressings. **Amenities:** A/C, cable TV w/movies, dataport, voice mail, in-rm safe. All units w/minibars, some w/terraces, some w/whirlpools. **Services:** ☉ ☞ VP 🚐 ☒ ↺ Twice-daily maid svce, social director, masseur, children's program, babysitting. **Facilities:** 🛋 ☒2 🏋 975 💻 ⚒ 4 restaurants, 5 bars (1 w/entertainment), games rm, spa, sauna, steam rm, whirlpool, beauty salon, washer/dryer. Whirlpool will accommodate up to 40 people. Tower is topped by a revolving lounge. **Rates:** Peak (Dec 15–Apr 15) $219–$259 S or D; $259–$1,000 ste; $219–$259 cottage/villa. Extra person $15. Children under age 18 stay free. Lower rates off-season. AP and MAP rates avail. Parking: Outdoor, $6/day. AE, CB, DC, DISC, MC, V.

### ≣≣≣ Lago Mar
1700 S Ocean Lane, 33316; tel 954/523-6511; fax 954/524-6627. 10 acres. Architecturally impressive Mediterranean-styled hotel set amid lush tropical plantings, with beautiful fountains surrounded by wrought-iron benches and flower beds. **Rooms:** 176 rms, stes, and effic. CI 3pm/CO noon. Great attention to detail in rooms and suites. Tailored spreads, bed ruffles, bleached tropical colors, and fine furniture. **Amenities:** A/C, cable TV, refrig, voice mail. Some units w/terraces. **Services:** ✕ ☞ VP ☒ ↺ Car-rental desk, children's program, babysitting. **Facilities:** 🛋 ⚓4 🏋

200 💻 ⚒ 4 restaurants, 2 bars (w/entertainment), 1 beach (ocean), volleyball, games rm, snorkeling, playground, washer/dryer. Hammocks under palms. Super-clean beach. **Rates:** Peak (Dec 15–May 1) $90–$185 S or D; $120–$395 ste; $130–$290 effic. Lower rates off-season. Parking: Indoor/outdoor, free. AE, DC, MC, V.

### ≣≣≣ Marriott's Harbor Beach Resort
3030 Holiday Dr, 33316; tel 954/525-4000 or toll free 800/222-6543; fax 954/766-6152. At 17th St. 16 acres. Directly on the beach, it is likely the best of the local Marriotts, at least for overall beach atmosphere. Breezy tropical style throughout. **Rooms:** 624 rms and stes. CI 4pm/CO 11am. Nonsmoking rms avail. Rattan-furnished rooms with pastel colors. **Amenities:** A/C, dataport, voice mail, in-rm safe. All units w/minibars, some w/terraces, some w/whirlpools. **Services:** ☉ ☞ VP 🚐 ☒ ↺ Twice-daily maid svce, car-rental desk, social director, masseur, children's program, babysitting. Shuttle operates to Bonaventure Country Club for golf. **Facilities:** 🛋 🚲 ⛱ ▶ 🏋 💻 ⚒ 5 restaurants (*see* "Restaurants" below), 3 bars (1 w/entertainment), 1 beach (ocean), lifeguard, basketball, volleyball, board surfing, games rm, lawn games, snorkeling, spa, sauna, steam rm, whirlpool, beauty salon, day-care ctr, playground, washer/dryer. "Tropical lagoon" swimming pool boasts waterfalls and extensive landscaping. **Rates (BB):** Peak (June–Apr) $279–$339 S or D; $550–$1,800 ste. Lower rates off-season. AP and MAP rates avail. Parking: Indoor, $6/day. AE, CB, DC, DISC, EC, JCB, MC, V.

### ≣≣≣ Rolling Hills Hotel & Golf Resort
3501 W Rolling Hills Circle, 33328; tel 954/475-0400 or toll free 800/327-7735; fax 954/474-9967. I-95 to I-595 W. 150 acres. Set away from the beach area in its own enclave, the training camp headquarters for the Miami Dolphins has its own following for its golf courses. While its facilities are of resort status, the accommodations, maintenance, and service do not measure up, and resort ambience is lacking. **Rooms:** 290 rms and stes. Executive level. CI 3pm/CO noon. Nonsmoking rms avail. Clean and well-maintained rooms, with tropical decor. **Amenities:** A/C, cable TV w/movies, refrig, dataport, CD/tape player. All units w/terraces. Hair dryers, coffeemakers, VCRs and, refrigerators are available upon request. **Services:** ✕ ☞ VP 🚐 ☒ ↺ Twice-daily maid svce, car-rental desk, social director, babysitting. Complimentary coffee in lobby 6–10 am. **Facilities:** 🛋 ▶27 ⛱6 500 💻 ⚒ 3 restaurants, 2 bars, volleyball, games rm, whirlpool. Free access to nearby fitness center. **Rates:** Peak (Dec 21–Apr 7) $110 S or D; $155 ste. Extra person $5. Children under age 12 stay free. Lower rates off-season. AP and MAP rates avail. Parking: Outdoor, free. AE, CB, DC, DISC, MC, V.

## RESTAURANTS 🍴

### Aruba Beach Cafe
1 E Commercial Blvd, Lauderdale-by-the-Sea; tel 954/776-0001. **Caribbean.** An extremely popular open-air eatery

with pier views. The Caribbean-inspired menu includes such dishes as grouper fingers and Baja black-bean chili. **FYI:** Reservations not accepted. Children's menu. **Open:** Mon–Tues 11am–1am, Wed–Sat 11am–2am, Sun 8:30am–2am. **Prices:** Main courses $5–$19. AE, DC, DISC, MC, V. ▲ VP ♿

## Bimini Boat Yard
In Quay Shopping Center, 1555 SE 17th St Causeway; tel 954/525-7400. **New American.** An upscale eatery with water views, a yuppie crowd, and a rollicking Friday night happy hour. The menu includes fresh blackened mahimahi served with couscous and Jamaican jerk ribs. **FYI:** Reservations not accepted. Dancing/guitar/piano. **Open:** Mon–Thurs 11:30am–11pm, Fri 11:30am–11:30pm, Sat noon–11:30pm, Sun 10:30am–11pm. **Prices:** Main courses $15–$23. AE, MC, V. ▲ VP ♿

## Brasserie Max
In the Fashion Mall, 321 N University Dr, Plantation; tel 954/424-8000. 1 block N of Broward Blvd. **New American.** A cozy cafe with dark wood in the dining room and a brick wall in the appealing lounge. The menu offers such items as oak-grilled chicken and New York strip steak. **FYI:** Reservations not accepted. **Open:** Mon–Thurs 11:30am–10pm, Fri–Sat 11:30am–11pm, Sun 11am–9pm. **Prices:** Main courses $8–$15. AE, CB, DC, DISC, MC, V. ♿

## ♥ Burt & Jack's
Berth 23, Port Everglades; tel 954/522-5225. At the Port Everglades cruise ship terminal. **American/Greek.** A club-like restaurant with water views from all sides due to its location on Port Everglades Peninsula. Prime-cut steaks, baked veal chops with seasoned honey-wheat crumbs, Maine lobster, and pork chops with baked apples are all favorites. **FYI:** Reservations recommended. Piano. Jacket required. **Open:** Fri–Sat 5–11pm, Sun–Thurs 5–10pm. **Prices:** Main courses $15–$45. AE, CB, DC, DISC, MC, V. ♥ ▲ VP ♿

## ★ By Word of Mouth
3200 NE 12th Ave; tel 954/564-3663. **Continental.** A stylish, appealing bistro-style cafe that began as a catering company. The interior is attractively accented with fresh gladiolas. Regularly changing gourmet menu includes some of the best desserts in south Florida. **FYI:** Reservations recommended. Dress code. Beer and wine only. No smoking. **Open:** Lunch Mon–Fri 11am–3pm; dinner Wed–Sat 5–10pm. **Prices:** Main courses $19–$32. AE, CB, DC, DISC, MC, V. ♿

## Cafe de Paris
715 E Las Olas Blvd; tel 954/467-2900. **French.** Bedecked in wrought iron and green marble. Live piano music wafts through the air as you dine on entrees like scampi and baby rack of lamb. Fine wine list. **FYI:** Reservations recommended. Piano. Dress code. No smoking. **Open:** Lunch Mon–Sat 11:30am–2:30pm; dinner Sun–Thurs 5:30–10pm, Fri–Sat 5:30–11pm. Closed Aug. **Prices:** Main courses $11–$25; prix fixe $15–$25. AE, CB, DC, DISC, MC, V. ♥ ▲ ✓ ♿

## The Chart House
301 SW 3rd Ave; tel 954/523-0177. **Seafood/Steak.** Located in two of Fort Lauderdale's oldest homes, the Bryant Homes, located on the New River. Off-season, early-bird specials are available. Local seafood, prime rib, caesar salad, mud pie. **FYI:** Reservations recommended. Children's menu. **Open:** Daily 5–10pm. **Prices:** Main courses $14–$24. AE, CB, DC, DISC, MC, V. ▮ ▲ VP ♿

## Country Ham n' Eggs
4405 El Mar Dr, Lauderdale-by-the-Sea; tel 954/776-1666. **Diner.** Conveniently located close to the pier. Bright yellow booths, Formica tables. Serving meat loaf, burgers, sandwiches. **FYI:** Reservations not accepted. Beer and wine only. **Open:** Daily 7am–9pm. **Prices:** Main courses $9–$11. MC, V.

## Down Under
3000 E Oakland Park Blvd; tel 954/563-4123. **New American.** Copious floral arrangements, Victorian antiques, and garden rooms filled with lush, colorful foliage make this an inviting dining spot. The patio overlooks flower gardens and the Intracoastal Waterway. The menu includes Idaho trout and steak au poivre. **FYI:** Reservations accepted. **Open:** Peak (Sept–May) lunch Tues–Fri 11am–2pm; dinner Sun–Sat 5–11pm. **Prices:** Main courses $12–$28. AE, DC, MC, V. ▲ VP ♿

## 15th St Fisheries
1900 SE 15th St; tel 954/763-2777. **Seafood.** A Florida-casual waterside seafood eatery with dining both upstairs and down. The menu includes sautéed snapper, tuna filet mignon, blackened redfish, and Lake Superior whitefish. **FYI:** Reservations recommended. Children's menu. **Open:** Daily 11:30am–10pm. **Prices:** Main courses $11–$35; prix fixe $35. AE, CB, DC, DISC, MC, V. ▲ ▲ ✓ VP ♿

## French Quarter
215 SE 8th Ave; tel 954/463-8000. **Creole/French.** A lovely, romantic hideaway with stained glass and gardens. The country French interior with lush foliage has a garden-like atmosphere. Red snapper, beef Wellington, Dover sole are among the menu options. **FYI:** Reservations recommended. Piano. Jacket required. **Open:** Lunch Mon–Fri 11:30am–3pm; dinner Mon–Sat 5:30–11:30pm. **Prices:** Main courses $30–$40. AE, CB, DC, DISC, MC, V. ♥ ✓ ♿

## ★ Gibby's
2900 NE 12th Terrace; tel 954/565-2929. **Seafood/Steak.** A very busy yet low-key old-fashioned steak house with a brick interior. Specialties like baked stuffed salmon served in addition to steaks. **FYI:** Reservations recommended. Jacket required. **Open:** Mon–Fri 5–10pm, Sat–Sun 4:30–10pm. **Prices:** Main courses $15–$30. AE, DC, DISC, MC, V. ✓ VP ♿

## Houston's
In Del Mar Shopping Center, 1451 N Federal Hwy; tel 954/563-2226. 3 blocks N of Sunrise Blvd. **New American.** A dimly lit, romantic restaurant with an open kitchen and

cheerful staff. The menu offers a good selection of quality beef, fresh fish, and chicken. **FYI:** Reservations not accepted. **Open:** Sun–Thurs 11:30am–11pm, Fri–Sat 11:30am–midnight. **Prices:** Main courses $10–$20. AE, DC, DISC, MC, V.

### Il Tartuffo
2400 E Las Olas Blvd; tel 954/767-9190. **Italian.** Northern Italian favorites are served in a cozy, casual setting. Some dishes prepared in the woodburning oven. **FYI:** Reservations recommended. Beer and wine only. **Open:** Daily 5–11:30pm. **Prices:** Main courses $14–$30. AE, DC, MC, V.

### ♣ Indigo
In Riverside Hotel, 620 E Las Olas Blvd; tel 954/467-0671. 1 block E of US 1 and S of Broward Blvd at SE 4th St. **Indonesian.** Fun atmosphere (large blond-wood bar, yellow tile floors, black wrought-iron furniture) and a varied and imaginative menu influenced by the southeast Asian flavors of Singapore, Indonesia, and Malaysia make this one of the area's more attractive spots. Menu items range from coconut grilled chicken to Balinese lamb to smoked-tea duckling. **FYI:** Reservations recommended. Dress code. **Open:** Daily 7am–11pm. **Prices:** Main courses $9–$17. AE, DC, DISC, MC, V.

### La Coquille
1619 E Sunrise Blvd; tel 954/467-3030. Between 15th Ave and 16th Terrace. **French.** Traditional French cuisine is served in a charming, casual French-accented setting. Prix-fixe dinner includes wine. **FYI:** Reservations recommended. Beer and wine only. **Open:** Peak (Oct–May) lunch Fri 11:30am–2pm; dinner daily 5:30–10pm. Closed Aug. **Prices:** Main courses $15–$25; prix fixe $25. AE, MC, V. &

### La Ferme
1601 E Sunrise Blvd; tel 954/764-0987. **French.** A warm and inviting restaurant made up of a series of separate cozy rooms. Tables are covered with pink linen and lace. Lump crabmeat and avocado salad is a notable starter. Entrees include roasted duck served with apricot sauce, and filet mignon in a pepper and orange sauce. The dessert specialty is Grand Marnier soufflé. **FYI:** Reservations recommended. **Open:** Peak (Nov–May) daily 5:30–10pm. Closed Aug. **Prices:** Main courses $18–$30; prix fixe $18. AE, MC, V.

### ♣ Le Dome
333 Sunset Dr; tel 954/463-3303. **American/Continental.** A Provençal-style restaurant, reminiscent of an old-world château, atop an upscale condo. The interior is done in soft tones and is graced with fluted columns and lovely water views. The menu includes rack of lamb, 3-pound Maine lobster, and swordfish. There's a separate bar area and a full-time wine steward. **FYI:** Reservations recommended. Piano. Dress code. **Open:** Daily 6–10pm. **Prices:** Main courses $19–$28; prix fixe $25–$35. AE, CB, DC, DISC, MC, V.

### Left Bank
214 SE 6th Ave; tel 954/462-5376. 1 block N of Las Olas Blvd. **New American/French.** A romantic hideaway with a country French ambience. Chef Jean Claude, host of a cooking show on PBS, calls his fare "sunshine cuisine" (American/French with a Mediterranean flair). **FYI:** Reservations recommended. Dress code. Beer and wine only. **Open:** Daily 6–11pm. **Prices:** Main courses $18–$26; prix fixe $30. AE, CB, DISC, MC, V.

### Mai Kai
3599 N Federal Hwy; tel 954/563-3272. Between Oakland Park and Commercial Blvds. **American/Cantonese.** Entrees are served in a lavish South Seas setting with a casual atmosphere. Relax and enjoy a tropical drink and the nightly Polynesian Revue amid thatched roofs, torches, waterfalls, lagoons, lush gardens. **FYI:** Reservations recommended. Children's menu. **Open:** Sun–Thurs 5–10pm, Fri–Sat 5–11pm. **Prices:** Main courses $16–$30; prix fixe $10–$15. AE, DC, DISC, MC, V.

### ♣ Mark's Las Olas
1032 E Las Olas Blvd; tel 954/463-1000. **Regional American/Caribbean.** The open, postmodern dining room features blond wood and mahogany floors, an exhibition kitchen, and floor-to-ceiling windows. Friendly, experienced staff serve up the artful "Floribbean" creations of celebrated local chef Mark Militello. Menus change daily but are likely to include dishes such as crispy squid with Creole remoulade, sesame-seared dolphin, and charcoal-grilled lamb loin with Zinfandel sauce. Three-layer chocolate–peanut butter pie makes a delightfully decadent ending to any meal. **FYI:** Reservations recommended. Dress code. **Open:** Lunch Mon–Fri 11:30am–2:30pm; dinner Sun–Thurs 6–10:30pm, Fri–Sat 5:30–11:30pm. **Prices:** Main courses $11–$32. AE, CB, DC, MC, V.

### Newman's La Bonne Auberge
In 4300 Plaza, 4300 N Federal Hwy; tel 954/491-5522. **Continental/French.** A romantic, elegant bistro with a country French decor. Calf's liver, sautéed veal chops, fresh trout, large shrimps in saffron sauce. **FYI:** Reservations recommended. **Open:** Mon–Sat 5:30–10pm. Closed Aug. **Prices:** Main courses $15–$25. AE, DISC, MC, V.

### Old Florida Seafood House
1414 NE 26th St, Wilton Manors; tel 954/566-1044. 4 blocks S of Oakland Park Blvd. **Seafood.** This seafood palace, decorated with sunset murals and nautical embellishments, caters to an older crowd. The fish is fresh and the oyster bar menu offers raw specialties. **FYI:** Reservations not accepted. Children's menu. **Open:** Mon–Sat 5–10pm, Sun 4–9pm. **Prices:** Main courses $13–$26. AE, MC, V.

### Outback Steakhouse
1823 N Pine Island Rd, Plantation; tel 954/370-9956. **Steak.** Enjoy ribs, chicken, or the daily fish grilled to order as you relax in a spacious booth at this casual, comfortable eatery.

FYI: Reservations not accepted. Children's menu. Dress code. Additional location: 650 Riverside Dr, Coral Springs (tel 345-5965). **Open:** Mon–Thurs 4–10:30pm, Fri–Sat 4–11:30pm, Sun 4–10:30pm. **Prices:** Main courses $9–$19. AE, CB, DC, DISC, MC, V.

**Paesano**
1301 E Las Olas Blvd; tel 954/467-3266. **Italian.** A rather formal trattoria serving northern Italian fare. The menu features veal dishes, baked stuffed shrimp, and pasta Venetian. The adjacent bar area is less formal. **FYI:** Reservations recommended. Piano. Dress code. **Open:** Lunch Mon–Sat 11:30am–2:30pm; dinner Mon–Sat 5:30–10:30pm. **Prices:** Main courses $12–$28. AE, DISC, MC, V.

**Pier Restaurant**
2 E Commercial Blvd, Lauderdale-by-the-Sea; tel 954/776-1690. **American.** A popular '50s-style coffee shop with a nautical theme. A complete breakfast is available for $2.99. **FYI:** Reservations not accepted. No liquor license. **Open:** Daily 7am–4pm. **Prices:** Lunch main courses $5–$10. No CC.

**The Plum Room**
3001 E Oakland Park Blvd; tel 954/563-4168. At SW corner of Intracoastal Waterway. **New American/Continental.** This polished art deco restaurant with a wonderful collection of artwork is the perfect setting in which to enjoy unusual specialties like lobster à la whiskey, loin of Canadian elk, and wild African game pheasant. **FYI:** Reservations recommended. Harp. Jacket required. **Open:** Mon–Thurs 5–10pm, Fri–Sat 5–10:30pm. **Prices:** Main courses $24–$49. AE, CB, DC, DISC, MC, V.

**Primavera**
830 E Oakland Park Blvd; tel 954/564-6363. Between NE 6th Ave and Dixie Hwy. **Italian.** Specialties include veal chops with wild mushrooms, lobster with a light brandy and ginger sauce, and beef tenderloin sautéed in rosemary and balsamic vinaigrette. **FYI:** Reservations recommended. Children's menu. Jacket required. **Open:** Tues–Thurs 5–10pm, Fri–Sun 5–11pm. **Prices:** Main courses $15–$25. AE, CB, DC, DISC, MC, V.

**Ruth's Chris Steak House**
2525 N Federal Hwy; tel 954/565-2338. **Steak.** A basic, casual steakhouse with romantic lighting and a cozy lounge. Veal, chicken, and fish also served. **FYI:** Reservations recommended. **Open:** Mon–Sat 5–11pm, Sun 5–10pm. **Prices:** Main courses $18–$30. AE, CB, DC, MC, V.

**Seawatch**
6002 N Ocean Blvd; tel 954/781-2200. 1 mi N of Commercial Blvd on FL A1A. **Seafood/Steak.** This favorite beach area hideaway is situated in a two-story space complete with an upbeat nautical decor, great ocean views, and outdoor dining. The staff, dressed in striped sailor tops, serves a variety of seafood dishes and grilled specialties. **FYI:** Reserva-

tions accepted. Children's menu. **Open:** Lunch daily 11:30am–3:30pm; dinner daily 5–10pm. **Prices:** Main courses $13–$31. AE, MC, V.

**Sheffield's**
In Marriott's Harbor Beach Resort, 3030 Holiday Dr; tel 954/525-4000. **Continental.** Classy, formal setting. Continental dishes include beef Wellington and chateaubriand. Attentive service. **FYI:** Reservations recommended. **Open:** Peak (Sept–May) daily 6–10:30pm. **Prices:** Main courses $18–$26. AE, CB, DC, DISC, ER, MC, V.

**Stacey's Buffet**
4121 Pine Island Rd, Sunrise; tel 954/749-1521. At 44th St. **Buffet.** A cafeteria-style dining room with country-style decor. Popular menu items include roast turkey and roast prime rib; the buffet includes a variety of salads and soups. Large choice of desserts, ice cream. Great value, particularly for families. **FYI:** Reservations not accepted. Children's menu. No liquor license. **Open:** Daily 11am–8pm. **Prices:** Main courses $7. MC, V.

**Tien Hong Chinese Restaurant**
In Shoppes of McNab, 8006 W McNab Rd, North Lauderdale; tel 954/724-8118. 1 mi W of Rock Island Rd. **Chinese.** An attractive Asian restaurant serving healthy dishes and traditional Chinese specialties. The glass-block, mirrored interior is accented in soft blues and pinks. **FYI:** Reservations accepted. Children's menu. Beer and wine only. **Open:** Daily noon–10pm. **Prices:** Main courses $7–$12. AE, MC, V.

**Yesterday's**
3001 E Oakland Park Blvd; tel 954/561-4400. **New American/Continental.** Every table at this stunning three-tiered restaurant enjoys sweeping views of the Intracoastal Waterway. Both the dining room and the high-energy nightclub are popular with Palm Beach's jet set. Specialties include pistachio-encrusted dolphin sautéed with ginger and key lime–butter sauce. **FYI:** Reservations recommended. **Open:** Mon–Thurs 4:30–10pm, Fri–Sat 4:30–11pm, Sun 4:30–9pm. **Prices:** Main courses $9–$40; prix fixe $9–$16. AE, CB, DC, DISC, MC, V.

**Zanz Z Bar**
602 E Las Olas Blvd; tel 954/767-3377. **International.** This one-of-a-kind restaurant claims to be the only place offering South African fare in South Florida. A great placed to be "spotted," due to the leopard prints which dominate the jungle-like decor and servers outfits. The exotic menu features grilled filet of ostrich, grilled South African beef sausage, and corn porridge with tomato-onion gravy. Wide selection of South African wine and beer also available. **FYI:** Reservations recommended. Beer and wine only. **Open:** Sun–Thurs 11am–midnight, Fri–Sat 11am–2am. **Prices:** Main courses $10–$28. AE, CB, DC, DISC, ER, MC, V.

## ATTRACTIONS

### Museum of Discovery & Science
401 SW 2nd St; tel 954/467-6637. This interactive science museum features seven permanent exhibits, including Florida EcoScapes, KidScience, Space Base, and Choose Health. The Blockbuster IMAX Theater shows large-format films on a five-story screen. **Open:** Mon–Fri 10am–5pm, Sat 10am–8:30pm, Sun noon–5pm. $$$

### International Swimming Hall of Fame
1 Hall of Fame Dr; tel 954/462-6536. The world's largest repository of swimming memorabilia, with Olympic gold medals won by some of the sport's greats, as well as films, books, interactive video displays, and more. The complex also houses two Olympic-size swimming pools. **Open:** Daily 9am–7pm. $

### Bonnet House
900 N Birch Rd; tel 954/563-5393. A historic 35-acre subtropical plantation-style home and estate designed by Chicago muralist Frank Clay Bartlett and completed in 1921. Tours are given Tues–Fri at 10am and 1pm, Sun at 1 and 2pm. **Open:** May–Nov. $$$

### Broward Center for the Performing Arts
201 SW 5th Ave; tel 954/462-0222. Opened in 1991, this stunning $55-million complex contains both a 2,700-seat auditorium and a smaller 590-seat theater. The center attracts top opera, symphony, dance, and Broadway productions, as well as more modest-sized shows $$$$

### Ocean World
1701 SE 17th St; tel 954/525-6611 (recorded info). Six animal shows run continuously throughought the day. Performers range from dolphins and sea lions to river otters and exotic birds; also on view are tortoises, alligators, and tropical fish. A one-hour narrated sightseeing cruise along the Intracoastal Waterway departs three times each day (additional fee required). Snack bars, gift shop. **Open:** Daily 10am–6pm. $$$$

### Hugh Taylor Birch State Recreation Area
3109 E Sunrise Blvd; tel 954/564-4521. Almost 200 acres with access to the ocean. Swimming, fishing, canoe rentals, hiking/nature trails. **Open:** Daily 8am–sunset. $$

# Fort Myers

See also Captiva Island, Fort Myers Beach, Pine Island, Sanibel Island

Winter homes of Thomas Edison and Henry Ford are preserved in this southwestern city of 45,000. Established in 1841 as a US Army outpost, its entire downtown is listed on the National Register of Historic Places. **Information:** Lee County Visitors & Convention Bureau, 2180 1st St #100, PO Box 2445, Fort Myers, 33902 (tel 941/338-3500).

## HOTELS

### Best Western Robert E Lee Motor Inn
13021 N Cleveland Ave, North Fort Myers, 33903; tel 941/997-5511 or toll free 800/274-5511; fax 941/656-6962. Exit 26 off I-75. Some great river views from this property 1 mile from downtown Fort Myers. **Rooms:** 108 rms and stes. CI 3pm/CO 11am. Nonsmoking rms avail. Double rooms are large. **Amenities:** A/C, cable TV. All units w/terraces. **Services:** Facilities: 1 restaurant, 1 bar, whirlpool, washer/dryer. Lounge at the water's edge is a nice feature. **Rates:** Peak (Feb–Apr 15) $75 S; $80–$100 D; $125–$145 ste. Extra person $5. Children under age 19 stay free. Lower rates off-season. Parking: Outdoor, free. AE, CB, DC, DISC, MC, V.

### Courtyard by Marriott
4455 Metro Pkwy, 33901; tel 941/275-8600 or toll free 800/321-2211; fax 941/275-7087. Exit 22 off I-75; W 3 mi at Colonial Blvd. An oasis of good taste in a busy commercial district. The extensive lobby contains a fireplace, television parlor, and restaurant. **Rooms:** 149 rms and stes. CI 4pm/CO noon. Nonsmoking rms avail. Handsome rooms are carefully maintained and outfitted with tasteful appointments. **Amenities:** A/C, satel TV w/movies, dataport, voice mail. Some units w/terraces. Irons and ironing boards in all rooms. Refrigerators available free upon request. **Services:** Facilities: 1 restaurant (bkfst only), 1 bar, whirlpool, washer/dryer. **Rates:** Peak (Jan 20–Apr) $115–$130 S or D; $145–$160 ste. Children under age 18 stay free. Lower rates off-season. Parking: Outdoor, free. AE, DC, DISC, MC, V.

### Holiday Inn Central
2431 Cleveland Ave, 33901; tel 941/332-3232 or toll free 800/998-0466; fax 941/332-0590. 1 mi S of downtown Fort Myers. A mid-rise hotel with southwestern styling that is handy to downtown and the nearby mall. If you can live without a beach location, this is a good find. **Rooms:** 126 rms and stes. Executive level. CI 3pm/CO noon. Nonsmoking rms avail. Spiffy rooms are colorful and upbeat. **Amenities:** A/C, cable TV w/movies, dataport. Some units w/terraces. **Services:** Twice-daily maid svce. **Facilities:** 1 restaurant, 1 bar (w/entertainment). Complimentary use of next-door health facility. **Rates:** Peak (Jan 15–Apr) $119–$139 S or D; $260 ste. Children under age 19 stay free. Lower rates off-season. Parking: Outdoor, free. AE, CB, DC, DISC, JCB, MC, V.

### Holiday Inn Select
13051 Bell Tower Dr, 33907 (Southwest Florida Regional Airport); tel 941/482-2900 or toll free 800/HOLIDAY. Exit 21 off I-75 at intersection of Daniels Pkwy and Cleveland Ave. Right in the thick of a shopping center area and five minutes from a major mall, it's geared more toward business travelers than leisure guests. **Rooms:** 227 rms and stes. Executive level. CI 3pm/CO noon. Nonsmoking rms avail.

**Amenities:** 🔒 🛁 🖥 🍴 A/C, cable TV w/movies, refrig. Some units w/minibars. TV and radio speaker in bathroom. **Services:** ✕ 🍽 🚐 🧺 🍷 Twice-daily maid svce, car-rental desk. **Facilities:** 🏊 🏌 🎰 [450] 🖥 🏌 ♿ 1 restaurant, 1 bar (w/entertainment), games rm, washer/dryer. Impressive lobby area with marble sculptures and water fountain. **Rates:** Peak (Jan 15–Apr 15) $149 S or D; $169 ste. Extra person $10. Children under age 12 stay free. Lower rates off-season. Parking: Outdoor, free. AE, DC, DISC, MC, V.

### 🏨🏨 Holiday Inn SunSpree Resort

2220 W 1st St, 33901; tel 941/334-3434 or toll free 800/HOLIDAY; fax 941/334-3844. Take Virginia Ave off McGregor Blvd. Lush vegetation, cages of colorful birds, and a marble-and-coral lobby give this riverfront property a tropical feel. Caters to both business and leisure travelers. **Rooms:** 170 rms and stes. CI 3pm/CO 11am. Nonsmoking rms avail. **Amenities:** 🔒 🛁 🖥 🍴 A/C, cable TV w/movies, refrig, dataport, voice mail. Some units w/terraces, some w/whirlpools. **Services:** ✕ 🚐 🧺 🍷 Social director, masseur, children's program, babysitting. **Facilities:** 🏊 🏌 [300] ♿ 1 restaurant (*see* "Restaurants" below), 2 bars (1 w/entertainment), basketball, spa, beauty salon, day-care ctr, playground, washer/dryer. Waterfront restaurant, party cruises, and dockside theme nights. **Rates:** Peak (Jan–Apr) $119 S or D; $139–$169 ste. Children under age 19 stay free. Lower rates off-season. Parking: Outdoor, free. AE, DISC, MC, V.

### 🏨🏨🏨 Radisson Inn Fort Myers

12635 Cleveland Ave, 33907; tel 941/936-4300 or toll free 800/333-3333; fax 941/936-2058. At College Pkwy. A two-part property with older two-level, courtyard units around pool and executive-type accommodations in a midrise tower. **Rooms:** 224 rms and stes. CI 4pm/CO noon. Nonsmoking rms avail. **Amenities:** 🔒 🛁 A/C, cable TV, voice mail. **Services:** ✕ 🚐 🧺 🍷 **Facilities:** 🏊 🍽 [250] ♿ 2 restaurants, 2 bars, volleyball, washer/dryer. Nearby health club offers free access to guests. **Rates:** Peak (Feb 14–Apr 15) $119–$139 S or D; $149–$169 ste. Extra person $10. Children under age 17 stay free. Min stay special events. Lower rates off-season. Parking: Outdoor, free. AE, CB, DC, DISC, ER, JCB, MC, V.

### 🏨🏨🏨 Radisson Inn Sanibel Gateway

20091 Summerlin Rd, 33908; tel 941/466-1200 or toll free 800/333-3333; fax 941/466-3797. A smartly decorated establishment that manages to make the most of its off-beach location, with an inviting courtyard that provides a nice alternative for tired beachgoers. Fountain in registration area is a fun touch. **Rooms:** 157 stes. CI 3pm/CO noon. Nonsmoking rms avail. **Amenities:** 🔒 🛁 🍴 A/C, cable TV w/movies, refrig, in-rm safe. All suites have fold-out couches. **Services:** ✕ 🧺 🍷 🍽 Twice-daily maid svce. **Facilities:** 🏊 🏌 ♿ 1 restaurant, 1 bar, games rm, washer/dryer. **Rates:** Peak (Feb–Apr) $129–$149 ste. Children under age 18 stay free. Min stay special events. Lower rates off-season. Parking: Outdoor, free. Rates apply to up to four in a suite. AE, CB, DC, DISC, MC, V.

### 🏨🏨 Shell Point Village Guest House

15000 Shell Point Blvd, 33908; tel 941/466-1111; fax 941/454-2220. 1 mi E of the Sanibel tollgate. 75 acres. This hostelry in a Christian retirement village is certainly not for everyone, but it may appeal to those who desire a quiet retreat or vacation in a wholesome environment. No drinking or smoking is allowed, and there is no dancing in public. A security gate controlls access to the village. **Rooms:** 39 rms. CI 2pm/CO 11am. Nonsmoking rms avail. **Amenities:** A/C. No phone. **Services:** 🍷 **Facilities:** 🏊 🍽 2 🏌 [200] ♿ 1 restaurant, spa, beauty salon, washer/dryer. Mini-market and emergency medical care. Marina. **Rates:** Peak (Dec–Apr) $75 S; $85 D. Extra person $6. Children under age 18 stay free. Lower rates off-season. Parking: Outdoor, free. Senior and extended-stay discounts avail. MC, V.

### 🏨🏨🏨 Sheraton Harbor Place

2500 Edwards Dr, 33901; tel 941/337-0030 or toll free 800/833-1620; fax 941/337-1530. At Fort Myers Marina between the 2 bridges. This downtown waterfront high-rise offers a variety of accommodations and facilities capable of satisfying the needs of both business and leisure clients. **Rooms:** 416 rms and stes. Executive level. CI 3pm/CO noon. Nonsmoking rms avail. **Amenities:** 🔒 🛁 🖥 A/C, cable TV w/movies, dataport. **Services:** ✕ 🍽 🚐 🧺 🍷 Car-rental desk. **Facilities:** 🏊 🚲 🍽 🏌 [800] ♿ 1 restaurant, 3 bars (1 w/entertainment), games rm, whirlpool, washer/dryer. **Rates:** Peak (Feb 15–Mar) $120–$149 S; $130–$159 D; $130–$179 ste. Extra person $10. Lower rates off-season. Parking: Indoor, free. AE, DC, DISC, MC, V.

## MOTELS

### 🏨🏨 Hampton Inn Riverfront

13000 N Cleveland Ave, North Fort Myers, 33903; tel 941/656-4000 or toll free 800/HAMPTON; fax 941/656-1612. Exit 26 off I-75. Standard, bare-bones accommodations offering pleasant surroundings. **Rooms:** 121 rms. CI 3pm/CO noon. Nonsmoking rms avail. **Amenities:** 🔒 🛁 🖥 A/C, cable TV w/movies, dataport. **Services:** 🧺 🍷 **Facilities:** 🏊 [25] ♿ Washer/dryer. **Rates (CP):** Peak (Dec–Apr) $60–$70 S; $65–$75 D. Extra person $5. Children under age 18 stay free. Lower rates off-season. Parking: Outdoor, free. Senior discounts avail. AE, DC, DISC, MC, V.

### 🏨🏨 La Quinta Motor Inn

4850 S Cleveland Ave, 33907; tel 941/275-3300 or toll free 800/531-5900; fax 941/275-6661. On US 41 near Colonial Blvd. Southwestern motif is carried out in the nicely decorated lobby and rooms. **Rooms:** 130 rms. CI 3pm/CO 11am. Nonsmoking rms avail. **Amenities:** 🔒 🛁 A/C, cable TV w/movies, dataport. **Services:** 🧺 🍷 🍽 Twice-daily maid svce. **Facilities:** 🏊 [30] ♿ Washer/dryer. Guests receive discount at nearby fitness facility. **Rates (CP):** Peak (Feb–Apr) $94–$101 S; $104–$111 D. Extra person $10. Children under age 18 stay free. Lower rates off-season. Parking: Outdoor, free. AE, DISC, MC, V.

### Travelodge

2038 W 1st St, 33901; tel 941/334-2284 or toll free 800/578-7878; fax 941/334-2366. Downtown 1 block NW of McGregor Blvd. Renovation of rooms and pool area began in 1996 at this motel in transition. **Rooms:** 48 rms. CI 3pm/CO 11am. Nonsmoking rms avail. **Amenities:** 📺 ☎ 🖥 A/C, cable TV. Some units w/terraces. **Services:** 🛎 Twice-daily maid svce. **Facilities:** 🔲 ₺ **Rates:** $85 S; $95 D. Extra person $6. Children under age 18 stay free. Parking: Outdoor, free. AE, DC, DISC, MC, V.

### Wellesley Inn

4400 Ford St, 33916; tel 941/278-3949 or toll free 800/444-8888; fax 941/278-3670. Exit 22 off I-75. Basic lodgings, featuring an attractive lobby with marble floor and potted palms. **Rooms:** 106 rms and stes. CI 2pm/CO 11am. Nonsmoking rms avail. **Amenities:** 📺 ☎ 🖥 A/C, cable TV, refrig, VCR, in-rm safe. **Services:** ✕ 🛎 🕼 **Facilities:** 🔲 ₺ Washer/dryer. **Rates (CP):** Peak (Dec 20–Apr 20) $90 S; $100 D; $110–$140 ste. Extra person $10. Children under age 16 stay free. Lower rates off-season. Parking: Outdoor, free. AE, CB, DC, DISC, MC, V.

## RESORTS

### Admiral Lehigh Golf Resort

225 E Joel Blvd, Lehigh Acres, 33936; tel 941/369-2121 or toll free 800/843-0971; fax 941/368-1660. East of I-75 at exit 22. 500 acres. An affordable option for golf and tennis buffs, it has two parts: a hotel and a condominium community. Each has its own pool and access to two golf courses. Less stuffy, more friendly than its more prestigious counterparts on the coast. **Rooms:** 288 rms and effic. CI 3pm/CO 11am. Nonsmoking rms avail. Rooms overlook the courtyard or fairways. **Amenities:** 📺 ☎ A/C, cable TV. Some units w/terraces. **Services:** 🖐 🛎 Social director, masseur. **Facilities:** 🔲 🚲 🔲 ▶36 🏌4 🏊 220 ₺ 3 restaurants, 3 bars (1 w/entertainment), basketball, volleyball, games rm, racquetball, whirlpool, beauty salon, playground, washer/dryer. 9-hole miniature golf course. Fishing in the nearby lake. **Rates:** Peak (Jan 13–Apr 15) $74–$79 S or D; $125–$150 effic. Extra person $6. Children under age 19 stay free. Lower rates off-season. Parking: Outdoor, free. AE, DC, DISC, MC, V.

### Sanibel Harbour Resort & Spa

17260 Harbour Point Rd, 33908; tel 941/466-4000 or toll free 800/767-7777; fax 941/466-2150. East of Sanibel Causeway in Punta Rassa. 80 acres. This local favorite offers the most complete package in Fort Myers. Situated near Sanibel on extensively landscaped acreage, the resort exudes good taste without being too stuffy. Known for its dining, tennis, and spa facilities, it boasts dramatic views of the bay. **Rooms:** 340 rms, stes, and effic. CI 3pm/CO noon. Nonsmoking rms avail. All rooms are newly renovated and have water views. **Amenities:** 📺 ☎ 🍴 A/C, cable TV w/movies, dataport, voice mail, bathrobes. All units w/minibars, all w/terraces, some w/whirlpools. **Services:** 🍽 🔑 VP 🖐 🛎

Car-rental desk, social director, masseur, children's program, babysitting. Numerous young staffers are friendly and efficient. **Facilities:** 🔲 ⛰ 🔲 🏖 🔲 13 🏓 600 🔲 ₺ 4 restaurants, 4 bars (3 w/entertainment), 1 beach (bay), basketball, volleyball, games rm, racquetball, snorkeling, spa, sauna, steam rm, whirlpool, beauty salon, day-care ctr. **Rates:** Peak (Dec 20–Apr 20) $250–$290 S or D; $315 ste; $305–$420 effic. Children under age 18 stay free. Lower rates off-season. AP and MAP rates avail. Parking: Indoor, free. AE, CB, DC, DISC, MC, V.

## RESTAURANTS 🍴

### The Chart House

2024 W 1st St; tel 941/332-1881. **Seafood/Steak.** An excellent chain restaurant featuring map-topped tables, a central bar, and lovely water views. This location offers a popular salad bar as well as a few beef and chicken dishes to satisfy landlubbers. **FYI:** Reservations accepted. Children's menu. Dress code. **Open:** Mon–Fri 11:30am–10pm, Sat–Sun 4–10pm. **Prices:** Main courses $15–$24. AE, DISC, MC, V. 🏔 ❤ ₺

### Outback Steakhouse

In Bell Tower Shops, 12995 S Cleveland Ave; tel 941/936-1021. **Steak.** A casual eatery popular with families for the good value it offers. The varied menu features entrees like grilled baby-back ribs and 12-ounce center-cut sirloin. There is a bar area as well, with dark wood tables, booths, and a TV. **FYI:** Reservations not accepted. Children's menu. **Open:** Mon–Thurs 3:30–10:30pm, Fri–Sat 3–11:30pm, Sun noon–10:30pm. **Prices:** Main courses $9–$18. AE, CB, DC, DISC, MC, V. 🍴 ₺

### 🍸 Peter's La Cuisine

2224 Bay St (Downtown); tel 941/332-2228. Adjacent to the Harborside Convention Center. **Continental.** A retooled old warehouse provides the trendy digs for this upscale dining room. Specialties include lobster bisque, chateaubriand, and white-and-dark-chocolate mousse. The jazz club upstairs serves light fare from 5:30pm to midnight, and is a hip place to be seen. **FYI:** Reservations recommended. Blues/jazz. Dress code. **Open:** Lunch Mon–Fri 11:30am–2pm; dinner daily 5:30–9:30pm. **Prices:** Main courses $25–$30; prix fixe $45–$65. AE, MC, V. ₺

### ★ The Prawnbroker Restaurant and Fish Market

In Cypress Square, 13451 McGregor Blvd; tel 941/489-2226. **Seafood/Steak.** This seafood restaurant and fish shop is a good choice for families and the older crowd. A great value for fresh fish. **FYI:** Reservations recommended. Children's menu. **Open:** Mon–Sat 4–10pm, Sun 4–9pm. **Prices:** Main courses $13–$18. AE, MC, V. ₺

### Shooters Waterfront Cafe, USA

In Holiday Inn SunSpree Resort, 2220 W 1st St; tel 941/334-2727. Take Virginia Ave off McGregor Blvd. **New American.** Seared fresh tuna salad, grilled smoked turkey and Swiss sandwich, Cajun shrimp pizza, and grilled catch of the day are among the highlights on the all-day menu. Fine selection of wines by the glass. Jazz Brunch on Sundays, complimentary grand buffet during happy hour on Fridays. **FYI:** Reservations not accepted. Jazz/rock/salsa. Children's menu. **Open:** Mon–Thurs 7am–midnight, Sun 7am–11pm, Fri–Sat 7am–1am. **Prices:** Main courses $10–$16. AE, DISC, MC, V. ⬤ ⬛ ⬛ ⬛ &

### Smitty's
In Fort Myers Country Club, 3583 McGregor Blvd (Downtown); tel 941/939-7300. ½ mi W of the Caloosahatchee River Bridge. **Steak.** Smitty's has been a favorite local beefhouse since 1958, particularly for its special slow-roasted prime rib. The restaurant is also justly famous for its peppercorn dressing and yeasty rolls (both made on the premises). Brandy Alexander pie is a popular choice for dessert. **FYI:** Reservations recommended. Piano/singer. Children's menu. **Open:** Lunch Mon–Sat 11am–2:30pm; dinner Mon–Thurs 4:30–9:30pm, Fri–Sat 4:30–10pm, Sun 4:30–9pm; brunch Sun 11:30am–4:30pm. **Prices:** Main courses $10–$20. AE, MC, V. ⬛ ⬛ &

### Veranda
2122 2nd St; tel 941/332-2228. Across from City Hall. **Regional American/Continental.** Experience Southern comfort and elegance in an antique-filled Victorian house. Entrees include rack of New Zealand lamb, grilled grouper, and chicken jambalaya. Among dessert choices are Southern praline tart and peanut butter fudge pie. **FYI:** Reservations accepted. Children's menu. Dress code. No smoking. **Open:** Lunch Mon–Fri 11am–2:30pm; dinner Mon–Sat 5:30–11pm. **Prices:** Main courses $14–$27. AE, MC, V. ⬤ ⬛ ⬛ ⬛ ⬛ &

## ATTRACTIONS 📷

### Edison Winter Home
2350 McGregor Blvd; tel 941/334-3614. Regularly scheduled tours are conducted of inventor Thomas Alva Edison's winter retreat, in which he lived with his wife and their family until his death in 1931. Tour includes a visit to the gardens of the estate, with wild orchids and an enormous banyan tree that Edison grew from a seedling; the laboratory, which contains the original equipment used for his rubber research from 1928 to 1931; and the museum, with vintage light bulbs, phonographs, early movie projectors, and other interesting gadgets and memorabilia. **Open:** Mon–Sat 9am–4pm, Sun 12:30–4pm. $$$

### Ford Winter Home
2350 McGregor Blvd; tel 941/332-6634. "Mangoes," industrialist Henry Ford's winter home, is next door to the Edison home and was purchased so the two friends could be neighbors. Tours are given of the interior of the house, which contains 1920s-style furnishings, and of the grounds. **Open:** Mon–Sat 9am–4pm, Sun noon–4pm. $$$

### Fort Myers Historical Museum
2300 Peck St; tel 941/332-5955. Artifacts, graphic depictions, and photos present the history of Fort Myers, from the Calusa and Seminole civilizations to the first European settlers and beyond. There are scale models, a collection of Ethel Cooper glass, and the "Esperanza," the last (and longest) of the plush Pullman railroad cars, which is parked outside the museum. **Open:** Tues–Fri 9am–4pm, Sat 10am–4pm. $

### Burroughs Home
2505 1st St; tel 941/332-6125. A 1901 Georgian revival mansion. "Living history" tours are conducted by the two Burroughs sisters, local historians who dress up in period fashion and talk to visitors about life in the mansion. The garden overlooks the Caloosahatchee River. **Open:** Nov–Apr, Mon–Fri 10am–4pm, Sun noon–4pm. $

### Calusa Nature Center and Planetarium
3450 Ortiz Ave; tel 941/275-3435. Nature trails wind through over 100 acres of pine flatwoods and cypress swamp. Visitors can also visit the aviary, live reptile exhibit, freshwater aquarium, and museum store. Planetarium features star and laser shows. **Open:** Mon–Sat 9am–5pm, Sun 11am–5pm. $

### Six Mile Cypress Slough Preserve
Penzance Crossing and Six Mile Cypress Pkwy; tel 941/338-3300. Visitors can walk along a mile-long boardwalk through this 2,000-acre wetland ecosystem, exploring southwest Florida's diverse flora and fauna. Subtropical ferns, wild orchids, and such birds as herons, egrets, spoonbills, and storks. **Open:** Daily 8am–5pm. $

# Fort Myers Beach

A small bridge along County Rd 865 connects mainland southwest Florida with this Gulf beach town, where population has nearly doubled (to 10,000 permanent residents) since the 1980 census. Free trolleys travel between the beach and Fort Myers. A November sand-sculpting contest has amateur and masters' divisions. **Information:** Lee County Visitors & Convention Bureau, 2180 1st St #100, PO Box 2445, Fort Myers, 33902 (tel 941/338-3500).

## HOTELS 🏨

### ▤▤ Days Inn at Lover's Key
8701 Estero Blvd, 33931; tel 941/765-4422 or toll free 800/325-2525; fax 941/765-4422. 7 mi S of Sky Bridge. This architecturally unremarkable high-rise offers a private beach with a view of the bridge at Big Bonita Pass, and water activities. The sunsets make up somewhat for the dull decor. **Rooms:** 110 effic. CI 3pm/CO 11am. Nonsmoking rms avail. All rooms look out at the water. **Amenities:** 🅰 🅱 A/C, cable TV, refrig, in-rm safe. All units w/terraces. **Services:** 🛎 🖐 Complimentary cocktails served at sunset. **Facilities:** 🎣 ⚠ &

1 beach (bay), washer/dryer. Private concession rents bikes and watersports equipment. **Rates (CP):** Peak (Dec 17–31/ Feb–Apr 13) $159–$189 effic. Extra person $10. Children under age 12 stay free. Lower rates off-season. Parking: Outdoor, free. AE, DC, DISC, MC, V.

### ≡≡≡ Holiday Inn

6890 Estero Blvd, 33931; tel 941/463-5711 or toll free 800/ HOLIDAY; fax 941/463-7038. 4½ mi S of Sky Bridge. Appealing for its sunny, landscaped pool area wrapped by a one- and two-story section, with some rooms opening directly to the pool. **Rooms:** 103 rms, stes, and effic. CI 3pm/CO noon. No smoking. **Amenities:** 🛏 ⚱ A/C, cable TV w/movies, refrig. Some units w/terraces. **Services:** ✗ ⌂ ⌐ Babysitting. **Facilities:** 🛠 ▩ ⌐40⌐ ⚱ 1 restaurant, 2 bars (1 w/entertainment), 1 beach (ocean), games rm, lawn games, washer/dryer. Thatched umbrellas and lounge chairs beside pool. **Rates:** Peak (Feb–Apr) $141–$186 S or D; $325 ste; $186 effic. Extra person $6. Children under age 18 stay free. Lower rates off-season. Parking: Outdoor, free. AE, CB, DC, DISC, ER, JCB, MC, V.

### ≡≡≡ Pointe Estero

6640 Estero Blvd, 33931; tel 941/765-1155 or toll free 800/ 237-5141; fax 941/765-0657. South end of Estero Island. An attractive, upscale, slender condominium high-rise on the beach. Boasts a sunny freeform pool and deck enhanced by foliage. **Rooms:** 60 effic. CI 3pm/CO 10am. One- or two-bedroom condos feature large marble whirlpool bathroom tubs. **Amenities:** 🛏 ⚱ 🖭 A/C, cable TV, VCR. All units w/terraces, some w/fireplaces, all w/whirlpools. **Services:** ⌂ ⌐ Children's program, babysitting. Maid service available at $25 charge. **Facilities:** 🛠 △ ⚱1 ⌷ ⚱ 1 beach (ocean), whirlpool, washer/dryer. Independent vendor operates watersports on beach. Barbecue grills available. **Rates:** Peak (Feb–Apr) $189–$329 effic. Children under age 18 stay free. Min stay. Lower rates off-season. Parking: Outdoor, free. Charges are per unit, not per person. DISC, MC, V.

### ≡≡≡ Santa Maria All-Suite Resort

7317 Estero Blvd, 33931; tel 941/765-6700 or toll free 800/ 765-6701; fax 941/765-6909. 5 mi S of Sky Bridge. Condominium resort on a canal is minutes away from Gulf beaches and boasts a full-service marina. **Rooms:** 55 effic. CI 3pm/ CO 10am. Tastefully appointed one-, two-, and three-bedroom units have tropical decor. **Amenities:** 🛏 ⚱ 🖭 A/C, cable TV, refrig. All units w/terraces. Irons and ironing boards in all rooms. **Services:** ⌐ Maid service available for extra charge. **Facilities:** 🛠 △ Volleyball, sauna, whirlpool, washer/dryer. **Rates:** Peak (Dec 20–Apr 15) $99–$140 effic. Min stay. Lower rates off-season. Parking: Outdoor, free. Charges are per unit, not per person. DISC, MC, V.

### ≡≡ Seawatch-on-the-Beach

6550 Estero Blvd, 33931; tel 941/463-4469 or toll free 800/ 448-2736; fax 941/463-3926. 5 mi S of Sky Bridge. Considered a frontrunner in the condo market, a hotel away from the center of beach activity but still convenient to it. **Rooms:** 42 effic. CI 3pm/CO 10am. Units have one or two bedrooms and are decorated with designer style. **Amenities:** 🛏 ⚱ 🖭 A/C, cable TV, refrig, VCR. All units w/terraces, all w/whirlpools. **Services:** ⌐ Children's program. **Facilities:** 🛠 ▩ 1 bar, 1 beach (ocean), games rm, whirlpool, washer/ dryer. Nearby health club offers free access to guests. No restaurant on premises. **Rates:** Peak (Feb 17–Apr 12) $210– $235 effic. Children under age 18 stay free. Min stay peak. Lower rates off-season. Parking: Outdoor, free. Charges are per unit, not per person. AE, DISC, MC, V.

## RESORTS

### ≡≡≡ Best Western Pink Shell Beach Resort

275 Estero Blvd, 33931; tel 941/463-6181 or toll free 800/ 237-5786; fax 941/481-4947. North end of Estero Island. 12 acres. This sprawling complex fronts the best of both island water worlds with Gulf and bay views at the quiet, north end of Fort Myers Beach. It boasts a wide, sugar-sand beach and extensive recreational activities. **Rooms:** 162 effic; 46 cottages/villas. CI 4pm/CO 11am. Nonsmoking rms avail. All units have kitchen facilities. **Amenities:** 🛏 ⚱ 🖭 A/C, cable TV, refrig, VCR, in-rm safe. All units w/terraces. **Services:** ⌐ Social director, children's program, babysitting. Grocery/deli offers free morning coffee and newspaper. Boat excursions have shelling, nature, or fishing focus. **Facilities:** 🛠 ⚲⚱ △ ▯ ⌐35⌐ 2 restaurants, 2 bars, 1 beach (ocean), volleyball, board surfing, games rm, playground, washer/dryer. Outdoor dining room features lovely bay views. **Rates:** Peak (Feb–Apr) $214–$335 effic; $199–$360 cottage/villa. Extra person $5– 10. Children under age 18 stay free. Min stay special events. Lower rates off-season. Parking: Outdoor, free. AE, DC, DISC, MC, V.

### ≡≡ Lani Kai Island Resort

1400 Estero Blvd, 33931 (Times Square); tel 941/463-3111 or toll free 800/237-6133; fax 941/463-2986. Mid Estero Island. The center of beach action and partying on Fort Myers Beach, it appeals to families and, during spring break, the college crowd. **Rooms:** 100 rms and effic. CI 3pm/CO 11am. Nonsmoking rms avail. Maintenance is not quite up to par, and a committee must have decorated—too many patterns and colors are used in the units. Rooms have great views, however, and good-sized decks, from which you can hear the waves crashing below. **Amenities:** 🛏 A/C, cable TV, refrig. All units w/terraces. **Services:** ✗ ⌐ Twice-daily maid svce, social director, children's program, babysitting. **Facilities:** 🛠 ⚲⚱ △ ⌐100⌐ ⚱ 1 restaurant, 5 bars (3 w/entertainment), 1 beach (ocean), volleyball, games rm, beauty salon, day-care ctr, playground, washer/dryer. **Rates:** Peak (Dec 16–Apr) $150 S or D; $170–$195 effic. Extra person $10. Children under age 12 stay free. Min stay special events. Lower rates off-season. Parking: Outdoor, free. CB, DC, DISC, MC, V.

## RESTAURANTS 🍽

### Anthony's on the Gulf

3040 Estero Blvd; tel 941/463-2600. **Italian/Seafood.** Excellent informal dining overlooking the water. The food is basic—but good—Italian, with veal, chicken, and seafood dishes dominating the reasonably priced menu. **FYI:** Reservations not accepted. Children's menu. **Open:** Daily 11:30am–11pm. **Prices:** Main courses $13–$17. AE, DISC, MC, V. 🏛 🖼 &

### The Bridge

708 Fisherman's Wharf; tel 941/765-0050. **Seafood/Steak.** This waterside restaurant, a comfortable, open room furnished in wood, is popular with locals and tourists alike. The dinner menu abounds with beef and seafood dishes, including Maine lobster. Sandwiches and salads are available at lunch. **FYI:** Reservations accepted. Children's menu. **Open:** Mon–Thurs 11:30am–10pm, Fri–Sat 11:30am–11pm, Sun 10:30am–midnight. **Prices:** Main courses $9–$18. AE, DC, MC, V. 🖼 &

### Channel Mark

19001 San Carlos Blvd; tel 941/463-9127. 1¼ mi N of the Skybridge. **Italian/Seafood.** Diners may choose to sit at a table inside the light, airy dining room or outdoors overlooking the water. The menu includes sandwiches, fresh local seafood, and pasta-seafood combinations. **FYI:** Reservations not accepted. Children's menu. **Open:** Daily 11am–11pm. **Prices:** Main courses $12–$25. AE, DC, DISC, MC, V. 🏛 🖼 VP &

### Gulf Shore Restaurant

1270 Estero Blvd; tel 941/463-9551. **Seafood/Steak.** A basic waterside eatery with a simple menu featuring seafood and steaks. An adjacent bar, the Cottage, serves light meals and caters to a college crowd. **FYI:** Reservations accepted. Children's menu. **Open:** Daily 7am–10pm. **Prices:** Main courses $10–$16. AE, MC, V. 🖼 🗹

### Skipper's Galley Restaurant

3040 Estero Blvd; tel 941/463-6139. 2 mi SE of beach on Fla 865. **Seafood/Steak.** A nautical, wood-furnished eatery with a relaxed atmosphere and a great view of the beach. The menu offers fresh seafood, prime beef, veal Oscar, and the special dish, chicken Skipper. **FYI:** Reservations not accepted. Children's menu. **Open:** Daily 4–10pm. **Prices:** Main courses $17–$24. AE, DISC, MC, V. 🖼 🗹 &

### Snug Harbor Waterfront Restaurant & Cafe

645 San Carlos Blvd; tel 941/463-8077. Under the high bridge. **Seafood/Steak.** This old favorite waterside eatery has been recently revitalized with a bright, white interior. The restaurant has lunch and dinner hours, but the Cafe, which huddles casually around the bar and spills onto the outdoor dock, serves the same menu continuously. The well-rounded menu includes sandwiches, seafood, steak, and pasta. **FYI:**

Reservations not accepted. Children's menu. **Open:** Daily 11:30am–2am. **Prices:** Main courses $12–$18. AE, DISC, MC, V. 🏛 🖼

# Fort Pierce

See also Jensen Beach, Port St Lucie, Stuart, Vero Beach

Haitians add spice to this southeastern coastal city of 164,000, founded in 1838 as an Army headquarters. Visitors come to bet on jai alai or dive shipwrecks in an underwater park. **Information:** St Lucie County Chamber of Commerce, 2200 Virginia Ave, Fort Pierce, 34982 (tel 561/595-9999).

## HOTEL 🏨

### 🛏 Econo Lodge

7050 Okeechobee Rd, PO Box 1, 34945; tel 561/465-8600 or toll free 800/424-4777. Exit 65 off I-95. A bare-bones pit stop for motorists, adequate for an overnight stay but otherwise charmless. **Rooms:** 60 rms. CI 2pm/CO 11am. Nonsmoking rms avail. **Amenities:** 🛁 A/C, cable TV w/movies. **Services:** 🛎 **Rates:** Peak (Dec–Apr) $55 S or D. Extra person $5. Children under age 18 stay free. Lower rates off-season. Parking: Outdoor, free. AE, DISC, MC, V.

## MOTELS

### 🛏🛏 Days Inn South Hutchinson Island

1920 Seaway Dr, 34949; tel 561/461-8737 or toll free 800/447-4732; fax 561/460-2218. 2½ mi E of US 1. Set on the Intracoastal Waterway, 350 feet from the beach. Units face pool, grounds, or Intracoastal. **Rooms:** 31 rms and stes. CI 2pm/CO 11am. Nonsmoking rms avail. **Amenities:** 🛁 A/C, cable TV w/movies. Some units w/terraces. **Facilities:** 🏊 & Washer/dryer. **Rates:** Peak (Dec–Apr) $95–$135 S or D; $107–$125 ste. Extra person $10. Children under age 13 stay free. Lower rates off-season. Parking: Outdoor, free. AE, CB, DC, DISC, JCB, MC, V.

### 🛏 Edgewater Motel and Apartments

1156 Seaway Dr, 34949; tel 561/468-3555 or toll free 800/433-0004. At Seaway Dr and Alhambra St. A plain mom-and-pop operation located on the inlet, with standard motel rooms and a few efficiencies or units with a separate bedroom and dining and living areas. Affiliated with the pricier Harbor Light Inn next door (see below). **Rooms:** 14 rms and effic. CI 1pm/CO 11am. Nonsmoking rms avail. **Amenities:** 🛁 A/C, cable TV, refrig. **Services:** 🛎 **Facilities:** 🏊 Whirlpool, washer/dryer. Boat dock available by reservation. **Rates:** Peak (Dec 20–Apr) $55 S or D; $65 effic. Extra person $10. Children under age 14 stay free. Min stay special events. Lower rates off-season. Parking: Outdoor, free. AE, DC, DISC, MC, V.

### 🛏 Harbor Light Inn

1160 Seaway Dr, 34949; tel 561/468-3555. Located on Fort Pierce Inlet, this low-key hotel with an appealing nautical theme is a good choice for boating and fishing enthusiasts, as it offers boat slips and a pier for fishing. **Rooms:** 21 rms and effic. CI 1pm/CO 11am. Nonsmoking rms avail. Simply decorated, adequate rooms. **Amenities:** 🛏 A/C, cable TV, refrig. Some units w/terraces. **Services:** 🛎 **Facilities:** 🦽 ♿ Whirlpool, washer/dryer. **Rates:** Peak (Dec 20–Apr) $95 S or D; $100 ste. Extra person $10. Children under age 14 stay free. Min stay special events. Lower rates off-season. Parking: Outdoor, free. AE, DC, DISC, MC, V.

## RESTAURANTS 🍴

### Captain's Galley
827 N Indian River Dr; tel 561/466-8495. **New American/Seafood.** Cheerful, colorful eatery offering such selections as blackened grouper and New York strip steak prepared to order. All entrees include soup or salad, potato or rice, and vegetables. **FYI:** Reservations not accepted. Children's menu. Beer and wine only. **Open:** Peak (Jan–Apr) Mon–Sat 7am–9pm, Sun 7am–noon. **Prices:** Main courses $10–$15. MC, V. 📷 ♿

### Mangrove Mattie's
1640 Seaway Dr; tel 561/466-1044. **American/Seafood.** An open, airy eatery with Casablanca-style ceiling fans and a jungle of plants. Menu specialties include baked mahimahi and prime rib. **FYI:** Reservations recommended. Children's menu. **Open:** Daily 11:30am–10pm. **Prices:** Main courses $13–$20. AE, DC, DISC, MC, V. 🖼 📷 ♿

### PV Martin's
5150 N FL A1A; tel 561/465-7300. **New American.** Most customers recommend reserving a window table at this lovely oceanfront restaurant. Menu highlights include leg of lamb, roast beef, and a selection of seafood dishes. The Friday night seafood buffet is a good value. **FYI:** Reservations recommended. Guitar. Children's menu. **Open:** Lunch Mon–Sat 11am–3:30pm; dinner Mon–Sat 5–10pm, Sun 3–10pm; brunch Sun 10:30am–2:30pm. **Prices:** Main courses $11–$20. AE, MC, V. 🖼 📷 ♿

### Sevenseas Restaurant
2041 Seaway Dr; tel 561/466-0311. **Seafood/Steak.** A lively, casual seafood restaurant at the ocean that's a popular hangout for locals. Outdoor diners are entertained by a live band. **FYI:** Reservations accepted. Big band. Beer and wine only. **Open:** Daily 11am–11pm. **Prices:** Main courses $6–$17. DISC, MC, V. 🍴

### Theo Thudpucker's Raw Bar & Seafood
2025 Seaway Dr; tel 561/465-1078. **Seafood/Steak.** A casual spot with interesting decor—the ceiling is covered with autographed money and a hanging alligator. Menu offerings include stuffed grouper, captain's platters, and a selection of daily specials. **FYI:** Reservations not accepted. Beer and wine only. **Open:** Mon–Thurs 11:30am–9:30pm, Fri–Sat 11:30am–11pm, Sun 1–9:30pm. **Prices:** Main courses $9–$24. MC, V.

## ATTRACTIONS 📷

### Underwater Demolition Team–SEAL Museum
3300 N FL A1A; tel 561/489-3597 or 595-1570. This tribute to the US Navy Underwater Demolition Team and their successors, the SEAL (sea, air, and land) teams, is located in Pepper Park on Hutchinson Island, where the first "frogmen" began their training. Dioramas trace the history of these naval commandos; exhibits show diving gear, weapons, and other equipment used. **Open:** Tues–Sat 10am–4pm, Sun noon–4pm. $

### Fort Pierce Inlet State Recreation Area
905 Shorewinds Dr; tel 561/468-4007. This park located off FL A1A consists of 343 ocean-fronted acres, offering swimming, fishing, and nature trails. $$

# Fort Walton Beach

See also Destin, Niceville

Once a Confederate outpost, today a resort town of 22,000 on Florida's northern Gulf coast. Indian Temple Mound Museum recalls centuries past. Catamarans fly at the Hog's Breath Hobie Regatta in May. Grayton Beach and Seaside are part of the Beaches of South Walton district. **Information:** Fort Walton Beach Chamber of Commerce, 34 Miracle Strip Pkwy, PO Drawer 640, Fort Walton Beach, 32549 (tel 904/244-8191).

## HOTELS 🏨

### 🏖 Carousel Beach Resort
571 Santa Rosa Blvd, 32548; tel 904/243-7658 or toll free 800/523-0208; fax 904/244-4330. 1 mi S of US 98. Noteworthy for beachfront rooms that offer great views of the ocean and dunes—just as well since most of the rooms themselves are nothing to look at, although ongoing post-hurricane renovations may bring improvements. Strict management policy contains several caveats; ask about them before reserving. **Rooms:** 105 rms, stes, and effic. CI 2pm/CO 11am. Nonsmoking rms avail. **Amenities:** 🛏 ♿ A/C, cable TV, refrig. All units w/terraces. **Services:** 🛎 🛎 Babysitting. **Facilities:** 🦽 ♿ 1 bar (w/entertainment), 1 beach (ocean), lifeguard, washer/dryer. **Rates:** Peak (Mar–Sept 6) $75–$90 S or D; $110–$180 ste; $95–$105 effic. Extra person $10. Children under age 12 stay free. Lower rates off-season. Parking: Outdoor, free. AE, DC, DISC, MC, V.

### 🏖 Marina Bay Resort
80 Miracle Strip Pkwy (US 98), 32548; tel 904/244-5132; fax 904/244-0491. A waterside hotel (facing an inlet rather than the Gulf) with enough activities to keep a family occupied. **Rooms:** 120 effic. CI 3pm/CO 10am. Nonsmoking rms avail. Lodgings are plain-jane but well-equipped. **Amenities:** 🛏 A/C, cable TV. Some units w/terraces. **Services:** 🛎 🛎 Babysitting. **Facilities:** 🦽 🚲 💯 ♿ 1 restaurant, 1 bar

(w/entertainment), basketball, volleyball, games rm, lawn games, whirlpool, washer/dryer. Dull dining room. **Rates:** Peak (May 23–Sept 2) $59–$119 effic. Children under age 18 stay free. Min stay peak. Lower rates off-season. Parking: Outdoor, free. AE, CB, DC, DISC, MC, V.

## INN

### ⊟⊟⊟⊟ Josephine's French Country Inn
101 Seaside Ave, PO Box 4767, Seaside, 32459 (Beaches of South Walton); tel 904/231-1940 or toll free 800/848-1840. Exit C-30A off US 98. Meticulously decorated rooms in a Victorian-inspired manor house and nearby guest houses. Unsuitable for children under 12. **Rooms:** 11 rms and stes. CI 4pm/CO 11am. No smoking. Furnished with period reproductions and a few antiques. **Amenities:** 🛏 🔥 ▣ A/C, cable TV, refrig, VCR. All units w/terraces, all w/fireplaces. All rooms have microwaves. **Services:** 🚐 🔔 **Facilities:** 🚲 🛎 & 1 restaurant (bkfst and dinner only), guest lounge w/TV. **Rates (BB):** $130–$190 D; $195–$225 ste. Extra person $20. Parking: Outdoor, free. Senior and government discounts avail. MC, V.

## RESORT

### ⊟⊟⊟⊟ Seaside Cottage Rental Agency
County Rd 30A and Quincy Circle, PO Box 4730, Seaside, 32459; tel 904/231-1320 or toll free 800/277-TOWN; fax 904/231-2219. Off US 98 and follow the three-umbrellas signs to Seaside. 78 acres. Walking and biking outstrip cars as the preferred mode of transport in this all-inclusive resort community. Restaurants, concerts, shopping, and art galleries all lie within a 10-minute walk of your cottage, suite, or motel-style room. And, of course, that stunning white beach lies at the end of the boardwalk at the foot of the Gulf of Mexico. **Rooms:** 26 rms and stes; 244 cottages/villas. Executive level. CI 4pm/CO 11am. Nonsmoking rms avail. Accommodations range from the funky 1950's-style Motor Court to the luxuriously furnished Classic Cottages. Most units are individually owned, so each reflects the owner's preferences and tastes. All units have balconies with Gulf views, private patios, or wrapped porches with large porch swings and rocking chairs. **Amenities:** 🛏 🔥 ▣ A/C, cable TV, refrig, VCR, CD/tape player. All units w/terraces, some w/fireplaces, some w/whirlpools. Classic Cottage rentals include daily housekeeping and nightly turndown service, continental breakfast delivered to cottage, fresh flowers, welcome basket (with wine), and butler service. **Services:** ✕ 🛎 🚐 🖥 🔔 🐾 Twice-daily maid svce, social director, children's program, babysitting. **Facilities:** 🍴 🚲 △ 🔲 🎿 🐾⁶ 🛶 100 & 5 restaurants, 2 bars (1 w/entertainment), 1 beach (ocean), basketball, volleyball, board surfing, lawn games, snorkeling, playground, washer/dryer. Lawn games and beach service in season. **Rates:** Peak (May 22–Aug 21) $125 S or D; $150–$225 ste; $205–$925 cottage/villa. Min stay special events.

Lower rates off-season. Parking: Outdoor, free. Security deposit of $200 plus a $10 non-refundable processing fee. Extended-stay discounts avail. AE, DC, DISC, MC, V.

## RESTAURANTS 🍴

### Bud & Alley's Restaurant
County Rd 30A, Seaside; tel 904/231-5900. Off US 98. **Mediterranean/Southern.** Seaside's first restaurant (opened in 1986) is still number one to its steady patrons. In addition to its own herb garden and wine cellar, Bud & Alley's now has a gazebo on the Gulf and open-air rooftop dining with live jazz under the stars throughout the summer. The menu varies depending on availability and freshness of ingredients, but will usually include an eclectic selection of Italian and continental dishes, and the freshest local seafood. **FYI:** Reservations recommended. Jazz. No smoking. **Open:** Peak (June–Aug) lunch Wed–Mon 11:30am–3pm; dinner Sun–Thurs 6–9:30pm, Fri–Sat 6–10pm. Closed Nov–Dec. **Prices:** Main courses $15–$20. MC, V. 🏞

### ♣ Criolla's
170 E County Rd 30A, Grayton Beach; tel 904/267-1267. Off US 98. **Caribbean/Eclectic.** Chef Johnny Earles calls his dishes "Contemporary Equatorial," which can be anything from grilled-tenderloin chili between layers of masa steamed in banana leaves to cobia *arroz con gandules* (grilled cobia with pigeon peas and rice, red chile soffrito, roast corn and green chile mofongo, and rock shrimp–scallion salsa verde). The Caribbean-inspired decor fits the food; there's also an extensive wine list. **FYI:** Reservations recommended. No smoking. **Open:** Peak (Jan 15–Nov) Mon–Sat 5:30–10pm. Closed Dec–mid-Jan. **Prices:** Main courses $20–$27. DISC, MC, V. &

### Shades
Seaside Center, Seaside; tel 904/231-1950. **American.** In another life, this was a rustic house built in the small town of Chattahoochee at the turn of the century. Some 70 years later, it was moved here to Seaside and reborn as this quaint eatery. The menu offers basic fare: stacked-high sandwiches, spicy chicken wings, burgers, and fried seafood platters. There are 61 types of beer to wash it all down. Live music on the outdoor deck in summer. **FYI:** Reservations not accepted. Rock. Children's menu. Beer and wine only. **Open:** Daily 7am–10pm. Closed 2 weeks in Jan. **Prices:** Main courses $5–$17. MC, V. &

## ATTRACTIONS 📷

### US Air Force Armament Museum
Eglin Air Force Base; tel 904/882-4189. Displays include reconnaisance, fighter, and bomber planes; a fighter-cockpit simulator; and a collection of war films, photographs, rockets, bombs, and missiles. **Open:** Daily 9:30am–4:30pm. **Free**

### Indian Temple Mound and Museum
139 SE Miracle Strip Pkwy (US 98); tel 904/243-6521. One of the largest ceremonial mounds ever discovered near

saltwater, dating back to around AD 1400. The adjacent museum houses artifacts testifying to 12,000 years of Native American settlement of the Choctawhatchee Bay region. **Open:** Peak (June–Aug) Mon–Sat 9am–4pm. Reduced hours off-season. **$**

### Focus Center

139 Brooks St; tel 904/664-1261. A hands-on museum with over 250 exhibits which explore various subjects in the world of science. Topics include the Human Body, Physics, "Bubblology," and much more. Geared for children of all ages. **Open:** Peak (June–Aug) daily 1–5pm. Reduced hours off-season. **$**

### Gulfarium

1010 Miracle Strip Pkwy SE (US 98); tel 904/244-5169. One of the nation's original marine parks, featuring dolphin, sea lion, and scuba diving shows. Other exhibits showcase gray seals, otters, alligators, Ridley turtles, penguins, tropical birds, and numerous fish. **Open:** Daily 9am–sunset. **$$$$**

### Eden State Gardens and Mansion

Point Washington; tel 904/231-4214. The white-columned, two-story Wesley Mansion contains period architectural details and is furnished with 18th-century antiques, among other items. The mansion stands amid huge moss-draped oaks, and the gardens are filled with azaleas, camellias, and other typical Southern flowers. Mansion tours given hourly Thurs–Mon 9am–4pm. **Open:** Park, daily 8am–sunset. **$**

### Grayton Beach State Recreation Area

357 Main Park Rd, Santa Rosa Beach; tel 904/231-4210. Part of the Beaches of South Walton district, this outstanding park has a self-guided, 1.5-mile nature trail that traverses salt marsh, 40-foot-high sand dunes, and natural Florida scrub. The park also contains pine forests and the scenic Western Lake, with boat ramp. Swimming, fishing, camping, and picnicking permitted. **Open:** Daily 8am–sunset. **$$**

# Fruitland Park

## ATTRACTION 🏛

### Lake Griffin State Recreation Area

3089 US 441/27; tel 352/787-7402. This 427-acre park encompasses mostly floating marsh and islands. Fishing, boating, canoe rentals, camping, nature trails. **$$**

# Gainesville

University of Florida students constitute half of this city's 35,000 residents. Sights include outstanding natural history and art museums plus the Fred Bear Museum, dedicated to archery since prehistoric times. **Information:** Gainesville Area Chamber of Commerce, 300 E University Ave, PO Box 1187, Gainesville, 32602 (tel 352/334-7100).

## HOTELS 🏨

### ≡≡ Holiday Inn University Center

1250 W University Ave, 32601; tel 352/376-1661 or toll free 800/HOL-IDAY; fax 352/336-8717. Exit 76 off I-75. At NW 13th St. This well-kept hotel is centrally located and within walking distance to the University of Florida. **Rooms:** 167 rms and stes. Executive level. CI 2pm/CO noon. Nonsmoking rms avail. **Amenities:** 🛋 🦮 🎙 A/C, cable TV w/movies. **Services:** ✕ 🚗 🖼 🛎 Car-rental desk. **Facilities:** 🛗 📷450 🦽 1 restaurant, 1 bar. **Rates:** Peak (Aug–Dec) $85 S or D; $106 ste. Extra person $7. Children under age 18 stay free. Min stay special events. Lower rates off-season. Parking: Indoor/outdoor, free. AE, CB, DC, DISC, MC, V.

### ≡≡ Radisson Hotel

2900 SW 13th St, 32608; tel 352/377-4000 or toll free 800/344-5866; fax 352/371-1159. Exit 74 off I-75, 2 mi NE on US 331, then ½ mi N on US 441. This hotel, located on a scenic wildlife preserve, caters to the business traveler. **Rooms:** 197 rms and stes. CI 3pm/CO noon. Nonsmoking rms avail. **Amenities:** 🛋 🦮 A/C, cable TV w/movies. All units w/terraces. **Services:** ✕ 🚗 🖼 🛎 Car-rental desk, babysitting. **Facilities:** 🛗 📷1000 🦽 1 restaurant, 1 bar (w/entertainment), washer/dryer. **Rates (BB):** $79 S or D; $159 ste. Min stay special events. Parking: Outdoor, free. AE, DC, DISC, JCB, MC, V.

### ≡≡ Residence Inn by Marriott

4001 SW 13th St, 32608; tel 352/371-2101 or toll free 800/331-3131; fax 352/371-2101. Exit 74 off I-75. 2 mi NE on US 331. For the more independent traveler who desires a complete home-like atmosphere in overnight or extended stay lodging. **Rooms:** 80 rms, stes, and effic. CI 3pm/CO noon. Nonsmoking rms avail. Self-contained units vary in size from studios to large suites with separate bedrooms. **Amenities:** 🛋 🦮 🎙 A/C, cable TV w/movies, refrig. All units w/fireplaces, some w/whirlpools. **Services:** 🖼 🛎 🛍 **Facilities:** 🛗 📷30 🦽 Basketball, volleyball, whirlpool, washer/dryer. **Rates (CP):** $99 S; $125 D; $99–$125 effic. Min stay special events. Parking: Outdoor, free. AE, CB, DC, DISC, MC, V.

## MOTELS

### ≡≡ Cabot Lodge

3726 SW 40th Blvd, 32608; tel 352/375-2400 or toll free 800/843-8735; fax 352/335-2321. Exit 75 off I-75. A relaxing, home-like atmosphere. The comfortable atrium with central fireplace, antler chandeliers, and unique wooden end tables is the perfect place to unwind. **Rooms:** 208 rms. Executive level. CI 3pm/CO 11am. Nonsmoking rms avail. **Amenities:** 🛋 🦮 A/C, cable TV w/movies. Some units w/terraces. **Services:** 🖼 🛎 Babysitting. Evening activities include a two-hour cocktail reception with popcorn. **Facilities:** 🛗

[50] & 1 bar. **Rates (CP):** $66–$81 S or D. Extra person $7. Min stay special events. Parking: Outdoor, free. AE, DC, DISC, MC, V.

### 🏳🏳 Fairfield Inn
6901 NW 4th Blvd, 32607; tel 352/332-8292 or toll free 800/228-2800; fax 352/332-8292. Exit 76 off I-75. Modest accommodations; friendly atmosphere. **Rooms:** 135 rms. CI 3pm/CO noon. Nonsmoking rms avail. **Amenities:** 🔟 🐾 A/C, cable TV w/movies, dataport. **Services:** 🛎 🍴 🐾 **Facilities:** 🏊 & **Rates (CP):** $45–$48 S; $55–$57 D. Extra person $3. Children under age 18 stay free. Min stay wknds and special events. Parking: Outdoor, free. AE, DC, DISC, MC, V.

### 🏳🏳🏳 Holiday Inn West
7417 NW 8th Ave, 32605; tel 352/332-7500 or toll free 800/551-8206; fax 352/332-0487. Exit 76 off I-75. Very well-preserved establishment built in the 1970s but with modern guest-room decor and ample meeting facilities. **Rooms:** 280 rms. CI 3pm/CO noon. Nonsmoking rms avail. Bathrooms are in need of renovation. **Amenities:** 🔟 🐾 A/C, cable TV w/movies, dataport, voice mail. **Services:** ✗ 🛎 🍴 Babysitting. **Facilities:** 🏊 [450] 1 restaurant, 1 bar (w/entertainment), washer/dryer. **Rates:** Peak (Feb 16–May 19/Sept–Nov) $89–$139 S or D. Extra person $7. Children under age 18 stay free. Min stay special events. Lower rates off-season. Parking: Outdoor, free. AE, CB, DC, DISC, ER, JCB, MC, V.

### 🏳🏳 Howard Johnson Lodge
7400 NW 8th Ave, 32605; tel 352/332-3200 or toll free 800/IGO-HOJO; fax 352/332-5500. Exit 76 off I-75. With its convenient location, this is an acceptable choice for long or short stays, business or pleasure. **Rooms:** 64 rms. CI 2pm/CO noon. Nonsmoking rms avail. **Amenities:** 🔟 🐾 A/C, cable TV w/movies. Some units w/terraces. **Services:** 🍴 🐾 **Facilities:** 🏊 & Playground, washer/dryer. **Rates:** Peak (Sept–Dec) $30–$38 S; $33–$45 D. Children under age 18 stay free. Min stay special events. Lower rates off-season. Parking: Outdoor, free. AE, DC, DISC, MC, V.

### 🏳 La Quinta Inn
920 NW 69th Terrace, 32605; tel 352/332-6466 or toll free 800/591-5900; fax 352/332-7074. Exit 76 off I-75. Economical lodging without frills or fanfare. **Rooms:** 134 rms and stes. CI 3pm/CO noon. Nonsmoking rms avail. **Amenities:** 🔟 🐾 A/C, cable TV w/movies. Some units w/terraces. **Services:** 🛎 🍴 🐾 **Facilities:** 🏊 [50] & **Rates (CP):** Peak (Aug–Nov) $60–$84 S or D; $95–$107 ste. Extra person $10. Children under age 18 stay free. Min stay special events. Lower rates off-season. Parking: Outdoor, free. AE, CB, DC, DISC, EC, MC, V.

### RESTAURANT 🍽
**Sovereign**
12 SE 2nd Ave; tel 352/378-6307. Exit 76 off I-75. **Continental.** An attractive, romantic restaurant housed in a converted carriage barn. Menu options range from fresh floun-

der to beef Wellington; choose the white-chocolate cheesecake as a postscript. **FYI:** Reservations recommended. Piano. **Open:** Mon–Thurs 5:30–10pm, Fri–Sat 5:30–11pm. Closed Aug 7–21. **Prices:** Main courses $15–$27. AE, CB, DC, MC, V. ❤

### ATTRACTIONS 🏛
**Samuel P Harn Museum of Art**
SW 34th St at Hull Rd; tel 352/392-9826. Located on the University of Florida campus, this is one of the largest of Florida's art museums. Exhibitions in 1997 will include contemporary American landscape painting, traditional African art, photography, and American craft. **Open:** Tues–Fri 11am–5pm, Sat 10am–5pm. **Free**

**Fred Bear Museum**
4600 SW 41st Blvd (Fred Bear Dr); tel 352/376-2411. This natural history museum exhibits ancient archery and bowhunting artifacts, including a broadhead arrow tip dating from 2700 BC. On display are more than 100 mounted animals, as well as Native American artwork. **Open:** Wed–Sun 10am–6pm. **$$**

**Marjorie Kinnan Rawlings State Historic Site**
County Rd 325, Hawthorne; tel 352/466-3672. This typical 1930s Florida farmstead located 11 miles south of Gainesville was the home of the Pulitzer Prize–winning author of *The Yearling* and *Cross Creek*. Tours include the house and the surrounding citrus grove and are limited to 10 persons per tour. Thurs–Sun, tours at 10 and 11 am, and on the hour 1–4pm. Closed Aug–Sept and some hols. **$**

# Grayton Beach
See Fort Walton Beach

# Gulf Breeze
This town of 6,000 occupies an island south of Pensacola in Florida's far western Panhandle. The town itself offers a combination zoo and botanical gardens; a toll bridge leads further south to picnic and camping areas within Gulf Islands National Seashore. **Information:** Gulf Breeze Area Chamber of Commerce, PO Box 337, Gulf Breeze, 32562 (tel 904/932-7888).

### HOTEL 🏨
### 🏳🏳 Holiday Inn Bay Beach
51 Gulf Breeze Pkwy, 32561; tel 904/932-2214 or toll free 800/HOLIDAY; fax 904/932-0932. Chase St exit off I-10. Pleasant hotel with beautiful scenic bay views. **Rooms:** 168 rms. CI 3pm/CO 11am. Nonsmoking rms avail. Eight bay-view rooms are extra large and have superior views. **Amenities:** 🔟 🐾 A/C, cable TV w/movies. All units w/ter-

races. **Services:** ✗ 🚐 🖼 🎧 Complimentary cocktails served Mon–Thurs 5–7pm. **Facilities:** 🎣 🛏150 1 restaurant, 1 beach (bay), washer/dryer. **Rates:** Peak (Apr 28–Sept 9) $69–$89 S or D. Extra person $10. Children under age 18 stay free. Min stay peak. Lower rates off-season. Parking: Outdoor, free. AE, DC, MC, V.

## RESTAURANT 🍽

### Chris' Seafood Grille
47 Gulf Breeze Pkwy; tel 904/934-3500. Beaches exit off I-110. **Seafood/Steak.** There's no better place in the area to watch the sun sink slowly into the bay than from the decks at Chris'. With deliciously prepared fresh seafood and an atmosphere that caters to both families and couples, Chris' is a year-round favorite. **FYI:** Reservations accepted. Children's menu. Beer and wine only. **Open:** Peak (Mar–Oct) Wed–Mon 11am–9:30pm, Sun 11am–2:30pm. **Prices:** Main courses $6–$17. AE, CB, DC, DISC, MC, V. 🏔 🍷

## ATTRACTIONS 🖼

### The ZOO
5701 Gulf Breeze Pkwy; tel 904/932-2229. More than 700 animals make their home within this 50-acre zoo and botanical garden, not the least of which is Colossus, one of the largest gorillas in captivity. The Safari Line, a 20-minute miniature train tour through a wildlife preserve, allows visitors a look at free-roaming animals. The giraffe feeding tower allows guests a rare face-to-face meeting. Elephant shows and elephant rides; petting zoo. Restaurant and snack shop. **Open:** Daily 9am–5pm. **$$$**

### Gulf Islands National Seashore
1801 Gulf Breeze Pkwy; tel 904/934-2600. Established in 1971, the protected beach area actually stretches from Gulfport, Mississippi to Destin, Florida, providing a natural environment for at least 280 different species of birds. Pristine white sand beaches and rolling sand dunes await visitors, who can enjoy swimming, boating, fishing, picnicking, camping, and ranger-led walks. The seashore area also contains Fort Pickens and Fort Barrancas (see below) as well as other historic fortifications on the grounds of the Naval Air Station. **Open:** Daily sunrise–sunset. **$$**

### Fort Barrancas
Tel 904/455-5167. Located on the grounds of the Naval Air Station. Originally built by the Spanish in the 16th century and later fortified by the British in the 19th century, the fort has been authentically restored and preserved. Visitors can stroll nature trails and picnic in the surrounding area. Guided tours available. **Open:** Peak (Apr–Oct) daily 9:30am–5pm. Reduced hours off-season. **Free**

### Fort Pickens
Tel 904/934-2600. Located across the bay from Fort Barrancas at the western tip of Santa Rosa Island are the substantial remains of this slave-built fort. Dating from the 1830s, it was meant to protect Pensacola from seaborne attack. Chief Geronimo was imprisoned here during the 1880s along with a group of fellow Apaches. A small museum details the history of the structure, as well as the flora and fauna of the national seashore area. Guided tours available. **Free**

# Haines City

See also Davenport

Smack in the middle of the state's foremost citrus-growing area, this town of 12,000 doubles in population with Northern retirees during winter. Great fresh-water fishing at myriad lakes. Baseball's Kansas City Royals train at Baseball City Stadium, 10 miles north of town on US 27. **Information:** Haines City Chamber of Commerce, 908 US 27 N, PO Box 986, Haines City, 33845 (tel 941/422-3751).

## RESORT 🏨

### ⬛⬛⬛ Grenelefe Golf and Tennis Resort
3200 State Rd 546, 33844; tel 941/422-7511 or toll free 800/237-9549; fax 941/421-5000. 6 mi E of Haines City. 1,000 acres. A villa resort that's a golfer's paradise. The modern facilities sparkle and the extensive grounds are expertly manicured. **Rooms:** 400 stes; 500 cottages/villas. CI 3pm/CO 11am. Nonsmoking rms avail. Each villa is fully equipped with kitchen and views of the fairways. **Amenities:** 🛁 🍽 A/C, cable TV w/movies, refrig. All units w/terraces. **Services:** ✗ 🍷 VP 🖼 🎧 Car-rental desk, masseur, babysitting. **Facilities:** 🎣 🚲 🏊 ▶54 🎾 🏐11 🏌9 ⛳ 🏌1600 💻 ♿ 3 restaurants, 1 bar (w/entertainment), games rm, lawn games, spa, sauna, whirlpool, playground, washer/dryer. Lake, nature trails. Miniature golf. **Rates:** Peak (Feb–Apr) $180–$300 ste; $220 cottage/villa. Extra person $20. Children under age 18 stay free. Lower rates off-season. AP and MAP rates avail. Parking: Outdoor, free. AE, MC, V.

# Highland Beach

See Delray Beach

# Hollywood

See also Hollywood Beach

Large numbers of French Canadians winter in this city of 124,000, on the ocean south of Fort Lauderdale. Visitors may choose to sample Seminole culture, play bingo, or explore the shops along the three-mile boardwalk. **Information:** Greater Hollywood Chamber of Commerce, 4000 Hollywood Blvd # 265-S, Hollywood, 33021 (tel 954/985-4000).

## HOTEL 🛏

### ≝≝≝ Holiday Inn

2905 Sheridan St at I-95, 33020; tel 954/925-9100 or toll free 800/480-7623; fax 954/925-5512. Exit 24 off I-95. This recently built hotel caters to a business clientele but emphasizes its resort-like grounds with innovative landscaping. **Rooms:** 150 rms and stes. Executive level. CI 3pm/CO noon. Nonsmoking rms avail. Large, bright and smartly decorated rooms. **Amenities:** 🛏 ⚴ 🍽 A/C, cable TV w/movies, dataport, voice mail. Some units w/terraces. **Services:** ✕ 🖙 🚐 🖂 ↵ Car-rental desk, social director, babysitting. **Facilities:** 🛁 🛎 🏊 🖵 ⚵ 1 restaurant, 1 bar, spa, whirlpool. **Rates:** Peak (Dec–Apr) $135 S or D; $175–$225 ste. Extra person $10. Children under age 18 stay free. Lower rates off-season. Parking: Outdoor, free. AE, CB, DC, DISC, MC, V.

## RESTAURANTS 🍴

### ★ Martha's

6024 N Ocean Dr; tel 954/923-5444. At the foot of the Dania Beach Blvd bridge. **American.** A comfortable eatery with views of the Intracoastal Waterway through floor-to-ceiling windows. The menu includes pancooked Florida snapper and grilled tuna. Sitting atop Martha's is Martha's Tropical Grill, featuring "Floribbean" fare with a changing menu appealing to a younger crowd. **FYI:** Reservations recommended. Big band. Children's menu. Dress code. **Open:** Lunch Mon–Sat 11:30am–3:30pm; dinner Mon–Thurs 4pm–midnight, Fri–Sat 4pm–1am; brunch Sun 11am–3pm. **Prices:** Main courses $15–$38. AE, CB, DC, DISC, MC, V. 💟 🏞 💟 🆅🅿 ⚵

### Wan's Mandarin House

In Sheridan Park Plaza, 3331 Sheridan St; tel 954/963-6777. 1 mile W of I-95. **Chinese.** Basic Chinese eatery serving traditional Szechuan cuisine. The lunch combination specials, which include selections like honey-garlic chicken and chicken curry, are both delightful and a good value. Food can be ordered spicy hot or mild. **FYI:** Reservations accepted. **Open:** Mon–Thurs 11:30am–10pm, Fri–Sat 11:30am–10:30pm, Sun 1–10pm. **Prices:** Main courses $8–$18. AE, DISC, MC, V. ⚵

## ATTRACTION 🏛

### Graves Museum of Archeology & Natural History

481 S Federal Hwy; tel 954/925-7770. Features artifacts of the Maya, the Inca, and the Aztec such as pottery, metals, and textiles. Egyptian temple replica; tribal masks, wood carvings, and textiles from Africa; tools and fossils from prehistoric Florida. **Open:** Tues–Sat 10am–4pm, Sun 1–4pm. **$$**

# Hollywood Beach

## HOTELS 🛏

### ≝≝ Holiday Inn SunSpree Resort

2711 S Ocean Dr, 33019; tel 954/923-8700 or toll free 800/237-4667; fax 954/923-7059. ½ mi N of Hallandale Beach Blvd. On a clean stretch of beach, it has remade itself since changing owners and sports a new look. **Rooms:** 200 rms and effic. CI 4pm/CO 11am. Nonsmoking rms avail. Rooms overlook the pool and ocean. **Amenities:** 🛏 ⚴ 🍽 A/C, cable TV w/movies, refrig. Some units w/terraces. **Services:** ✕ 🆅🅿 🖂 ↵ Car-rental desk, social director, children's program, babysitting. **Facilities:** 🛁 🛎 🏖 ⚵ 1 restaurant, 1 bar (w/entertainment), 1 beach (ocean), games rm, playground, washer/dryer. Children under 12 eat free in restaurant. **Rates:** Peak (Dec–Apr) $149–$209 S or D; $169–$229 effic. Extra person $10. Lower rates off-season. Parking: Outdoor, free. AE, DC, DISC, MC, V.

### ≝≝≝ Hollywood Beach Resort Hotel

101 N Ocean Dr, Hollywood, 33019; tel 954/921-0990 or toll free 800/331-6103; fax 954/920-9480. Exit 24 off I-95. Dating back to 1925, this historic oceanfront art deco hotel was recently renovated. **Rooms:** 360 stes and effic. Executive level. CI 4pm/CO 11am. Nonsmoking rms avail. Floral and rattan decor throughout. **Amenities:** 🛏 ⚴ 🍽 A/C, cable TV, refrig, in-rm safe. Some units w/terraces. All units include full kitchens. **Services:** 🖙 🆅🅿 🚐 🖂 ↵ Masseur. **Facilities:** 🛁 🚲 ⛰ 🎱 🎿 ⚓ 🐟 🛎 🏖 🖵 ⚵ 2 restaurants, 2 bars (w/entertainment), 1 beach (ocean), lifeguard, volleyball, board surfing, games rm, racquetball, snorkeling, spa, sauna, whirlpool, beauty salon, playground, washer/dryer. **Rates:** Peak (Dec 22–Apr 17) $190–$210 ste; $104–$142 effic. Children under age 18 stay free. Min stay special events. Lower rates off-season. Parking: Outdoor, $6/day. AE, CB, DC, DISC, MC, V.

## ATTRACTION 🏛

### Hollywood Beach Boardwalk

Hollywood. This paved beach path runs from Sheridan St to Georgia St. It is 3 miles long and 27 feet wide, and is packed with retirement-age residents and French Canadian tourists who take their daily strolls past the path's gift shops, cafes, and restaurants. The boardwalk also has a bicycling lane and in-line skate rentals.

# Homestead

After Hurricane Andrew's direct hit in April 1992, this city (and its namesake Air Force base) has been on the rebound. Highlights include the hand-built Coral Castle and Biscayne Underwater National Park (9 mi E of town). **Information:**

Greater Homestead–Florida City Chamber of Commerce, 43 N Krome Ave, Historic Old Town Hall, Homestead, 33030 (tel 305/247-2332).

## REFRESHMENT STOP ▽

### Robert Is Here Fruit Stand & Farm
19200 SW 344th St; tel 305/246-1592. **Fruit Stand.** Wide selection of fresh fruits and vegetables as well as freshly canned goods. Fresh fruit milkshakes come in a variety of flavors, from key lime to strawberry. **Open:** Peak (Dec–Apr) daily 8am–7pm. No CC.

## ATTRACTIONS 🖼

### Coral Castle
28655 S Dixie Hwy; tel 305/248-6344. This roofless, prehistoric-looking structure was carved out of massive slabs of coral rock by one man over the course of 20 years. The solitary Latvian immigrant used handmade tools to fashion chairs, tables, and beds for his home, and even constructed a nine-ton gate that you can swivel with just a finger! **Open:** Daily 9am–6pm. $$$

### Orchid Jungle
26715 SW 157th Ave; tel 305/247-1990. One of the world's largest outdoor orchid gardens showcasing a wide variety of rare tropical flora, including rare palms. Many varieties are offered for sale, and there is a gift shop. **Open:** Daily 10am–5pm. $$

### Preston B Bird/Mary Heinlein Fruit & Spice Park
24801 SW 187th Ave; tel 305/247-5727. This 30-acre living plant museum shows off more than 200 species of tropical plants and 500 varieties of fruits, nuts, and spices from around the world. A shop sells dried and canned fruits and spices, horticultural supplies, and books. **Open:** Daily 10am–5pm. $

### Biscayne National Underwater Park
9700 SW 328th St; tel 305/230-7275. This is America's largest underwater park; only 10 percent of its 181,500 acres are above the surface. On dry land is a visitor center, which has exhibits, videos, and a slide presentation. A boardwalk connects the mainland with a rock jetty, from which fishing is permitted. A three-hour glass-bottom boat tour departs at 10am for a trip out to the coral reef and its colorful variety of marine life, and a snorkeling and scuba diving expedition departs at 1:30pm (fees required). Reservations are recommended for all tours; phone 230-1100 for further details. **Open:** Daily 8am–5:30pm. **Free**

# Homosassa

About 2,000 permanent residents inhabit this Citrus County town in northwest peninsular Florida. Most outsiders come for Homosassa Springs, a state park with an awesome underwater observatory.

## HOTEL 🏨

### ≡≡ Ramada Inn Homosassa
4076 S Suncoast Blvd, 34448; tel 352/628-4311; fax 352/628-4311. A restful spot on a busy commercial strip. The lobby has two antique automobiles. Good for children. **Rooms:** 105 rms and stes. CI 3pm/CO 11am. Nonsmoking rms avail. **Amenities:** 🖥 A/C, cable TV. Some units w/terraces. **Services:** ✗ ⬭ ⬭ **Facilities:** 🖼 🏓 🗲2 ⛺30 ⬭ 1 restaurant, 1 bar, games rm, playground. **Rates:** Peak (Dec–Mar) $69–$79 S or D; $179–$200 ste. Extra person $10. Children under age 12 stay free. Lower rates off-season. Parking: Outdoor, free. DC, DISC, MC, V.

## MOTEL

### ≡≡ Riverside Inn Resort
FL 490, PO Box 258, 34487; tel 352/628-2474 or toll free 800/442-2040; fax 352/628-5208. Family-operated local staple. **Rooms:** 79 rms and effic. CI 4pm/CO 11am. Nonsmoking rms avail. Deluxe riverside rooms. **Amenities:** 🖥 A/C, TV. **Services:** ⬭ ⬭ **Facilities:** 🖼 ⛰ 🏓 🗲2 ⛺150 ⬭ 1 restaurant, 1 bar (w/entertainment), games rm, snorkeling, washer/dryer. **Rates:** $69–$79 S or D; $89 effic. Extra person $7. Children under age 12 stay free. Min stay wknds. Parking: Outdoor, free. AE, CB, DC, DISC, MC, V.

## ATTRACTION 🖼

### Fort Cooper State Park
3100 S Old Floral City Rd, Inverness; tel 352/726-0315. This 700-acre day-use park sits on the site of Fort Cooper, which was built during the Second Seminole War; one wall of the fort has been reconstructed. Canoe and paddleboat rentals are available. Swimming, fishing, camping, nature trails. **Open:** Peak (May–Aug) daily 8am–sunset. Reduced hours off-season. $

# Indialantic

Linked to the southeast Florida mainland by a bridge from Melbourne, this beach town is home to about 2,900 people. FL A1A is the main drag, bisecting the long, narrow island between the Atlantic and the Indian River.

## HOTELS 🏨

### ≡≡ Holiday Inn–Melbourne Oceanfront
2605 N FL A1A, 32903; tel 407/777-4100 or toll free 800/HOLIDAY; fax 407/773-6132. Double-tower oceanfront property, perfectly suitable for beachgoers. **Rooms:** 299 rms and stes. CI 4pm/CO noon. Nonsmoking rms avail. **Amenities:** 🖥 🐾 🖵 A/C, cable TV w/movies. Some units w/terraces. **Services:** ✗ 🖛 ⓋⓅ 🚗 ⬭ ⬭ ⬭ Children's program, babysitting. **Facilities:** 🖼 🗲6 ⛺600 ⬭ 1 restaurant, 2 bars (w/entertainment), 1 beach (ocean), lawn games, whirlpool, washer/dryer. Pool receives some shade from the

hotel's towers. **Rates:** Peak (Feb–Apr/June–Aug) $110–$130 S or D; $170 ste. Children under age 18 stay free. Lower rates off-season. Parking: Outdoor, free. AE, CB, DC, DISC, JCB, MC, V.

### ▤▤▤ Melbourne Beach Hilton Oceanfront

3003 N FL A1A, 32903; tel 407/777-5000 or toll free 800/624-0073; fax 407/777-3713. This high-rise set on pretty landscaped grounds stands head and shoulders above other hotels on the beach, both literally and figuratively. The snazzy architecture is a welcome change from most humdrum beach offerings. **Rooms:** 118 rms and stes. CI 3pm/CO noon. Nonsmoking rms avail. **Amenities:** 📧 🕭 📺 A/C, cable TV w/movies. All units w/terraces. **Services:** ✗ ⬜ 🛎 Children's program. Water sports rentals available on beach through independent vendor. **Facilities:** 🛥 🚲 ⛱ 📺 350 🕭 1 restaurant, 3 bars (1 w/entertainment), 1 beach (ocean), lawn games. **Rates:** Peak (Jan–Apr) $130–$160 S or D. Children under age 18 stay free. Lower rates off-season. MAP rates avail. Parking: Outdoor, free. AE, DC, DISC, MC, V.

### ▤▤ Quality Suites Oceanside

1665 N FL A1A, 32903; or toll free 800/876-4222; fax 407/768-2438. Twin-tower facility is joined by low-rise public area. **Rooms:** 208 stes. CI 3pm/CO noon. Nonsmoking rms avail. **Amenities:** 📧 🕭 A/C, cable TV w/movies, VCR, CD/tape player, in-rm safe. All units w/minibars, all w/terraces. **Services:** ⬜ 🛎 🛎 Masseur, babysitting. Breakfast buffet served daily. **Facilities:** 🛥 📺 75 🕭 1 restaurant, 1 bar, 1 beach (ocean), games rm, lawn games, whirlpool, washer/dryer. The restaurant offers pool and ocean views. **Rates (CP):** Peak (Feb–Apr/May–Aug) $109–$149 ste. Extra person $10. Children under age 18 stay free. Lower rates off-season. Parking: Outdoor, free. AE, CB, DC, DISC, ER, JCB, MC, V.

## RESTAURANT 🍽

### Villa Palma

111 5th Ave; tel 407/951-0051. At 6th Ave. **Northern Italian.** A cozy, romantic, Euro-style eatery. This award winning restaurant is filled with works of art and maintains a comfortable, homestyle atmosphere. The diverse menu includes stuffed chicken rollatini, fish, a lobster speciality called Zuppa de Pesce, and a variety of pasta dishes. **FYI:** Reservations accepted. Beer and wine only. **Open:** Sun–Thurs 5–10pm, Fri–Sat 5–10:30pm. **Prices:** Main courses $11–$28. AE, DISC, MC, V. 💟 🕭

# Indian Rocks Beach

Lots of motels, cottages, restaurants, and souvenir shops line of streets of this town of 4,000, which is on the same barrier island as St Petersburg Beach. **Information:** Gulf Beaches on Sand Key Chamber of Commerce, 105 5th Ave, Indian Rocks Beach, 34635 (tel 813/595-4575).

## MOTEL 🏨

### ▤▤ Pelican East & West

108 21st Ave, 34635; tel 813/595-9741. At 1st St, ½ block E of Gulf Blvd. Very attractive facility with private beach. **Rooms:** 13 rms, stes, and effic. CI 2pm/CO 10:30am. No smoking. Most units have kitchens. **Amenities:** 🕭 📺 A/C, cable TV, refrig. No phone. **Services:** 🛎 **Facilities:** 1 beach (ocean). **Rates:** Peak (Jan 15–Apr) $30–$45 S or D; $55–$70 ste; $35–$50 effic. Extra person $3. Lower rates off-season. Parking: Outdoor, free. MC, V.

## RESTAURANT 🍽

### Crabby Bill's Seafood Restaurant

401 Gulf Blvd; tel 813/595-4825. **Seafood.** An informal eatery offering a variety of seafood platters. Stone crab claws are a specialty. **FYI:** Reservations accepted. Children's menu. **Open:** Mon–Thurs 11:30am–10pm, Fri–Sat 11:30am–11pm, Sun noon–10pm. **Prices:** Main courses $5–$25. AE, MC, V. 💟 🕭

# Indian Shores

Thanks to supporters of the nonprofit Suncoast Seabird Sanctuary, more than 40 species of birds (including cormorants, white herons, and brown pelicans) thrive in this St Petersburg suburb. The Sanctuary's private Tiki Gardens are a Polynesian escape for humans too. **Information:** Gulf Beaches on Sand Key Chamber of Commerce, 501 150th Ave, Madeira Beach, 33708 (tel 813/391-7373).

## RESTAURANT 🍽

### Scandia

19829 Gulf Blvd; tel 813/595-5525. Between Park Blvd and FL 688. **Scandinavian.** If a Viking came for dinner, he would be right at home in this Scandinavian-inspired restaurant. Specialties include stuffed filet of sole with a delightful seafood dressing, and roasted leg of lamb served with mint jelly. **FYI:** Reservations accepted. Children's menu. **Open:** Tues–Sat 11:30am–9pm, Sun noon–8pm. Closed Aug 26–Sept 30. **Prices:** Main courses $6–$20. DISC, MC, V. 💟 🕭

## ATTRACTION 🏛

### Suncoast Seabird Sanctuary

18328 Gulf Blvd; tel 813/391-6211. The largest wild-bird hospital in the United States, the sanctuary is dedicated to the rescue, treatment, recuperation, and release of sick and injured wild birds. Visitors are free to wander around this tree-lined open-air sanctuary and photograph the wide variety of birds. Tours Wed and Sun at 2pm. **Open:** Daily 9am–sunset. **Free**

# Islamorada

Third town heading south through the Keys. Charter boats abound at Whale Harbor Marina. Visitors can swim with dolphins at Theater of the Sea or boat south to Indian Key historic site and the virgin tropics of Lignumvitae ("wood of life") Key. **Information:** Islamorada Chamber of Commerce, PO Box 915, Islamorada, 33036 (tel 305/664-4503).

## HOTELS 🏨

### 📇📇📇 Chesapeake Resort

83409 Overseas Hwy, PO Box 909, 33036; tel 305/664-4662 or toll free 800/338-3395; fax 305/664-8595. At MM 83.5 on US 1. This family-run facility attracts seclusion-seekers desiring attractive accommodations set on tropical grounds. **Rooms:** 14 cottages/villas. CI 3pm/CO 11am. **Amenities:** 🛏 🏖 A/C, cable TV w/movies, refrig, in-rm safe. All units w/terraces, some w/whirlpools. Some have cooking facilities. **Services:** 🛎 Babysitting. **Facilities:** 🎣 ⛰ 🍸1 ⛳ 🏊50 1 beach (ocean), lawn games, spa, whirlpool, playground, washer/dryer. **Rates:** Peak (Dec–Apr) $155–$500 cottage/villa. Extra person $15. Children under age 12 stay free. Min stay special events. Lower rates off-season. Parking: Indoor/outdoor, free. AE, DISC, MC, V.

### 📇📇 Holiday Isle Beach Resorts & Marina

Overseas Hwy MM 84, 33036; tel 305/664-2321 or toll free 800/327-7070; fax 305/664-2703. A large hotel drawing watersports enthusiasts and sun-seekers. **Rooms:** 175 rms, stes, and effic. CI 3:30pm/CO 11am. Nonsmoking rms avail. Clean, brightly-colored units. **Amenities:** 🛏 A/C, cable TV w/movies, in-rm safe. Some units w/terraces, 1 w/whirlpool. **Services:** 🛎 **Facilities:** 🎣 ⛰ 🍸 🛥 ⛳ 🏊135 ⛳ 9 restaurants, 11 bars (4 w/entertainment), 1 beach (ocean), snorkeling, playground, washer/dryer. Beach area has thatched umbrella tables. Volleyball. **Rates:** Peak (Dec–Apr) $90–$175 S or D; $225–$395 ste; $190–$210 effic. Extra person $10–$15. Children under age 18 stay free. Min stay wknds and special events. Lower rates off-season. Parking: Outdoor, free. AE, CB, DC, DISC, MC, V.

## MOTELS

### 📇📇 Breezy Palms Resort

Overseas Hwy MM 80, PO Box 767, 33036 (Oceanside); tel 305/664-2361; fax 305/664-2572. Varied accommodations, many with excellent water views. Casual atmosphere throughout. **Rooms:** 39 rms, stes, and effic; 1 cottage/villa. CI 3pm/CO 11am. **Amenities:** 🛏 A/C, cable TV w/movies, refrig. Some units w/terraces. **Services:** 🛎 **Facilities:** 🎣 ⛰ 🏊 1 beach (ocean), volleyball, snorkeling, washer/dryer. **Rates:** Peak (Dec 16–Apr 20) $75 S or D; $90–$180 ste; $80 effic; $130 cottage/villa. Extra person $10. Children under age 12 stay free. Min stay special events. Lower rates off-season. Parking: Outdoor, free. AE, DISC, MC, V.

### 📇 Islander Motel

Overseas Hwy MM 82.1, PO Box 766, 33036; tel 305/664-2031; fax 305/664-5503. 20 acres. Solid offering with a family atmosphere. **Rooms:** 114 rms and effic. CI 3pm/CO 11am. **Amenities:** 🛏 A/C, cable TV, refrig. All units w/terraces. **Services:** 🛎 **Facilities:** 🎣 🏊50 ⛳ 1 beach (ocean), basketball, volleyball, washer/dryer. Saltwater and freshwater pools. Tennis nearby. **Rates (CP):** Peak (Dec 15–Apr 14) $71–$77 S or D; $77–$95 effic. Extra person $7. Children under age 12 stay free. Min stay special events. Lower rates off-season. Parking: Outdoor, free. AE, CB, DC, MC, V.

### 📇📇 Pelican Cove Resort

84457 Old Overseas Hwy, MM 84.5, 33036; tel 305/664-4435 or toll free 800/445-4690; fax 305/664-5134. Set on the water, with a clean, sandy beach. **Rooms:** 63 rms, stes, and effic. CI 4pm/CO 11am. **Amenities:** 🛏 🏖 🍽 A/C, cable TV, refrig. All units w/terraces, some w/whirlpools. **Services:** 🛎 Babysitting. **Facilities:** 🎣 ⛰ 🍸 🍸1 ⛳ 1 restaurant (lunch only), 1 bar, 1 beach (ocean), volleyball, whirlpool, playground. **Rates (CP):** Peak (Dec 15–Apr 15) $165–$285 S or D; $285 ste; $185 effic. Extra person $15. Children under age 16 stay free. Min stay peak, wknds, and special events. Lower rates off-season. Parking: Outdoor, free. AE, MC, V.

### UNRATED Sunset Inn Resort

Overseas Hwy MM 82.2, PO Box 269, 33036; tel 305/664-3454 or toll free 800/558-9409; fax 305/664-3390. Basic rooms, friendly atmosphere. **Rooms:** 60 rms, stes, and effic. CI 2pm/CO 11am. **Amenities:** 🛏 A/C, cable TV. Some units w/terraces. **Services:** 🛎 🍽 **Facilities:** 🎣 2 restaurants (lunch and dinner only). **Rates:** Peak (Dec–Apr) $129–$225 S or D; $129–$225 ste; $59–$89 effic. Extra person $5. Children under age 12 stay free. Lower rates off-season. Parking: Outdoor, free. AE, DISC, MC, V.

## RESORT

### 📇📇📇 Cheeca Lodge

Overseas Hwy MM 82, PO Box 527, 33036; tel 305/664-4651 or toll free 800/327-2888; fax 305/664-2893. 27 acres. An extensive resort complex that is one of the Keys' most enduring facilities. It comprises about two dozen buildings housing first-rate accommodations and handsome public areas. Served by dedicated young staff. **Rooms:** 203 rms and stes. Executive level. CI 4pm/CO 11am. Nonsmoking rms avail. **Amenities:** 🛏 🏖 🍽 🍷 A/C, cable TV, VCR, bathrobes. All units w/minibars, some w/terraces, 1 w/whirlpool. **Services:** ✗ 🔑 📺 🚗 📠 🛎 Social director, masseur, children's program, babysitting. **Facilities:** 🎣 ⛳ ⛰ 🍸9 🎿 🏊6 🛥 🏊350 ⛳ 3 restaurants (see "Restaurants" below), 2 bars, 1 beach (ocean), basketball, volleyball, board surfing, lawn games, snorkeling, playground. **Rates:** Peak (Dec 20–Apr) $240–$585 S or D; $315–$1,000 ste. Extra person $25. Children under age 18 stay free. Lower rates off-season. AP and MAP rates avail. Parking: Indoor/outdoor, free. AE, CB, DC, DISC, MC, V.

## RESTAURANTS

### Atlantic's Edge

In Cheeca Lodge, Overseas Hwy MM 82; tel 305/664-4651. **New American.** Upscale eatery where wraparound windows provide great views of private beaches and the ocean beyond. Menu highlights include a selection of fresh fish prepared blackened, grilled, or braised, filet of beef, jumbo sea scallops, and cheese-filled saffron pasta spirals. **FYI:** Reservations recommended. Children's menu. Dress code. **Open:** Peak (Labor Day–Mem Day) dinner daily 5:30–11pm; brunch Sun 11am–3pm. **Prices:** Main courses $20–$38; prix fixe $34–$42. AE, CB, DC, DISC, MC, V. 

### ★ Lazy Days Oceanfront Bar and Seafood Grill

Overseas Hwy MM 79.5; tel 305/664-5256. **Seafood/Steak.** A relaxed restaurant with a maritime theme and great water views. Extensive seafood menu. **FYI:** Reservations accepted. **Open:** Tues–Sun 11:30am–10pm. **Prices:** Main courses $12–$22. AE, DISC, MC, V. 

### ⑤ Manny and Isa's Kitchen

Overseas Hwy MM 81.6 PO Box 826; tel 305/664-5019. **Cuban.** Opened over a dozen years ago as a small shop selling key lime pie and conch chowder, this pint-size place now sells a variety of "Florribean" dishes: pork chops with black beans and rice, lobster enchiladas, and Cuban-style sandwiches. Fresh-made sangria is also a specialty. **FYI:** Reservations not accepted. Children's menu. Beer and wine only. **Open:** Wed–Mon 11am–9pm. Closed Oct–Nov 15. **Prices:** Main courses $3–$17. MC, V. 

### Papa Joe's

Overseas Hwy MM 79.7; tel 305/664-8109. **Seafood/Steak.** Basic, dark restaurant and bar, with lovely water and marina views. Fish is prepared broiled, fried, or sautéed; stone-crab claws are always available. **FYI:** Reservations accepted. Children's menu. **Open:** Lunch Wed–Mon 11am–3:30pm; dinner Wed–Mon 4:30–10pm. **Prices:** Main courses $9–$19. AE, MC, V. 

## ATTRACTION

### Theater of the Sea

Overseas Hwy MM 84.5; tel 305/664-2431. One of the world's oldest marine parks, featuring dolphin and sea lion shows, guided marine exhibit, and bottomless boat ride. **Open:** Daily 9:30am–4pm. $$$$

# Isle of Capri

## RESTAURANT

### ♣ Blue Heron Inn

387 Capri Blvd; tel 941/394-6248. **Eclectic.** Watch the sun set over the marina and the rest of Johnson Bay as you dine. Many fresh fish specialties are offered on the rotating menu, which is changed every two weeks. **FYI:** Reservations recom-mended. Dress code. Beer and wine only. **Open:** Peak (Oct–Apr) Mon–Sat 5:30–10pm. Closed Aug–Sept. **Prices:** Main courses $33–$37. AE, MC, V. 

# Jacksonville

See also Atlantic Beach, Jacksonville Beach, Ponte Vedra Beach

This growing metropolis of 1 million boasts one of the NFL's newest expansion teams, the Jaguars, and two major Navy bases. Ninety miles south of Georgia and 10 miles from the Atlantic, its treasures include the Cummer Gallery of Art and a November jazz festival. **Information:** Jacksonville & the Beaches Convention & Visitors Bureau, 3 Independent Dr, Jacksonville, 33202 (tel 904/798-9148).

## PUBLIC TRANSPORTATION

**Jacksonville Transit Authority Buses** Operate 4am–2am; hours vary, depending on route. Local fare 60¢ adults, 45¢ teens under 17 with student ID, children and seniors free. Buses to beach $1.10. For information call 904/630-3100.

## HOTELS

### AmeriSuites Jacksonville

8277 Western Way Circle, 32256; tel 904/737-4477 or toll free 800/833-1516; fax 904/739-1649. Baymeadows Rd exit off I-95. Contemporary-style tourist hotel. **Rooms:** 112 stes. CI 2pm/CO 11am. Nonsmoking rms avail. **Amenities:** A/C, cable TV, refrig, VCR. Some units have bathroom TVs. **Services:** Manager's reception on Tuesday evenings. **Facilities:** Washer/dryer. Free passes available to nearby fitness center. **Rates (CP):** $59–$134 ste. Extra person $10. Children under age 18 stay free. **Parking:** Outdoor, free. AE, CB, DC, DISC, ER, JCB, MC, V.

### Comfort Suites Hotel

8333 Dix Ellis Trail, 32256; tel 904/739-1135 or toll free 800/228-5150; fax 904/731-0752. Exit 100 off I-95. SW of Baymeadows Rd exit. The lobby, which features a tile floor, potted trees, and a wicker-furnished seating area, provides a comfortable introduction to the modest suites within. **Rooms:** 128 rms and stes. Executive level. CI 3pm/CO 11am. Nonsmoking rms avail. Units have sleeper sofas and large bathrooms. **Amenities:** A/C, cable TV, refrig. Some units w/terraces. **Services:** Car-rental desk, babysitting. Evening cocktail reception. **Facilities:** Lawn games, whirlpool, washer/dryer. **Rates (CP):** Peak (Feb–Apr/June–Aug) $64–$84 S; $74–$94 D; $79–$109 ste. Children under age 18 stay free. Lower rates off-season. **Parking:** Outdoor, free. AE, DC, DISC, MC, V.

### Courtyard by Marriott

4600 San Pablo Rd, 32224; tel 904/223-1700 or toll free 800/321-2211; fax 904/223-1026. Butler Blvd exit off I-95. Guests are primarily those with business at the Mayo Clinic next door. **Rooms:** 146 rms and stes. CI 3pm/CO noon.

Nonsmoking rms avail. **Amenities:** ▨ ☖ ▦ A/C, cable TV w/movies. Some units w/terraces. **Services:** ◩ ↵ Babysitting. **Facilities:** ▥ ▨ ☖ Whirlpool, day-care ctr, washer/dryer. Trademark courtyard with pool. **Rates:** $103–$123 S; $113–$133 D; $115–$125 ste. Children under age 18 stay free. Parking: Outdoor, free. AE, CB, DC, DISC, MC, V.

### ▤▤ DoubleTree Hotel
4700 Salisbury Rd, 32256; tel 904/281-9700 or toll free 800/222-8733; fax 904/281-1957. Exit 101 off I-95. Popular with both business travelers and families, who like to take advantage of its attractive pool, whirlpool, and fitness facility. Near downtown. **Rooms:** 167 rms and stes. CI 3pm/CO 1pm. Nonsmoking rms avail. **Amenities:** ▨ ☖ A/C, cable TV w/movies. Some rooms have refrigerators. **Services:** ✕ ◩ ↵ **Facilities:** ▥ ▨ ▦ ☖ 1 restaurant, 1 bar, whirlpool. **Rates:** $129 S or D; $149 ste. Extra person $10. Children under age 16 stay free. Parking: Outdoor, free. AE, DC, DISC, MC, V.

### ▤▤▤ Embassy Suites
9300 Baymeadows Rd, 32256; tel 904/731-3555 or toll free 800/851-4185; fax 904/731-4972. Exit 100 off I-95. Its richly decorated lobby leads out to a lush courtyard traversed by terraced walkways and graced with waterfalls. **Rooms:** 210 stes. CI 3pm/CO noon. Nonsmoking rms avail. **Amenities:** ▨ ☖ ▦ A/C, cable TV w/movies, refrig, dataport, voice mail. All units w/minibars, some w/terraces, 1 w/whirlpool. 2 TVs. **Services:** ✕ ▰ ◩ ↵ Complimentary evening cocktail reception. **Facilities:** ▥ ▨ ▦ ☖ 1 restaurant, 1 bar (w/entertainment), sauna, steam rm, whirlpool, washer/dryer. **Rates (CP):** $99–$115 ste. Extra person $10. Children under age 12 stay free. Min stay special events. Parking: Outdoor, free. AE, DISC, JCB, MC, V.

### ▤▤▤ Holiday Inn Airport
I-95 at Airport Rd, 32218 (Jacksonville Int'l Airport); tel 904/741-4404 or toll free 800/HOLIDAY; fax 904/741-4907. Exit 27 off I-95. A snazzy airport choice that's convenient to the interstate and noteworthy for its Holidome recreation center attached to the two- and six-story structure. **Rooms:** 489 rms. CI 11am/CO noon. Nonsmoking rms avail. Modern accommodations are kept commendably neat and clean. **Amenities:** ▨ ☖ A/C, cable TV, in-rm safe. **Services:** ✕ ▰ ▰ ◩ ↵ ◁ Car-rental desk, babysitting. **Facilities:** ▥ ▨ ▦ ☖ 1 restaurant, 2 bars (1 w/entertainment), games rm, sauna, washer/dryer. **Rates:** $62–$86 S or D. Extra person $4. Children under age 18 stay free. Parking: Outdoor, free. AE, DC, DISC, JCB, MC, V.

### ▤▤ Holiday Inn Baymeadows
9150 Baymeadows Rd, 32256; tel 904/737-1700 or toll free 800/HOLIDAY; fax 904/737-0207. Exit 100 off I-95. With ample banquet facilities and an inexpensive family restaurant, this is a reliable spot for business travelers and families. **Rooms:** 249 rms. Executive level. CI 3pm/CO noon. Nonsmoking rms avail. **Amenities:** ▨ ☖ ▦ A/C, cable TV w/movies, dataport. **Services:** ✕ ▦ ◩ ↵ ◁ **Facilities:** ▥

▨ ▦ ☖ 1 restaurant, 2 bars, washer/dryer. **Rates:** $79–$89 S or D. Extra person $5. Children under age 18 stay free. Parking: Outdoor, free. AE, CB, DC, DISC, EC, MC, V.

### ▤▤ Homewood Suites
8737 Baymeadows Rd, 32256; tel 904/733-9299 or toll free 800/CALL HOME; fax 904/448-5889. Baymeadows Rd exit off I-95. Take hard right off ramps. Comfortable, clean suites. **Rooms:** 116 stes and effic. CI 3pm/CO noon. Nonsmoking rms avail. Rooms offer modern decor, full kitchens, and separate sleeping areas. **Amenities:** ▨ ☖ ▦ A/C, cable TV, refrig, dataport, VCR, voice mail. Some units w/terraces, some w/fireplaces. **Services:** ◩ ↵ ◁ Babysitting. Complimentary evening beverages; free daily newspaper. Staff will shop for groceries. **Facilities:** ▥ ▨ ▦ ▣ ☖ Whirlpool, washer/dryer. **Rates (CP):** $70–$155 ste; $70–$155 effic. Children under age 18 stay free. Min stay special events. Parking: Outdoor, free. AE, CB, DC, DISC, EC, MC, V.

### ▤▤▤ Jacksonville Marriott at Southpoint
4670 Salisbury Rd, 32256; tel 904/296-2222 or toll free 800/228-9290; fax 904/296-7561. Butler Rd exit off I-95. This high-rise hotel, just minutes from the beach and downtown attractions, is a top choice in the area. Plushly furnished marble-floored lobby lends a polished look. The fine staff has a knack for pleasing guests. **Rooms:** 256 rms and stes. CI 3pm/CO noon. Nonsmoking rms avail. Handsomely decorated rooms with mahogany furnishings. **Amenities:** ▨ ☖ A/C, cable TV. Some units w/whirlpools. **Services:** ✕ ▰ ▦ ▰ ◩ ↵ Babysitting. **Facilities:** ▥ ▨ ▦ ▣ ☖ 1 restaurant (see "Restaurants" below), 1 bar, sauna, steam rm, whirlpool. Health club has excellent facilities, better than you're likely to find at other hotels in this category. **Rates:** Peak (Aug–Dec/Jan–Apr) $139 S; $159 D; $195–$295 ste. Extra person $10. Children under age 18 stay free. Lower rates off-season. Parking: Outdoor, free. AE, CB, DC, DISC, MC, V.

### ▤▤▤ Omni Jacksonville Hotel
245 Water St, 32202; tel 904/355-6664 or toll free 800/THE OMNI; fax 904/791-4809. From I-95 Riverside Ave exit to US 17N. Located across from Jacksonville Landing and its dining, shopping, and entertainment options, this is one of the city's major downtown hotels, a spectacle of glass, polished wood, and marble. **Rooms:** 354 rms and stes. Executive level. CI 3pm/CO noon. Nonsmoking rms avail. Rollaway beds available for a fee. **Amenities:** ▨ ☖ ▯ A/C, cable TV w/movies, voice mail. All units w/minibars. Fax machines in all "club level" rooms. **Services:** ✕ ▦ ▰ ◩ ↵ Babysitting. Discounts offered to 2 area golf courses. **Facilities:** ▥ ▨ ▦ 1 restaurant, 1 bar. Use of YMCA facilites for $5. **Rates:** $129–$149 S; $139–$159 D; $350–$500 ste. Extra person $10. Children under age 17 stay free. Min stay special events. Parking: Indoor/outdoor, $3–$6/day. AE, CB, DC, DISC, JCB, MC, V.

### ≡≡≡ Radisson Riverwalk Hotel

1515 Prudential Drive, 32207; tel 904/396-5100 or toll free 800/333-3333; fax 904/396-7154. Exit 107 off I-95, S side of St Johns River. This five-story hotel sports a nautical look, with its huge ship-like lobby with exposed pipes and corrugated tin ceiling. **Rooms:** 323 rms and stes. Executive level. CI 3pm/CO noon. Nonsmoking rms avail. **Amenities:** 🛍 🕭 📺 🍽 A/C, cable TV w/movies, dataport, voice mail. Some units w/terraces. **Services:** ✕ 🚐 ⊠ 🗍 Twice-daily maid svce, car-rental desk, babysitting. **Facilities:** 🛍 ⛱ 🎱 🎱 🖥 3 restaurants, 1 bar (w/entertainment). **Rates:** Peak (Jan–Mar) $139–$159 S; $149–$169 D; $179–$475 ste. Extra person $10. Children under age 18 stay free. Min stay special events. Lower rates off-season. Parking: Outdoor, free. AE, CB, DC, DISC, ER, JCB, MC, V.

### ≡≡ Ramada Inn Mandarin Conference Center

3130 Hartley Rd, 32257; tel 904/268-8080 or toll free 800/2-RAMADA; fax 904/262-8718. Exit 2 off I-295, at San Jose Blvd. Known for the professional attention and service provided conference-goers. **Rooms:** 152 rms, stes, and effic. CI 3pm/CO noon. Nonsmoking rms avail. **Amenities:** 🛍 🕭 A/C, cable TV. **Services:** ✕ ⊠ 🗍 ⊲ **Facilities:** 🛍 ⛱ 🕭 1 restaurant, 2 bars (w/entertainment), whirlpool, washer/dryer. Comedy club. Restaurant features all-you-can-eat buffets. **Rates (CP):** $54–$67 S; $59–$72 D; $120–$150 ste; $125–$155 effic. Extra person $5. Children under age 18 stay free. Min stay special events. Parking: Outdoor, free. AE, CB, DC, DISC, MC, V.

### ≡≡ Residence Inn by Marriott

8365 Dix Ellis Trail, 32256; tel 904/733-8088 or toll free 800/331-3131; fax 904/731-8354. Exit 100 off I-95. Comfortable, condominium-style accommodations. **Rooms:** 112 effic. CI noon/CO noon. Nonsmoking rms avail. Full kitchen, living area, sleeping area or separate bedrooms. **Amenities:** 🛍 🕭 📺 A/C, cable TV, refrig, voice mail. Some units w/fireplaces. Microwaves; irons and ironing boards. **Services:** ⊠ 🗍 ⊲ Car-rental desk, babysitting. **Facilities:** 🛍 ⛱ 🕭 Lawn games, whirlpool, washer/dryer. **Rates (CP):** $179 effic. Children under age 18 stay free. Parking: Outdoor, free. AE, CB, DC, DISC, JCB, MC, V.

## MOTELS

### ≡ Econo Lodge

5221 W University Blvd, 32216; tel 904/737-1690 or toll free 800/553-2666; fax 904/448-5638. Exit 102 off I-95. Basic budget accommodations. **Rooms:** 180 rms. CI 3pm/CO noon. Nonsmoking rms avail. **Amenities:** 🛍 A/C, cable TV w/movies. **Services:** 🗍 **Facilities:** 🛍 ⛱ 1 restaurant, washer/dryer. **Rates:** Peak (Mar–Sept/Oct–Jan) $36–$46 S; $41–$51 D. Lower rates off-season. Parking: Outdoor, free. AE, DISC, MC, V.

### ≡≡ Fairfield Inn

8050 Baymeadow Circle W, 32256; tel 904/739-0739 or toll free 800/228-2800. Exit 100 off I-95. Located in a peaceful, quiet corner of town, right next to a PGA golf course. **Rooms:** 102 rms and stes. CI 3pm/CO noon. Nonsmoking rms avail. Nicely maintained rooms and public spaces. Some loft suites offer kitchenettes. **Amenities:** 🛍 🕭 A/C, cable TV w/movies, dataport. Some units w/terraces, some w/whirlpools. **Services:** ⊠ 🗍 **Facilities:** 🛍 🎱 🕭 Basketball, whirlpool, washer/dryer. **Rates:** $72–$125 ste. Children under age 18 stay free. Parking: Outdoor, free. AE, CB, DC, DISC, MC, V.

### ≡ Motel 6

8285 Dix Ellis Trail, 32256; tel 904/731-8400; fax 904/730-0781. Exit 100 off I-95. Strictly "no frills" accommodations. **Rooms:** 109 rms. CI 2pm/CO noon. Nonsmoking rms avail. Plain but adequate. **Amenities:** 🛍 A/C, satel TV w/movies, dataport. **Services:** 🗍 **Facilities:** 🛍 Guest privileges available at nearby gym. **Rates:** $32 S; $36 D. Extra person $4. Children under age 18 stay free. Min stay special events. Parking: Outdoor, free. AE, CB, DC, DISC, MC, V.

### ≡≡ Ramada Inn South

5624 Cagle Rd, 32211; tel 904/737-8000 or toll free 800/2-RAMADA; fax 904/448-8624. Exit 103 off I-95. In a convenient location off the interstate. A good value. **Rooms:** 110 rms. CI 1:30pm/CO noon. Nonsmoking rms avail. **Amenities:** 🛍 🕭 A/C, cable TV. **Services:** ⊠ ⊲ **Facilities:** 🛍 🕭 🕭 1 restaurant, 1 bar (w/entertainment), washer/dryer. **Rates:** $37 S; $43 D. Children under age 18 stay free. Parking: Outdoor, free. AE, CB, DC, DISC, MC, V.

## RESTAURANTS 🍴

### Banyan's

In the Jacksonville Marriott at Southpoint, 4670 Salisbury Rd; tel 904/296-2222. **New American.** A casual, family-style restaurant. The breakfast buffet offers a wide selection at a low price. Dinner entrees include Caribbean-grilled mahimahi. **FYI:** Reservations accepted. Children's menu. **Open:** Breakfast Mon–Sat 6:30–10:30am, Sun 7–10:30am; lunch daily 11am–2pm; dinner Sun–Thurs 5–10pm, Fri–Sat 5–11pm; brunch Sun 10:30am–2pm. **Prices:** Main courses $6–$17. AE, DC, DISC, MC, V. 🖤 ⛱

### Cafe Carmon

1986 San Marco Blvd; tel 904/399-4488. Between Carlo St and Waldo Ave. **New American.** Casual restaurant located in the heart of the San Marco shopping district. Be prepared to wait for your freshly prepared dinner, which might be potato-encrusted salmon over a garlic–sour cream sauce with carmelized onions and red-pepper strips. Afterward, you can sip a cappuccino on the patio and enjoy one of the many decadent desserts such as peanut butter pie with Oreo crust. **FYI:** Reservations accepted. Children's menu. Beer and wine only. **Open:** Mon–Thurs 11am–11pm, Fri–Sat 11am–midnight, Sun 11am–9pm. **Prices:** Main courses $7–$19. AE, DC, DISC, MC, V. 🍰 ⛱

## The Chart House
In St John's Place, 1501 Riverplace Blvd; tel 904/398-3353. **Seafood/Steak.** A casual steak house located in the heart of the shopping district. The attractive black-and-white decor is accented by ceiling fans and exposed brick. Every table has river views. The salad bar has more than 60 items from which to choose. On weekend evenings this place is jammed with moviegoers who come in afterward for dessert and coffee. **FYI:** Reservations recommended. **Open:** Sun–Thurs 5–10pm, Fri–Sat 5–11pm. **Prices:** Main courses $14–$39. AE, DC, DISC, MC, V. 🖼️ 📷 ♿

## Chili's Grill & Bar
In Baymeadow Commons Shopping Center, 9500 Baymeadows Rd; tel 904/739-2476. **Southwestern.** Locals love the lounge here, with its foliage and tiled table tops. Burger platters, chicken, and caesar salad are good values. **FYI:** Reservations not accepted. Children's menu. **Open:** Mon–Thurs 11am–11pm, Fri–Sat 11am–midnight, Sun 11am–10:30pm. **Prices:** Main courses $6–$10. AE, DC, DISC, MC, V. ♿

## Mozzarella's Cafe
In Jacksonville Landing, 2 Independent Dr, Suite 201; tel 904/353-4503. **Italian.** Comfortable, with good views of the St Johns River. Menu highlights include gourmet pizzas as well as the Southwestern grilled catch of the day. **FYI:** Reservations not accepted. Children's menu. **Open:** Sun–Thurs 11am–10pm, Fri–Sat 11am–midnight. **Prices:** Main courses $4–$14. AE, CB, DC, DISC, MC, V. ⛴️

## Ruby Tuesday
In Jacksonville Landing, 2 Independent Dr; tel 904/358-7737. **New American.** This riverside restaurant offers beautiful views from its wrap-around windows. The menu includes baby back ribs, fajitas, and sonara chicken pasta. **FYI:** Reservations not accepted. Children's menu. **Open:** Mon–Thurs 11am–11pm, Fri–Sat 11am–midnight, Sun 11am–10pm. **Prices:** Main courses $7–$14. AE, CB, DC, DISC, MC, V. ♿

# ATTRACTIONS 📷

## Jacksonville Museum of Science & History
1025 Museum Circle; tel 904/396-7062. This hands-on interactive children's museum located on the Riverwalk focuses on science and northern Florida history. Exhibits include a small aviary of Florida songbirds and a 10,000-gallon aquarium. Planetarium shows for adults and children are scheduled daily. **Open:** Mon–Fri 10am–5pm, Sat 10am–6pm, Sun 1–6pm. **$$**

## Jacksonville Museum of Contemporary Art
4160 Boulevard Center Dr; tel 904/398-8336. On permanent display is a notable collection of modern works by Picasso, Lichtenstein, and Nevelson, among others. There's also an impressive gallery of pre-Columbian artifacts. Changing exhibits present the latest in painting, drawing, photography, and sculpture. **Open:** Tues–Wed and Fri 10am–4pm, Thurs 10am–10pm, Sat–Sun 1–5pm. **$**

## Jacksonville Landing
2 Independent Dr; tel 904/353-1188. A dining, shopping, and entertainment center on the north bank of the St Johns River, home to street performers, festivals, concerts, and other special events. The complex offers over 65 shops plus a market with open-air stalls displaying an array of meats, cheeses, fresh seafood, baked goods, flowers, and produce. **Open:** Mon–Thurs 10am–8pm, Fri–Sat 10am–9pm, Sun noon–5:30pm. **Free**

## Riverwalk
851 N Market St; tel 904/396-4900. This 1.2-mile wooden boardwalk on the south bank of the St Johns River is one of Jacksonville's most popular attractions, the scene of numerous festivals and special events throughout the year. Food vendors and restaurants line the route. At the west end is the massive Friendship Fountain, particularly pretty at night, when it is illuminated with colored lights. **Free**

## Cummer Gallery of Art
829 Riverside Ave; tel 904/356-6857. Set amidst stunning formal gardens with fountains and reflecting pools, the museum boasts collections of 18th-century Meissen porcelain and 18th- and 19th-century American landscapes and portraits by the likes of Thomas Eakins, Winslow Homer, John Singer Sargent, and Frederic Remington. **Open:** Tues 10am–9:30pm, Wed–Fri 10am–4pm, Sat noon–5pm, Sun 2–5pm. **$**

## Jacksonville Zoological Garden
8605 Zoo Rd; tel 904/757-4462 or 757-4463. Lushly landscaped zoo exhibiting over 700 mammals, birds, and reptiles, many of them in large, natural enclosures that simulate native habitats. Breeding programs involve such endangered species as the white rhino and the Florida panther. At the Educational Center (open weekends and holidays only, 10am–4pm), hands-on exhibits offer the opportunity to examine birds' eggs and nests, peer at insects through a microscope, or touch a giraffe vertebra or tiger skull. **Open:** Daily 9am–5pm. **$$$**

## Anheuser-Busch Brewery
111 Busch Dr; tel 904/751-8116. Visitors can tour the brewing and bottling facilities and learn about the company's history from its inception in 1852 to the present. Free samples of the final product in the Hospitality Room at the end of the tour. **Open:** Mon–Sat 9am–4pm. **$**

## Fort Caroline National Memorial
12713 Fort Caroline Rd; tel 904/641-7155. A triangular fort of earth and wood on the St Johns River protected the French outpost of La Carolinet during the European struggle for dominance in the New World. Arriving in 1564, the French colonists, mostly Huguenots, suffered great privation due to famine and Native American hostility. By 1565, seven

ships loaded with food and more settlers narrowly prevented the abandonment of the colony. But soon thereafter the colony was attacked and overrun by Spanish forces, who held Florida almost continuously for the next 250 years.

Today a replica of Fort Caroline near the original site is under the auspices of the National Park Service, as is the nearby 600-acre **Theodore Roosevelt Area,** beautiful woodland undisturbed since the Civil War. On a two-mile hike along a centuries-old park trail, you'll see a wide variety of birds (including owls, wood storks, and ospreys), wildflowers, and maritime hammock forest. There are picnic areas at the visitor center and at the trailhead.

Ranger-guided tours of Fort Caroline are given Sat–Sun at 1pm, followed by guided nature walks through Theodore Roosevelt Area at 2:30pm. **Open:** Daily 9am–5pm. **Free**

### Kingsley Plantation

11676 Palmetto Ave; tel 904/251-3537. About 60 slaves tended the 1,000 acres of Sea Island cotton, sugarcane, and other crops grown on this 19th-century plantation, located just off FL A1A. Visitors can tour the 2-story residence, kitchen house, barn/carriage house, and the remains of 23 slave cabins made of tabby, a kind of primitive concrete composed of sand, water, and crushed oyster shells. The National Park Service schedules programs daily; call ahead for times. **Open:** Daily 9am–5pm. **Free**

# Jacksonville Beach

See also Atlantic Beach, Jacksonville, Ponte Vedra Beach

This seaside town of 20,000, 12 miles east of downtown Jacksonville, offers broad beaches, a small commercial boardwalk, and the American Lighthouse Museum of nautical memorabilia, plus spring's annual Springin' the Blues music festival. **Information:** Jacksonville & the Beaches Convention & Visitors Bureau, 3 Independent Dr, Jacksonville, 33202 (tel 904/798-9148).

## HOTELS 🏨

### 📰 Comfort Inn Oceanfront

1515 N 1st St, 32250; tel 904/241-2311 or toll free 800/654-8776; fax 904/349-3830. Fronted by 3,000 feet of pristine white sand, this economical choice is very popular with families. **Rooms:** 180 rms and stes. CI 3pm/CO 11am. Nonsmoking rms avail. Many rooms with beach views. **Amenities:** 🛏 💧 A/C, cable TV. Some units w/terraces. **Services:** 🛎 🍴 **Facilities:** 🛗 ⛳ 🏊 ⅙ 1 restaurant (bkfst and lunch only), 1 bar (w/entertainment), 1 beach (ocean), games rm, lawn games, whirlpool. Large pool has rock waterfalls and sun deck. Restaurant and lounge have both beach and pool views. **Rates (CP):** Peak (Feb–Aug) $69–$175 S or D; $150–$195 ste. Children under age 18 stay free. Lower rates off-season. Parking: Outdoor, free. AE, CB, DC, DISC, ER, JCB, MC, V.

### 📰 Days Inn Oceanfront Resort

1031 S 1st St, 32250; tel 904/249-7231 or toll free 800/321-2037; fax 904/249-7924. Butler Blvd exit off I-95. Located directly on the beach, at dunes' edge, this facility boasts panoramic ocean views from all its rooms. **Rooms:** 155 rms and stes. CI 3pm/CO noon. Nonsmoking rms avail. **Amenities:** 🛏 A/C, cable TV. All units w/terraces. **Services:** ✕ 🛎 🍴 **Facilities:** 🛗 🏊 [250] ⅙ (bkfst and dinner only) 1 bar (w/entertainment), 1 beach (ocean), lifeguard, lawn games, washer/dryer. Beach volleyball. Poolside patio bar. Restaurant and lounge have ocean views. **Rates:** Peak (Mar–Sept) $69–$139 S or D; $185–$295 ste. Children under age 18 stay free. Lower rates off-season. Parking: Outdoor, free. AE, CB, DC, DISC, EC, ER, MC, V.

### UNRATED Holiday Inn SunSpree

1617 N 1st St, 32250; tel 904/249-9071 or toll free 800/590-4767; fax 904/241-4321. Off FL A1A S. The 7th floor, dedicated as meeting space, features floor-to-ceiling windows affording a panoramic ocean view. **Rooms:** 143 rms and effic. CI 3pm/CO 11am. Nonsmoking rms avail. **Amenities:** 🛏 💧 🍴 A/C, cable TV, refrig. All units w/terraces. **Services:** 🛎 🍴 🍷 Babysitting. **Facilities:** 🛗 🏊2 🍴 [250] ⅙ (bkfst and dinner only) 1 bar, 1 beach (ocean), lawn games, washer/dryer. **Rates (CP):** Peak (June–Aug) $60–$145 S or D; $125–$175 effic. Children under age 18 stay free. Lower rates off-season. Parking: Outdoor, free. EC, ER.

## ATTRACTION 🏛

### American Lighthouse Historical Society

1011 N 3rd St (FL A1A); tel 904/241-8845. Extensive collection of photographs, artifacts, and historical and technical data on more than 1,000 lighthouses in the United States. Artifacts, oil paintings, scale models, navigational aids, and blueprints help preserve the place of the lighthouse in American history. **Open:** Tues–Sat 10am–4pm. **Free**

# Jensen Beach

This yuppified town 120 miles north of Miami is home to 10,000 people. A bridge across Indian River reaches Hutchinson Island and the Atlantic; sea turtles hatch here during the summer. **Information:** Jensen Beach Chamber of Commerce, 1910 Jensen Beach Blvd, Jensen Beach, 34957 (tel 561/334-3444).

## HOTELS 🏨

### 📰 Courtyard by Marriott

10978 S Ocean Dr, 34957; tel 561/229-1000 or toll free 800/321-2211; fax 561/229-0253. 1 mi N of Jensen Beach Causeway. Popular with families for location near beachgoing and island activities. **Rooms:** 110 rms and stes. CI 3pm/CO noon. Nonsmoking rms avail. Contemporary appointments. Some rooms with ocean views. **Amenities:** 🛏 💧 🍴 A/C, cable TV w/movies. Some units w/terraces. **Services:**

✗ 🖼 ⤴ Babysitting. **Facilities:** 🖽 ⛺ 🖳 🔲150 ♿ 1 restaurant, 1 beach (ocean), board surfing, games rm, washer/dryer. **Rates:** Peak (Dec–Apr) $135–$175 S; $145–$185 D; $250–$350 ste. Extra person $10. Children under age 18 stay free. Lower rates off-season. Parking: Outdoor, free. AE, CB, DC, DISC, MC, V.

### 🏨 Holiday Inn Jensen Beach

3793 NE Ocean Blvd, 34957; tel 561/225-3000 or toll free 800/992-4747; fax 561/225-1956. Its beachfront location is the main appeal. **Rooms:** 181 rms and stes. CI 3pm/CO 11am. Nonsmoking rms avail. Well-maintained rooms. **Amenities:** 🛏 🍴 A/C, satel TV w/movies, in-rm safe. All units w/terraces. **Services:** ✗ 🖼 ⤴ Babysitting. **Facilities:** 🖽 🏊2 🎱 🖳 🔲200 ♿ 1 restaurant, 2 bars (1 w/entertainment), 1 beach (ocean), games rm, washer/dryer. Patio bar. **Rates:** Peak (Jan–Apr) $125–$150 S or D; $265–$415 ste. Extra person $10. Children under age 19 stay free. Min stay special events. Lower rates off-season. Parking: Indoor/outdoor, free. AE, CB, DC, DISC, JCB, MC, V.

## MOTEL

### 🏨 Hutchinson Inn

9750 S Ocean Dr, 34957; tel 561/229-2000; fax 561/229-8875. 2 mi N of Jensen Beach Causeway. A quiet beachfront hideaway. Brick walkways lead to the pastel two-story building, and the thick green lawns are dotted with white gazebos. The lobby, though tiny, is charming. **Rooms:** 21 rms and effic. CI 2pm/CO 11am. Nonsmoking rms avail. Accommodations vary from a handful with queen-size beds to efficiencies with more space to a single apartment suite. Most units offer a view of the pool and limited ocean vistas. **Amenities:** 🛏 🍴 🖥 A/C, cable TV w/movies, refrig. Some units w/terraces. **Services:** ⤴ **Facilities:** 🖽 1 beach (ocean), washer/dryer. Good swimming beach. **Rates:** Peak (Dec–Apr) $90 S or D; $150 effic. Extra person $15. Children under age 3 stay free. Lower rates off-season. Parking: Outdoor, free. AE, DISC, MC, V.

## RESTAURANTS 🍽

### Cafe Coconuts

In Island Shops, 4304 NE Ocean Blvd; tel 561/225-6006. Off Jensen Beach Causeway. **Seafood/Steak.** Casual, plant-filled restaurant. The early-bird dining specials offer terrific value. Surf-and-turf and baby-back ribs are mainstays. **FYI:** Reservations accepted. Dancing/jazz/piano. Children's menu. **Open:** Sun–Thurs 11:30am–10pm, Fri–Sat 11:30am–11pm. **Prices:** Main courses $11–$16. V. 🖭 ♿

### ★ Island Reef

10900 S Ocean Dr; tel 561/229-2600. 1 mi N of Jensen Beach Causeway. **Seafood/Steak.** A casual, tropical spot with great views, popular with locals and visitors alike. **FYI:** Reservations not accepted. Guitar. Children's menu. **Open:** Sun–Thurs 11:30am–9:30pm, Fri–Sat 11:30am–10pm. **Prices:** Main courses $8–$20. AE, DISC, MC, V. 🍽 🖼 🖭 VP

# Jupiter

Jupiter resident Burt Reynolds put this town of 28,000 on the map with two theaters, one in nearby Tequesta. A 130-year-old lighthouse still guides Atlantic sailors into the inlet 20 miles north of Palm Beach. **Information:** Jupiter-Tequesta-Juno Beach Chamber of Commerce, 800 N US 1, Jupiter, 33477 (tel 561/746-7111).

## MOTEL 🖽

### 🏨 Wellesley Inn

34 Fisherman's Wharf, 33477; tel 561/575-7201 or toll free 800/444-8888; fax 561/575-1169. Exit 59A off I-95. Caters to the budget-minded motorist. **Rooms:** 105 rms and stes. CI 2pm/CO 11am. Nonsmoking rms avail. **Amenities:** 🛏 🍴 A/C, cable TV w/movies. **Services:** ✗ 🖼 ⤴ **Facilities:** 🖽 🔲15 ♿ Washer/dryer. **Rates (CP):** Peak (Dec 20–Apr 1) $97 S or D; $116 ste. Extra person $6. Children under age 18 stay free. Lower rates off-season. Parking: Outdoor, free. AE, DC, DISC, MC, V.

## RESORT

### 🏨 Jupiter Beach Resort

5 N FL A1A at Indiantown Rd, 33477; tel 561/746-2511 or toll free 800/228-8810; fax 561/744-1741. The local showplace, in a convenient location directly on the beach and near area attractions. Inside are some delightful public areas. **Rooms:** 189 rms and stes. CI 4pm/CO noon. Nonsmoking rms avail. Some rooms offer pretty panoramic views. **Amenities:** 🛏 🍴 🖥 A/C, cable TV w/movies, bathrobes. All units w/minibars, all w/terraces. **Services:** ✗ VP 🖼 ⤴ Twice-daily maid svce, car-rental desk, babysitting. **Facilities:** 🖽 🚲 ⛺ 🏊 🖳 🔲500 ♿ 2 restaurants, 2 bars (1 w/entertainment), 1 beach (ocean), snorkeling, washer/dryer. **Rates:** Peak (Dec–Apr) $200–$340 S or D; $750–$1,000 ste. Extra person $25. Children under age 18 stay free. Lower rates off-season. Parking: Outdoor, free. AE, CB, DC, DISC, ER, JCB, MC, V.

## RESTAURANTS 🍽

### Chili's Grill & Bar

In the Shops at Jupiter, 65 US 1; tel 561/575-6900. **American/Southwestern.** A fun, casual eatery with comfortable booths, serving good food at affordable prices. Enjoy a variety of salads, soups, or burgers for lunch, or opt for the fajitas at dinner. Happy hour from opening until 7 pm daily. **FYI:** Reservations not accepted. Children's menu. **Open:** Mon–Thurs 11:15am–11pm, Fri–Sat 11:15am–midnight, Sun 11:15am–10:30pm. **Prices:** Main courses $5–$12. AE, DC, DISC, MC, V. ♿

### Cobblestone Cafe

In Gallery Square North, 383 Tequesta Dr, Tequesta; tel 561/747-4419. **New American.** This cozy, country-style cafe offers a variety of seafood dishes, from the fresh catch of the day to sautéed crab cakes. The regularly changing menu may also include grilled leg of lamb or veal medallions. **FYI:** Reservations recommended. Beer and wine only. No smoking. **Open:** Lunch Mon–Fri 11:30am–2:30pm; dinner daily 5:30–9:30pm. **Prices:** Main courses $14–$25. AE, DISC, MC, V. ♥ ♿

### The Crab House
1065 FL A1A Service Rd; tel 561/744-1300. Across from the Jupiter Lighthouse. **American/Seafood/Steak.** A tropically decorated, contemporary waterfront cafe serving Caribbean-inspired cuisine. Specialties include Mahi Orleans and Crab Reef Raff. **FYI:** Reservations not accepted. Children's menu. **Open:** Sun–Thurs 11:30am–10pm, Fri–Sat 11:30am–11pm. **Prices:** Main courses $11–$35. AE, CB, DC, DISC, MC, V. ♥ ♿

### Grayson's Log Cabin Restaurant
631 N FL A1A; tel 561/746-6877. Between US 1 and Indiantown Rd. **Barbecue/Seafood/Steak.** A rustic eatery serving hearty fare in a relaxing atmosphere. The menu offers traditional grilled and barbecued favorites like steaks, chicken, and spare ribs, as well as some seafood dishes. **FYI:** Reservations accepted. Children's menu. **Open:** Mon–Fri 11am–10pm, Sat–Sun 8am–10pm. **Prices:** Main courses $9–$19; prix fixe $10. AE, CB, DC, MC, V. ♥ ♿

### Schooners
1001 N FL A1A; tel 561/746-7558. **Seafood.** A casual grill with a nautical motif. Appetizers include crabmeat-stuffed mushrooms; fresh fish entrees might be swordfish, salmon, or snapper. The fish can be ordered broiled, blackened, or grilled. **FYI:** Reservations not accepted. Children's menu. **Open:** Sun–Thurs 11am–9:30pm, Fri–Sat 11am–10:30pm. **Prices:** Main courses $10–$20. AE, MC, V. ⛵ ♿

## ATTRACTIONS 📷

### Florida History Center & Museum
805 N US 1; tel 561/747-6639. In Burt Reynolds Park. Chronologically arranged exhibits in this museum relate to Jupiter and its vicinity, from fossil shells to Seminole utensils to Burt Reynolds's boots.

Nearby **Jupiter Inlet Lighthouse** is the oldest standing structure in the area. The 135-year-old lighthouse contains a museum and is open for tours. **Open:** Tues–Fri 10am–5pm, Sat–Sun 1–5pm. $

### Blowing Rocks Preserve
FL A1A, Jupiter Island. This wonderfully picturesque beach on Jupiter Island owes its beauty to a cluster of large rock formations. Although not recommended for swimming, it is a popular fishing spot. The preserve is a 10-minute drive from downtown Jupiter.

### Hobe Sound National Wildlife Refuge
Hobe Sound; tel 561/546-6141. Most of this 900-acre refuge is on the mainland, along US 1 near Hobe Sound, where visitors will find a museum and nature center. The remainder of the refuge covers the north end of Jupiter Island, which is closed to car traffic. Visitors to this portion of the refuge enjoy the island's three miles of undeveloped beach. Swimming, fishing, boating, hiking, nature trails. **Open:** Daily sunrise–sunset. $$

# Kennedy Space Center

For lodging and dining, see Cocoa, Cocoa Beach, Indialantic, Melbourne, Titusville

Located at Cape Canaveral on FL 405, 12 miles east of Titusville. The Kennedy Space Center Visitor Center (tel 407/452-2121) allows visitors to explore the past, present, and future of human endeavors in space. Many exhibits, movie presentations, and two major tours make up a full-day itinerary designed to inform and entertain.

The **Red Tour**, a double-decker bus ride, includes stops at the Space Shuttle launch complex, the massive Vehicle Assembly building, and more. The **Blue Tour** highlights the history of space exploration, traveling through Cape Canaveral Air Force Station to visit the Air Force Space Museum and the mission control center for the Mercury and Gemini programs. Both tours last about two hours and depart at regular intervals beginning at 9:30am, with the last tour departing two hours before dusk. Purchase tickets at the Ticket Pavilion as soon as you arrive.

Other features include "Satellites and You," a 50-minute voyage through a simulated space station explaining satellites and their uses; Explorer, a full-scale orbiter mock-up; the Galaxy Center, featuring three IMAX film presentations, a NASA art exhibit, and a walk-through model of the space station *Freedom*; Spaceport Theater; the Rocket Garden; and the Astronauts Memorial.

Also a part of the Space Center is the 140,000-acre **Merritt Island National Wildlife Refuge** (tel 407/861-0667), a pristine wilderness of dense woods, unspoiled beaches, and swampland that provides refuge for more than 500 species, many threatened or endangered. To find out about guided nature walks, interpretive programs, and self-guided hikes contact the Visitor Information Center, located 4 miles east of Titusville on FL 402 (open Mon–Fri 8am–4:30pm, Sat to 5pm). Note: There won't be enough time to see the refuge and the Space Center all in 1 day.

For tickets to a launch call Spaceport USA for current launch information (ext 260 to make reservations or fax 407/454-3211). Tickets are $7 adults, $4 children 3–11, under 3 free. Tickets may be reserved up to 7 days before a launch but must be picked up at least 2 days defore launch. A special bus takes observers to a site just 6 miles from the launch pad.

## HOTEL 🏨

### ≣≣ Holiday Inn Merritt Island
260 E Merritt Island Causeway, Merritt Island, 32952; tel 407/452-7711 or toll free 800/HOLIDAY. Exit 75 off I-95.

Casual, attractive lodging. **Rooms:** 128 rms. CI 3pm/CO noon. Nonsmoking rms avail. **Amenities:** 🔒 ⚡ A/C, cable TV. **Services:** ✗ 🚗 🖼 🛎 Car-rental desk. **Facilities:** 🏊 🍽 1 🟫 400 ⚡ 1 restaurant, 1 bar (w/entertainment). **Rates:** Peak (Feb–Apr/July–Aug) $59–$85 S or D. Extra person $8. Children under age 18 stay free. Lower rates off-season. AP and MAP rates avail. Parking: Outdoor, free. AE, CB, DC, DISC, ER, JCB, MC, V.

# Key Biscayne

This upscale community of 9,000 is linked to Miami by the Rickenbacker Causeway, making it a favorite among city professionals. Lots of sunning, swimming, fishing, and wind surfing take place at Crandon Park, Bill Baggs Recreation Area, and Cape Florida State Recreation Area. **Information:** Key Biscayne Chamber of Commerce, 95 W McIntyre St, Key Biscayne, 33149 (tel 305/361-5207).

## RESORT 🏨

### 🏳🏳🏳🏳 Sonesta Beach Resort
350 Ocean Dr, 33149; tel 305/361-2021 or toll free 800/SONESTA; fax 305/361-3096. Rickenbacker Causeway to Crandon Blvd. A full-service, top-notch resort located on the ocean side of Key Biscayne. The beaches are white, the water is clear and the on-site activities are abundant. The resort is located between the Bill Baggs Cape Florida State Park with its historic lighthouse, and Crandon Park & Marina with miles of winding bicycle paths. **Rooms:** 292 rms and stes; 3 cottages/villas. CI 3pm/CO noon. Nonsmoking rms avail. All 300 recently renovated rooms have either one king or two queen size beds. Also available are 15 one- and two-bedroom suites. Perfect for families, the three-bedroom vacation homes have screened in private heated swimming pools, two-line telephones, entertainment system, plus a washer and dryer. **Amenities:** 🔒 ⚡ 🛎 A/C, satel TV w/movies, dataport, voice mail, in-rm safe. All units w/minibars, all w/terraces. **Services:** 🍽 🗝 VP 🚗 🖼 🛎 Twice-daily maid svce, car-rental desk, social director, masseur, children's program, babysitting. **Facilities:** 🏊 🚲 ⛰ 🍽 18 🏖 ⚓ 🍸 🎾 🛥 🟫 630 💻 ⚡ 3 restaurants (see "Restaurants" below), 4 bars (1 w/entertainment), 1 beach (ocean), basketball, volleyball, games rm, snorkeling, spa, sauna, steam rm, whirlpool, beauty salon, playground. Olympic-size swimming pool and whirlpool spa overlook the ocean. **Rates:** Peak (Dec 15–Apr) $235–$325 D; $600–$1,200 ste; $800–$1,700 cottage/villa. Extra person $35. Children under age 12 stay free. Lower rates off-season. AP and MAP rates avail. Parking: Indoor/outdoor, free. AE, CB, DC, DISC, JCB, MC, V.

## RESTAURANTS 🍴

### The Dragons
In Sonesta Beach Resort, 350 Ocean Dr; tel 305/361-2021. **Chinese.** Standard Chinese restaurant. Extensive menu. **FYI:**
Reservations recommended. Children's menu. **Open:** Daily 5–11pm. **Prices:** Main courses $11–$18. AE, MC, V. 🖥 VP ⚡

### Rusty Pelican
3201 Rickenbacker Causeway; tel 305/361-3818. **Seafood/Steak.** A very romantic dining room with great ocean views. The menu offers seafood dishes, steaks, and an extensive wine selection. **FYI:** Reservations recommended. Violin. Children's menu. **Open:** Lunch Mon–Sat 11am–4pm; dinner Sun–Thurs 5–11pm, Fri–Sat 5pm–midnight; brunch Sun 10:30am–3pm. **Prices:** Main courses $16–$23; prix fixe $28. AE, CB, DC, DISC, MC, V. ♥ 🏞 ⚡

### ⭐ Sundays on the Bay
5420 Crandon Blvd; tel 305/361-6777. 3 mi E of toll plaza. **New American/Seafood.** An engaging attractive cafe furnished in white wrought iron and wicker. The eclectic menu offers a wide variety of dishes, including Caribbean bouillabaisse in natural broth and pan-roasted lamb shank on Tuscan beans. Oven-roasted red snapper with rum-glazed bananas and fried leeks is a favorite. **FYI:** Reservations recommended. **Open:** Lunch Mon–Sat 11:30am–3pm; dinner daily 6–11pm; brunch Sun 11:30am–3pm. **Prices:** Main courses $9–$18. AE, DC, MC, V. ♥

## ATTRACTIONS 📷

### Miami Seaquarium
4400 Rickenbacker Causeway; tel 305/361-5705. A marine-life park offering six different animal shows each day as well as marine exhibits and aquariums. Shows feature killer whales, sea lions, sharks, and Flipper, the dolphin star of the old television series. Visitors can also see manatees, sea turtles, exotic birds, and reptiles. **Open:** Daily 9:30am–6pm. **$$$$**

### First Street Beach
Crandon Blvd, bottom of Ocean Dr. Crandon Blvd, at the bottom of Ocean Dr. One of the area's best surfing beaches. No lifeguard.

### Crandon Park Beach
Offers 3 miles of oceanfront beach and 493 acres of park, with barbecue grills and soccer and softball fields. There is also a public 18-hole golf course, a tennis center, and a marina. **$**

### Bill Baggs Cape Florida State Park
1200 S Crandon Blvd; tel 305/361-5811. On the south end of Key Biscayne. Barbecue grills, picnic tables, and bicycle trails are among the recreational facilities available. Adjacent, narrow soft-sand beach is home of Cape Florida Lighthouse, with re-created lightkeeper's residence. **Open:** Daily sunrise–sunset. **$$**

# Key Largo

The island immortalized by Humphrey Bogart and Lauren Bacall in the 1948 movie of the same name. This first stop into the Keys attracts one million divers a year to John Pennekamp Coral Reef State Park. On land, highlights include a dolphin research center and a salvaged treasure museum. **Information:** Florida Keys Visitor Center, 105950 Overseas Hwy, Key Largo, 33037 (tel 305/451-1414 or toll free 800/822-1088).

## HOTELS 🏨

### ≣≣≣ Holiday Inn Key Largo Resort & Marina
99701 Overseas Hwy, MM 99.7, 33037; tel 305/451-2121 or toll free 800/843-5397; fax 305/451-5592. **Rooms:** 132 rms. CI 3pm/CO 11am. Nonsmoking rms avail. **Amenities:** 🛏 A/C, cable TV w/movies, voice mail. Some units w/minibars, some w/terraces. **Services:** ✗ 🖨 🛎 Babysitting. **Facilities:** 🎱 ⛱ 🏊 🛦 1 restaurant, 2 bars, games rm, snorkeling, whirlpool. **Rates:** Peak (Dec–Apr) $129–$199 S or D. Extra person $10. Children under age 18 stay free. Min stay special events. Lower rates off-season. Parking: Outdoor, free. AE, CB, DC, DISC, MC, V.

### ≣≣≣ Marina Del Mar Bayside Resort
99500 Overseas Hwy, MM 99.5, PO Box 1050, 33037; tel 305/451-4450 or toll free 800/242-5229; fax 305/451-9650. This sibling of the Marina Del Mar Resort and Marina (see below) is set back from the highway in a three-story, coral-colored building. **Rooms:** 56 rms and stes. CI 3pm/CO 11am. Nonsmoking rms avail. Standardized rooms with tropical decor; some have bayviews. **Amenities:** 🛏 A/C, cable TV. Some units w/terraces. **Services:** 🛎 **Facilities:** 🎱 🛦 1 restaurant (lunch and dinner only), 1 bar, 1 beach (bay), lawn games. Guests can use health club facilities and washers/dryers at nearby Marina Del Mar Resort and Marina. **Rates:** Peak (Dec–Apr) $99–$169 S or D; $199–$269 ste. Children under age 18 stay free. Min stay special events. Lower rates off-season. Parking: Outdoor, free. AE, DC, DISC, MC, V.

### ≣≣ Marina Del Mar Resort and Marina
527 Caribbean Dr, MM 94, 33037; tel 305/451-4107 or toll free 800/451-3483; fax 305/451-1891. Family-oriented four-story property boasts the largest pool in the Upper Keys. **Rooms:** 76 rms, stes, and effic. CI 3pm/CO 11am. Nonsmoking rms avail. Studios have Murphy beds. **Amenities:** 🛏 📺 A/C, cable TV, refrig. Some units w/terraces. **Services:** 🛎 **Facilities:** 🎱 ⛱ 🏊 🛁 🚐 1 restaurant (lunch and dinner only), 2 bars (1 w/entertainment), snorkeling, whirlpool, washer/dryer. Open-air bar overlooks marina. **Rates (CP):** Peak (Dec–Apr) $99–$169 S or D; $149–$329 ste; $139–$329 effic. Children under age 18 stay free. Min stay special events. Lower rates off-season. Parking: Outdoor, free. AE, CB, DC, DISC, JCB, MC, V.

## LODGE

### UNRATED Jules' Undersea Lodge
51 Shoreland Dr, PO Box 3330, 33037; tel 305/451-2353; fax 305/451-4789. MM 103.2. Originally built as a research lab in the 1970s, this small underwater compartment now operates as a single-room hotel. The lodge rests on pillars on the ocean floor; to get inside, guests swim under the structure and pop up into the unit through a four-by-six-foot "moon pool." Most popular with diving honeymooners and other active and romantic couples. Reserve as far in advance as possible. **Rooms:** 1 stes. CI open/CO open. No smoking. The 300-foot-deep underwater suite consists of a bedroom and galley, and sleeps up to six. **Amenities:** 🛏 ⛄ A/C, refrig, VCR. No TV. **Services:** ✗ Dinner is delivered to your door in a waterproof container. **Facilities:** 🏊 Snorkeling. **Rates (MAP):** $195 ste. Parking: Outdoor, free. AE, DISC, MC, V.

## RESORTS

### ≣≣≣ Marriott's Key Largo Bay Beach Resort
103800 Overseas Hwy MM 103.5, 33037; tel 305/453-9393 or toll free 800/932-9332; fax 305/453-0093. **Rooms:** 145 rms and stes. CI 3pm/CO noon. Nonsmoking rms avail. **Amenities:** 🛏 ⛄ 🍴 A/C, cable TV w/movies, in-rm safe. All units w/minibars, some w/terraces, some w/whirlpools. **Services:** 🛎 Babysitting. **Facilities:** 🎱 🚴 ⛱ 🏊 🚐 🛦 2 restaurants, 3 bars (1 w/entertainment), 1 beach (ocean), games rm, snorkeling, spa, whirlpool, washer/dryer. **Rates:** Peak (Dec–Apr) $129–$259 S or D; $295–$350 ste. Extra person $25. Children under age 18 stay free. Lower rates off-season. Parking: Indoor/outdoor, free. AE, DC, DISC, MC, V.

### ≣≣≣≣ Ocean Reef Club
31 Ocean Reef Dr, 33037; tel 305/367-2611 or toll free 800/741-REEF; fax 305/367-5860. 4,000 acres. A beautifully landscaped and well-managed resort complex with a variety of accommodations and strict security. An ideal family vacation spot. Nonmember guests may be sponsored for their first visit by the hotel's membership department, but subsequent visits must be at the sponsorship of a member. **Rooms:** 199 rms, stes, and effic; 112 cottages/villas. CI 3pm/CO noon. Nonsmoking rms avail. **Amenities:** 🛏 ⛄ 📺 🍴 A/C, cable TV w/movies, voice mail. All units w/minibars, all w/terraces, some w/whirlpools. **Services:** ✗ 🚗 🖨 🛎 Car-rental desk, masseur, children's program, babysitting. **Facilities:** 🎱 🚴 ⛱ 🏌 ⛵ 🏊 🚐 🖥 🛦 4 restaurants, 3 bars (1 w/entertainment), 1 beach (ocean), lifeguard, basketball, games rm, lawn games, spa, whirlpool, beauty salon, playground, washer/dryer. Manmade beach. Fishing village. **Rates:** Peak (Dec 18–Apr 14) $310–$410 S or D; $560–$1,750 ste; $390–$610 effic; $315–$980 cottage/villa. Extra person $20. Children under age 16 stay free. Min stay peak. Lower rates off-season. AP and MAP rates avail. Parking: Indoor/outdoor, free. AE, DC, DISC, MC, V.

≣≣≣ **Sheraton Key Largo Resort**
97000 S Overseas Hwy MM 97, 33037; tel 305/852-5553 or toll free 800/826-1006; fax 305/852-8669. 13 acres. A stylish facility that blends in with the natural surroundings and offers spectacular sunset views. **Rooms:** 200 rms and stes. CI 3pm/CO 11am. Nonsmoking rms avail. Upper floors offer the best views. **Amenities:** 🚽 🅰 🖲 A/C, cable TV w/movies. All units w/minibars, all w/terraces, some w/whirlpools. **Services:** ✗ ☞ VP 🚙 ⛵ 🐬 Masseur, children's program, babysitting. **Facilities:** 🛎 ⛰ 🌊 ⚓ 🚣 🎱 ⛵ 400 ⛳ 2 restaurants, 3 bars (2 w/entertainment), 1 beach (ocean), volleyball, games rm, whirlpool, beauty salon. **Rates:** Peak (Dec 19–Apr) $240–$425 S or D; $425 ste. Extra person $15. Children under age 17 stay free. Lower rates off-season. AP and MAP rates avail. Parking: Outdoor, free. AE, DC, DISC, MC, V.

## ATTRACTIONS 🖼

### Seven-Mile Bridge
Overseas Hwy MM 40–47. The Keys' most celebrated span rests on 546 concrete piers and rises to a 72-foot crest, the highest point in the Keys. The first bridge was constructed here in 1910, built to carry Henry Flagler's railroad track, which ran all the way to Key West. Most of the bridge was destroyed by a hurricane in 1935, but you can still see portions of the original track bed running for miles alongside the modern span that was constructed 10 years later.

### John Pennekamp Coral Reef State Park
Overseas Hwy MM 102.5; tel 305/451-1202. One of the largest and most popular parks in the Keys. The visitor center houses a 30,000-gallon saltwater marine aquarium surrounded by various educational exhibits and screens movies about the area's natural resources and the coral reef. There are two small, manmade beach areas; a concessionaire operates glass-bottom boat tours and snorkeling and scuba trips to the reef. Swimming, sailboat and canoe rentals, nature trails, camping. **Open:** Daily 8am–sunset. $$

# Key West

Favored by presidents and artists from Ernest Hemingway to native "conchhead" Jimmy Buffett, the southernmost point in the United States juxtaposes idyllic homes with utilitarian motels, tin-roof shacks with chic resorts, and historicity with tropical kitsch. Numerous magicians, jugglers, acrobats, and mimes perform at the nightly Mallory Pier Sunset Celebration. **Information:** Key West Chamber of Commerce, 402 Wall St, PO Box 984, Key West, 33040 (tel 305/294-2587).

## HOTELS 🏨

### ≣≣ Bayside Key West Resort Hotel
3444 N Roosevelt Blvd, 33040; tel 305/296-7593 or toll free 800/888-3233; fax 305/294-5246. US 1 to Roosevelt Blvd. Close to a public beach, this upbeat facility features rooms, suites, and penthouses. **Rooms:** 64 rms, stes, and effic. CI 2pm/CO 11am. Nonsmoking rms avail. Rooms are moderately sized and adequately furnished, with Key West decor. Some have views of the Gulf. **Amenities:** 🚽 🅰 A/C, cable TV, in-rm safe. Some units w/minibars, some w/terraces. **Services:** ⛵ 🐬 Babysitting. **Facilities:** 🛎 20 ⛳ **Rates (CP):** $99–$149 S or D; $149–$229 ste; $149–$229 effic. Children under age 16 stay free. Min stay special events. Lower rates off-season. Parking: Outdoor, free. AE, CB, DC, DISC, MC, V.

### ≣≣≣ The Gardens Hotel
526 Angela St, 33040; tel 305/294-2661 or toll free 800/526-2664; fax 305/292-1007. 1 block N of Duval St. A sophisticated hotel with the feel of a West Indian plantation house. Not recommended for children under 18. **Rooms:** 17 rms and stes. Executive level. CI 3pm/CO noon. No smoking. Rooms are beautifully appointed, each with its individual charm. **Amenities:** 🚽 🅰 🖲 🍽 A/C, cable TV w/movies, refrig, in-rm safe, bathrobes. All units w/minibars, all w/terraces, all w/whirlpools. **Services:** ☞ ⛵ Twice-daily maid svce. **Facilities:** 🛎 1 bar, whirlpool. **Rates (CP):** Peak (Dec–Apr) $225–$315 S or D; $435–$625 ste. Min stay peak, wknds, and special events. Lower rates off-season. Parking: Outdoor, free. AE, MC, V.

### ≣≣ Holiday Inn Beachside
3841 N Roosevelt Blvd, 33040; tel 305/294-2571 or toll free 800/HOLIDAY; fax 305/296-5659. A pleasant facility consisting of a two-story section that wraps around a landscaped pool, and a four-story building that faces the water and houses deluxe rooms. **Rooms:** 222 rms and stes. CI 3pm/CO noon. Nonsmoking rms avail. **Amenities:** 🚽 🅰 A/C, cable TV, in-rm safe. Some units w/terraces. **Services:** ✗ ⛵ Car-rental desk. **Facilities:** 🛎 🚲 ⛰ 🌊 2 600 ⛳ 1 restaurant, 1 bar, 1 beach (bay), snorkeling, whirlpool, washer/dryer. **Rates:** Peak (Feb–Apr) $125–$240 S or D; $175–$275 ste. Children under age 19 stay free. Lower rates off-season. Parking: Outdoor, free. AE, DC, DISC, JCB, V.

### ≣≣ Holiday Inn La Concha Hotel
430 Duval St, 33040; tel 305/296-2991 or toll free 800/745-2191; fax 305/294-3283. Situated in the heart of Key West's restaurants, bars, and shops. Guests can enjoy great sunset views from the rooftop lounge. **Rooms:** 160 rms and stes. Executive level. CI 4pm/CO 11am. Nonsmoking rms avail. **Amenities:** 🚽 🅰 🍽 A/C, cable TV w/movies. Some units w/minibars, some w/terraces. **Services:** ✗ ☞ ⛵ 🐬 Babysitting. **Facilities:** 🛎 300 ⛳ 2 restaurants, 4 bars. **Rates:** Peak (Dec–Apr) $175–$235 S or D; $240–$300 ste. Extra person $15. Children under age 16 stay free. Min stay special events. Lower rates off-season. Parking: Outdoor, free. AE, CB, DC, DISC, JCB, MC, V.

### ≣≣≣ Hyatt Key West
601 Front St, 33040; tel 305/296-9000 or toll free 800/233-1234; fax 305/292-1038. This hotel, known for beautiful sunset views, offers guests many amenities in a waterfront

setting. Staff is very friendly and accommodating. **Rooms:** 120 rms and stes. Executive level. CI 4pm/CO noon. Nonsmoking rms avail. Tastefully appointed rooms. **Amenities:** 🛎 🧖 📺 🍴 A/C, refrig, dataport, voice mail, in-rm safe, bathrobes. All units w/minibars, all w/terraces, some w/whirlpools. **Services:** ✕ 🆅🅿 🖼 🛎 Twice-daily maid svce, car-rental desk, social director, masseur, babysitting. **Facilities:** 🏊 🚲 ⛰ ⚓ 🛥 🛶 60 👟 2 restaurants, 2 bars (1 w/entertainment), 1 beach (ocean), snorkeling, spa, sauna, whirlpool, beauty salon. **Rates:** Peak (Dec–Apr) $280–$340 S or D; $360–$660 ste. Extra person $45. Children under age 18 stay free. Min stay special events. Lower rates off-season. Parking: Outdoor, free. AE, MC, V.

### ▤▤▤ Marriott's Reach Resort

1435 Simonton St, 33040; tel 305/296-5000 or toll free 800/874-4118; fax 305/296-2830. A nice beachfront hotel in an unusually tranquil setting. **Rooms:** 149 rms and stes. Executive level. CI 4pm/CO 11am. Nonsmoking rms avail. **Amenities:** 🛎 🧖 🍴 A/C, satel TV w/movies, refrig, voice mail, in-rm safe, bathrobes. All units w/minibars, all w/terraces, some w/whirlpools. **Services:** ✕ 🖥 🆅🅿 🍴 🖼 🛎 Car-rental desk, social director, masseur, babysitting. **Facilities:** 🏊 ⛰ 🛶 80 👟 2 restaurants, 3 bars (2 w/entertainment), 1 beach (ocean), spa, sauna, steam rm, beauty salon. Guests may use facilities at nearby Marriott's Casa Marina Resort. **Rates:** Peak (Dec–Apr) $305–$350 S or D; $350–$490 ste. Extra person $35. Children under age 18 stay free. Min stay special events. Lower rates off-season. AP and MAP rates avail. Parking: Indoor, free. AE, CB, DC, DISC, MC, V.

### ▤▤ Ocean Key House Suite Resort and Marina

Zero Duval St, 33040 (Old Town); tel 305/296-7201 or toll free 800/328-9815; fax 305/292-7685. In a prime location, this is ideal for those who appreciate independent living in an upscale environment. A good family offering. **Rooms:** 100 rms, stes, and effic. CI 4pm/CO noon. Nonsmoking rms avail. Many units have ocean views. **Amenities:** 🛎 🧖 📺 🍴 A/C, cable TV, refrig, VCR, bathrobes. Some units w/minibars, some w/terraces, some w/whirlpools. **Services:** ✕ 🖥 🖼 🛎 Babysitting. **Facilities:** 🏊 🍴 🛶 30 👟 1 bar (w/entertainment), snorkeling. **Rates:** Peak (Dec–Apr) $160 S or D; $345–$700 ste; $345–$700 effic. Extra person $25. Children under age 18 stay free. Min stay wknds. Lower rates off-season. Parking: Indoor/outdoor, free. AE, CB, DC, DISC, MC, V.

### ▤▤▤ The Pier House

1 Duval St, 33040 (Old Town); tel 305/296-4600 or toll free 800/327-8340; fax 305/296-7569. Elegant, comfortable rooms with a variety of views and amenities. **Rooms:** 142 rms and stes. Executive level. CI 4pm/CO noon. Nonsmoking rms avail. Rooms vary from simple business-class to luxurious. About two dozen overlook the pool. **Amenities:** 🛎 🧖 📺 🍴 A/C, cable TV w/movies, refrig. All units w/minibars, all w/terraces, some w/fireplaces, some w/whirlpools. **Services:** ✕ 🖥 🖼 🛎 Twice-daily maid svce, social director, masseur,

children's program, babysitting. **Facilities:** 🏊 🚲 🍴 🎾 🛶 175 👟 4 restaurants, 5 bars (3 w/entertainment), 1 beach (ocean), snorkeling, spa, sauna, steam rm, whirlpool, beauty salon. First-rate spa and fitness facilities are ideal for those who enjoy a little pampering. **Rates:** Peak (Dec–Apr) $275–$435 S or D; $450–$950 ste. Extra person $35. Children under age 18 stay free. Min stay wknds and special events. Lower rates off-season. AP and MAP rates avail. Parking: Outdoor, free. AE, CB, DC, DISC, MC, V.

### ▤▤▤ Sheraton Suites Key West

2001 S Roosevelt Blvd, 33040; tel 305/292-9800 or toll free 800/325-3535; fax 305/294-6009. The area's newest hotel, located opposite Key West's best swimming beach and away from downtown district. Beautifully landscaped grounds and outdoor dining courtyard. Architecture is attempt at turn-of-the-century Key West look. **Rooms:** 180 stes. CI 3pm/CO 11am. Nonsmoking rms avail. All are two-room suites, with tropical decor and upscale appointments. **Amenities:** 🛎 🧖 📺 🍴 A/C, cable TV w/movies. All units w/minibars, some w/terraces, some w/whirlpools. **Services:** ✕ 🖥 🍴 🖼 🛎 Social director, babysitting. Free shuttle to Old Town. Free newspaper daily. **Facilities:** 🏊 🛶 60 👟 1 restaurant, 2 bars, whirlpool, washer/dryer. Atmospheric dining room decorated in fish-market motif. **Rates (BB):** Peak (Dec–Apr) $380–$450 ste. Extra person $25. Children under age 18 stay free. Lower rates off-season. Parking: Outdoor, free. AE, CB, DC, DISC, ER, JCB, MC, V.

## MOTELS

### ▤ Best Western Key Ambassador Resort Inn

3755 S Roosevelt Blvd, 33040; tel 305/296-3500 or toll free 800/432-4315; fax 305/296-9961. Pleasant low-rise with spacious grounds, located opposite the seawall and away from the downtown crush. **Rooms:** 100 rms. CI 3pm/CO noon. Standard budget rooms. **Amenities:** 🛎 🧖 A/C, cable TV w/movies, refrig. All units w/minibars, all w/terraces. **Services:** 🛎 **Facilities:** 🏊 Washer/dryer. **Rates (CP):** Peak (Dec–Mar) $130–$185 S or D. Extra person $10. Children under age 18 stay free. Lower rates off-season. Parking: Outdoor, free. AE, CB, DC, DISC, MC, V.

### ▤▤ Comfort Inn

3824 N Roosevelt Blvd, 33040; tel 305/294-3773 or toll free 800/695-5150; fax 305/294-3773. Neatly landscaped facility offering comfortable rooms. Short drive to historic district; convenient to restaurants. **Rooms:** 100 rms. CI 2pm/CO 11am. Nonsmoking rms avail. **Amenities:** 🛎 🧖 A/C, cable TV w/movies, refrig, in-rm safe. **Services:** 🛎 Babysitting. **Facilities:** 🏊 🚲 👟 Games rm, washer/dryer. **Rates (CP):** Peak (Dec–Apr) $110–$275 S or D. Extra person $10. Children under age 18 stay free. Min stay special events. Lower rates off-season. Parking: Outdoor, free. AE, CB, DC, DISC, ER, JCB, MC, V.

### ≣≣ Econo Lodge Resort of Key West

3820 N Roosevelt Blvd, 33040; tel 305/294-5511 or toll free 800/553-2666; fax 305/296-1939. Budget property. Rooms were recently renovated. **Rooms:** 145 rms, stes, and effic. CI 3pm/CO 11am. Nonsmoking rms avail. The decor is better than you'd expect from a motel in this price category. **Amenities:** 🗄 🕭 A/C, cable TV. **Services:** ✗ ⫝ **Facilities:** 🔢 ⅙ 1 restaurant, 1 bar (w/entertainment), washer/dryer. **Rates:** Peak (Dec–Apr) $150–$300 S or D; $170–$400 ste; $160–$350 cottage/villa. Extra person $10. Children under age 18 stay free. Min stay special events. Lower rates off-season. Parking: Outdoor, free. AE, CB, DC, DISC, ER, JCB, MC, V.

### ≣≣ Fairfield Inn by Marriott

2400 N Roosevelt Blvd, 33040; tel 305/296-5700 or toll free 800/843-5888; fax 305/292-9840. US 1 S to Roosevelt Blvd. An unusually nice chain motel, in a quiet spot yet close to Historic District action. **Rooms:** 132 rms and stes. CI 3pm/CO 11am. Nonsmoking rms avail. **Amenities:** 🗄 A/C, cable TV w/movies. **Services:** ⫝ Babysitting. **Facilities:** 🔢 ⅙ 1 bar, washer/dryer. **Rates (CP):** Peak (Dec–May) $129–$169 S or D; $149–$209 ste. Extra person $10. Children under age 18 stay free. Lower rates off-season. Parking: Outdoor, free. AE, DISC, MC, V.

### ≣≣ Hampton Inn

2801 N Roosevelt Blvd, 33040; tel 305/294-2917 or toll free 800/394-1634; fax 305/296-0211. Clean and reliable accommodations a short drive from Old Town. **Rooms:** 157 rms and stes. CI 3pm/CO noon. Nonsmoking rms avail. **Amenities:** 🗄 A/C, cable TV w/movies. 1 unit w/whirlpool. **Services:** 🖾 ⫝ ⫝ Babysitting. **Facilities:** 🔢 △ ⟨30⟩ ⅙ 1 bar, whirlpool, washer/dryer. Discounts available at nearby gym. **Rates (CP):** Peak (Dec–Apr) $129–$149 S or D; $250 ste. Children under age 18 stay free. Min stay special events. Lower rates off-season. Parking: Indoor/outdoor, free. AE, CB, DC, DISC, MC, V.

### ≣≣ Key Wester Resort Inn & Villas

3675 S Roosevelt Blvd, 33040; or toll free 800/477-8888; fax 305/296-5671 Ext 419. Off US 1 S. An array of low-rise buildings sprinkled roadside, near a public beach area. Limited landscaping. **Rooms:** 93 rms, stes, and effic; 12 cottages/villas. CI 2pm/CO 11am. Nonsmoking rms avail. **Amenities:** 🗄 A/C, cable TV. **Services:** ⫝ **Facilities:** 🔢 ⟨60⟩ 1 restaurant (bkfst and lunch only), 1 bar, games rm, sauna, washer/dryer. **Rates:** Peak (Dec–May) $59–$115 S or D; $99–$185 ste; $115–$155 effic; $99–$185 cottage/villa. Extra person $10. Children under age 17 stay free. Min stay special events. Lower rates off-season. Parking: Outdoor, free. AE, CB, DC, DISC, MC, V.

### ≣≣ Quality Inn of Key West

3850 N Roosevelt Blvd, 33040; tel 305/294-6681 or toll free 800/533-5024; fax 305/294-5618. A solid middle-grade operation. Gleaming lobby has lots of sunlight. **Rooms:** 148 rms, stes, and effic. CI 3pm/CO 11am. Nonsmoking rms avail. New tower building houses upgraded rooms, some with Gulf views. **Amenities:** 🗄 🕭 🖬 A/C, cable TV. Some units w/terraces. Guests can play Nintendo in their rooms through the hotel's entertainment center, Lodgenet. **Services:** ✗ ⫝ **Facilities:** 🔢 ⅙ 1 restaurant, 1 bar, washer/dryer. **Rates:** Peak (Dec 26–Mar 28) $145–$220 S or D; $256 ste; $225 effic. Extra person $10–$20. Children under age 18 stay free. Min stay special events. Lower rates off-season. Parking: Outdoor, free. AE, CB, DC, DISC, JCB, MC, V.

### ≣≣ Ramada Inn at Key's Inn

3420 N Roosevelt Blvd, 33040; tel 305/294-5541 or toll free 800/330-5541; fax 305/294-7932. US 1 to Roosevelt Blvd. Basic motel located on Key West's commercial strip. A good value for those who don't mind a short drive to the Historic District. **Rooms:** 104 rms, stes, and effic. CI 3pm/CO 11am. Nonsmoking rms avail. **Amenities:** 🗄 🕭 A/C, cable TV. **Services:** ✗ ⫝ ⫝ Babysitting. **Facilities:** 🔢 ⟨100⟩ ⅙ 1 restaurant, 2 bars (1 w/entertainment), games rm, washer/dryer. Tiki bar in large pool area. **Rates:** Peak (Dec–Apr) $140–$170 S or D; $190 ste; $200 effic. Extra person $10. Children under age 18 stay free. Min stay special events. Lower rates off-season. Parking: Outdoor, free. AE, CB, DC, DISC, JCB, MC, V.

### ≣≣ Santa Maria Motel

1401 Simonton St, 33040; tel 305/296-5678 or toll free 800/821-5397; fax 305/294-0010. An art deco motel, just a half-block to the beach and handy to restaurants. Spacious lobby. **Rooms:** 50 rms and effic. CI 2:30pm/CO noon. Nonsmoking rms avail. Units are cool and comfortable. **Amenities:** 🗄 A/C, cable TV. Some units w/terraces. **Services:** ⫝ Babysitting. **Facilities:** 🔢 1 bar. **Rates:** Peak (Dec–Apr) $125–$155 S or D; $145 effic. Extra person $20. Children under age 12 stay free. Min stay special events. Lower rates off-season. Parking: Outdoor, free. AE, DC, DISC, MC, V.

### ≣≣ South Beach Oceanfront Motel

508 South St, 33040; tel 305/296-5611 or toll free 800/354-4455; fax 305/294-8272. A beachside property popular among the younger crowd. Beach affords good swimming. **Rooms:** 47 rms, stes, and effic. CI 2pm CI 1pm/CO 11am. Nonsmoking rms avail. **Amenities:** 🗄 🖬 A/C, cable TV, refrig, in-rm safe. Some units w/terraces. **Services:** 🖾 ⫝ Babysitting. **Facilities:** 🔢 🚲 1 beach (ocean), snorkeling. 150-foot pier for sunbathing. **Rates:** Peak (Dec–Apr) $107–$205 S or D; $107–$205 ste; $107–$205 effic. Extra person $15. Children under age 17 stay free. Min stay special events. Lower rates off-season. Parking: Outdoor, free. AE, MC, V.

### ≣≣ Southernmost Motel in the USA

1319 Duval St, 33040; tel 305/296-6577 or toll free 800/354-4455; fax 305/294-8272. Handsomely outfitted, near the beach. **Rooms:** 127 rms and effic. CI 1pm/CO 11am. No smoking. Fine accommodations; some open to pool. **Amenities:** 🗄 🕭 A/C, cable TV, in-rm safe. Some units w/terraces. **Services:** ☍ 🖾 ⫝ Babysitting. **Facilities:** 🔢 🚲

30 ⬚ ⅍ 2 bars, whirlpool. **Rates:** Peak (Dec–Apr) $99–$175 S or D; $185 effic. Extra person $15. Children under age 17 stay free. Min stay wknds. Lower rates off-season. Parking: Outdoor, free. AE, MC, V.

## INNS

### The Curry Mansion Inn

511 Caroline St, 33040; tel 305/294-5349 or toll free 800/ 253-3466; fax 305/294-4093. This former mansion, listed on the National Register of Historic Places, is a popular sightseeing attraction (see also "Attractions" below) as well as a notable bed-and-breakfast. The inn is furnished with antiques in the main inn and wicker pieces in the annex; the lobby has beautiful hardwood floors and a tiled fireplace. Within walking distance of historic attractions, shopping, Mallory Square. **Rooms:** 29 rms and stes. CI 2pm/CO 11am. Nonsmoking rms avail. The few original mansion guest rooms are preferable to the annex rooms. **Amenities:** 🔳 ⅍ A/C, cable TV, refrig. Some units w/terraces, some w/whirlpools. **Services:** 🔺 Wine/sherry served. **Facilities:** 🔳 ⅍ Whirlpool, washer/dryer, guest lounge. Guests receive passes to Casa Marina's beach or to beach at Pier House Beach Club, a block away. **Rates (CP):** Peak (Dec–Apr) $200 S or D; $250 ste. Extra person $25. Children under age 16 stay free. Min stay special events. Lower rates off-season. Higher rates for special events/hols. Parking: Outdoor, free. AE, CB, DC, DISC, JCB, MC, V.

### Heron House

512 Simonton St, 33040; tel 305/294-9227 or toll free 800/ 294-1644; fax 305/294-5692. These four homes, set around a brick courtyard with a lush pool, date back to 1856. Unsuitable for children under 12. **Rooms:** 23 rms and stes. CI 1pm/CO 11am. Many rooms open onto the courtyard. **Amenities:** 🔳 ⅍ A/C, cable TV, refrig. Some units w/terraces, 1 w/whirlpool. **Facilities:** 🔳 ⅍ Guest lounge. Breakfast bar. **Rates (BB):** Peak (Dec–Apr) $125–$165 D; $195–$280 ste. Extra person $20. Min stay special events. Lower rates off-season. Higher rates for special events/hols. AE, CB, DC, MC, V.

### Island City House Hotel

411 William St, 33040; tel 305/294-5702 or toll free 800/ 634-8230; fax 305/294-1289. Consists of three guest houses dating back to the 1880s. Lush tropical gardens. **Rooms:** 24 stes and effic. CI 2pm/CO 11am. All suites, some with marble baths, are furnished with antiques, hardwood floors, and paddle fans. **Amenities:** 🔳 🔲 A/C, cable TV, refrig. Some units w/terraces. **Services:** 🔲 🔲 Breakfast buffet served on courtyard patio. **Facilities:** 🔳 🔲 Whirlpool. **Rates (CP):** Peak (Dec–Apr) $165–$250 ste; $165–$275 effic. Extra person $20. Children under age 12 stay free. Min stay special events. Lower rates off-season. Higher rates for special events/hols. CB, DC, DISC, MC.

### La Mer

506 South St, 33040; tel 305/296-5611; fax 305/294-8272. An early-1900s Victorian clapboard home on the beach, this is a lovely, upscale property. No children under 16. **Rooms:** 66 rms, stes, and effic. CI 1pm/CO 11am. Nonsmoking rms avail. Pleasant, spacious country inn–style rooms with ceiling fans and attractive appointments. **Amenities:** 🔳 ⅍ 🔲 A/C, cable TV, in-rm safe. All units w/minibars, some w/terraces. **Services:** 🔺 Afternoon tea and wine/sherry served. **Facilities:** 1 beach (ocean), guest lounge. Guests have access to pools at Southernmost Motel and South Beach Oceanfront Motel. **Rates (CP):** Peak (Dec–Apr) $175–$210 S or D; $175 ste. Extra person $10. Min stay special events. Lower rates off-season. Higher rates for special events/hols. Parking: Outdoor, free. AE, MC, V.

### The Marquesa Hotel

600 Fleming St, 33040; tel 305/292-1919 or toll free 800/ 869-4631; fax 305/294-2121. Luxurious, finely restored clapboard Victorian home with plush furnishings. Charming and delightful. **Rooms:** 27 rms and stes. CI 3pm/CO noon. Each room or suite is different, most with gilded mirrors, original art, and fresh flowers. **Amenities:** 🔳 ⅍ A/C, cable TV w/movies, in-rm safe, bathrobes. All units w/minibars, some w/terraces. **Services:** ✗ VP 🔺 Twice-daily maid svce, wine/ sherry served. **Facilities:** 🔳 1 restaurant (dinner only; see "Restaurants" below), 1 bar, guest lounge. First-rate restaurant. **Rates:** Peak (Dec–Apr) $185–$265 S or D; $265–$280 ste. Extra person $15. Min stay wknds. Lower rates off-season. Higher rates for special events/hols. Parking: Outdoor, free. AE, CB, DC, MC, V.

### Simonton Court Historic Inn and Cottages

320 Simonton St, 33040; tel 305/294-6386 or toll free 800/ 944-2687; fax 305/293-8446. A lovely courtyard setting and unique rooms make this a real find for those in search of quirky-yet-quaint Key West atmosphere. Unsuitable for children under 18. **Rooms:** 20 rms and stes; 6 cottages/villas. CI 2pm/CO 11am. Each unit is uniquely outfitted. **Amenities:** 🔳 ⅍ 🔲 🔲 A/C, cable TV, refrig, VCR, in-rm safe. All units w/minibars, some w/terraces, some w/whirlpools. **Services:** Twice-daily maid svce. **Facilities:** 🔳 Whirlpool, washer/ dryer. **Rates:** Peak (Dec–Apr) $150 S or D; $175 ste; $280 cottage/villa. Extra person $10. Min stay peak and special events. Lower rates off-season. Parking: Outdoor, $5/day. AE, DISC, MC, V.

### Wicker Guesthouse

913 Duval St, 33040; tel 305/296-4275 or toll free 800/ 880-4275; fax 305/294-7240. This Caribbean-style guesthouse offers comfortable rooms in the heart of Duval Street action. It is particularly appealing to value-oriented families. **Rooms:** 20 rms and stes. CI 1pm/CO 11am. Some rooms share living space and kitchen. Rooms are appointed with lots of wicker furnishings. **Amenities:** 🔲 A/C, cable TV, refrig, in-rm safe. No phone. Some units w/minibars, some w/terraces. Only some rooms with TV. **Services:** 🔲 Babysitting.

**Facilities:** On-site children's playhouse. Communal kitchen facilities; TV lounge. **Rates (CP):** Peak (Dec–Apr) $75 S or D; $95–$155 ste. Extra person $15. Children under age 2 stay free. Min stay peak and special events. Lower rates off-season. Higher rates for special events/hols. Parking: Outdoor, free. AE, CB, DC, DISC, MC, V.

## RESORT

### ☰☰☰ Marriott's Casa Marina Resort

1500 Reynolds St, 33040; tel 305/296-3535 or toll free 800/228-9290, 800/626-0777, 800/235-4837 in FL; fax 305/296-9960. At Flagler Ave. This historic property, built in the 1920s by railroad tycoon Henry Flagler, is one of the Keys' most enduring and romantic spots. It is set on a huge swath of oceanfront and has some of the most charming public areas south of Miami. **Rooms:** 311 rms and stes. Executive level. CI 4pm/CO 11am. No smoking. Ongoing renovations should bring up the standard of rooms. The historic hotel's structure renders some rooms quite small. **Amenities:** A/C, cable TV w/movies, refrig, dataport, voice mail, in-rm safe, bathrobes. All units w/minibars, some w/terraces. **Services:** ✕ ➡ VP 🚗 ◺ ↵ Twice-daily maid svce, social director, masseur, children's program, babysitting. **Facilities:** 🛼 ⚠ 🎣 🐬 🎱 500 ⚓ 2 restaurants, 2 bars (1 w/entertainment), 1 beach (ocean), volleyball, spa, sauna, whirlpool, beauty salon. **Rates:** Peak (Dec–Apr) $290–$348 S or D; $355–$720 ste. Extra person $10. Children under age 18 stay free. Min stay peak and special events. Lower rates off-season. Parking: Outdoor, free. AE, CB, DC, DISC, MC, V.

## RESTAURANTS 🍴

### Bagatelle

115 Duval St; tel 305/296-6609. **Caribbean.** Gingerbread-style architectural details ornament this casually elegant eatery. The menu features fresh local seafood prepared with a tropical flair, such as sautéed grouper with macadamia crust in a mango-butter sauce. Expansive veranda. **FYI:** Reservations recommended. Children's menu. **Open:** Peak (Dec–Apr) lunch daily 11:30am–3pm; dinner daily 5:30–9:45pm. **Prices:** Main courses $15–$24. AE, CB, DC, DISC, MC, V.

### ♥ Café des Artistes

1007 Simonton St; tel 305/294-7100. **French.** A lovely cafe with contemporary works of art covering its walls. The house specialty is Lobster Tango Mango. An extensive wine list is available. **FYI:** Reservations recommended. **Open:** Daily 6–11pm. **Prices:** Main courses $23–$36. AE, MC, V. ♥

### ♥★ Café Marquesa

In the Marquesa Hotel, 600 Fleming St; tel 305/292-1244. 1 block E of Duval St. **New American/Eclectic.** A smart, colorful, sophisticated cafe with a formal atmosphere and menu. **FYI:** Reservations recommended. No smoking. **Open:** Peak (Dec–Apr) daily 6–11pm. **Prices:** Main courses $17–$28. AE, MC, V. ⚫

### $★ Half Shell Raw Bar

231 Margaret St; tel 305/294-7496. **Seafood.** This appealing place, catering to tourists and locals alike, is decorated with license plates from all 50 states. You can sit at a picnic table and enjoy the catch of the day or oysters on the half-shell. **FYI:** Reservations not accepted. Children's menu. **Open:** Mon–Thurs 11am–10:30pm, Fri–Sat 11am–11pm, Sun noon–10:30pm. **Prices:** Main courses $5–$20; prix fixe $9–$20. DISC, MC, V. ⚓ 🖼

### Jimmy Buffett's Margaritaville Cafe

500 Duval St; tel 305/292-1435. **New American.** A collegiate-style eatery frequented by a generally young crowd. The menu includes salads, burgers, fish sandwiches, and the catch of the day, prepared deep-fried or grilled. Ben & Jerry's ice cream is available for dessert. **FYI:** Reservations not accepted. Big band. **Open:** Sun–Thurs 11am–2am, Fri–Sat 11am–4am. **Prices:** Main courses $10–$14. AE, MC, V.

### Kelly's Caribbean Bar and Grill and Brewery

301 Whitehead St; tel 305/293-8484. **Caribbean.** One of the few microbreweries in the Florida Keys. Indoor tables are available, but most patrons seem to prefer the tree-shaded outdoor dining area. The lunch menu includes cold curried seafood salad with mango chutney. Dinner entrees might include grilled jerk chicken breast with tamarind sweet-and-sour sauce. **FYI:** Reservations accepted. Cabaret/jazz. Children's menu. **Open:** Peak (Jan 15–May 15) Mon–Sat 11am–1am, Sun noon–1am. **Prices:** Main courses $10–$15. AE, DISC, MC, V. ⚫

### La-Te-Da's

1125 Duval St; tel 305/296-6706. **Seafood/Steak.** A beautiful, colorful little cafe with a great bar. Steaks, pastas, seafood dishes. Intimate outdoor dining available. **FYI:** Reservations accepted. **Open:** Lunch daily 9am–3pm; dinner Mon–Sat 6–11pm. **Prices:** Main courses $25. AE, DISC, MC, V. ⚓ ⚫

### ★ Louie's Backyard

700 Waddell Ave; tel 305/294-1061. **Caribbean/Eclectic.** This appealing open-air waterfront cafe is perfect for a casual lunch, a romantic dinner, or just a nightcap. The creative menu includes New Zealand venison, grouper, and wonderful salads. **FYI:** Reservations recommended. Dress code. **Open:** Peak (Oct–Aug) daily 11:30am–2am. **Prices:** Main courses $25–$35. AE, DC, MC, V. ▮ ⚓ 🖼

### Papa's Banyan Tree Cafe

217 Duval St; tel 305/293-7880. **New American.** A huge gumbo-limbo tree provides shade at this outdoor cafe. The simple lunch menu includes pizzas and burgers. For dinner, surf-and-turf and the catch of the day, served blackened, baked, or jerk-style, are available. **FYI:** Reservations not accepted. Children's menu. Beer and wine only. **Open:** Daily 8:30am–midnight. **Prices:** Main courses $10–$24. AE, CB, DC, DISC, MC, V. ⚓ ☑ ⚫

### $⭐ Pepe's
806 Caroline St; tel 305/294-7192. 4 blocks E of Duval St. **American.** Established in 1909, this local landmark serves up traditional American fare in a down-home setting. Nightly entrees include fresh fish, steaks, and pork chops. Friendly service and a loyal local clientele add to the jovial, come-as-you-are atmosphere. **FYI:** Reservations not accepted. Children's menu. **Open:** Daily 6:30am–10:30pm. **Prices:** Main courses $11–$20. AE, DISC, MC, V.

### Square One
In Duval Square, 1075 Duval St; tel 305/296-4300. **New American.** A beautiful, elegant dining room filled with floral murals. Before dinner, you can enjoy cocktails on the terrace. Fresh fish and pasta are featured on the contemporary menu. **FYI:** Reservations recommended. Piano. **Open:** Peak (Dec–May) daily 6:30–11pm. **Prices:** Main courses $15–$24. AE, DISC, MC, V. 🅥 &

### Yo Saké
722 Duval St; tel 305/294-2288. **Japanese.** Delicate lighting and cool, lively ambience. Favorites include seafood combo, beef Yakiniku, and sushi. **FYI:** Reservations accepted. Beer and wine only. **Open:** Daily 6–11pm. **Prices:** Main courses $13–$18. AE, CB, DC, DISC, MC, V.

## ATTRACTIONS 🏛

### Ernest Hemingway House Museum
907 Whitehead St; tel 305/294-1575. The Nobel Prize–winning author owned this beautiful Spanish colonial house from 1931 until his death in 1961. It was here that he wrote such novels as *For Whom the Bell Tolls*, *Death in the Afternoon*, and *To Have and Have Not*, and the short stories "The Snows of Kilimanjaro" and "The Short, Happy Life of Francis Macomber." Built in 1851, the house was one of the first in Key West to be fitted with indoor plumbing. Today, it contains many personal possessions as well as dozens of six-toed cats, said by some to be descendants of a feline family that was here in Hemingway's day. **Open:** Daily 9am–5pm. $$$

### Little White House
111 Front St; tel 305/294-9911. Built in 1890 as the residence of the naval base commandant, the house has been restored to its 1940s appearance. President Harry Truman spent 11 working vacations here, which is how the house came by its name. Guided tours include a look at original Truman furnishings and memorabilia. **Open:** Daily 9am–5pm. $$$

### Audubon House and Gardens
205 Whitehead St; tel 305/294-2116. The restored three-story house, surrounded by lush tropical gardens, features the master artist's original etchings and a large collection of lithographs. The house also holds a collection of porcelain birds and period furnishings. **Open:** Daily 9:30am–5pm. $$$

### Curry Mansion
511 Caroline St; tel 305/294-5349. Built in 1855 for William Curry, Florida's first millionaire, this "conch-style" house is a tribute to the early days of Key West and is listed in the National Register of Historic Places. Inside are an eclectic mix of stylish furnishings (including a Frank Lloyd Wright–designed lamp), Tiffany glass, mahogany paneling, and Audubon prints. Part of the mansion operates as a bed-and-breakfast (see above). **Open:** Daily 10am–5pm. $$

### East Martello Museum and Gallery
3501 S Roosevelt Blvd; tel 305/296-3913. Housed in a pre–Civil War fort, the museum's various exhibits and artifacts illustrate Key West's history of shipwrecks, pirates, sponging, and cigar-making. Works of local artists are also displayed. **Open:** Daily 9am–5pm. $$

### Key West Lighthouse Museum
938 Whitehead St; tel 305/294-0012. Built in 1847, this historic brick lighthouse has 88 steps leading to the top. The observation level provides a panoramic view of the Keys. **Open:** Daily 9:30am–5pm. $$

### Key West Cemetery
Margaret and Angela Sts. This decidedly unsolemn cemetery of above-ground vaults (a high water table and rocky soil prevent traditional below-ground interment) is worth a stroll. Many memorials are marked with amusing nicknames or tongue-in-cheek epitaphs like "I told you I was sick" or one widow's "At least I know where he's sleeping tonight."

### Mel Fisher Maritime Heritage Museum
200 Greene St; tel 305/294-2633. Some of the $400 million in treasure from the sunken Spanish galleons *Atocha* and *Santa Margarita* are displayed here, as well as authentic cannons, historic weapons, and other artifacts. **Open:** Daily 9:30am–5pm. $$$

# Kissimmee

This central Florida city of 33,000 emphasizes both its nearness and its contrast to Disney life. Guests may choose to stroll Old Town's brick streets; enjoy Arabian, Wild West, or medieval dinner theaters; hoot at rodeos and bluegrass; visit museums celebrating Chinese culture, Elvis, orchids, or Tupperware. **Information:** Kissimmee–St Cloud Convention & Visitors Bureau, 1925 E Irlo Bronson Memorial Hwy, PO Box 422007, Kissimmee, 34742 (tel 407/847-5000).

## HOTELS 🏛

### ≡≡ Best Western Eastgate
5565 W Irlo Bronson Memorial Pkwy, 34746; tel 407/396-0707 or toll free 800/223-5361; fax 407/396-6644. Exit 25A off I-4. A good family value, it's set back from the road and fronted by a small pond. Central courtyard has pool and whirlpool. **Rooms:** 403 rms. CI 4pm/CO noon. Nonsmoking rms avail. The choicest units are those facing the courtyard,

but they tend to be more noisy. **Amenities:** 🔒 A/C, in-rm safe. **Services:** 🔑 🚐 ⟳ ⟳ Car-rental desk, babysitting. **Facilities:** 🏠 📺2 1 restaurant, basketball, games rm, whirlpool, playground. **Rates:** Peak (Dec 18–Aug 22) $42–$99 S or D. Children under age 17 stay free. Min stay peak and special events. Lower rates off-season. Parking: Outdoor, free. AE, CB, DC, DISC, MC, V.

### 🏨🏨 Courtyard by Marriott

7675 W Irlo Bronson Memorial Hwy, 34747; tel 407/396-4000 or toll free 800/568-3352; fax 407/396-0714. Exit 25B off I-4. Bright, cheerful five-story hotel ideally suited for familes. Close to all the action. **Rooms:** 198 rms and stes. CI 3pm/CO noon. Nonsmoking rms avail. Most rooms have fold-out sofas and can accommodate up to four people. **Amenities:** 🔒 ⚬ 📺 A/C, cable TV w/movies, in-rm safe. **Services:** 🚐 🛎 ⟳ Car-rental desk, babysitting. Free transportation to all Disney parks. **Facilities:** 🏠 🏊 🍴75 ⟳ 1 restaurant (bkfst only), 1 bar, games rm, whirlpool, playground, washer/dryer. **Rates:** Peak (Feb–Apr/June–Aug/Dec) $79–$99 S or D; $89–$109 ste. Children under age 18 stay free. Min stay special events. Lower rates off-season. Parking: Outdoor, free. AE, CB, DC, DISC, JCB, MC, V.

### 🏨🏨 Days Inn Maingate West

7980 W Irlo Bronson Memorial Hwy, 34747; tel 407/396-8000 or toll free 800/327-9173, 800/432-9926 in FL; fax 407/396-6542. Exit 25B off I-4. **Rooms:** 321 rms and stes. CI 3pm/CO 11am. Nonsmoking rms avail. **Amenities:** 🔒 ⚬ A/C, cable TV. **Services:** 🚐 🛎 ⟳ Car-rental desk, babysitting. **Facilities:** 🏠 🍴25 ⟳ 1 restaurant, games rm, playground, washer/dryer. **Rates:** Peak (June–Aug) $89 S or D; $129 ste. Children under age 18 stay free. Lower rates off-season. Parking: Outdoor, free. AE, CB, DC, DISC, EC, ER, MC, V.

### 🏨🏨🏨 Hilton Inn Gateway

7470 W Irlo Bronson Memorial Hwy, 34747; tel 407/396-4400 or toll free 800/327-9170; fax 407/396-4320. Exit 25B off I-4. Attractive, well-maintained hotel set away from the commercial strip. The original courtyard building has been recently augmented by a mid-rise tower with larger rooms and suites. **Rooms:** 500 rms and stes. CI 4pm/CO noon. Nonsmoking rms avail. Tower rooms are newer and more attractive. Nice views. **Amenities:** 🔒 ⚬ A/C, cable TV w/movies, refrig, dataport. **Services:** ✕ 🚐 🛎 ⟳ Car-rental desk. Free coffee in the deli every morning. **Facilities:** 🏠 🍴 🍴900 ⟳ 1 restaurant (bkfst and dinner only), 1 bar (w/entertainment), basketball, games rm, lawn games, playground, washer/dryer. **Rates:** Peak (Feb–Apr/June–Aug/Dec) $95–$125 S or D; $225–$300 ste. Children under age 18 stay free. Min stay peak and special events. Lower rates off-season. AP and MAP rates avail. Parking: Outdoor, free. AE, CB, DC, DISC, JCB, MC, V.

### 🏨🏨 Holiday Inn Hotel & Suites

5678 Irlo Bronson Memorial Hwy, 32804; tel 407/396-4488 or toll free 800/FON-KIDS; fax 407/396-8915. Exit 25A off I-4. Bright, cheerful hotel with a strong emphasis on kids' activities. **Rooms:** 614 rms and stes. CI 4pm/CO 11am. Nonsmoking rms avail. Poolside units offer direct access to courtyard. "Kids" suites have separate rooms for children and feature different themes. **Amenities:** 🔒 ⚬ 📺 A/C, cable TV, refrig, dataport, VCR, in-rm safe. **Services:** ✕ 🚐 🛎 ⟳ ⟳ Car-rental desk, children's program, babysitting. **Facilities:** 🏠 📺2 ⚬ 2 restaurants, 2 bars, basketball, volleyball, games rm, whirlpool, day-care ctr, playground, washer/dryer. **Rates:** Peak (Feb–Apr/June–Aug 14/Dec 22–31) $85–$105 S or D; $125–$195 ste. Extra person $6. Children under age 19 stay free. Lower rates off-season. Parking: Outdoor, free. AE, CB, DC, DISC, JCB, MC, V.

### 🏨🏨 Holiday Inn Maingate West

7601 Black Lake Rd, 34747; tel 407/396-1100 or toll free 800/ENJOY FL; fax 407/396-0689. 2½ mi W of exit 25B off I-4. Draws many families, who come for the varied facilities and the kids-under-12-eat-free policy. Glittering atrium lobby. **Rooms:** 287 rms. CI 4pm/CO 11am. Nonsmoking rms avail. **Amenities:** 🔒 ⚬ A/C, cable TV, VCR, in-rm safe. **Services:** ✕ 🔑 🚐 🛎 ⟳ Car-rental desk, babysitting. **Facilities:** 🏠 🚲 🍴150 ⚬ 1 restaurant, 1 bar, games rm, lawn games, washer/dryer. **Rates:** Peak (June–Sept) $119–$105 S or D. Children under age 18 stay free. Lower rates off-season. AP rates avail. Parking: Outdoor, free. AE, CB, DC, DISC, EC, MC, V.

### 🏨🏨 Howard Johnson Fountain Park Plaza Hotel

5150 W Irlo Bronson Memorial Hwy, 34746; tel 407/396-1111 or toll free 800/327-9179; fax 407/396-1607. A range of accommodations housed in both mid-rise and high-rise buildings, with attractive public areas and lovely manicured grounds. **Rooms:** 400 rms and stes. CI 4pm/CO 11am. Nonsmoking rms avail. **Amenities:** 🔒 ⚬ A/C, cable TV, dataport, VCR, in-rm safe. Some units w/minibars, all w/terraces. **Services:** ✕ 🚐 🛎 ⟳ Car-rental desk, babysitting. **Facilities:** 🏠 ⚠ 🏊9 📺4 🍴 🍴125 ⚬ 1 restaurant (bkfst and dinner only), 1 bar, basketball, games rm, lawn games, sauna, whirlpool, playground, washer/dryer. **Rates:** Peak (Feb–Apr/June–Aug) $75–$85 S or D; $99–$119 ste. Extra person $10. Children under age 18 stay free. Min stay special events. Lower rates off-season. Parking: Outdoor, free. AE, CB, DC, DISC, JCB, MC, V.

### 🏨🏨🏨 Hyatt Orlando

6375 W Irlo Bronson Memorial Hwy, 34747; tel 407/396-5000 or toll free 800/233-1234; fax 407/396-5090. Exit 25A off I-4. Situated on expansive grounds in an area of many hotels and restaurants, this complex offers an attractive package of facilities, services, and recreational diversions. This is a suburban version of a Hyatt hotel: comfortable and subdued. **Rooms:** 922 rms and stes. Executive level. CI 4pm/CO noon. Nonsmoking rms avail. **Amenities:** 🔒 ⚬ A/C, cable

TV w/movies, dataport, voice mail, in-rm safe. All units w/terraces, some w/whirlpools. **Services:** X ⊷ VP ▦ ▦ ▱ Car-rental desk, babysitting. **Facilities:** ▦ ▦ 3 ▦ 2000 ▯ & 3 restaurants, 2 bars (1 w/entertainment), games rm, whirlpool, beauty salon, playground, washer/dryer. **Rates:** Peak (Jan–May 14/Dec 21–Dec 31) $139–$154 S or D; $180–$480 ste. Children under age 18 stay free. Min stay special events. Lower rates off-season. MAP rates avail. Parking: Outdoor, free. AE, CB, DC, DISC, MC, V.

### Meliá Orlando Suites & Villas Hotel

4787 W Irlo Bronson Memorial Hwy, 34746; tel 407/ 397-0555 or toll free 800/292-9765; fax 407/397-1968. Exit 25A off I-4. Spacious two-level townhouses on lovely, manicured grounds provide a quiet getaway for families. **Rooms:** 150 cottages/villas. CI 3pm/CO 11am. Nonsmoking rms avail. Each unit has two bathrooms and sofabeds. Tasteful, traditional decor. **Amenities:** ▦ ▯ ▦ ⊓ A/C, cable TV w/movies, refrig, in-rm safe. All units w/terraces. **Services:** X ⊷ ▦ ▱ Car-rental desk, masseur, babysitting. Mostly bilingual (English/Spanish) staff. **Facilities:** ▦ ▦ ▦ ▦ ▦ & 1 restaurant, 1 bar, basketball, volleyball, games rm, racquetball, squash, whirlpool, playground, washer/dryer. A mini-grocery store stocks essentials; supermarkets are nearby. **Rates (CP):** Peak (Dec 21–Jan 8/Feb 14–Apr 16) $140–$210 cottage/villa. Children under age 18 stay free. Lower rates off-season. Parking: Outdoor, free. AE, CB, DC, DISC, MC, V.

### Nikki Bird Resort Holiday Inn

7300 Irlo Bronson Memorial Hwy, 34747; tel 407/396-7300 or toll free 800/621-9378; fax 407/396-7555. Exit 25 B off I-4. Busy hotel with well-kept grounds and lots of activities for families. **Rooms:** 529 rms. CI 4pm/CO 11am. Nonsmoking rms avail. **Amenities:** ▦ ▯ ⊓ A/C, cable TV w/movies, refrig, in-rm safe. All rooms with microwaves. **Services:** X ▦ ▱ Car-rental desk, babysitting. Free shuttle to Disney parks. **Facilities:** ▦ ▦ 3 & 2 restaurants, 1 bar, games rm, whirlpool, playground, washer/dryer. Popular 1950s-style diner. **Rates:** Peak (Feb–Apr/Nov 11–Dec/June–Aug) $89–$115 S or D. Children under age 18 stay free. Lower rates off-season. Parking: Outdoor, free. AE, CB, DC, DISC, JCB, MC, V.

### Orlando–Kissimmee Gateway Hilton Inn

7470 W Irlo Bronson Memorial Hwy, 34747; tel 407/ 396-4400 or toll free 800/327-9170; fax 407/396-4320. Exit 25B off I-4. One of the area's favorites, providing good value for families. **Rooms:** 500 rms. CI 4pm/CO 11am. Nonsmoking rms avail. **Amenities:** ▦ ▯ A/C, cable TV w/movies, refrig, in-rm safe. Some rooms have microwaves. **Services:** X ▦ ▦ ▱ Car-rental desk. **Facilities:** ▦ ▦ 1000 & 1 restaurant (bkfst and dinner only), 3 bars (1 w/entertainment), games rm, lawn games, washer/dryer. **Rates:** Peak (Jan–Mar/June–July) $55–$125 S or D. Extra person $15. Children under age 18 stay free. Lower rates off-season. AP rates avail. Parking: Indoor/outdoor, free. AE, CB, DC, DISC, ER, JCB, MC, V.

### Radisson Inn Maingate

7501 W Irlo Bronson Memorial Hwy, 34747; tel 407/ 396-1400 or toll free 800/333-3333; fax 407/396-0660. Exit 25B off I-4. Two modern seven-story buildings connected by a restaurant and registration area. The Radisson caters to corporate clients as well as families, and offers more style than similarly priced hotels nearby. **Rooms:** 580 rms and stes. CI 3pm/CO noon. Nonsmoking rms avail. **Amenities:** ▦ ▯ A/C, dataport, voice mail, in-rm safe. Some units w/minibars, 1 w/whirlpool. **Services:** X ▦ ▦ ▱ ◈ Car-rental desk, children's program, babysitting. Free shuttle to Disney parks and Universal Studios. **Facilities:** ▦ ▦ 2 ▦ 400 & 1 restaurant, 1 bar, basketball, volleyball, games rm, whirlpool, playground, washer/dryer. Courtyard. **Rates:** Peak (Dec/ July–Aug/Feb–Apr) $69–$89 S or D; $129–$210 ste. Extra person $10. Children under age 18 stay free. Lower rates off-season. Parking: Outdoor, free. AE, CB, DC, DISC, JCB, MC, V.

### Ramada Resort Maingate

2950 Reedy Creek Blvd, 34747; tel 407/396-4466 or toll free 800/ENJOY FL; fax 407/396-6418. Exit 25B off I-4. Pleasant family hotel with a functional, contemporary lobby. **Rooms:** 391 rms and stes. CI 4pm/CO noon. Nonsmoking rms avail. **Amenities:** ▦ ▯ A/C, cable TV, VCR, in-rm safe. **Services:** X ▦ ▦ ▱ Car-rental desk, babysitting. **Facilities:** ▦ ▦ ▦ 200 & 1 restaurant, 2 bars, games rm, washer/ dryer. **Rates:** Peak (Feb–Aug) $79–$85 S; $89–$95 D; $195– $350 ste. Extra person $10. Children under age 18 stay free. Lower rates off-season. Parking: Outdoor, free. AE, CB, DC, DISC, MC, V.

### Residence Inn by Marriott on Lake Circle

4786 W Irlo Bronson Memorial Hwy, 34746; tel 407/ 396-2056 or toll free 800/468-3027; fax 407/396-2906. US 192 exit off I-4. Set on a pretty lake, these family-oriented accommodations afford privacy and style as well as some wonderful views. Popular with longer-term visitors. **Rooms:** 159 stes. CI 4pm/CO 11am. Nonsmoking rms avail. Each unit has a fully equipped kitchen, including dishwasher and utensils. **Amenities:** ▦ ▯ ▦ A/C, cable TV w/movies, refrig, dataport, in-rm safe. Some units w/terraces, all w/fireplaces. **Services:** X ▦ ▦ ▱ Babysitting. Staff can do guests' grocery shopping. **Facilities:** ▦ △ ▦ ▦ 80 & 1 restaurant (bkfst only), 1 bar (w/entertainment), basketball, volleyball, games rm, lawn games, whirlpool, playground, washer/dryer. **Rates (CP):** Peak (Feb–Apr) $119–$189 ste. Children under age 12 stay free. Lower rates off-season. Parking: Outdoor, free. AE, CB, DC, DISC, JCB, MC, V.

### Sheraton Inn Lakeside

7769 W Irlo Bronson Memorial Hwy, 34747; tel 407/ 396-2222 or toll free 800/848-0801; fax 407/239-2650. Exit 25B off I-4. One of the area's more attractive properties, helped by regular renovations. Close to Disney World's main gate but away from the hyper-commercialism of the neon strip, its lakeside locale helps create a soothing atmosphere.

**Rooms:** 651 rms. CI 4pm/CO 11am. Nonsmoking rms avail. Comfortable rooms in pleasing designs are warm and restful. **Amenities:** 🛎 ⚒ A/C, cable TV, refrig, voice mail, in-rm safe. **Services:** ✕ 🚐 ☒ ⌟ Car-rental desk, children's program, babysitting. Free shuttle to all Disney parks and Universal Studios. **Facilities:** 🏊 △ 🎳 🏓2 ⚒ 2 restaurants (bkfst and dinner only), 3 bars, basketball, volleyball, games rm, lawn games, playground, washer/dryer. **Rates:** Peak (Feb 10–Apr 14/June 15–Aug 20/Dec) $89–$129 S or D. Extra person $10. Children under age 17 stay free. Lower rates off-season. Parking: Outdoor, free. AE, CB, DC, DISC, EC, ER, JCB, MC, V.

## MOTELS

### ▤ Colonial Motor Lodge

1815 W Vine St, 34741; tel 407/847-6121 or toll free 800/325-4348, 800/432-3052 in FL; fax 407/847-0728. A family-run enterprise that's been in business for nearly a quarter-century. **Rooms:** 123 rms and effic. CI 1pm/CO 11am. Nonsmoking rms avail. Rooms were last renovated in 1992. **Amenities:** 🛎 A/C, cable TV w/movies, in-rm safe. **Services:** ☒ ⌟ Car-rental desk. **Facilities:** 🏊 ⚒ Washer/dryer. **Rates:** Peak (Feb–Apr/June–Aug/Dec) $20–$80 S or D; $35–$100 effic. Extra person $5. Children under age 18 stay free. Lower rates off-season. Parking: Outdoor, free. AE, CB, DC, DISC, MC, V.

### ▤▤ Comfort Inn Maingate

7571 W Irlo Bronson Memorial Hwy, 34747; tel 407/396-7500 or toll free 800/223-1628, 800/432-0887 in FL; fax 407/396-7497. Exit 25B off I-4. Clean, spiffy-looking standard motel accommodations in two-story peach stucco buildings. **Rooms:** 281 rms. CI 3pm/CO 11am. Nonsmoking rms avail. Garden rooms face a lawn with a gazebo. **Amenities:** 🛎 A/C, cable TV. **Services:** 🚐 ☒ ⌟ 🍴 Car-rental desk, babysitting. **Facilities:** 🏊 ⚒ 1 restaurant (bkfst and dinner only), 1 bar, games rm, playground, washer/dryer. **Rates:** Peak (Feb–Apr/June–Aug/Dec 20–Jan 1) $41–$70 S or D. Extra person $6. Children under age 18 stay free. Lower rates off-season. Parking: Outdoor, free. AE, CB, DC, DISC, EC, ER, JCB, MC, V.

### ▤▤ Econo Lodge Maingate Hawaiian Resort

7514 W Irlo Bronson Memorial Hwy, 34747; tel 407/396-2000 or toll free 800/365-6935; fax 407/396-1295. Exit 25B off I-4. Basic but pleasant budget lodging. **Rooms:** 445 rms and stes. CI 4pm/CO 11am. Nonsmoking rms avail. **Amenities:** 🛎 A/C, cable TV, dataport, VCR, in-rm safe. 1 unit w/terrace. **Services:** 🚐 ☒ ⌟ Car-rental desk, babysitting. Staff provides minimal assistance. **Facilities:** 🏊 🏊200 ⚒ 1 restaurant, 2 bars (1 w/entertainment), games rm, whirlpool, playground, washer/dryer. **Rates:** Peak (Dec 22–Jan 1/Feb–Apr/June–Aug) $49–$79 S or D; $89–$125 ste. Extra person $10. Children under age 12 stay free. Min stay peak. Lower rates off-season. Parking: Outdoor, free. AE, CB, DC, DISC, EC, ER, JCB, MC, V.

### ▤ Howard Johnson Inn Maingate

6051 W Irlo Bronson Memorial Hwy, 34747; tel 407/396-1748 or toll free 800/288-4678; fax 407/649-8642. Exit 25A off I-4. A five-story family hotel offering reasonable comfort in plain surroundings for a fair price. **Rooms:** 367 rms, stes, and effic. CI 4pm/CO noon. Nonsmoking rms avail. **Amenities:** 🛎 A/C, cable TV w/movies, in-rm safe. **Services:** ☒ ⌟ Babysitting. Complimentary shuttle to all Disney parks. Complimentary morning coffee. **Facilities:** 🏊 ⚒ 1 bar, games rm, whirlpool, playground, washer/dryer. **Rates:** Peak (Dec 20–31/Feb–Apr/June–Aug) $75 S or D; $95–$105 ste; $85 effic. Extra person $6. Children under age 18 stay free. Lower rates off-season. Parking: Outdoor, free. AE, CB, DC, DISC, MC, V.

### ▤▤ Ramada Plaza Resort Maingate

2900 Parkway Rd, 34747; tel 407/396-7000 or toll free 800/634-4774; fax 407/396-6792. Exit 25 off I-4 W. Some nice architectural touches provide a look that's less routine than many comparable properties. **Rooms:** 718 rms. CI 3pm/CO noon. Nonsmoking rms avail. **Amenities:** 🛎 ⚒ A/C, cable TV, in-rm safe. **Services:** ✕ ☒ ⌟ Car-rental desk. **Facilities:** 🏊 🏓2 🏊650 ⚒ 1 restaurant, 2 bars, games rm, lawn games, sauna, whirlpool, playground, washer/dryer. **Rates:** Peak (June–Aug/Dec 21–31) $67–$145 S or D. Children under age 18 stay free. Lower rates off-season. MAP rates avail. Parking: Outdoor, free. AE, CB, DC, DISC, EC, ER, JCB, MC, V.

## RESORT

### ▤▤▤ Orange Lake Country Club

8505 W Irlo Bronson Memorial Hwy, 34747; tel 407/239-0000 or toll free 800/877-6522; fax 407/239-5119. A low-key spread set in a rural-like setting; makes an ideal choice for families who want everything under one roof but still need to stay on budget. The colorful main clubhouse building houses the registry, dining facilities, and many activities. **Rooms:** 168 stes. CI 4pm/CO 10am. Nonsmoking rms avail. **Amenities:** 🛎 ⚒ 📺 A/C, cable TV, VCR, voice mail. Some units w/minibars. **Services:** ✕ 🚐 ☒ ⌟ Car-rental desk, social director, children's program, babysitting. **Facilities:** 🏊 △ 🎳 ⛳27 ⚒6 🏊10 🎣 🍴 🏊60 4 restaurants, 2 bars (1 w/entertainment), 1 beach (lake shore), games rm, racquetball, sauna, beauty salon, playground, washer/dryer. **Rates:** Peak (Jun–Aug/Feb–Apr) $120 ste. Children under age 18 stay free. Lower rates off-season. Parking: Outdoor, free. AE, DC, MC, V.

## ATTRACTIONS 📷

### Flying Tigers Warbird Air Museum

231 N Hoagland Blvd; tel 407/933-1942. This "working museum" focuses on the restoration of vintage aircraft to flying condition. Most aircraft are from the World War II era, with a few more modern and some antique planes as well; one

plane dates from 1929. Guided tours include the restoration area, where visitors can watch work in progress. **Open:** Mon–Sat 9am–5:30pm, Sun 9am–5pm. **$$$**

## Florida Splendid China

3000 Splendid China Blvd; tel 407/396-7111. Located off US 192. Opened in late 1993, this 76-acre cultural theme park re-creates elements of the land and culture of China. It is a near-duplicate of the original Splendid China near Hong Kong, which debuted in 1989. There are reproductions of more than 60 of China's most famous historic sites, all built to various scales using authentic materials and adorned with painstaking detail. More than 100 Chinese artisans spent 2 years working in Florida to complete the project. Among the sites are the half-mile-long scale replica of the Great Wall, made up of 6.5 million hand-laid miniature bricks; the Forbidden City and its 9,999-room Imperial Palace; a 35-foot-tall version of the Leshan Grand Buddha; and more than 1,000 miniature copies of the 6,000-odd "Terra Cotta Warriors" that were unearthed in China in 1974.

**Suzhou Gardens,** the park's entrance area, replicates the main street of this eastern China urban area known as the "water city" or "the Venice of China," as it was in 1300. Here visitors can view a 13-minute orientation film. Throughout the park, Chinese acrobats, folk dancers, singers, and other traditional performers entertain; martial arts and Mongolian wrestling are also demonstrated. Chinese silk-makers, tapestry weavers, and other artisans create their wares. Afternoon performances are staged hourly in the 1,000-seat Temple of Light amphitheater. A parade steps off at 6:30pm and a finale performance is staged at Suzhou Gardens to close out the day. **Open:** Daily 9:30am–9:30pm. **$$$$**

## Water Mania

6073 W Irlo Bronson Memorial Hwy; tel 407/396-2626. This 38-acre water park offers a variety of aquatic thrill rides and attractions. Body-surf in the Whitecaps continuous wave pool or dare to try the Wipe Out surfing ride; plummet down spiraling water slides and steep flumes; or enjoy a whitewater tubing adventure. Small children have pint-size slides and pools to frolic in. Adjoining miniature-golf course and wooded picnic area with arcade games, beach, and volleyball. **Open:** Daily. Call for hours. **$$$$**

## Green Meadows Farm

Poinciana Blvd; tel 407/846-0770. Two-hour guided tours bring visitors in close contact with more than 200 farm animals, including pigs, cows, goats, sheep, donkeys, turkeys, and geese. Geared toward children of all ages, the farm also has a milking cow, pony rides, and a tractor-drawn hayride. Picnic area; snack and souvenir shop. **Open:** Daily 9:30am–4pm. **$$$$**

# Lake Buena Vista

See also Orlando

Orlando gets all the credit, but this central Florida city west of I-4 is the real home of Walt Disney World Resort—the Magic Kingdom, Epcot, Disney-MGM Studios, and the adjacent theme hotels and other attractions. (Believe it or not, the city only has 1,700 permanent residents!)

## PUBLIC TRANSPORTATION

**Disney Shuttles** Unlimited complimentary service via bus, monorail, ferry, and water taxi between all Disney resorts and official hotels and all three Disney parks from two hours before opening to two hours after closing. Also free to Disney Village Marketplace, Typhoon Lagoon, Pleasure Island, and Fort Wilderness. Disney properties also offer transport to other area attractions; fees vary.

## HOTELS 🏨

### ≣≣ Comfort Inn Lake Buena Vista

8442 Palm Pkwy, 32830; tel 407/239-7300 or toll free 800/999-7300; fax 407/239-7740. Exit 27 off I-4. Two V-shaped buildings rising five stories contain numerous rooms for the vacationing family on a budget. Sturdy and functional rooms and public areas; some renovating is underway. **Rooms:** 640 rms. CI 3pm/CO 11am. Nonsmoking rms avail. **Amenities:** 🔒 A/C, cable TV w/movies, in-rm safe. **Services:** ⊠ ⤵ ⇦ Babysitting. Free shuttle to Disney parks. **Facilities:** 🔓 ♿ 1 restaurant (bkfst and dinner only), 1 bar, games rm, washer/dryer. Affordable, buffet-style breakfast and dinner. Kids under 11 eat free with paying adult. **Rates:** $69 D. Extra person $6. Children under age 18 stay free. Min stay peak. Parking: Outdoor, free. AE, CB, DC, DISC, MC, V.

### ≣≣ Disney's All-Star Sports Resort

3499 W Buena Vista Dr, PO Box 10100, 32830; tel 407/939-5000; fax 407/939-7333. US 192 exit off I-4; follow signs for Disney Resorts. One of Disney's newest entries in the hotel scene, this sports-themed hotel is part of a budget complex that also includes the All-Star Music Resort. Rooms are housed in ten buildings with baseball, basketball, football, surfing, and tennis themes. **Rooms:** 3,840 rms. CI 3pm/CO 11am. Nonsmoking rms avail. Some rooms are a hike from the parking lot. **Amenities:** 🔒 ♨ A/C, cable TV w/movies, refrig, voice mail, in-rm safe. **Services:** ✕ 🖦 ⊠ ⤵ Twice-daily maid svce, social director, babysitting. **Facilities:** 🔓 ♿ 2 bars, games rm, playground, washer/dryer. One pool has a surfing theme and two 38-foot shark fins; the other is shaped like a baseball diamond with an "outfield" sun deck. Guests receive preferred tee times at Disney golf courses elsewhere. **Rates:** Peak (Dec 24–Jan 1/Feb–Apr/June–Aug) $69–$79 S or D. Extra person $8. Children under age 17 stay free. Lower rates off-season. Parking: Outdoor, free. AE, DC, DISC, MC, V.

### ≣≣≣ Disney's Caribbean Beach Resort

900 Cayman Way, PO Box 10100, 32830-0100; tel 407/934-3400; fax 305/820-8190. US 192 exit off I-4; follow signs for Disney Resorts. Each of the five clusters of attractive, coral-colored two-story buildings surrounding the large, duck-filled lake is designed with its own Caribbean island theme. Custom House lobby is decked with potted palms and overhead fans. **Rooms:** 1,700 rms. CI 3pm/CO 11am. Nonsmoking rms avail. Many rooms offer lake views. **Amenities:** ☎ ♨ ☷ A/C, cable TV w/movies, voice mail. All units w/minibars, some w/terraces. **Services:** ✗ ☕ ⚓ ♫ Babysitting. **Facilities:** ⛳ ⚲ △ ☒ ዦ 1 restaurant, 2 bars, 7 beaches (lake shore), lifeguard, games rm, whirlpool, playground, washer/dryer. Marina. Guests receive preferred tee times at Disney golf courses. **Rates:** Peak (Dec 24–Jan 1/Feb–Apr/June–Aug) $55–$125 S or D; $200 ste. Extra person $12. Children under age 12 stay free. Lower rates off-season. AP rates avail. Parking: Outdoor, free. AE, DC, DISC, MC, V.

### ≣≣≣ Disney's Dixie Landings Resort

1251 Dixie Dr, PO Box 10100, 32830; tel 407/934-6000; fax 407/934-5777. Family complex with the look of an Old South plantation. Its landscaping is quite elaborate, and there's a fun, colorful outdoor area. Linked to other Disney resorts by a launch. **Rooms:** 2,048 rms. CI 3pm/CO 11am. Nonsmoking rms avail. Cleverly conceived rooms with log beds and other cute design elements create a wholesome look. **Amenities:** ☎ ♨ A/C, cable TV w/movies, voice mail, in-rm safe. **Services:** ☕ ⚓ △ ♫ Babysitting. **Facilities:** ⛳ ⚲ △ ☒ ☒ ዦ 2 restaurants (see "Restaurants" below), 1 bar (w/entertainment), games rm, whirlpool, playground, washer/dryer. Guests receive preferred tee times at Disney golf courses. Dining choices are arranged like a food court. **Rates:** Peak (Feb–Aug) $123–$153 S or D. Extra person $12. Children under age 18 stay free. Lower rates off-season. Parking: Outdoor, free. AE, MC, V.

### ≣≣≣ Disney's Port Orleans Resort

2201 Orleans Dr, PO Box 10100, 32830; tel 407/824-2900; fax 407/354-1866. US 192 exit off I-4; follow signs for Disney Resorts. A cluster of three-story pastel buildings decked out in French Quarter motif. **Rooms:** 1,008 rms. CI 3pm/CO 11am. Nonsmoking rms avail. Accommodations, though not as posh as those at the more expensive Disney resorts, are comfortable. **Amenities:** ☎ ♨ A/C, cable TV w/movies, voice mail. Some units w/terraces. **Services:** ⚓ △ ♫ Babysitting. Boats escort guests to Pleasure Island and other Disney spots from the dock. **Facilities:** ⛳ ⚲ △ ዦ 1 restaurant (see "Restaurants" below), 2 bars, lifeguard, games rm, whirlpool, playground, washer/dryer. Guests receive preferred tee times at Disney golf courses. **Rates:** Peak (Dec 24–Jan 1/June–Aug) $95–$134 S or D. Extra person $12. Children under age 17 stay free. Lower rates off-season. AP and MAP rates avail. Parking: Outdoor, free. AE, MC, V.

### ≣≣≣ DoubleTree Guest Suites Resort

2305 Hotel Plaza Blvd, 32830; tel 407/934-1000 or toll free 800/424-2900; fax 407/934-1008. Exit 27 off I-4. Attractive hotel with marble lobby. **Rooms:** 229 stes. CI 4pm/CO 11am. Nonsmoking rms avail. **Amenities:** ☎ ♨ ☷ ♫ A/C, cable TV w/movies, refrig, dataport, in-rm safe. Some units w/terraces. Microwaves, sofa beds. TVs in bathrooms. **Services:** ✗ ☕ ⚓ △ ♫ Car-rental desk, babysitting. Free shuttle to all Disney parks. **Facilities:** ⛳ ⚲ ╘ 80 ☐ ዦ 1 restaurant, 2 bars, volleyball, games rm, whirlpool, playground, washer/dryer. **Rates:** Peak (Feb–Apr/Dec) $149–$249 ste. Extra person $20. Children under age 18 stay free. Min stay peak. Lower rates off-season. MAP rates avail. Parking: Outdoor, free. AE, CB, DC, DISC, EC, JCB, MC, V.

### ≣≣≣ Embassy Suites Resort Lake Buena Vista

8100 Lake Ave, 32836; tel 407/239-1144 or toll free 800/257-8483; fax 407/239-1718. Exit 27 off I-4. One of the chain's newest area hotels, this peach-shaded building is constructed around an atrium, where breakfast and social-hour cocktails are served on granite tables. **Rooms:** 280 stes. CI 3pm/CO noon. Nonsmoking rms avail. Airy decor. **Amenities:** ☎ ♨ ☷ ♫ A/C, cable TV w/movies, refrig, VCR, in-rm safe. Some units w/terraces. **Services:** ✗ ☕ VP ⚓ △ ♫ Car-rental desk, social director, children's program, babysitting. **Facilities:** ⛳ ☒ ⚲ ╘ 300 ዦ 1 restaurant, 3 bars, games rm, lawn games, spa, sauna, steam rm, whirlpool, daycare ctr, playground, washer/dryer. **Rates (BB):** Peak (Dec 24–31/mid-Feb–mid-Apr/mid-June–mid-Aug) $139–$189 ste. Children under age 18 stay free. Lower rates off-season. Parking: Outdoor, free. AE, CB, DISC, JCB, MC, V.

### ≣≣≣ Grosvenor Resort at WDW Village

1850 Hotel Plaza Blvd, 32830; tel 407/828-4444 or toll free 800/624-4109; fax 407/828-8192. Exit 27 off I-4. Attractive accommodations in courtyard rooms or 19-story tower. **Rooms:** 626 rms and stes. CI 3pm/CO 11am. Nonsmoking rms avail. **Amenities:** ☎ ♨ ☷ ♫ A/C, cable TV w/movies, refrig, dataport, VCR, voice mail, in-rm safe. All units w/minibars, some w/whirlpools. Irons and ironing boards. **Services:** ✗ VP ⚓ △ ♫ Car-rental desk, babysitting. Free transportation to Disney parks, night shuttle to Pleasure Island. Disney characters come to breakfast three times a week. **Facilities:** ⛳ ☒ ⚲ ╘ 1200 ዦ 2 restaurants, 3 bars (1 w/entertainment), basketball, volleyball, games rm, lawn games, whirlpool, playground, washer/dryer. Cafe open 24 hours. Guests can use Buena Vista Palace facilities. **Rates:** Peak (Dec 15–31/June–Aug) $110–$160 S or D; $225–$500 ste. Children under age 18 stay free. Min stay peak. Lower rates off-season. AP and MAP rates avail. Parking: Outdoor, free. AE, CB, DC, DISC, ER, JCB, MC, V.

### ≣≣≣ Hilton at Walt Disney World Village

1751 Hotel Plaza Blvd, 32830; tel 407/827-4000 or toll free 800/782-4414; fax 407/827-6369. Exit 27 off I-4. This sleek contemporary hotel is a leader in this resort hotel district. Its public areas are adorned with marble and rich fabrics. Within walking distance to village shops and Pleasure Island activities. **Rooms:** 814 rms and stes. Executive level. CI 3pm/CO 11am. Nonsmoking rms avail. All units are in top form. Alcove guest rooms are ideal for families who need a crib or playpen area. **Amenities:** 🔒 🍸 🖥 A/C, cable TV w/movies. All units w/minibars, some w/terraces. **Services:** ✗ 🚪 VP 🚐 ⬜ ↲ Car-rental desk, children's program, babysitting. **Facilities:** 🏊 🎾 🛎 2300 🖥 ♿ 4 restaurants, 3 bars, games rm, lawn games, sauna, steam rm, whirlpool, beauty salon, playground, washer/dryer. Guests receive preferred tee times at Disney golf courses. **Rates:** Peak (Jan–mid-May/late Dec) $180–$225 S or D; $459–$1,500 ste. Extra person $20. Children under age 18 stay free. Lower rates off-season. Parking: Outdoor, free. AE, CB, DC, DISC, MC, V.

### UNRATED Holiday Inn Crown Royal Plaza

1905 Hotel Plaza Blvd, 32830; tel 407/828-2828 or toll free 800/248-7890; fax 407/827-6338. Exit 27 off I-4. This 17-story hotel has just undergone a multimillion-dollar renovation and upgrade. Very popular with families—you can watch Magic Kingdom fireworks from your balcony here. **Rooms:** 394 rms and stes. Executive level. CI 3pm/CO 11am. Nonsmoking rms avail. Newly redecorated rooms feature pastel colors and upgraded furnishings. **Amenities:** 🔒 🍸 🖥 A/C, cable TV, dataport, VCR, in-rm safe. Some units w/minibars, all w/terraces, some w/whirlpools. Refrigerators available on request. **Services:** ✗ VP 🚐 ⬜ ↲ Car-rental desk, babysitting. Free transport to and from all Walt Disney World parks. **Facilities:** 🏊 🎾 ♣4 🏊4 🛎 500 ♿ 1 restaurant, 2 bars, games rm, spa, sauna, whirlpool, washer/dryer. **Rates:** Peak (Feb–Apr/Dec) $90–$190 D; $500–$700 ste. Children under age 18 stay free. Lower rates off-season. AP and MAP rates avail. Parking: Outdoor, free. AE, CB, DC, DISC, EC, MC, V.

### ☰☰☰ Holiday Inn SunSpree Lake Buena Vista

13351 FL 535, 32821; tel 407/239-4500 or toll free 800/FON-MAXX; fax 407/239-7713. Exit 27 off I-4. Gated hotel is always busy with families with small children, who seemingly overtake the public areas and terrace. Many activities for kids. **Rooms:** 507 rms and stes. CI 3pm/CO 11am. Nonsmoking rms avail. Oversize guest rooms, all done with a sturdy but cheerful decor, are big enough for children to play in. **Amenities:** 🔒 🍸 🖥 🍴 A/C, cable TV, refrig, VCR, in-rm safe. **Services:** ✗ 🚪 🚐 ↲ Car-rental desk, social director, children's program, babysitting. State-licensed child care for ages 2–12 from 8am–midnight. **Facilities:** 🏊 🛎 ♿ 2 restaurants, 1 bar, games rm, whirlpool, day-care ctr, playground. **Rates:** Peak (Dec–Apr/June–Aug) $79–$119 S or D; $138–$168 ste. Children under age 19 stay free. Lower rates off-season. Parking: Outdoor, free. AE, CB, DC, DISC, ER, MC, V.

### ☰☰ Howard Johnson Park Square Inn and Suites

8501 Palm Pkwy, 32830; tel 407/239-6900 or toll free 800/635-8684; fax 407/239-1287. Exit 27 off I-4. **Rooms:** 222 rms and stes. CI 4pm/CO 11am. Nonsmoking rms avail. **Amenities:** 🔒 🍸 🖥 A/C, cable TV w/movies, refrig, in-rm safe. Some units w/terraces. **Services:** ✗ 🚪 🚐 ⬜ ↲ Car-rental desk, babysitting. **Facilities:** 🏊 100 ♿ 1 restaurant (bkfst and dinner only), 1 bar, games rm, whirlpool, playground, washer/dryer. **Rates:** Peak (Jan–Apr/June–Sept) $65–$105 S or D; $95–$135 ste. Extra person $10. Children under age 18 stay free. Lower rates off-season. Parking: Outdoor, free. AE, CB, DC, DISC, EC, ER, JCB, MC, V.

### ☰☰☰ Lake Buena Vista Resort & Suites–Days Inn

12205 Apopka Vineland Rd, 32836; tel 407/239-0444 or toll free 800/423-3297; fax 407/239-1778. Exit 27 off I-4. More upscale than a typical Days Inn, this is the company's flagship property in the Orlando/Kissimmee area, with four six-story buildings overlooking the pool. **Rooms:** 490 rms and stes. CI 4pm/CO 11am. Nonsmoking rms avail. **Amenities:** 🔒 A/C, cable TV, voice mail, in-rm safe. Some units w/terraces. **Services:** ✗ 🚐 ⬜ ↲ Car-rental desk, babysitting. Free shuttle to all Disney parks. **Facilities:** 🏊 200 ♿ 2 restaurants, 1 bar, games rm, playground, washer/dryer. **Rates:** Peak (Dec 19–Jan/Feb–Apr 15/June 15–Aug) $79–$119 S or D; $109–$159 ste. Extra person $10. Children under age 18 stay free. Lower rates off-season. Parking: Outdoor, free. AE, CB, DC, DISC, EC, JCB, MC, V.

### ☰☰☰ Travelodge Hotel WDW Village

2000 Hotel Plaza Blvd, 32830; tel 407/828-2424 or toll free 800/348-3765; fax 407/828-8933. Exit 27 off I-4. Spiffy and immaculate lakefront property, far better than most in the chain (it's the flagship hotel). Designed to evoke a Caribbean plantation manor house. **Rooms:** 325 rms and stes. CI 3pm/CO 11am. Nonsmoking rms avail. Many accommodations offer views of Lake Buena Vista from furnished terraces. **Amenities:** 🔒 🍸 🖥 🍴 A/C, cable TV w/movies, voice mail, in-rm safe. All units w/minibars, all w/terraces. Free newspaper delivered to room weekdays. **Services:** ✗ 🚐 ⬜ ↲ Car-rental desk, babysitting. Free transport to and from all Walt Disney World parks. **Facilities:** 🏊 100 ♿ 2 restaurants, 2 bars (1 w/entertainment), games rm, playground, washer/dryer. **Rates:** Peak (Feb–Apr/June–Aug/Dec) $119–$169 S or D; $199–$299 ste. Children under age 18 stay free. Lower rates off-season. AP and MAP rates avail. Parking: Outdoor, free. AE, CB, DC, DISC, ER, JCB, MC, V.

### ☰☰ Wyndham Garden Hotel

8688 Palm Pkwy, 32830; tel 407/239-8500 or toll free 800/228-2846; fax 407/239-8591. Exit 27 off I-4. An artfully designed building with attractive landscaping. **Rooms:** 167 rms and stes. CI 3pm/CO 11am. Nonsmoking rms avail. **Amenities:** 🔒 🍸 🖥 🍴 A/C, cable TV w/movies, dataport. **Services:** ✗ 🚪 🚐 ⬜ ↲ Babysitting. Free shuttle to Magic Kingdom. **Facilities:** 🏊 🛎 120 ♿ 1 restaurant (bkfst and dinner only), 1 bar, games rm, whirlpool, washer/dryer. **Rates:** Peak (Jan 10–Apr 15/Dec 23–Jan 2) $74–$104 S or D; $135 ste. Extra person $10. Children under age 18 stay free. Lower rates off-season. MAP rates avail. Parking: Outdoor, free. AE, CB, DC, DISC, JCB, MC, V.

# RESORTS

### ≣≣≣≣ Buena Vista Palace–WDW Village

1900 Buena Vista Dr, 32830; tel 407/827-2727 or toll free 800/327-2990; fax 407/827-6034. Exit 27 off I-4. A dazzling multi-winged high-rise that soars above Walt Disney World Village. Arriving guests will not be disappointed as they approach the impressive circular drive entry and the dozen-story atrium that sparkles with polished surfaces. Well-heeled families and foreigners make up much of the business. **Rooms:** 1,014 rms and stes. CI 3pm/CO 11am. Nonsmoking rms avail. Tasteful accommodations offer views of Lake Buena Vista or the vast Disney complex. **Amenities:** 🛗 ⚿ A/C, cable TV w/movies, in-rm safe. All units w/minibars, all w/terraces, some w/whirlpools. Some units have coffeemakers. **Services:** ⎟◎⎟ ⌂ VP 🚗 ⎣ ⏧ Car-rental desk, children's program, babysitting. The eager-to-please staff scurries to assist arrivals. **Facilities:** 🏋 🚲 ⚠ 🍴3 🏓 ▢2000 ⌨ ⛴ 5 restaurants (see "Restaurants" below), 4 bars (3 w/entertainment), games rm, whirlpool, beauty salon, playground, washer/dryer. Guests receive preferred tee times at Disney golf courses. **Rates:** Peak (Feb–Apr/June–Aug/Dec) $169–$250 S or D; $290–$455 ste. Extra person $15. Children under age 18 stay free. Lower rates off-season. Parking: Outdoor, free. AE, CB, DC, DISC, MC, V.

### ≣≣≣ Disney's Beach Club Resort

1800 Epcot Resorts Blvd, PO Box 10100, 32830; tel 407/934-8000; fax 407/463-3315. US 192 exit off I-4; follow signs for Disney Resorts. 56 acres. This Victorian-inspired complex faced with clapboard is positioned around a lake and accessed via a palm-lined drive. The sun-dappled lobby is graced with wicker and rattan furnishings amid tall potted palms. **Rooms:** 630 rms and stes. Executive level. CI 3pm/CO 11am. Nonsmoking rms avail. Charming rooms furnished in bleached woods. **Amenities:** 🛗 ⚿ A/C, cable TV, voice mail, in-rm safe. All units w/minibars, all w/terraces. **Services:** ⎟◎⎟ ⌂ VP 🚗 ⎣ ⏧ Masseur, children's program, babysitting. **Facilities:** 🏋 ⚠ �

 🏊 🍴2 🏓 ▢1000 ⌨ ⛴ 6 restaurants, 5 bars, 1 beach (lake shore), volleyball, games rm, lawn games, sauna, steam rm, whirlpool, beauty salon, day-care ctr, playground, washer/dryer. Guests receive preferred tee times at Disney golf courses. Guests share some facilities, including restaurant, with the Disney Yacht Club Resort next door. **Rates:** Peak (Dec 17–31/Feb–Apr/June–Aug 17) $240–$390 S or D; $410 ste. Extra person $15. Children under age 18 stay free. Lower rates off-season. AP and MAP rates avail. Parking: Outdoor, free. AE, MC, V.

### ≣≣≣ Disney's Contemporary Resort

4600 N World Dr, PO Box 10100, 32830; tel 407/824-1000; fax 407/824-3539. US 192 exit off I-4; follow signs for Disney Resorts. One of Disney's original Magic Kingdom offerings and still very popular, this architecturally interesting double-sloped high-rise is suitable for any Disney junkie. It's on the monorail line; trains pass through the center

atrium. **Rooms:** 1,051 rms and stes. CI 3pm/CO 11am. Nonsmoking rms avail. Rooms decorated in desert tones, with art deco furnishings. **Amenities:** 🛗 ⚿ A/C, TV, voice mail. Some units w/terraces. **Services:** ⎟◎⎟ ⌂ VP 🚗 ⎣ ⏧ Children's program, babysitting. **Facilities:** 🏋 ⚠ 🏊 🎿 🏓 ▢5000 ⌨ ⛴ 4 restaurants (see "Restaurants" below), 3 bars, 1 beach (lake shore), games rm, lawn games, sauna, beauty salon, day-care ctr, playground, washer/dryer. The concierge level enjoys private lakeview lounge. Guests receive preferred tee times at Disney golf courses. **Rates:** Peak (Dec 24–Jan 1/Feb–Apr/June–Aug) $215–$320 S or D; $690–$1,195 ste. Extra person $15. Children under age 17 stay free. Lower rates off-season. AP and MAP rates avail. Parking: Outdoor, free. AE, MC, V.

### ≣≣≣≣ Disney's Grand Floridian Beach Resort

4401 Floridian Way, PO Box 10100, 32830; tel 407/824-3000; fax 407/824-3186. US 192 exit off I-4; follow signs for Disney Resorts. 40½ acres. The choicest of the Disney hotels, designed with much flair and imagination in turn-of-the-century style and without the heavy-handed commercialism of some of the other Disney properties. The lobby is nothing short of stunning and is staffed by a spirited team of Disney troupers who glide guests through registration. **Rooms:** 900 rms and stes. Executive level. CI 3pm/CO 11am. Nonsmoking rms avail. Graciously styled, luxuriously furnished accommodations. Rooms facing away from the courtyard and toward the lagoon are quietest. **Amenities:** 🛗 ⚿ 🗞 A/C, cable TV, dataport, voice mail, in-rm safe, bathrobes. All units w/minibars, all w/terraces, some w/whirlpools. **Services:** ⎟◎⎟ ⌂ VP ⎣ ⏧ Twice-daily maid svce, children's program, babysitting. **Facilities:** 🏋 ⚠ 🏊 ▶36 🎿 🏓 ▢2000 ⌨ ⛴ 6 restaurants, 2 bars (1 w/entertainment), 1 beach (lake shore), lifeguard, games rm, lawn games, whirlpool, beauty salon, day-care ctr, playground, washer/dryer. Guests receive preferred tee times at Disney golf courses. **Rates:** Peak (Christmas/Feb–Apr/June–Aug) $290–$490 S or D; $580 ste. Extra person $15. Children under age 17 stay free. Min stay peak. Lower rates off-season. AP and MAP rates avail. Parking: Outdoor, free. AE, MC, V.

### ≣≣≣ Disney's Polynesian Resort

1600 Seven Seas Dr, PO Box 10100, 32840; tel 407/824-2000; fax 407/824-3174. US 192 exit off I-4; follow signs for Disney Resorts. Polynesian-themed facility filled with gardens and lagoons and tropical foliage; one of the original Magic Kingdom properties. It's linked to Epcot and the Magic Kingdom by monorail. **Rooms:** 853 rms and stes. Executive level. CI 3pm/CO 11am. Nonsmoking rms avail. Fine selection of accommodations may offer lagoon or garden views. **Amenities:** 🛗 ⚿ A/C, cable TV, voice mail. Some units w/terraces. **Services:** ✗ ⌂ VP 🚗 ⎣ ⏧ Children's program, babysitting. **Facilities:** 🏋 ⚠ ▶99 🎿 ⛴ ▢90 ⛴ 3 restaurants (see "Restaurants" below), 4 bars, 1 beach (lake shore), games rm, lawn games, day-care ctr, playground, washer/dryer. Guests receive preferred tee times at Disney golf courses. **Rates:** Peak (Dec 24–Jan 1/Feb–Apr/June–Aug) $42–$63 S; $50–$73 D; $60–$85 ste. Extra person $6. Children under age 17 stay free. Lower rates off-season. Parking: Outdoor, free. AE, CB, DC, DISC, MC, V.

### ≣≣≣≣ Disney's Wilderness Lodge

901 W Timberline Dr, 32830; tel 407/824-3200; fax 407/824-3232. US 192 exit off I-4; follow signs for Disney Resorts. A wonderful new Disney hotel evocative of those grand turn-of-the-century lodges found in North American national parks. Design incorporates beautiful chandeliers, totem poles, and an 80-foot fireplace depicting the sedimentary rock layers of the Grand Canyon. The grounds feature beautiful 340-acre Bay Lake, replicas of Yellowstone fossils, volcanic craters, spewing geysers, and a waterfall. **Rooms:** 728 rms and stes. CI 3pm/CO 11am. Nonsmoking rms avail. Walls are adorned with Native American tribal friezes and landscape paintings. **Amenities:** 🛋 ♨ A/C, cable TV, voice mail, in-rm safe. All units w/terraces, some w/whirlpools. **Services:** ✕ ⓥ🄿 🚐 ⛱ 🛎 Car-rental desk, masseur, babysitting. **Facilities:** 🅖 🚴 ⚠ 🄳 🏌 🄺 🖳6 🛶 🍴 ⛳30 ⌨ 👟 3 restaurants (*see* "Restaurants" below), 2 bars, 1 beach (lake shore), lifeguard, volleyball, games rm, spa, whirlpool, beauty salon, playground, washer/dryer. Watersports on lake. **Rates:** Peak (Mar–July/Nov–Dec) $179–$225 S or D; $260–$290 ste. Extra person $15. Children under age 3 stay free. Lower rates off-season. AP and MAP rates avail. Parking: Outdoor, free. AE, MC, V.

### ≣≣≣ Disney's Yacht Club Resort

1700 Epcot Resorts Blvd, PO Box 10100, 32830; tel 407/934-7000; fax 407/934-3450. US 192 exit off I-4; follow signs for Disney Resorts. 56 acres. This large and impressive resort, which shares its 25-acre lake, facilities, and gorgeous landscaping with the adjacent Beach Club (see listing above), evokes a luxurious turn-of-the-century New England yacht club. The five-story, gray-clapboard building houses a magnificent, plush lobby. **Rooms:** 630 rms and stes. Executive level. CI 3pm/CO 11am. Nonsmoking rms avail. Handsome nautical decor and quality furnishings. French doors open onto porches and balconies. **Amenities:** 🛋 ♨ A/C, cable TV, voice mail, in-rm safe. All units w/minibars, all w/terraces. **Services:** ⑩ ☎ ⓥ🄿 🚐 ⛱ 🛎 Masseur, children's program, babysitting. **Facilities:** 🅖 ⚠ 🄳 🄺 🖳7 🍴 ⛳4000 ⌨ 👟 6 restaurants (*see* "Restaurants" below), 5 bars, 1 beach (lake shore), volleyball, games rm, lawn games, spa, sauna, steam rm, whirlpool, beauty salon, playground, washer/dryer. Bar has its own fireplace. Guests receive preferred tee times at Disney golf courses. **Rates:** Peak (Dec 17–31/Feb–Apr/June–Aug 17) $240–$390 S or D; $410 ste. Extra person $15. Children under age 18 stay free. Lower rates off-season. AP and MAP rates avail. Parking: Outdoor, free. AE, MC, V.

### ≣≣≣≣ Walt Disney World Dolphin

1500 Epcot Resorts Blvd, 32830; tel 407/934-4000 or toll free 800/325-3535; fax 407/934-4884. US 192 exit off I-4; follow signs for Epcot Resorts. Larger-than-life and whimsically designed, from architect Michael Graves. Managed by Sheraton. The coral and turquoise facade is centered on a 27-story pyramid, which is flanked by 11-story wings topped by 56-foot twin dolphin sculptures. There are cascading fountains throughout the property and numerous works of art in the colorful, if sometimes dizzying, public areas. **Rooms:** 1,509 rms and stes. Executive level. CI 3pm/CO 11am. Nonsmoking rms avail. Playful decor. **Amenities:** 🛋 ♨ 📺 ⛱ A/C, cable TV w/movies, dataport, voice mail, in-rm safe. All units w/minibars, some w/terraces. **Services:** ⑩ ☎ ⓥ🄿 🚐 ⛱ 🛎 Car-rental desk, social director, masseur, children's program, babysitting. **Facilities:** 🅖 ⚠ 🄺 🖳4 🍴 ⛳9400 ⌨ 👟 7 restaurants, 3 bars (1 w/entertainment), 1 beach (lake shore), lifeguard, volleyball, games rm, lawn games, spa, sauna, steam rm, whirlpool, beauty salon, playground, washer/dryer. Guests receive preferred tee times at Disney golf courses. **Rates:** Peak (Feb 12–Apr 22) $270–$380 S or D; $450 ste. Children under age 18 stay free. Lower rates off-season. AP and MAP rates avail. Parking: Outdoor, free. AE, CB, DC, DISC, ER, JCB, MC, V.

### ≣≣≣ Walt Disney World Swan

1200 Epcot Resorts Blvd, 32830; tel 407/934-3000 or toll free 800/248-7926; fax 407/934-4499. Follow signs for Epcot Resorts. Managed by Westin Hotels, this hard-to-miss, glamorous highrise with giant swans atop its roof is a big hit. Designed by Michael Graves, it allows both large groups and individuals to coexist in harmony, and the crack staff works hard to ensure that goal is achieved. **Rooms:** 758 rms and stes. Executive level. CI 3pm/CO 11am. Nonsmoking rms avail. Flashy, innovatively designed rooms. **Amenities:** 🛋 ♨ 📺 ⛱ A/C, cable TV w/movies, dataport, voice mail, in-rm safe, bathrobes. All units w/minibars, some w/terraces, some w/whirlpools. **Services:** ⑩ ☎ ⓥ🄿 🚐 ⛱ 🛎 Car-rental desk, masseur, babysitting. **Facilities:** 🅖 ⚠ 🄺 🖳6 🍴 ⛳2800 ⌨ 👟 3 restaurants (*see* "Restaurants" below), 3 bars (1 w/entertainment), 1 beach (lake shore), lifeguard, volleyball, games rm, spa, sauna, whirlpool, beauty salon, playground. Guests receive preferred tee times at Disney golf courses. **Rates:** Peak (Jan 28–Apr/Christmas) $280–$370 S or D; $320–$1,750 ste. Extra person $25. Children under age 12 stay free. Lower rates off-season. AP and MAP rates avail. Parking: Outdoor, free. AE, CB, DC, MC, V.

## RESTAURANTS 🍴

### Ariel's

In Disney's Yacht Club Resort, 1700 Epcot Resorts Blvd; tel 407/934-1279. **Seafood/Steak.** This restaurant, decorated in "mermaid" hues of seafoam green, peach, and coral, offers elegant dining in a room adorned with crisp, white table linens, seashell-motif china, and attractively shaded lamps. Menu changes daily. Popular dishes include shellfish paella and Maine lobster baked with crabmeat. Extensive, award-winning wine list. For priority seating, call 407/WDW-DINE.

**FYI:** Reservations not accepted. Children's menu. No smoking. **Open:** Daily 6–10pm. **Prices:** Main courses $18–$47. AE, MC, V. 🖤 &

### ♥ Arthur's 27
In Buena Vista Palace–WDW Village, 1900 Buena Vista Dr; tel 407/827-3450. **International.** This elegant restaurant, located at the top of the hotel, offers spectacular views of Walt Disney World Village. Specialties include fillet of beef with glazed shallots, pecans, and a roquefort-port sauce. A daily selection of fresh fish and lobster is prepared each evening. **FYI:** Reservations accepted. Piano/singer. Dress code. **Open:** Daily 6–10:30pm. **Prices:** Main courses $23–$35. AE, CB, DC, DISC, MC, V. ❤ 🔺 VP &

### Artist's Point
In Disney's Wilderness Lodge, 901 W Timberline Dr; tel 305/824-3200. **Regional American.** One of Disney's classiest and most popular dining spots. Windows overlook Bay Lake and western murals adorn the walls. Grilled steak, seafood, wild game are the dinner highlights; breakfast with the Disney characters is held daily. Vegetarian menu available. For priority seating, call 407/WDW-DINE. **FYI:** Reservations not accepted. Children's menu. No smoking. **Open:** Breakfast daily 7:30–11:30am; dinner daily 5:30–10pm. **Prices:** Main courses $15–$26. AE, MC, V. 📷 VP &

### Boatwrights Dining Hall
In Disney's Dixie Landings Resort, 1251 Dixie Dr; tel 407/934-6000. **Cajun/Seafood/Steak.** Dine in a 19th-century maritime atmosphere. The interior has two large fireplaces and is decorated with antique boatbuilding tools. Patrons can enjoy slowly roasted prime rib, blackened chicken sandwich, or blackened shrimp, scallops, or catfish, all served over brown-buttered pasta in creamy garlic sauce. **FYI:** Reservations accepted. Comedy/guitar/singer. Children's menu. No smoking. **Open:** Breakfast daily 7–11:30am; dinner daily 5–10pm. **Prices:** Main courses $7–$18. AE, MC, V. 📷 VP &

### Bonfamille's Cafe
In Disney's Port Orleans Resort, 2201 Orleans Dr; tel 407/934-5000. Off Bonnet Creek Pkwy. **American/Creole.** A family-oriented restaurant serving breakfast and dinner only. Notable selections from the menu are the family salad, jambalaya with jumbo shrimp, and blackened sea scallops over Mardi Gras pasta. The Scat Cats Club offers musical entertainment in the evening. **FYI:** Reservations accepted. Piano. Children's menu. No smoking. **Open:** Breakfast daily 7–11:30am; dinner daily 5–10pm. **Prices:** Main courses $9–$17. AE, MC, V. &

### Cape May Cafe
In Disney's Yacht Club Resort, 1700 Epcot Resorts Blvd; tel 407/934-8000. **Continental/Seafood.** Casual family restaurant featuring a nightly clambake buffet with peel-and-eat shrimp, steamed clams and mussels, and fresh fish. At breakfast, kids can visit with their favorite Disney characters. For priority seating, call 407/WDW-DINE. **FYI:** Reservations not

accepted. No smoking. **Open:** Peak (Nov–Jan) breakfast daily 7:30–11am; dinner daily 5:30–9:30pm. **Prices:** Prix fixe $19. AE, MC, V. 📷 &

### Chef Mickey's
Walt Disney World Village; tel 407/828-3859. **New American.** Where else can you have Mickey Mouse prepare your lunch? The children's menu offers a variety of dishes for young ones, all at $4.95; grown-ups might enjoy the rib-eye steak, barbecue ribs, or king crab legs. **FYI:** Reservations accepted. Children's menu. No smoking. **Open:** Breakfast daily 9–11:30am; lunch daily 11:30am–2pm; dinner daily 5–10pm. **Prices:** Main courses $13–$25. AE, DISC, MC, V. 📷 &

### $ Chef Mickey's Buffet
In Disney's Contemporary Resort, 4600 N World Dr; tel 407/824-3238. **Buffet.** A bright, casual, buffet-style eatery with umbrella-covered tables and indoor gardens. The extensive buffet includes prime rib, seafood, a salad bar, and desserts. Popular with families for its festive atmosphere and good value. Kids will enjoy the daily breakfasts with Disney characters. **FYI:** Reservations not accepted. Children's menu. No smoking. **Open:** Breakfast daily 7:30–11:30am; dinner daily 5:30–9:30pm. **Prices:** Prix fixe $5–$15. AE, MC, V. 📷 VP &

### Fireworks Factory
1630 Buena Vista Dr; tel 407/934-8989. On Pleasure Island. **American.** A casual eatery with exposed brick, neon lights, and explosives theme. Video games will entertain the young ones while you wait for your table. Dine on dishes such as Vermont pork chops, applewood-smoked baby-back ribs, Pacific shrimp salad. **FYI:** Reservations recommended. Children's menu. **Open:** Daily 11am–2am. **Prices:** Main courses $13–$22. AE, MC, V. &

### Garden Grove Café/Gulliver's
In the Walt Disney World Swan, 1200 Epcot Resorts Blvd; tel 407/934-1618. **Seafood/Steak.** A comfortable restaurant with wicker furniture, potted palms, and a domed ceiling. House specialties are prime rib, baked stuffed Maine lobster, and broiled salmon fillet with hollandaise sauce. Dine with your favorite Disney characters on Monday, Thursday, and Friday evenings, or breakfast with them on Wednesday and Saturday mornings. **FYI:** Reservations accepted. Guitar. Children's menu. **Open:** Breakfast daily 6:30–11am; lunch daily 11am–2pm; dinner daily 5:30–11pm. **Prices:** Main courses $19–$29. AE, CB, DC, MC, V. 🖤 VP &

### $ Jungle Jim's
In Walt Disney World Village, PO Box 22821; tel 407/827-1257. **New American.** A fun, safari-themed bar and restaurant with stools shaped like elephant feet and murals of jungle animals. The fare includes hamburgers, salads, chicken burgers, and spare ribs. **FYI:** Reservations not accepted. Children's menu. **Open:** Daily 11am–2am. **Prices:** Main courses $6–$20. AE, CB, DC, DISC, MC, V. 📷 &

★ **Papeete Bay Verandah**
In Disney's Polynesian Resort, 1600 Seven Seas Dr; tel 407/824-1391. **Polynesian.** Curiously decorated Polynesian-style dining room. Breakfast is attended by Minnie Mouse and other Disney characters. **FYI:** Reservations accepted. Children's menu. **Open:** Breakfast Sun 7:30–11am, Mon–Sat 7:30–10:30am; dinner daily 5:30–10pm. **Prices:** Main courses $12–$20. AE, CB, DC, DISC, MC, V. 🎦 VP ♿

**Portobello Yacht Club**
1650 Buena Vista Dr; tel 407/934-8888. On Pleasure Island. **Northern Italian.** Another soon-to-be classic Disney restaurant. The menu offers a variety of Italian-inspired specialties, including crispy thin-crust pizza, jumbo Alaskan red king crab served with pasta, and boneless chicken breast marinated in olive oil, garlic, and fresh rosemary. **FYI:** Reservations not accepted. Children's menu. **Open:** Daily 11:30am–midnight. **Prices:** Main courses $13–$23. AE, MC, V. ♿

**Watercress Cafe**
In Buena Vista Palace–WDW Village, 1900 Buena Vista Dr; tel 407/827-3440. **American.** A casual eatery in one of the area's best hotels, where you can enjoy views of Lake Buena Vista while you dine. A dinner buffet is available for $13; kids eat for $6. Disney characters make regular appearances here on Sundays 8–10am. The bakery operates around the clock. **FYI:** Reservations not accepted. Children's menu. **Open:** Daily 6am–midnight. **Prices:** Main courses $10–$15. AE, CB, DC, DISC, MC, V. 🏞 VP ♿

**Whispering Canyon Cafe**
In Disney's Wilderness Lodge, 901 W Timberline Dr; tel 305/824-3200. **Regional American/Barbecue.** A fun, relaxed restaurant. Dine at a large table with an oversized lazy susan at its center that spins food in your direction. The prix-fixe dinner for children is $6.50. Guests receive souvenir menu personalized with their name. **FYI:** Reservations not accepted. Children's menu. No smoking. **Open:** Breakfast daily 7–11am; lunch daily 11:30am–3pm; dinner daily 5–10pm. **Prices:** Prix fixe $17–$19. AE, MC, V. 🎦 VP ♿

**Yachtsman Steakhouse**
In Disney's Yacht Club Resort, 1700 Epcot Resorts Blvd; tel 407/934-3415. **Steak.** Wood floors, a beamed ceiling, and an open kitchen help to create a warm, comfortable atmosphere. Beef is the specialty; there's even a beef-aging room in which you can watch the chef cut the high-quality meats. The chef offers a few seafood specialties as well. Extensive wine list. For priority seating, call 407/WDW-DINE. **FYI:** Reservations not accepted. Children's menu. No smoking. **Open:** Daily 5:30–10pm. **Prices:** Main courses $17–$27. AE, MC, V. ♿

## ATTRACTIONS 🏛

### Walt Disney World
One of the world's most famous vacation spots, Walt Disney World sprawls across 43 square miles of central Florida just southwest of Orlando, at I-4 and FL 535. In addition to its three main theme parks (Magic Kingdom, Epcot Center, and Disney–MGM Studios), visitors can check out the seven unique clubs at Pleasure Island, the waves at Typhoon Lagoon, or the shops at Disney Village Marketplace; sing around a campfire at Fort Wilderness; or experience a number of other varied amusements. Both within and around the parks, there are manmade beaches, tranquil lakes, five golf courses, dinner shows, conservation areas, and several elegant and imaginative hotels.

Walt Disney World offers a variety of ticket options. The five-day World Hopper provides unlimited admission on any five days you choose to any (or all) of the three major theme parks, plus admission to Pleasure Island, Blizzard Beach, Typhoon Lagoon, River Country, and Discovery Island for seven consecutive days after first day of use at a major theme park. A four-day Park Hopper gives unlimited admission for four days at just the three major parks. A four-day Value Pass gives you one day at each of the three major parks plus a fourth-day return to one of them (your choice). One Day/One Park tickets also available. For general information contact Walt Disney World (tel 407/824-4321), PO Box 10000, Lake Buena Vista, FL 32830. For reservations at Disney hotels, call 407/W-DISNEY or write to the address above.

### Magic Kingdom
Centered around Cinderella Castle and its medieval spires, the Magic Kingdom consists of seven "lands" offering themed attractions, specialty merchandise, and food: **Main Street USA,** a Disney-style depiction of small-town America at the turn of the century; **Adventureland,** an exotic and mysterious jungle; **Frontierland,** a celebration of America's frontier origins; **Liberty Square,** a tribute to colonial times; **Fantasyland,** an area of fairy tales brought to life; **Mickey's Toontown Fair,** the all-new home of Mickey, Minnie, and friends; and **Tomorrowland,** a futuristic land focusing on outer space.

Among the most popular attractions are The ExtraTERRORestrial Alien Encounter (Tomorrowland), a spine-tingling encounter with a visitor from another galaxy; Space Mountain (Tomorrowland), an indoor roller coaster through darkest space; Splash Mountain (Frontierland), a log flume ride based on the Disney film *Song of the South;* and The Legend of the Lion King (Fantasyland), a live stage show with puppetry, music, and special effects based on Disney's animated classic.

### Epcot Center
There's something new around every corner at Epcot, the ever-changing Walt Disney World theme park of discovery. On one side of Epcot Future World, guests are "shrinking" in their seats at Honey, I Shrunk the Audience. Across the way, at Innoventions, Epcot guests are trying the latest technologies, including the internet and virtual reality. On the east side of Future World, guests can take a crash course in energy at the Universe of Energy's Ellen Energy Crisis.

The other side of the park consists of World Showcase, an international fellowship of nations celebrating the distinctive sights, sounds, and cuisines of 11 nations. Each pavilion is a celebration of the nation's life, culture, and heritage. Each night prior to closing, Illuminations, a popular laser, light, and fireworks show choreographed to classical music, takes place around World Showcase lagoon.

### Disney–MGM Studios

Opened in 1989, Disney's third major theme park invites visitors into the magical realms of the cinema, blending amusement park elements with actual working TV and movie production facilities. Attractions include adventure rides, stage shows, and a backstage studio tour.

Highlights include the Twilight Zone Tower of Terror, which takes riders on a terrifying 13-floor drop at speeds faster than the force of gravity. Marvel as the first full-length computer-animated film comes to life in Disney's Toy Story Parade, performing daily on Hollywood Boulevard. See real movie action as the backstage studio tour takes you into the middle of an avalanche, an oil fire, and a flash flood—courtesy of Catastrophe Canyon. Kermit the Frog and his friends star in Jim Henson's Muppet Vision 3-D, while Star Tours combines high-tech film and exhilarating flight simulation technology. The Indiana Jones Epic Stunt Spectacular demonstrates incredible, death-defying movie stunts and The Magic of Disney Animation allows guests to learn about animation and watch real Disney animators at work.

Guests can also plunge into fabulous fantasy at The Voyage of the Little Mermaid or see a Disney classic come to life with Beauty and the Beast—Live on Stage. Live stage show The Hunchback of Notre Dame pays tribute to Disney's newest movie hero.

### Pleasure Island

A 6-acre entertainment complex with 7 clubs, 4 unique restaurants, trendy shops, and a 10-screen movie theater. Dance clubs include **Mannequins Dance Palace** (under 21 not admitted), a glitzy, high-tech club; **8 TRAX** (under 21 not admitted), a 1970s-themed club; and the all-ages **Rock & Roll Beach Club,** with live bands performing oldies and current pop tunes. (Visitors under age 18 must be accompanied by an adult after 7pm, when the clubs open for the night.)

In addition, guests can enjoy the **Pleasure Island Jazz Company,** with live jazz and blues music; the **Neon Armadillo Music Saloon,** with the best in country music; the **Comedy Warehouse,** featuring top name comedians and a resident improvisational troupe; and the **Adventurers Club,** a theatrically stuffy English gentlemen's club offering improvisational comedy shows in the main salon and cabaret performances in the library. In addition, live bands perform nightly at the outdoor **West End Stage.**

### Typhoon Lagoon

This large water park features water slides, streams, rapids, tidal pools, waterfalls, and an enormous man-made lagoon equipped with a powerful wave generator. Preceded by a foghorn blast, six-foot waves surge across the length of the lagoon, but are engineered to dissipate quickly as they approach the shoreline. Castaway Creek is a meandering, 2,000-foot river for tubing; Shark Reef provides free snorkeling equipment and instruction for a 15-minute swim through a 362,000-gallon simulated coral reef; and Ketchakiddie Creek is a section of mini-slides, pools, and fountains reserved for small children.

### River Country

River Country was Disney's first water park. Smaller than Typhoon Lagoon, it was based on the theme of a rural swimming hole. It features two corkscrew slides, ropes and booms to swing from, manmade boulders serving as diving platforms, and a tubing stream. A 350-yard boardwalk nature trail winds through a cypress swamp.

### Discovery Island

A lush, 11-acre island conservation area and zoological sanctuary, Discovery Island offers nature trails, an enormous, walk-through aviary, and three live shows featuring birds of prey, trained exotic birds, and reptiles native to Florida. Specimens cared for range from exotic birds and miniature deer to alligators. Plants and trees along the trails are marked with explanatory placards. Access to Discovery Island is by boat from Frontierland (Magic Kingdom).

### Blizzard Beach

Whether it's bobsledding down the "snowy" slopes of Mount Gushmore or plunging straight down Summit Plummet at 55 mph, Walt Disney World guests get all the spine-chilling thrills of a northern ski resort. But the new 66-acre Blizzard Beach water adventure park is strictly tropical and the ice is limited to the soft drinks.

# Lake City

## HOTEL 🏨

### ≣≣ Holiday Inn

US 90 at I-75, PO Box 1239, 32056; tel 904/752-3901 or toll free 800/HOLIDAY; fax 904/775-1027. Exit 82 off I-75. Basic, familiar motel with the traditional look of the chain. **Rooms:** 227 rms and stes. CI 3pm/CO noon. Nonsmoking rms avail. **Amenities:** 🛁 ⚙ A/C, cable TV. **Services:** ✕ ⊠ ⊒ **Facilities:** 🔲 ⛖ ₺ 1 restaurant, 1 bar, washer/dryer. **Rates:** Peak (June–Aug) $55 S; $61 D; $125 ste. Lower rates off-season. Parking: Outdoor, free. AE, DC, DISC, MC, V.

# Lakeland

### See also Winter Haven

The 60-shop antiques district in this central Florida city of 73,000 is a big draw, as are lakeside parks and Frank Lloyd Wright architecture at Florida Southern College.

**Information:** Lakeland Area Chamber of Commerce, 35 Lake Morton Dr, PO Box 3607, Lakeland, 33802 (tel 941/688-8551).

## HOTELS 🏨

### ▤▤▤ Four Points Hotel by ITT Sheraton
4141 S Florida Ave, 33813; tel 941/647-3000 or toll free 800/325-3535; fax 941/644-0467. Exit 18 off I-4. Modern facility with adjacent multi-level parking garage. **Rooms:** 140 rms and stes. CI 2pm/CO 11am. Nonsmoking rms avail. **Amenities:** 🛏 ⚙ 📺 A/C, cable TV w/movies. Some units w/minibars. **Services:** ✕ VP 🖼 🕭 **Facilities:** 🏋 ▦ 480 🖥 ᕦ 1 restaurant, 1 bar (w/entertainment), sauna, steam rm, whirlpool. Top-floor conference room offers grand views. **Rates:** Peak (Jan–Apr) $96–$116 S or D; $116–$126 ste. Extra person $10. Children under age 18 stay free. Lower rates off-season. Parking: Indoor/outdoor, free. AE, CB, DC, DISC, MC, V.

### ▤▤ Holiday Inn South
3405 S Florida Ave, 33803; tel 941/646-5731 or toll free 800/833-4902; fax 941/646-5215. Updated facility is top-notch for the chain. Attracts many families, but business clientele will find many amenities suited to their needs. **Rooms:** 171 rms and stes. CI 3pm/CO noon. No smoking. **Amenities:** 🛏 ⚙ 📺 ☎ A/C, cable TV w/movies. Some units w/minibars. **Services:** ✕ 🖼 🕭 Children's program, babysitting. **Facilities:** 🏋 75 ᕦ 1 restaurant, 1 bar (w/entertainment), whirlpool. **Rates (CP):** Peak (Jan–May) $78–$88 S or D; $78 ste. Extra person $10. Children under age 18 stay free. Lower rates off-season. Parking: Outdoor, free. AE, CB, DC, DISC, JCB, MC, V.

### ▤▤ Ramada Inn
3260 US 98 N, 33805; tel 941/688-8080; fax 941/688-8080 ext 152. Exit 18 off I-4. Standard Ramada attracting a mainly business clientele. **Rooms:** 153 rms and stes. CI 3pm/CO noon. Nonsmoking rms avail. **Amenities:** 🛏 A/C, cable TV w/movies. **Services:** ✕ 🖼 🕭 🕭 **Facilities:** 🏋 📺 300 ᕦ 1 restaurant, 1 bar, washer/dryer. **Rates:** $59–$89 S; $69–$99 D; $100–$175 ste. Children under age 18 stay free. Parking: Outdoor, free. AE, DC, DISC, MC, V.

# Lake Wales

Famous for Bok Tower, a 57-bell carillon in 157 acres of gardens, this central Florida town of 10,000 also has its City Hall and commercial district listed on the National Register of Historic Places. **Information:** Lake Wales Area Chamber of Commerce, 340 W Central Ave, PO Box 191, Lake Wales, 33859 (tel 941/676-3445).

## HOTEL 🏨

### ▤▤ Chalet Suzanne Country Inn
3800 Chalet Suzanne Dr, 33853; tel 941/676-6011 or toll free 800/433-6011; fax 941/676-1814. Off US 27, 4 mi N of Lake Wales. A winding road lined with orange groves leads to this complex of dollhouse-like buildings with pastel coloring, gingerbread detailing, and whimsical hand-painted signage. The inn overlooks a small lake, rose garden with benches, and courtyard. **Rooms:** 32 rms, stes, and effic. CI 3pm/CO noon. All distinctly decorated with pretty chintzes and some antiques. **Amenities:** 🛏 ⚙ A/C, cable TV, bathrobes. Some units w/terraces, some w/whirlpools. **Services:** ✕ 🖼 🕭 🕭 Social director, masseur, babysitting. **Facilities:** 🏋 ▦ 🏊 50 ᕦ 1 restaurant (see "Restaurants" below), 1 bar, volleyball, lawn games, washer/dryer. Private airstrip with helicopter landing facilities. **Rates (BB):** $135–$195 S or D; $195 ste; $155 effic. Extra person $12. Children under age 2 stay free. AP and MAP rates avail. Parking: Outdoor, free. AE, CB, DC, DISC, JCB, MC, V.

## RESTAURANTS 🍴

### ♟ Chalet Suzanne
In Chalet Suzanne Country Inn, 3800 Chalet Suzanne Dr; tel 941/676-6011. 4 mi N of Lake Wales. **American.** This highly acclaimed spot has been attracting visitors from near and far since 1931. Soup bowls and plates are made in the ceramic salon on the premises, and the recipes supposedly haven't changed in over 60 years. Chicken Suzanne and shrimp curry are popular entree choices; all-inclusive six-course dinners are also offered. **FYI:** Reservations recommended. Piano. Children's menu. Dress code. **Open:** Tues–Sun 8am–9pm. **Prices:** Prix fixe $57–$75. AE, CB, DC, DISC, MC, V. ▮

### Vinton's
229 E Stuart Ave; tel 941/676-8242. 15 mi W of US 27. **Regional American.** The Creole-inspired menu outshines the decor at this popular family-owned restaurant. Try the shrimp jambalaya or one of the other Southern-style seafood dishes. **FYI:** Reservations recommended. Dress code. **Open:** Peak (Aug–Apr) lunch Mon–Fri 11:30am–2pm; dinner Mon–Sat 6–10pm. **Prices:** Main courses $15–$28. AE, CB, DC, MC, V. ♥ ᕦ

## ATTRACTION 🏛

### Bok Tower Gardens
1151 Tower Blvd; tel 941/676-1408. The focal point of the gardens is its 205-foot tower, which contains a 57-bell carillon. The resident carillonneur performs daily at 3pm. At the visitors center, guests can enjoy hands-on exhibits and a video depicting the construction of the tower, which is closed to the public. Formal gardens and paths, nature trails, picnic area, restaurant. Guided tours daily, Jan–Apr at noon and 2pm. **Open:** Daily 8am–5pm. **$$**

# Leesburg

In February, this central Florida town of 15,000 draws hundreds to its Megabucks BASS Tournament. Area lakes also yield perch and catfish. Venetian Gardens, on Lake Harris, provides freshwater swimming, boat ramps, tennis courts, and a cultural center. **Information:** Leesburg Area Chamber of Commerce, PO Box 490309, Leesburg, 34749 (tel 352/787-2131).

## MOTEL ▦

### ⊫ Shoney's Inn
1308 N 14th St, 34748; tel 352/787-1210 or toll free 800/222-2222; fax 352/365-0163. At jct US 27 and US 441. Variety of accommodations set amongst palm trees. **Rooms:** 130 rms. CI 3pm/CO 11am. Nonsmoking rms avail. **Amenities:** ▦ A/C, cable TV w/movies. **Services:** ⊠ ⌂ **Facilities:** ⊡ ⌂ ⊡ & 1 bar, washer/dryer. Boat ramp and dock. **Rates:** Peak (Nov–Mar) $42 S or D. Children under age 18 stay free. Lower rates off-season. Parking: Outdoor, free. AE, CB, DC, DISC, MC, V.

## RESTAURANT ▥

### Vic's Embers
7940 US 441; tel 352/728-8989. 4½ miles SE of jct US 27. **Seafood/Steak.** The atmosphere is casual and a bit rustic. Dishes include a variety of beef entrees, chops, pasta, and fish of the day. **FYI:** Reservations not accepted. Guitar/piano. Children's menu. **Open:** Dinner Mon–Sat 4:30pm–2am, Sun 4:30–9:30pm; brunch Sun 11:30am–2:30pm. **Prices:** Main courses $10–$14. MC, V. ▣ ▣ &

# Lido Beach

The John Ringling Causeway leads from Sarasota to this crescent-shaped island between Sarasota Bay and the Gulf.

## HOTELS ▦

### ⊫⊫ Harley Sandcastle
1540 Ben Franklin Dr, 34236; tel 941/388-2181 or toll free 800/321-2323; fax 941/388-2655. A low-rise family-style property located directly on Lido Beach; enjoys a fine reputation both as a family spot and a romantic haven for couples. **Rooms:** 179 rms. CI 3pm/CO 11am. **Amenities:** ▦ ⌂ ⌐ A/C, cable TV, refrig, in-rm safe. Some units w/terraces. **Services:** ✕ ⊠ ⌂ **Facilities:** ⊡ ⊕ ⚠ ▣ ▣ & 1 restaurant, 2 bars (1 w/entertainment), 1 beach (ocean), board surfing, games rm, washer/dryer. **Rates:** Peak (Jan–May) $139–$210 S or D. Extra person $15. Children under age 18 stay free. Lower rates off-season. Parking: Outdoor, free. AE, CB, DC, DISC, ER, MC, V.

### ⊫⊫ Holiday Inn Lido Beach
233 Ben Franklin Dr, 34236; tel 941/388-5555 or toll free 800/892-9174; fax 941/388-4321. Exit 39 off I-75. Two blocks from shops, restaurants, and nightlife on St Armand's Circle. **Rooms:** 140 rms and stes. CI 3pm/CO noon. No smoking. Some rooms have Gulf views. **Amenities:** ▦ ⌂ A/C, cable TV w/movies. Some units w/minibars, all w/terraces, some w/whirlpools. **Services:** ✕ ⊶ ⊠ ⌂ Babysitting. **Facilities:** ⊡ ▣ & 1 restaurant, 2 bars (1 w/entertainment), washer/dryer. **Rates:** Peak (Dec–May) $159–$184 S or D; $199 ste. Extra person $10. Children under age 17 stay free. Lower rates off-season. Parking: Outdoor, free. JCB, MC, V.

## MOTELS

### ⊫⊫ Azure Tides
1330 Ben Franklin Dr, 34236; tel 941/388-2101. 2½ mi S of Ringling Causeway. A pleasant low-key operation, located right on the beach. **Rooms:** 66 rms and effic. CI 3pm/CO noon. Nonsmoking rms avail. **Amenities:** ▦ ⌂ A/C, cable TV w/movies, refrig, voice mail. Some units w/terraces. **Services:** ⊠ ⌂ Babysitting. **Facilities:** ⊡ 1 bar, 1 beach (ocean). The outdoor beach bar is open to guests as well as other beachgoers. **Rates:** Peak (Dec–May) $100 S or D; $160–$220 effic. Lower rates off-season. Parking: Outdoor, free. AE, DC, DISC, MC, V.

### ⊫⊫⊫ Half Moon Beach Club
2050 Ben Franklin Dr, 34236; tel 941/388-3694 or toll free 800/358-3245; fax 941/388-1938. Exit 39 off I-75. A beach-side establishment catering to the comfort of beachgoers. Guests enjoy magnificent sunsets from the beach deck and private balconies. **Rooms:** 85 rms and stes. CI 3pm/CO 11am. **Amenities:** ▦ ⌂ ▣ ⌐ A/C, cable TV w/movies, refrig. All units w/minibars, all w/terraces. **Services:** ✕ ⊠ ⌂ Babysitting. Beach attendant offers towels, beverages, and ice cream. **Facilities:** ⊡ ⊕ ▣ & 1 restaurant, 1 bar (w/entertainment), 1 beach (ocean), volleyball, washer/dryer. **Rates:** Peak (Feb–Apr) $110–$155 S or D; $175 ste. Extra person $6. Children under age 17 stay free. Min stay special events. Lower rates off-season. Parking: Outdoor, free. AE, DC, DISC, ER, MC, V.

# Lighthouse Point

Ten miles north of Fort Lauderdale, this small town takes its name from a 130-foot lighthouse built in 1907 to mark the Florida reef at Hillsboro Inlet.

## RESTAURANTS ▥

### Cafe Arugula
In 3110 Plaza, 3110 N Federal Hwy; tel 954/785-7732. ¼ mi S of Sample Rd on US 1. **Regional American.** An innovative restaurant that prepares many items on its oak grill. Specialties include salmon fillet with arugula-butter sauce. **FYI:**

Reservations recommended. Dress code. Beer and wine only. **Open:** Sun–Thurs 5:30–10pm, Fri–Sat 5:30–10:30pm. **Prices:** Main courses $14–$28. AE, DC, DISC, MC, V. ♿

### Cafe Grazia

3850 N Federal Hwy; tel 954/942-7207. 1 block N of Sample Road on US 1. **Italian.** A traditional eatery that is truly Italian in both flavor and decor. The dining room is filled with red tablecloths, wine bottles, and Italian music. The menu includes pasta dishes, pizzas, bean and pasta soup, and lasagna. **FYI:** Reservations accepted. Children's menu. **Open:** Lunch Mon–Fri 11:30am–2:30pm; dinner Sun–Thurs 4:30–10pm, Fri–Sat 4:30–11pm. **Prices:** Main courses $9–$17; prix fixe $12–$17. AE, MC, V. ♿ ☑

### ★ Cap's Place Island

In Lighthouse Point Marina, 2765 NE 28th Court; tel 954/941-0418. The restaurant's launch takes guests from Cap's Dock, next to the marina. **American.** The appealing shanty, with a simple, rustic decor and marina views, offers fresh seafood and other items; however, it is most noted for its fresh hearts of palm. The restaurant, located on the National Register of Historic Places, is reached via a launch that is on call to bring guests from the marina. Call ahead. **FYI:** Reservations recommended. Children's menu. **Open:** Sun–Thurs 5:30–10pm, Fri–Sat 5:30–11pm. **Prices:** Main courses $15–$30. AE, MC, V. 🍺 🏞

# Little Torch Key

## MOTEL 🏨

### 🛏 Parmers Place Inc

565 Barry Ave, PO Box 430665, 33043; tel 305/872-2157; fax 305/872-2014. MM 28.5. Modest but comfortable cottages available in a variety of configurations. Every unit is different: Some face the water while others are just a short walk away. **Rooms:** 44 rms, stes, and effic. CI 3pm/CO 11am. Nonsmoking rms avail. Sparsely decorated but very clean. Some cottages have small kitchenettes, while others hold just a bedroom. **Amenities:** ☕ A/C, cable TV. No phone. All units w/terraces. **Services:** 🚐 🍴 Babysitting. **Facilities:** 🏠 ⚠ 🗑 🏊 ♿ Lawn games, snorkeling, washer/dryer. **Rates (CP):** Peak (Dec 22–Apr/July–Aug) $66–$85 S or D; $115–$190 ste; $85–$115 effic. Extra person $13. Min stay special events. Lower rates off-season. Parking: Outdoor, free. AE, DISC, MC, V.

## RESORT

### 🛏🛏🛏🛏 Little Palm Island

28500 Overseas Hwy MM 28.5, PO Box 1036, 33042; tel 305/872-2524 or toll free 800/843-8567; fax 305/872-4843. 15 min boat ride from Little Torch Key. 5 acres. Romantic and secluded on its own private island, this is an exclusive, affluent adult sanctuary featuring top-of-the-line suites. Chil-

dren under 12 not permitted. **Rooms:** 30 stes. Executive level. CI 3pm/CO 11am. All units have outdoor showers. **Amenities:** 🗑 🍷 A/C, in-rm safe, bathrobes. No phone or TV. All units w/minibars, all w/terraces, all w/whirlpools. **Services:** ✕ 🔑 🚐 Twice-daily maid svce, social director, masseur. Hourly launch operates 7:30am–10:30 pm. **Facilities:** 🏠 ⚠ 🗑 🎿 🏌 🏊 🛶 🎣 1 restaurant, 2 bars (1 w/entertainment), 1 beach (ocean), snorkeling, sauna, beauty salon, washer/dryer. **Rates:** Peak (Dec 22–Mar) $425–$645 ste. Min stay wknds and special events. Lower rates off-season. AP and MAP rates avail. Parking: Outdoor, free. AE, DISC, MC, V.

# Live Oak

## ATTRACTION 🏛

### Suwannee River State Park

20185 County Rd 132; tel 904/362-2746. This tranquil, 1,800-acre park is at the halfway point of the Suwannee River Canoe Trail, which begins in Georgia. Within the park are earthworks remaining from a Confederate fortification overlooking the river. Boat ramp, hiking trails, picnic area, campground (no pets allowed in campground). **Open:** Daily 8am–sunset. $

# Longboat Key

This upscale community of 2,700 occupies the northern tip of a Gulf Coast barrier island by the same name, across Sarasota Bay from Bradenton. Great fishing and shelling via plentiful charter boats. **Information:** Longboat Key Chamber of Commerce, 5360 Gulf of Mexico Dr #107, Longboat Key, 34228 (tel 941/383-2466).

## HOTELS 🏨

### 🛏🛏🛏 Harbour Villa Club at the Buccaneer

615 Dream Island Rd, 34228; tel 941/383-9544 or toll free 800/433-5298; fax 941/383-8028. Overlooking Sarasota Bay is this complex of tastefully designed 2-bedroom units. **Rooms:** 38 cottages/villas. CI 4pm/CO 10AM. Nonsmoking rms avail. **Amenities:** 🛁 ☕ 🗑 A/C, cable TV, refrig. All units w/terraces. **Services:** 🗑 🍴 **Facilities:** 🏠 Whirlpool, washer/dryer. On-site marina. **Rates:** Peak (Dec–May) $1,730–$1,850 cottage/villa. Min stay. Lower rates off-season. Parking: Outdoor, free. Rates per week, based on seven-night minimum stay MC, V.

### 🛏🛏 Holiday Inn Longboat Key

4949 Gulf of Mexico Dr, 34228; tel 941/383-3771 or toll free 800/HOLIDAY; fax 941/383-7871. Exit 39 off I-75. Fresh, tropical-looking hotel, with its own private beach. **Rooms:** 146 rms and stes. CI 3pm/CO 11am. Nonsmoking rms avail. Many offer views of the ocean. **Amenities:** 🛁 ☕

A/C, cable TV. Some units w/terraces, some w/whirlpools. **Services:** ✕ 🛏 ⬜ 🗒 Babysitting. **Facilities:** 🎿 🚴 ⚠ 🖼4 🏊 🖳 📞 400 🔶 3 restaurants, 2 bars (1 w/entertainment), 1 beach (ocean), games rm, sauna, whirlpool. **Rates:** Peak (Jan–Apr) $167–$194 S; $177–$204 D; $206 ste. Extra person $10. Children under age 18 stay free. Lower rates off-season. Parking: Outdoor, free. AE, CB, DC, DISC, JCB, MC, V.

### 🏴🏴🏴 Longboat Key Hilton Beach Resort

4711 Gulf of Mexico Dr, 34228; tel 941/383-2451 or toll free 800/282-3046; fax 941/383-7979. Arranged in a handful of architecturally pleasing buildings standing parallel to the beach. Natural woods used both inside and out; surrounded by manicured landscaping. **Rooms:** 102 rms and stes. CI 3pm/CO 11am. Nonsmoking rms avail. **Amenities:** 🛏 🔰 📺 🍴 A/C, cable TV w/movies, voice mail, in-rm safe. All units w/minibars, all w/terraces. **Services:** ✕ ⬜ 🗒 Babysitting. **Facilities:** 🎿 🚴 ⚠ 🖼1 150 🔶 1 restaurant, 2 bars (1 w/entertainment), 1 beach (ocean), volleyball. **Rates (AP):** Peak (Dec–Apr) $175–$265 S or D; $250–$350 ste. Extra person $25. Children under age 18 stay free. Min stay wknds and special events. Lower rates off-season. AP and MAP rates avail. Parking: Outdoor, free. AE, CB, DC, DISC, EC, MC, V.

## RESORTS

### 🏴🏴🏴 The Colony Beach & Tennis Resort

1620 Gulf of Mexico Dr, 34228; tel 941/383-6464 or toll free 800/4 COLONY; fax 941/383-7549. 18 acres. Beach lovers will relish their stay in this gated enclave of taste and simplicity. So will families, who seem to get special attention. The large, super-friendly staff seems like it was hand-picked from Disney. **Rooms:** 235 stes. CI 4pm/CO 11am. **Amenities:** 🛏 🔰 📺 🍴 A/C, cable TV w/movies, refrig, dataport, voice mail, in-rm safe. All units w/terraces. **Services:** ✕ 🛏 VP 🚗 ⬜ 🗒 Car-rental desk, social director, masseur, children's program, babysitting. **Facilities:** 🎿 🚴 ⚠ 🏊 🏐17 🖼4 🏊 📞 150 🔶 3 restaurants, 1 bar (w/entertainment), 1 beach (ocean), basketball, volleyball, snorkeling, spa, sauna, steam rm, whirlpool, playground, washer/dryer. **Rates:** Peak (Oct–Apr) $305–$495 ste. Extra person $16. Children under age 18 stay free. Min stay special events. Lower rates off-season. Parking: Outdoor, free. Units priced according to proximity to beach. AE, CB, DC, DISC, EC, JCB, MC, V.

### 🏴🏴🏴 Resort at Longboat Key Club

301 Gulf of Mexico Dr, PO Box 15000, 34228; tel 941/383-8821 or toll free 800/237-8821; fax 941/383-0359. 410 acres. Catering to the country-club set, this upmarket resort offers accommodations of varying sizes and shapes. **Rooms:** 225 rms and stes. CI 3pm/CO 11am. **Amenities:** 🛏 🔰 📺 🍴 A/C, cable TV, refrig, voice mail, in-rm safe. All units w/minibars, all w/terraces. **Services:** ✕ 🛏 VP ⬜ 🗒 Twice-daily maid svce, car-rental desk, masseur, children's program, babysitting. Professional staff addresses guests needs adequately and with good cheer. **Facilities:** 🎿 🚴 ⚠ 🏌45 🖼 🏊32

🖳 📞 150 ⬜ 🔶 5 restaurants, 4 bars (2 w/entertainment), 1 beach (ocean), basketball, volleyball, snorkeling, spa, sauna, washer/dryer. **Rates:** Peak (Mar–Apr) $250–$320 S or D; $360–$710 ste. Extra person $15. Children under age 18 stay free. Min stay special events. Lower rates off-season. Parking: Outdoor, free. AE, CB, DC, MC, V.

## RESTAURANTS 🍴

### The Chart House

210 Gulf of Mexico Dr; tel 941/383-5593. **Seafood/Steak.** The open kitchen, the comfortable bar area, the wicker furnishings, and the terrific ocean view unite to create a charming, casual atmosphere. Besides steak and prime rib, there's lobster tail, swordfish, mahimahi, stone crab, and salmon. Salad bar. **FYI:** Reservations recommended. **Open:** Dinner daily 5–10pm. **Prices:** Main courses $18–$24. AE, DISC, MC, V. 🖼 🔶

### Moore's Stone Crab

800 Broadway; tel 941/383-1748. At Gulf of Mexico Dr at north end of Longboat Key. **Seafood.** A casual restaurant and bar overlooking Sarasota Bay. Popular menu items are scallops, shrimp, oysters, Florida lobster, and stone-crab claws. **FYI:** Reservations not accepted. Children's menu. **Open:** Sun–Thurs 11:30am–9pm, Fri–Sat 11:30am–9:30pm. Closed May 16–Oct 14. **Prices:** Main courses $7–$24. MC, V. 🖼 🔶

# Long Key

## ATTRACTION 🏛

### Long Key State Recreation Area

Overseas Hwy MM 68; tel 305/664-4815. This 1,000-acre park features a specially marked canoe trail to guide explorers through some of its wetlands. There are several picnic areas, as well as swimming, fishing, canoe rentals, hiking, beachfront camping, and nature trails. **$$**

# Madeira Beach

One of many small municipalities that hug the Gulf Coast beaches north of Tampa, home to about 4,200 residents and Europa Cruise's "sail-to-nowhere" gambling boats. An October seafood festival draws thousands. **Information:** Gulf Beaches on Sand Key Chamber of Commerce, 501 150th Ave, Madeira Beach, 33708 (tel 813/391-7373).

## HOTELS 🏨

### 🏴🏴 Holiday Inn Madeira Beach

15208 Gulf Blvd, 33708; tel 813/393-4012 or toll free 800/HOLIDAY; fax 813/392-2275. At 150th Ave. A welcome break from this high traffic area. Preferred among repeat guests for its ample beach frontage and waterfront activities. **Rooms:** 148 rms and stes. CI 4pm/CO 11am. Nonsmoking rms avail. **Amenities:** 🔒 🐾 A/C, cable TV w/movies. Some units w/terraces. **Services:** ✕ 🖼 🔌 Babysitting. Car rentals and sightseeing are arranged by the staff. **Facilities:** 🎣 🚐 ⅖ ⅖ 1 restaurant, 2 bars (1 w/entertainment), 1 beach (ocean), games rm, washer/dryer. Beach cabanas and boats available, as are nearby fishing charters. Poolside bar. **Rates:** Peak (Mar–Apr) $114–$129 S or D; $314 ste. Extra person $10. Children under age 12 stay free. Lower rates off-season. Parking: Outdoor, free. AE, CB, DC, DISC, MC, V.

**☰☰☰ North Redington Beach Hilton Resort**
17120 Gulf Blvd, North Redington Beach, 33708; tel 813/391-4000 or toll free 800/221-2424; fax 813/391-4000 ext 7777. 3 mi N of Treasure Island. The ocean laps up against this delightful first-class hotel. A fine upmarket choice. Neatly attired staff, too. **Rooms:** 125 rms and stes. CI 3pm/CO 11am. Nonsmoking rms avail. **Amenities:** 🔒 🐾 📺 A/C, cable TV w/movies. All units w/minibars, all w/terraces. **Services:** ✕ 🔑 VP 🖼 🔌 Babysitting. **Facilities:** 🎣 ⚠ 🚐 ⅖ 1 restaurant, 2 bars (1 w/entertainment), 1 beach (ocean). **Rates:** Peak (Feb–Apr) $125–$195 S or D; $555–$670 ste. Children under age 18 stay free. Lower rates off-season. Parking: Indoor/outdoor, free. AE, DC, DISC, MC, V.

**☰ Shoreline Island Resort Motel**
14200 Gulf Blvd, 33708; tel 813/397-6641 or toll free 800/635-8373; fax 813/393-9157. Exit 15 off I-275 S. An all-adult resort community. **Rooms:** 69 rms and effic. CI 3pm/CO 11am. Nonsmoking rms avail. **Amenities:** 🔒 🐾 📺 A/C, cable TV w/movies, refrig. Some units w/terraces. Gulf-front units have companion recliners. **Facilities:** 🎣 1 beach (ocean), washer/dryer. **Rates:** Peak (Jan 26–Apr 26) $80 S or D; $198 effic. Lower rates off-season. Parking: Outdoor, free. AE, DC, DISC, EC, MC, V.

## RESTAURANTS 🍴

**Friendly Fisherman**
150 128th Ave; tel 813/391-6025. At Gulf Blvd. **Seafood.** Before you dine, sample one of this waterfront eatery's drink specials, like the melon breezer or the lime freeze. For dinner, you can dive into Cajun shrimp, grouper nuggets, or deviled crab. **FYI:** Reservations not accepted. Children's menu. **Open:** Daily 7am–10pm. **Prices:** Main courses $7–$14. DISC, MC, V. ⬛ ⅖

**Lobster Pot**
17814 Gulf Blvd, Redington Shores; tel 813/391-8592. ½ mi S of Park Blvd. **Seafood.** This romantic lobster house with a nautical motif is widely known for the quality of its fare. Choose from a variety of seafood entrees. **FYI:** Reservations recommended. Children's menu. **Open:** Mon–Thurs 4:30–10pm, Fri–Sat 4:30–11pm. **Prices:** Main courses $13–$26. AE, DISC, MC, V. 🖼 ⬛ ⅖

**Shells**
17855 Gulf Blvd, Redington Shores; tel 813/393-8990. Just north of 175th St. **Seafood.** This waterfront restaurant offers

diners a casual, nautical atmosphere and lovely views. Fish dishes may be ordered blackened, fried, or char-grilled. A great value for large groups or families. Tuesday is Lobster Night. **FYI:** Reservations not accepted. Children's menu. **Open:** Sun–Thurs 11:30am–10pm, Fri–Sat 11:30am–11pm. **Prices:** Main courses $7–$23. AE, DISC, MC, V. 🖼 ⅖

**The Wine Cellar**
17307 Gulf Blvd, North Redington Beach; tel 813/393-3491. 2 mi N of Treasure Island. **Continental.** Formal dining room, offering German-influenced continental cuisine. Seafood includes fresh salmon fillet, lobster tails, and Dover sole. The beef Wellington gets high marks. **FYI:** Reservations recommended. Children's menu. **Open:** Mon–Sat 4:30pm–late, Sun 4pm–late. **Prices:** Main courses $7–$28. AE, CB, DC, DISC, ER, MC, V. ⬛ VP ⅖

## ATTRACTIONS 🏛

**John's Pass Village and Boardwalk**
12901 Gulf Blvd; tel toll free 800/944-1847. This rustic Florida fishing village lies on the southern edge of Madeira Beach, where the waters of Boca Ciega Bay meet the Gulf. More than 100 merchants ply their wares here, but the focal point is the large fishing pier and marina, where you can watch commercial and charter fishing boats unloading their daily catch, or sign up for a day's fishing trip on a party boat. Jet-ski rentals and sunset sailboat rides also available. **Open:** Most shops open daily 9am–9pm. **Free**

**Captain Hubbard's Marina**
150 128th Ave; tel 813/393-1947 or 392-0167. Known as a "fish famous" spot, the marina is the focal point of John's Pass, a huge recreational village perched on pilings where Boca Ciega Bay meets the gulf. Sailings daily: half-day trips, 8am–1pm and 1–6pm; full-day trips, 8am–6pm; overnight trips, Tues and Fri departing 8pm. **$$$$**

**Redington Long Pier**
17490 Gulf Blvd (at 175th Ave), Redington Shores; tel 813/391-9398. Extending 1,021 feet into the Gulf of Mexico, the pier is popular with fishermen and sightseers alike. There are rod rentals, bait and tackle, fish-cleaning facilities, and a snack bar. **Open:** Daily 24 hours. **$$**

# Maitland

Lakes Maitland, Sybelia, Lily, and Minehaha surround this residential community of 9,000 five miles north of Orlando, home to a Holocaust memorial center. The Maitland Art Center (listed on the National Register) hosts "All That Jazz" in March; a July art festival draws thousands. **Information:** Maitland–South Seminole Chamber of Commerce, 110 N Maitland Ave, Maitland, 32751 (tel 407/644-0741).

## RESTAURANTS 🍴

### Antonio's Lafiamma
611 S Orlando Ave; tel 407/645-5523. At Maitland Ave.
**Northern Italian.** A stylishly contemporary restaurant with floor-to-ceiling windows overlooking Lake Lily. A variety of pasta dishes, such as bow-tie pasta with scallops tossed in homemade pesto, is available. The deli downstairs offers outdoor dining. **FYI:** Reservations accepted. **Open:** Lunch Mon–Fri 11:30am–2:30pm; dinner Mon–Thurs 5–10pm, Fri–Sat 5–11pm. **Prices:** Main courses $9–$22. AE, DC, DISC, MC, V. 🏞 &

### The Bubble Room
1351 S Orlando Ave; tel 407/628-3331. Lee Rd exit off I-4. **American.** A whimsical 1940s-style restaurant full of kitschy memorabilia, like a vintage jukebox, "bubbling" Christmas lights, and a train that circles the entire dining room. "Bubble Scouts" wearing ridiculous hats keep the enormous portions coming. The huge, homemade desserts are a must. **FYI:** Reservations not accepted. Children's menu. **Open:** Lunch daily 11:30am–4pm; dinner Sun–Thurs 5–10pm, Fri–Sat 5–11pm. **Prices:** Main courses $13–$27. AE, CB, DISC, MC, V. &

# Manalapan

See Palm Beach

# Marathon

Connecticut fishermen settled here in 1818; Bahamians followed. Today, the self-styled "Heart of the Keys" (equidistant to Key Largo and Key West) offers exceptional natural history and children's museums and a prestigious dolphin research center. **Information:** Greater Marathon Chamber of Commerce, 12222 Overseas Hwy, Marathon, 33050 (tel 305/743-5417).

## HOTELS 🏨

### ≝≝≝ Banana Bay Resort & Marina
4590 Overseas Hwy, MM 49.5, 33050; tel 305/743-3500 or toll free 800/226-2621; fax 305/743-2670. A resorty place with handsome accommodations. **Rooms:** 60 rms. CI 3pm/CO 11am. Rooms are decorated with plants, wicker wing chairs, ceiling fans, shutters, bed ruffles, and matching fabrics. **Amenities:** 🛏 👓 🖙 A/C, cable TV, refrig. Some units w/terraces. **Services:** 🚗 🛎 Babysitting. **Facilities:** 🛝 👓 ⚠ 🔲 📞2 🛶 🔲75 & 1 restaurant (lunch and dinner only), 2 bars (w/entertainment), 1 beach (ocean), lawn games, snorkeling, whirlpool, washer/dryer. Small man-made beach. Para-sailing offered seasonally. **Rates (CP):** Peak (Dec–Apr) $95–$195 S or D. Extra person $10. Children under age 5 stay free. Min stay peak, wknds, and special events. Lower rates off-season. Parking: Outdoor, free. AE, CB, DC, DISC, EC, MC, V.

### ≝≝≝ Faro Blanco Marine Resort
Overseas Hwy MM 48.5, 33050; tel 305/743-9018 or toll free 800/759-3276; fax 305/743-2918. Unique, commendable offering comprising cottages, rooms in two-story barges docked in the marina, three-bedroom condominiums, and two apartments in a lighthouse on the pier. **Rooms:** 95 cottages/villas. Executive level. CI 2pm/CO 11am. **Amenities:** 🛏 🖙 A/C, cable TV, refrig. Some units w/minibars, some w/terraces, 1 w/whirlpool. **Services:** 🚗 🛎 🌭 Babysitting. **Facilities:** 🛝 👓 ⚠ 🔲 🔲50 & 4 restaurants, 4 bars (1 w/entertainment), snorkeling, playground, washer/dryer. **Rates:** Peak (Dec 20–Apr) $65–$233 cottage/villa. Extra person $10. Children under age 6 stay free. Min stay peak and special events. Lower rates off-season. Parking: Indoor/outdoor, free. AE, DISC, MC, V.

## RESORTS

### ≝≝≝ Hawk's Cay Resort & Marina
Overseas Hwy MM 61, 33050; tel 305/743-7000 or toll free 800/432-2242; fax 305/743-5215. 10 mi N of Marathon Airport. 60 acres. A good family facility; operates a dolphin research program on the premises with 14 dolphins and daily shows offered free to guests and visitors. **Rooms:** 176 rms and stes; 18 cottages/villas. CI 3pm/CO 11am. Nonsmoking rms avail. **Amenities:** 🛏 👓 🖙 A/C, cable TV w/movies, refrig. All units w/terraces, 1 w/whirlpool. **Services:** ✕ 🍴 🚗 🖼 🛎 Social director, children's program, babysitting. **Facilities:** 🛝 👓 ⚠ 🔲 ▶18 🏌 🔲8 🛶 🔲175 🖥 & 4 restaurants, 2 bars (w/entertainment), 1 beach (ocean), basketball, volleyball, games rm, lawn games, snorkeling, whirlpool, playground. **Rates:** Peak (Dec 18–Apr 13) $195–$345 S or D; $380–$850 ste. Extra person $25. Children under age 16 stay free. Min stay special events. Lower rates off-season. AP rates avail. Parking: Outdoor, free. AE, DC, DISC, MC, V.

### ≝≝≝ Sombrero Resort & Lighthouse Marina
19 Sombrero Blvd, 33050; tel 305/743-2250 or toll free 800/433-8660; fax 305/743-2998. Modern, well-maintained facility. **Rooms:** 122 stes and effic. CI 2pm/CO 11am. Nonsmoking rms avail. Gray and blue decor, Formica-covered furniture. Large showers with seats. **Amenities:** 🛏 🖙 A/C, cable TV, refrig, voice mail. All units w/terraces. **Services:** 🛎 **Facilities:** 🛝 🔲 📞2 🔲2 🔲60 1 restaurant (dinner only), 2 bars (1 w/entertainment), games rm, snorkeling, sauna, washer/dryer. Golf across the street. Sunny pool has inviting bar. **Rates (CP):** Peak (Dec–Apr) $125–$165 ste; $160–$180 effic. Extra person $10. Children under age 12 stay free. Lower rates off-season. Parking: Outdoor, free. AE, DC, MC, V.

## RESTAURANT 🍴

### Banana Cabana

In Banana Bay Resort & Marina, 4590 Overseas Hwy MM 49.5; tel 305/289-1232. **Eclectic/Seafood.** Grilled-to-order prime rib and fresh local seafood draw in the guests at this oasis for good food, friendly service, and pleasant atmosphere. **FYI:** Reservations accepted. Children's menu. **Open:** Daily 11:30am–10pm. **Prices:** Main courses $11–$23. AE, CB, DC, DISC, MC, V. 🚢 ⚭

## ATTRACTIONS 🏛

### Museum of Natural History

5550 Overseas Hwy, MM 50.5; tel 305/743-9100. This small museum displays dozens of local historical artifacts, including shell tools and pottery from pre-Columbian native tribes and booty from one of America's oldest shipwrecks. Other exhibits focus on the Keys' natural habitats, including a coral reef tank that holds sharks, lobsters, and tropical fish, and a "touch" tank, where visitors can handle rays, starfish, and other safe sea creatures. Outside, visitors are encouraged to explore the museum's quarter-mile nature trail, which winds through rare tropical palm hammock. **Open:** Mon–Sat 9am–5pm, Sun noon–5pm. **$$**

### Dolphin Research Center

Overseas Hwy MM 59, Marathon Shores; tel 305/289-1121. This not-for-profit organization helps visitors learn about and interact with dolphins and other sea creatures. The more in-depth (and much more expensive) DolphinInsight program includes a guided tour of the facility and open-air workshops on dolphin physiology and basic training techniques. Visitors are given the opportunity to touch and communicate with dolphins using a variety of hand signals. The center also operates a swim-with-the-dolphins program called Dolphin Encounter (reservations required up to a month in advance). Basic tours run daily at 10 and 11am and at 12:30, 2, and 3:30pm. **$$$**

# Marco Island

The only inhabited island among the Ten Thousand Islands off southwest Florida, its first residents were members of the Calusa tribe, who came here 3,500 years ago. Its 38 square miles feature a renowned archeological site, exceptional shelling, fishing, golf and tennis, trolley tours, and remnants of a purportedly haunted tower. **Information:** Marco Island Area Chamber of Commerce, 1102 N Collier Blvd, Marco Island, 33937 (tel 941/394-7549).

## HOTELS 🏨

### 🏳🏳 Eagle's Nest Beach Resort

410 S Collier Blvd, 33927; tel 941/237-8906; fax 941/642-1599. Exit 15 off I-75, S on Rte 951, mid-beach. 5 acres. Unpretentious condo complex offering daily and weekly rentals. Outlying units to supplement the 12-story tower, where most guests stay. **Rooms:** 96 effic. CI 3pm/CO 10am. Tastefully appointed one- and two-bedroom units have full, modern kitchens. **Amenities:** 🏨 👁 📺 A/C, cable TV w/movies, refrig, VCR. All units w/terraces, all w/whirlpools. **Services:** 🛎 Social director, masseur, children's program, babysitting. **Facilities:** 🏊 ⚠ 🏀 🍴 50 1 beach (ocean), volleyball, games rm, racquetball, spa, whirlpool, washer/dryer. Scuba lessons offered. **Rates:** Peak (Dec 20–Apr 15) $199–$299 effic. Min stay. Lower rates off-season. Parking: Outdoor, free. Rooms rent on a Fri-to-Fri basis. AE, DISC, MC, V.

### 🏳🏳🏳 Marco Bay Resort

1001 N Barfield Dr, 33937; tel 941/394-8881 or toll free 800/228-0661; fax 941/394-8909. Exit 15 off I-75. Go south on FL 951 to the island and make a right at the first traffic light. A major condo complex drawing snowbirds who come for more than just a few days and desire a self-sufficient arrangement, while still being just a mile to shopping and beach. **Rooms:** 109 stes. CI 4pm/CO 11am. Nonsmoking rms avail. **Amenities:** 🏨 👁 📺 A/C, cable TV w/movies, refrig. All units w/terraces. **Services:** 🛎 **Facilities:** 🏊 🍴 2 200 ⚭ 2 restaurants, 1 bar, whirlpool, washer/dryer. On-site marina. **Rates:** Peak (Jan–Apr) $110–$190 ste. Children under age 18 stay free. Lower rates off-season. Parking: Indoor/outdoor, free. AE, MC, V.

## RESORTS

### 🏳🏳🏳🏳 Marco Island Hilton Beach Resort

560 S Collier Blvd, 33937; tel 941/394-2511 or toll free 800/445-8667; fax 941/642-2672. Exit 15 off I-75. 23 acres. A leader among the beachfront hotels, this shining facility boasts trend-setting design and excellent maintenance. **Rooms:** 298 rms and stes. Executive level. CI 3pm/CO noon. Nonsmoking rms avail. Recently redecorated rooms feature bright floral patterns and sleeper sofa. **Amenities:** 🏨 👁 📺 🍷 A/C, cable TV w/movies, refrig, dataport, voice mail, in-rm safe. All units w/minibars, all w/terraces, some w/whirlpools. All rooms have kitchenettes (sink, hot plate, kettle, microwave). TV, phone, double vanities, and marble shower in bathroom. **Services:** ✕ 🔑 VP 🖼 🛎 Twice-daily maid svce, social director, masseur, children's program, babysitting. Valet service. **Facilities:** 🏊 ⚠ 🏀 3 🍴 500 💻 ⚭ 2 restaurants, 2 bars (w/entertainment), 1 beach (ocean), lifeguard, volleyball, games rm, spa, sauna, whirlpool. **Rates:** Peak (Dec 20–Apr 27) $189–$339 S or D; $379–$389 ste. Extra person $20–$25. Children under age 18 stay free. Lower rates off-season. Parking: Outdoor, free. AE, CB, DC, DISC, MC, V.

### 🏳🏳🏳 Marriott's Marco Island Resort

400 S Collier Blvd, 33937; tel 941/394-2511 or toll free 800/228-9290; fax 941/642-2672. Off FL 951. 12 acres. This sprawling establishment consists of two nine-story towers and two A-frame wings fronted by beachfront courtyards. Popu-

lar with couples, families, and groups. **Rooms:** 735 rms and stes. CI 3pm/CO noon. Nonsmoking rms avail. All units have Gulf views. **Amenities:** 🛁 🐶 🖥 🍷 A/C, cable TV, dataport, voice mail. All units w/minibars, all w/terraces. Irons and ironing boards in every room. Two-bedroom suites have microwaves and refrigerators. **Services:** ✕ 🛏 VP 🚗 🖼 🛎 Twice-daily maid svce, car-rental desk, social director, masseur, children's program, babysitting. Beach strollers for rent. **Facilities:** 🏃₃ 🚲 ⛲ ▶₁₈ ☂₁₂ 🎱₄ 🏋 🍽 🛖 1500 💻 ⬇ 5 restaurants (*see* "Restaurants" below), 5 bars (2 w/entertainment), 1 beach (ocean), basketball, volleyball, games rm, whirlpool, beauty salon, day-care ctr, playground, washer/dryer. Miniature-golf course, chic shopping arcade, small grocery. Golf course is an 8-mile drive off-island from the resort. **Rates:** Peak (Dec 20–Apr 15) $260–$365 S or D; $550–$890 ste. Extra person $15. Children under age 18 stay free. Lower rates off-season. Parking: Outdoor, free. AE, CB, DC, DISC, MC, V.

### ≣ ≣ ≣ Radisson Suite Beach Resort

600 S Collier Blvd, 33937; tel 941/394-4100 or toll free 800/814-0633; fax 941/394-0419. Exit 15 off I-75. 6 acres. A colorful, first-rate operation with luscious landscaped grounds, an attractive pool area, and a good selection of dining and recreational options. **Rooms:** 269 rms and effic. Executive level. CI 4pm/CO noon. Nonsmoking rms avail. Efficiencies are quite roomy. **Amenities:** 🛁 🐶 🖥 A/C, cable TV w/movies, refrig, dataport, voice mail, in-rm safe. All units w/terraces. **Services:** 🛏 🚗 🖼 🛎 Car-rental desk, social director, children's program, babysitting. **Facilities:** 🏃₁ ⛲ 🎱₂ 🛖 500 ⬇ 3 restaurants, 2 bars (1 w/entertainment), 1 beach (ocean), basketball, games rm, whirlpool, day-care ctr. **Rates:** Peak (Feb–Apr) $219 S or D; $249–$459 effic. Extra person $15–$25. Children under age 12 stay free. Lower rates off-season. Parking: Indoor/outdoor, free. Efficiency rates apply to up to four guests (for one-bedroom unit) or six guests (for two-bedroom unit). AE, CB, DC, DISC, MC, V.

## RESTAURANTS 🍴

### Cafe de Marco

In Port of Marco Shopping Village, 244 Palm St; tel 941/394-6262. **Seafood.** A garden-style cafe with wicker appointments, mint-colored tablecloths, and a fresh spring ambiance. Enjoy the giant prawns or one of the fresh fish dishes served from the daily menu. **FYI:** Reservations recommended. Children's menu. Beer and wine only. **Open:** Lunch Wed–Fri 11:30am–2:30pm; dinner daily 5–10pm. **Prices:** Main courses $16–$26. AE, MC, V. 🍸

### Captain's Corner Restaurant & Lounge

In Chamber of Commerce Plaza, 1106½ N Collier Blvd; tel 941/394-8887. **Seafood.** Dine indoors or on the enclosed porch overlooking Cedar Bay and the marina. The casual, comfortable eatery offers a lobster buffet and lots of local seafood. **FYI:** Reservations recommended. Dancing/piano.

Children's menu. **Open:** Lunch daily noon–2:30pm; dinner daily 4:30–10pm. **Prices:** Main courses $13–$21. MC, V. 🏞 ⬇

### The Dining Room at Heritage Square

1000 N Collier Blvd; tel 941/394-2221. **French.** A small, offbeat cafe where the kitchen is in view of the dining room. Chilled curried apple soup, fish of the day, rabbit Dijon, and coq au vin are among the featured dishes. **FYI:** Reservations recommended. Jacket required. Beer and wine only. **Open:** Mon–Sat 5:30–10pm. Closed July–Sept. **Prices:** Main courses $18–$26. AE, DC, DISC, MC, V. 🅥 VP ⬇

### Olde Marco Inn

100 Palm St; tel 941/394-3131. **New American.** Established in 1883, this antiquated inn once rented rooms for $1 per day. Today, you can enjoy fine dining here amid 150-year-old Audubon prints and other period antiques, including the 2,000-piece prism-and-cranberry-glass chandelier. **FYI:** Reservations accepted. **Open:** Lunch Mon–Fri 11:30am–2pm; dinner daily 5:30–10pm. **Prices:** Main courses $13–$25. AE, CB, DC, DISC, MC, V.

### Snook Inn

1215 Bald Eagle Dr; tel 941/394-3313. On the corner of Palm St and Bald Eagle Dr. **Seafood.** Rustic Florida setting. The grouper sandwich is the house specialty. **FYI:** Reservations not accepted. Children's menu. **Open:** Peak (Dec–May) daily 11am–10pm. **Prices:** Main courses $8–$18. AE, MC, V. 🏞 👨‍👩‍👧 ⬇

### ✴ Stan's Idle Hour Seafood Restaurant

1 Harbor Place; tel 941/394-3041. **Seafood/Steak.** Enjoy fresh ocean treats at this fun and funky '60s-inspired eatery. (Stan, the owner, looks as if that era was mighty good to him.) Sample grilled shrimp and the softshell crabs. The outdoor bar shouldn't be missed. The patio hosts a party and show on Sundays. Open only on weekends in August. **FYI:** Reservations accepted. Big band. Children's menu. **Open:** Tues–Sun 11am–10pm. **Prices:** Main courses $11–$19. DISC, MC, V. 🏞 ⬇

### Voyager Steak & Seafood

In Marriott's Marco Island Resort and Golf Club, 400 S Collier Blvd; tel 941/394-2511. **Seafood/Steak.** Lunch buffet and Sunday brunch draw locals and hotel guests. Pasta, seafood, and steaks are served in a large dining room with a view of the pool. **FYI:** Reservations recommended. Children's menu. **Open:** Lunch Mon–Fri 11:30am–2pm; dinner daily 5–10pm; brunch Sun 10am–2pm. **Prices:** Main courses $13–$20. AE, CB, DC, DISC, MC, V. 💟 ⬇

## ATTRACTION 💼

### Ted Smallwood's Store

Chololoskee Island; tel 941/695-2989. Located on Chololoskee Island, just south of Everglades City, this is one of southwestern Florida's oldest buildings, dating back to pioneer days. It has been converted to a museum and gift shop.

The rustic store was also once a Native American trading post. **Open:** Peak (Dec–Apr) daily 10am–5pm. Reduced hours off-season. **$**

# Marianna

This is a Deep South town, flavored by nearby Alabama and Georgia. Confederate Park includes a monument to residents who defended the town against the Union Army in 1864. Florida Caverns, three miles south of town, offers guided tours. **Information:** Marianna Chamber of Commerce, 2928 Jefferson St, PO Box 130, Marianna, 32447 (tel 904/ 482-8061).

## MOTEL 🏨

**UNRATED Ramada Limited**
4655 US 90 E, PO Box 979, 32446; tel 904/526-3251 or toll free 800/HOLIDAY; fax 904/482-6223. Exit 21 off I-10. Standard, affordable lodging. **Rooms:** 80 rms. CI 2pm/CO noon. Nonsmoking rms avail. **Amenities:** 🕾 🗘 A/C, cable TV, dataport. **Services:** 🖃 🗘 🖎 **Facilities:** 🚣 ⌐100⌐ **Rates:** $49 S or D. Extra person $5. Children under age 18 stay free. Parking: Outdoor, free. AE, DC, DISC, MC, V.

## ATTRACTION 🖼

**Florida Caverns State Park**
3345 Caverns Rd; tel 904/482-9598. An intriguing series of caves 65 feet underground decorated with stalagmites, limestone stalactites, columns, and other striking formations. Chambers include the Waterfall Room, the Cathedral Room, and the Wedding Room, so-called for its ornate wedding cake appearance. Guided ranger tours cover about a half-mile of illuminated passageways. The park also offers swimming, fishing, horseback-riding (stables are available), and camping. The 50-mile Chipola River Canoe Trail begins in the park. **Open:** Daily 8am–sunset. **$$**

# Marineland

## HOTEL 🏨

**≣≣≣ Quality Inn Marineland**
9507 Ocean Shore Blvd, 32086; tel 904/471-1222 or toll free 800/824-4218; fax 904/471-3352. Exit 93E off I-95 S. A beachfront family hotel located at the entrance to Marineland park. **Rooms:** 125 rms and stes. CI 3pm/CO 11am. Nonsmoking rms avail. **Amenities:** 🕾 A/C, cable TV. Some units w/terraces. **Services:** 🗘 **Facilities:** 🚣 🖾 ⌐200⌐ 🕭 2 restaurants, 1 bar, 1 beach (ocean), lawn games, playground, washer/dryer. Pool with neighboring kiddie pool receives sun throughout the day. Tennis courts across the street. **Rates:** Peak (Feb–Apr/May–Aug) $74–$104 S or D; $225–$350 ste.

Extra person $5. Children under age 18 stay free. Lower rates off-season. Parking: Outdoor, free. AE, DC, DISC, MC, V.

## ATTRACTION 🖼

**Marineland of Florida**
9507 Ocean Shore Blvd (FL A1A); tel 904/471-1111. The first marinelife park to successfully maintain dolphins in a manmade environment and achieve a successful birth in captivity, this was, in pre-Disney days, Florida's most popular attraction. Dolphins and California sea lions perform for crowds in the huge circular oceanarium. Also on view are sharks, moray eels, barracudas, and many other saltwater and freshwater fish; rare and beautiful sea shells are displayed in the Margaret Herrick Shell Museum. A 3-D film called *Sea Dream* is shown throughout the day at the Aquarius Theater. Restaurant and snack bars on premises. **Open:** Daily 9am–5:30pm. **$$$$**

# Matlacha

## RESTAURANT 🍴

**Snook Harbour Inn**
At the foot of Matlacha Bridge; tel 941/283-1131. **Seafood.** Dine indoors or out in a relaxing setting offering great views of the water. The weekend seafood buffet is a good value. Desserts are made on the premises. **FYI:** Reservations not accepted. Children's menu. Beer and wine only. **Open:** Daily 11am–10pm. **Prices:** Main courses $8–$19. AE, MC, V. No CC. 🍴 🖼 🕭

# Melbourne

See also Indialantic

Home of the Sea Turtle Preservation Society, this east coast city of 60,000 is 40 miles south of Kennedy Space Center. Tourists can visit botanical gardens or Liberty Bell Memorial Museum, bet on greyhounds or cross the Indian River to Spanish treasure wrecks and a historic pier at Melbourne Beach. **Information:** Melbourne–Palm Bay and the Beaches Convention & Visitors Bureau, 1005 E Strawbridge Ave, Melbourne, 32901 (tel 407/724-5400).

## HOTELS 🏨

**≣≣ Courtyard by Marriott**
2101 W New Haven Ave, 32904; tel 407/724-6400 or toll free 800/321-2211; fax 407/984-4006. Exit 71 off 95. Attractive hotel featuring neatly landscaped grounds and an attentive, friendly staff. **Rooms:** 146 rms and stes. CI 3pm/ CO noon. Nonsmoking rms avail. **Amenities:** 🕾 🗘 A/C, cable TV w/movies, dataport, voice mail. Some units w/terraces. **Services:** ✕ 🚐 🖃 🗘 **Facilities:** 🚣 🛎 ⌐50⌐ 🕭 1 restaurant

(bkfst only), 1 bar, whirlpool, washer/dryer. **Rates:** Peak (Dec–Apr) $59–$84 S; $59–$89 D; $99–$109 ste. Extra person $4. Children under age 18 stay free. Lower rates off-season. Parking: Outdoor, free. AE, DC, DISC, MC, V.

### ≣≣≣ Melbourne Airport Hilton

200 Rialto Place, 32901; tel 407/768-0200 or toll free 800/437-8010; fax 407/984-2528. Exit 71 off I-95. A classy place with a smart, modern style. The glass-and-concrete high-rise is not on the beach, but it offers many of the facilities of a first-class hotel. **Rooms:** 240 rms and stes. CI 3pm/CO noon. Nonsmoking rms avail. **Amenities:** ☎ ⚗ A/C, cable TV w/movies. Some units w/minibars, some w/terraces, some w/whirlpools. **Services:** ✗ ▣ 🚗 ▣ ⌂ Car-rental desk, babysitting. **Facilities:** ⚡ ▣ 🛵 ▣ 800 ⬜ ⚭ 1 restaurant, 2 bars, games rm, whirlpool, playground, washer/dryer. The sports bar is immensely popular. **Rates:** Peak (Jan–Apr) $119–$139 S or D; $229–$279 ste. Children under age 18 stay free. Lower rates off-season. Parking: Outdoor, free. AE, CB, DC, DISC, ER, JCB, MC, V.

### ≣≣≣ Radisson Suite Hotel Oceanfront

3101 N FL A1A, 32903; tel 407/773-9260 or toll free 800/333-3333; fax 407/777-3190. Exit 71 off I-95. An ocean-front high-rise. **Rooms:** 166 stes. CI 4pm/CO noon. Non-smoking rms avail. Some rooms have bunk beds for families. **Amenities:** ☎ ▣ A/C, cable TV, refrig, VCR, voice mail, in-rm safe. All units w/terraces. Suites have whirlpool tubs. **Services:** ✗ ▣ ⌂ Children's program, babysitting. **Facilities:** ⚡ ▣ 150 ⚭ 1 restaurant, 2 bars (1 w/entertainment), 1 beach (ocean), board surfing, whirlpool, washer/dryer. Dinner and breakfast buffets. **Rates:** Peak (Jan–May) $109–$199 ste. Extra person $10. Children under age 18 stay free. Lower rates off-season. MAP rates avail. Parking: Outdoor, free. AE, CB, DC, DISC, ER, JCB, MC, V.

## MOTELS

### ≣≣ Budgetel Inn

7200 George T Edwards Dr, 32940; tel 407/242-9400 or toll free 800/4-BUDGET; fax 407/242-9440. Exit 73 off I-95. Basic accommodations geared toward the business traveler or families on a budget. **Rooms:** 107 rms. CI 2pm/CO noon. Nonsmoking rms avail. Cheerful, contemporary room decor. **Amenities:** ☎ ⚗ ▣ A/C, cable TV w/movies, dataport. **Services:** ▣ ⌂ ⚭ Babysitting. **Facilities:** ⚡ 12 ⚭ Washer/dryer. Use of nearby health club for an additional fee. **Rates (CP):** Peak (Jan–Mar) $40–$46 S; $49–$56 D. Children under age 19 stay free. Lower rates off-season. Parking: Outdoor, free. AE, CB, DC, DISC, MC, V.

### ≣≣ Comfort Inn of Melbourne

8298 N Wickham Rd, 32940; tel 407/255-0077 or toll free 800/554-5188; fax 407/259-9633. Exit 73 off I-95. A superior selection in this chain. Hotel receives many guests from the nearby performing arts center. Close to zoo and Florida Marlins spring training camp. **Rooms:** 134 rms and stes. CI 3pm/CO 11am. Nonsmoking rms avail. **Amenities:** ☎ A/C,

cable TV w/movies, voice mail. 1 unit w/minibar, 1 w/whirlpool. Some suites equipped with computer/fax/modem/printer/copier. **Services:** ✗ ▣ ⌂ Babysitting. **Facilities:** ⚡ 30 ⚭ 1 bar (w/entertainment). Use of nearby health club for an additional fee. **Rates (BB):** Peak (Feb–Apr) $45–$65 S; $50–$65 D; $85–$250 ste. Extra person $10. Children under age 19 stay free. Lower rates off-season. Parking: Outdoor, free. AE, CB, DC, DISC, MC, V.

### ≣≣ Holiday Inn West

4500 W New Haven Ave, 32904; tel 407/724-2050 or toll free 800/HOLIDAY; fax 407/723-2040. Exit 71 off I-95. Above average accommodations geared to corporate guests. **Rooms:** 100 rms. CI 1pm/CO 11am. Nonsmoking rms avail. Very attractive oak furnishings. **Amenities:** ☎ ⚗ A/C, cable TV. Some units w/terraces. **Services:** ✗ ▣ ⌂ ⚭ **Facilities:** ⚡ 10 ⚭ 1 restaurant, 1 bar, washer/dryer. Guest privileges at nearby Gold's Gym. **Rates:** Peak (Jan–Mar) $95 S or D. Extra person $8. Children under age 18 stay free. Lower rates off-season. Parking: Outdoor, free. AE, CB, DC, DISC, JCB, MC, V.

### ≣≣ Melbourne Harbor Suites Hotel

1207 E New Haven Ave, 32901; tel 407/723-4251 or toll free 800/242-4251; fax 407/768-1227. Exit 71 off I-95. Located in the downtown historic shopping district next to the marina, this comfortable, clean all-suite motel is one hour from Disney World and Kennedy Space Center. **Rooms:** 50 stes and effic. CI 1pm/CO 11am. Nonsmoking rms avail. All rooms are equipped with full kitchens or kitchenettes. The most interesting room is the fourth-floor lighthouse suite. **Amenities:** ☎ ▣ A/C, cable TV, refrig. Some units w/terraces, 1 w/whirlpool. **Services:** 🚗 ⌂ Free coffee and danish served daily in the tiny front lobby. **Facilities:** ⚡ ⚭ 1 restaurant (bkfst and lunch only), beauty salon, washer/dryer. **Rates (CP):** Peak (Jan 15–Mar) $85–$125 ste; $45–$65 effic. Children under age 14 stay free. Lower rates off-season. Parking: Outdoor, free. AE, DISC, MC, V.

## RESTAURANTS 🍴

### Cooker Bar and Grille

1510 W New Haven Ave; tel 407/727-8448. 2 blocks E of Wickam Rd and W New Haven Ave. **Regional American.** A dark wood-trimmed dining room and a cozy sports bar with two TV screens. The menu offers steaks, ribs, and prime rib; specialties include Cajun catfish fillet. Sunday brunch 11am–3pm. **FYI:** Reservations not accepted. Children's menu. **Open:** Mon–Thurs 11am–10:30pm, Fri–Sat 11am–11:30pm, Sun 11am–10pm. **Prices:** Main courses $7–$14. AE, CB, DC, DISC, MC, V. ⚭

### The 812 Rendez Vous

812 E New Haven Ave; tel 407/676-4007. E of Waverly St and W of Municipal St. **New American.** Excellent variety of healthy and flavorful dishes, served up in ample portions. **FYI:** Reservations accepted. Beer and wine only. No smoking.

**Open:** Lunch Tues–Sat 11:30am–2:30pm; dinner Thurs–Sat 6am–9pm. Closed Aug 1–15. **Prices:** Main courses $5–$8. AE, DISC, MC, V.

**Shells**
1490 W New Haven Ave; tel 407/722-1122. **Seafood.** Popular seafood eatery with nautical decor accented with fish logos and neon lights around the bar. **FYI:** Reservations not accepted. Children's menu. **Open:** Dinner Mon–Thurs 4–10pm, Fri–Sat 4–11pm, Sun noon–10pm. **Prices:** Main courses $5–$11. AE, DISC, MC, V. 👫 &

**Strawberry Mansion**
1218 E New Haven Ave; tel 407/723-1900. **American.** Housed in an elegant, restored Victorian home. The old-fashioned setting is an ideal one in which to enjoy traditional continental cuisine. Classical music wafts through the several dining rooms as you dine. Menu highlights include the fresh fish of the day, crab cakes, steak Oscar, and a variety of veal dishes. **FYI:** Reservations accepted. **Open:** Daily 8am–10pm. **Prices:** Main courses $11–$19. AE, MC, V. 🍴

## ATTRACTIONS 🏛

**Brevard Art Center and Museum (BACAM)**
1463 Highland Ave; tel 407/242-0737. This community-oriented museum offers both visual arts and physical science programming. The art galleries present a rotating schedule of visual art exhibits; the science museum offers hands-on, interactive exhibits for children of all ages. **Open:** Tues–Sat 10am–5pm, Sun 1–5pm. $

**Space Coast Science Center**
1510 Highland Ave; tel 407/259-5572. A "playground" of hands-on exhibits dealing with science and technology. Exhibits, which are changed every few months, have included "Invaders," dealing with exotic flora and fauna in Florida, and "The Art of Design," exploring the boundaries between science and art. A nature room has local animals on view. **Open:** Tues–Sat 10am–5pm, Sun noon–5pm. $

# Merritt Island

See Kennedy Space Center

# Miami

See also Coral Gables, Fort Lauderdale, Homestead, Key Biscayne, Miami Int'l Airport, Miami Beach, Sunny Isles, Surfside

A world-class city with an urban, Latin beat. Its combination of culture (universities, symphonies, opera, ballet, museums), sports (major league football, basketball, hockey, baseball, two horse tracks, two jai alai frontons, and a greyhound track), and shopping (open-air Bayside Marketplace, Mayfair and CocoWalk in the Grove) offers something for everyone.

Must-sees include Little Havana, circa-1916 Vizcaya, Seaquarium, and the cage-less Metrozoo. **Information:** Greater Miami Convention & Visitors Bureau, 701 Brickell Ave #2700, Miami, 33131 (tel 305/539-3000).

### PUBLIC TRANSPORTATION

**Metrorail** Operates 6am–12:40am. Runs north–south between downtown Miami and the city's southern suburbs, including Coral Gables and Coconut Grove. Fare is $1.25; transfers are 25¢. For information call 305/638-6700.

**Metromover** Operates 6am–12:40am. Single-train car connects with Metrorail at Government Center and circles city's downtown area. Fare 25¢. For information call 305/638-6700 or 375-5675.

## HOTELS 🏨

**☰☰☰ Biscayne Bay Marriott Hotel & Marina**
1633 N Bayshore Dr, 33132 (Downtown); tel 305/374-3900 or toll free 800/228-9290; fax 305/375-0597. A deluxe high-rise with commanding views from most rooms of downtown Miami, Miami Beach, or the Port of Miami. Its public areas are glossy and sleek. **Rooms:** 603 rms and stes. Executive level. CI 4pm/CO noon. Nonsmoking rms avail. Beautifully decorated rooms in sophisticated tones and patterns. **Amenities:** 🛏 ⚐ A/C, cable TV w/movies. All units w/minibars, some w/terraces. **Services:** ✕ ☞ VP ⬧ ↵ Car-rental desk. **Facilities:** 🎱 🏌 🏊 & 1 restaurant, 2 bars, games rm, whirlpool, beauty salon. **Rates:** Peak (Dec–Apr) $145–$165 S or D; $400–$800 ste. Children under age 18 stay free. Lower rates off-season. Parking: Indoor, $7/day. AE, CB, DC, DISC, ER, JCB, MC, V.

**☰☰☰ Don Shula's Hotel & Golf Club**
Main St, Miami Lakes, 33014; tel 305/821-1150 or toll free 800/247-4852; fax 305/819-8298. Owned by Miami Dolphins coach Don Shula, it does a brisk business with athletic types and others who don't mind being 20 minutes out of the downtown loop. The facility is comprised of a main inn and other units at the golf course, where most of the athletic facilities are located. Traditional golfing attire is worn by some staff. **Rooms:** 301 rms and stes. Executive level. CI 3pm/CO noon. No smoking. **Amenities:** 🛏 ⚐ A/C, cable TV w/movies, refrig. Some units w/minibars, some w/terraces. **Services:** ✕ ☞ ⬧ ↵ Car-rental desk, babysitting. **Facilities:** 🎱 ▶18 🏌 🏊 🏊12 🏌 🏊500 💻 & 4 restaurants, 3 bars (1 w/entertainment), racquetball, squash, spa, sauna, steam rm, whirlpool, playground. Restaurant and lounge have rows of TV monitors so diners and drinkers don't miss any of the football action. **Rates:** Peak (Jan 11–Feb 28) $154 S or D; $164 ste. Extra person $10. Children under age 18 stay free. Lower rates off-season. Parking: Outdoor, free. AE, DC, DISC, MC, V.

**☰☰☰☰ Grand Bay Hotel**
2669 S Bayshore Dr, 33133 (Coconut Grove); tel 305/858-9600 or toll free 800/327-2788; fax 305/859-2026. Striking hotel with Aztec pyramid architecture and stepped

balconies overlooking Biscayne Bay. The lobby is lavishly done in marble and gleaming wood paneling and furnished with antiques and elaborate chandeliers. **Rooms:** 184 rms and stes. CI 3pm/CO noon. Nonsmoking rms avail. Some rooms have uninspired layouts and furnishings, but a recent redecorating and refurbishing has spruced up many of them. Spacious suites, some with grand pianos, are individually designed with exotic themes (e.g., Mandarin, Marrakech, Safari). **Amenities:** ☎ ⚬ ◥ A/C, cable TV w/movies, dataport, VCR, CD/tape player, bathrobes. All units w/minibars, all w/terraces, some w/fireplaces, some w/whirlpools. All rooms with fax machines; bathroom TVs in suites. **Services:** ○ ☞ VP ⚐ ↵ ◁ Twice-daily maid svce, car-rental desk, masseur, babysitting. Arriving guests are offered fresh orange juice or champagne. **Facilities:** ⚐ ⚑ ▣ ⚏ & 2 restaurants (see "Restaurants" below), 2 bars (1 w/entertainment), spa, sauna, steam rm, whirlpool, beauty salon. Poolside grill on rooftop. **Rates:** Peak (Jan–Mar) $285–$325 S or D; $350–$1,100 ste. Children under age 18 stay free. Min stay special events. Lower rates off-season. Parking: Indoor, $11/day. AE, CB, DC, DISC, EC, JCB, MC, V.

### ≣≣≣ HJ Occidental Plaza Hotel

100 SE 4th St, 33131 (Downtown); tel 305/374-5100 or toll free 800/521-5100; fax 305/381-9826. At 1st Ave SE. A high-rise with an impressive marbled lobby and other stylish public areas. **Rooms:** 224 rms and stes. Executive level. CI 3pm/CO noon. Nonsmoking rms avail. Suites come in an assortment of configurations. **Amenities:** ☎ ⚬ ◥ A/C, cable TV w/movies, dataport, voice mail, in-rm safe. All units w/minibars. **Services:** ✗ ☞ VP ⚐ ↵ ◁ Twice-daily maid svce, car-rental desk, social director, masseur, babysitting. **Facilities:** ⚐ ⚑ ▣ ⚏ & 1 restaurant, 2 bars, washer/dryer. **Rates:** Peak (Jan–Apr) $115–$160 S or D; $165 ste. Extra person $20. Children under age 12 stay free. Lower rates off-season. Parking: Outdoor, $10/day. AE, CB, DC, DISC, MC, V.

### ≣≣≣ Hotel Mayfair House

3000 Florida Ave, 33133 (Coconut Grove); tel 305/441-0000 or toll free 800/433-4555, 800/341-0809 in FL; fax 305/447-9173. This upscale fantasyland, with its phantasmagoric facade, is an integral part of a three-story atrium shopping mall. Grotto-like lobby has sit-down reception desks to the left and a cozy lounge to the right furnished with antiques and decorative glass. **Rooms:** 182 stes. CI 3pm/CO 1pm. Nonsmoking rms avail. Rooms, which are lined up on open corridors around the atrium (picking up some extraneous noises), have spacious, off-center layouts and feature carved-mahogany trim, Tiffany-style glass, and art deco furnishings. Many suites have antique grand pianos. **Amenities:** ☎ ⚬ ◥ A/C, cable TV w/movies, refrig, dataport, VCR, bathrobes. Some units w/terraces, some w/whirlpools. TV in bathrooms; central stereo system with three music channels. Japanese kimonos. **Services:** ○ ☞ VP ↵ ◁ Twice-daily maid svce, car-rental desk, social director, masseur, babysitting. Compli-

mentary orange juice and champagne in reception area. **Facilities:** ⚐ ▣ ⚏ & 2 restaurants, 2 bars (1 w/entertainment), spa, sauna, steam rm, whirlpool, beauty salon. Rooftop garden has pool w/lifeguard, spa, sundeck, and bar. **Rates:** Peak (Dec 16–Apr) $230–$450 ste. Extra person $35. Children under age 12 stay free. Min stay special events. Lower rates off-season. Parking: Indoor, $14/day. AE, CB, MC, V.

### ≣≣ Howard Johnson Hotel

1100 Biscayne Blvd, 33132 (Downtown); tel 305/358-3080 or toll free 800/654-2000; fax 305/358-8631. Exit 3-E off I-95. This seven-story hotel has easy access to the interstate, and is within walking distance of Bayside Marketplace. **Rooms:** 115 rms. CI 3pm/CO noon. Nonsmoking rms avail. Front rooms are larger and better furnished. **Amenities:** ☎ A/C, cable TV. All units w/terraces. **Services:** ✗ ☞ ↵ ◁ Car-rental desk, babysitting. Shuttle to Port of Miami. **Facilities:** ⚐ ⚏ & 1 restaurant, 1 bar, washer/dryer. **Rates:** Peak (Dec–Apr) $65–$99 S or D. Children under age 18 stay free. Min stay special events. Lower rates off-season. Parking: Outdoor, free. AE, CB, DC, DISC, MC, V.

### ≣≣≣≣ Hyatt Regency Miami

400 SE 2nd Ave, 33131 (Downtown); tel 305/358-1234 or toll free 800/233-1234; fax 305/358-0529. Exit 3 off I-95. On the river, this sleek high-rise is a staple in the convention market; it adjoins the convention center. Soaring atrium is polished up for a clean, efficient look. **Rooms:** 615 rms and stes. Executive level. CI 3pm/CO noon. Nonsmoking rms avail. **Amenities:** ☎ ⚬ ◥ A/C, cable TV w/movies, dataport, in-rm safe. All units w/terraces. **Services:** ✗ ☞ VP ⚐ ↵ ◁ Twice-daily maid svce, car-rental desk, babysitting. City's water taxi stops at hotel's dock. **Facilities:** ⚐ ⚏ ▣ & 1 restaurant, 1 bar (w/entertainment). Restaurants get over-taxed during big events. **Rates:** Peak (Dec–Apr) $135–$160 S; $145–$170 D; $250 ste. Extra person $25. Children under age 18 stay free. Lower rates off-season. Parking: Indoor/outdoor, $11/day. AE, CB, DC, DISC, MC, V.

### ≣≣ Marina Park Hotel Miami

340 Biscayne Blvd, 33132 (Downtown); tel 305/371-4400 or toll free 800/526-5655; fax 305/372-2862. Exit 5 off I-95. Pleasant, middle-grade accommodations near access to cruise ships. **Rooms:** 198 rms and stes. CI 3pm/CO noon. Nonsmoking rms avail. **Amenities:** ☎ A/C, cable TV, in-rm safe. **Services:** ✗ ☞ ↵ ◁ Car-rental desk, social director. **Facilities:** ⚐ ⚏ & 1 restaurant, 1 bar. **Rates:** Peak (Dec–Mar) $105–$115 S or D; $135 ste. Extra person $10. Children under age 12 stay free. Min stay special events. Lower rates off-season. Parking: Outdoor, $9/day. AE, DC, DISC, MC, V.

## RESORTS

### ≣≣≣ Doral Golf Resort and Spa

4400 NW 87th Ave, 33178; tel 305/592-2000 or toll free 800/713-6725, 800/367-2826 in FL; fax 305/594-4682. At

36th St. 650 acres. A golfer's paradise and a tennis buff's demi-paradise, but otherwise an ordinary spot for everyone else. With its location, low-flying jets can at times mar the tranquility. Popular for business meetings. **Rooms:** 694 rms and stes. CI 4pm/CO 11am. Nonsmoking rms avail. Recent renovations have transformed guest rooms into light, airy & spacious accommodations. Some have views of only other rooms or pathways. Second-floor rooms are best bets (higher ceilings, more security). **Amenities:** 🏠 🍸 A/C, cable TV w/movies, refrig, dataport, VCR, CD/tape player, voice mail, in-rm safe. Some units w/minibars, some w/terraces. **Services:** 🍴 🔑 📺 🚗 📠 🛎 Twice-daily maid svce, car-rental desk, social director, masseur, babysitting. Shuttle to Doral at Miami Beach. **Facilities:** 🏌 🚵 🏊 ►81 🎾15 🛶 🖥1200 💻 ♿ 6 restaurants, 2 bars (1 w/entertainment), basketball, games rm, lawn games, racquetball, spa, sauna, steam rm, whirlpool, beauty salon, day-care ctr, playground, washer/dryer. European-style spa, a short walk away through landscaped gardens. Well-equipped business center. **Rates:** Peak (Dec 20–Apr 16) $225–$370 S or D; $395–$1,280 ste. Extra person $35. Children under age 16 stay free. Min stay special events. Lower rates off-season. Parking: Outdoor, $9/day. AE, CB, DC, DISC, MC, V.

#### 🏨🏨🏨🏨 The Fisher Island Club

1 Fisher Island Dr, Fisher Island, 33109; tel 305/535-6020 or toll free 800/537-3708; fax 305/535-6003. Fisher Island exit off MacArthur Causeway then by car ferry (every 15 minutes) from the island's private dock. 216 acres. If you're looking for security, resorts and hideaways don't come more secure than this one. On a private island only a few miles from downtown Miami, it is accessible only by private launch and private car ferry (or, rather, limo ferry). The swank, full-service suites are augmented by a restored, antique-filled Vanderbilt mansion and its attendant cottages. **Rooms:** 60 stes; 4 cottages/villas. CI 3pm/CO noon. Nonsmoking rms avail. Rooms and suites echo the style and decor of a Mediterranean resort; apartments date from the 1980s and sport California contemporary decor, some with views of the sea and cruise ships. Some self-contained cottages have private patios and spas. **Amenities:** 🏠 🍸 📺 A/C, cable TV w/movies, refrig, dataport, VCR, CD/tape player, voice mail, in-rm safe, bathrobes. All units w/minibars, some w/terraces, some w/fireplaces, some w/whirlpools. Ceiling fans in rooms and suites. Every guest room comes with golf cart for getting around the island. Bedside carafe of sherry. **Services:** 🍴 🔑 📺 🚗 📠 🛎 Twice-daily maid svce, car-rental desk, social director, masseur, babysitting. **Facilities:** 🏌 🚵 ⛰ 🏊 ►9 🏖 🛥1 🎾18 🛶 🏐40 ♿ 5 restaurants, 2 bars (w/entertainment), 1 beach (ocean), spa, sauna, steam rm, whirlpool, beauty salon, day-care ctr, playground, washer/dryer. Marina can handle luxury yachts up to 200 feet. Acclaimed full-service Spa Internazionale includes private rooms for VIP pampering. Posh restaurant in library of mansion; four other moderately priced dining spots throughout the island. **Rates:** Peak (Nov–

Apr) $425–$1,400 ste; $525 cottage/villa. Children under age 12 stay free. Min stay special events. Lower rates off-season. Parking: Outdoor, free. Quoted rates do not include daily membership fee of $25 per room. AE, CB, DC, DISC, MC, V.

## RESTAURANTS 🍴

### Cafe de Sol

In Crowne Plaza Miami, 1601 Biscayne Blvd; tel 305/374-0000. **International/Latin.** An upbeat, tropical atmosphere sets the tone for diners to enjoy fresh seafood, attractive fruit platters, pasta buffet, and Latin-flavored dishes. **FYI:** Reservations accepted. Piano. Dress code. **Open:** Breakfast Mon–Sat 7–11:30am; lunch Mon–Sat 11:30am–5pm; dinner daily 5:30–10pm; brunch Sun 11:30am–3pm. **Prices:** Main courses $7–$19. AE, CB, DC, DISC, MC, V. 📺 ♿

### Cafe Europa

3159 Commodore Plaza (Coconut Grove); tel 305/448-5723. **Continental/French.** A traditional French creperie where you can dine outdoors or inside the casual, softly toned cafe. **FYI:** Reservations accepted. **Open:** Sun–Thurs 5pm–1am, Fri–Sat 5pm–2am. **Prices:** Main courses $9–$20. AE, DC, DISC, MC, V. 🏖

### Casa Juancho

2436 SW 8th St (Little Havana); tel 305/642-2452. **Spanish.** Traditional Spanish appointments as well as nightly performing Spanish musicians give this eatery an authentic flavor. The menu offers mixed seafood in vinaigrette, fresh shrimp in hot garlic sauce, and fried calamari rings. **FYI:** Reservations recommended. Piano/singer. Dress code. **Open:** Mon–Fri noon–midnight, Sat–Sun noon–1am. **Prices:** Main courses $12–$27. AE, MC, V. 💟 📺 ♿

### The Chart House

51 Chart House Dr (Coconut Grove); tel 305/856-9741. Off Bayshore Dr near the Grand Bay Hotel. **Seafood/Steak.** Great food, service, and views are available at this solid oceanside eatery. **FYI:** Reservations recommended. **Open:** Lunch Mon–Fri 11am–2:30pm; dinner Mon–Sat 5:30–11pm, Sun 5–10pm. **Prices:** Main courses $18–$23. AE, CB, DC, DISC, MC, V. 🏞 📺 ♿

### ⭐ The Crab House

1551 79th Street Causeway; tel 305/868-7085. **Seafood.** Enjoy lovely views of Biscayne Bay while you feast on selections from the fresh seafood bar. **FYI:** Reservations not accepted. Children's menu. **Open:** Mon–Thurs 11:30am–11pm, Sat noon–12pm, Sun noon–11pm. **Prices:** Main courses $11–$20. AE, DISC, MC, V. 🏞 💟 📺 ♿

### Crocodile Cantina

In Bayside Marketplace, 401 Biscayne Blvd (Downtown); tel 305/374-7417. **Mexican/Southwestern.** A casual, family-oriented dining spot with a festive atmosphere. Standard Mexican fare like chili, nachos, salads, and burritos is served at basic wooden tables. **FYI:** Reservations accepted. **Open:** Daily 11am–midnight. **Prices:** Main courses $4–$15. AE, CB, DC, DISC, MC, V. 🛥 📷 ♿

### East Coast Fisheries
360 W Flagler St; tel 305/377-2529. **Seafood.** This combination fish market/restaurant has a rustic atmosphere, an open kitchen, an extensive seafood menu, and views of the river. Rock lobster and lobster tails are house specialties. **FYI:** Reservations accepted. Beer and wine only. **Open:** Daily 11am–11pm. **Prices:** Main courses $14–$30. AE, MC, V. 📷 📷

### ⑤ Fish Bone Grille
650 S Miami Ave; tel 305/530-1915. **Seafood.** Basic, unpretentious eatery serving great seafood at outstanding prices. The chef's specialty is classic cioppino with homemade cornbread. **FYI:** Reservations accepted. Beer and wine only. **Open:** Peak (Dec–Apr) Mon–Thurs 11:30am–10pm, Fri 11:30am–11pm, Sat 5:30–11pm. **Prices:** Main courses $9–$16. AE, CB, DC, DISC, MC, V. ♿

### Fish Peddler
8699 Biscayne Blvd; tel 305/757-0648. At 87th St. **American.** Specialties at this relaxed surf-and-turf eatery with a maritime theme include grilled Florida swordfish, black grouper à la Française and live Maine lobster. The menu also features a variety of chicken and pastas. Both the food and the service enjoy excellent reputations. **FYI:** Reservations accepted. Children's menu. **Open:** Sun–Thurs 11am–9:30pm, Fri–Sat 11am–10pm. **Prices:** Main courses $12–$17. AE, DISC, MC, V. 📷 ♥ ♿

### ★ Flemming
8611 SW 136th St; tel 305/232-6444. **Scandinavian.** A simple, warm restaurant with glass block walls. Dishes include swordfish, Norwegian salmon, and Grandfather's Duck Danoise. **FYI:** Reservations recommended. Dress code. **Open:** Tues–Sun 5:30–10:30pm. Closed Mid-July–mid-Aug. **Prices:** Main courses $9–$20. AE, MC, V. ♿

### Fuddruckers
In Mayfair Shops, 3444 Main Hwy (Coconut Grove); tel 305/442-8164. **Burgers.** An open, self-serve establishment catering to families and seniors. The menu offers burgers and fish; lots of toppings are available to dress up your selection. **FYI:** Reservations not accepted. Children's menu. **Open:** Daily 11am–2am. **Prices:** Main courses $4–$9. AE, MC, V. 📷

### ★ Grand Cafe
In Grand Bay Hotel, 2669 S Bayshore Dr (Coconut Grove); tel 305/858-9600. **New American/Seafood.** Accented with pink linen and soft decor, this lovely restaurant is a special place for a romantic interlude. Entrees include seared Pacific salmon served with Japanese Ikura salmon caviar, annatto-marinated breast of chicken, and spiced tenderloin of beef with grilled wild mushrooms and crispy foie gras. The chef can prepare most entrees to dietary specifications. **FYI:**

Reservations recommended. Piano. Children's menu. Jacket required. No smoking. **Open:** Breakfast daily 7–11:30am; lunch Mon–Sat 11:30am–3pm; dinner Sun–Thurs 6–11pm, Fri–Sat 6–11:30pm; brunch Sun 11:30am–3pm. **Prices:** Main courses $21–$38. AE, CB, DC, DISC, MC, V. ♥ 🆅🅿 ♿

### ★ Green Street Cafe
3468 Main Hwy (Coconut Grove); tel 305/444-0244. **American/Mediterranean.** A casual indoor/outdoor eatery situated at the epicenter of the Grove—the corner of Main Hwy and Commodore Plaza—in a great location for people watching. Menu emphasizes pizzas baked in an oak-burning oven, an array of pastas with specialty sauces, and grilled hamburgers. Only sidewalk cafe in the area with a full bar. **FYI:** Reservations not accepted. Children's menu. **Open:** Daily 7am–midnight. **Prices:** Main courses $9–$14. AE, DC, MC, V. 🛥 ♿

### ★ Hard Rock Cafe
In Bayside Marketplace, 401 Biscayne Blvd (Downtown); tel 305/377-3160. **New American.** This festive international chain restaurant, housed in a distinctive circular building with a vintage pink Cadillac suspended over its entryway, offers spectacular views of downtown Miami, beautiful Biscayne Bay, and the popular Bayside Marketplace. The menu features substantial burgers, barbecued chicken, smoked ribs, fajitas, vegetarian entrees, salads, soups, and desserts, all at moderate prices. **FYI:** Reservations not accepted. Rock. Children's menu. **Open:** Daily 11am–2am. **Prices:** Main courses $6–$17. AE, DC, MC, V. 📷 🆅🅿 ♿

### ★ Johnny Rockets Hamburgers
3036 Grand Ave (Coconut Grove); tel 305/444-1000. **Diner.** A fun, popular diner-style joint. This is a branch of the original Johnny Rockets located on Melrose Avenue in Los Angeles. Burgers, fries, shakes, and malts are staples; you can even order a peanut butter and jelly sandwich. **FYI:** Reservations not accepted. Rock. Beer only. No smoking. **Open:** Sun–Wed 11am–1am, Thurs–Sat 11am–3am. **Prices:** Main courses $3–$6. MC, V. 📷 ♿

### ★ Kaleidoscope
3112 Commodore Plaza; tel 305/446-5010. Off Bay Shore Dr. **New American/Caribbean.** An engaging, attractive cafe furnished in white wrought iron and wicker. Its location, overlooking a bustling street. The eclectic menu offers a wide variety of dishes, including Caribbean Bouillabaisse in Natural Broth and Pan Roasted Lamb Shank on Tuscan Beans. The Oven Roasted Red Snapper with Rum Glazed Bananas and Fried Leeks is a favorite. **FYI:** Reservations recommended. **Open:** Lunch daily 11:30am–3pm; dinner daily 6–11pm; brunch Sun 11:30am–3pm. **Prices:** Main courses $13–$20. AE, DC, DISC, MC, V. ♥ 🛥

### Las Tapas
In Bayside Marketplace, 401 Biscayne Blvd (Downtown); tel 305/372-2737. **Spanish.** Authentic Spanish artifacts, fabrics, and furniture adorn this attractive restaurant serving Spanish

cuisine with a South Florida twist. Diners can sample many of the house specialties by ordering a variety of appetizer-size portions. The relaxing outdoor terrace has full bar and food service. **FYI:** Reservations accepted. Guitar/singer. **Open:** Sun–Thurs 11:30am–midnight, Fri–Sat 11:30am–1am. **Prices:** Main courses $15–$20. AE, DISC, MC, V.

**Los Ranchos**
In Bayside Marketplace, 401 Biscayne Blvd (Downtown); tel 305/375-8188. **Steak/Nicaraguan.** A Nicaraguan chain restaurant with floor-to-ceiling windows overlooking the port of Miami. It has garnered awards for its cuisine, which features mostly Central American beef dishes. **FYI:** Reservations accepted. Singer. Children's menu. **Open:** Daily 11:30am–11:30pm. **Prices:** Main courses $10–$23. AE, CB, DC, MC, V.

**Mike Gordon's**
1201 NE 79th St; tel 305/751-4429. **Seafood.** A landmark Miami restaurant with a beautiful waterfront location. Enjoy views of the waterfowl and boats while you dine on any one of a variety of pastas and seafood dishes. **FYI:** Reservations accepted. Children's menu. Dress code. **Open:** Daily noon–10pm. **Prices:** Main courses $14–$20. AE, CB, DC, DISC, MC, V.

**★ Señor Frog's**
3008 Grand Ave (Coconut Grove); tel 305/448-0990. **Mexican.** Twentysomethings regularly converge at this fun, lively spot. Choose among 14 varieties of chili, along with traditional Mexican-American entrees, all served with rice and beans. **FYI:** Reservations not accepted. Latin. **Open:** Sun–Wed 11:30am–1am, Thurs–Sat 11:30am–2am. **Prices:** Main courses $6–$12. AE, CB, DC, MC, V.

**Shucker's Bar & Grill**
In Inn on the Bay, 1819 79th St; tel 305/866-1570. Exit 9 off I-95. **Barbecue/Seafood.** A nautically themed eatery with great water and marina views as well as pleasant outdoor dining. The menu boasts lots of seafood and poultry in addition to select daily specials. **FYI:** Reservations accepted. **Open:** Daily 11:30am–1am. **Prices:** Main courses $6–$13. AE, DISC, MC, V.

**Snappers Bar and Grill**
In Bayside Marketplace, 401 Biscayne Blvd (Downtown); tel 305/379-0605. **Seafood.** Enjoy lovely ocean views at this pleasant, laid-back seafood eatery. **FYI:** Reservations not accepted. Rock. Children's menu. **Open:** Sun–Thurs 11am–11pm, Fri–Sat 11am–midnight. **Prices:** Main courses $10–$18. AE, CB, DC, DISC, MC, V.

**Tuscany Trattoria**
3484 Main Hwy (Coconut Grove); tel 305/445-0022. Next to Coconut Grove Playhouse. **Italian.** Attractive, brick-accented interior with fireplace. Pasta and fish dishes. **FYI:** Reservations accepted. Beer and wine only. **Open:** Daily 11:30am–midnight. **Prices:** Main courses $7–$20. AE, DC, DISC, MC, V.

**$ Versailles**
3535 SW 8th St (Little Havana); tel 305/444-0240. **Cuban.** This casual Latin restaurant, specializing in fried fish and Cuban dishes, sparkles with crystal, chandeliers, and mirrors. **FYI:** Reservations accepted. **Open:** Mon–Thurs 8am–2am, Fri 8am–4am, Sat–Sun 8am–5am. **Prices:** Main courses $6–$15. AE, CB, DC, DISC, MC, V.

## ATTRACTIONS

**Miami Museum of Science and Space Transit Planetarium**
280 S Miami Ave (Coconut Grove); tel 305/854-4247 (museum) or 854-2222 (planetarium). Features over 150 hands-on exhibits exploring the mysteries of the universe. The adjacent Space Transit Planetarium presents astronomy and rock music laser shows. Virtual-reality basketball and five high-speed internet terminals are open to the public. The in-house observatory is free and open to the public on Saturday evenings. **Open:** Daily 10am–6pm. **$$$**

**Historical Museum of Southern Florida**
101 W Flagler St (Downtown); tel 305/375-1492. Part of the Metro-Dade Cultural Center, which also houses the Center for Fine Arts and the Dade County Public Library, this museum's primary exhibit is "Tropical Dreams," a state-of-the-art, chronological history of the past 10,000 years in South Florida. Hands-on displays, audio-visual presentations, and hundreds of artifacts. **Open:** Mon–Wed and Fri–Sat 10am–5pm, Thurs 10am–9pm, Sun noon–5pm. **$$**

**Villa Vizcaya**
3251 S Miami Ave (Coconut Grove); tel 305/579-2708. Italian Renaissance-style villa (1916) surrounded by 10 acres of beautiful formal gardens. Antiques adorn 34 of the 70 rooms, which are filled with examples of decorative art from the 15th to 19th centuries. Outside, the gardens are accented with statuary, fountains, balustrades, and decorative urns, and front an enormous swath of Biscayne Bay. **Open:** Daily 9:30am–4:30pm. **$$$**

**The Barnacle**
3485 Main Hwy (Coconut Grove); tel 305/448-9445. The former home of naval architect and early settler Ralph Middleton Munroe, the Barnacle was built in 1891 and occupied by the family until 1973. The furnishings are mostly original and date from the 1920s. Some of Munroe's ship drawings can be seen. Tours Thurs–Mon at 10:30am, 1pm, and 2:30pm. Schedule may vary. **$**

**Cuban Museum of Arts and Culture**
1300 SW 12th Ave (Little Havana); tel 305/858-8006. This unique museum displays significant works reflecting the main historical currents in Cuban art. Paintings and drawings add up to only about 200, but they are well selected and representative of a wide range of styles. **Open:** Tues–Fri 11am–5pm, Sat–Sun 1–5pm. **$**

### American Police Hall of Fame and Museum

3801 Biscayne Blvd; tel 305/573-0202. More than 10,000 items relating to police work, ranging from weapons and uniforms to squad cars and execution devices. Guests may study a "crime scene" for clues and are awarded a certificate if they solve the crime. A memorial lists the names of more than 5,000 US police officers killed in the line of duty. **Open:** Daily 10am–5pm. **$$$**

### Miami Metrozoo

12400 SW 152nd St (at SW 124th Ave); tel 305/251-0400 or 251-0401. This huge 290-acre complex is completely cageless; animals are separated from people by moats. Highlights include 2 rare white Bengal tigers, a 1.5-acre free-flight tropical aviary, a monorail "safari," and one of the few koala bear exhibits in America. There's a newly designed petting zoo as well. **Open:** Daily 9:30am–5:30pm. **$$**

### Parrot Jungle and Gardens

11000 SW 57th Ave; tel 305/666-7834. This 60-year-old park features birds of nearly every description, as well as alligators, tortoises, and iguanas. Continuous shows in Parrot Bowl Theater star performing parrots, roller-skating cockatoos, and card-playing macaws. Other attractions include a wildlife show, "Primate Experience," and a children's playground and petting zoo. **Open:** Daily 9:30am–6pm. **$$$$**

### Monkey Jungle

14805 SW 216th St; tel 305/235-1611. There are no cages to restrain the antics of monkeys, gorillas, and chimpanzees, but screened-in trails that wind through acres of "jungle" give visitors ample protection. Four different shows that feature performing primates rotate on a 30-minute cycle. Also on view are such species as golden lion tamarins and Asian macaques. **Open:** Daily 9:30am–5pm. **$$$$**

### Club Nautico of Coconut Grove

2560 S Bayshore Dr (Coconut Grove); tel 305/858-6258. Rental of high-quality power boats for fishing, waterskiing, diving, and cruising on the bay or ocean. All boats are equipped with Coast Guard–approved VHF radios and safety gear. Half- and full-day rentals. **Open:** Mon–Fri 9am–5pm, Sat–Sun 8am–5pm. **$$$$**

### Heritage Miami II

Topsail Schooner, Bayside Marketplace Marina, 401 Biscayne Blvd (Downtown); tel 305/442-9697. Two-hour cruises aboard Miami's only tall ship pass by Villa Vizcaya, Coconut Grove, and Key Biscayne, and provide great views of the Miami skyline. **Open:** September–May. Call for schedule. **$$$$**

### Dade County Auditorium

2901 W Flagler St; tel 305/547-5414. This intimate, 2,500-seat facility is home to the Greater Miami Opera, the Miami Ballet Company, and the Concert Association of Greater Miami. **Open:** Sept–July; call for performance schedule.

### Miami Arena

721 NW 1st Ave; tel 305/577-HEAT. The NBA's Miami Heat hold court here from November to April. **$$$$**

### Pro Player Stadium

2269 NW 199th St; tel 305/620-5000. Formerly known as Joe Robbie Stadium. The Miami Dolphins (NFL) play their home games here from August to December.

### Flagler Greyhound Track

401 NW 38th Court; tel 305/649-3000. Some of the nation's top dogs are featured at this high-stakes track, which hosts the $110,000 International Classic. Post times are 7:30pm daily and 12:30pm Tues, Thurs, Sat, and some hols. **Open:** May–June and Sept–Oct. **$**

### Miami Jai Alai Fronton

3500 NW 37th Ave; tel 305/633-6400. This is America's oldest jai alai fronton, built in 1926. Approximately 13 matches are scheduled every evening. **$**

# Miami Int'l Airport

## HOTELS 🏨

### 🛏🛏 Airport Regency Hotel

1000 NW LeJeune Rd, Miami, 33126; tel 305/441-1600 or toll free 800/367-1039, 800/432-1192 in FL; fax 305/443-0766. 1 mi S of airport terminal entrance. Mostly a layover hotel for both passengers and airline crews, with a mishmash of decor and some spotty housekeeping. **Rooms:** 176 rms. CI noon/CO noon. Nonsmoking rms avail. Room decor runs the gamut from the Kennedy Administration to the Reagan years. **Amenities:** 🛏 A/C, cable TV w/movies. All units w/terraces. **Services:** ✕ 🚐 ⊠ ⊄ Car-rental desk, babysitting. Security cameras for added safety. **Facilities:** 🎱 100 1 restaurant, 2 bars (1 w/entertainment), games rm, washer/dryer. **Rates:** Peak (Dec–Apr) $85–$95 S; $95–$105 D. Extra person $10. Children under age 16 stay free. Lower rates off-season. Parking: Outdoor, free. AE, CB, DC, DISC, EC, ER, MC, V.

### 🛏🛏🛏 Crown Sterling Suites

3974 NW South River Dr, Miami Springs, 33142; tel 305/634-5000 or toll free 800/772-3787; fax 305/635-9499. ¾ mi N of airport terminal on FL 953. The sporty look of this all-suites arrangement is a nice alternative to some of the humdrum offerings an airport tends to attract. **Rooms:** 316 stes. CI 3pm/CO noon. Nonsmoking rms avail. **Amenities:** 🛏 ⚷ 🖥 A/C, cable TV w/movies, refrig, voice mail. All units w/terraces. Microwaves. **Services:** ✕ 🚐 ⊠ ⊄ **Facilities:** 🎱 300 ⚷ 1 restaurant, 1 bar, washer/dryer. **Rates (BB):** Peak (Feb) $159–$169 ste. Extra person $10. Children under age 12 stay free. Lower rates off-season. Parking: Outdoor, free. AE, DC, DISC, MC, V.

### ☰☰ Days Inn Miami Airport

3401 NW LeJeune Rd, Miami, 33142; tel 305/871-4221 or toll free 800/325-2525; fax 305/871-3933. Renovation underway as new owners put their own brand on this property. **Rooms:** 155 rms. CI noon/CO noon. Nonsmoking rms avail. Rooms to be updated, but present condition is adequate. **Amenities:** 🛏 A/C, cable TV w/movies. **Services:** 🚗 🖼 🍴 🐾 Children's program. **Facilities:** 🛗 🏊 ₁₅₀ Ꮭ 1 restaurant. **Rates:** Peak (Dec 15–Apr 15) $69 S; $79 D. Extra person $10. Children under age 18 stay free. Lower rates off-season. Parking: Outdoor, free. AE, DC, DISC, MC, V.

### ☰☰☰ Holiday Inn LeJeune Centre

950 NW Le Jeune Rd, Miami, 33126; tel 305/446-9000 or toll free 800/428-9582; fax 305/441-0725. 1 mi S of airport terminal entrance. A good value that is smart, attractive, and reliable. The responsive management keeps this place looking sharp. **Rooms:** 304 rms and stes. Executive level. CI 2pm/CO noon. Nonsmoking rms avail. **Amenities:** 🛏 🏊 A/C, cable TV w/movies. **Services:** ✕ 🚗 🖼 🍴 Children's program. **Facilities:** 🛗 Ꮭ ₄₀₀ Ꮬ 1 restaurant, 1 bar, sauna, steam rm, washer/dryer. Fenced-in parking lot is patrolled by security. **Rates:** Peak (Dec 1–Apr 15) $149–$169 S; $169–$179 D; $221 ste. Extra person $10. Children under age 19 stay free. Min stay special events. Lower rates off-season. Parking: Outdoor, free. AE, DC, DISC, MC, V.

### ☰☰☰ Hotel Sofitel Miami

5800 Blue Lagoon Dr, Miami, 33126; tel 305/262-9049 or toll free 800/258-4888; fax 305/261-7871. Off FL 836 W, at NW 57th Ave. This high-rise establishment brings a distinctive, French look to the airport hotel community. Beautifully adorned public areas exhibit a flair for the dramatic. A seasoned staff brings everything together. **Rooms:** 281 rms and stes. CI 3pm/CO noon. Nonsmoking rms avail. **Amenities:** 🛏 🍴 A/C, cable TV w/movies, refrig, voice mail. Some units w/minibars, some w/terraces. **Services:** 🍽 🖚 📺 🚗 🖼 🍴 🐾 Car-rental desk, masseur, babysitting. **Facilities:** 🛗 🏊 🍴 ₂ Ꮭ ₆₀₀ Ꮬ 2 restaurants, 1 bar (w/entertainment), games rm. **Rates:** Peak (Oct–Apr) $185 S; $195 D; $225–$450 ste. Extra person $50. Children under age 12 stay free. Lower rates off-season. Parking: Outdoor, free. Romance packages available. AE, CB, DC, DISC, MC, V.

### ☰☰☰ Miami Airport Marriott

1201 NW LeJeune Rd, Miami, 33126; tel 305/649-5000 or toll free 800/228-9290; fax 305/642-3369. A first-rate operation, accessible via a security-controlled gate. Recreational diversions helps keep layover guests and others here for longer stays content. **Rooms:** 365 rms and stes. Executive level. CI 3pm/CO noon. Nonsmoking rms avail. **Amenities:** 🛏 🏊 🍴 A/C, cable TV, voice mail, bathrobes. **Services:** ✕ 🖚 🚗 🖼 🍴 🐾 Babysitting. **Facilities:** 🛗 🏊 🍴 ₂ ₈ Ꮭ ₃₆₀ Ꮬ 2 restaurants, 2 bars (1 w/entertainment), games rm, racquetball, spa, whirlpool, beauty salon, washer/dryer. **Rates:** Peak

(Sept–May) $150 S or D; $395 ste. Children under age 19 stay free. Lower rates off-season. Parking: Outdoor, free. AE, CB, DC, DISC, MC, V.

### ☰☰☰ Miami International Airport Hotel

NW 20th St and Le Jeune Rd, PO Box 997510, Miami, 33299; tel 305/871-4100 or toll free 800/327-1276; fax 305/871-0800. Part of the airport terminal, a hectic location at the best of times and a nightmare for anyone arriving by car. Best suited for those requiring lodging close to gates for early-morning departures or late-night arrivals. **Rooms:** 263 rms and stes. Executive level. CI 3pm/CO noon. Nonsmoking rms avail. Half the rooms overlook the runways and tarmac. **Amenities:** 🛏 🏊 🍴 A/C, cable TV w/movies, bathrobes. Some units w/whirlpools. **Services:** ✕ 🖼 🍴 **Facilities:** 🛗 🏊 🍴 ₄₀₀ 💻 Ꮬ 2 restaurants, 2 bars (1 w/entertainment), racquetball, sauna, steam rm, whirlpool. **Rates:** Peak (Sept–Feb) $115–$125 S; $130–$170 D; $225 ste. Extra person $10. Children under age 12 stay free. Lower rates off-season. Parking: Outdoor, $6/day. AE, CB, DC, DISC, MC, V.

### ☰☰☰ Radisson Mart Plaza Hotel

711 NW 72nd Ave, Miami, 33126; tel 305/261-3800 or toll free 800/333-3333; fax 305/261-7665. At Collins Ave. A smart, attractive hotel with a capable staff, attached to the Merchandise Mart. **Rooms:** 334 rms and stes. Executive level. CI 3pm/CO noon. Nonsmoking rms avail. Recently renovated rooms offer dark floral print spreads and drapes. **Amenities:** 🛏 🏊 A/C, cable TV w/movies, dataport, voice mail. **Services:** ✕ 🖚 📺 🚗 🖼 🍴 Twice-daily maid svce, car-rental desk. **Facilities:** 🛗 🏊 ₃₀₀₀ 💻 Ꮬ 2 restaurants, 2 bars (1 w/entertainment), games rm, spa, sauna, steam rm, whirlpool, beauty salon. **Rates:** Peak (Jan–Mar) $149–$159 S or D; $169 ste. Children under age 18 stay free. Min stay special events. Lower rates off-season. AP rates avail. Parking: Outdoor, free. AE, CB, DC, DISC, MC, V.

### ☰☰ Ramada Hotel Miami International Airport

3941 NW 22nd St, 33142; tel 305/871-1700 or toll free 800/272-6232; fax 305/871-4830. Basic airport hotel catering to business travelers. **Rooms:** 272 rms and stes. CI 9am/CO noon. Nonsmoking rms avail. **Amenities:** 🛏 🏊 🍴 A/C, satel TV. Some units w/terraces, 1 w/whirlpool. **Services:** ✕ 🚗 🖼 🍴 🐾 Car-rental desk. **Facilities:** 🛗 ₃₀₀ Ꮬ 1 restaurant, 1 bar, games rm, sauna, steam rm, whirlpool. **Rates:** Peak (Mar 1–Apr 15) $79–$89 S; $89–$99 D; $129 ste. Extra person $10. Children under age 18 stay free. Lower rates off-season. Parking: Indoor/outdoor, free. AE, CB, DC, DISC, EC, ER, JCB, MC, V.

### ☰☰ Residence Inn by Marriott

1212 NW 82nd Ave, Miami, 33126; tel 305/591-2211 or toll free 800/331-3131; fax 305/591-0902. At 12th St. Nearby air traffic makes this location noisy; however, accommodations are more than adequate. **Rooms:** 112 stes. CI 3pm/CO noon. Nonsmoking rms avail. **Amenities:** 🛏 🏊 🍴 A/C, satel TV w/movies, refrig. Some units w/terraces, some w/fireplaces. **Services:** [icons] **Facilities:** [icons] Basketball, whirlpool, washer/dryer. **Rates:** Peak (Jan–Apr) $139 ste. Children under age 12 stay free. Lower rates off-season. Parking: Outdoor, free. AE, DC, DISC, EC, MC, V.

### ☰☰☰ Sheraton Gateway
3900 NW 21st St, Miami, 33142; tel 305/871-3800 or toll free 800/325-3535; fax 305/871-0447. Located in a modern, elongated building; it's due respect for its attention to maintenance and housekeeping. **Rooms:** 408 rms and stes. Executive level. CI 3pm/CO noon. Nonsmoking rms avail. Popular with business folk, who usually book the upper floors where rooms are equipped with extra phones, irons and ironing boards, and coffeemakers. **Amenities:** [icons] A/C, cable TV w/movies. Some units w/whirlpools. **Services:** [icons] Babysitting. **Facilities:** [icons] 1 restaurant, 1 bar (w/entertainment), games rm, sauna, steam rm, whirlpool. **Rates:** Peak (Jan–Mar) $165 S or D; $350 ste. Children under age 19 stay free. Lower rates off-season. Parking: Indoor/outdoor, free. AE, DC, DISC, ER, MC, V.

# Miami Beach

See also Sunny Isles

The historic art deco district of this city, on a sandbar off the coast of Miami (between 6th and 23rd Sts), includes more than 1,000 architectural gems and hundreds of beautiful people flocking to its fashionable cafes, clubs, and boutiques. A trace of its Jewish-retiree heritage remains, and arty festivals are constant. **Information:** Greater Miami Convention & Visitors Bureau, 701 Brickell Ave #2700, Miami, 33131 (tel 305/539-3000).

## HOTELS 🏨

### ☰☰☰ The Alexander All-Suite Luxury Hotel
5225 Collins Ave, 33140; tel 305/865-6500 or toll free 800/327-6121; fax 305/864-8525. Across from the Intracoastal Waterway. A luxury address, featuring beautifully decorated public areas with fine sculptures, paintings, and antiques, and panoramic views from the upper floors. **Rooms:** 150 stes. Executive level. CI 3pm/CO noon. Nonsmoking rms avail. Suites are independently owned so decor is varied. Most are spacious and luxurious. **Amenities:** [icons] A/C, cable TV w/movies, refrig, in-rm safe. All units w/minibars, some w/terraces, some w/whirlpools. **Services:** [icons] Twice-daily maid svce, masseur, babysitting. Chefs will cook for guests privately in suites. **Facilities:** [icons] 2 restaurants (see "Restaurants" below), 1 bar, 1 beach (ocean), volleyball, sauna, steam rm, whirlpool, beauty salon. **Rates:** Peak (Apr 14–Dec 22) $310–$950 ste. Extra person $35. Children under age 17 stay free. Lower rates off-season. Parking: Indoor, free. AE, MC, V.

### ☰☰ Avalon Hotel
700 Ocean Dr, 33139 (South Beach); tel 305/538-0133 or toll free 800/933-3306; fax 305/534-0258. Visually striking, with classic art deco look. Modest lobby. **Rooms:** 108 rms. CI 3pm/CO 11am. Nonsmoking rms avail. Rooms with familiar art deco style. A complimentary bottle of Avalon water is placed in each room upon arrival. **Amenities:** [icons] A/C, cable TV, refrig, VCR, CD/tape player, voice mail, in-rm safe. **Services:** [icons] Car-rental desk. **Facilities:** [icons] 1 restaurant (dinner only), 1 bar (w/entertainment), 1 beach (ocean), lifeguard. Atmospheric outdoor cafe. **Rates (CP):** Peak (Dec 23–Apr 3) $115–$165 S or D. Extra person $10. Children under age 12 stay free. Lower rates off-season. Parking: Outdoor, $8/day. AE, CB, DC, DISC, MC, V.

### ☰☰ Boulevard Hotel & Cafe
740 Ocean Dr, 33139 (South Beach); tel 305/532-0376; fax 305/674-8179. Blends well with the art deco delights, with accommodations dressed in pastel, of course. **Rooms:** 37 rms and stes. CI 2pm/CO 11am. Nonsmoking rms avail. **Amenities:** [icons] A/C, cable TV, in-rm safe. Some units w/minibars, 1 w/whirlpool. **Services:** [icons] Twice-daily maid svce, car-rental desk. **Facilities:** [icons] 1 restaurant, 1 bar, 1 beach (ocean), lifeguard. Playground across the street, gym nearby. **Rates (BB):** Peak (Dec–Apr) $140–$155 S or D; $235–$575 ste. Children under age 18 stay free. Min stay special events. Lower rates off-season. AE, DC, MC, V.

### ☰☰ Cardoza Hotel
1300 Ocean Dr, 33139 (South Beach); tel 305/535-6500 or toll free 800/782-6500; fax 305/532-3563. One of the art deco district's sharpest and most notable properties. Owned by pop star Gloria Estéfan. **Rooms:** 42 rms and stes. CI 3pm/CO noon. Nonsmoking rms avail. Room decor features bright jazzy colors. Spacious suites have cedar closets; some have two baths. **Amenities:** [icons] A/C, cable TV w/movies, refrig, VCR, CD/tape player, voice mail, in-rm safe. All units w/minibars, some w/terraces, some w/whirlpools. **Services:** [icons] Car-rental desk. **Facilities:** 1 restaurant (lunch and dinner only), 1 bar (w/entertainment). **Rates (CP):** Peak (Dec–Apr) $120–$145 S or D; $210–$385 ste. Extra person $15. Children under age 12 stay free. Lower rates off-season. Parking: Outdoor, $14/day. AE, CB, DC, DISC, MC, V.

### ☰☰☰ Casa Grande Suite Hotel
834 Ocean Dr, 33139 (South Beach); tel 305/672-7003 or toll free 800/688-7678; fax 305/673-3669. Stylish, large accommodations. **Rooms:** 33 stes. CI 3pm/CO noon. Nonsmoking rms avail. Units have full kitchens, beautifully tiled baths, large closets, mahogany beds. **Amenities:** [icons] A/C, cable TV, refrig, dataport, VCR, CD/tape player, voice mail, in-rm safe, bathrobes. Some units w/terraces. **Services:** [icons] Twice-daily maid svce, car-rental desk, social director, masseur, babysitting. **Facilities:** 1 restaurant, 1 bar, 1 beach (ocean), lifeguard. **Rates:** Peak (Dec–Apr) $185–

$325 ste. Extra person $15. Children under age 18 stay free. Min stay wknds and special events. Lower rates off-season. AE, CB, DC, DISC, MC, V.

### ▤▤ Cavalier Hotel

1320 Ocean Dr, 33139 (South Beach); tel 305/534-2135 or toll free 800/338-9076; fax 305/531-5543. Historic hotel (built in 1936) that was among the first Ocean Drive art deco properties to undergo extensive renovation. This architectural gem has beautifully restored period furnishings and an ultra-contemporary style. **Rooms:** 44 rms and stes. CI 3pm/CO noon. Nonsmoking rms avail. **Amenities:** 🛗 ⚬ A/C, cable TV w/movies, VCR, CD/tape player, voice mail, in-rm safe. All units w/minibars. **Services:** ✗ ☛ 💶 🛆 ⎐ Car-rental desk, babysitting. Newspaper provided daily. **Facilities:** ⟨15⟩ 1 beach (ocean), lifeguard. **Rates:** Peak (Oct–June) $145 S or D; $375 ste. Extra person $15. Children under age 12 stay free. Min stay wknds and special events. Lower rates off-season. Parking: Outdoor, $14/day. AE, CB, DC, DISC, MC, V.

### ▤ The Clay Hotel and International Hostel

1438 Washington Ave, 33139 (South Beach); tel 305/534-2988 or toll free 800/379-CLAY; fax 305/673-0346. Divided into a 60-room hotel and a 238-bed dormitory style youth hostel. Suggested for the young and young-at-heart on a budget. Public areas always bustling with activity. Walking distance to beach, bars, and restaurants. **Rooms:** 298 rms. CI 1pm/CO noon. Nonsmoking rms avail. Very basic and frill-less rooms. More deluxe rooms, for higher prices, are available for extended stays. **Amenities:** 🛗 A/C, refrig. No TV. Some units w/terraces. **Services:** 🚐 🛆 **Facilities:** ⅙ 1 restaurant, washer/dryer. Inexpensively priced restaurant is usually busy. **Rates:** Peak (Dec 15–Apr 15) $35–$40 S; $38–$48 D. Extra person $8. Children under age 6 stay free. Lower rates off-season. JCB, MC, V.

### ▤▤▤ Delano

1685 Collins Ave, 33139 (South Beach); tel 305/672-2000 or toll free 800/555-5001; fax 305/673-0888. I-95 to I-395 at 17th St. In a striking departure for South Beach, there are no pastels at this new hotel—white-on-white is the color scheme throughout. The lobby resembles a breezeway adorned by long white draperies, and stretches from the street to a garden terrace and then spills down to the borderless pool. **Rooms:** 208 rms and stes. CI 3pm/CO noon. Nonsmoking rms avail. Rooms are entirely white, including the furniture. All rooms contain large old-fashioned bathtubs with hand-held showers. To add a dab of color, a green apple is placed on its own pedestal in your room each day. **Amenities:** 🛗⚬🍽 A/C, cable TV w/movies, dataport, VCR, CD/tape player, voice mail, in-rm safe. All units w/minibars, some w/terraces. **Services:** ⎟⊙⎟ ☛ 💶 🛆 ⎐ Twice-daily maid svce, car-rental desk, social director, masseur, children's program, babysitting. **Facilities:** ⟨⟩ 📷 ▾ ⟨150⟩ ▯ ⅙ 4 restaurants, 3 bars, 1 beach (ocean), lifeguard, sauna, steam rm, whirlpool, playground. Beach activities available through concessions locat-

ed in front of the hotel. **Rates:** Peak (Dec–Apr) $200–$250 S or D; $550–$600 ste. Children under age 12 stay free. Min stay special events. Lower rates off-season. AE, CB, DC, DISC, MC, V.

### ▤▤ Dezerland Surfside Beach Hotel

8701 Collins Ave, 33154; tel 305/865-6661 or toll free 800/331-9346 in the US, 800/331-9347 in Canada; fax 305/866-2630. A fun hotel with a 1950s-automobile theme in a tropical setting. Mint-condition cars are scattered about the floors. **Rooms:** 225 rms. CI 3pm/CO noon. Nonsmoking rms avail. Rooms are comfortable and in good condition. **Amenities:** 🛗 ⚬ A/C, cable TV w/movies. Some units w/terraces. **Services:** ✗ ⎐ Babysitting. **Facilities:** ⟨⟩ ⚠ ⟨250⟩ 1 restaurant, 3 bars, 1 beach (ocean), lifeguard, games rm, whirlpool, washer/dryer. Fishing and scuba diving can be arranged. **Rates:** Peak (Dec 16–Apr 15) $80–$125 S or D. Extra person $9. Children under age 18 stay free. Lower rates off-season. Parking: Outdoor, free. AE, CB, DC, DISC, MC, V.

### ▤▤▤ Doral Ocean Beach Resort

4833 Collins Ave, 33140; tel 305/532-3600 or toll free 800/233-6725; fax 305/534-7409. The beachside sibling to the redoubtable Doral Resort and Country Club, offering a wide range of facilities for the sports enthusiast. **Rooms:** 422 rms, stes, and effic. CI 3pm/CO noon. Nonsmoking rms avail. Rooms are decorated in pastel seashore colors. **Amenities:** 🛗 ⚬ 🍽 A/C, cable TV w/movies, voice mail. All units w/minibars, some w/whirlpools. **Services:** ✗ ☛ 💶 🛆 ⎐ Car-rental desk, social director, masseur, children's program, babysitting. Chilled champagne awaits arrivals. Housekeeping routinely ask guests if they desire afternoon service. Shuttle bus goes to other Doral properties for golf. **Facilities:** ⟨⟩ 🚲 ⚠ 📷 🏊² ▾ ▾ ⟨2000⟩ ⅙ 2 restaurants, 3 bars, 1 beach (ocean), games rm, snorkeling, whirlpool, beauty salon. Beach cabanas. **Rates:** $220–$325 S or D; $625–$875 ste; $1,000–$2,000 effic. Extra person $20–$40. Children under age 13 stay free. Lower rates off-season. Parking: Indoor, $9/day. AE, CB, DC, DISC, EC, ER, JCB, MC, V.

### ▤▤ The Dorchester

1850 Collins Ave, 33139 (South Beach); tel 305/534-6971 or toll free 800/327-4739; fax 305/673-1006. Convenient to SoBe beach, activities, and nightlife. **Rooms:** 94 rms and effic. CI 2pm/CO noon. Rooms are quieter than at many art deco district hotels. **Amenities:** 🛗 🍽 A/C, TV, refrig. Some units w/terraces, 1 w/whirlpool. **Services:** ⎐ Car-rental desk. **Facilities:** ⟨⟩ ▾ ⟨30⟩ Games rm, day-care ctr. A coffeeshop is planned. **Rates:** Peak (Dec–mid-Apr) $70–$85 S; $79–$90 D; $85 ste; $79–$90 effic. Children under age 14 stay free. Lower rates off-season. Parking: Outdoor, $5/day. AE, CB, DC, EC, MC, V.

### ▤▤ Eden Roc Resort and Spa

4525 Collins Ave, 33140; tel 305/531-0000 or toll free 800/327-8337; fax 305/531-6959. N of I-95 at Arthur Godfrey

Rd. Showy 1950s charmer, with a fanciful pink pastel, Morris Lapidus–designed lobby. Offers unusually spacious accommodations. **Rooms:** 350 rms and stes. CI 3pm/CO noon. Nonsmoking rms avail. Some units have 1½ baths and extra-large closets. **Amenities:** 🛏 Ⓐ A/C, cable TV w/movies, in-rm safe. All units w/minibars, some w/terraces, some w/whirlpools. **Services:** ✕ 🗝 ⓋⓅ 🖼 ⌔ Car-rental desk. **Facilities:** 🖼 ⚠ 🔟 ⌔ 1 restaurant (*see* "Restaurants" below), 2 bars, 1 beach (ocean). Porch Restaurant affords diners underwater view through glass sides of the adjacent swimming pool. **Rates:** Peak (Dec 15–Apr) $195 S or D; $275 ste. Extra person $20. Children under age 18 stay free. Lower rates off-season. Parking: Indoor, $8.50/day. AE, CB, DC, DISC, MC, V.

### Essex House Hotel

1001 Collins Ave, 33139 (South Beach); tel 305/534-2700 or toll free 800/553-7739; fax 305/532-3827. At 10th St. Plush, romantic art deco hotel, located one block from the beach. Tastefully done lobby is outfitted with leather appointments, piano, Oriental vases, and silk flower arrangements. Relaxing courtyard encircled by stucco wall, with palms and plants. **Rooms:** 57 rms and stes. CI 3pm/CO noon. Nonsmoking rms avail. Solid oak furnishings, fine linens, and pastel colors. **Amenities:** 🛏 Ⓠ A/C, cable TV. **Services:** 🗝 🚐 🖼 ⌔ Car-rental desk, social director, babysitting. **Rates (CP):** Peak (Jan–Mar) $125–$145 S or D; $155–$300 ste. Extra person $20. Lower rates off-season. AE, DC, MC, V.

### Golden Sands

6901 Collins Ave, 33141; tel 305/866-8734 or toll free 800/932-0333 in the US, 800/423-5170 in Canada; fax 305/866-0187. Smallish lobby is redeemed by the attractive guest rooms. **Rooms:** 98 rms and effic. CI 11am/CO noon. Nonsmoking rms avail. Pastel decor, airy appointments, new wallpaper. Some rooms have ocean views. **Amenities:** 🛏 A/C, cable TV, refrig. **Services:** ✕ 🖼 ⌔ Car-rental desk, babysitting. Staff will arrange sports activities. **Facilities:** 🖼 🚴 ⚠ 🔟 ⌔ 🥄 🍴 1 restaurant, 2 bars (w/entertainment), 1 beach (ocean), games rm, snorkeling, beauty salon. Cozy restaurant has pool views. **Rates:** Peak (Dec 20–Apr 5) $47–$77 S or D; $57–$120 effic. Children under age 18 stay free. Lower rates off-season. Parking: Indoor/outdoor, $5/day. AE, MC, V.

### The Governor Hotel

435 21st St, 33139 (South Beach); tel 305/532-2100 or toll free 800/542-0444; fax 305/532-9139. In a quiet neighborhood close to the beach action. The modest accommodations are fine for those with minimal expectations. **Rooms:** 124 rms and effic. CI 2pm/CO 11am. Nonsmoking rms avail. **Amenities:** 🛏 A/C, cable TV w/movies. Some units w/terraces. **Services:** ✕ 🖼 ⌔ Babysitting. **Facilities:** 🖼 1 restaurant, 1 bar, washer/dryer. Lounge area in lobby has piano and pool table. **Rates:** Peak (Dec 20–Apr 10) $85 S or D; $125 effic. Extra person $10. Children under age 17 stay free. Lower rates off-season. Parking: Outdoor, free. AE, CB, DC, DISC, MC, V.

### Holiday Inn Newport Pier Resort

16701 Collins Ave, 33160; tel 305/949-1300 or toll free 800/327-5476, 800/826-5319 in FL; fax 305/956-2733. Tropical-themed property offering an abundance of activities. Super-friendly staff. **Rooms:** 355 rms and stes. CI 3pm/CO noon. Nonsmoking rms avail. Crisp, newly renovated rooms. **Amenities:** 🛏 Ⓠ A/C, cable TV, refrig, in-rm safe. Some units w/terraces. **Services:** ✕ 🗝 ⓋⓅ 🖼 ⌔ 🥄 Car-rental desk, social director, masseur, children's program, babysitting. **Facilities:** 🖼 ⚠ 🔟 ⌔ 🥄 🔟 ⌔ 4 restaurants, 4 bars (2 w/entertainment), 1 beach (ocean), lifeguard, board surfing, games rm, snorkeling, spa, whirlpool, beauty salon, washer/dryer. **Rates:** Peak (Dec–Apr 15) $135–$165 S or D; $195–$235 ste. Extra person $10. Children under age 19 stay free. Lower rates off-season. AP and MAP rates avail. Parking: Indoor/outdoor, $4/day. AE, CB, DC, DISC, EC, JCB, MC, V.

### Holiday Inn Oceanside Convention Inn

2201 Collins Ave, 33139 (South Beach); tel 305/534-1511 or toll free 800/356-6902; fax 305/532-1403. Popular for its oceanfront location, this full-service, 12-story hotel fronts the boardwalk and is a popular rendezvous for both convention delegates and avid beachgoers. **Rooms:** 357 rms and stes. CI 3pm/CO noon. Nonsmoking rms avail. Some rooms have ocean views. **Amenities:** 🛏 Ⓠ A/C, cable TV w/movies. **Services:** ✕ 🖼 ⌔ Car-rental desk. **Facilities:** 🖼 🏊 🔟 ⌔ 1 restaurant, 2 bars (1 w/entertainment), 1 beach (ocean), games rm, whirlpool, washer/dryer. **Rates:** Peak (Dec–Apr) $109–$119 S; $124–$134 D; $280–$360 ste. Extra person $15. Children under age 10 stay free. Lower rates off-season. Parking: Indoor, $6/day. AE, DC, DISC, EC, MC, V.

### Hotel Astor

956 Washington Ave, 33139 (South Beach); tel 305/531-8081 or toll free 800/270-4981; fax 305/531-3193. At 9th St. One of the finest South Beach Deco renovations to date. Unfailing attention to detail in a boutique setting make this a truly unique hotel. **Rooms:** 42 rms and stes. Executive level. CI 3pm/CO noon. Nonsmoking rms avail. Rooms exude quiet elegance. **Amenities:** 🛏 Ⓠ 🍴 A/C, cable TV w/movies, refrig, dataport, VCR, CD/tape player, voice mail, in-rm safe, bathrobes. All units w/minibars, 1 w/terrace, 1 w/whirlpool. **Services:** ✕ 🗝 ⓋⓅ 🖼 Twice-daily maid svce, car-rental desk. 24-hour concierge will try to accommodate any request. **Facilities:** 🖼 ⌔ 1 restaurant (*see* "Restaurants" below), 2 bars. **Rates:** $120 S or D; $210–$450 ste. Extra person $35. Min stay wknds and special events. Parking: Outdoor, $3/day. AE, MC, V.

### The Indian Creek Hotel

2727 Indian Creek Dr, 33140; tel 305/531-2727; fax 305/531-5651. 1 block W of Collins Ave. Friendly staff and art deco antiques add to this Miami Beach landmark. **Rooms:** 61 rms and stes. CI 3pm/CO noon. Nonsmoking rms avail. **Amenities:** 🛏 Ⓠ A/C, satel TV w/movies, voice mail. Suites feature sofas with double beds and two phones. Some have dataports. **Services:** ✕ ⬜ ⌐ Babysitting. **Facilities:** 🔥 [50] 1 restaurant, 1 bar. **Rates:** Peak (Oct–Apr) $100–$110 D; $190 ste. Extra person $10. Lower rates off-season. Parking: Outdoor, free. AE, MC, V.

### ⬛ Kenmore Hotel
1050 Washington Ave, 33139 (South Beach); tel 305/674-1930; fax 305/534-6591. At 10th St. Traditional art deco hotel. **Rooms:** 60 rms and stes. CI 3pm/CO noon. Clean, sparsely decorated rooms have some period furnishings in 1930s style; rooms with pool and patio views are best. **Amenities:** 🔧 A/C, TV, refrig, voice mail. Some units w/minibars. **Services:** ⚷ 🚗 ⬜ Car-rental desk, social director, babysitting. **Facilities:** 🔥 [15] **Rates (CP):** Peak (Nov 15–Apr) $89 S or D; $99 ste. Extra person $20. Children under age 12 stay free. Lower rates off-season. AE, CB, DC, DISC, MC, V.

### ⬛⬛ Kent Hotel
1131 Collins Ave, 33139 (South Beach); tel 305/531-6771; fax 305/531-0720. Comfortable art deco hotel in a fine location. Garden setting with trees, plants, and umbrella tables. Security bars protect the ground floor. **Rooms:** 54 rms and stes. CI 3pm/CO noon. Nonsmoking rms avail. Cozy pastel colors used throughout. **Amenities:** 🔧 A/C, TV. All units w/minibars. **Services:** ⚷ 🚗 ⬜ ⌐ 🔧 Car-rental desk, masseur. **Facilities:** [20] 🖥 **Rates:** Peak (Nov–May) $95–$135 S or D; $175 ste. Extra person $10. Children under age 12 stay free. Min stay special events. Lower rates off-season. Parking: Outdoor, $10/day. AE, CB, DC, DISC, MC, V.

### ⬛⬛ The Leslie
1244 Ocean Dr, 33139 (South Beach); tel 305/534-2135 or toll free 800/338-9076; fax 305/531-5543. One of the district's most popular historic hotels, it was among the first Ocean Drive properties to undergo extensive renovation. Small and quiet, with a distinct art deco design on the outside and an art nouveau interior. Within walking distance of some of the best restaurants and clubs. **Rooms:** 43 rms and stes. CI 3pm/CO noon. Nonsmoking rms avail. Suites with ocean views have lots of windows to take in Ocean Drive color. **Amenities:** 🔧 A/C, cable TV, VCR, CD/tape player, voice mail, in-rm safe. All units w/minibars. **Services:** ✕ ⚷ VP 🚗 ⬜ ⌐ Car-rental desk, babysitting. **Facilities:** [25] 🔥 1 restaurant, 2 bars, 1 beach (ocean), lifeguard. **Rates:** Peak (Oct–Apr) $105–$135 S or D; $225 ste. Extra person $15. Children under age 12 stay free. Min stay wknds and special events. Parking: Outdoor, $10/day. AE, CB, DC, DISC, MC, V.

### ⬛⬛ The Marlin
1200 Collins Ave, 33139 (South Beach); tel 305/673-8770 or toll free 800/338-9076; fax 305/673-9609. At 12th St. Garners much local attention for its rock-and-roll clientele. Beautifully lit, powder blue exterior, but relatively simple rooms. **Rooms:** 12 stes. CI 3pm/CO noon. **Amenities:** 🔧 🖥 A/C, cable TV w/movies, refrig, VCR, CD/tape player,

voice mail, in-rm safe, bathrobes. All units w/minibars. **Services:** ✕ ⚷ VP 🚗 ⬜ ⌐ Car-rental desk, masseur. **Facilities:** [15] 🖥 1 bar. Guests receive discounts at nearby health club. **Rates (CP):** Peak (Jan–Apr) $200–$325 ste. Extra person $15. Children under age 5 stay free. Min stay special events. Lower rates off-season. Parking: Outdoor, $10/day. AE, CB, DC, DISC, MC, V.

### ⬛⬛ Marseilles Hotel
1741 Collins Ave, 33139 (South Beach); tel 305/538-5711 or toll free 800/327-4739; fax 305/673-1006. Well priced, basic lodging in a good people-watching location in the heart of the art deco district. **Rooms:** 115 rms, stes, and effic. CI 3pm/CO noon. Nonsmoking rms avail. Pastel colors, rattan appointments. **Amenities:** 🔧 A/C, cable TV, refrig, in-rm safe. **Services:** ⚷ ⬜ ⌐ Car-rental desk. **Facilities:** 🔥 [125] 1 restaurant (bkfst and dinner only), 1 bar, 1 beach (ocean), lifeguard. Outdoor bar. **Rates:** Peak (Dec 16–Apr 15) $85 S or D; $115 ste; $110 effic. Extra person $10. Children under age 8 stay free. Lower rates off-season. Parking: Outdoor, $6/day. AE, CB, DC, DISC, MC, V.

### ⬛⬛ Park Central Hotel
640 Ocean Dr, 33139 (South Beach); tel 305/538-1611 or toll free 800/727-5236; fax 305/534-7520. Pretty art deco hotel harks back to 1937, when it was built. It is still in need of some improvement, but it has the right idea for a solid start. The lobby is decorated with black-and-white photos from the 1930s. South Beach atmosphere makes up for relative lack of facilities. **Rooms:** 117 rms and stes. CI 3pm/CO noon. Rooms are pleasant and simple. **Amenities:** 🔧 🔊 A/C, cable TV, refrig, dataport, voice mail, in-rm safe. **Services:** ✕ ⚷ 🚗 ⬜ ⌐ Car-rental desk. **Facilities:** 🔥 🖥 [50] 1 restaurant, 2 bars. Juice bar offers fresh and delicious fruit or vegetable smoothies. **Rates:** Peak (Jan–Apr) $125–$175 S or D; $175–$225 ste. Extra person $10. Children under age 12 stay free. Min stay wknds and special events. Lower rates off-season. Parking: Outdoor, $9/day. AE, DC, MC, V.

### ⬛ Park Washington Hotel
1020 Washington Ave, 33139 (South Beach); tel 305/532-1930; fax 305/672-6706. At 10th St. Geared toward tourists, the Park Washington is one of the better values in South Beach. **Rooms:** 30 rms and stes. CI 3pm/CO noon. Clean, comfortable rooms. **Amenities:** 🔧 A/C, TV, refrig, voice mail. 1 unit w/minibar. **Services:** ⚷ 🚗 ⬜ Car-rental desk, babysitting. **Facilities:** 🔥 **Rates (CP):** Peak (Nov 15–Apr) $59–$89 S or D; $119 ste. Extra person $20. Children under age 12 stay free. Lower rates off-season. AE, CB, DC, DISC, MC, V.

### ⬛⬛ Ritz Plaza Hotel
1701 Collins Ave, 33139 (South Beach); tel 305/534-3500 or toll free 800/522-6400; fax 305/531-6928. At 17th St. A better-than-average art deco hotel and a prime address for beach action. You might see models posing in the hotel's

backyard. **Rooms:** 132 rms and stes. CI 3pm/CO noon. Nonsmoking rms avail. **Amenities:** 🔲 🔾 ▣ A/C, cable TV, voice mail, in-rm safe. **Services:** ✗ VP 🚗 🗺 🗘 🗘 Babysitting. **Facilities:** 🗒 ᵺ 250 2 restaurants, 2 bars, 1 beach (ocean), spa. **Rates:** Peak (Oct–Apr) $145–$185 S or D; $275–$450 ste. Children under age 17 stay free. Lower rates off-season. Parking: Outdoor, $6/day. AE, CB, DC, DISC, MC, V.

### ⬛⬛⬛ The Shelborne Beach Hotel
1801 Collins Ave, 33139 (South Beach); tel 305/531-1271 or toll free 800/327-8757; fax 305/531-2206. At 18th St. A one-time headquarters for beauty pageants in the 1940s and '50s, the hotel has retained its original look, including a very appealing marbled entry and a curved staircase in the lobby. Staff is friendly and attentive. **Rooms:** 185 rms and stes. Executive level. CI 3pm/CO noon. Nonsmoking rms avail. Suites offer exceptional decor, black leather sofas, full kitchens, dining areas with glass-block partitions, den, and bedroom. Balconies provide views of SoBe, downtown, or the beach. **Amenities:** 🔲 🔾 ▣ A/C, cable TV w/movies, refrig. 1 unit w/minibar, some w/terraces. **Services:** ✗ 🗝 VP 🗺 🗘 Car-rental desk, babysitting. **Facilities:** 🗒 △ ᵺ 400 🔾 1 restaurant, 2 bars, 1 beach (ocean), lifeguard, volleyball, spa, sauna, whirlpool, beauty salon, washer/dryer. **Rates:** Peak (Apr 16–Dec 14) $120–$180 S or D; $350–$480 ste. Extra person $10. Children under age 17 stay free. Min stay special events. Lower rates off-season. AP and MAP rates avail. Parking: Outdoor, $8/day. AE, MC, V.

### ⬛⬛⬛ Shore Club Hotel
1901 Collins Ave, 33139 (South Beach); tel 305/672-0303 or toll free 800/327-8330; fax 305/672-6287. At 19th St. Larger-than-average rooms and large meeting facilities attract convention-goers and families like. **Rooms:** 106 rms. CI 3pm/CO noon. Nonsmoking rms avail. All units are clean and comfortable, though decor is a bit dark. **Amenities:** 🔲 A/C, cable TV w/movies. Some units w/terraces. **Services:** VP 🗺 🗘 🗘 Twice-daily maid svce, babysitting. **Facilities:** 🗒 △ 225 1 bar, 1 beach (ocean), lifeguard, day-care ctr. Fax service on request. **Rates (CP):** Peak (Oct–May) $110–$180 S or D. Extra person $25. Children under age 18 stay free. Min stay special events. Lower rates off-season. Parking: Outdoor, $10/day. AE, CB, DC, DISC, MC, V.

### ⬛⬛ Sol Miami Beach
3925 Collins Ave, 33140; tel 305/531-3534 or toll free 800/531-3534; fax 305/531-1765. 2 blocks S of I-95. One of the largest of Miami Beach's "painted ladies," catering to an international (mostly Latin American and European) clientele. **Rooms:** 271 rms and stes. CI 3pm/CO noon. Nonsmoking rms avail. Rooms are modest, but comfortable and clean. **Amenities:** 🔲 A/C, cable TV w/movies, refrig, in-rm safe. Some units w/minibars, some w/fireplaces. **Services:** ✗ 🗝 VP 🗺 🗘 Masseur. **Facilities:** 🗒 ᵺ 150 🔾 2 restaurants, 2 bars, 1 beach (ocean), beauty salon, washer/dryer. **Rates:**

Peak (Jan–Apr) $95–$130 S or D; $130 ste. Extra person $15. Children under age 16 stay free. Min stay special events. Lower rates off-season. Parking: Outdoor, free. AE, MC, V.

### ⬛⬛ The Surfcomber
1717 Collins Ave, 33139 (South Beach); tel 305/532-7715 or toll free 800/336-4264 in the US, 800/446-4264 in Canada; fax 305/532-7280. At 18th St. A friendly staff welcomes guests at this art deco district standby. Ongoing renovations to rooms. **Rooms:** 192 rms and effic. CI 3pm/CO noon. Nonsmoking rms avail. "Evergreen" rooms (with air- and water-filtration systems) available on request. **Amenities:** 🔲 A/C, cable TV w/movies, voice mail, in-rm safe. Some units w/terraces. **Services:** 🗝 VP 🗘 Car-rental desk. **Facilities:** 🗒 150 2 restaurants (lunch and dinner only), 1 bar, 1 beach (ocean). **Rates (BB):** Peak (Apr 16–Dec 14) $70–$110 S or D; $75 effic. Extra person $10. Children under age 12 stay free. Min stay special events. Lower rates off-season. Parking: Outdoor, $9/day. AE, CB, DC, DISC, MC, V.

### ⬛⬛ Waldorf Towers Hotel
860 Ocean Dr, 33139 (South Beach); tel 305/531-7684 or toll free 800/933-2332; fax 305/672-6836. Classic local styling, with wicker ceiling fans and potted tropical plants in the lobby. **Rooms:** 45 rms and stes. CI 3pm/CO noon. Nonsmoking rms avail. Rooms decorated in seascape colors with light, comfortable furnishings. **Amenities:** 🔲 🍴 A/C, cable TV w/movies. Some units w/minibars. **Services:** 🗝 VP 🚗 🗺 🗘 🗘 Car-rental desk, masseur. **Facilities:** 10 1 restaurant, 1 bar, 1 beach (ocean), lifeguard. Nearby health club offers discount. **Rates:** Peak (Dec 15–Apr 15) $109–$149 S or D; $199 ste. Extra person $10. Children under age 12 stay free. Min stay special events. Lower rates off-season. AE, CB, DC, DISC, MC, V.

## MOTELS
### ⬛⬛ Best Western Surf Vista
18001 Collins Ave, N Miami Beach, 33160; tel 305/932-1800 or toll free 800/992-4786; fax 305/935-5575. Exit 13 off I-95, at 18th St. A basic, well-maintained family-oriented beach motel. **Rooms:** 120 rms. Executive level. CI 2pm/CO noon. Nonsmoking rms avail. Rooms lack frills, but are quite large. **Amenities:** 🔲 A/C, cable TV, refrig. All units w/terraces, 1 w/whirlpool. **Services:** ✗ 🗝 🗺 🗘 Car-rental desk. **Facilities:** 🗒 50 1 restaurant, 1 bar, 1 beach (ocean), lifeguard, games rm, washer/dryer. **Rates:** Peak (Dec–Apr) $90–$135 S or D. Extra person $10. Children under age 12 stay free. Min stay special events. Lower rates off-season. Parking: Outdoor, free. AE, CB, DC, DISC, MC, V.

### ⬛ The New Waterside Inn
2360 Collins Ave, 33139; tel 305/538-1951; fax 305/531-3217. Just outside the official art deco district, it provides comfortable rooms without fanfare. Popular with European tourists. **Rooms:** 80 rms. CI 11am/CO 11am. Nonsmoking rms avail. **Amenities:** 🔲 A/C, cable TV. **Services:** 🗘 🗘 Car-rental desk. Continental breakfast ($2.50) served

poolside. **Facilities:** ⬚ ⬚ ⬚ Washer/dryer. Fax machine in lobby for guest use. **Rates:** Peak (Dec 15–Apr 15) $40–$65 S; $50–$80 D. Extra person $10. Children under age 12 stay free. Lower rates off-season. Parking: Outdoor, free. AE, CB, DC, JCB, MC, V.

### ⬚ Paradise Inn Motel
8520 Harding Ave, 33141; tel 305/865-6216; fax 305/865-9028. Exit 13 off I-95. One of the area's original motels, intended for budget-minded guests who want basic, clean accommodations close to the beach. **Rooms:** 96 rms and effic. CI open/CO noon. **Amenities:** ⬚ ⬚ A/C, cable TV w/movies, refrig, in-rm safe. **Services:** ⬚ ⬚ Coffee available mornings. Uniformed security patrols at night. **Facilities:** ⬚ Washer/dryer. **Rates (CP):** Peak (Dec–Apr) $32–$48 S; $36–$52 D; $36–$60 effic. Extra person $3. Children under age 12 stay free. Lower rates off-season. Parking: Outdoor, free. AE, CB, DC, DISC, ER, MC, V.

## RESORTS

### ⬚⬚⬚ Fontainebleau Tower
4441 Collins Ave, 33140; tel 305/538-2000 or toll free 800/548-8886; fax 305/673-5351. 20 acres. A magnet for the old and new in-crowd and a staple of the beach scene, this elaborate, always-bustling complex harks back to the forgotten heyday of 1950s Miami Beach. Often a stop for tourists, even if they're not staying here. **Rooms:** 1,207 rms and stes. CI 3pm/CO 11am. Nonsmoking rms avail. Handsome rooms. **Amenities:** ⬚ ⬚ A/C, cable TV w/movies, refrig. Some units w/minibars, some w/terraces. **Services:** ✕ ⬚ ⬚ ⬚ ⬚ ⬚ Car-rental desk, masseur, children's program, babysitting. Business center operates six days per week. Pets under 20 lbs permitted for $20/day. **Facilities:** ⬚ ⬚ ⬚ ⬚ ⬚ ⬚ ⬚ ⬚ ⬚ ⬚ 9 restaurants, 2 bars (w/entertainment), 1 beach (ocean), lifeguard, board surfing, games rm, lawn games, spa, sauna, steam rm, whirlpool, beauty salon, playground. **Rates:** Peak (Nov–May) $200–$295 S; $225–$320 D; $430–$720 ste. Extra person $25. Children under age 18 stay free. Lower rates off-season. Parking: Indoor, $10/day. AE, CB, DC, DISC, EC, JCB, MC, V.

### ⬚⬚⬚⬚ Sheraton Bal Harbour Resort
9701 Collins Ave, Bal Harbour, 33154; tel 305/865-7511 or toll free 800/999-9898; fax 305/864-2601. Exit 13 off I-95. 11 acres. A major force in the hotel market north of Miami Beach, featuring a fancy lobby and recently renovated rooms. **Rooms:** 668 rms and stes; 26 cottages/villas. CI 3pm/CO noon. Nonsmoking rms avail. **Amenities:** ⬚ ⬚ ⬚ ⬚ ⬚ A/C, cable TV w/movies, refrig, dataport, VCR, CD/tape player, voice mail, in-rm safe, bathrobes. Some units w/minibars, some w/terraces, some w/whirlpools. **Services:** ⬚ ⬚ ⬚ ⬚ ⬚ ⬚ ⬚ Twice-daily maid svce, car-rental desk, social director, masseur, children's program, babysitting. Security guards patrol beach and outdoor shower areas. **Facilities:** ⬚ ⬚ ⬚ ⬚ ⬚ ⬚ ⬚ ⬚ ⬚ ⬚ ⬚ ⬚ 4 restaurants, 2 bars (1 w/entertainment), 1 beach (ocean), lifeguard, basketball,

volleyball, board surfing, racquetball, snorkeling, sauna, steam rm, whirlpool, day-care ctr, playground. **Rates:** Peak (Jan–Mar) $200–$450 S or D; $550 ste; $450 cottage/villa. Extra person $25. Children under age 17 stay free. Min stay special events. Lower rates off-season. AE, CB, DC, DISC, MC, V.

## RESTAURANTS ⬚

### A Fish Called Avalon
In Avalon Hotel, 700 Ocean Dr (South Beach); tel 305/532-1727. **Seafood.** Porch dining adds to the appeal of this upscale eatery. Continental fare changes nightly but always includes fresh local fish, pastas, and local stone crabs (in season). Nightly live music rounds out the evening. **FYI:** Reservations recommended. Jazz. Children's menu. **Open:** Peak (Dec–Apr) Tues–Thurs 6pm–midnight, Fri–Sat 6pm–1am, Sun 6pm–midnight. **Prices:** Main courses $15–$21. AE, MC, V. ⬚ ⬚ ⬚

### Astor Place Bar & Grill
In Hotel Astor, 956 Washington Ave (South Beach); tel 305/672-7217. **New American.** The sleek atrium setting is in keeping with Hotel Astor's quiet art deco elegance. The menu offers an eclectic mix of tropical and Southwestern-style entrees: jerk grilled tuna, grilled anchovy-rubbed pork chops. **FYI:** Reservations accepted. **Open:** Peak (Nov–Apr) Sun–Thurs 7:30am–midnight, Fri–Sat 7:30am–1am. **Prices:** Main courses $14–$25. AE, DC, DISC, MC, V. ⬚ ⬚

### Caffè Milano
850 Ocean Dr (South Beach); tel 305/532-0707. **Italian.** Whether you opt for outdoor or indoor candlelit dining, this classic Italian bistro offers style and substance. Menu highlights include braised osso buco *al Milanese* and several risottos, as well as nightly specials. **FYI:** Reservations recommended. **Open:** Lunch daily noon–5pm; dinner Mon–Thurs 6pm–midnight, Fri–Sun 6pm–1am. **Prices:** Main courses $14–$26. AE, DC, DISC, MC, V. ⬚ ⬚ ⬚

### Casona De Carlitos
2236 Collins Ave; tel 305/534-7013. **Italian/South American/Steak.** A casual dining room with an Argentine-Italian menu published in various languages. Entrees include baked fish in bleu-cheese sauce, chicken oreganato in wine, and a number of grilled meats. **FYI:** Reservations not accepted. Beer and wine only. **Open:** Sun–Fri 11:30am–12:30am, Sat 11:30am–1:30am. **Prices:** Main courses $11–$21. AE, DC, DISC, MC, V. ⬚ ⬚

### ⬚ China Grill Miami Beach
404 Washington Ave; tel 305/534-2211. At 5th St. **International.** Famous for family-size portions of inventive "world cuisine" utilizing spices, ingredients, and techniques culled from around the globe. The 12,000-sq-ft restaurant includes an intimate champagne, sake, and vodka bar. Specialties of the house include lobster pancakes, wasabi-crusted grouper, and spice-rubbed pork loin in papaya-berry salsa. **FYI:** Reser-

vations recommended. Dress code. **Open:** Lunch Mon–Fri 11:45am–5pm; dinner Sun–Thurs 6pm–midnight, Fri–Sat 6pm–1am. **Prices:** Main courses $19–$52. AE, CB, DC, DISC, MC, V. 📷 VP &

### Colony Bistro
In Colony Hotel, 736 Ocean Dr (South Beach); tel 305/673-6776. **New American/Caribbean.** A sophisticated, romantic bistro. Entrees might include grilled pompano with seaweed salad, sticky rice, and red curry–coconut mushrooms. **FYI:** Reservations recommended. **Open:** Lunch daily 11:30am–3pm; dinner Mon–Fri 6–11pm, Sat–Sun 6pm–midnight. **Prices:** Main courses $14–$25. AE, DC, MC, V. ❤ VP &

### ✹ Compass Cafe & Market
In Waldorf Towers Hotel, 860 Ocean Dr (South Beach); tel 305/673-5890. **American.** This breezy cafe with indoor and outdoor rattan seating is a great spot for people watching. Menu selections range from salads and burgers to pastas, stir-fry and fresh seafood. The basement market offers a good selection of wines, deli sandwiches, snacks, and magazines. **FYI:** Reservations not accepted. **Open:** Peak (Dec–Apr) daily 8am–1am. **Prices:** Main courses $8–$20. AE, MC, V. 🍔 VP

### Dominique's
In The Alexander All-Suite Luxury Hotel, 5225 Collins Ave; tel 305/861-5252. **Continental/French.** An opulent ocean-side restaurant serving adventurous, French-inspired cuisine. Dine among antiques, Persian rugs, and lush foliage, on selections including buffalo sausage, alligator scaloppine, and fresh rattlesnake salad. The less adventurous might choose one of the steaks or the rack of lamb. **FYI:** Reservations accepted. Piano. **Open:** Peak (Dec–Apr) breakfast daily 7–11:30am; lunch daily 11:30am–3pm; dinner Sun–Thurs 6–11pm, Fri–Sat 5–11pm. **Prices:** Main courses $13–$28; prix fixe $19–$22. AE, DC, MC, V. ❤ VP &

### Escopazzo
1311 Washington Ave (South Beach); tel 305/674-9450. **Italian.** A cozy, romantic Italian restaurant featuring a distinguished menu and wine list. **FYI:** Reservations recommended. Beer and wine only. **Open:** Sun–Thurs 6pm–midnight, Fri–Sat 6pm–1am. **Prices:** Main courses $13–$25. AE, CB, DC, MC, V. ❤ VP

### ✦ The Forge
432 Arthur Godfrey Rd; tel 305/538-8533. **American.** An elegant restaurant of several rooms adorned with oak paneling and artwork. The chef prepares fish, veal, poultry and beef specialties, many on the oak grill. **FYI:** Reservations accepted. Piano. **Open:** Daily 6pm–midnight. **Prices:** Main courses $18–$65. AE, CB, DC, DISC, MC, V. ❤ VP &

### ✹ Joe's Stone Crab
227 Biscayne St; tel 305/673-0365. 6 blocks S of FL A1A. **Regional American/Seafood.** A simply decorated landmark eatery whose stone crabs have been drawing crowds for decades. Other fish and seafood dishes, all prepared to order,

are also available. **FYI:** Reservations not accepted. **Open:** Lunch Tues–Sat 11:30am–2pm; dinner Sun–Thurs 5–10pm, Fri–Sat 5–11pm. Closed May 15–Oct 15. **Prices:** Main courses $5–$37. AE, CB, DC, MC, V. 📷 VP &

### ✦ Lure
805 Lincoln Rd (South Beach); tel 305/538-5873. Near Lincoln Theater. **Pan-Asian.** The decor here (designed by the same team who did the ultratrendy Nemo) is dark and eclectic, with touches like live goldfish swimming in miniature bowls on the downstairs tables. Renowned chef Scott Howard turns out specialties such as curried seared tuna and sautéed black Keys grouper, and the extensive and carefully selected wine list ensures the perfect marriage of wine and food. Service is attentive, and surprisingly unpretentious. **FYI:** Reservations recommended. Jazz. **Open:** Peak (Dec–Apr) lunch Wed–Fri 11:30am–3:30pm, Sat–Sun 1–5pm; dinner Mon–Thurs 6pm–midnight, Fri–Sat 6pm–1am, Sun 6–11pm. **Prices:** Main courses $14–$21. AE, MC, V. ♥ &

### Mezzaluna
In Casa Grande Suite Hotel, 834 Ocean Dr (South Beach); tel 305/674-1330. **Italian.** Dine indoors or out at this Italianate art deco restaurant with butter-yellow walls and a sophisticated menu. **FYI:** Reservations accepted. Jazz/piano/singer. **Open:** Sun–Thurs noon–midnight, Fri–Sat noon–4am. **Prices:** Main courses $7–$19. AE, CB, DC, DISC, MC, V. VP &

### ✦ Mezzanotte
1200 Washington Ave (South Beach); tel 305/673-4343. **Italian.** An open, airy restaurant with tile floors and black lacquered chairs serving a traditional Italian menu. **FYI:** Reservations recommended. No smoking. **Open:** Sun–Thurs 6pm–midnight, Fri–Sat 6pm–2am. **Prices:** Main courses $12–$27. AE, CB, DC, DISC, MC, V. 📷 VP &

### Nemo
100 Collins Ave (South Beach); tel 305/532-4550. At 1st St. **Continental/Asian.** Sleek surroundings, a world-class menu, and uncommonly friendly service make this one of the hottest newcomers in SoBe. Nightly entree selections include seared Chilean sea bass and grilled Angus sirloin, as well as a variety of similarly daring specials. A comprehensive wine list showcases some of California's finest, while the open kitchen lets diners look in on the magic. **FYI:** Reservations recommended. **Open:** Peak (Dec–Apr) lunch Mon–Fri noon–3pm; dinner Mon–Fri 7pm–midnight, Sat 6pm–midnight, Sun 6–11pm; brunch Sun noon–4pm. **Prices:** Main courses $16–$21. AE, MC, V. 🍔 VP &

### ✹ News Cafe
800 Ocean Dr (South Beach); tel 305/538-6397. **New American/Cafe.** This trendy hangout serves healthy entrees, a variety of green salads, both meat and cheese sandwiches, and a selection of coffee drinks. **FYI:** Reservations not accepted. No smoking. **Open:** Daily 24 hrs. **Prices:** Main courses $7–$14. AE, CB, DC, DISC, MC, V. 🕔 VP &

### ★ Norma's

646 Lincoln Rd (South Beach); tel 305/532-2809. **Caribbean.** Caribbean art and great music add to the breezy atmosphere of this down-home Caribbean cafe. Friendly management will help guests choose between such entrees as Rasta Chicken and curried shrimp. **FYI:** Reservations not accepted. Blues. Children's menu. **Open:** Peak (Dec–Apr) lunch Tues–Sat noon–5pm; dinner Tues–Thurs 6–11pm, Fri–Sat 6pm–midnight, Sun 6–10:30pm. **Prices:** Main courses $13–$26. AE, DC, DISC, MC, V. ᕫ

### Pacific Time

915 Lincoln Rd (South Beach); tel 305/534-5979. Between Jefferson and Michigan Aves. **Pacific Rim.** Your senses will be dazzled with the flavors of the ocean at this inventive seafood eatery. Fish and chips take on new meaning here—tuna is prepared tartare and served with Idaho potato chips. Some poultry and beef selections are available. **FYI:** Reservations recommended. **Open:** Sun–Thurs 6–11pm, Fri–Sat 6–midnight. **Prices:** Main courses $17–$32; prix fixe $20. AE, DC, MC, V. ♥ ᕫ

### Palace Bar & Grill

1200 Ocean Dr; tel 305/531-9077. **Cafe.** The diner-style menu includes burgers, salads, sandwiches, and steaks. **FYI:** Reservations not accepted. **Open:** Peak (Nov–Apr) Sun–Thurs 8am–2am, Fri–Sat 8am–3am. **Prices:** Main courses $11–$16. AE, MC, V.

### Pineapples

530 Arthur Godfrey Rd; tel 305/532-9731. **New American/Health/Spa.** Plain-looking health food restaurant serving sandwiches and fresh juices as well as meal-size salads, stir-fries, and such dishes as chicken with pineapple sauce, and mahimahi with kiwi sauce. **FYI:** Reservations accepted. Beer and wine only. No smoking. **Open:** Sun–Thurs 11:30am–9pm, Fri 11:30am–2:30am. **Prices:** Main courses $8–$20. AE, DISC, MC, V. 🗹

### ★ South Pointe Seafood House and Brewing Co

1 Washington Ave; tel 305/673-1708. **New American/Seafood.** A casual waterfront restaurant with great views and affordable prices. The county's only microbrewery/pub. **FYI:** Reservations accepted. Children's menu. **Open:** Lunch Mon–Sat 11:30am–3pm; dinner Mon–Thurs 5–11pm, Fri–Sat 5pm–midnight, Sun 5–10pm; brunch Sun 10:30am–2:30pm. **Prices:** Main courses $14–$25. AE, CB, DC, DISC, MC, V. 🏔 🗹 ᕫ

### ★ The Strand

671 Washington Ave (South Beach); tel 305/532-2340. **Regional American/French.** An old standby, with a large, open dining room and candlelit tables. Attracts a lively, fashionable crowd that comes for the boisterous bar scene and the comfort food prepared with a twist. **FYI:** Reservations recommended. **Open:** Sun–Thurs 7pm–midnight, Fri–Sat 7pm–1am. **Prices:** Main courses $13–$23. AE, CB, DC, DISC, MC, V. ♥ 🏔 VP

### Thai Toni

890 Washington Ave (South Beach); tel 305/538-8424. **Thai.** Thai food prepared with a tropical twist is served in an attractive, informal setting at this trendy eatery. **FYI:** Reservations accepted. Beer and wine only. **Open:** Sun–Thurs 5:30–11pm, Fri–Sat 5:30pm–midnight. **Prices:** Main courses $8–$19. AE, MC, V. ⊡ VP ᕫ

### ⑤ Toni's Sushi Bar

1208 Washington Ave; tel 305/673-9368. **Japanese.** Decorated like a traditional Samurai mansion. Specialties include grilled chicken breast with fresh mushroom sauce. Extensive sushi bar. Combination plates available. **FYI:** Reservations accepted. Beer and wine only. **Open:** Sun–Thurs 6pm–midnight, Fri–Sat 6pm–1am. **Prices:** Main courses $10–$18. AE, MC, V. VP ᕫ

### Wolfie's

2038 Collins Ave; tel 305/538-6626. **American/Jewish.** The mauve-and-green decor is pure Miami, but the bagels, cold smoked-fish platters, and overstuffed deli sandwiches are pure New York. The bakery displays an assortment of tempting cakes, pies, and pastries. **FYI:** Reservations not accepted. Children's menu. Beer and wine only. **Open:** Daily 24 hrs. **Prices:** Main courses $7–$16. DISC, MC, V. 🕧 🗹 ᕫ

### ♣ Yuca South Beach

501 Lincoln Rd (South Beach); tel 305/532-YUCA. **Cuban.** This Cuban-style bistro with a distinct Miami twist hearkens back to the heyday of Havana. The "haute Cuban" menu includes entrees like plantain-coated dolphin and grilled marinated pork tenderloin. Sauces are delicate and well-balanced. There's a hip Latin dance club upstairs. **FYI:** Reservations recommended. Dancing. Additional location: 177 Giralda, Coral Gables (tel 444-4448). **Open:** Peak (Dec–Apr) lunch Mon–Sat noon–5pm; dinner Mon–Thurs 5–11pm, Fri–Sat 5pm–midnight, Sun 6–11pm; brunch Sun noon–4pm. **Prices:** Main courses $15–$31. AE, CB, DC, DISC, MC, V. ⌂ 🗹 VP ᕫ

## ATTRACTIONS 🏛

### Lummus Park Beach

Ocean Dr (South Beach). Runs along Ocean Drive from about 6th to 14th St in the art deco district. Popular spot for topless sunbathing. Rest rooms, showers, playgrounds, food concession, lifeguards, boat rentals. **Free**

### Bass Museum of Art

2121 Park Ave (South Beach); tel 305/673-7530. European paintings, sculptures, and tapestries from the Renaissance, baroque, rococo, and modern periods make up the bulk of the small permanent collection. Temporary exhibitions alternate between traveling shows and rotations of the Bass's stock. Built from coral rock in 1930, the museum sits in the middle of six landscaped, tree-topped acres. **Open:** Tues–Sat 10am–5pm, Sun 1–5pm; 2nd and 4th Wed of month 1–9pm. **$$**

## Art Deco District Tours

(South Beach); tel 305/672-2014. The Miami Design Preservation League sponsors tours of Miami Beach's famous art deco district, which encompasses about 800 buildings from the 1920s and 1930s. Many of the buildings were rescued from demolition, renovated and repainted in the bright pastel colors that have become characteristic of the area. The revitalized district now houses numerous shops, hotels, restaurants, and nightclubs. Walking and bicycle tours do not follow a specific route, but take in a number of noteworthy sights. Walking tours (90 minutes) depart Saturday at 10:30am from the Art Deco Welcome Center at 1001 Ocean Dr. Bicycle tours depart Sunday 10:30am from the Cycles on the Beach Shop at 1421 Washington Ave; bikes can be rented. **Open:** Call for schedule. **$$**

## Colony Theater

1040 Lincoln Rd; tel 305/674-1026. Renovated to become the architectural showpiece of the art deco district, this 465-seat theater hosts performances by nationally known theatre, music, dance, comedy, and film events. **Open:** Call for schedule. **$$$$**

## Jackie Gleason Theater of the Performing Arts

1700 Washington Ave (South Beach); tel 305/673-7300. This newly renovated theater, which seats 2,700, provides a venue for big-budget Broadway shows, classical music concerts, opera, and dance performances. **Open:** Call for schedule.

## Kelley Fishing Fleet

Haulover Marina, 10800 Collins Ave; tel 305/945-3801. Half-day, full-day, and night fishing aboard diesel-powered "party boats" reaps fish like snapper, sailfish, and mackerel. Reservations recommended. **Open:** Daily. Call for hours. **$$$$**

## Charter Boat *Helen C*

Haulover Marina, 10800 Collins Ave; tel 305/947-4081. A 55-foot, twin-engine fishing charter equipped for "monster" fish, such as sailfish, tuna, dolphin, and kingfish. Split parties arranged or private charters available. **$$$$**

# Naples

Its 20,000 residents enjoy more than 250 performances yearly amid art and sculpture at the Philharmonic Center. There's also fishing, golfing, museums for automobiles and Collier County history, and the 3,000-strong Teddy Bear Museum. **Information:** Naples Area Chamber of Commerce, 3620 Tamiami Trail N, Naples, 33940 (tel 941/262-6141).

## HOTELS 🏨

### 🏢🏢 Comfort Inn

1221 5th Ave S, 33940; tel 941/649-5800 or toll free 800/382-7941; fax 941/619-0523. Exit 16 off I-75. From Pine Ridge Rd W turn left onto Goodlette Rd and proceed to 5th Ave. A waterfront lodging at an affordable price. Close to area beaches and shopping. **Rooms:** 101 rms. CI 3pm/CO noon. Nonsmoking rms avail. **Amenities:** 🏠 ♨ A/C, cable TV, refrig. Some units w/minibars. **Services:** 🛏 Babysitting. **Facilities:** 🛗 🏊 30 ♿ Washer/dryer. **Rates (CP):** Peak (Dec 21–Apr 21) $129–$149 S or D. Extra person $5. Children under age 18 stay free. Lower rates off-season. Parking: Outdoor, free. AE, CB, DC, DISC, MC, V.

### 🏢🏢 Hampton Inn

3210 Tamiami Trail N, 33940; tel 941/261-8000 or toll free 800/732-4667; fax 941/261-7802. Exit 16 off I-75. Handsome new construction; good, predictable accommodations. **Rooms:** 107 rms and stes. CI 2pm/CO noon. Nonsmoking rms avail. **Amenities:** 🏠 A/C, cable TV w/movies, refrig. **Services:** 📠 🛏 Free local calls. **Facilities:** 🛗 🏊 40 ♿ **Rates (CP):** Peak (Dec–Apr) $99 S; $109 D; $200 ste. Extra person $10. Children under age 18 stay free. Lower rates off-season. Parking: Outdoor, free. AE, CB, DC, DISC, MC, V.

### 🏢🏢🏢 Inn of Naples

4055 Tamiami Trail N, 33940; tel 941/649-5500 or toll free 800/237-8858; fax 941/649-5500. Exit 16 off I-75. A good value for those who don't require a beachfront location. Its architecture, featuring Spanish and Mediterranean accents, lends an appealing look. **Rooms:** 64 rms. CI 3pm/CO noon. Nonsmoking rms avail. **Amenities:** 🏠 ♨ 📷 A/C, cable TV w/movies, refrig, VCR, in-rm safe. All units w/minibars, all w/terraces. **Services:** ✕ 📠 🛏 **Facilities:** 🛗 🏊 25 ♿ 1 restaurant, 1 bar, whirlpool. Guests have access to a nearby golf course and fitness club for a fee. **Rates (CP):** Peak (Jan–Apr) $134–$160 S or D. Extra person $10. Children under age 18 stay free. Lower rates off-season. Parking: Outdoor, free. AE, DC, DISC, MC, V.

### 🏢🏢 Park Shore Resort Hotel

600 Neopolitan Way, 33940; tel 941/263-2222 or toll free 800/548-2077; fax 941/263-0946. 2 blocks W of US 41. Handsome four-story complex. Wicker-furnished lobby has lodge-like atmosphere. **Rooms:** 156 stes. CI 3pm/CO 11am. All units have two baths, tropical-style furniture, and ceiling fans. **Amenities:** 🏠 ♨ 📷 A/C, cable TV, refrig. Some units w/minibars, all w/terraces. **Services:** ✕ 🛏 Children's program, babysitting. **Facilities:** 🛗 🏊 4 ♿ 1 restaurant (lunch and dinner only), 1 bar, lawn games, racquetball, whirlpool, washer/dryer. **Rates:** Peak (Dec–Apr) $189 ste. Extra person $10. Children under age 18 stay free. Lower rates off-season. Parking: Outdoor, free. AE, MC, V.

### 🏢🏢🏢 Port of the Islands Resort & Marina

25000 Tamiami Trail E, ; tel 941/394-3101 or toll free 800/237-4173; fax 941/394-4335. 20 mi S of Naples. Boasts a spacious lobby with Spanish patterns, Mexican tile, potted palms, and a huge fireplace. **Rooms:** 187 rms, stes, and effic. CI 3pm/CO noon. Nonsmoking rms avail. **Amenities:** 🏠 ♨ 📷 A/C, cable TV w/movies. **Services:** ✕ 🛏 **Facilities:** 🛗 🚲 🎣 🏊 4 📷 2 🚤 300 ♿ 2 restaurants, 2 bars (1 w/entertainment), lawn games, playground, washer/dryer. **Rates:** Peak (Dec–

Apr) $95 S or D; $135 ste; $120 effic. Extra person $10. Children under age 16 stay free. Lower rates off-season. Parking: Outdoor, free. AE, DC, DISC, MC, V.

### ≣≣≣ Quality Inn Golf & Country Club
4100 Golden Gate Pkwy, 33999; tel 941/455-1010 or toll free 800/277-0017; fax 941/455-4038. Exit 15 off I-75. A golfing favorite; draws a sedate crowd. **Rooms:** 181 rms, stes, and effic. CI 3pm/CO noon. Nonsmoking rms avail. Cheerful rooms. Some overlook the golf course. **Amenities:** ☎ A/C, cable TV w/movies. Some units w/terraces. **Services:** ⚐ ⌂ **Facilities:** ⌐ ►₁₈ ⚲² ⊑₁₅₀ 1 restaurant, 2 bars (1 w/entertainment), whirlpool. **Rates:** Peak (Jan–Apr) $59–$115 S or D; $99–$179 ste; $79–$139 effic. Extra person $8. Children under age 18 stay free. Lower rates off-season. Parking: Outdoor, free. AE, DC, DISC, MC, V.

### ≣≣ Quality Inn Gulfcoast
2555 Tamiami Trail N, 33940; tel 941/261-6046 or toll free 800/330-0046; fax 941/261-5742. Exit 16 off I-75. An inviting, updated facility with a popular pool bar and Japanese steak house. **Rooms:** 121 rms. CI 2pm/CO noon. Nonsmoking rms avail. **Amenities:** ☎ ⚙ ▣ A/C, cable TV w/movies, in-rm safe. **Services:** ⌂ Babysitting. **Facilities:** ⌐ ⊑₅₀ & 2 restaurants, 2 bars (1 w/entertainment), games rm. Pool bar under a thatched hut attracts locals and guests alike for its jukebox and wide-screen TV. **Rates (CP):** Peak (Jan–Apr) $80–$90 S; $95–$100 D. Extra person $5. Children under age 18 stay free. Lower rates off-season. Parking: Outdoor, free. AE, CB, DC, DISC, ER, JCB, MC, V.

### ≣≣ Vanderbilt Inn on the Gulf
11000 Gulf Shore Dr, 33963; tel 941/597-3157 or toll free 800/643-8654; fax 941/597-3099. Exit 17 off I-75. 5½ mi W of I-75. This classic, constantly updated offering is appealing for its beach locale and informality. **Rooms:** 147 rms and effic. CI 3pm/CO 11am. Nonsmoking rms avail. **Amenities:** ☎ ⚙ A/C, satel TV w/movies, refrig, dataport, in-rm safe. Some units w/terraces. **Services:** ✕ ⌂ Car-rental desk, babysitting. **Facilities:** ⌐ ⊖ ◬ ⊑₄₀ & 2 restaurants, 2 bars (w/entertainment), 1 beach (ocean), volleyball, washer/dryer. **Rates:** Peak (Feb–Apr) $170–$180 S or D; $280 effic. Extra person $10. Children under age 18 stay free. Min stay special events. Lower rates off-season. Parking: Outdoor, free. AE, CB, DC, DISC, MC, V.

## MOTELS

### ≣≣ Best Western Naples Inn
2329 9th Street N, 33940 (Old Naples); tel 941/261-1148 or toll free 800/243-1148; fax 941/262-4684. At US 41 N and Mooringline Dr. Lovely fish pond and grounds offer respite from a busy, central location of this motel. **Rooms:** 80 rms and stes. CI 3pm/CO 11am. Nonsmoking rms avail. Microwaves. **Amenities:** ☎ ⚙ ▣ A/C, cable TV w/movies, refrig, VCR, voice mail, in-rm safe. All units w/terraces. **Services:** ⚐ ⌂ Social director. **Facilities:** ⌐ Washer/dryer. **Rates**

(CP): Peak (Feb–Mar) $159 S or D; $179 ste. Extra person $10. Children under age 18 stay free. Lower rates off-season. Parking: Outdoor, free. AE, CB, DC, DISC, MC, V.

### ≣≣ Cove Inn Resort & Marina
1191 8th St S, 33940; tel 941/262-7161 or toll free 800/255-4365; fax 941/261-6905. Exit 15 off I-75. An older motel with a homey, friendly feel and great views of the marina. Recently refurbished lobby. **Rooms:** 75 rms and effic. CI 3pm/CO 11am. Rooms are individually owned and decorated, most with views of the harbor. **Amenities:** ☎ ⚙ A/C, cable TV, refrig. All units w/terraces. **Services:** ⚐ ⌂ Babysitting. **Facilities:** ⌐ ⊑₁₂ 3 restaurants (see "Restaurants" below), 3 bars, beauty salon, washer/dryer. Full-service marina. **Rates:** Peak (Dec 19–Apr) $108–$120 S or D; $121–$150 effic. Extra person $10. Children under age 16 stay free. Lower rates off-season. Parking: Outdoor, free. AE, DC, DISC, MC, V.

### ≣≣ Holiday Inn
1100 9th St N, 33940 (Old Naples); tel 941/262-7146 or toll free 800/465-4329; fax 941/261-3809. A convenient location and the tropical pool area make this a well-chosen resting spot. **Rooms:** 137 rms. CI 4pm/CO noon. Nonsmoking rms avail. **Amenities:** ☎ ⚙ ▣ A/C, cable TV. **Services:** ✕ ⚐ ⌂ ⚑ Newspapers delivered daily to rooms. **Facilities:** ⌐ & 1 restaurant, 1 bar (w/entertainment), games rm. **Rates:** Peak (Dec 25–Apr) $120–$129 S or D. Extra person $10. Children under age 12 stay free. Min stay special events. Lower rates off-season. Parking: Outdoor, free. AE, DC, DISC, MC, V.

### ≣ Trails End Motel
309 9th St S, 33940; tel 941/262-6336 or toll free 800/247-5307; fax 941/262-3381. 1 mi N of FL 84 on US 41. Very affordable, basic lodging. Walk to nearby shopping district. **Rooms:** 50 rms. CI noon/CO 11am. Nonsmoking rms avail. **Amenities:** ☎ ⚙ A/C, cable TV, refrig. **Services:** ⌂ ⚑ **Facilities:** ⌐ ⊖ & Washer/dryer. **Rates:** Peak (Feb) $80–$94 S or D. Extra person $6. Children under age 16 stay free. Lower rates off-season. Parking: Outdoor, free. AE, DISC, MC, V.

### ≣≣ Wellesley Inn
1555 5th Ave S, 33942; tel 941/793-4646 or toll free 800/444-8888; fax 941/793-5248. 1 mi S on US 41 from FL 84. A stylish and inviting lobby, but rooms are just standard. **Rooms:** 105 rms and stes. CI 1pm/CO 11am. Nonsmoking rms avail. **Amenities:** ☎ ⚙ A/C, cable TV. **Services:** ✕ ⚐ ⌂ ⚑ Babysitting. **Facilities:** ⌐ ⊑₁₅ & **Rates (CP):** Peak (Dec 20–Apr 26) $150 S or D; $150 ste. Children under age 18 stay free. Lower rates off-season. Parking: Outdoor, free. AE, CB, DC, DISC, MC, V.

## RESORTS

### ≣≣≣≣ Edgewater Beach Hotel
1901 Gulf Shore Blvd N, 33940; tel 941/262-6511 or toll free 800/821-0196; fax 941/262-1243. 3½ mi N of down-

town. 4 acres. Quaint resort with gingerbread-trimmed balconies and newly revamped condominiums. A resplendent marble lobby welcomes guests. **Rooms:** 124 effic. CI 3pm/CO noon. Nonsmoking rms avail. Typical decor consists of floral designs, saltillo tile, rattan furnishings, and silk plants. **Amenities:** 🛅 🕭 📠 🍴 A/C, cable TV w/movies, refrig, in-rm safe. All units w/terraces. Minibars available. **Services:** ✕ 🗝 📺 🏖 ↩ Twice-daily maid svce, car-rental desk, social director, masseur, babysitting. **Facilities:** 🏋 🚲 ⛰ 🐟4 ⛵ 🍴 🎱 🏊100 ♿ 2 restaurants, 3 bars (1 w/entertainment), 1 beach (ocean), games rm. Pleasant outdoor cafe with iron chairs, umbrellas, and views of the Gulf. Rooftop restaurant offers more formal dining. **Rates:** Peak (Dec 22–Apr 20) $240–$550 effic. Children under age 18 stay free. Min stay special events. Lower rates off-season. Parking: Outdoor, free. Rates are per unit, maximum occupancy of four for one bedroom, six for two bedroom. AE, CB, DC, DISC, MC, V.

### ☰☰☰ La Playa Beach & Racquet Inn

9891 Gulf Shore Dr, 33963; tel 941/597-3123 or toll free 800/237-6883, 800/237-6883, 800/282-4423 in FL; fax 941/597-6278. Exit 17 off I-75. 6 mi W of I-75. 5 acres. High-class renovations and a newly widened beach make this older resort one of the best in the area. Staff is friendly and attentive. **Rooms:** 174 rms and stes. CI 3pm/CO noon. Nonsmoking rms avail. Recently redone rooms with tropical-print bedspreads and elegant, white-marble baths. **Amenities:** 🛅 🕭 🍴 A/C, cable TV w/movies, refrig, in-rm safe. All units w/terraces. **Services:** 🗝 📺 🏖 ↩ Car-rental desk, children's program, babysitting. **Facilities:** 🏋 ⛰ 🐟4 🍴 🏊500 ♿ 1 restaurant, 1 bar (w/entertainment), 1 beach (ocean). **Rates:** Peak (Dec 16–Apr 7) $195–$345 S or D; $650–$995 ste. Extra person $15. Children under age 19 stay free. Min stay special events. Lower rates off-season. Parking: Indoor/outdoor, $5–$10/day. AE, CB, DC, DISC, EC, MC, V.

### ☰☰☰ Naples Bath & Tennis Club

4995 Airport Rd N, ; tel 941/261-5777 or toll free 800/225-9692; fax 941/649-2072. ½ mi S of Pine Ridge. 23 acres. Expansive grounds and a multitude of tennis courts are good evidence this facility caters to the athletic guest. Security-controlled gate entrance. **Rooms:** 40 effic. CI 3pm/CO 11am. Units are privately owned and decorated. **Amenities:** 🛅 🕭 📠 A/C, cable TV, refrig. All units w/terraces. **Services:** ↩ 🕭 Masseur. **Facilities:** 🏋 🐟28 🎱10 🍴 🏊2000 2 restaurants, 2 bars, squash, spa, sauna, steam rm, whirlpool, washer/dryer. Junior Olympic-sized pool. **Rates:** Peak (Dec 16–Apr 23) $180–$235 effic. Min stay. Lower rates off-season. Parking: Outdoor, free. AE, CB, DC, DISC, MC, V.

### ☰☰☰ Naples Beach Hotel and Golf Club

851 Gulf Shore Blvd N, 33940; tel 941/261-2222 or toll free 800/237-7600; fax 941/237-7600. At S Golf Dr. 135 acres. This Naples classic has a fresh coat of paint and its beach has recently been widened. The expansive lobby still impresses and its restaurants and golf course are still worthy. **Rooms:**

315 rms and effic. Executive level. CI 4pm/CO noon. Nonsmoking rms avail. All rooms have been recently renovated, many in beach cabana decor. **Amenities:** 🛅 🕭 A/C, cable TV w/movies. Some units w/minibars, some w/terraces. **Services:** 📺 🏖 ↩ Social director, children's program, babysitting. **Facilities:** 🏋 🚲 ⛰ ⛳18 🐟4 ⛵ 🏊250 ♿ 3 restaurants, 2 bars (1 w/entertainment), 1 beach (ocean), games rm, beauty salon, day-care ctr. Sundays are pool party day, and twice weekly a big band performs for dinner dances. **Rates:** Peak (Dec 17–Apr 13) $195–$295 S or D; $270–$425 effic. Extra person $15. Children under age 13 stay free. Min stay special events. Lower rates off-season. MAP rates avail. Parking: Outdoor, free. Kids 17 and under stay free with parents (off-season only). AE, CB, DC, DISC, MC, V.

### ☰☰☰☰ The Registry Resort

475 Seagate Dr, 33940 (Pelican Bay); tel 941/597-3232 or toll free 800/247-9810; fax 941/597-3197. Exit 16 off I-75. 25 acres. Contemporary-styled 18-story tower set amongst gardens and a mangrove preserve. Impressive marble-and-crystal lobby. Great for tennis players, beach or spa lovers. **Rooms:** 474 rms and stes. CI 3pm/CO 11am. Nonsmoking rms avail. Spacious rooms, with great views from upper levels. **Amenities:** 🛅 🕭 🍴 A/C, cable TV, CD/tape player, voice mail, in-rm safe, bathrobes. All units w/minibars, all w/terraces, some w/whirlpools. **Services:** 🍽 🗝 📺 🚐 🏖 ↩ Twice-daily maid svce, car-rental desk, social director, masseur, children's program, babysitting. Shuttle tram to beach. **Facilities:** 🏋 🚲 ⛰ 🎾 🐟10 🎱5 🍴 🏊1200 🖥 ♿ 5 restaurants (see "Restaurants" below), 3 bars (2 w/entertainment), 1 beach (ocean), basketball, volleyball, board surfing, games rm, snorkeling, spa, sauna, steam rm, whirlpool, beauty salon. Guaranteed tee times at nearby golf courses. Rental canoes for paddling through mangrove preserve. The elegant Lafite restaurant serves fine local cuisine; there's also an ice cream parlor and snack bar on the beach. **Rates:** Peak (Jan–Apr 15) $295–$385 S or D; $495–$675 ste. Lower rates off-season. AP and MAP rates avail. Parking: Indoor/outdoor, free. Rates are for four people per unit, and vary by floor and view. AE, DC, DISC, MC, V.

### ☰☰☰☰☰ The Ritz-Carlton Naples

280 Vanderbilt Beach Rd, 33963 (Vanderbilt Beach); tel 941/598-3300 or toll free 800/241-3333; fax 941/598-6690. Exit 17 off I-75. 13 acres. A modern version of 1920s splendor. Located right on the edge of seemingly endless white beach, this pink palace is filled with original art, chandeliers, and lofty salons with sumptuous draperies. **Rooms:** 463 rms and stes. Executive level. CI 3pm/CO noon. Nonsmoking rms avail. Spacious and efficient rooms with refined furnishings, refurbished in 1995. **Amenities:** 🛅 🕭 🍴 A/C, cable TV w/movies, in-rm safe, bathrobes. All units w/minibars, all w/terraces. **Services:** 🍽 🗝 📺 🚐 🏖 ↩ Twice-daily maid svce, car-rental desk, masseur, children's program, babysitting. Responsive, attentive service; staff-to-room ratio of two to one. **Facilities:** 🏋 🚲 ⛰ 🎿 🍴 🏊1000 🖥

& 4 restaurants (*see* "Restaurants" below), 6 bars (2 w/entertainment), 1 beach (ocean), games rm, sauna, steam rm, whirlpool, beauty salon. First-rate tennis facility and fitness center/spa. Golf privileges at nearby clubs, with priority tee times. Elegant though expensive dining, offered indoors and out. **Rates:** Peak (Jan–Apr 27) $325–$595 S or D; $850 ste. Extra person $15. Children under age 18 stay free. Min stay special events. Lower rates off-season. Parking: Indoor/outdoor, $12/day. AE, CB, DC, DISC, MC, V.

### ≡≡≡ World Tennis Center & Resort

4800 Airport–Pulling Rd, 33942; tel 941/263-1900 or toll free 800/292-6663, 800/292-6663 in the US, 800/621-6665 in Canada; fax 941/649-7855. Exit 16 off I-75. An all-condo resort for the tennis enthusiast. Extensive grounds and modern facilities. **Rooms:** 148 effic. CI 3pm/CO 11am. **Amenities:** 🛎 🐕 🖵 🍴 A/C, TV. All units w/terraces. **Services:** 🛎 🍴 🐕 Social director, children's program, babysitting. Daily maid service offered for fee. **Facilities:** 🏂 🏊 🎣6 🏖10 🏓 🏌40 & 1 restaurant, 1 bar (w/entertainment), sauna, whirlpool, washer/dryer. **Rates:** Peak (Feb–Apr) $160 effic. Extra person $15. Lower rates off-season. Parking: Outdoor, free. AE, DISC, MC, V.

## RESTAURANTS 🍴

### Backstage Tap & Grill

In Waterside Shops, 5535 Tamiami Trail N; tel 941/598-1300. Exit 16 off I-75 At the corner of US 41 and Seagate Dr. **Burgers/Seafood.** This show-themed restaurant has a jazzy decor featuring stage lighting, director's chairs, and posters from Broadway musicals. Its equally jazzy menu features items like the Backstage Burger. Live classical jazz is featured Thursday, Friday, and Saturday nights. **FYI:** Reservations not accepted. Beer and wine only. **Open:** Mon–Sat 7:30am–midnight, Sun 7:30am–10pm. **Prices:** Main courses $4–$9. AE, DISC, MC, V. 🍽 &

### Bayside

In the Village on Venetian Bay, 4270 Gulfshore Blvd N; tel 941/649-5552. **Mediterranean.** Blue wicker, white columns and walls, lush plants, and water views set the mood at this tropical-style restaurant. The lunch fare includes soups (such as black bean with chorizo), salads, pizza, and sandwiches; dinner will often consist of pastas, oak-grilled meats, and inventive seafood specialties. **FYI:** Reservations recommended. Piano. Children's menu. Dress code. No smoking. **Open:** Daily 11:30am–11pm. **Prices:** Main courses $16–$28. AE, CB, DC, DISC, MC, V. 🏞 VP &

### Chardonnay

2331 Tamiami Trail; tel 941/261-1744. **French.** Enjoy a romantic evening in this glass-enclosed dining room. A favorite dish is the duck pâté studded with pistachio nuts, the chef's special appetizer. **FYI:** Reservations recommended. Dress code. **Open:** Peak (Easter) daily 5:30–10pm. Closed Aug–Labor Day. **Prices:** Main courses $17–$29. AE, DC, MC, V. VP &

### ⭐ Chef's Garden

In Third Street Shopping Plaza, 1300 3rd St S; tel 941/262-5500. At 13th Ave. **New American/Continental.** Mirrored walls, french doors, and wicker furnishings adorn this attractive dining room. The menu focuses on jazzed-up versions of continental classics, such as grilled veal chop filled with prosciutto, fontina, and spinach. Pasta, seafood, and vegetarian dishes round out the menu. **FYI:** Reservations recommended. Piano/singer. Children's menu. Dress code. **Open:** Peak (Nov–Apr) lunch Mon–Sat 11:30am–2:30pm; dinner daily 6–9:30pm. **Prices:** Main courses $18–$29. AE, DC, DISC, MC, V. 🍽 VP &

### Ciao

835 4th Ave S; tel 941/263-3889. Near US 41. **Italian.** Well-known for its wonderful Italian cuisine. Try the linguine with lobster and baby shrimp sautéed in olive oil, spinach, and garlic. **FYI:** Reservations recommended. Beer and wine only. No smoking. **Open:** Daily 5:30–10pm. Closed July–Aug. **Prices:** Main courses $12–$26. AE, CB, DC, DISC, MC, V. &

### Coffee Shop

In the Cove Inn, 1191 8th St S; tel 941/262-7161. At Broad Ave and 9th St. **Coffeehouse.** A traditional coffee shop with the expected decor and menu. Counter service. **FYI:** Reservations not accepted. No liquor license. **Open:** Daily 7am–1:30pm. **Prices:** Lunch main courses $2–$7. No CC. &

### The Dining Room

In The Ritz-Carlton Naples, 280 Vanderbilt Beach Rd (Vanderbilt Beach); tel 941/598-3300. 9 mi N of downtown Naples; exit 17 off I-7 Go west on Vanderbilt Beach Rd. **New American/Mediterranean/Seafood.** Elegant French provincial ambience, with low lighting. Gulf shrimp with garlic and shiitake mushrooms, tournedos of beef Rossini, Madeira sauce, and coconut crème brûlée with key-lime tuile are among the inventive specialties. **FYI:** Reservations recommended. Piano. Children's menu. Jacket required. No smoking. **Open:** Tues–Sun 7–10pm. Closed May–Nov. **Prices:** Main courses $30–$41. AE, CB, DC, DISC, MC, V. 💗 VP &

### The Dock at Crayton Cove

12th Ave S on Naples Bay; tel 941/263-9940. **American.** A surf-and-turf restaurant located at the Naples City Dock. **FYI:** Reservations not accepted. Children's menu. **Open:** Mon–Sat 11am–midnight, Sun 10am–midnight. **Prices:** Main courses $9–$16. AE, MC, V. 🍽 🏞 &

### The English Pub

2408 Linwood Ave; tel 941/774-2408. **British/Pub.** British pub fare is served up in this traditionally styled tavern, decorated with hundreds of labels from beers of yesteryear. The menu includes fish and chips, steak pies, and Yorkshire pudding. A large array of imported beers is available. **FYI:** Reservations not accepted. Karaoke. Children's menu. Beer and wine only. **Open:** Mon–Thurs 11am–midnight, Fri 11am–2am, Sat noon–2am. **Prices:** Main courses $9–$15. AE, CB, DC, DISC, MC, V. 📷 💌

### The Key Wester Fish & Pasta House

In Old Naples Seaport, 1001 10th Ave S; tel 941/649-7770. **Seafood/Pasta.** Enjoy the harbor view from any table in the second-level dining room or first-level bar. The creative Key West–style menu ranges from coconut-fried shrimp to meat ravioli and Cuban pork. A light menu is served between meals. Sunday champagne jazz brunch. **FYI:** Reservations recommended. Jazz/piano. **Open:** Sun–Thurs 11am–10pm, Fri–Sat 11am–11pm. **Prices:** Main courses $13–$20. AE, CB, DC, DISC, MC, V. 🚢 🖼 💟 VP ♿

### ♣ Lafite

In The Registry Resort, 475 Seagate Dr; tel 941/597-3232. **New American/Continental.** Feast on Dover sole or rack of lamb in one of several beautifully decorated dining rooms. If you're feeling extravagant, you can sample 50-year-old cognac for $100 per glass. A harpist entertains diners on the weekends. **FYI:** Reservations recommended. Jacket required. No smoking. **Open:** Peak (Nov–Apr) daily 6–10pm. **Prices:** Main courses $26–$35; prix fixe $37. AE, DC, DISC, MC, V. 💟 VP ♿

### L & N Seafood Grill

In Gateway of Naples, 2184 Tamiami Trail N; tel 941/649-1141. Golden Gate Pkwy at Tamiami Trail. **Seafood.** A casual, three-tiered restaurant with ceiling fans, nautical overtones, and great river views. The grilled catch of the day might be tuna, salmon, grouper, or halibut. **FYI:** Reservations not accepted. Children's menu. **Open:** Sun–Thurs 11:30am–10pm, Fri–Sat 11:30am–11pm. **Prices:** Main courses $5–$24. AE, CB, DC, DISC, MC, V. 🖼 💟 ♿

### L'Auberge

602 5th Ave S; tel 941/261-8148. **French.** The sidewalk seating at this simple French cafe in the shopping district offers great opportunities for people watching. Most local diners come casual for lunch, slightly more dressy for dinner. The menu includes a variety of classic chicken, veal, and lamb dishes. **FYI:** Reservations recommended. Dress code. Beer and wine only. No smoking. **Open:** Lunch daily 11am–2pm; dinner daily 5:30–9pm. **Prices:** Main courses $18–$23. AE, MC, V. 🚢 💟

### Margaux's Restaurant

3080 Tamiami Trail N; tel 941/434-2773. **Country French.** Floral prints abound in this romantic dining room, which features a country-French menu and rich desserts. **FYI:** Reservations accepted. Children's menu. Beer and wine only. **Open:** Lunch Mon–Fri 11:30am–2pm; dinner daily 5:30–9pm. **Prices:** Main courses $13–$19. AE, MC, V. 💟 ♿

### Merriman's Wharf

In Old Marine Marketplace at Tin City, 1200 5th Ave S; tel 941/261-1811. At jct US 41 and Goodlett Road. **New American/Seafood/Steak.** Enjoy the friendly nautical atmosphere and views of the river while you dine. A variety of seafood is available, but the specialty here is prime rib. **FYI:** Reservations not accepted. Children's menu. **Open:** Mon–Sat 11am–10pm, Sun noon–10pm. **Prices:** Main courses $17–$35. AE, DC, DISC, MC, V. 🖼 ♿

### Michelbob's

371 Airport Rd; tel 941/843-RIBS. Opposite Naples Airport. **Barbecue.** The eating is hearty and the setting casual. Unfinished wood and early Coca-Cola advertisements decorate the room. Nationally celebrated for the quality of its ribs and other barbecued meats. **FYI:** Reservations not accepted. Guitar/singer. Children's menu. No smoking. **Open:** Fri–Sat 11am–10pm, Sun 8:30am–9pm, Mon–Thurs 11am–9pm. **Prices:** Main courses $8–$19. AE, DC, MC, V. 💟 ♿

### Old Naples Pub

In Robinson Court, 255 13th Ave S; tel 941/649-8200. **Burgers/Pub.** Dining tables surround the central bar at this tavern-style restaurant. Outdoor seating is under cover. Popular dishes include caesar salad with chicken. Live jazz is performed on Sunday; during the week, you can enjoy board games or darts. **FYI:** Reservations not accepted. Beer and wine only. **Open:** Daily 11am–midnight. **Prices:** Main courses $5–$9. AE, DC, DISC, MC, V. 🚢 ♿

### Peppino's Cafe

In Naples Plaza, 2041 9th St N; tel 941/263-4191. **Italian.** Old-world Italian-style eatery, with pictures of stars and the proprietor's family and friends adorning the walls. Standard Italian fare. **FYI:** Reservations not accepted. Beer and wine only. **Open:** Mon–Fri 11am–10pm, Sat–Sun 4–10pm. **Prices:** Main courses $9–$18. AE, CB, DC, DISC, MC, V.

### Plum's Cafe

8920 Tamiami Trail N; tel 941/597-8119. Exit 16 off I-75, W on Pine Ridge Rd. **Cafe/Italian.** Sandwiches, salads, and other light fare are prepared in an open kitchen. **FYI:** Reservations not accepted. Children's menu. **Open:** Peak (Oct–Apr) Mon–Sat 11:30am–10pm, Sun 5–10pm. **Prices:** Main courses $9–$17. AE, DC, DISC, MC, V. 💟 VP ♿

### St George and the Dragon

936 5th Ave; tel 941/262-6546. **Seafood/Steak.** Ships' lanterns provide dim lighting by which to enjoy the famous conch chowder, succulent prime rib, juicy steaks, and grilled catch of the day. The lunch menu offers soups, salads, burgers, and smaller portions of the dinner selections. **FYI:** Reservations not accepted. Jacket required. **Open:** Peak (Jan–Mar) Mon–Sat 11am–10pm, Sun 5–9pm. **Prices:** Main courses $11–$30. AE, DC, MC, V. VP ♿

### ♣ Sign of the Vine

980 Solana Rd; tel 941/261-6745. 1 mi S of Seagate Dr. **Eclectic.** The romantic ambience of this former private home, with vines wrapped in white lights and a porch furnished with white wicker, will become apparent even before you enter its doors. Seasonally changing menu features the likes of duck, pasta, and salmon. **FYI:** Reservations

recommended. Dress code. Beer and wine only. **Open:** Peak (Nov–June) Mon–Sat 6–10pm. **Prices:** Main courses $28–$49. AE. ⬤ 🔳 ♿

### Silver Spoon Cafe
In Waterside Shops at Pelican Bay, 5375 Tamiami Trail N Ste 210; tel 941/591-2123. **New American/Italian.** Clean cafe-style restaurant, decorated in a contemporary black-and-white scheme, looking out at the mall and its small waterfall. Sandwiches, salads, grilled fish of the day, chicken pot pie, delightful desserts. **FYI:** Reservations accepted. Children's menu. **Open:** Sun–Thurs 11am–10pm, Fri–Sat 11am–11pm. **Prices:** Main courses $7–$14. AE, DISC, MC, V. ◲♿

### Villa Pescatore
8920 Tamiami Trail N; tel 941/597-8119. Exit 16 off I-75. **Italian/Seafood.** Enjoy pasta and fish dishes amid floral prints and wicker furniture. Soft music and lighting help to create a relaxed atmosphere. **FYI:** Reservations recommended. Children's menu. Dress code. **Open:** Peak (Sept–May) daily 6–10pm. **Prices:** Main courses $18–$25. AE, DC, DISC, MC, V. ⬤ 🆅🅿 ♿

### The Whistle Stop Steakhouse
In Waterloo Station, 200 Goodlette Rd S; tel 941/263-8440. **Seafood/Steak.** Railroad memorabilia and wall murals recall the site's previous life. The popular lunch salad bar is presented in an old train car, and you can board a vintage caboose out back. **FYI:** Reservations not accepted. Piano. Children's menu. Dress code. **Open:** Mon–Sat 11am–midnight. **Prices:** Main courses $12–$17. AE, DC, DISC, MC, V. ◲♿

## ATTRACTIONS 🏛

### Jungle Larry's Zoological Park at Caribbean Gardens
1590 Goodlette Rd; tel 941/262-5409. Acres of lush vegetation and lakes provide a natural home for a collection of endangered species from around the world. Visitors can take guided boat tours and natural walking trails through the park. Wild animal shows, petting zoo, and playground. Concessions, gift shop. **Open:** Daily 9:30am–5:30pm. $$$$

### Collier County Museum
3301 Tamiami Trail E; tel 941/774-8476. Permanent exhibits trace the last 10,000 years in the history of Florida's last frontier. The five-acre historical park includes native Florida gardens, restored buildings, an archeological lab, swamp buggy, and steam logging locomotive. Special events include the two-day Old Florida Festival, held each November. **Open:** Mon–Fri 9am–5pm. **Free**

### Conservancy Nature Center
14th Ave N; tel 941/262-0304. Located off Goodlette-Frank Rd, the center features the Natural Science Museum, with serpentarium, sea turtle tank, and daily presentations; an aviary with bald eagles and other birds; a wildlife rehabilitation center; 45-minute guided boat tours through a man-

grove swamp; and nature trails. **Open:** Peak (Jan–Mar) Mon–Fri 9am–4:30pm, Sat 9am–4:30pm, Sun 1–5pm. Reduced hours off-season. $

### Briggs Nature Center
401 Shell Island Rd; tel 941/775-8569. Situated within the Rookery Bay National Estuarine Research Reserve just south of Naples. Visitors can observe a great variety of birds and other wildlife in their natural habitat along the half-mile boardwalk. Arrangements can be made for canoe and boat tours. Hours vary, call ahead. **Open:** Peak (Jan–Mar) Mon–Sat 9–4:30pm, Sun 1–5pm. Reduced hours off-season. $$$$

### Teddy Bear Museum
2511 Pine Ridge Rd; tel 941/598-2711. Some 2,000 teddy bears from around the world are imaginatively and humorously displayed. There is a collection of antique stuffed bears as well. Adjoining gift shop. **Open:** Peak (Dec–Apr) Mon 10am–5pm, Wed–Sat 10am–5pm, Sun 1–5pm. Reduced hours off-season. $$$

### Collier-Seminole State Park
20200 Tamiami Trail E; tel 941/394-3397. Many species of birds inhabit these 6,000 acres adjoining the Big Cypress Swamp. A concession boat tour is offered along the Blackwater River, and there's a primitive campsite for those who would rather canoe it themselves. Swimming, fishing, boating, canoe rentals, hiking, and nature trails also available. **Open:** Daily 8am–sunset. $$

### Corkscrew Swamp Sanctuary
375 Sanctuary Rd; tel 941/657-3771. Located 20 mi NE of Naples off County Rd 846. This natural preserve is maintained by the National Audubon Society and contains the largest ancient bald cypress forests in the United States. A two-mile-long boardwalk winds through the forest, marshes, and pine flatwoods. Alligators, wood storks, otters, wading birds, and wild orchids are all found on the sanctuary grounds. **Open:** Peak (Dec–Apr) daily 7am–5pm. Reduced hours off-season. $$$

# New Smyrna Beach
Midway down Florida's Atlantic coast with about 17,500 residents, this community is where Orlando goes to swim. Greek, Italian, and Minorcan immigrants built this town in the late 1700s. **Information:** Southeast Volusia Chamber of Commerce, 115 Canal St, New Smyrna Beach, 32168 (tel 904/428-2449).

## HOTELS 🏨

### 🔳🔳 Islander Beach Resort
1601 S Atlantic Ave, 32169; tel 904/427-3452; fax 904/426-5606. Exit 56 off I-4. This seven-story time-share facility situated on the beach features self-contained accommodations ranging from studios to one- and two-bedroom units. **Rooms:** 114 effic. CI 4pm/CO 10am. **Amenities:** 🔳 🕐 🔳

A/C, cable TV, refrig, VCR. Some units w/terraces. **Services:** Car-rental desk, social director, children's program, babysitting. **Facilities:** 1 restaurant (lunch and dinner only), 1 bar (w/entertainment), 1 beach (ocean), lifeguard, games rm, whirlpool, washer/dryer. Discounts available at nearby golf course. **Rates:** Peak (Dec–Apr/June–Aug) $70–$120 effic. Children under age 18 stay free. Min stay. Lower rates off-season. Parking: Outdoor, free. AE, DISC, MC, V.

### Riverview Hotel

103 Flagler Ave, 32169; tel 904/428-5858 or toll free 800/945-7416; fax 904/423-8927. Nicely furnished lodge on the Indian River; a popular rendezvous for the boating crowd, who moor at the dock to dine in the restaurant. **Rooms:** 18 rms and stes. CI 2pm/CO noon. Nonsmoking rms avail. **Amenities:** A/C, cable TV. All units w/terraces. **Services:** Babysitting. **Facilities:** 1 restaurant (lunch and dinner only), 1 bar (w/entertainment), washer/dryer. **Rates (CP):** $80 S; $80–$125 D; $150 ste. Extra person $10. Children under age 6 stay free. Min stay special events. Parking: Outdoor, free. AE, DC, DISC, MC, V.

## MOTEL

### Coastal Waters Inn

3509 S Atlantic Ave, 32169; tel 904/428-3800 or toll free 800/321-7882; fax 904/423-5002. Exit 56 off I-4. A pleasant facility on the beach, with both standard motel rooms and units with kitchens. **Rooms:** 40 rms and effic. CI 3pm/CO 11am. There are three rooms considered oceanfront. **Amenities:** A/C, cable TV, refrig. Some units w/terraces. **Services:** **Facilities:** 1 beach (ocean). **Rates:** Peak (Dec–Sept) $49–$99 S or D; $79–$169 effic. Extra person $7.50. Children under age 12 stay free. Lower rates off-season. Parking: Outdoor, free. MC, V.

## RESTAURANTS

### ★ JB's Fish Camp

859 Pompano Ave; tel 904/427-5747. 5 mi S of New Smyrna Beach; exit 56 off I-4. **Regional American/Seafood.** This waterside restaurant offers a New Zealand scallops, fresh flounder, and lobster tails. Live band with vocalist entertains diners. **FYI:** Reservations not accepted. **Open:** Mon–Fri 11:30am–9pm, Sat–Sun 11:30am–10:30pm. **Prices:** Main courses $6–$18. AE, CB, MC, V.

### ♣ Riverview Charlie's

101 Flagler Ave; tel 904/428-1865. New Smyrna exit off I-95. **American/Seafood.** A waterside restaurant with a traditional menu offering fresh seafood dishes, freshly made pasta, and black Angus beef. You can sit on the patio and watch the sun set as you dine. **FYI:** Reservations accepted. Big band. Children's menu. **Open:** Sun–Thurs 11:30am–10pm Fri–Sat 11:30am–11pm. **Prices:** Main courses $12–$23. AE, DISC, MC, V.

# Niceville

Eglin Air Force Base surrounds this western Panhandle town of 11,000, which averages less rain each year than any other place in Florida. Choctawhatchee Bay yields tons of mullet for autumn's annual Boggy Bayou Mullet Festival. **Information:** Niceville–Valparaiso Bay Area Chamber of Commerce, 170 N John Sims Pkwy, 32580 (tel 904/678-2323).

## RESORT

### Bluewater Bay Resort

1950 Bluewater Blvd, 32578; tel 904/897-3613 or toll free 800/874-2128; fax 904/897-2424. 2,000 acres. Individually-owned one-, two-, and three-bedroom condo units, efficiencies, and studios, with views of either the fairways or the bay. Daily and weekly rental units are interspersed with year-round residential neighborhoods. **Rooms:** 100 rms, stes, and effic. Executive level. CI 3pm/CO 11am. Nonsmoking rms avail. **Amenities:** A/C, cable TV, refrig, dataport, voice mail. Some units w/terraces, some w/fireplaces. Since the condos have individual owners, some of them have "little extras" like full stereo systems, VCRs, fireplaces, and whirlpool tubs. **Services:** Social director, children's program, babysitting. **Facilities:** 36 7 12 150 1 restaurant, 1 bar (w/entertainment), 1 beach (bay), volleyball, lawn games, racquetball, snorkeling, playground, washer/dryer. Biking and hiking trails; 120-slip deep-water marina, picnic area. Unfortunately, there are no trolleys to shuttle guests around. **Rates:** Peak (Mar–May/Oct) $65–$120 S or D; $120–$215 ste; $90–$205 effic. Children under age 18 stay free. Min stay wknds and special events. Lower rates off-season. AP rates avail. Parking: Outdoor, free. Golf, tennis, and family packages avail. AE, CB, DC, DISC, MC, V.

## ATTRACTION

### Rocky Bayou State Recreation Area

Tel 904/833-2144. Located north of Destin, this park encompasses over 350 acres for swimming, fishing, boating, camping, and picnicking. **Open:** Daily 8am–dusk. $

# North Miami

## RESORT

### Turnberry Isle Resort & Club

19999 W Country Club Dr, 33180; tel 305/932-6200 or toll free 800/327-7028; fax 305/933-6554. Exit 20 off I-95. 300 acres. A three-part resort consisting of the Country Club, surrounded by two golf courses and featuring new seven-story wing and a Mediterranean-style courtyard; the Yacht Club and Marina, located beside the Intracoastal Waterway, with a circular five-story hotel; and the Beach Club, situated on the Atlantic Ocean. **Rooms:** 340 rms and stes. CI 4pm/

CO noon. Nonsmoking rms avail. Country Club rooms have clay tile floors, small balconies, and ceiling fans, for a cool, elegant Mediterranean flavor; they are convenient for golfers and tennis players. Yacht Club rooms, recently upgraded, have a no-nonsense 1960s ambience with a few contemporary touches and are popular with celebrities seeking seclusion and anonymity. **Amenities:** 🛎🕹🍸A/C, cable TV w/movies, dataport, VCR, voice mail, in-rm safe, bathrobes. All units w/minibars, all w/terraces, some w/whirlpools. Country Club rooms have bath slippers and umbrella in closet, small TV in bathroom. Cellular phones can be rented. **Services:** 🍽🔑 📺 📪 🛗 Twice-daily maid svce, car-rental desk, social director, masseur, children's program, babysitting. Free shuttle between hotels and Beach Club and mall. **Facilities:** 🏊🚲 ⚠🗻▶36 🎿 🖥24 🍺🛎🔢 🖥 ♿ 5 restaurants, 6 bars (2 w/entertainment), 1 beach (ocean), lifeguard, basketball, board surfing, racquetball, snorkeling, spa, sauna, steam rm, whirlpool, beauty salon, washer/dryer. Helipad on property. Cabanas at Beach Club, beverage service on beach. Tennis courts supervised by Fred Stolle; two golf courses designed by Robert Trent Jones. Marina for 110 boats up to 200 feet in length. Spa at Yacht Club includes healthy and relaxing treatments such as shiatsu and Dead Sea mud packs. **Rates:** Peak (Dec 22–Apr) $295–$405 S or D; $475–$2,100 ste. Extra person $30. Children under age 18 stay free. Min stay special events. Lower rates off-season. Parking: Outdoor, free. AE, CB, DC, DISC, EC, ER, MC, V.

## RESTAURANTS 🍴

### ♥★ Mark's Place
2286 NE 123rd St; tel 305/893-6888. At Bay Shore Ave. **New American.** A bright, stylish, trendy restaurant with an open kitchen. The innovative daily menu is prepared from local fresh fish and produce. **FYI:** Reservations recommended. **Open:** Sun–Thurs 6–10pm, Fri–Sat 6–11pm. **Prices:** Main courses $17–$32. AE, DC, MC, V. 📺♿

### Outback Steakhouse
3161 NE 163rd St; tel 305/944-4329. Between Biscayne Blvd and Intracoastal Waterway. **Steak.** A casual, Australian-themed steak house with whirling ceiling fans, serving chicken, ribs, and steaks. **FYI:** Reservations not accepted. Children's menu. **Open:** Mon–Thurs 4–10:30pm, Fri 4–11:30pm, Sat 3:30–11:30pm, Sun 3–10:30pm. **Prices:** Main courses $8–$18. AE, DC, DISC, MC, V. ♿

### Roadhouse Grill
12599 Biscayne Blvd; tel 305/893-7433. At NE 126th St. **Steak.** A bucket of peanuts awaits you when you arrive at your table in this neon-lit establishment. Steaks, ribs, chicken, salads. A butcher shop is on the premises. **FYI:** Reservations not accepted. Children's menu. **Open:** Daily 11am–11pm. **Prices:** Main courses $10–$18. AE, CB, DISC, MC, V. ♿

# Ocala
See also Silver Springs

Florida's only quarter-horse wagering track is located in this central Florida city situated amid rolling hills and thoroughbred farms. Once an Indian trading post, it was the flash point for the second Seminole War (1835–1842). **Information:** Ocala–Marion County Chamber of Commerce, 110 E Silver Springs Blvd, PO Box 1210, Ocala, 34478 (tel 352/629-8051).

## HOTELS 🏨

### 🏁🏁 Holiday Inn West
3621 W Silver Springs Blvd, PO Box 3308, 32678; tel 352/629-0381 or toll free 800/HOLIDAY; fax 352/629-0381 ext 51. Exit 69 off FL 40. This modern hotel caters to business travelers and large groups and has good resources for staging business meetings and conventions. **Rooms:** 270 rms and stes. CI 2pm/CO noon. Nonsmoking rms avail. **Amenities:** 🛎 A/C, cable TV w/movies. **Services:** ✕🚐📺📪🛗 **Facilities:** 🏊🔢450 ♿ 1 restaurant, 1 bar (w/entertainment), washer/dryer. **Rates:** Peak (Jan–Apr) $55 S or D; $99 ste. Children under age 18 stay free. Lower rates off-season. Parking: Outdoor, free. AARP discounts available. AE, DC, DISC, MC, V.

### 🏁🏁🏁 Ocala–Silver Springs Hilton
3600 SW 36th Ave, 34474; tel 352/854-1400 or toll free 800/445-8667; fax 352/854-4010. Exit 68 off I-75. The premier hotel in Ocala. Marble floors, potted palms, and chandeliers grace the lobby. **Rooms:** 198 rms and stes. CI 3pm/CO 11am. Nonsmoking rms avail. **Amenities:** 🛎🕹📺 A/C, cable TV w/movies. Some units w/terraces. **Services:** ✕📺📪 Babysitting. **Facilities:** 🏊🛎🔢300 ♿ 1 restaurant, 1 bar, whirlpool. The lobby lounge with baby grand piano is a great place for an evening cocktail; there's an English-style pub, too. **Rates:** Peak (Jan–Mar 15) $99–$119 S or D; $150–$295 ste. Children under age 18 stay free. Min stay special events. Lower rates off-season. Parking: Outdoor, free. AE, CB, DC, DISC, MC, V.

### 🏁🏁 Ramada Inn Steinbrenner's
3810 NW Blitchton Rd, 32675; tel 352/732-3131 or toll free 800/2-RAMADA; fax 352/732-5692. At US 27 and I-75. Colonial-inspired design, smart layout, and lush landscaping. This moderately priced establishment offers a relaxed ambience for both businesspeople and vacationers. **Rooms:** 124 rms. CI 2pm/CO noon. Nonsmoking rms avail. **Amenities:** 🛎🕹 A/C, cable TV. **Services:** ✕📺📪🛗 Babysitting. **Facilities:** 🏊🛎🔢800 1 restaurant, 1 bar (w/entertainment), whirlpool, playground, washer/dryer. **Rates:** Peak (Jan–April) $65 S or D. Extra person $10. Children under age 18 stay free. Lower rates off-season. Parking: Outdoor, free. AE, CB, DC, DISC, MC, V.

## MOTELS

### ⫤⫤ Days Inn
3811 NW Blitchton Rd, 34482; tel 352/629-7041 or toll free 800/325-2525; fax 352/629-1026. Exit 70 (US 27) off I-75. A clean, no-frills motel offering good value and convenient interstate access. **Rooms:** 64 rms and stes. CI 3pm/CO noon. Nonsmoking rms avail. **Amenities:** 🛏 A/C, cable TV w/movies. Some units w/terraces, 1 w/whirlpool. Suites have microwaves and refrigerators. **Services:** ⊃ ⫩ Free coffee in lobby 24 hours. **Facilities:** ⟦⟧ ⟦40⟧ ⟐ Lawn games, playground, washer/dryer. **Rates (CP):** Peak (Jan–Mar/Christmas) $50–$55 S or D; $65–$75 ste. Extra person $5. Children under age 17 stay free. Lower rates off-season. Parking: Outdoor, free. AE, CB, DC, DISC, MC, V.

### ⫤⫤ Days Inn Ocala
3620 W Silver Springs Blvd, 32674; tel 352/629-0091 or toll free 800/333-3333; fax 352/867-8399. Exit 69 off I-75. Two buildings flank a handsome registration area with soaring ceiling and knotted pine accents. Friendly, accommodating staff. **Rooms:** 100 rms and stes. CI 2pm/CO 11am. Nonsmoking rms avail. **Amenities:** 🛏 A/C, cable TV. Some units w/terraces. **Services:** ⊃ ⫩ **Facilities:** ⟦⟧ ⟦135⟧ ⟐ 1 restaurant, 1 bar (w/entertainment), washer/dryer. **Rates:** $49–$55 S or D; $99 ste. Children under age 18 stay free. Parking: Outdoor, free. AE, CB, DC, DISC, MC, V.

### ⫤⫤ Quality Inn
3767 NW Blitchton Rd, 32675; tel 352/732-2300 or toll free 800/221-2222; fax 352/351-0153. Exit 70 off I-75. An older but adequately maintained two-story property, handy to the highway. **Rooms:** 120 rms. CI 1pm/CO 11am. Nonsmoking rms avail. **Amenities:** 🛏 A/C, cable TV. **Services:** ✕ ⊃ ⫩ **Facilities:** ⟦⟧ ⟦76⟧ ⟐ 1 restaurant (bkfst and dinner only), 1 bar (w/entertainment), washer/dryer. **Rates:** Peak (mid-Dec–Apr) $35–$55 S or D. Lower rates off-season. Parking: Outdoor, free. AE, CB, DC, DISC, EC, ER, JCB, MC, V.

## RESTAURANT 🍽

### Bella Luna Cafe
3425 SW College Rd; tel 352/237-9155. Exit 68 off I-75. **Italian.** Specialties include brick-oven pizza, snapper with artichoke hearts and wild mushrooms, and calamari fra diavolo. Excellent homemade desserts, including low-fat selections. **FYI:** Reservations accepted. Children's menu. **Open:** Lunch Mon–Sat 11am–2:30pm, Sun 11am–4pm; dinner daily 4–10pm. **Prices:** Main courses $11–$16. AE, DISC, MC, V. ⟐

# Orlando

For Walt Disney World, see Lake Buena Vista. See also Altamonte Springs, Davenport, Haines City, Kissimmee, Maitland, Sanford, Winter Park

Since Walt Disney World was announced in 1966, the former Fort Gatlin has metamorphosed from a sleepy citrus-and-cattle backwater to a tourist mecca of 173,000 permanent residents. Downtown's Church Street Station is a carnival of restaurants. Also home to Sea World, Gatorland, and the NBA's Orlando Magic. **Information:** Orlando–Orange County Convention & Visitors Bureau, 7208 Sand Lake Rd #300, Orlando, 32819 (tel 407/363-5800).

## PUBLIC TRANSPORTATION

**Mears Transportation Group** operates buses from most major Orlando-area hotels to Cypress Gardens, Kennedy Space Center, Universal Studios, Sea World, and Church Street Station. Call 407/423-5566 for more information.

## HOTELS 🏨

### ⫤⫤ Best Western Plaza International
8738 International Dr, 32819; tel 407/395-8195 or toll free 800/654-7160; fax 407/352-8196. Exit 29 off I-4. Popular for its reasonable rates and wide variety of accommodations. **Rooms:** 672 rms, stes, and effic. CI 4pm/CO 11am. Nonsmoking rms avail. **Amenities:** 🛏 ⟐ A/C, cable TV, VCR, in-rm safe. Some units w/whirlpools. **Services:** ✕ ▭ �car ▱ Car-rental desk, babysitting. **Facilities:** ⟦⟧ ⟐ 1 bar, games rm, whirlpool, washer/dryer. Spacious deck with lounge chairs. **Rates:** Peak (Feb–Apr/June–Aug) $65–$85 S or D; $85–$105 ste; $75–$90 effic. Children under age 18 stay free. Lower rates off-season. Parking: Outdoor, free. AE, CB, DC, DISC, MC, V.

### ⫤⫤⫤ Clarion Plaza Hotel
9700 International Dr, 32819; tel 407/352-9700 or toll free 800/363-9700; fax 407/351-9111. Exit 29 off I-4. A large and bustling hotel next to the Orlando Convention Center. Popular with groups. **Rooms:** 810 rms and stes. CI 3pm/CO noon. Nonsmoking rms avail. Decor has some warm touches, such as bordered ceilings and bed ruffles. **Amenities:** 🛏 ⟐ A/C, cable TV w/movies, in-rm safe. **Services:** ✕ ▭ ⟦VP⟧ 🚗 ▱ ⊃ Car-rental desk, masseur, children's program, babysitting. **Facilities:** ⟦⟧ ⟦3000⟧ 💻 ⟐ 3 restaurants, 2 bars (1 w/entertainment), games rm, whirlpool, washer/dryer. Deli. **Rates:** Peak (Jan–Mar/June–Oct) $135–$155 S or D; $310–$680 ste. Children under age 18 stay free. Lower rates off-season. MAP rates avail. Parking: Outdoor, free. AE, CB, DC, DISC, JCB, MC, V.

### ⫤⫤ Courtyard by Marriott International Drive
8600 Austrian Court, 32819; tel 407/351-3306 or toll free 800/321-2211; fax 407/351-1933. Exit 29 off I-4. Located in a secluded complex of hotels and restaurants off International Drive, the Courtyard occupies a tan stucco four-story building with a green tile roof. Out front are lush tropical

plantings; the expertly landscaped courtyard features a gazebo. **Rooms:** 151 rms and stes. CI 4pm/CO 1pm. Nonsmoking rms avail. Tasteful accommodations furnished with mahogany pieces. **Amenities:** A/C, cable TV w/movies. Some units w/terraces. **Services:** **Facilities:** [35] Games rm, whirlpool, washer/dryer. **Rates:** Peak (Jan–Apr) $99–$109 S or D; $139–$149 ste. Extra person $10. Children under age 18 stay free. Lower rates off-season. Parking: Outdoor, free. AE, CB, DC, DISC, MC, V.

### Courtyard by Marriott Orlando Airport
7155 N Frontage Rd, 32812; tel 407/240-7200 or toll free 800/321-2211; fax 407/240-8962. Chosen by many businesspeople for its proximity to the airport. **Rooms:** 149 rms and stes. CI 3pm/CO noon. Nonsmoking rms avail. **Amenities:** A/C, cable TV w/movies. Some units w/terraces. **Services:** Car-rental desk, babysitting. **Facilities:** [50] 1 restaurant (bkfst only), 1 bar, whirlpool, washer/dryer. Guests can receive passes for Bally's Fitness Center and can use the tennis courts and pool at the Orlando Airport Marriott. **Rates:** Peak (Jan–Apr) $99–$109 S; $109–$119 D; $129–$137 ste. Extra person $10. Children under age 18 stay free. Lower rates off-season. AP and MAP rates avail. Parking: Outdoor, free. AE, DC, DISC, MC, V.

### Days Inn Convention Center–Seaworld
9990 International Dr, 32819; tel 407/352-8700 or toll free 800/224-5055; fax 407/363-3965. Exit 28 off I-4. **Rooms:** 223 rms. CI 4pm/CO noon. Nonsmoking rms avail. **Amenities:** A/C, cable TV w/movies, in-rm safe. **Services:** Babysitting. **Facilities:** [12] Playground, washer/dryer. **Rates:** Peak (Feb–Apr/June–Aug/Dec) $59–$84 S; $69–$94 D. Extra person $6. Children under age 18 stay free. Lower rates off-season. Parking: Outdoor, free. AE, CB, DC, DISC, ER, JCB, MC, V.

### Days Inn International Drive
7200 International Dr, 32819; tel 407/351-1200 or toll free 800/224-5057; fax 407/363-1182. Exit 29 off I-4. Standard operation with rates a bit high for what is offered. **Rooms:** 245 rms. CI 3pm/CO noon. Nonsmoking rms avail. **Amenities:** A/C, cable TV w/movies. **Services:** Car-rental desk, babysitting. **Facilities:** [50] 1 restaurant (bkfst only), games rm, playground, washer/dryer. **Rates:** Peak (July–Aug/Dec 20–Feb) $74–$84 S or D. Children under age 18 stay free. Lower rates off-season. Parking: Outdoor, free. AE, CB, DC, DISC, MC, V.

### Delta Orlando Resort
5715 Major Blvd, 32819; tel 407/351-3340 or toll free 800/634-4763; fax 407/351-5117. A long-established facility offering an array of diversions for guests. **Rooms:** 800 rms and stes. CI 4pm/CO 11am. Nonsmoking rms avail. **Amenities:** A/C, cable TV w/movies, in-rm safe. All units w/terraces. Some rooms with coffeemakers. Refrigerators available on request. **Services:** Car-rental desk, children's program, babysitting. **Facilities:** [800] 3

restaurants, 3 bars (1 w/entertainment), games rm, sauna, whirlpool, playground, washer/dryer. **Rates:** Peak (Feb–Mar) $118–$158 S or D; $109–$250 ste. Children under age 18 stay free. Lower rates off-season. Parking: Outdoor, free. AE, CB, DC, DISC, MC, V.

### DoubleTree Guest Suites Orlando Airport
7550 Augusta National Dr, 32822; tel 407/240-5555 or toll free 800/424-2900; fax 407/240-1300. Airport exit off FL 528. A fine alternative to Lake Buena Vista hotels when those are all booked by Disney-bound vacationers. Joggers can often be seen circling the attractive pond in front of the hotel. **Rooms:** 150 stes. CI 3pm/CO 11am. Nonsmoking rms avail. Breezily decorated two-room suites. **Amenities:** A/C, cable TV w/movies, refrig, dataport, voice mail. All units w/minibars, some w/terraces. **Services:** Babysitting. **Facilities:** [75] 1 restaurant, 1 bar, games rm, whirlpool, washer/dryer. **Rates:** Peak (Jan–Apr/June–Sept 15/Dec) $149 ste. Children under age 18 stay free. Lower rates off-season. Parking: Outdoor, free. AE, CB, DC, DISC, MC, V.

### Embassy Suites International Drive
8250 Jamaican Court, 32819; tel 407/345-8250 or toll free 800/327-9797; fax 407/352-1463. Exit 29 off I-4. ¼ mi S of Sand Lake Rd. Stands out from the lackluster offerings on this drive. Suite configuration surrounds atrium. **Rooms:** 246 stes. CI 3pm/CO noon. Nonsmoking rms avail. **Amenities:** A/C, cable TV, refrig, in-rm safe. **Services:** Car-rental desk, babysitting. Attentive service. **Facilities:** [280] 1 bar, games rm, sauna, steam rm, whirlpool, washer/dryer. **Rates (BB):** Peak (Dec–Apr/June–Aug) $125–$175 ste. Lower rates off-season. Parking: Outdoor, free. AE, CB, DC, DISC, JCB, MC, V.

### Embassy Suites Orlando South
8978 International Dr, 32819; tel 407/352-1400 or toll free 800/EMBASSY; fax 407/363-1120. Exit 29 off I-4. Another in the chain of quality all-suites hotels, this one is housed in a Mediterranean-influenced, eight-floor building containing the trademark atrium. **Rooms:** 249 rms. CI 3pm/CO noon. Nonsmoking rms avail. **Amenities:** A/C, cable TV w/movies, refrig. **Services:** Car-rental desk, children's program, babysitting. Social-hour cocktails served in the atrium. **Facilities:** [400] 1 restaurant, 2 bars, games rm, spa, sauna, steam rm, whirlpool, washer/dryer. **Rates (BB):** Peak (Feb–Apr/Aug–Dec) $149–$179 S or D. Extra person $15. Children under age 18 stay free. Lower rates off-season. Parking: Outdoor, free. AE, CB, DC, DISC, MC, V.

### Enclave Suites at Orlando
6165 Carrier Dr, 32819; tel 407/351-1155 or toll free 800/457-0077; fax 407/352-7292. Exit 28 off I-4. A complex of three buildings offering a residential look; handy to International Drive restaurants and souvenir shopping. **Rooms:** 321 stes and effic. CI 3pm/CO 11am. Nonsmoking rms avail.

**Amenities:** 🔒 💧 📻 A/C, cable TV w/movies, refrig, in-rm safe. All units w/minibars, all w/terraces. Fully-equipped kitchens. **Services:** ✗ 🔑 🚗 🛅 🍴 Car-rental desk, babysitting. **Facilities:** 🏠 🏊 📺 🏓 🔵200 💻 ♿ 1 beach (lake shore), games rm, whirlpool, playground, washer/dryer. **Rates (CP):** Peak (Jan–Apr/June–Aug) $79–$125 ste; $125–$160 effic. Children under age 18 stay free. Lower rates off-season. Parking: Outdoor, free. AE, CB, DC, DISC, MC, V.

### 🇺🇸🇺🇸 Hampton Inn Universal Studios

7110 S Kirkman Rd, 32819; tel 407/345-1112 or toll free 800/763-1100; fax 407/352-6591. Within driving (but not walking) distance to Universal Studios, this small, scaled-down hotel offers basic rooms and friendly service. **Rooms:** 170 rms and stes. CI 3pm/CO 11am. Nonsmoking rms avail. **Amenities:** 🔒 💧 A/C, cable TV, refrig. Some units w/whirlpools. Microwaves. **Services:** 🔑 🛅 Car-rental desk. **Facilities:** 🏠 🏓 🔵35 ♿ Games rm, washer/dryer. **Rates (CP):** Peak (Christmas/June–Aug) $77 S or D; $109 ste. Children under age 18 stay free. Lower rates off-season. Parking: Outdoor, free. AE, DC, DISC, MC, V.

### 🇺🇸🇺🇸 Hawthorn Suites Hotel

6435 Westwood Blvd, 32821; tel 407/351-6600 or toll free 800/527-1133; fax 407/351-1977. Exit 28 off I-4. Offers generally attractive suites in an informal setting, with a sunny furnished deck around the pool. A good choice for value-conscious families who need a little extra space. **Rooms:** 150 stes. CI 4pm/CO 11am. Nonsmoking rms avail. **Amenities:** 🔒 💧 📻 A/C, cable TV w/movies, refrig, dataport, VCR, CD/tape player. All units have microwaves, ovens, stoves, dishwashers, and icemakers. **Services:** ✗ 🛅 🍴 Car-rental desk, babysitting. Free shuttle to Disney parks. **Facilities:** 🏠 🏓 🔵35 ♿ 1 bar, games rm, whirlpool, playground, washer/dryer. 24-hour convenience store. **Rates (CP):** Peak (Dec/Feb–Apr) $109–$185 ste. Children under age 18 stay free. Lower rates off-season. Parking: Outdoor, free. AE, CB, DC, DISC, MC, V.

### 🇺🇸🇺🇸🇺🇸 Holiday Inn International Drive

6515 International Dr, 32819; tel 407/351-3500; fax 407/351-9196. Exit 30A off I-4. Placed squarely in the midst of the International Drive bustle, this large operation features an atrium soaring 14 floors and a tropical-accented lobby. **Rooms:** 652 rms and stes. Executive level. CI 4pm/CO 11am. Nonsmoking rms avail. **Amenities:** 🔒 💧 📻 🍴 A/C, cable TV w/movies, refrig, dataport, voice mail, in-rm safe. Some units w/terraces. Microwaves. **Services:** ✗ 🔑 🚗 🛅 🍴 Car-rental desk, babysitting. The staff sometimes hosts barbecues on the pool terrace. **Facilities:** 🏠 🏊 🏓 🔵1500 💻 ♿ 2 restaurants, 2 bars (1 w/entertainment), basketball, volleyball, games rm, lawn games, whirlpool, playground, washer/dryer. **Rates:** Peak (Feb–Apr/June) $109 S or D; $200–$400 ste. Children under age 18 stay free. Lower rates off-season. AP and MAP rates avail. Parking: Outdoor, free. AE, CB, DC, DISC, ER, JCB, MC, V.

### 🇺🇸🇺🇸🇺🇸 Holiday Inn Orlando International Airport

5750 T G Lee Blvd, 32822; tel 407/851-6400 or toll free 800/HOLIDAY; fax 407/240-3717. A subdued hotel with an upscale look. Marble lobby. **Rooms:** 290 rms. CI 3pm/CO noon. Nonsmoking rms avail. Well-appointed guest rooms. **Amenities:** 🔒 💧 📻 A/C, cable TV w/movies. **Services:** ✗ 🔑 VP 🛅 🍴 Car-rental desk, babysitting. **Facilities:** 🏠 📺4 🏓 🔵300 💻 ♿ 1 restaurant, 1 bar, games rm, lawn games, sauna, whirlpool, washer/dryer. **Rates:** Peak (Jan–Mar) $105–$115 S or D. Extra person $10. Children under age 18 stay free. Lower rates off-season. Parking: Outdoor, free. AE, CB, DC, DISC, MC, V.

### 🇺🇸🇺🇸 Holiday Inn Winter Park

626 Lee Rd, 32810; tel 407/645-5600 or toll free 800/HOLIDAY; fax 407/740-7912. Exit 46 off I-4. This five-story hotel with easy interstate access has recently completed guest room updating. **Rooms:** 200 rms. CI 3pm/CO noon. Nonsmoking rms avail. **Amenities:** 🔒 💧 A/C, cable TV w/movies. **Services:** ✗ 🚗 🛅 🍴 Car-rental desk. **Facilities:** 🏠 🏓 🔵75 1 restaurant, 1 bar, games rm, washer/dryer. Comedy club operates several nights per week. **Rates:** Peak (Jan–Apr) $70–$80 S or D. Extra person $5. Children under age 19 stay free. Lower rates off-season. Parking: Outdoor, free. AE, CB, DC, DISC, JCB, MC, V.

### 🇺🇸🇺🇸🇺🇸 Hyatt Orlando International Airport

9300 Airport Blvd, 32827; tel 407/825-1234 or toll free 800/233-1234; fax 407/856-1672. Airport exit off FL 528. This hotel sparkles at every turn. Rooms are sophisticated and stylish; the staff is gracious and seasoned. This is just what Orlando needs, a civil spot to light where children probably won't be underfoot. **Rooms:** 446 rms. Executive level. CI 3pm/CO noon. Nonsmoking rms avail. **Amenities:** 🔒 💧 🍴 A/C, cable TV w/movies. All units w/terraces. **Services:** 🍽 🔑 VP 🚗 🛅 🍴 Car-rental desk, masseur, babysitting. **Facilities:** 🏓 🔵800 💻 ♿ 2 restaurants, 1 bar, games rm, whirlpool, beauty salon. **Rates:** Peak (Jan–Apr) $165 S; $190 D. Extra person $25. Children under age 18 stay free. Lower rates off-season. AP and MAP rates avail. Parking: Indoor/outdoor, $11/day. AE, DC, DISC, JCB, MC, V.

### 🇺🇸🇺🇸 La Quinta Inn International Drive

8300 Jamaican Court, 32819; tel 407/351-1660 or toll free 800/531-5900; fax 407/351-9264. Exit 29 off I-4. A notch or two above the others in this chain; situated in the convenient and more desirable Plaza International section of International Drive. **Rooms:** 200 rms. CI 4pm/CO noon. Nonsmoking rms avail. **Amenities:** 🔒 💧 A/C, cable TV w/movies, refrig. **Services:** ✗ 🔑 🚗 🛅 🍴 🐕 Car-rental desk, babysitting. **Facilities:** 🏠 ♿ 1 restaurant, 1 bar, whirlpool, washer/dryer. **Rates:** Peak (Jan–Apr) $55–$65 S; $65–$75 D. Extra person $8. Children under age 18 stay free. Lower rates off-season. Parking: Outdoor, free. AE, CB, DC, DISC, EC, MC, V.

### 🎚🎚 Las Palmas Hotel

6233 International Dr, 32819; tel 407/351-3900 or toll free 800/327-2114; fax 407/352-5597. Exit 30A off I-4. In the thick of International Drive's vast commercial strip stands this routine four-story hotel. **Rooms:** 262 rms. CI 3pm/CO noon. Nonsmoking rms avail. **Amenities:** 📞 🐾 A/C, cable TV, in-rm safe. **Services:** ✗ 🖥 🚗 🖼 🔧 Car-rental desk, babysitting. **Facilities:** 🏊 250 💻 ♿ 1 restaurant, 1 bar, games rm, washer/dryer. Lounge sometimes offers entertainment. **Rates:** Peak (June–Aug) $59–$89 S or D. Extra person $5. Children under age 17 stay free. Lower rates off-season. MAP rates avail. Parking: Outdoor, free. AE, CB, DC, DISC, MC, V.

### 🎚🎚🎚 Orlando Airport Marriott

7499 Augusta National Dr, 32822; tel 407/851-9000 or toll free 800/228-9290; fax 407/857-6211. Surrounded by neatly trimmed landscaping, this first-class hotel is fronted by a pond and offers guests a fresh look at traditional stylings in its public areas and rooms. **Rooms:** 484 rms and stes. CI 3pm/CO noon. Nonsmoking rms avail. **Amenities:** 📞 🐾 A/C, cable TV w/movies. **Services:** ✗ 🖥 VP 🚗 🖼 🔧 Car-rental desk, babysitting. **Facilities:** 🏊 🎿 🏌 🎾 1500 💻 ♿ 2 restaurants, 3 bars, games rm, lawn games, sauna, steam rm, whirlpool, washer/dryer. **Rates:** Peak (Jan–Apr) $175 S or D; $185 ste. Children under age 18 stay free. Lower rates off-season. AP and MAP rates avail. Parking: Outdoor, free. AE, DC, DISC, MC, V.

### 🎚🎚🎚 Orlando Marriott

8001 International Dr, 32819; tel 407/351-2420 or toll free 800/228-9290, 800/421-8001 in FL; fax 407/351-5016. Exit 29 off I-4. At Sand Lake Rd. This busy property on extensive grounds is a haven for families. Its low-rise design provides an almost suburban feel, even though the surrounding area is unrelentingly commercial. **Rooms:** 1,054 rms, stes, and effic. CI 4pm/CO 11am. Nonsmoking rms avail. **Amenities:** 📞 🐾 🍽 A/C, cable TV w/movies, dataport, voice mail, in-rm safe. Some units w/terraces. **Services:** ✗ 🚗 🖼 🔧 Car-rental desk, babysitting. More staff would help ease service glitches. **Facilities:** 🏊 🎾 🏌 1000 💻 ♿ 3 restaurants, 4 bars (1 w/entertainment), basketball, volleyball, games rm, whirlpool, beauty salon, playground, washer/dryer. **Rates:** Peak (Jan–May) $89–$129 S or D; $150–$350 ste. Children under age 18 stay free. Lower rates off-season. Parking: Outdoor, free. AE, CB, DC, DISC, ER, JCB, MC, V.

### 🎚🎚🎚 Orlando Renaissance Hotel Int'l Airport

5445 Forbes Place, 32812; tel 407/240-1000 or toll free 800/228-9898; fax 407/240-1005. Off FL 528. **Rooms:** 300 rms and stes. CI 3pm/CO noon. Nonsmoking rms avail. **Amenities:** 📞 🐾 🍽 A/C, cable TV w/movies. All units w/minibars. **Services:** ✗ 🖥 VP 🚗 🖼 🔧 Car-rental desk, babysitting. **Facilities:** 🏊 🏌 450 💻 ♿ 2 restaurants, 1 bar, games rm, whirlpool. **Rates:** Peak (Jan–Apr) $145 S; $175 D;

$300 ste. Extra person $15. Children under age 18 stay free. Lower rates off-season. AP and MAP rates avail. Parking: Outdoor, free. AE, DC, DISC, ER, MC, V.

### 🎚🎚🎚🎚 The Peabody Orlando

9801 International Dr, 32819; tel 407/352-4000 or toll free 800/42-DUCKS; fax 407/351-0073. A true tour de force, one of the most architecturally pleasing hotels in Orlando. This deluxe establishment pampers guests with gracious service and fine facilities. The skylit atrium lobby is a showcase for live orchids, palms, bamboo, ficus, and magnolia trees. The hotel is probably best known for the daily duck march to and from the lobby fountain, staged at 11am and 5pm. **Rooms:** 891 rms and stes. Executive level. CI 3pm/CO noon. Nonsmoking rms avail. Luxurious rooms with bamboo and bleached-wood furnishings. **Amenities:** 📞 🐾 🍽 A/C, cable TV w/movies, dataport, VCR, voice mail. All units w/minibars, some w/terraces. **Services:** 🍽 🖥 VP 🚗 🖼 🔧 Car-rental desk, social director, masseur, babysitting. **Facilities:** 🏊 🎿 🎾 🏌 3000 💻 ♿ 3 restaurants (see "Restaurants" below), 3 bars (1 w/entertainment), games rm, spa, sauna, steam rm, whirlpool, beauty salon. **Rates:** Peak (Jan/Sept–Oct) $185–$250 S or D; $400–$1,350 ste. Children under age 18 stay free. Lower rates off-season. Parking: Outdoor, free. AE, CB, DC, DISC, EC, ER, JCB, MC, V.

### 🎚🎚 Quality Inn International Drive

7600 International Dr, 32819; tel 407/351-1600 or toll free 800/825-7600; fax 407/352-5328. Exit 29 off I-4. Offers good location, well-maintained grounds, and adequate accommodations at very competitive rates. **Rooms:** 728 rms. CI 3pm/CO 11am. Nonsmoking rms avail. **Amenities:** 📞 🐾 A/C, cable TV w/movies. **Services:** 🚗 🖼 🔧 🛎 Car-rental desk, babysitting. **Facilities:** 🏊 ♿ 1 restaurant, 1 bar, games rm, washer/dryer. **Rates:** Peak (June–Aug) $55 S or D. Children under age 18 stay free. Lower rates off-season. Parking: Outdoor, free. AE, CB, DC, DISC, EC, ER, JCB, MC, V.

### 🎚🎚 Quality Inn Plaza

9000 International Dr, 32819; tel 407/345-8585 or toll free 800/999-8585; fax 407/352-6839. Exit 29 off I-4. A huge complex with a city of rooms attracting an unending stream of families for its rates and simple comforts served up in a no-nonsense way. **Rooms:** 1,020 rms. CI 3pm/CO 11am. Nonsmoking rms avail. **Amenities:** 📞 A/C, cable TV, in-rm safe. Refrigerators may be rented from an independent vendor. **Services:** ✗ 🚗 🖼 🔧 🛎 Car-rental desk, babysitting. **Facilities:** 🏊 ♿ 1 restaurant (bkfst and dinner only), 1 bar, games rm, washer/dryer. **Rates:** Peak (June–Aug) $30–$55 S or D. Children under age 18 stay free. Lower rates off-season. Parking: Outdoor, free. AE, CB, DC, DISC, ER, JCB, MC, V.

### 🎚🎚 Quality Suites International Drive Area

7400 Canada Ave, 32819; tel 407/352-2598 or toll free 800/228-2027; fax 407/352-2598. 8 mi W of Orlando, exit 29 off I-4. Attractive suites, fine for families. **Rooms:** 154 stes. CI

3pm/CO 11am. Nonsmoking rms avail. **Amenities:** 🔲 🔥 A/C, cable TV w/movies, refrig, VCR, CD/tape player. Microwaves. **Services:** ✗ 🔲 🔲 🔲 🔲 Cocktail hour 5:30–7:30pm. TGI Fridays provides room service. **Facilities:** 🔲 🔲 🔲 🔥 Games rm, whirlpool, playground, washer/dryer. **Rates (BB):** Peak (Dec 20–31/Feb 11–Apr 16/Mid-June–Aug) $139 ste. Children under age 18 stay free. Lower rates off-season. Parking: Outdoor, free. AE, CB, DC, DISC, JCB, MC, V.

### 🔳🔳 Radisson Barcelo Hotel

8444 International Dr, 32819; tel 407/345-0505 or toll free 800/304-8000; fax 407/352-5894. Exit 29 off I-4. Handsome five-story structure with well-chosen appointments and a friendly staff. The impressive lobby and other public areas are presented with flair and imagination. **Rooms:** 299 rms. CI 4pm/CO noon. Nonsmoking rms avail. **Amenities:** 🔲 🔥 A/C, cable TV, refrig, in-rm safe. **Services:** ✗ 🔲 🔲 🔲 Car-rental desk, babysitting. **Facilities:** 🔲 🔲 🔲 🔲 🔥 1 restaurant, 2 bars, games rm, lawn games, racquetball, squash, whirlpool, playground, washer/dryer. Pool bar. **Rates:** Peak (Dec–Apr/June–Aug) $79–$99 S; $89–$109 D. Extra person $10. Children under age 12 stay free. Lower rates off-season. MAP rates avail. Parking: Outdoor, free. AE, CB, DC, DISC, ER, JCB, MC, V.

### 🔳🔳🔳 Radisson Hotel Orlando Airport

5555 Hazeltine National Dr, 32812; tel 407/856-0100 or toll free 800/333-3333; fax 407/855-7991. Airport exit off FL 528. Stylish commercial hotel receiving more business guests than families. **Rooms:** 357 rms and stes. CI 3pm/CO noon. Nonsmoking rms avail. **Amenities:** 🔲 🔥 A/C, cable TV w/movies. Some units w/terraces. **Services:** ✗ 🔲 🔲 🔲 Car-rental desk, babysitting. **Facilities:** 🔲 🔲 🔲 🔥 1 restaurant, 1 bar, games rm, whirlpool. **Rates:** Peak (Jan–Apr) $129–$139 S or D; $259 ste. Extra person $15. Children under age 18 stay free. Lower rates off-season. AP and MAP rates avail. Parking: Outdoor, free. AE, DC, DISC, MC, V.

### 🔳🔳🔳 Radisson Inn Lake Buena Vista

8686 Palm Pkwy, 32836; tel 407/239-8400 or toll free 800/333-3333; fax 407/239-8025. Exit 27 off I-4. Smartly styled hotel in fine shape, with an efficient staff. Good value. **Rooms:** 200 rms. CI 3pm/CO noon. Nonsmoking rms avail. **Amenities:** 🔲 🔥 A/C, cable TV. Some units w/minibars, all w/terraces. **Services:** ✗ 🔲 🔲 🔲 Car-rental desk, babysitting. **Facilities:** 🔲 🔥 1 restaurant, 1 bar, games rm, playground. **Rates:** Peak (Dec 24–31/June–Aug) $109–$139 S or D. Lower rates off-season. AP and MAP rates avail. Parking: Outdoor, free. AE, DC, DISC, MC, V.

### 🔳🔳🔳 Radisson Plaza Hotel Orlando

60 S Ivanhoe Blvd, 32804; tel 407/425-4455 or toll free 800/333-3333; fax 407/843-0262. Exit 42 off I-4. A downtown high-rise receiving many commercial guests and convention delegates. **Rooms:** 337 rms and stes. Executive level. CI 3pm/CO 11am. Nonsmoking rms avail. **Amenities:** 🔲 🔥 🔲 🔲 A/C, cable TV w/movies, bathrobes. All units w/minibars.

**Services:** ✗ 🔲 VP 🔲 🔲 🔲 Car-rental desk, babysitting. **Facilities:** 🔲 🔲 🔲 🔲 🔥 1 restaurant, 1 bar (w/entertainment), lawn games, sauna, whirlpool. **Rates:** Peak (Jan–May) $119–$140 S or D; $150–$400 ste. Extra person $15. Children under age 18 stay free. Lower rates off-season. Parking: Indoor, $5.50/day. AE, CB, DC, DISC, MC, V.

### 🔳🔳🔳🔳 Renaissance Orlando Resort

6677 Sea Harbor Dr, 32821; tel 407/351-5555 or toll free 800/327-6677; fax 407/351-9994. Exit 28 off I-4. A grand offering in a striking setting opposite Sea World. Spectacular atrium is lush with tropical foliage, fountains, a stocked fish pond, and antique Italian aviary with working parts. Courteous staff. **Rooms:** 780 rms and stes. Executive level. CI 3pm/CO noon. Nonsmoking rms avail. Some rooms have french doors opening out to atrium. **Amenities:** 🔲 🔥 🔲 A/C, cable TV w/movies, dataport, voice mail, in-rm safe. All units w/minibars, some w/terraces, 1 w/whirlpool. Complimentary coffee/tea and newspaper with wake-up call. **Services:** 🔲 🔲 VP 🔲 🔲 🔲 Twice-daily maid svce, car-rental desk, social director, masseur, babysitting. Complimentary champagne at check-in. **Facilities:** 🔲 🔲 🔲 🔲 🔲 🔲 🔥 4 restaurants (*see* "Restaurants" below), 3 bars (1 w/entertainment), basketball, volleyball, games rm, spa, sauna, steam rm, whirlpool, beauty salon, day-care ctr, playground. Preferred tee times, discounts at International Golf Course nearby. **Rates:** Peak (Jan–Apr 15) $179–$219 S or D; $350–$500 ste. Children under age 18 stay free. Lower rates off-season. Parking: Outdoor, free. AE, CB, DC, DISC, MC, V.

### 🔳🔳 Residence Inn by Marriott

8800 Meadow Creek Dr, 32821; tel 407/239-7700 or toll free 800/331-3131; fax 407/239-7605. Exit 27 off I-4. A former apartment building redesigned to offer all the amenities of home. Popular for longer-term stays. **Rooms:** 688 stes. CI 4pm/CO 11am. Nonsmoking rms avail. **Amenities:** 🔲 🔥 🔲 A/C, cable TV w/movies, refrig, dataport, VCR, voice mail, in-rm safe. All units w/terraces. Full kitchens. **Services:** 🔲 🔲 🔲 🔲 🔲 Masseur, children's program, babysitting. **Facilities:** 🔲 🔲 🔲 🔲 🔲 🔲 🔥 2 restaurants, basketball, volleyball, games rm, whirlpool, playground, washer/dryer. Guests have use of Orlando World Center facilities. **Rates (CP):** Peak (Jan–Apr/July–Aug) $189–$259 ste. Children under age 18 stay free. Min stay. Lower rates off-season. Parking: Outdoor, free. AE, CB, DC, DISC, ER, MC, V.

### 🔳🔳 Residence Inn Orlando Attraction Center

7975 Canada Ave, 32819; tel 407/345-0117 or toll free 800/227-3978; fax 407/352-2689. Exit 29 off I-4. These well-outfitted suites receive many guests for long stays. **Rooms:** 176 stes. CI 3pm/CO 11am. Nonsmoking rms avail. Attractive upholstery and appointments. **Amenities:** 🔲 🔥 🔲 A/C, cable TV w/movies, refrig, in-rm safe. All units w/terraces, some w/fireplaces. **Services:** ✗ 🔲 🔲 🔲 Car-rental desk, babysitting. **Facilities:** 🔲 🔲 🔥 Lawn games, whirlpool, washer/dryer. **Rates (CP):** Peak (Christmas–Apr/July–Aug)

$104–$189 ste. Children under age 12 stay free. Lower rates off-season. Parking: Outdoor, free. AE, CB, DC, DISC, JCB, MC, V.

### ☰☰☰ Sheraton Plaza Hotel at the Florida Mall

1500 Sand Lake Rd, 32809; tel 407/859-1500 or toll free 800/231-7883; fax 407/855-1585. High-rise features a food court. **Rooms:** 496 rms and stes. CI 3pm/CO noon. Nonsmoking rms avail. **Amenities:** ☎ ♨ ▨ A/C, cable TV w/movies. Some units w/terraces, some w/whirlpools. **Services:** ✕ ☞ 🚐 ☒ ↻ Car-rental desk. **Facilities:** ⛶ ⛳ ▦900 ⛁ ᶘ 2 restaurants, 1 bar, games rm, spa, sauna, whirlpool, beauty salon. **Rates:** $145–$225 S; $155–$250 D; $350 ste. Children under age 17 stay free. AP and MAP rates avail. Parking: Outdoor, free. AE, CB, DC, DISC, MC, V.

### ☰☰☰ Sheraton World

10100 International Dr, 32821; tel 407/352-1100 or toll free 800/327-0363, 800/327-0363, 800/341-4292 in FL; fax 407/352-3679. Exit 28 off I-4. Nearly two dozen buildings spread out over extensive grounds, though none are too far from parking or the pool and courtyard areas. Within walking distance of Sea World. **Rooms:** 788 rms and stes. CI 3pm/CO 11am. Nonsmoking rms avail. **Amenities:** ☎ ♨ ▨ A/C, cable TV w/movies, refrig, dataport, voice mail, in-rm safe. Some units w/minibars, some w/terraces, some w/whirlpools. **Services:** ✕ ☞ 🚐 ☒ ↻ ⇲ Car-rental desk, social director, masseur, children's program, babysitting. **Facilities:** ⛶ ⛳ ▦5 ⛳ ▦1600 ⛁ ᶘ 2 restaurants, 3 bars (1 w/entertainment), basketball, games rm, lawn games, spa, whirlpool, playground, washer/dryer. **Rates:** Peak (Jan–May) $130 S or D; $150 ste. Extra person $10. Children under age 17 stay free. Min stay special events. Lower rates off-season. AP and MAP rates avail. Parking: Outdoor, free. AE, CB, DC, DISC, MC, V.

### ☰☰☰ Summerfield Suites Hotel

8480 International Dr, 32806; tel 407/352-2400 or toll free 800/833-4353; fax 407/352-4631. Exit 27 off I-4. Fairly new, occupies a five-story building with Southwestern architectural overtones. **Rooms:** 146 stes. CI 4pm/CO 11am. Nonsmoking rms avail. Rooms situated around an attractive courtyard. **Amenities:** ☎ ♨ ▨ A/C, cable TV w/movies, refrig, dataport, VCR, voice mail, in-rm safe. All rooms have fully equipped kitchens. **Services:** ☒ ↻ Car-rental desk, masseur, babysitting. Coffee and tea available at all times in lobby. **Facilities:** ⛶ ⛳ ▦55 1 bar, games rm, whirlpool, washer/dryer. **Rates (CP):** Peak (Mar 23–Apr 11/Dec 25–Jan 2) $189–$219 ste. Children under age 18 stay free. Min stay peak. Lower rates off-season. Parking: Outdoor, free. AE, CB, DC, DISC, JCB, MC, V.

### ☰☰☰ Twin Towers Hotel & Convention Center

5780 Major Blvd, 32819; tel 407/351-1000 or toll free 800/327-2110; fax 407/363-0106. Exit 30A off I-4. Large hotel located opposite Universal Studios. Public areas are spacious. **Rooms:** 740 rms and stes. CI 3pm/CO 11am. Nonsmoking

rms avail. Accommodations are larger since balconies were eliminated and extra space added to rooms during a major overhaul in the early 1990s. **Amenities:** ☎ ♨ A/C, cable TV w/movies. **Services:** ⦿ ☞ VP ☒ ↻ Twice-daily maid svce, car-rental desk. **Facilities:** ⛶ ⛳ ▦2000 ⛁ ᶘ 2 restaurants, 3 bars (2 w/entertainment), games rm, sauna, whirlpool, beauty salon, playground, washer/dryer. **Rates:** Peak (Jan–Apr) $119 S or D; $370–$900 ste. Extra person $15. Children under age 17 stay free. Lower rates off-season. Parking: Outdoor, free. AE, CB, DC, DISC, EC, MC, V.

### ☰☰☰ Westgate Lakes Resort

10000 Turkey Lake Rd, 32819; tel 407/345-0000 or toll free 800/424-0708; fax 407/345-5384. Exit 29 off I-4. 97 acres. Luscious lakeside setting provides the atmosphere of a private retreat. The smart lobby has courtyard views. **Rooms:** 369 cottages/villas. CI 4pm/CO noon. Nonsmoking rms avail. **Amenities:** ☎ ♨ ▨ ᕯ A/C, cable TV w/movies, refrig, in-rm safe. All units w/terraces. **Services:** ☞ ☒ ↻ Children's program, babysitting. **Facilities:** ⛶ ⚲ ⛵ ⛸ ⛹ ◗ ◖ ⛳ ▦300 ᶘ 1 restaurant, 2 bars, 1 beach (lake shore), games rm, whirlpool, day-care ctr, playground, washer/dryer. **Rates:** Peak (Dec/June–Aug) $110–$235 cottage/villa. Children under age 18 stay free. Lower rates off-season. Parking: Outdoor, free. AE, CB, DC, DISC, MC, V.

## MOTELS

### ☰☰ Country Hearth Inn

9861 International Dr, 32819; tel 407/352-0008 or toll free 800/447-1890; fax 407/352-5449. Exit 28 off I-4. Located across from the Orange County Convention Center, this property deserves high praise for pleasant, homey surroundings. The country decor and the down-home hospitality are a pleasant change from the usual in this area. Among its fans are returning retirees and families. **Rooms:** 150 rms. CI 3pm/CO noon. Nonsmoking rms avail. **Amenities:** ☎ ♨ A/C, cable TV w/movies, refrig, in-rm safe. **Services:** ✕ 🚐 ☒ ↻ Car-rental desk, babysitting. **Facilities:** ⛶ ▦300 ᶘ 1 restaurant (bkfst and dinner only), 1 bar, games rm, washer/dryer. **Rates (CP):** Peak (Feb–Apr/June–July/Oct–Nov) $89–$99 S; $99–$130 D. Children under age 12 stay free. Lower rates off-season. AP rates avail. Parking: Outdoor, free. AE, CB, DC, DISC, ER, MC, V.

### ☰☰ Fairfield Inn International Dr

8342 Jamaican Court, 32819; tel 407/363-1944; fax 407/363-1944. Exit 29 off I-4. Budget offering provides good value. **Rooms:** 134 rms. CI 3pm/CO noon. Nonsmoking rms avail. **Amenities:** ☎ ♨ A/C, cable TV w/movies. **Services:** ☞ ☒ ↻ Babysitting. **Facilities:** ⛶ ᶘ **Rates (CP):** Peak (Dec/June–Aug) $70 S or D. Lower rates off-season. Parking: Outdoor, free. AE, DC, DISC, MC, V.

### ☰ Inns of America

8222 Jamaican Court, 32819; tel 407/345-1172 or toll free 800/826-0778; fax 407/352-2801. Exit 29 off I-4. Right on International Dr. Appeals to value-conscious families; close to area attractions and food outlets. **Rooms:** 121 rms. CI 4pm/CO 11am. Nonsmoking rms avail. **Amenities:** 🔔 A/C, cable TV w/movies, in-rm safe. **Services:** 🚗 🗲 Car-rental desk, babysitting. **Facilities:** ⛳ ♿ Washer/dryer. **Rates (CP):** Peak (Dec 20–Jan 1/Mar–Apr) $60–$80 S or D. Children under age 18 stay free. Lower rates off-season. Parking: Outdoor, free. AE, MC, V.

### ≣≣ Orlando Vacation Resort

1403 US 27 N, Clermont, 34711; tel 352/394-6171 or toll free 800/874-9064; fax 352/394-1069. 1 mi N of FL 192. Informal, welcoming motel convenient to all Magic Kingdom attractions. **Rooms:** 233 rms. CI 3pm/CO noon. **Amenities:** 🔔 A/C, TV. **Services:** 🚗 🗲 Babysitting. **Facilities:** ⛳ 🖼15 📷100 ♿ 1 restaurant, 1 bar, games rm, lawn games, washer/dryer. **Rates:** Peak (Feb 15–Mar/June 15–Aug) $51–$55 S or D. Extra person $5. Children under age 17 stay free. Lower rates off-season. Parking: Outdoor, free. AE, CB, DC, DISC, EC, MC, V.

### ≣ Red Roof Inn

9922 Hawaiian Court, 32819; tel 407/352-1507 or toll free 800/THE-ROOF; fax 407/352-5550. Exit 28 off I-4. Next to the convention center. Economical, basic accommodations. **Rooms:** 134 rms. CI 3pm/CO 11am. Nonsmoking rms avail. **Amenities:** 🔔 🖉 A/C, cable TV w/movies. **Services:** 🗲 🗲 Babysitting. **Facilities:** ⛳ ♿ Whirlpool, washer/dryer. **Rates:** $73 S or D. Children under age 18 stay free. Parking: Outdoor, free. AE, CB, DC, DISC, MC, V.

### ≣≣ Wynfield Inns Westwood

6263 Westwood Blvd, 32821; tel 407/345-8000 or toll free 800/346-1551; fax 407/345-1508. Exit 28 off I-4. Close to Sea World and the Plaza International action, this decent hotel offers good room quality, but nondescript, limited public areas. **Rooms:** 299 rms. CI 3pm/CO 11am. Nonsmoking rms avail. **Amenities:** 🔔 🖉 A/C, cable TV w/movies, voice mail, in-rm safe. 1 unit w/minibar. **Services:** 🖼 🗲 Car-rental desk. Free shuttle to Disney parks and Sea World. Complimentary coffee and tea 24 hours in the lobby. **Facilities:** ⛳ 🖼12 ♿ 1 restaurant, 1 bar, games rm, washer/dryer. **Rates:** Peak (Jan–Mar/June–Aug) $72–$80 D. Extra person $5. Children under age 17 stay free. Min stay peak. Lower rates off-season. Parking: Outdoor, free. AE, CB, DC, DISC, MC, V.

## INN

### ≣ Courtyard at Lake Lucerne

211 N Lucerne Circle E, 32801; tel 407/648-5188 or toll free 800/444-5289; fax 407/246-1368. A stylish downtown inn that incorporates an interesting mix of Victorian and art deco styles in its three separate buildings embracing a brick courtyard. **Rooms:** 22 rms and stes. CI 3pm/CO 11am. Nonsmoking rms avail. **Amenities:** 🔔 🖉 A/C, cable TV. Some units w/terraces, some w/whirlpools. **Services:** 🗲 **Facilities:** 📷100 Guest lounge. **Rates (CP):** $65–$85 S; $85 D. Extra person $15. Parking: Outdoor, free. AE, DC, MC, V.

## RESORTS

### ≣≣≣≣ Hyatt Regency Grand Cypress

1 Grand Cypress Blvd, 32836; tel 407/239-1234 or toll free 800/233-1234; fax 407/239-3800. 1,500 acres. Impressive resort with fantastic grounds and deluxe accommodations. The atrium lobby houses a mini–rain forest, with stone-bedded streams and live birds in cages. Outside are lovely flower beds, rock gardens, brooks, and sculpture, as well as scores of palm, cypress, oak, and pine trees; swans and sailboats grace a picturesque lake. **Rooms:** 750 rms and stes. Executive level. CI 4pm/CO noon. Nonsmoking rms avail. Newly redecorated rooms feature gorgeous furnishings and pastel color schemes. Mediterranean-style villas have fully equipped kitchens and feature large picture windows overlooking the golf course. **Amenities:** 🔔 🖉 🍽 A/C, cable TV w/movies, dataport, voice mail, in-rm safe, bathrobes. All units w/minibars, all w/terraces, 1 w/whirlpool. **Services:** 🍽 🖼 VP 🚗 🖼 🗲 Car-rental desk, masseur, children's program, babysitting. **Facilities:** ⛳ 🖼 🛆 🏊 ▶45 🏖 🖼 🎿 🖼6 🖼6 🖼 🖼 📷2500 🖳 ♿ 5 restaurants (see "Restaurants" below), 5 bars (2 w/entertainment), 1 beach (lake shore), volleyball, games rm, lawn games, racquetball, snorkeling, spa, sauna, steam rm, whirlpool, beauty salon, day-care ctr, playground. Lagoon-like swimming pool with waterfalls and waterslides. Jack Nicklaus–designed golf course. Helipad. **Rates:** Peak (Jan–May/Sept–Dec) $210–$370 S or D; $650–$2,500 ste. Children under age 18 stay free. Lower rates off-season. Parking: Indoor/outdoor, free. AE, CB, DC, DISC, EC, ER, JCB, MC, V.

### ≣≣≣ Marriott's Orlando World Center

8701 World Center Dr, 32821; tel 407/239-4200 or toll free 800/621-0638; fax 407/238-8777. Exit 26A off I-4. 200 acres. This enormous, grand resort hotel is a city unto itself, with various towers and sections augmented by elaborate landscaping and surrounded by a golf course. Little wonder the resort is one of the top venues in Florida for meetings and conventions; it's also a great choice for tourists. **Rooms:** 1,500 rms and stes. CI 4pm/CO 11am. Nonsmoking rms avail. **Amenities:** 🔔 🖉 📻 🍽 A/C, satel TV w/movies, dataport, voice mail, in-rm safe. All units w/minibars, all w/terraces. **Services:** 🍽 🖼 VP 🚗 🖼 🗲 Car-rental desk, social director, masseur, children's program, babysitting. **Facilities:** ⛳ ▶18 🖼 🖼8 🖼 📷6100 🖳 ♿ 6 restaurants (see "Restaurants" below), 3 bars (2 w/entertainment), basketball, volleyball, games rm, spa, sauna, steam rm, whirlpool, beauty salon, playground, washer/dryer. Vast public areas, and enough leisure diversions to make guests content to stay on the grounds. **Rates:** Peak (Nov–Dec/Feb–Apr) $169–$199 S or D; $250–$500 ste. Children under age 5 stay free. Min stay. Lower rates off-season. MAP rates avail. Parking: Outdoor, free. AE, CB, DC, DISC, EC, ER, JCB, MC, V.

# RESTAURANTS 🍴

### 🌶 Atlantis
In Stouffer Renaissance Orlando Resort, 6677 Sea Harbor Dr; tel 407/351-5555 ext 2720. Exit 28 off I-4. **Seafood.** An elegant dining room with mahogany-paneled walls, fresco ceilings, crystal chandelier, and etched glass accents. Award-winning fare includes lobster bisque with truffles, pasta-crusted salmon fillet, and pepper-seared yellowfin tuna. Crackerjack staff knows the fine points of good service. **FYI:** Reservations recommended. Harp. Dress code. **Open:** Mon–Sat 6–10pm. **Prices:** Main courses $21–$29. AE, CB, DC, DISC, MC, V. 🌐 VP &

### Ⓢ B-Line Diner
In The Peabody Orlando, 9801 International Dr; tel 407/352-4000. Exit 29 off I-4. **Diner.** An old-time rock 'n' roll cafe, this stylish take on a '50s diner serves inventive food and terrific desserts all night long. The menu includes fountain favorites and blue plate specials. **FYI:** Reservations not accepted. Children's menu. **Open:** Daily 24 hrs. **Prices:** Main courses $9–$17. AE, DC, DISC, MC, V. 🕤 VP &

### ★ Enzo's
In the Market Place Shopping Center, 7600 Dr Phillips Blvd; tel 407/351-1187. **Italian.** A classic Italian trattoria with peach walls hung with fine art prints. Always bustling and extremely popular. **FYI:** Reservations accepted. Children's menu. Beer and wine only. **Open:** Lunch daily 11:30am–4:30pm; dinner Mon–Thurs 4:30–10pm, Fri–Sat 4:30–11pm. **Prices:** Main courses $8–$13. AE, DISC, MC, V. &

### 🌶 Hemingway
In Hyatt Regency Grand Cypress, 1 Grand Cypress Blvd; tel 407/239-3854. **Seafood.** A beautiful dining room with a tropical atmosphere, lots of plants and flowers, and a great view from every table. An attentive staff serves dishes from the impressive seafood menu. Apple pie à la mode is a popular postscript to an elegant meal. **FYI:** Reservations accepted. Children's menu. **Open:** Lunch Tues–Sat 11:30am–2:30pm; dinner Tues–Sat 6–10:30pm. **Prices:** Main courses $20–$28. AE, CB, DC, DISC, ER, MC, V. ▲▲ VP &

### JW Steakhouse
In Marriott's Orlando World Center, 8701 World Center Dr, Lake Buena Vista; tel 407/239-4200. **Steak.** This casual, clubhouse-like dining room offers steaks and seafood. The jumbo shrimp and the pan-seared crab cakes are favorite appetizers. **FYI:** Reservations accepted. Children's menu. **Open:** Lunch daily 11am–5pm; dinner daily 6–10pm. Closed Aug. **Prices:** Main courses $15–$38. AE, CB, DC, DISC, ER, MC, V. ▲▲ VP &

### La Normandie
2021 E Colonial Dr; tel 407/896-9976. Exit 41 off I-4 Between Bumby St and Mills St. **French.** Enjoy classic northern French cuisine in this attractive country-style restaurant named for its owners' home region. There is a minimum charge of $9 per person. **FYI:** Reservations recommended. Dress code. No smoking. **Open:** Lunch Mon–Fri 11:30am–2pm; dinner Mon–Sat 5–10pm, Sun 5–8pm; brunch Sun 11:30am–2pm. **Prices:** Main courses $14–$23; prix fixe $25–$34. AE, CB, DC, DISC, MC, V. 🔲 &

### ★ Le Coq au Vin
4800 S Orange Ave; tel 407/851-6980. **French.** A comfortable, stylish cafe with a relaxed, home-like atmosphere serving country French cuisine prepared with a regional twist. The menu regularly includes local seafood and French favorites like coq au vin and sweetbreads. **FYI:** Reservations recommended. Beer and wine only. **Open:** Lunch Tues–Fri 11:30am–2pm; dinner Tues–Sun 5:30–10pm. **Prices:** Main courses $14–$22. AE, CB, DC, MC, V. &

### Linda's Lacantina
4721 E Colonial Dr; tel 407/894-4491. At Humphrey Ave. **Italian/Seafood.** The open dining room, outfitted with exposed brick, hanging plants, and red tablecloths, is a suitable environment in which to enjoy hearty fare from a conventional Italian-American menu. Satisfied customers have been coming back to Linda's for steaks and seafood for over 35 years. **FYI:** Reservations recommended. Children's menu. **Open:** Tues–Sat 4:30–11pm. **Prices:** Main courses $8–$21. AE, DISC, MC, V. 🔲 &

### Mikado Japanese Steakhouse
In Marriott's Orlando World Center, 8701 World Center Dr; tel 407/239-4200. Exit 26A off FL 53. **Japanese/Steak.** An elegant Japanese steak house adorned with attractive foliage and artwork. Choose from fillet of salmon, lobster tails, or filet mignon, all prepared with a pan-Asian flair. Sushi bar. **FYI:** Reservations accepted. **Open:** Daily 6–10pm. **Prices:** Main courses $16–$29. AE, CB, DC, DISC, ER, MC, V. VP &

### Ming Court
9188 International Dr; tel 407/351-9988. Exit 29 off I-4. **Chinese.** A casual restaurant preparing traditional east Asian cuisine at affordable prices. The variety of entrees ranges from curried chicken to the Szechuan platter with seasonal vegetables. **FYI:** Reservations accepted. Children's menu. **Open:** Lunch daily 11am–2:30pm; dinner daily 4:30pm–midnight. **Prices:** Main courses $10–$19; prix fixe $25–$50. AE, CB, DC, DISC, MC, V. 🚗 &

### ★ Pebbles
In Crossroads Shopping Center, 12551 FL 535, Lake Buena Vista; tel 407/827-1111. **New American/Californian.** A casual, tropical restaurant offering a creative menu. The bar features live entertainment Thursday, Friday, and Saturday nights. **FYI:** Reservations not accepted. Children's menu. **Open:** Sun–Thurs 11am–11pm, Fri–Sat 11am–midnight. **Prices:** Main courses $10–$20. AE, MC, V. &

### Straub's Fine Seafood
5101 E Colonial Dr; tel 407/273-9330. **Seafood.** A wide variety of fresh fish dishes served in a tropical dining room adorned with hanging shell lights. **FYI:** Reservations recom-

mended. Children's menu. **Open:** Mon–Thurs 4:30–10pm, Fri–Sat 4:30–11pm, Sun 4:30–10pm. **Prices:** Main courses $11–$27. AE, CB, DC, MC, V. ☑ ♿

## ATTRACTIONS 📷

### Universal Studios Florida
1000 Universal Studios Plaza; tel 407/363-8000. A state-of-the-art theme park built around a working motion picture and TV production studio, Universal Studios Florida uses thrilling rides and cutting-edge special effects in 10 major attractions to introduce visitors to the world of moviemaking. Major attractions are *ET Adventure*, which transports visitors to ET's home planet; *Back to the Future*, where riders join Doc Brown in pursuing the evil Biff through time; **Kongfrontation,** with an attack by the giant ape himself; and **Earthquake,** the Big One, replete with splitting sidewalks, bursting water mains, and an exploding propane truck.

New additions include **Terminator 2 3-D** (a virtual-reality adventure starring Arnold Schwarzenegger) and **Day in the Park with Barney.**

Other features include stage shows, filmings of movie and TV productions, and Hanna-Barbera cartoon characters. There are over 25 shops and numerous restaurants, including Mel's Drive-In from the film *American Graffiti* as well as a Hard Rock Cafe. **Open:** Daily 9am–sunset. $$$$

### Sea World
7007 Sea World Dr; tel 407/351-3600. This popular, 175-acre marine-life park explores the world of the deep, combining entertainment with promoting wildlife conservation awareness. Its landscaped grounds include a 17-acre lagoon and a lush tropical rain forest.

Major shows and attractions include **Mission: Bermuda Triangle,** a high-definition film coupled with flight simulator technology that takes visitors on an exciting underwater mission; **Monster Marsh,** a re-created Mesozoic swamp, complete with life-size, animated robotic dinosaurs, that teaches awareness of endangered species; **Shamu: Close Up!,** a multipurpose habitat and research facility that gives visitors a close look at how killer whales interact; **Big Splash Bash,** a fast-paced song-and-dance extravaganza with an aquatic theme; **Mermaids, Myths & Monsters,** a nighttime show combining music, fireworks, and laser graphic images projected onto a 60-foot "waterscreen"; and a killer whale show highlighted by an underwater "ballet."

Other favorites include Hotel Clyde and Seamore, a comedy show starring sea lions, otters, and walruses; the Gold Rush Ski Show, with acrobatics set to hoedown music; Penguin Encounter, with hundreds of Arctic and Antarctic specimens; and Dolphin Community Pool, where guests can feed and pet bottlenose dolphins. There is also a revolving 400-foot Sky Tower, a Polynesian Luau Dinner, and guided behind-the-seas tours. **Open:** Daily, 9am–7pm. $$$$

### Church Street Station
129 W Church St; tel 407/422-2434. A popular downtown dining, shopping, and entertainment complex. A city block's worth of cobblestone streets and authentic turn-of-the-century buildings house a variety of Victoranesque establishments adorned with magnificent woodwork, stained glass, ornate chandeliers, and authentic antiques.

Highlights include **Rosie O'Grady's Good Time Emporium,** an 1890s-style gambling hall/saloon; **Cheyenne Saloon and Opera House,** a three-tiered country-and-western dance hall; the **Orchid Garden Ballroom,** a setting of wrought iron and marble featuring rock-and-roll oldies; **Apple Annie's Courtyard,** evocative of a Victorian tropical garden; **Phineas Phogg's Balloon Works,** a high-energy dance club with an aviation theme; **Crackers Oyster Bar;** and **Lili Marlene's Aviator's Pub & Restaurant,** embellished with World War I memorabilia. There are several shows featured nightly, from live bands to cancan girls. Also Commander Ragtime's Midway of Fun, Food and Games, with a huge video arcade, a food court, and 50 specialty shops in the Church Street Exchange. **Open:** Daily 11am–11pm. $$$$

### New Orlando Science Center
810 E Rollins St; tel 407/896-7151. The 193,000-sq-ft New Orlando Science Center, due to open in spring 1997, will house 10 themed exhibit halls with hundreds of interactive exhibits for both children and adults. Visitors can peer inside a sinkhole as it swallows a house, become a particle of food and travel through the organs of the human body, or draw imaginary landscapes using high-tech computers. The new Center will have a large-scale Science Adventure Theater, five Discovery Lab classrooms, a restaurant, two science-oriented gift shops, an IMAX theater, and a planetarium. Call ahead to confirm new location. **Open:** Mon–Thurs and Sat 9am–5pm, Fri 9am–9pm, Sun noon–5pm. $$$

### Orlando Museum of Art
2416 N Mills Ave (in Loch Haven Park); tel 407/896-4231. A permanent collection of 19th- and 20th-century American art, pre-Columbian artifacts, and African objects is presented on a rotating basis. Guided tours, children's workshops, gallery talks. **Open:** Tues–Sat 9am–5pm, Sun noon–5pm. $$

### Terror on Church Street
135 S Orange Ave; tel 407/649-FEAR or 649-1912. Housed in a converted old building in downtown Orlando, this attraction uses high technology, cinematic special effects, theatrical techniques, and even climate control to provide a terrifying journey through a maze of more than 20 elaborately detailed rooms, or "sets," each with its own horrific theme. The sets are populated by assorted monsters and chainsaw-wielding maniacs that can spring up almost anywhere—the actors are encouraged to improvise. People enter in groups of 8; the tour lasts about 25 minutes, but there are "chicken-out" exits for the faint of heart. **Open:** Sun–Thurs 7am–midnight, Fri–Sat 7am–1am. $$$$

## Harry P Leu Gardens

1730 N Forest Ave; tel 407/246-2620. This 56-acre botanical garden showcases a magnificent array of flowering trees, orchids, perennials, wildflowers, camelias, azaleas, roses, and more. There are also specialty gardens, such as the Xerophyte Garden and Mary Jane's Rose Garden, which contains more than 70 varieties. The Leu House Museum is a turn-of-the-century farmhouse, restored and furnished to reflect the 1910–1930 period; guided tours are available. **Open:** Daily 9am–5pm. $

## Gatorland

14501 S Orange Blossom Trail; tel 407/855-5496. Founded in 1949 with a handful of alligators living in huts and pens, this facility has grown to accommodate 5,000 alligators and crocodiles on a 55-acre spread. A 2,000-foot boardwalk winds through a cypress swamp and a 10-acre breeding marsh with an observation tower. There are three shows scheduled throughout the day: Gator Jumparoo, The Snakes of Florida, and Gator Wrestlin'. Picnic facilities, restaurant, gift shop. **Open:** Daily 8am–sunset. $$$$

## Wet 'n' Wild

6200 International Dr; tel 407/351-WILD. Among the highlights of this water park are Surf Lagoon, which sports four-foot waves; Bomb Bay, a 76-foot vertical drop into a target pool; and Black Hole, a 500-foot, 2-person raft ride in total darkness propelled by a 1,000-gallon-per-minute blast of water. Elaborate children's area features mini-versions of the popular adult rides plus the Fuji Flyer toboggan ride. **Open:** Daily. Call for hours. $$$$

## Orlando Arena

600 W Amelia St; tel 407/849-2020. The NBA's Orlando Magic play basketball here November–April, and the Tampa Bay Lightning hockey team has a few of its home games here as well. $$$$

# Ormond Beach

The Casements, the restored home of John D Rockefeller, is now used as the cultural center for this affluent resort community of 31,000, immediately north of Daytona Beach between the ocean and the Halifax River. **Information:** Ormond Beach Chamber of Commerce, 165 W Granada Blvd, PO Box 874, Ormond Beach, 32175 (tel 904/677-3454).

## HOTEL 🏨

### ≡≡ Maverick Resort

485 S Atlantic Ave, 32176; tel 904/672-3550. Exit 88 off US 40. Pleasant time-share accommodations housed in a mid-rise building on the ocean. Popular with families. **Rooms:** 138 effic. CI 3pm/CO 10am. **Amenities:** 🛏 🛁 🖵 A/C, cable TV, refrig. All units w/terraces. **Services:** 🖵 Children's program, babysitting. **Facilities:** 🔓 ⛳ 1 restaurant, 1 beach (ocean),

lifeguard, games rm, spa, sauna, whirlpool, playground, washer/dryer. **Rates:** $110 effic. Children under age 18 stay free. Parking: Outdoor, free. AE, MC, V.

## MOTELS

### ≡≡ Casa Del Mar

621 S Atlantic Ave, 32176; tel 904/672-4550 or toll free 800/245-1590; fax 904/672-1418. This pleasant, modest facility receives many repeat guests. **Rooms:** 151 effic. CI 3pm/CO 11am. Nonsmoking rms avail. Florida-tropical decor. Oceanfront units are spacious. **Amenities:** 🛏 🛁 🖵 A/C, cable TV, refrig, in-rm safe. All units w/terraces. **Services:** ✕ 🖼 🖵 **Facilities:** 🔓 🖾 50 🛁 1 restaurant (bkfst and lunch only), 2 bars, 1 beach (ocean), lifeguard, games rm, whirlpool, washer/dryer. Guests often gather in the sitting area of the lobby to converse or watch TV. **Rates:** Peak (Feb–Mar/June–Aug) $78–$130 effic. Extra person $10. Children under age 16 stay free. Min stay special events. Lower rates off-season. Parking: Indoor/outdoor, free. AE, DC, DISC, MC, V.

### UNRATED Granada Inn

51 S Atlantic Ave, 32176; tel 904/672-7550 or toll free 800/228-8089, 800/237-6865 in Canada. A low-key and folksy favorite among the senior set, who often come for long stays. **Rooms:** 192 rms, stes, and effic. CI 4pm/CO 11am. Plain decor. **Amenities:** 🛏 🛁 A/C, cable TV. All units w/terraces. **Services:** ✕ 🖼 🖵 Children's program, babysitting. **Facilities:** 🔓 🖾 200 🛁 1 restaurant, 2 bars, 1 beach (ocean), lifeguard, games rm, whirlpool, washer/dryer. **Rates:** Peak (Feb 10–Apr 10) $68–$98 S or D; $96–$138 ste; $114–$130 effic. Extra person $6. Children under age 16 stay free. Min stay peak. Lower rates off-season. Parking: Outdoor, free. AE, DC, DISC, MC, V.

### ≡≡ Ivanhoe Beach Resort

205 S Atlantic Ave, 32176; tel 904/672-6711 or toll free 800/874-9910; fax 904/676-9494. On FL A1A ½ mi S of jct FL 40. A mid-rise hotel directly on the beach, noteworthy for its variety of accommodations. **Rooms:** 147 rms, stes, and effic. CI 2pm/CO 11am. Nonsmoking rms avail. Generally well-tended units are sometimes a mishmash of decor. **Amenities:** 🛏 A/C, cable TV, refrig, in-rm safe. All units w/terraces. **Services:** 🖼 🖾 🖵 Children's program. **Facilities:** 🔓 65 🛁 1 restaurant (bkfst and lunch only), 1 bar, 1 beach (ocean), lifeguard, games rm, washer/dryer. **Rates:** Peak (July/Feb/Mar) $50–$75 S or D; $70–$105 ste; $55–$80 effic. Extra person $5. Children under age 18 stay free. Min stay special events. Lower rates off-season. Parking: Indoor/outdoor, free. AE, MC, V.

## RESTAURANTS 🍴

### Bennigan's

890 S Atlantic Ave; tel 904/673-3691. At Harvard Blvd. **American.** A simple American restaurant and bar with a casual atmosphere and a varied menu. You'll find potato skins, chicken fingers, salads, sandwiches, pastas, and steaks

here. **FYI:** Reservations not accepted. Children's menu. **Open:** Daily 11am–2am. **Prices:** Main courses $6–$11. AE, DC, DISC, MC, V. &

### Julian's
88 S Atlantic Ave; tel 904/677-6767. 1 block S of FL 40. **American.** You can choose from a variety of charbroiled poultry or beef entrees as well as from an extensive selection of seafood dishes. **FYI:** Reservations accepted. Piano. **Open:** Daily 4–11pm. **Prices:** Main courses $8–$23. AE, DISC, MC, V. &

### La Crepe en Haut
In Fountain Square Shops, 142 E Granada Blvd; tel 904/673-1999. At Vining Court. **French.** Attentive service is part of the fine dining experience here. Specialties include the Cajun sampler with chicken, shrimp, oysters, and sausage; and mushroom ravioli in cream sauce. **FYI:** Reservations recommended. **Open:** Lunch Tues–Fri 11:30am–2:30pm; dinner Tues–Sun 5:30–10pm. **Prices:** Main courses $21–$33. AE, MC, V.

### Sophie Kay's Coffee Tree Family Restaurant
100 S Atlantic Ave; tel 904/677-0300. At Bosarvey Dr. **American.** This casual and old-fashioned coffee shop–style restaurant can serve patrons in booths or at the counter. Variety of items to choose from, including veal, beef, and seafood dishes. Special entrees and sandwiches are offered daily. **FYI:** Reservations not accepted. Children's menu. Beer and wine only. **Open:** Daily 7am–10pm. **Prices:** Main courses $5–$9. AE, CB, DC, DISC, MC, V. &

## ATTRACTIONS 🖼

### The Casements
25 Riverside Dr; tel 904/676-3216. Guided tours are offered of this three-story villa that was once the winter home of billionaire John D Rockefeller. The house presently serves as a cultural and civic center. With a Hungarian folk art and costume collection as well as an exhibit of Boy Scout memorabilia. Tours are Mon–Fri 10am–2:30pm, Sat 10–11:30am. **Free**

### Birthplace of Speed Museum
160 E Granada Blvd; tel 904/672-5657. The history of beach racing is chronicled. Antique cars, automotive memorabilia, photographs. **Open:** Tues–Sat 1–5pm. **$**

# Palm Beach

**See also Boca Raton, Riviera Beach, West Palm Beach**

Winter home of the rich and famous, this city of 65,000 midway down the Atlantic coast boasts mansions like Mar-A-Lago. Flagler Museum honors Florida's east-coast railroad baron. Flagler's sumptuous Breakers Hotel—built in 1901, destroyed by fire, rebuilt in 1926—is listed on the National Register of Historic Places. **Information:** Palm Beach Chamber of Commerce, 45 Cocoanut Row, Palm Beach, 33480 (tel 561/655-3282).

## HOTELS 🏨

### ≡≡ Best Western Seaspray Inn
123 Ocean Ave, Palm Beach Shores, 33404; tel 561/844-0233 or toll free 800/330-0233; fax 561/844-9885. Blue Heron Blvd exit off I-95. A pretty establishment on the oceanfront with a pleasant pool area. **Rooms:** 50 rms and effic. CI 2pm/CO 11am. Nonsmoking rms avail. **Amenities:** 🛏 A/C, cable TV. Some units w/terraces. **Services:** 🛎 🧹 Babysitting. **Facilities:** 🏖 & 2 restaurants, 2 bars (1 w/entertainment), 1 beach (ocean). **Rates:** Peak (Feb 13–Apr 9) $110–$140 S or D; $120–$150 effic. Extra person $10. Children under age 18 stay free. Lower rates off-season. Parking: Indoor/outdoor, free. AE, DC, DISC, MC, V.

### ≡≡≡ Chesterfield Hotel
363 Coconut Row, 33480; tel 561/659-5800 or toll free 800/243-7871; fax 561/659-6707. Between Australian and Chilean Aves. A dignified yet stylish choice, with some whimsical touches inside. **Rooms:** 53 rms and stes. CI 4pm/CO noon. Nonsmoking rms avail. Individually decorated, functional rooms and suites. **Amenities:** 🛏 🍸 🍽 A/C, cable TV w/movies, bathrobes. **Services:** ✗ 🔑 VP 🖼 🧹 Babysitting. **Facilities:** 🏖 50 & 1 restaurant, 1 bar (w/entertainment). **Rates:** Peak (Dec–Mar) $185–$280 S or D; $375–$800 ste. Extra person $10. Children under age 17 stay free. Lower rates off-season. AE, CB, DC, DISC, MC, V.

### ≡≡≡ The Colony Hotel
155 Hammon Ave, 33480; tel 561/655-5430 or toll free 800/521-5525; fax 561/832-7318. Maintains a loyal following (including some celebrities) in this fashionable neighborhood. Attentive, respectful service. **Rooms:** 81 rms and stes; 10 cottages/villas. CI 4pm/CO noon. Nonsmoking rms avail. Some guest rooms are not up to par considering the rates, but the higher-end accommodations are well done, and suites are fitted with superior appointments. **Amenities:** 🛏 🍸 A/C, cable TV w/movies, in-rm safe, bathrobes. Some units w/terraces, some w/fireplaces, some w/whirlpools. **Services:** 🍽 🔑 VP 🚐 🖼 🧹 🧹 Twice-daily maid svce, car-rental desk, masseur, children's program, babysitting. **Facilities:** 🏖 🍴 450 & 1 restaurant (see "Restaurants" below), 1 bar (w/entertainment), spa, sauna, beauty salon. **Rates:** Peak (Dec–Apr) $190–$275 S or D; $360–$450 ste; $750–$1,000 cottage/villa. Extra person $10. Children under age 16 stay free. Lower rates off-season. AP and MAP rates avail. Parking: Outdoor, $6/day. AE, CB, DC, EC, MC, V.

### ≡≡ Days Inn Oceanfront Resort
2700 Ocean Dr, Riviera Beach, 33404 (Singer Island); tel 561/848-8661 or toll free 800/325-2525; fax 561/844-0999. A decent choice right on the ocean, a half-block from Ocean Mall. For those not-particularly-demanding guests who appreciate casual surroundings where the kids roam freely.

**Rooms:** 165 rms and effic. CI 4pm/CO noon. Nonsmoking rms avail. **Amenities:** 🔒 A/C, cable TV, in-rm safe. All units w/terraces. **Services:** ✗ 🖊 ↩ ⬳ Babysitting. **Facilities:** 🏋 🛏 ⅙ 1 restaurant, 2 bars (1 w/entertainment), 1 beach (ocean), whirlpool, washer/dryer. **Rates:** Peak (Dec–Apr) $116–$156 S or D; $199 effic. Extra person $10. Children under age 12 stay free. Lower rates off-season. Parking: Outdoor, free. AE, CB, DC, DISC, EC, ER, JCB, MC, V.

### ≣≣≣ Embassy Suites Resort

181 Ocean Ave, Palm Beach Shores, 33404 (Singer Island); tel 561/863-4000 or toll free 800/328-2289; fax 561/845-3245. Blue Heron Blvd exit off I-95. Geared toward families and those who want a little spa pampering, instead of the business clientele who are the traditional market for this chain. The waterfront location allows for a multitude of activities, especially for children. **Rooms:** 254 stes. CI 3pm/CO noon. Nonsmoking rms avail. **Amenities:** 🔒 🛁 🖥 ⌿A/C, cable TV w/movies, refrig, VCR, voice mail. **Services:** ✗ 🖊 VP 🖊 ↩ Car-rental desk, social director, masseur, children's program, babysitting. Evening cocktail service. **Facilities:** 🏋 🚲 🛏 🛏 ⅙ 1 restaurant, 2 bars (1 w/entertainment), 1 beach (ocean), lifeguard, games rm, sauna, whirlpool, day-care ctr, playground, washer/dryer. **Rates (BB):** Peak (Dec–Apr) $229–$299 ste. Extra person $15. Children under age 12 stay free. Lower rates off-season. Parking: Outdoor, $5/day. Package plans include spa programs or golf. AE, CB, DC, DISC, JCB, MC, V.

### ≣≣ Heart of Palm Beach Hotel

160 Royal Palm Way, 33480; tel 561/655-5600 or toll free 800/523-5377; fax 561/832-1201. Between S County Rd and Ocean Blvd. A two- and three-story building, within walking distance to the beach and four blocks north of Worth Ave shopping. **Rooms:** 88 rms and stes. CI 3pm/CO noon. Nonsmoking rms avail. Some rooms face the pool and deck area. **Amenities:** 🔒 A/C, cable TV, refrig, voice mail. Some units w/terraces. **Services:** ✗ 🖊 🖊 ↩ ⬳ Babysitting. **Facilities:** 🏋 🚲 🛏 2 restaurants, 1 bar. **Rates:** Peak (Dec 15–Apr 30) $99–$199 S or D; $225–$250 ste. Extra person $15. Children under age 18 stay free. Lower rates off-season. Parking: Indoor/outdoor, free. AE, CB, DC, MC, V.

### ≣≣ Howard Johnson Hotel

2870 S Ocean Blvd, 33480; tel 561/582-2581 or toll free 800/654-2000; fax 561/582-7189. Exit 93 off FL Tpk. Not on the beach, but it's an easy walk to it. There are some quite charming rooms that you might not expect in a place of this grade. **Rooms:** 98 rms and stes. CI 2pm/CO noon. Nonsmoking rms avail. **Amenities:** 🔒 A/C, cable TV w/movies, in-rm safe. Some units w/terraces. **Services:** ✗ 🖊 ↩ **Facilities:** 🏋 🚲 🛏 ⅙ 1 restaurant, 2 bars, washer/dryer. **Rates:** Peak (Dec–Apr) $102–$120 S or D; $300 ste. Extra person $10. Children under age 12 stay free. Lower rates off-season. Parking: Outdoor, free. AE, CB, DC, DISC, MC, V.

### ≣≣ Palm Beach Hawaiian Ocean Inn

3550 S Ocean Blvd, 33480; tel 561/582-5631 or toll free 800/457-5631; fax 561/582-5631. 2 mi S of Lake Worth Bridge. A modest family operation with light Hawaiian touches. **Rooms:** 58 rms, stes, and effic. CI 2pm/CO 11am. Nonsmoking rms avail. **Amenities:** 🔒 A/C, cable TV, refrig, in-rm safe. **Services:** ✗ 🚐 🖊 ↩ Car-rental desk, babysitting. **Facilities:** 🏋 🚲 ⅙ 1 restaurant, 1 bar (w/entertainment), 1 beach (ocean), games rm, washer/dryer. The patio and dining room can get hectic during peak times. **Rates:** Peak (Jan–Apr) $100 S or D; $124–$180 ste; $109 effic. Extra person $5. Children under age 18 stay free. Lower rates off-season. Parking: Outdoor, free. AE, CB, DC, DISC, MC, V.

### ≣≣≣ Palm Beach Hilton

2842 S Ocean Blvd, 33480; tel 561/586-6542 or toll free 800/433-1718; fax 561/585-0188. ½ mi N of Lake Worth Bridge. Upscale resort feel; makes efficient use of its limited grounds. **Rooms:** 134 rms and stes. CI 3pm/CO noon. Nonsmoking rms avail. **Amenities:** 🔒 🛁 ⌿ A/C, cable TV w/movies, refrig. All units w/minibars, some w/terraces, some w/whirlpools. **Services:** ✗ 🖊 VP 🖊 ↩ Car-rental desk, masseur, babysitting. **Facilities:** 🏋 🚲 ⚠ 🛏 🛏 2 restaurants, 2 bars (1 w/entertainment), 1 beach (ocean), snorkeling, sauna, whirlpool. The pool is surrounded by the parking lot area. **Rates:** Peak (Dec–Apr) $235–$295 S or D; $475–$855 ste. Extra person $25. Children under age 18 stay free. Min stay special events. Lower rates off-season. Parking: Outdoor, $5/day. AE, DC, DISC, MC, V.

### ≣≣≣ Plaza Inn

215 Brazilian Ave, 33480; tel 561/832-8666 or toll free 800/233-2632; fax 561/835-8776. 1 block S of Royal Palm Way at S County Rd. Located in an art deco building one block from the ocean, this luxurious boutique hotel exudes European charm. **Rooms:** 50 rms and stes. CI 2pm/CO noon. Nonsmoking rms avail. Accommodations in front are particularly attractive and romantic and are worth the extra cost. **Amenities:** 🔒 A/C, cable TV, refrig. **Services:** ✗ 🖊 🖊 ↩ ⬳ Babysitting. **Facilities:** 🏋 ⅙ 1 restaurant (bkfst only), 1 bar, whirlpool. **Rates (BB):** Peak (Dec 15–Apr) $125–$195 S or D; $225 ste. Extra person $15. Children under age 18 stay free. Min stay special events. Parking: Outdoor, free. AE, MC, V.

### ≣≣≣ Radisson Resort Singer Island

3200 N Ocean Dr, Singer Island, 33404; tel 561/842-6171 or toll free 800/327-0522; fax 561/848-6842. Blue Heron Blvd exit off I-95. Floor-to-ceiling windows in the tropically decorated units ensure guests won't miss a sunrise. **Rooms:** 202 rms and stes. Executive level. CI 3pm/CO noon. Nonsmoking rms avail. **Amenities:** 🔒 🛁 A/C, cable TV w/movies, in-rm safe. All units w/terraces. **Services:** ✗ 🚐 ↩ Car-rental desk, babysitting. **Facilities:** 🏋 🎿 🛏 1 restaurant, 3 bars (1 w/entertainment), 1 beach (ocean), lifeguard, games rm, snorkeling, washer/dryer. Sports bar opens in afternoons for pizza and happy-hour drinks. **Rates:** Peak (Dec–Apr) $95–

$159 S or D; $99–$180 ste. Children under age 18 stay free. Lower rates off-season. AP and MAP rates avail. Parking: Outdoor, free. AE, DC, DISC, JCB, MC, V.

## MOTELS

### ☰ Beachcomber Sea Cay Motor Apartments

3024 S Ocean Blvd, 33480; tel 561/585-4646. Three low-rise buildings set on landscaped grounds, with an attractive beachside pool and sunning area. **Rooms:** 50 rms and effic. CI 1pm/CO noon. Some rooms with showers only. Jalousie windows let in cool ocean breeze. **Amenities:** ☎ A/C, cable TV, refrig. Some units w/terraces. **Services:** ⌣ **Facilities:** ⛵ 1 beach (ocean), lawn games, washer/dryer. Pool is saltwater. Barbecue grills. **Rates:** Peak (Jan–Apr) $80–$150 S or D; $100–$205 effic. Extra person $10. Children under age 18 stay free. Lower rates off-season. Parking: Outdoor, free. AE, DISC, MC, V.

### ☰☰ Rutledge Inn

3730 Ocean Dr, Singer Island, 33404; tel 561/848-6621 or toll free 800/348-7946; fax 561/840-1787. Blue Heron Blvd exit off I-95. Comfortable oceanfront accommodations in a seaside setting. Good beach. **Rooms:** 60 rms, stes, and effic. CI 2pm/CO noon. **Amenities:** ☎ ▣ A/C, cable TV, refrig. All units w/terraces. **Facilities:** ⛵ 1 bar, 1 beach (ocean), lifeguard. Eye-level wall blocks sunbathers on the deck from strong breezes. **Rates:** Peak (Feb–Mar) $80–$86 S or D; $200 ste; $90–$98 effic. Extra person $6. Children under age 18 stay free. Lower rates off-season. Parking: Outdoor, free. AE, DISC, MC, V.

## RESORTS

### ☰☰☰☰ The Breakers

1 S County Rd, 33480; tel 561/655-6611 or toll free 800/833-3141; fax 561/659-8403. Exit 52A off I-95. 140 acres. The owners have done a commendable job preserving this historic 70-year-old beauty, with its palazzo-like facade and twin belvedere towers, by gently adapting the interiors to modern tastes—sometimes successfully (like adding eight much-needed elevators), sometimes by sacrificing grandeur. A popular rendezvous for business meetings, the hotel's innate graciousness is sometimes swamped by the hordes of temporary exhibits and omnipresent name tags. **Rooms:** 572 rms and stes. Executive level. CI 4pm/CO noon. Nonsmoking rms avail. Lodgings vary considerably in size and view. **Amenities:** ☎ ♨ ☖ A/C, cable TV, dataport, voice mail, in-rm safe, bathrobes. All units w/minibars, some w/terraces, some w/whirlpools. Guests with hearing problems will welcome the special beds with vibrating wakeup pads. **Services:** ☉ ☞ VP 🚐 ☒ ⌣ Twice-daily maid svce, car-rental desk, social director, masseur, children's program, babysitting. Personable staff sometimes overwhelmed by number of guests. **Facilities:** ⛵ ☍ △ ▤ ▶18 ☒ ⚑9 ⚑5 ☷ ☲1400 ▯ ☖ ☕ 5 restaurants (see "Restaurants" below), 3 bars (2 w/entertainment), 1 beach (ocean), lifeguard, volleyball, games rm, lawn

games, snorkeling, sauna, steam rm, whirlpool, beauty salon, day-care ctr, playground. Outstanding sports facilities, though beach is small for a luxury seaside resort. Pool and beach cabanas available. Fitness center offers such services as crania sacral massage and lymphodrain treatments. **Rates:** Peak (Dec 18–Apr) $295–$565 S or D; $495 ste. Extra person $25. Children under age 17 stay free. Min stay peak. Lower rates off-season. AP and MAP rates avail. Parking: Outdoor, $8/day. AE, CB, DC, DISC, MC, V.

### ☰☰☰☰ Four Seasons Ocean Grand

2800 S Ocean Blvd, 33480; tel 561/582-2800 or toll free 800/332-3442, 800/332-3442 in the US, 800/268-6282 in Canada; fax 561/547-1557. 5 mi S of downtown Palm Beach. 6 acres. The limited grounds and the five-story condo facade belie a lobby lavishly coated with marble and a spacious lounge/library facing a patio with a fountain. **Rooms:** 211 rms and stes. CI 4pm/CO noon. Nonsmoking rms avail. Efficiently laid-out rooms feature beachy colors and fine fabrics, as well as dazzlingly mirrored bathrooms. **Amenities:** ☎ ♨ ☖ A/C, cable TV w/movies, dataport, voice mail, in-rm safe, bathrobes. All units w/minibars, all w/terraces. Bathrooms with TV and telephone. **Services:** ☉ ☞ VP ☒ ⌣ ⌤ Twice-daily maid svce, car-rental desk, masseur, children's program, babysitting. Top-flight staff. **Facilities:** ⛵ ☍ ♦ ☷ ☲600 ▯ ☕ 2 restaurants (see "Restaurants" below), 2 bars (w/entertainment), 1 beach (ocean), spa, sauna, steam rm, whirlpool, beauty salon, day-care ctr. Well-equipped clubroom for kids with professional staff. The Ocean Bistro has canopied, poolside terrace that recalls the French Riviera, while The Restaurant serves innovative cuisine in an elegant setting. **Rates:** Peak (Dec 15–Apr 15) $320–$500 S or D; $1,500–$1,800 ste. Extra person $30. Children under age 17 stay free. Lower rates off-season. Parking: Indoor/outdoor, $12/day. AE, CB, DC, DISC, EC, ER, JCB, MC, V.

### ☰☰☰☰ The Ritz-Carlton Palm Beach

100 S Ocean Blvd, Manalapan, 33462; tel 561/533-6000 or toll free 800/241-3333; fax 561/588-4202. Exit 46 off I-95. 7 acres. Designed in a six-story, Mediterranean-style double-U facing the ocean, topped with faux bell towers. Furnished in true Ritz-Carlton fashion with polished wood paneling, museum-caliber art, and high-ceilinged salons with crystal chandeliers and elegantly draped windows. **Rooms:** 270 rms and stes. Executive level. CI 3pm/CO noon. Nonsmoking rms avail. Rooms are gracious, refined, and comfortable; best bets for families are ground-floor "minimum" rooms opening directly to a quiet, green courtyard. Extra-large, marble-clad bathrooms with twin vanities. **Amenities:** ☎ ♨ ☖ A/C, cable TV w/movies, dataport, in-rm safe, bathrobes. All units w/minibars, all w/terraces, 1 w/fireplace. Terraces have dining table and chairs. All rooms have two-line phones. **Services:** ☉ ☞ VP 🚐 ☒ ⌣ Twice-daily maid svce, car-rental desk, masseur, children's program, babysitting. Brisk, competent, professional service. Outstanding Ritz Kids programs (with club room and tennis clinics). **Facilities:** ⛵ ☍ △

🐴3 🐴4 🖥 🎛 💻 ⚓ 3 restaurants (*see* "Restaurants" below), 3 bars (w/entertainment), 1 beach (ocean), board surfing, snorkeling, spa, sauna, steam rm, whirlpool, beauty salon, day-care ctr. Sculpted pool area with private cabanas. Golf privileges at nearby courses. **Rates:** Peak (Jan–Apr 27/Dec 16–31) $325–$650 S or D; $890 ste. Children under age 18 stay free. Min stay peak. Lower rates off-season. Parking: Indoor, $12/day. Rates vary by room location and floor. AE, CB, DC, DISC, EC, ER, JCB, MC, V.

# RESTAURANTS 🍽

## Anchor Inn
2412 Floral Rd, Lantana; tel 561/965-4794. Exit 45 off I-95 ½ mi W of I-95. **Seafood/Steak/Pasta.** A casual, nautically styled seafood palace where you can watch the sun set over Lake Osborne as you dine. The menu includes the ocean catch of the day, a variety of seafood platters, and steaks. A good value. **FYI:** Reservations accepted. Children's menu. **Open:** Daily 5–9:30pm. **Prices:** Main courses $10–$23. AE, MC, V. 🏔 💟 ⚓

## Bice
313½ Worth Ave; tel 561/835-1600. **Northern Italian.** Cheery pastel-yellow tablecloths and bright flowers decorate the modern dining room of this upscale Milan-based chain. The daily menu includes pasta, veal, chicken, and seafood specialties. **FYI:** Reservations recommended. Jacket required. **Open:** Peak (Sept–May) lunch daily noon–5pm; dinner daily 6–11pm. **Prices:** Main courses $7–$28. AE, DC, MC, V. 🏛 VP ⚓

## Bistro
In the Brazilian Court Hotel, 301 Australian Ave; tel 407/655-7740. Between Coconut Row and Hibiscus Ave. **New American.** Contemporary American cuisine, including the catch of the day, is served on marble-topped tables in this historic hotel dining room. Tropical prints and lush garden views abound. **FYI:** Reservations recommended. Piano. Children's menu. **Open:** Breakfast daily 7–11am; lunch daily 11am–2:30pm; dinner daily 6–10pm. **Prices:** Main courses $19–$32. AE, CB, DC, DISC, MC, V. VP ⚓

## 🌱 Cafe L'Europe
321 S County Rd; tel 561/655-4020. 5 blocks N of Worth Ave. **French.** The ambiance of this Palm Beach landmark is gracious, not imposing. And despite its soaring ceilings and grand-scale murals, patrons enjoy a high level of intimacy. Lunch might include miniature seashell pasta salad with chicken and vegetables in balsamic vinegar dressing, or lobster-corn pancakes with sautéed sea scallops; dinner might start with baked goat cheese salad with raspberry-walnut dressing, then progress to sautéed potato-crusted Florida snapper. A dedicated pastry chef bakes chocolate cakes and fruit tarts daily. **FYI:** Reservations recommended. Jacket required. **Open:** Dinner Mon–Sat 5:30pm–1am. **Prices:** Main courses $28–$60. AE, DC, MC, V. ♥ VP ⚓

## 🌱 Centennial
In The Breakers, 45 Cocoanut Row; tel 561/659-8460. 2 blocks S of Royal Poinciana Way. **Continental.** The Breakers celebrated its 100th anniversary with the opening of this extraordinary new dining salon inspired by the elegance of the late Victorian era. The intimate setting resembles a private home more than it does an eatery: rich mahogany appointments, marble-top tables, velvet sofas, lace curtains, and silver-and-crystal table settings. **FYI:** Reservations accepted. Jacket required. No smoking. **Open:** Tues–Sun 7pm–1am. **Prices:** Prix fixe $75. AE, CB, DC, DISC, MC, V. ♥ ⚓

## Charley's Crab
456 S Ocean Ave; tel 561/659-1500. ¹⁄₁₀ mi S of Royal Palm Way. **Seafood.** A tavern-style restaurant with beautiful ocean views. A good value for families, Sunday brunchers, and seafood lovers. **FYI:** Reservations recommended. Children's menu. **Open:** Lunch Mon–Sat 11:30am–3:30pm; dinner Sun–Thurs 5–10pm, Fri–Sat 5–11pm; brunch Sun 10:30am–2:30pm. **Prices:** Main courses $22–$35. AE, CB, DC, DISC, MC, V. 🏔 💟 VP ⚓

## ★ Chuck & Harold's
207 Royal Poinciana Way; tel 561/659-1440. ⅓ mile E of Flagler Memorial Bridge on FL A1A. **New American.** A fun, stylish cafe with a loyal clientele of both tourists and locals. Tuscan black-bean soup, gazpacho for appetizers; fresh grilled or broiled fish, lobster, chicken, and pastas for main courses. Different lunch specials are offered daily. **FYI:** Reservations recommended. Dancing/jazz. Children's menu. Dress code. **Open:** Daily 7:30am–1am. **Prices:** Main courses $13–$28. AE, DC, DISC, MC, V. 🎭 💟 VP ⚓

## De Cesare's
639 US 1, North Palm Beach; tel 561/848-1400. ¼ mile N of N Lake Blvd. **New American.** A casual eatery where the walls are decorated with photos of golf pros. Pastas and prime rib. **FYI:** Reservations not accepted. Children's menu. **Open:** Mon–Sat 11am–11pm, Sun noon–11pm. **Prices:** Main courses $10–$18. AE, DC, DISC, MC, V. 💟 VP ⚓

## E R Bradley's Saloon
111 Bradley Place; tel 561/833-3520. At Royal Palm Way. **American.** An intimate cafe with marble-topped tables, ceiling fans, and an outdoor patio. For lunch, there is caesar, conch, or basic house salad. The dinner menu includes grilled swordfish, sautéed chicken breast, and steaks. **FYI:** Reservations accepted. Children's menu. **Open:** Mon–Fri 11am–3am, Sat–Sun 10am–3am. **Prices:** Main courses $5–$18. AE, DISC, MC, V. 🍷 🏛 ⚓

## ★ Francoise's Place
336 Royal Poinciana Way; tel 561/832-4800. **Continental.** An upscale eatery catering to the local jet set and young up-and-comers. Patrons come here as much to see and be seen as to eat and drink. Enjoy cocktails at the bar or dine on the continental cuisine. Late evening big band music on Wednesdays. **FYI:** Reservations recommended. Big band/

jazz. Jacket required. **Open:** Peak (Oct–May) Tues–Sun 5:30pm–3am. **Prices:** Main courses $11–$17; prix fixe $20. MC, V. 🔲 VP &

### Green's Pharmacy
151 N County Rd; tel 561/832-9171. **American.** A traditional black-and-white-tiled coffee shop with an open kitchen serving sandwiches, soups, and salads. Patrons are seated in booths or at the counter. **FYI:** Reservations not accepted. No liquor license. **Open:** Mon–Sat 7am–5pm, Sun 7am–2pm. **Prices:** Lunch main courses $4–$7. AE, DISC, MC, V. &

### Jo's Restaurant
200 Chilian Ave; tel 561/659-6776. At County Rd. **French.** A cozy, antique-filled bistro, located in Palm Beach's historic district, serving a traditional menu. **FYI:** Reservations recommended. Beer and wine only. **Open:** Lunch Mon–Sat 11:30am–3pm; dinner Mon–Sat 6–10pm. **Prices:** Main courses $22–$30. AE, MC, V. &

### ♥ Le Bateau
In the Esplanade, 150 Worth Ave; tel 561/655-9999. **Continental/French.** Overlooking Palm Beach's exclusive Esplanade is Palm Beach's newest fine French restaurant. Le Bateau offers a discriminating menu of continental cuisine that is matched only by the bistro's striking decor. Well worth the calories! **FYI:** Reservations recommended. Jacket required. No smoking. **Open:** Mon–Sat 11:30am–10:30pm, Sun 4–9pm. **Prices:** Main courses $19–$33. AE, DISC, MC, V. 💗 VP &

### The Polo Restaurant
In the Colony Hotel, 155 Hammon Ave; tel 561/655-5430. **Continental.** The look is lively but mannered, with white shutters and an elegant bar partially overlooking the pool. The menu includes lobster linguine, yellowtail snapper, and penne with vodka and prosciutto. **FYI:** Reservations recommended. Piano. Jacket required. **Open:** Daily 7am–midnight. **Prices:** Main courses $17–$30. AE, CB, DC, MC, V. 💗 VP &

### ⑤ The Restaurant
In The Ritz-Carlton Palm Beach, 100 S Ocean Blvd, Manalapan; tel 561/540-4833. 8 mi S of downtown Palm Beach on FL A1A. **Eclectic/Mediterranean.** Refined oceanfront dining on a spacious terrace or indoors behind an arc of floor-to-ceiling windows set off with sumptuous drapes, sconce candelabra and Ritz-Carlton's trademark clubby decor. A recent menu ranged from chilled cantaloupe-and-honeydew soup to Loxahatchee goat-cheese napoleon, from baked fillet of grouper with seared basil and risotto cake to five-spice breast of duck with sweet-potato egg roll. **FYI:** Reservations recommended. Piano. Children's menu. Dress code. **Open:** Daily 7am–10:30pm. **Prices:** Main courses $20–$25. AE, CB, DC, DISC, ER, MC, V. 💗 🛥 🔲 VP &

### ♥ The Restaurant
In the Four Seasons Ocean Grand, 2800 S Ocean Blvd; tel 561/582-2800. 5 mi S of Downtown Palm Beach. Go east on Southern Blvd across the Intracoastal Waterway. **Southeast-** ern. Innovative cuisine served in a refined, pillared setting enhanced with antiques and chinoiserie. Much-lauded chef Hubert de Marais makes regular use of local produce and ingredients (like hearts of palm from a Seminole reservation and goat cheese from Loxahatchee). He even has his own orchard and herb garden on the premises. Typical dishes include stone-ground grits cake with ruby chard, yellowtail snapper with tangelo sauce, fire-roasted tenderloin of beef with Oregon morels, and ginger-buttermilk wrap cake. Exceptional wine list; enthusiastic staff. **FYI:** Reservations recommended. Piano. Jacket required. No smoking. **Open:** Tues–Sun 6–10pm. **Prices:** Main courses $27–$34. AE, CB, DC, DISC, ER, MC, V. 💗 🛥 VP &

### Shakespeare's
7306 Lake Worth Rd, Lake Worth; tel 561/967-4852. **Seafood/Steak.** A comfortable grill with a library theme, done in lots of brick and wood. Specials are offered daily. **FYI:** Reservations accepted. Big band. Children's menu. **Open:** Lunch Mon–Sat 11:30am–2:30pm, Sun 1–4pm; dinner Sun–Thurs 4–10pm, Fri–Sat 4–11pm. **Prices:** Main courses $9–$26. AE, DC, DISC, MC, V. 🔲 &

### Ta-boo
221 Worth Ave; tel 561/835-3500. **Southwestern.** A smart, casual, yet elegant grill with a southwestern-style menu. Grilled fish, veal, steaks, Maine lobster, and pasta. Try one of their trademark exotic cocktails. **FYI:** Reservations recommended. Dancing/piano. Dress code. **Open:** Lunch daily 11:30am–5pm; dinner daily 5–11pm; brunch Sun 11:30am–2pm. **Prices:** Main courses $20–$25. AE, CB, DC, MC, V. VP &

### Testa's
221 Royal Poinciana Way; tel 561/832-0992. **Continental.** An upbeat eatery overlooking Royal Poinciana Way. Freshwater fish, pasta, and seafood selections are offered daily. **FYI:** Reservations recommended. Children's menu. **Open:** Daily 7am–midnight. **Prices:** Main courses $12–$25. AE, DC, DISC, MC, V. 🛥 🔲 VP &

## ATTRACTIONS 🏛

### Marinelife Center of Juno Beach
1200 US 1, Juno Beach; tel 561/627-8280. Located in Loggerhead Park, a public beachfront park in Juno Beach, this combination ecology museum and nature trail focuses on South Florida's unique ecosystem. Hands-on exhibits, outdoor trails through dune vegetation, and live, endangered sea turtles. **Open:** Tues–Sat 10am–3pm, Sun 10am–noon. **Free**

### John D MacArthur Beach State Park
10900 FL 703, North Palm Beach; tel 561/624-6950. This large day-use park off FL A1A has about two miles of oceanfront beach. The nature center (open Wed–Mon 9am–5pm) shows a movie about the park and has several exhibits on the flora and fauna of the area. Swimming, fishing, nature trails. **Open:** Daily 8am–sunset. $$

### Henry Morrison Flagler Museum
Coconut Row and Whitehall Way; tel 561/655-2833. Henry Flagler, co-founder of the Standard Oil Company, probably had a greater influence on South Florida's development than any other individual. The museum that now bears his name was originally a mansion called Whitehall, built by Flagler in 1901 and restored to its original opulence in 1960. Also on display is Flagler's luxurious personal railroad car, "The Rambler," dating from 1886. **Open:** Tues–Sat 10am–5pm, Sun noon–5pm. **$$$**

### Society of the Four Arts
Four Arts Plaza; tel 561/655-7226. This cultural complex is made up of a museum, theater, library, and auditorium. Plays, movies, local art exhibits. **Open:** Dec–Apr, Mon–Sat 10am–5pm, Sun 2–5pm. **$**

# Palm Beach Gardens

## HOTEL 🏨

### ☰☰☰ Embassy Suites
4350 PGA Blvd, 33410; tel 561/622-1000 or toll free 800/362-2279; fax 561/626-4860. PGA Blvd exit off I-95. Convenient to highways and local attractions. Stylish layout, including a soaring lobby featuring a pond with three resident swans. This is one of the more sophisticated all-suites properties on the market. **Rooms:** 160 stes. CI 3pm/CO noon. Nonsmoking rms avail. **Amenities:** 🛁 🔥 📺 🍷 A/C, cable TV w/movies, refrig. All units w/minibars, some w/whirlpools. **Services:** ✕ 🍴 🚐 🧺 🛎 Car-rental desk, masseur, children's program, babysitting. **Facilities:** 🏋️ 🏊 💇 🍴 1 restaurant, 1 bar, games rm, spa, sauna, steam rm, whirlpool, beauty salon, washer/dryer. **Rates (BB):** Peak (Dec–Apr) $165–$195 ste. Extra person $10. Children under age 17 stay free. Lower rates off-season. Parking: Indoor/outdoor, free. AE, DC, DISC, MC, V.

## RESORT

### ☰☰☰ PGA National Resort and Spa
400 Ave of the Champions, 33418; tel 561/627-2000 or toll free 800/633-9150; fax 561/622-0261. PGA Blvd exit off I-95. 2,300 acres. A massive and impressive resort that receives many groups and conventions, but also hosts its share of individual golfers and tennis enthusiasts. Cheerful staff. **Rooms:** 339 rms and stes; 79 cottages/villas. CI 3pm/CO noon. Nonsmoking rms avail. Accommodations include cottage-like arrangements that provide extra space. Some rooms are a hike from the lobby. **Amenities:** 🛁 🔥 🍷 A/C, cable TV w/movies, in-rm safe. All units w/minibars, all w/terraces. **Services:** ✕ 🍴 📶 🚐 🧺 🛎 Car-rental desk. **Facilities:** 🏋️ 🚴 ⛳ 🏊 🎾 💇 🍴 6 restaurants, 6 bars (1 w/entertainment), 1 beach (lake shore), games rm, lawn games, racquetball, spa, sauna, steam rm, whirlpool, beauty salon, washer/dryer. **Rates:** Peak (Dec–

Apr) $219–$249 S or D; $340–$745 ste; $305 cottage/villa. Extra person $30. Children under age 18 stay free. Lower rates off-season. Parking: Outdoor, $5/day. AE, DC, DISC, ER, JCB, MC, V.

## RESTAURANTS 🍽

### Bistro Zenith
In Harbor Financial Center, 180 Rue de la Mer; tel 407/627-0000. At PGA Blvd and Prosperity Rd. **New American.** A lovely restaurant with a cool, casual atmosphere and an open kitchen. Choose the appetizing grilled swordfish, slow-roasted duckling, or veal meat loaf. **FYI:** Reservations recommended. Children's menu. **Open:** Lunch Mon–Fri 11:30am–2:30pm; dinner Sun–Thurs 5:30–10pm, Fri–Sat 5:30–11pm; brunch Sun 11am–2:30pm. **Prices:** Main courses $11–$22. AE, DISC, MC, V. 🅥🅟 &

### ★ Cafe Chardonnay
In Garden Square Shoppes, 4533 PGA Blvd, North Palm Beach; tel 561/627-2662. **Regional American.** An casual, upscale cafe with funky decor and a comfortable bar area. The inventive menu concentrates on lighter fare and includes pasta, beef, and seafood dishes. **FYI:** Reservations recommended. Children's menu. Dress code. Beer and wine only. **Open:** Lunch Mon–Fri 11:30am–2:30pm; dinner Mon–Sun 5:30–10pm. **Prices:** Main courses $16–$27; prix fixe $24. AE, DC, MC, V. &

### Crab Catcher
In the PGA National Resort and Spa, 400 Ave of the Champions, Palm Beach Gardens; tel 561/627-2000. Exit 57B off I-95. **Seafood.** Dine while seated in luxurious wingbacked leather chairs or a velvet-cushioned booth. Typical dishes include roasted half-duck, sautéed red snapper, and beef tenderloin. **FYI:** Reservations recommended. Piano. No smoking. **Open:** Dinner Mon–Sat 5:30–10pm. **Prices:** Main courses $11–$20; prix fixe $30–$50. AE, DISC, MC, V. 🅥🅟 &

### ★ No Anchovies! Neighborhood Pastaria
In PGA Plaza, 2650 PGA Blvd, Palm Beach Gardens; tel 561/622-7855. Exit 57B off I-95 at Prosperity Farms Rd. **Italian.** In addition to a full pizza menu, No Anchovies! features pastas, eggplant dishes, lasagna, and an extensive dessert menu. **FYI:** Reservations not accepted. Children's menu. Additional location: 1901 Palm Beach Lakes Blvd, West Palm Beach (tel 407/684-0040). **Open:** Lunch Mon–Sat 11:30am–2:30pm; dinner Sun–Thurs 5–10:30pm, Fri–Sat 5–11pm. **Prices:** Main courses $7–$16. AE, DISC, MC, V. 🖼 &

### Waterway Cafe
2300 PGA Blvd, Palm Beach Gardens; tel 561/694-1700. Between Prosperity Rd and US 1. **American.** An open-air, nautically themed restaurant located on the Intracoastal Waterway, serving a variety of beef, pasta, and seafood dishes. While the dining room is firmly planted on solid ground, the bar is located on an adjacent floating boat; in

addition to cocktails, a limited bar menu, including chicken wings and burgers, is served there. **FYI:** Reservations not accepted. Big band/reggae. Children's menu. **Open:** Mon–Thurs 11:30am–10pm, Fri–Sat 11:30am–11pm. **Prices:** Main courses $6–$19. AE, MC, V. 🏛 🖼 ▼ VP &

# Palm Harbor

See Dunedin

# Panama City

See also Panama City Beach

This Bay County seat of 34,000 has a commercial port and busy pleasure boat docks. Midway across Florida's Panhandle, it was named in 1906 after the Central American canal then under construction. Tyndal Air Force Base and St Andrews State Recreation Center are nearby. **Information:** Bay County Chamber of Commerce, 235 W 5th St, PO Box 1850, Panama City, 32402 (tel 904/785-5206).

## RESTAURANTS 🍴

### Harbour House
In the Ramada Inn, 3001A W 10th St; tel 904/785-9053. **New American.** Outdoor dining on open-air deck offers lovely views of St Andrews Bay. The standard menu includes prime rib, charcoal-broiled steaks, and fresh Gulf seafood; there's also a salad bar. **FYI:** Reservations accepted. Dancing/piano. **Open:** Daily 6am–10pm. **Prices:** Main courses $9–$17. AE, CB, DC, DISC, MC, V. 🏛 ▼ &

### Pappy's German Restaurant and Oyster Bar
In St Andrews Marina, 1000 Bayview Ave; tel 904/785-6611. **German/Seafood.** Tiny (only four tables!) older restaurant with lots of local atmosphere. Typical German fare—sauerbraten, knockwurst, and some local seafood—can be washed down with imported German brews. **FYI:** Reservations not accepted. Beer and wine only. **Open:** Mon–Sat 11am–10pm. Closed Aug 1–14. **Prices:** Main courses $8–$10. MC, V. 🖼

## ATTRACTIONS 🖼

### Junior Museum of Bay County
1731 Jenks Ave; tel 904/769-6128. Exhibits include a Florida pioneer log cabin, a grist and cane mill, and Native American artifacts from nearby archeological digs. Also on site: a re-created 1880s farm where visitors can feed chickens and ducks, a nature trail with an elevated walkway, and science exhibits. **Open:** Tues–Fri 10am–4:30pm, Sat 10am–4pm. **Free**

### Dead Lakes State Recreation Area
Wewahitchka; tel 904/639-2702. Located 20 mi E of Panama City off FL 71, near the Apalachicola River and Apalachicola National Forest. Along the nature trails, pine, magnolia, and cypress trees border wetlands where visitors can spot alligators and other critters. Fishing, boating, and overnight camping available. **Open:** Daily 8am–sunset. $$$

# Panama City Beach

On a barrier island south of Panama City, this town's attractions range from Captain Anderson's Shell Island Tours to Zoo World. Twenty-seven miles of white Gulf beaches draw crowds during spring break. Kids like the Miracle Strip Amusement Park. **Information:** Panama City Beach Convention & Visitors Bureau, 12015 Front Beach Rd, PO Box 9473, Panama City Beach, 32417 (tel 904/234-6575).

## HOTELS 🏨

### 🛏🛏🛏 Holiday Inn SunSpree Resort
11127 Front Beach Rd, 32407; tel 904/234-1111 or toll free 800/633-0266; fax 904/235-1907. Just off Thomas Dr gulfside. This curved, 15-story beach hotel offers all Gulf-front rooms. Its dramatic, tropical lobby has a waterfall. **Rooms:** 342 rms. Executive level. CI 4pm/CO 11am. Non-smoking rms avail. Attractive, spacious rooms have Gulf views from balconies. **Amenities:** 🛁 👗 📺 🍷 A/C, cable TV w/movies, refrig. All units w/terraces, some w/whirlpools. **Services:** ✕ ➡ 🧺 🛎 Social director, children's program. **Facilities:** 🗝 🏐 🛏 & 1 restaurant, 2 bars (w/entertainment), 1 beach (ocean), basketball, volleyball, sauna, steam rm, playground, washer/dryer. Extra-large pool and lounge area. **Rates:** Peak (Mem Day–Labor Day) $139 S; $149 D. Children under age 12 stay free. Min stay special events. Lower rates off-season. Parking: Outdoor, free. AE, CB, DC, DISC, MC, V.

### 🛏🛏🛏 Ramada Inn Beach & Convention Center
12907 Front Beach Rd, 32407; tel 904/234-1700 or toll free 800/633-0266; fax 904/235-2700. On US 98, 3½ mi W of Hathaway Bridge. Modest facility catering to beachgoers. **Rooms:** 147 rms. CI 4pm/CO 11am. Nonsmoking rms avail. **Amenities:** 🛁 👗 A/C, cable TV. All units w/terraces. **Services:** ✕ 🧺 🛎 ✂ Babysitting. **Facilities:** 🗝 🏐 🛏 & 1 restaurant, 3 bars (1 w/entertainment), 1 beach (ocean), games rm, sauna, washer/dryer. Waves lap against the tiki bar. **Rates:** Peak (Mar–Aug) $99–$139 S; $149–$159 D. Extra person $10. Children under age 16 stay free. Min stay wknds. Lower rates off-season. Parking: Outdoor, free. AE, CB, DC, EC, JCB, MC, V.

### 🛏 The Sandpiper Beacon
17403 Front Beach Rd, 32413; tel 904/234-2154 or toll free 800/488-8828; fax 904/233-0278. A three-story complex with wide variety of accommodations, from small motel-style rooms to two-bedroom units sleeping up to ten people. (The latter units are especially popular at spring break). The already-cramped lobby will be hard-pressed to cope when 80

to 100 additional rooms are completed. **Rooms:** 155 rms, stes, and effic. CI 4pm/CO 11am. Nonsmoking rms avail. **Amenities:** 🛏 A/C, cable TV, refrig, in-rm safe. Some units w/terraces. **Services:** 🚗 🛒 🍴 🛎 Babysitting. **Facilities:** 🎣 ⚠ 🅿 ⚐ 1 restaurant, 1 bar (w/entertainment), 1 beach (ocean), lifeguard, volleyball, games rm, lawn games, whirlpool, playground, washer/dryer. Tiki beach bar. **Rates:** Peak (July–Labor Day) $89–$99 S or D; $99 ste; $99–$119 effic. Children under age 18 stay free. Min stay special events. Lower rates off-season. Parking: Outdoor, free. AE, DISC, MC, V.

## MOTELS

### ≣ Rendezvous Beach Resort

17281 Front Beach Rd, 32407; tel 904/234-8841 or toll free 800/874-6617. ½ block W of FL 79. Guests are likely to keep their eyes on the Gulf views rather than the interiors, at least until the post-hurricane renovations are completed and the corridors and walkways get spruced up. **Rooms:** 72 rms, stes, and effic. CI 3pm/CO 11am. **Amenities:** 🛏 A/C, cable TV, refrig. All units w/terraces. **Services:** 🛒 🍴 Babysitting. **Facilities:** 🎣 ⚐ 1 restaurant, 1 bar, 1 beach (ocean), lifeguard, whirlpool, washer/dryer. **Rates:** Peak (May 23–Sept 3) $60–$80 S or D; $95–$105 ste; $95–$105 effic. Extra person $5. Children under age 12 stay free. Lower rates off-season. Parking: Outdoor, free. AE, DISC, MC, V.

### ≣ Sunset Inn

8109 Surf Dr, 32408; tel 904/234-7370; fax 904/234-7370 ext 303. At Joan Ave. Family-oriented beachfront lodging. **Rooms:** 50 rms and effic. CI 2pm/CO 10am. Nonsmoking rms avail. Rooms are large and modestly furnished; some are recently redecorated. **Amenities:** 🛏 📺 A/C, cable TV, refrig. All units w/terraces. **Services:** 🍴 **Facilities:** 🎣 ⚐ 1 beach (ocean), washer/dryer. **Rates:** Peak (May 26–Labor Day) $53–$98 S or D; $60–$98 effic. Extra person $5. Children under age 18 stay free. Lower rates off-season. Parking: Outdoor, free. DISC, MC, V.

## RESORTS

### ≣≣≣ Edgewater Beach Resort

11212 Front Beach Rd, 32407; tel 904/235-4044. Large resort complex includes three high-rise towers as well as low condominium sections, half on the beautiful beach, half on the golf course. Spectacular beachfront swimming lagoon features cascading waterfalls and an island. Garden landscaping with palm trees. **Rooms:** 525 effic. CI 4pm/CO 10am. Nonsmoking rms avail. Spacious one- to three-bedroom apartments come with fully equipped kitchen and living and dining areas. **Amenities:** 🛏 📻 📺 A/C, cable TV w/movies, refrig, voice mail. All units w/terraces. Apartments have washers and dryers. **Services:** ✕ 🖥 🚗 🍴 Children's program, babysitting. **Facilities:** 🎣 🅿9 🏊12 🍴200 ⚐ 3 restaurants, 2 bars (1 w/entertainment), 1 beach (ocean), games rm, whirlpool, beauty salon, washer/dryer. **Rates:** Peak (May–

Sept) $165 effic. Children under age 18 stay free. Min stay special events. Lower rates off-season. Parking: Outdoor, free. AE, DC, DISC, MC, V.

### ≣≣≣≣ Marriott's Bay Point Resort

4200 Marriott Dr, 32411; tel 904/234-3307 or toll free 800/874-7105; fax 904/233-1308. Off Thomas Dr. 1,100 acres. Bordered by St Andrews Bay and Grand Lagoon, this top golf-and-tennis resort serves as a classy respite from the honky-tonk community nearby. The outstanding coral stucco hotel is surrounded by gardens, palm trees, oaks, and magnolias. A window wall in the three-story lobby looks out to pretty water views. **Rooms:** 355 rms and stes. CI 4pm/CO 11am. Nonsmoking rms avail. Spacious, well-maintained guest rooms. **Amenities:** 🛏 🍷 📺 🍷 A/C, cable TV w/movies, refrig, voice mail. All units w/minibars, all w/terraces, some w/fireplaces, some w/whirlpools. **Services:** ✕ 🖥 VP 🚗 🛒 🍴 🛎 Car-rental desk, social director, masseur, children's program, babysitting. **Facilities:** 🎣 🚲 ⚠ 🅿36 🎾 ⛳8 🏊4 🏌 ⚐ 1000 ⚐ 4 restaurants, 4 bars (2 w/entertainment), 1 beach (bay), basketball, volleyball, board surfing, games rm, snorkeling, spa, whirlpool, beauty salon, washer/dryer. **Rates:** Peak (March 3–Nov 16) $180–$210 S or D; $220–$400 ste. Extra person $20. Children under age 18 stay free. Min stay. Lower rates off-season. Parking: Outdoor, free. AE, CB, DC, DISC, ER, MC, V.

## RESTAURANTS 🍴

### Billy's

3000 Thomas Dr; tel 904/235-2349. **Seafood.** Billy's is hard to spot, but if you're looking to slurp some oysters and chug down an ice-cold longneck, this is the place. Besides oysters (be sure to heed the warning about eating them raw), Billy's serves up blue crab, Florida lobster, Gulf shrimp, and other local seafood favorites. **FYI:** Reservations not accepted. Beer and wine only. **Open:** Daily 11am–10pm. Closed Thanksgiving–Feb. **Prices:** Main courses $5–$15. AE, DISC, MC, V.

### Boar's Head Restaurant

17290 Front Beach Rd; tel 904/234-6628. **New American/British.** The pub-style decor of this comfortable establishment sets the stage for a British-inspired menu. Specialties include prime rib of beef with Yorkshire pudding on the side. Extensive wine list. A local favorite for over 15 years. **FYI:** Reservations accepted. Dancing/guitar/singer. Children's menu. **Open:** Peak (Mem Day–Labor Day) daily 4:30–10pm. Closed Christmas week. **Prices:** Main courses $13–$24. MC, V. 🍴 ⚐

### ⑤ Cajun Inn

In The Shoppes at Edgewater, 477 Beckrich Rd; tel 904/235-9987. **Cajun/Seafood.** Mardi Gras posters and paraphernalia provide a festive, down-home atmosphere. Owner/chef Kenny Gilmore specializes in Louisiana favorites done up with Cajun flair: crawfish and po' boys are especially popular. Six Bayou Country luncheon specials are available daily, and come with either curly or Cajun fries, boiled potatoes or corn-on-the-cob, a slab of Cajun bread, and a tall glass of iced tea. **FYI:** Reservations not accepted. Children's menu. Beer and wine only. **Open:** Daily 11am–11pm. **Prices:** Main courses $4–$14. AE, CB, DC, DISC, MC, V. ◘ &

### Captain Anderson's Restaurant
5551 N Lagoon Dr; tel 904/234-2225. **Seafood/Steak.** Since 1953, owners Johnny and Jimmy Petronis have kept a hawk eye on every aspect of this award-winning restaurant. In addition to the freshest seafood, you're sure to find a wide variety of steaks and pasta dishes on the menu. Views are terrific from every table—come early to see the fishing boats unload their catch. **FYI:** Reservations not accepted. Children's menu. **Open:** Daily 4–10pm. Closed Nov–Feb. **Prices:** Main courses $11–$21. AE, DISC, MC, V. ▨ &

### Mariner Restaurant
9104 Front Beach Rd; tel 904/234-8450. 2 mi W of Hathaway Bridge. **Seafood/Buffet.** Panama City Beach loves its retirees, and retirees love the Mariner for its all-you-can-eat seafood buffet. The buffet price is reasonable at $6, and you can add crab or lobster for an additional $6 to $9. **FYI:** Reservations not accepted. Children's menu. **Open:** Peak (Mar–Sept) daily 11am–10pm. **Prices:** Main courses $10–$21. AE, DISC, MC, V. &

### Montego Bay Seafood House and Oyster Bar
4920 Thomas Dr; tel 904/234-8686. **Seafood/Steak.** Small, rather plain member of a local seafood chain. Very popular for its $4 lunch specials and dinnertime Captain's Catch Seafood Platters, stacked high with a variety of favorites and served with a savory hot gumbo and crisp salad. Parking is woefully inadequate. **FYI:** Reservations not accepted. Children's menu. Beer and wine only. Additional location: 477 Beckrich Rd (tel 233-6033). **Open:** Daily 11am–11pm. **Prices:** Main courses $7–$13. AE, DISC, MC, V.

## ATTRACTIONS ▥

### Museum of Man in the Sea
17314 Back Beach Rd; tel 904/235-4101. Among the diving-related exhibits are artifacts recovered from shipwrecks, including items from the Spanish galleon *Atocha* (a 25-minute video chronicles its discovery) and relics from the early days of scuba diving. Also displays on oceanography, marine life, and underwater archeology. **Open:** Daily 9am–5pm. $$.

### Gulf World
15412 Front Beach Rd; tel 904/234-5271. Set in a land-scaped tropical garden, this marine park has continuously running shows starring porpoises, sea lions, and parrots, and is home to penguins, sea turtles, alligators, and other creatures. Visitors can also witness shark feedings, scuba demonstrations, and underwater shows. **Open:** Peak (Mem Day–Labor Day) daily 9am–7pm. Reduced hours off-season. $$$$

### Zoo World Zoological & Botanical Park
9008 Front Beach Rd (US 98); tel 904/230-0096. More than 100 species live here in re-created natural habitats, including many rare and endangered animals. Visitors can see orang-utans and other primates, big cats, and reptiles. **Open:** Daily 9am–sunset. $$$

### Miracle Strip Amusement Park
12000 Front Beach Rd; tel 904/234-5810. A family-oriented park with nine acres of rides and attractions, food concessions, and a full-service snack bar. **Open:** Peak (June–Labor Day) Mon–Fri 6–11:30pm, Sat 1–11:30pm, Sun 3–11:30pm. Reduced hours off-season. Closed Labor Day–mid-Mar. $$$$

### Shipwreck Island Water Park
12000 Front Beach Rd; tel 904/234-0368. A six-acre water park built around a tropical theme. Highlights include 1,600-foot river for tubing, Speed Slide, Tree Top Drop, wave pool, and children's activity area. Lifeguard. **Open:** Peak (June–Labor Day) daily 10:30am–5:30pm. Reduced hours off-season. Closed Sept–mid-April. $$$$

### Captain Anderson's Marina
5550 N Lagoon Dr; tel 904/234-3435. This double-decker offers several day-trip excursions to Shell Island, an uninhabited natural preserve offering terrific opportunities for shell collecting, swimming, and sunbathing on the brilliant white sand beach. Tours leave daily at 9am and 1pm. **Open:** Mar–Oct. Call for cruise schedule. $$$

### St Andrews State Recreation Area
4415 Thomas Dr; tel 904/233-5140. Located 3 mi E of Panama City Beach. This area of over 1,000 acres of dazzling beaches topped by towering sand dunes also features pine woodlands and the Grand Lagoon. Activities include swimming, scuba diving, boating, fishing from piers and jetties, picnicking, and camping. **Open:** Daily 8am–sunset. $$

# Pensacola

See also Gulf Breeze, Pensacola Beach

This city of 60,000 is half an hour east of Alabama in Florida's far western Panhandle. Historic Pensacola Village commemorates Spanish, French, and English colonization of the area during the 18th century. **Information:** Pensacola Area Chamber of Commerce, 1401 E Gregory St, Pensacola, 32501 (tel 904/434-1234).

## HOTELS ▥

### ≣≣ Days Inn Downtown
710 N Palafox St, 32501; tel 904/438-4922 or toll free 800/329-7466; fax 904/438-7999. Cervantes St exit off I-110. An economically priced, well-kept older facility, close to the historic district. **Rooms:** 156 rms. CI 3pm/CO noon. Non-smoking rms avail. **Amenities:** ▥ A/C, satel TV w/movies, in-rm safe. **Services:** ✕ ▨ ▧ ▨ **Facilities:** ▧ [75] 1 restaurant. **Rates:** Peak (Easter–Labor Day) $45–$56 S or D. Extra

person $5. Children under age 18 stay free. Min stay special events. Lower rates off-season. Parking: Outdoor, free. AE, CB, DC, DISC, MC, V.

### ≣≣ New World Landing
600 S Palafox St, 32501; tel 904/432-4111; fax 904/435-8939. Garden St exit off I-110. Attractive hotel designed with natural woods and brick and overseen by a dedicated staff. **Rooms:** 16 rms and stes. CI 2pm/CO noon. Nonsmoking rms avail. Rooms are individually decorated. **Amenities:** 🛏 ⚗ ☎ A/C, cable TV. **Services:** ✗ ⊠ ⊲ **Facilities:** ⌷1000⌷ ⚐ 1 restaurant (lunch and dinner only; see "Restaurants" below), 1 bar. **Rates:** $70 S; $80 D; $125 ste. Extra person $10. Children under age 18 stay free. Parking: Outdoor, free. AE, MC, V.

### ≣≣≣ Pensacola Grand Hotel
200 E Gregory St, 32501; tel 904/433-3336 or toll free 800/348-3336; fax 904/432-7572. Garden St exit off I-110. Unique hotel in the Seville Historic District on the site of the former L & N Train Depot, built in 1912. The beautifully restored grand lobby, which incorporates the antiquated station, contains an ornate railroad clock, the original oak stair rails, mosaic tile floors, and antique furniture. The 2-story glass galleria links the historic depot to the modern 15-floor tower housing guest rooms. **Rooms:** 212 rms and stes. Executive level. CI 3pm/CO 1pm. Nonsmoking rms avail. Executive floors have city views. **Amenities:** 🛏 ⚗ ☎ ⚐ A/C, cable TV. Some units w/minibars, some w/whirlpools. **Services:** ✗ 🚐 ⊠ ⊲ ⚐ Car-rental desk, babysitting. **Facilities:** ⌷ 🏊 ⌷600⌷ ⚐ 1 restaurant, 2 bars, games rm. **Rates:** $85–$90 S; $90–$100 D; $204 ste. Extra person $10. Min stay. Parking: Outdoor, free. AE, CB, DC, DISC, MC, V.

### ≣≣ Residence Inn
7230 Plantation Rd, 32504; tel 904/479-1000 or toll free 800/331-3131; fax 904/477-3399. Exit 5 off I-110. Residential-style living; units have kitchens and living and sleeping areas. Handy to the interstate and University Mall. **Rooms:** 64 stes. CI noon/CO noon. Nonsmoking rms avail. **Amenities:** 🛏 ⚗ ☎ A/C, cable TV, refrig. 1 unit w/minibar, some w/terraces, all w/fireplaces. **Services:** ✗ ⊠ ⊲ Babysitting. **Facilities:** ⌷ ⌷40⌷ ⚐ Sauna, washer/dryer. **Rates (CP):** $92–$118 ste. Children under age 18 stay free. Parking: Outdoor, free. AE, DC, DISC, MC, V.

## MOTELS

### ≣≣≣ Best Western Perdido Key Beach
13585 Perdido Key Dr, 32507 (Perdido Key); tel 904/492-2755 or toll free 800/554-8879; fax 904/492-9587. Located on a pristine island west of Pensacola, this family-friendly motel is near the preserved beaches of the Gulf Islands National Seashore and Big Lagoon State Recreation Area. **Rooms:** 100 rms. CI 4pm/CO 11am. Nonsmoking rms avail. **Amenities:** 🛏 ⚗ A/C, cable TV, refrig. Microwaves. **Services:** ⊠ ⊲ Fishing charters can be arranged. **Facilities:** ⌷ ⌷25⌷ Games rm, whirlpool, playground, washer/dryer.

Restaurants nearby. **Rates (CP):** Peak (Mar–Sept) $75 S; $90 D. Extra person $10. Children under age 18 stay free. Min stay special events. Lower rates off-season. Parking: Outdoor, free. Golf packages avail. AE, DC, DISC, MC, V.

### ≣≣ Hampton Inn University Mall
7330 Plantation Rd, 32514; tel 904/477-3333 or toll free 800/426-7866; fax 904/477-8163. Exit 5 off I-10. Fairly priced middle-grade choice. Mall and restaurants are within walking distance. **Rooms:** 124 rms. CI 3pm/CO noon. Nonsmoking rms avail. **Amenities:** 🛏 ⚗ ☎ A/C, satel TV w/movies, dataport. Complimentary morning coffee and newspaper. **Services:** ✗ 🚐 ⊠ ⊲ Room service and airport transportation offered through nearby Holiday Inn. **Facilities:** ⌷12⌷ Guests have access to the pool at the Holiday Inn next door. **Rates (CP):** Peak (Mar–Sept 4) $70 S; $76 D. Extra person $6. Children under age 18 stay free. Min stay special events. Lower rates off-season. Parking: Outdoor, free. AE, DC, DISC, MC, V.

### ≣≣ Holiday Inn Express
6501 Pensacola Blvd, 32505; tel 904/476-7200 or toll free 800/HOLIDAY; fax 904/476-1277. Exit 3A off I-10. Basic motel. Offers rates lower than traditional Holiday Inns. **Rooms:** 214 rms. CI 3pm/CO noon. Nonsmoking rms avail. **Amenities:** 🛏 ⚗ ☎ A/C, satel TV w/movies. 1 unit w/minibar. **Services:** ⊠ ⊲ **Facilities:** ⌷ ⌷200⌷ ⚐ Washer/dryer. **Rates (CP):** Peak (May–Sept) $85 S or D. Extra person $6. Children under age 18 stay free. Lower rates off-season. Parking: Indoor, free. AE, DC, DISC, MC, V.

### ≣≣≣ Holiday Inn University Mall
7200 N Plantation Rd, 32514; tel 904/474-0100 or toll free 800/465-4329; fax 904/477-9821. Exit 5 off I-110. A very nice stopover, equally appropriate for businesspeople and families. Although it sits next to I-10, a dense line of trees muffles traffic noise. **Rooms:** 152 rms. CI 3pm/CO noon. Nonsmoking rms avail. **Amenities:** 🛏 ⚗ ☎ A/C, satel TV w/movies. Complimentary 24-hour coffee and morning newspaper. **Services:** ✗ 🚐 ⊠ ⊲ **Facilities:** ⌷ ⌷200⌷ 1 restaurant, 2 bars (1 w/entertainment), washer/dryer. Comedy club 3 times a week. **Rates (BB):** $77 S or D. Extra person $6. Children under age 21 stay free. Min stay special events. Parking: Outdoor, free. AE, DC, DISC, MC, V.

### ≣≣≣ Ramada Inn Bayview
7601 Scenic Hwy, 32504; tel 904/477-7155 or toll free 800/282-1212. Exit 6 off I-10. Despite the name, most rooms here have views of parking lots rather than the bay. Still, it's convenient and quiet, and the service is friendly and professional. **Rooms:** 50 rms and stes. CI 3pm/CO noon. Nonsmoking rms avail. **Amenities:** 🛏 ⚗ ☎ A/C, cable TV w/movies. All units w/terraces. **Services:** ✗ 🚐 ⊠ ⊲ ⚐ **Facilities:** ⌷ 🏊 ⌷80⌷ ⚐ 1 restaurant, 1 bar (w/entertainment), whirlpool. **Rates:** Peak (May 24–Aug) $48–$62 S;

$54–$68 D; $90 ste. Extra person $6. Children under age 18 stay free. Lower rates off-season. Parking: Outdoor, free. AE, CB, DC, DISC, MC, V.

### ▤▤ Ramada Inn North

6550 Pensacola Blvd, 32505; tel 904/477-0711 or toll free 800/838-7642; fax 904/477-0711 ext 602. Good, no-nonsense accommodations. **Rooms:** 106 rms and stes. CI 3pm/CO noon. Nonsmoking rms avail. **Amenities:** 🛏 👜 📺 🍴A/C, cable TV, voice mail. Some units w/minibars, some w/terraces. **Services:** ✗ 🚗 🖼 🍸 Babysitting. **Facilities:** 🏊 🏊 & 1 restaurant, 1 bar, washer/dryer. **Rates:** Peak (Apr–Sept) $50–$60 S; $60–$74 D; $99 ste. Extra person $10. Children under age 18 stay free. Min stay special events. Lower rates off-season. Parking: Outdoor, free. AE, CB, DC, DISC, ER, JCB, MC, V.

### ▤ Red Roof Inn

7340 Plantation Rd, 32504; tel 904/476-7960 or toll free 800/THE-ROOF. Exit 5 off I-110. Budget-minded motel sufficient for overnight stays. **Rooms:** 108 rms. CI open/CO noon. Nonsmoking rms avail. **Amenities:** 🛏 A/C, satel TV w/movies. All units w/terraces. **Services:** 🍸 🖥 **Facilities:** & **Rates:** Peak (Mar–Sept) $45 S; $52 D. Extra person $6. Children under age 18 stay free. Lower rates off-season. Parking: Outdoor, free. AE, CB, DC, DISC, MC, V.

### ▤▤ Seville Inn

223 E Garden St, 32501; tel 904/433-8331 or toll free 800/277-7275; fax 904/432-6849. Garden St exit off I-110. Downtown location is convenient for commercial travelers as well as families. **Rooms:** 125 rms. CI 3pm/CO 11am. Nonsmoking rms avail. **Amenities:** 🛏 🍴A/C, cable TV. **Services:** 🚗 🖼 🍸 🖥 **Facilities:** 🏊 💯 & Washer/dryer. **Rates:** Peak (May–Aug) $39–$59 S; $44–$69 D. Extra person $10. Children under age 18 stay free. Min stay special events. Lower rates off-season. Parking: Outdoor, free. AE, DC, DISC, MC, V.

### ▤▤ Shoney's Inn

8086 N Davis Hwy, 32504; tel 904/484-8070 or toll free 800/222-2222; fax 904/484-3853. Exit 5 off I-10. Satisfactory for a short stay. **Rooms:** 115 rms. CI 3pm/CO noon. Nonsmoking rms avail. **Amenities:** 🛏 A/C, satel TV w/movies. **Services:** 🖼 🍸 **Facilities:** 🏊 💯 1 restaurant, washer/dryer. **Rates (BB):** Peak (May–Sept 5) $68 S; $74 D. Extra person $6. Children under age 18 stay free. Min stay special events. Lower rates off-season. Parking: Outdoor, free. AE, DC, DISC, MC, V.

## RESTAURANTS 🍴

### ✸ The Ale House

In Harbour Village at Pitt Slip Marina, 600 S Barracks St; tel 904/435-9719. Garden St exit off I-110. **American.** Enjoy some of the best views in the area of the Seville Historic District, Pitt Slip Marina, and Pensacola Bay. The menu is a crowd-pleaser, too, with everything from New Orleans muffulettas and fresh seafood to gigantic sandwiches and imported beer. **FYI:** Reservations accepted. Jazz. Children's menu. **Open:** Sun–Wed 11am–1am, Thurs–Sat 11am–2am. **Prices:** Main courses $7–$14. AE, MC, V. 📷

### $ ✸ Hopkin's Boarding House

900 N Spring St; tel 904/438-3979. Cervantes St exit off I-110. **American/Southern.** Since 1949, Hopkin's has been serving up traditional cooking. Platters are piled high with seasonal southern-style vegetables from nearby farms. Tuesday is famous as Fried Chicken Day, and you're likely to be served fried fish on Friday. (All dinners include beverage and dessert.) Rocking chairs and park benches lining the huge wrapped veranda make the wait for seating almost pleasant. **FYI:** Reservations not accepted. No liquor license. No smoking. **Open:** Breakfast Tues–Sun 7–9:30am; lunch Tues–Sun 11am–2pm; dinner Tues–Fri 5:15–7:30pm. Closed Dec 25–Jan 1. **Prices:** Main courses $7. No CC. 📷

### ♣ Jamie's

424 E Zaragoza St; tel 904/434-2911. Garden St exit off I-110. **French.** An elegant dining room in the Seville Historic District. Among the gourmet favorites are grilled lamb chops laced with mint-mustard sauce. For a luscious dessert, try the white-chocolate Grand Marnier mousse. **FYI:** Reservations recommended. Guitar. Dress code. Beer and wine only. **Open:** Lunch Tues–Sat 11:30am–2:30pm; dinner Mon–Sat 6–10pm. **Prices:** Main courses $18–$22. AE, DISC, MC, V. ♥ 🍷

### ✸ McGuire's Irish Pub & Brewery

600 E Gregory St (East Hill); tel 904/433-6789. Cervantes or Gregory St exit off I-110. **Seafood/Steak.** A Gaelic-style tavern where you'll find steak, seafood dishes, and pub fare at fair prices. **FYI:** Reservations not accepted. Guitar/karaoke/singer. Children's menu. **Open:** Daily 11am–11pm. **Prices:** Main courses $15–$20. AE, MC, V. 🍷 📷 📷

### ♣ New World Landing Restaurant

In New World Landing, 600 S Palafox St; tel 904/434-7736. Garden St exit off I-110. **Regional American/Seafood/Steak.** Charming restaurant in an old brick building, with dining rooms recalling different periods in Pensacola's colorful history. Chandeliers, antique furnishings, and rich wood paneling enhance the setting. Dine on seafood in wine or butter sauce, or on prime rib, steak, or veal. **FYI:** Reservations recommended. Children's menu. **Open:** Lunch Tues–Fri 11am–2pm; dinner Tues–Sat 5:30–9:30pm. **Prices:** Main courses $10–$20. AE, MC, V. ♥ 📧 &

### The Oyster Bar

In the Oyster Bar/Shelter Cove Marina, 13700 River Rd, Perdido Key; tel 904/492-0192. Under the Perdido Key bridge. **Barbecue/Seafood.** The Oyster Bar comes highly recommended for views of the Intracoastal Waterway; outdoor dining even allows patrons to commune with pelicans and dolphins. "Fresh from the Gulf" seafood dominates the menu. **FYI:** Reservations recommended. Children's menu.

Additional location: 709 N Navy Blvd, Pensacola (tel 455-3925). **Open:** Peak (Apr–Oct) Tues–Thurs 11am–10:30pm, Fri–Sat 11am–11pm. **Prices:** Main courses $8–$21. AE, CB, DC, DISC, MC, V. 🍽 🏔 💟

### ♥ Skopelos on the Bay
670 Scenic Hwy; tel 904/432-6565. Cervantes St exit off I-110. **Seafood/Steak.** One of the area's finest dining experiences, featuring Greek-inspired seafood dishes such as scampi Cervantes (sautéed fillet of scampi stuffed with crabmeat) and grouper served with tomato sauce and roasted eggplant. **FYI:** Reservations recommended. Children's menu. Dress code. **Open:** Lunch Fri 11:30am–2:30pm; dinner Tues–Sat 5–10:30pm. **Prices:** Main courses $14–$20. AE, DISC, MC, V. 🍸 ⚅

### The Yacht Restaurant and Lounge
In Pitt Slip Marina, 600 S Barracks St, Slip No 1; tel 904/432-3707. Chase St exit off I-110. **Regional American.** Enjoy an elegant dinner aboard the *Good Neighbor,* a 153-foot yacht once owned by Carl Fisher (of Body by Fisher fame) and now permanently moored at Pitt Slip Marina. **FYI:** Reservations recommended. **Open:** Peak (Mem Day–Labor Day) Tues–Sun 6–10pm, Fri 11am–2:30pm, Sun 11:30am–2:30pm. **Prices:** Main courses $10–$18. AE, DISC, MC, V. 🍴 🏔

## ATTRACTIONS 📷

### Historic Pensacola Village and the T T Wentworth Jr Florida State Museum
330 S Jefferson St; tel 904/444-8905. **Historic Pensacola Village** includes the Museum of Industry, which contains a historic saw mill; The Museum of Commerce, with many of the storefronts and shop fittings of turn-of-the-century Pensacola; the Second Spanish period Charles Lavalle House (1805); the elegant Victorian period Dorr House (1871); and the Julee Cottage (1805), which houses an exhibit on African American history in west Florida.

The landmark Renaissance Revival–style **Wentworth Museum** (1907), originally the city hall, contains an eclectic collection of objects and memorabilia pertaining to the art, archeology, and history of west Florida. The third floor of the Wentworth houses the **Discovery Children's Museum.**

Combination tickets to the village and the museum are good for two days, and can be purchased at the museum or at the Village Ticket and Information Center (205 E Zaragoza St). **Open:** Peak (Easter to Labor Day) daily 10am–4pm. Reduced hours off-season. **$$$**

### OTHER ATTRACTIONS

### Pensacola Museum of Art
407 S Jefferson St; tel 904/432-6247. Housed in a two-story Mission Revival building that was once used as the city jail, the museum features permanent and changing exhibits ranging from European masters to the avant-garde. **Open:** Tues–Fri 10am–5pm, Sat 10am–4pm, Sun 1–4pm. **$**

### Civil War Soldiers Museum
108 S Palafox Place; tel 904/469-1900. Life-size dioramas, paintings, and artifacts dealing with the Civil War. The bookstore features more than 500 titles, as well as art prints, period music, and such souvenirs as Confederate soldiers' caps. **Open:** Mon–Sat 10am–4:30pm. **$$**

### National Museum of Naval Aviation
1750 Radford Blvd, Ste C; tel 904/452-3604. One of the world's largest air and space museums and located at the world's largest air station, this major attraction traces the history and development of Navy, Marine Corps, and Coast Guard aviation. Nearly 100 historic aircraft are on display, from biplanes and blimps to such space-age craft as the Skylab command module and an F-14 Tomcat fighter plane. The museum is also home to memorabilia, scale models, and high-tech photography. **Open:** Daily 9am–5pm. **Free**

### Palafox Historic District
Tel 904/444-8905. Formerly Old Pensacola's harborfront commercial center, this area features fine Spanish Renaissance–style buildings. At one time the area had such outstanding hotels as the San Carlos, at Palafox and Garden Sts, once considered one of the South's finest but closed for many years. Other structures have been restored, though, including the ornate **Saenger Theater,** with wrought-iron balconies, now the base of the Pensacola Symphony Orchestra. **Plaza Ferdinand VII,** part of Pensacola's first settlement, is a National Historic Landmark. At a ceremony here in 1821 Gen Andrew Jackson formally accepted Florida into the United States. His statue commemorates the event. **Free**

### North Hill Preservation District
Tel 904/444-8905. Located just north of the Palafox Historic District, this 50-block district contains more than 500 homes built for Pensacola's professional classes between 1870 and 1930. Homes in this fashionable, tree-studded area reflect a wide variety of architectural styles—Tudor revival, neoclassical, Queen Anne, Victorian, and art moderne are just some. **Free**

### Bay Bluffs Park
Scenic Hwy (US 90) and Summit. Part of the Scenic Highway, where US 90 heads northeast to Tallahassee, the park offers 20 acres of nature trails and boardwalks. An elevated boardwalk descends stunning red bluffs, which afford spectacular views of Pensacola Bay.

# Pensacola Beach

## HOTELS 🏨

### ▰▰▰ Best Western Pensacola Beach
16 Via de Luna Dr, 32561; tel 904/934-3300 or toll free 800/934-3301; fax 904/934-9780. Beaches exit off I-110. 2 acres. A first-class facility offering large, sunlit rooms and fun, beach-inspired furnishings. Post-hurricane renovations

have brought lush new landscaping. **Rooms:** 122 rms. CI 3pm/CO 11am. Nonsmoking rms avail. All rooms face the Gulf. **Amenities:** 🔒 ⚴ ▣ A/C, cable TV w/movies, voice mail. Some units w/terraces. Microwaves. **Services:** ➖ ⌣ **Facilities:** 🔒 200 1 beach (ocean), washer/dryer. Cabana bar on beach. **Rates (CP):** Peak (Apr–Sept 5) $105–$115 S or D. Children under age 18 stay free. Lower rates off-season. Parking: Outdoor, free. AE, DC, DISC, MC, V.

### 📶📶📶 Clarion Suites Resort

20 Via de Luna Dr, 32561; tel 904/932-4300 or toll free 800/874-5303; fax 904/934-9112. Beaches exit off I-110. An upscale choice appropriate for couples, families, and business travelers. Units are built like pastel-colored cottages, where entryways and windows are well spaced and angled for privacy, and all have gorgeous Gulf views. **Rooms:** 86 stes. CI 3pm/CO 11am. Nonsmoking rms avail. All suites have water views. **Amenities:** 🔒 ⚴ ▣ A/C, cable TV, refrig. Some units w/terraces. All suites have 2 TVs and 2 telephones. **Services:** ➖🖂⌣ Twice-daily maid svce, babysitting. **Facilities:** 🔒 ⟊ 500 ▭ 1 beach (ocean), washer/dryer. **Rates (CP):** Peak (Apr–Sept 3) $131–$161 ste. Extra person $10. Children under age 18 stay free. Min stay special events. Lower rates off-season. Parking: Outdoor, free. AE, DC, DISC, JCB, MC, V.

### 📶📶📶 Comfort Inn

40 Fort Pickens Rd, 32561; tel 904/934-5400 or toll free 800/934-5470; fax 904/932-7210. Beaches exit off I-110. Right off Pensacola Beach Blvd across from Casino Beach parking lot. Very nice spot on Little Sabine Bay, offering great sunset views from the pool area or bayside rooms. **Rooms:** 100 rms. CI 3pm/CO 11am. Nonsmoking rms avail. Upper floors have views of the bay and the Gulf. **Amenities:** 🔒 ▣ A/C, cable TV w/movies, refrig. Some units w/terraces. All rooms have microwaves. *USA Today* provided to guests on request daily. **Services:** ➖🖂⌣ Coffee provided in lobby 24 hours. **Facilities:** 🔒 ⟊ 60 ⛷ 1 beach (bay). **Rates (CP):** Peak (Apr–Sept 5) $89–$99 S or D. Extra person $10. Children under age 18 stay free. Min stay special events. Lower rates off-season. Parking: Outdoor, free. Fourth-floor "panorama" rooms—with views of the harbor, the bay, and the Gulf—are $10 extra. Government, corporate, senior, and military rates avail. AE, CB, DC, DISC, MC, V.

### 📶📶📶 Hampton Inn

2 Via de Luna, 32561; tel 904/932-6800 or toll free 800/HAMPTON; fax 904/932-6833. Beaches exit off I-110. On Pensacola Beach's main commercial strip, about ½ mile from the island toll booth. This new structure in the beach's main core area looks a bit foreboding, but inside, guests are treated to beautifully furnished rooms and plenty of extras. Nice views of either Santa Rosa Sound or the Gulf add to the Hampton's appeal. **Rooms:** 181 rms. CI 4pm/CO 11am. Nonsmoking rms avail. **Amenities:** 🔒 ⚴ A/C, cable TV w/movies, refrig. Some units w/terraces. All rooms have microwaves and wet bars. **Services:** 🗝 ➖🖂⌣ Free local

calls. **Facilities:** 🔒2 200 ⛷ 1 beach (ocean), washer/dryer. Dazzling Gulf-front beach. Both pools front the Gulf. **Rates (CP):** Peak (May–Sept 2) $95–$125 S; $101–$131 D. Children under age 18 stay free. Min stay special events. Lower rates off-season. Parking: Outdoor, free. Senior discounts avail. AE, CB, DC, DISC, MC, V.

## MOTEL

### 📶 Five Flags Motel

299 Fort Pickens Rd, 32561; tel 904/932-3586; fax 904/934-0257. Beaches exit off I-110. For the family that absolutely has to stay on the beach, this budget motel is a no-frills option. **Rooms:** 50 rms. CI 3pm/CO 11am. **Amenities:** 🔒 A/C, cable TV. All units w/terraces. **Facilities:** 🔒 1 beach (ocean). Gulfside outdoor pool is heated during March and April. **Rates:** Peak (May–Sept 4) $75 S or D. Min stay special events. Lower rates off-season. Parking: Outdoor, free. AE, DISC, MC, V.

## RESTAURANT 🍴

### 🍷 Jubilee Topside

In Quietwater Beach Boardwalk, 400 Quietwater Beach Rd; tel 904/934-3108. Garden St exit off I-110. **Seafood/Steak.** Most of the dining areas at this beachside restaurant/entertainment complex are very casual, and the cooking is consistently top-notch. Lunch and dinner in the pub-style Beachside Cafe offers a varied menu of fish and deli sandwiches, nachos, pasta, and salads, while the elegant Topside Restaurant excels in mesquite-grilled steaks and seafood specialties like Chicken de Luna (topped by chunks of sautéed crabmeat). **FYI:** Reservations recommended. **Open:** Peak (June–Aug) Sun–Thurs 6–10pm, Fri–Sat 5–11pm, Sun 9am–3pm. **Prices:** Main courses $11–$20. AE, DC, DISC, MC, V. ♥

# Perdido Key

See Pensacola

# Pine Island

See also Captiva Island, Sanibel Island

## RESTAURANT 🍴

### The Bokeelia Bootlegger

In Harborside at Four Winds Marina, 16501 Stringfellow Rd, Bokeelia; tel 941/283-4301. Northern end of Pine Island. **Seafood.** A colorful mural and harbor view brighten a modest dining room where fresh seafood dominates the menu. **FYI:** Reservations accepted. Children's menu. **Open:** Peak (mid-Dec–Apr) daily 11:30am–9pm. Closed Aug–Sept. **Prices:** Main courses $8–$21. AE, DISC, MC, V. 🏔 ⛷

# Pompano Beach

Harness racing, community theater, and boat charters on the Intracoastal Waterway are a few options in this resort city five miles north of Fort Lauderdale. Goodyear blimps dock here, and Quiet Waters Park offers boatless water-skiing via moving cables. **Information:** Greater Pompano Beach Chamber of Commerce, 2200 E Atlantic Blvd, Pompano Beach, 33062 (tel 954/941-2940).

## HOTELS 🏨

### ▤▤▤ Beachcomber Hotel and Villas

1200 S Ocean Blvd, 33062; tel 954/941-7830 or toll free 800/231-2423; fax 954/942-7680. Exit 34A off I-95. Set on lush, tropical oceanside grounds, with a relaxed atmosphere enhanced by rattan-furnished lobby with fountain. **Rooms:** 138 rms, stes, and effic; 2 cottages/villas. CI 3pm/CO 11am. Nonsmoking rms avail. Generally large rooms, with ocean views, tropical colors, dust ruffles, and large baths. **Amenities:** 🛁 ♨ 📺 🍴 A/C, cable TV w/movies, refrig, in-rm safe. Some units w/terraces. **Services:** ✕ 🖼 🍹 Car-rental desk. **Facilities:** 🛥 ⬚100 ♿ 1 restaurant, 2 bars (1 w/entertainment), 1 beach (ocean), lawn games, playground, washer/dryer. **Rates:** Peak (Jan 16–Apr 15) $90 S or D; $185–$202 ste; $155 effic; $195–$254 cottage/villa. Extra person $10. Children under age 12 stay free. Min stay special events. Lower rates off-season. AP rates avail. Parking: Outdoor, free. AE, DC, DISC, MC, V.

### ▤▤ Holiday Inn Pompano Beach

1350 S Ocean Blvd, 33062; tel 954/941-7300 or toll free 800/332-2735; fax 954/941-7300 ext 7793. ¾ mi S of Atlantic Blvd (FL 814). Pleasant lodging straddles both sides of FL A1A. **Rooms:** 112 rms, stes, and effic; 21 cottages/villas. CI 2pm/CO 11am. Nonsmoking rms avail. **Amenities:** 🛁 ♨ A/C, cable TV w/movies, refrig. All units w/terraces. **Services:** ✕ 🖭 🖼 🍹 Social director, children's program, babysitting. Water taxi stops at Intracoastal Waterway dock. **Facilities:** 🛥 ⛰ 🍹3 🎣 🐟 ⬚110 ♿ 1 restaurant, 2 bars (1 w/entertainment), 1 beach (ocean), board surfing, games rm, lawn games, snorkeling, day-care ctr, washer/dryer. Guests receive discounts for nearby Gold's Gym. **Rates:** Peak (Dec–Apr) $130 S or D; $155 ste; $155 effic; $185 cottage/villa. Extra person $10. Children under age 19 stay free. Lower rates off-season. AP and MAP rates avail. Parking: Outdoor, free. AE, CB, DC, DISC, JCB, MC, V.

### ▤▤ Howard Johnson's Pompano Beach Resort

9 N Pompano Beach Blvd, 33062; tel 954/781-1300 or toll free 800/223-5844; fax 954/782-5585. Centrally located for the beach, shopping, and attractions. A fishing pier is up the street. **Rooms:** 104 rms and effic. CI 3pm/CO noon. Nonsmoking rms avail. Pastel decor and wicker headboards. Most rooms offer ocean views. **Amenities:** 🛁 ♨ A/C, cable TV w/movies. Some units w/terraces. Refrigerators available from front desk for $3 a day. **Services:** ✕ 🚐 🖼 🍹 Free

morning coffee and newspapers in lobby. **Facilities:** 🛥 1 restaurant, 1 bar, 1 beach (ocean), lifeguard, washer/dryer. **Rates:** Peak (Feb 1–Apr 9) $120–$170 S or D; $140 effic. Extra person $10. Children under age 18 stay free. Lower rates off-season. Parking: Indoor/outdoor, free. AE, CB, DC, DISC, MC, V.

### ▤▤▤ Santa Barbara Resort & Yacht Club

1301 S Ocean Blvd, 33062; tel 954/941-5566; fax 954/941-3010. I-95 to Atlantic Blvd. Situated between the ocean and the Intracoastal Waterway, this high-rise offers spectacular views from all its rooms. Completely renovated in 1995. **Rooms:** 90 stes. CI 4pm/CO 10am. Nonsmoking rms avail. Rooms are beautifully decorated in lush tropical prints and rattan furniture. **Amenities:** 🛁 ♨ 📺 A/C, cable TV w/movies, refrig, dataport, VCR, CD/tape player. All units w/terraces, all w/whirlpools. All units contain a hot tub, a wet bar, and a fully equipped kitchen. **Services:** 🖭 🍹 Social director, children's program, babysitting. **Facilities:** 🛥 ⬚50 ♿ 1 restaurant, 1 bar, 1 beach (ocean), games rm, whirlpool, washer/dryer. **Rates:** Peak (Dec–Apr) $199–$250 ste. Extra person $10. Children under age 18 stay free. Min stay. Lower rates off-season. Parking: Outdoor, free. AE, CB, DC, DISC, MC, V.

## RESORT

### ▤▤▤ Palm-Aire Spa, Resort & Club

2601 Palm-Aire Dr N, 33069; tel 954/972-3300 or toll free 800/272-5624; fax 954/968-2711. Exit 32 off I-95. 1,500 acres. Hidden in a private tropical setting, this resort offers an ideal balance of relaxation and recreation. **Rooms:** 100 rms and stes. CI 3pm/CO 11am. Nonsmoking rms avail. Some units include two full baths and a separate dressing area. **Amenities:** 🛁 📺 🍴 A/C, cable TV w/movies, refrig, dataport, VCR, CD/tape player. All units w/terraces, some w/whirlpools. **Services:** ✕ 🖭 VP 🚐 🖼 🍹 ⬚ Car-rental desk, social director, masseur, children's program, babysitting. **Facilities:** 🛥 🍹90 🏊 🎾37 🎳 ⬚400 ♿ 1 restaurant, 1 bar (w/entertainment), basketball, volleyball, games rm, racquetball, squash, spa, sauna, steam rm, whirlpool, beauty salon, playground, washer/dryer. Features 5 championship golf courses and a world-class spa. **Rates:** Peak (Dec 13–Apr) $129–$240 S or D; $300 ste. Extra person $10. Children under age 12 stay free. Lower rates off-season. Parking: Outdoor, free. Group rates avail; spa and golf packages avail. AE, CB, DC, DISC, MC, V.

## RESTAURANTS 🍴

### Cafe Maxx

2601 E Atlantic Blvd; tel 954/782-0606. **Regional American/Caribbean.** An inventive restaurant outfitted with fine woods, stylish appointments, iron ice cream parlor–style chairs, and an open kitchen. The menu includes sweet onion–crusted yellowtail snapper, lamb, and fillet of veal. **FYI:** Reservations recommended. Dress code. Beer and wine only.

**Open:** Sun–Thurs 5:30–10:30pm, Fri–Sat 5:30–11pm. **Prices:** Main courses $15–$32. AE, CB, DC, DISC, MC, V. [VP]

### Fisherman's Wharf
222 Pompano Beach Blvd; tel 954/941-5522. At Pompano Pier. **New American/Seafood.** A nautically themed haven for seafood lovers, with a big, bustling bar that invites you to linger. The separate dining room has ocean and pier views. Daily specials are offered on three separate chalkboards. Outdoor bar. **FYI:** Reservations not accepted. Big band/piano. Children's menu. **Open:** Sun–Thurs 11am–midnight, Fri–Sat 11am–1:30am. **Prices:** Main courses $9–$17. AE, CB, DC, DISC, ER, MC, V. 🛥️ 🏞️ ♨️ ♿

## ATTRACTIONS 🏛️

### Butterfly World
3600 W Sample Rd, Coconut Creek; tel 954/977-4400. Amid three acres of tropical gardens are thousands of brilliantly colored, exotic butterflies in all stages of life. Visitors can watch butterflies emerge from their cocoons. With an insectarium, butterfly museum, and gift shop. **Open:** Mon–Sat 9am–5pm, Sun 1–5 pm. Last admission at 4pm. **$$$**

### Goodyear Blimp Base
1500 NE 5th Ave; tel 954/946-8300. Base for the airship *Stars and Stripes,* which visitors may view when the ship is moored. **Free**

# Ponce Inlet

## ATTRACTION 🏛️

### Ponce de León Inlet Lighthouse
4931 S Peninsula Dr; tel 904/761-1821. This 175-foot-tall brick lighthouse, 15 miles south of Daytona Beach, dates from the mid-1880s and was in operation until 1970. It has since been restored and is now listed in the National Register of Historic Places. The head lighthouse keeper's cottage houses exhibits on navigational aids, marine biology, and ocean exploration. A climb to the top of the lighthouse provides a fantastic panoramic view. **Open:** Peak (May–Aug) daily 10am–9pm. Reduced hours off-season. **$$**

# Ponte Vedra Beach

Settled as a silica-mining town in the early 1900s, this deluxe northeast Florida beach community is now the headquarters for the Professional Golf Association and the Association of Tennis Professionals. The town is dominated by Sawgrass, a 4,000-home golf-course community.

## RESORTS 🏨

### ⬟⬟⬟ The Lodge and Bath Club
607 Ponte Vedra Blvd, 32082; tel 904/273-9500 or toll free 800/243-4304; fax 904/273-0210. In a beautiful location on the ocean. Elaborately decorated deluxe facility with Spanish mission accents. Public areas are delightful venues for relaxing and appreciating the ocean vistas. **Rooms:** 66 rms and stes. CI 4pm/CO noon. Nonsmoking rms avail. Handsome accommodations with some very fine appointments. **Amenities:** 🗄️ 🛁 🍽️ A/C, cable TV w/movies, in-rm safe, bathrobes. All units w/minibars, all w/terraces, some w/fireplaces, some w/whirlpools. **Services:** 🍽️ [VP] 🚐 🎿 🪃 Twice-daily maid svce, social director, masseur, children's program, babysitting. Expert staff. **Facilities:** 🏌️ 🚲 🏐 🎳 [700] 3 restaurants, 2 bars (1 w/entertainment), 1 beach (ocean), lifeguard, volleyball, sauna, steam rm, whirlpool. Restaurant and lounge are romantic settings at night. **Rates:** Peak (Mar–Apr 7) $169–$245 S or D; $309 ste. Min stay special events. Lower rates off-season. Parking: Indoor, free. AE, CB, DC, DISC, MC, V.

### ⬟⬟⬟ Marriott at Sawgrass Resort
1000 TPC Blvd, 32082; tel 904/285-7777 or toll free 800/457-GOLF; fax 904/285-0906. 4 mi S of Turner Butler Blvd on FL A1A. 60 acres. One of Marriott's prized resort facilities, and with good reason. Its manicured acres contain gorgeous golf greens, waterfalls, lakes, and lagoons spanned by graceful wooden bridges, while the hotel's deluxe lobby is a towering skylit atrium with a waterfall and lush tropical garden. **Rooms:** 515 rms, stes, and effic; 3 cottages/villas. CI 4pm/CO noon. Nonsmoking rms avail. Two spacious golf course villas and one ocean villa are available. **Amenities:** 🗄️ 🛁 🍽️ A/C, cable TV w/movies, dataport, voice mail. Some units w/minibars. **Services:** ✗ 📠 [VP] 🚐 🎿 🪃 ⛵ Social director, masseur, children's program, babysitting. Pets allowed in villa units only. **Facilities:** 🏌️ 🚲 🏐 ⛳36 ⛱️ 🎿 🏊12 🎳 [600] 🖥️ 2 restaurants (*see* "Restaurants" below), 4 bars (1 w/entertainment), volleyball, sauna, steam rm, whirlpool, day-care ctr, playground, washer/dryer. **Rates:** Peak (Feb 16–June 13) $219 S; $239 D; $269–$500 ste; $268–$577 cottage/villa. Extra person $20. Children under age 13 stay free. Min stay special events. Lower rates off-season. Parking: Outdoor, free. AE, CB, DC, DISC, ER, JCB, MC, V.

### ⬟⬟⬟ Ponte Vedra Inn & Club
200 Ponte Vedra Blvd, 32082; tel 904/285-1111 or toll free 800/234-7842; fax 904/285-2111. Butler Blvd exit off I-95. 300 acres. A wonderful, sprawling country club and spa in the area's high-rent shoreline district. Elegance abounds, from the manicured front lawn that doubles as a putting green to the charming lobby and adjoining Great Lounge, which features overstuffed sofas and armchairs and massive fireplaces all under a beamed cypress ceiling. **Rooms:** 222 rms, stes, and effic. CI 3pm/CO noon. Nonsmoking rms avail. Spacious, lovely rooms, some with four-poster or sleigh

beds. **Amenities:** 🛍 🕯 ⛉ 🍷 A/C, cable TV w/movies, refrig, dataport, voice mail, in-rm safe, bathrobes. All units w/mini-bars, all w/terraces, 1 w/whirlpool. **Services:** 🍽 ☎ 🆅🅿 🚐 🖨 🕳 Twice-daily maid svce, social director, masseur, children's program, babysitting. **Facilities:** 🔧 🚲 ⛰ 🏠 ▶36 🏊 🌊15 🏌 🐴 🍴450 🖥 4 restaurants, 4 bars (1 w/entertainment), 1 beach (ocean), lifeguard, volleyball, board surfing, spa, sauna, steam rm, whirlpool, washer/dryer. Dining rooms range from casual to formal. **Rates:** Peak (Mar–Nov) $170–$240 S or D; $240–$340 ste; $170–$240 effic. Extra person $9. Children under age 18 stay free. Lower rates off-season. Parking: Outdoor, free. AE, CB, DC, DISC, MC, V.

## RESTAURANT 🍴

**The Augustine Grille**
In the Marriott at Sawgrass Resort, 1000 TPC Blvd; tel 904/285-7777. Exit 101 off I-95. **New American.** Anthony Pels, a disciple of famed chef Wolfgang Puck, brings a distinctly California flair to the kitchen here. The decor is ultra-elegant but the dress code is "golf casual." The food and service are helping Pels develop a following among guests, golfers, and the local country-club crowd. **FYI:** Reservations recommended. Children's menu. **Open:** Mon–Thurs 6–10pm, Fri–Sat 6–11pm. **Prices:** Main courses $19–$29. AE, CB, DC, DISC, MC, V. 🆅🅿 ♿

# Port St Joe

## ATTRACTION 📷

**St Joseph Peninsula State Park**
Tel 904/227-1327. One of Florida's major scallop-gathering spots. Scallops can be found by snorkeling in the Gulf or they can be harvested along the beaches. Swimming, fishing, boating, hiking, camping, nature trails. **Open:** Daily 8am–sunset. $$

# Port St Lucie

Unspoiled beaches and unhurried golf are promised by this fast-growing city of nearly 66,000 residents. You'll also find freshwater fishing in the Indian and St Lucie Rivers, ocean fishing and diving charters, and the New York Mets in spring training. **Information:** St Lucie County Chamber of Commerce, PO Box 8209, Port St Lucie, 34985 (tel 561/595-9999).

## HOTELS 🏨

**Best Western Port St Lucie**
7900 US 1 S, 34952; tel 561/878-7600 or toll free 800/528-1234; fax 561/340-0422. Exit 63 off I-95. A modest offering on the highway. **Rooms:** 98 stes. CI 2pm/CO 11am. Nonsmoking rms avail. Guest rooms are oversized and have a

separate sitting area. **Amenities:** 🛍 A/C, cable TV w/movies. **Services:** 🕳 **Facilities:** 🔧 🍴50 ♿ 1 restaurant (lunch and dinner only), whirlpool, washer/dryer. **Rates (CP):** Peak (Dec–Apr) $59–$89 ste. Extra person $5. Children under age 18 stay free. Lower rates off-season. Parking: Outdoor, free. AE, CB, DC, DISC, MC, V.

**Holiday Inn Port St Lucie**
10120 S Federal Hwy, 34952; tel 561/337-2200 or toll free 800/HOLIDAY; fax 561/335-7872. Exit 63 off I-95, 1 mi S on US 1. Former Radisson Hotel offers modest rooms. Not on the beach, but convenient to island activities. **Rooms:** 142 rms and stes. CI 3pm/CO noon. Nonsmoking rms avail. **Amenities:** 🛍 🕯 ⛉ 🍷 A/C, cable TV w/movies. Some units w/whirlpools. **Services:** ✕ 🖨 🕳 Small staff is friendly and accommodating. **Facilities:** 🔧 🍴175 ♿ 1 restaurant, 1 bar, whirlpool, washer/dryer. **Rates:** Peak (Jan–Apr) $99 S or D; $109 ste. Extra person $10. Children under age 12 stay free. Lower rates off-season. Parking: Outdoor, free. AE, DC, DISC, MC, V.

## RESORT

**Club Med–The Sandpiper**
3500 Morningside Blvd, 34952; tel 561/335-4400 or toll free 800/CLUB MED; fax 561/335-9497. Off US 1. 1,000 acres. This large, all-inclusive family getaway offers plenty of sports and activities as well as programs for children. **Rooms:** 332 rms. CI 2pm/CO 11am. **Amenities:** 🛍 🍷 A/C, cable TV, refrig, in-rm safe. All units w/terraces. **Services:** ☎ 🚐 🖨 🕳 Car-rental desk, social director, children's program, babysitting. All-you-can-eat buffets served in the main dining room three times a day. **Facilities:** 🔧 ⛰ ▶45 🌊10 🏌 🐴 🏊 🍴150 ♿ 4 restaurants, 2 bars (w/entertainment), games rm, playground, washer/dryer. River beach. Full-service marina. **Rates (AP):** Peak (Dec–Apr) $210 S or D. Lower rates off-season. Parking: Outdoor, free. AE, MC, V.

# Punta Gorda

One of the nation's fastest-growing communities. Its Woman's Club and residential areas are historic landmarks. Fishing and shelling cruises depart from Fisherman's Village Marina; swamp buggy tours explore Telegraph Cypress Swamp. **Information:** Charlotte County Chamber of Commerce, 326 W Marion #112, Punta Gorda, 33950 (tel 941/639-2222).

## HOTELS 🏨

**Days Inn Punta Gorda**
26560 N Jones Loop Rd, 33950; tel 941/637-7200 or toll free 800/325-2525; fax 941/639-0848. Exit 28 off I-75. Best for overnight stays while on the move. Next door to fast-food outlets. **Rooms:** 73 rms and stes. CI 3pm/CO noon. Nonsmoking rms avail. **Amenities:** 🛍 A/C, cable TV w/movies.

**Services:** ⌁ ⌁ **Facilities:** 🏠 ♿ Whirlpool, washer/dryer. **Rates:** Peak (Dec–Apr) $100 S or D; $130 ste. Children under age 12 stay free. Lower rates off-season. Parking: Outdoor, free. AE, CB, DC, DISC, MC, V.

### ⬛⬛ Holiday Inn Waterfront

300 Retta Esplanade, 33950; tel 941/639-1165 or toll free 800/525-1022; fax 941/639-8116. Exit 29 off I-75. A well-regarded establishment in the heart of town. **Rooms:** 183 rms and stes. CI 3pm/CO noon. Nonsmoking rms avail. **Amenities:** 🔟 ♨ A/C, cable TV w/movies. Some units w/terraces, some w/whirlpools. **Services:** ✗ ⌁ ⌁ ⌁ **Facilities:** 🏠 [400] ♿ 1 restaurant, 2 bars (1 w/entertainment), whirlpool, washer/dryer. Pool looks over the private harborside pier. **Rates (CP):** Peak (Jan–Apr) $79–$89 S; $89–$99 D; $175 ste. Extra person $10. Children under age 18 stay free. Lower rates off-season. Parking: Outdoor, free. AE, MC, V.

### ⬛⬛ Howard Johnson Lodge

33 Tamiami Trail, 33950; tel 941/639-2167 or toll free 800/654-2000; fax 941/639-1707. Exit 29 off I-75. Conveniently located, with panoramic views of Charlotte Harbor. **Rooms:** 100 rms. CI 3pm/CO noon. Nonsmoking rms avail. Some rooms are only a few feet from the water's edge. **Amenities:** 🔟 A/C, cable TV w/movies. All units w/terraces. **Services:** ⌁ ⌁ ⌁ **Facilities:** 🏠 [25] 1 restaurant, 1 bar (w/entertainment), washer/dryer. **Rates:** Peak (Dec–Apr) $69–$74 S or D. Extra person $5. Children under age 12 stay free. Lower rates off-season. Parking: Outdoor, free. AE, DC, DISC, MC, V.

## RESTAURANTS 🍴

### Captain's Table

In Fishermen's Village, 1200 W Retta Esplanade; tel 941/637-1177. Exit 29 off I-75. **American/Seafood.** An upscale but casual restaurant offering spectacular sunset views, the best from Fisherman's Village Wharf. The menu features poultry, veal, fish, and Italian dishes. **FYI:** Reservations recommended. Piano. Children's menu. **Open:** Sun–Thurs 11am–9pm, Fri–Sat 11am–10pm. **Prices:** Main courses $8–$26. AE, DISC, MC, V. 🏔 ♿

### Village Oyster Bar

In Fishermen's Village, 1200 W Retta Esplanade; tel 941/637-1212. Exit 29 off I-75. **Burgers/Seafood.** This casual waterside stop on the Fisherman's Village Wharf pedestrian mall specializes in seafood. Food can be served at the outside bar. **FYI:** Reservations recommended. **Open:** Mon–Thurs 11:30am–8pm, Fri–Sat 11:30am–9pm, Sun noon–8pm. **Prices:** Main courses $7–$24. AE, DISC, MC, V. 🍴 🏔 🍷 ♿

## ATTRACTION 📷

### Babcock Wilderness Adventures

8000 FL 31; tel 941/338-6367 or 489-3911 (reservations). A 90-minute swamp-buggy tour through Telegraph Cypress Swamp and the surrounding woodlands of a 90,000-acre working ranch, conducted by an experienced naturalist. Passengers can see alligators, bison, panthers, wild boars, birds, and other wildlife in their natural habitat. Reservations are essential. Picnic facilities available. **$$$$**

# Riviera Beach

## HOTELS 🏨

### ⬛⬛⬛ Holiday Inn SunSpree

3700 N Ocean Dr, 33404 (Singer Island); tel 561/848-3888 or toll free 800/443-4077; fax 561/845-9754. N of Blue Heron Causeway. An eight-story establishment right on the beach, with a sunny pool area flanked on one side by palm trees and fronted by the beach. **Rooms:** 222 rms. CI 3pm/CO noon. Nonsmoking rms avail. **Amenities:** 🔟 ♨ 📺 A/C, cable TV w/movies, refrig. All units w/terraces. **Services:** ✗ 🔑 ⌁ ⌁ Masseur, children's program, babysitting. **Facilities:** 🏠 🚲 ⛱ [110] ♿ 1 restaurant, 2 bars (1 w/entertainment), 1 beach (ocean), lifeguard, board surfing, games rm, snorkeling, spa, washer/dryer. **Rates:** Peak (Dec–Apr) $139–$199 S or D. Children under age 12 stay free. Lower rates off-season. Parking: Outdoor, free. AE, CB, DC, MC, V.

### ⬛⬛⬛ Quality Resort

3800 N Ocean Dr, 33404; tel 561/848-5502 or toll free 800/765-5502; fax 561/863-6560. 8 mi NE of West Palm Beach. A three- and four-story property affording angled views of the ocean. **Rooms:** 125 rms and stes. CI 3pm/CO noon. Nonsmoking rms avail. **Amenities:** 🔟 📺 A/C, cable TV. All units w/terraces. **Services:** ✗ 🔑 ⌁ ⌁ Babysitting. **Facilities:** 🏠 🚲 ⛱ 🎾 ⛱ [200] ♿ 1 restaurant, 2 bars, 1 beach (bay), games rm, lawn games, snorkeling, spa, sauna, whirlpool. **Rates:** Peak (Feb–Apr) $125–$195 S or D; $200–$220 ste. Extra person $10. Children under age 18 stay free. Min stay special events. Lower rates off-season. Parking: Outdoor, free. AE, CB, DC, DISC, MC, V.

# St Armands Key

See Sarasota

# St Augustine

See also Marineland, Ponte Vedra Beach

Pedro Menendez de Aviles founded America's oldest city in 1565; three years later Sir Francis Drake sacked it. Today the northeast Florida town's treasures include Spanish fort Castillo de San Marcos; St George Street shopping; a Catholic basilica; and railroad magnate Henry Flagler's Spanish-style hotel, now a private college. **Information:** St Augustine & St Johns County Chamber of Commerce, One Riberia St, St Augustine, 32084 (tel 904/829-5681).

## HOTELS

### ≣≣ Comfort Inn
1111 Ponce de Leon Blvd, 32084; tel 904/824-5554 or toll free 800/221-2222; fax 904/829-2222. Exit 95 off I-95. In a quiet locale, minutes from area attractions. Spiffy rooms are housed in a two-story, tan stucco building with a Mission-style facade and terra cotta roof. **Rooms:** 85 rms and stes. CI 2pm/CO 11am. Nonsmoking rms avail. **Amenities:** A/C, cable TV. **Services:** **Facilities:** 1 bar, whirlpool, washer/dryer. **Rates (CP):** Peak (June–Aug) $70–$99 S; $73–$99 D; $125–$145 ste. Children under age 18 stay free. Lower rates off-season. Parking: Outdoor, free. AE, CB, DC, DISC, JCB, MC, V.

### ≣≣ Holiday Inn Downtown
1300 Ponce de Leon Blvd, 32084; tel 904/824-3383 or toll free 800/HOLIDAY; fax 904/829-0668. FL 16 exit off I-95. A well-tended establishment located in the old Spanish Quarter. **Rooms:** 122 rms. CI 3pm/CO noon. Nonsmoking rms avail. **Amenities:** A/C, cable TV. **Services:** Car-rental desk. **Facilities:** 1 restaurant (bkfst and dinner only), 1 bar. The family-style restaurant is very reasonably priced. **Rates:** Peak (June–Aug) $66–$110 S or D. Children under age 18 stay free. Lower rates off-season. Parking: Outdoor, free. AE, CB, DC, DISC, MC, V.

### ≣≣ Holiday Inn St Augustine Beach
860 A1A Beach Blvd, 32084; tel 904/471-2555 or toll free 800/465-4329; fax 904/461-8450. Exit 93 off I-95. Beachfront hotel near area attractions. **Rooms:** 151 rms. CI 3pm/CO noon. Nonsmoking rms avail. Ocean views from balconies. **Amenities:** A/C, cable TV, VCR. All units w/terraces. **Services:** Babysitting. **Facilities:** 1 restaurant, 2 bars (1 w/entertainment), 1 beach (ocean), lawn games, washer/dryer. Beachfront tiki bar. Extra-large pool surrounded by lounge chairs is steps from the beach. **Rates:** Peak (June–Aug) $127 S or D. Extra person $5. Children under age 18 stay free. Lower rates off-season. Parking: Outdoor, free. AE, CB, DC, DISC, JCB, MC, V.

### ≣≣ Howard Johnson Resort Hotel
300 A1A Beach Blvd, 32084; tel 904/471-2575 or toll free 800/752-4037; fax 904/471-1247. FL 260E exit off I-95. A two-story oceanfront facility set on spacious grounds. **Rooms:** 144 rms. CI 3pm/CO 11am. Nonsmoking rms avail. **Amenities:** A/C, cable TV w/movies. **Services:** Car-rental desk. **Facilities:** 1 restaurant, 1 bar (w/entertainment), 1 beach (ocean), volleyball, games rm, lawn games, whirlpool, playground, washer/dryer. **Rates:** Peak (June–Aug) $63–$130 S or D. Children under age 18 stay free. Lower rates off-season. Parking: Outdoor, free. AE, DISC, MC, V.

### ≣≣ Quality Inn Alhambra
2700 Ponce de Leon Blvd, 32084; tel 904/824-2883 or toll free 800/223-4153; fax 904/825-0976. Exit FL 16 off I-95. Designed in an architectural style imitative of nearby historic

buildings. The warm lobby features chandeliers and a vaulted ceiling. **Rooms:** 77 rms and stes. Executive level. CI 3pm/CO noon. Nonsmoking rms avail. **Amenities:** A/C, cable TV. Some units w/whirlpools. **Services:** **Facilities:** 1 restaurant, whirlpool. **Rates:** Peak (Feb 15–Sept 8) $42–$135 S or D; $125–$250 ste. Extra person $5–$10. Children under age 18 stay free. Min stay special events. Lower rates off-season. Parking: Outdoor, free. AE, CB, DC, DISC, EC, ER, JCB, MC, V.

## MOTELS

### ≣≣ Howard Johnson
137 San Marco Ave, 32084; tel 904/824-6181 or toll free 800/654-2000; fax 904/825-2774. Exit 95 off I-95. A downtown motel offering basic amenities. Acceptable for its location and rates. **Rooms:** 77 rms and effic. CI 3pm/CO 11am. Nonsmoking rms avail. **Amenities:** A/C, cable TV. Some units w/whirlpools. **Services:** Car-rental desk. **Facilities:** 1 restaurant, 1 bar, whirlpool, washer/dryer. Ample parking for large vehicles. **Rates (CP):** Peak (June–Aug) $49–$99 S or D; $59–$199 effic. Children under age 18 stay free. Lower rates off-season. Parking: Outdoor, free. AE, DC, DISC, MC, V.

### ≣ La Fiesta Oceanside Inn
810 A1A Beach Blvd, 32084; tel 904/471-2220 or toll free 800/852-6390; fax 904/471-0186. Cheerful two-story beachfront property, with tan stucco walls and terra cotta roof. **Rooms:** 36 rms. CI 3pm/CO 11am. Some rooms have ocean views. The two ocean-view bridal suites have king-size beds and extra-large tubs. **Amenities:** A/C, cable TV, refrig. Some units w/terraces. **Services:** Babysitting. **Facilities:** 1 restaurant (bkfst only), 1 beach (ocean), playground, washer/dryer. **Rates:** Peak (Feb 10–Sept 10) $75–$130 S or D. Extra person $5. Min stay special events. Lower rates off-season. Parking: Outdoor, free. DC, DISC, MC, V.

### ≣≣ Ramada Inn
116 San Marco Ave, 32084; tel 904/824-4352 or toll free 800/575-5289; fax 904/824-2745. Exit 95 off I-95. At Old Mission Rd. Standard motel units housed in a five-story Mission-style stucco building with arched entranceway and terra cotta roof. Close to historic district. **Rooms:** 100 rms. CI 2pm/CO 11am. Nonsmoking rms avail. **Amenities:** A/C, cable TV. **Services:** **Facilities:** 1 restaurant, 1 bar, whirlpool. **Rates:** Peak (June–Aug) $100 S or D. Extra person $7. Children under age 18 stay free. Lower rates off-season. Parking: Outdoor, free. AE, CB, DC, DISC, MC, V.

## INN

### ≣≣ The Kenwood Inn
38 Marine St, 32084; tel 904/824-2116; fax 904/824-1684. This old Victorian woodframe house, painted in pale peach with white trim, has served as a boarding house or inn since the late 19th century; it's listed on the National Register of

Historic Places. Offers gracious Southern style and hospitality. Unsuitable for children under 8. **Rooms:** 14 rms and stes. CI 2pm/CO 11am. No smoking. Each room uniquely and beautifully decorated, some with mahogany canopied beds. **Amenities:** ☖ ☲ ☌ A/C, cable TV. No phone. Some units w/terraces, some w/fireplaces. **Services:** ☺ ☛ ☒ Afternoon tea and wine/sherry served. Continental breakfast can be taken in a parlor with lace-curtained bay windows and a fireplace; in a wicker-furnished sun room; or on the front porch. **Facilities:** ☖ Guest lounge w/TV. Secluded garden courtyard with fishpond, flower beds, and pecan tree. Small swimming pool with sundeck planted with hibiscus. **Rates (CP):** $65–$85 S; $75–$105 D; $105–$135 ste. Extra person $10. Min stay wknds and special events. Parking: Outdoor, free. DISC, MC, V.

## RESORT

≣≣≣ **Ponce de León Golf & Conference Resort**
4000 US 1 N, 32095; tel 904/824-2821 or toll free 800/ 228-2821; fax 804/824-8254. Exit 95 off I-95. 350 acres. Set on minimally landscaped but extensive grounds, with a beautiful championship golf course designed by Donald Ross in 1916. **Rooms:** 193 rms and stes. CI 3pm/CO noon. Nonsmoking rms avail. Traditionally furnished accommodations; may be a bit of a hike from the registration lobby. **Amenities:** ☎ ☲ A/C, cable TV. Some units w/terraces. **Services:** ☒ ☒ ☺ Children's program, babysitting. **Facilities:** ☖ ►18 ☍6 ⌷400 ☖ 1 restaurant, 1 bar (w/entertainment). **Rates:** Peak (Feb–May/Sept–Dec 15) $119 S or D; $129–$159 ste. Extra person $10. Children under age 18 stay free. Min stay special events. Lower rates off-season. AP and MAP rates avail. Parking: Outdoor, free. AE, DC, DISC, MC, V.

## RESTAURANTS ☖

### Creekside Dinery
160 Nix Boat Yard Rd; tel 904/829-6113. **Regional American.** A lovely restaurant with a cedar-lined interior augmented with plants and brightly colored table linens. The screened patio overlooks a creek and boats. Seafood includes pan-broiled oysters, crab cakes, scallops, and the catch of the night. **FYI:** Reservations not accepted. **Open:** Daily 5–10pm. Closed June–Aug. **Prices:** Main courses $7–$14. AE, DISC, MC, V. ☖ ☖

### Fiddler's Green
2750 Anahma Dr; tel 904/824-8897. **Seafood.** A rustically elegant dining room with cedar paneling, beamed, knotty pine ceilings, and two stone fireplaces. Most tables have a view of both the marsh and the ocean beyond. The fresh catch of the day could be snapper, grouper, or tuna. All entrees include vegetables and bread or potatoes. **FYI:** Reservations recommended. **Open:** Sun–Thurs 5–9pm, Fri–Sat 5–10pm. **Prices:** Main courses $8–$16; prix fixe $15–$20. AE, CB, DC, DISC, MC, V. ☖ ☖ ☖

### Florida Cracker Cafe
81 St George St; tel 904/829-0397. **Regional American.** A breezy, light cafe with french doors leading to an outdoor dining patio. The house specialties include crab cakes, coconut-fried shrimp, and the fish platter, served blackened or broiled. **FYI:** Reservations not accepted. Guitar/singer. Beer and wine only. **Open:** Mon–Thurs 11am–4pm, Fri–Sat 11am–9pm, Sun 11am–8pm. **Prices:** Main courses $8–$14. DISC, MC, V. ☖ ☖

### Gypsy Cab Company
828 Anastasia Blvd; tel 904/824-8244. Between White and Comares Sts. **Eclectic.** A funky eatery serving original "urban cuisine." Typical entrees might include blackened salmon with herbed citrus butter, or New York strip with peppercorn Gorgonzola glaze. **FYI:** Reservations not accepted. Children's menu. Beer and wine only. **Open:** Lunch Mon 11am–3pm, Wed–Sun 11am–3pm; dinner Sun–Thurs 5:30–10pm, Fri–Sat 5:30–11pm. **Prices:** Main courses $10–$17. AE, DISC, MC, V. ☖

### La Parisienne
60 Hypolita St; tel 904/829-0055. 3 blocks W of Avenida Menendez. **French.** An intimate, Euro-style dining room situated in the heart of the historic district. Duck salad with raspberry vinaigrette is a special appetizer, shrimp scampi a favorite entree. Steaks are prepared with selection of sauces. **FYI:** Reservations recommended. Beer and wine only. No smoking. Additional location: Seaside Plaza (tel 471-5914). **Open:** Lunch Tues–Sun 11am–3pm; dinner Tues–Sat 5:30–9pm. Closed Sept 1–21. **Prices:** Main courses $14–$18. AE, DISC, MC, V. ☖

### Oscar's Old Florida Grill
614 Euclid Ave; tel 904/829-3794. **Seafood.** A very casual restaurant with pine-planked floors and a pitched ceiling, housed in an old fish camp. Dine inside or at riverside picnic tables outdoors. Fresh specialties include fried shrimp, crab patties, or the catch of the day; all are served with fries, coleslaw, and homemade sauces. **FYI:** Reservations not accepted. Beer and wine only. **Open:** Wed–Thurs 5–9pm, Fri 5–10pm, Sat noon–10pm, Sun noon–9pm. **Prices:** Main courses $6–$15. MC, V. ☖ ☖

### Raintree
102 San Marco Ave; tel 904/824-7211. At Bernard St. **Eclectic.** This 1879 converted Victorian home, a cozy restaurant with a lovely garden, is one of the city's most romantic eateries. Popular dishes include beef Wellington, veal Oscar, and live Maine lobster, prepared steamed or broiled. More than 300 wines are available. A courtesy car provides transportation from local hotels. **FYI:** Reservations accepted. Children's menu. **Open:** Daily 5–9:30pm. **Prices:** Main courses $11–$20. AE, MC, V. ☖ ☖ ☖ ☖

### Salt Water Cowboy's
299 Dondanville Rd; tel 904/471-2332. **Barbecue/Seafood.** Arrive early and watch the sun set over the saltwater marsh as

you dine. In addition to the wonderful variety of seafood dishes, barbecued specialties are available. **FYI:** Reservations not accepted. **Open:** Daily 5–10pm. **Prices:** Main courses $8–$14. AE, MC, V. 🚗 ▨ ఽ

### Schmagel's Bagels
69 Hypolita St; tel 904/824-4444. 2 blocks W of St George St. **Deli.** A basic coffee shop with only five booths inside. The shaded patio tables are perfect for enjoying a fresh bagel and a cup of coffee outside. Twelve bagel varieties are usually available; sandwiches are prepared on homemade bread or on the bagel of your choice. **FYI:** Reservations not accepted. No liquor license. No smoking. **Open:** Mon–Sat 7:30am–3pm, Sun 8:30am–2pm. **Prices:** Lunch main courses $1–$5. No CC. 🚗 ఽ

## ATTRACTIONS 🏛

### SPANISH QUARTER MUSEUM

#### Restored Spanish Quarter
Entrance at 33 St George St between Cuna and Orange Sts; tel 904/825-6830. This two-block area south of the City Gate on the east side of St George Street aims to create the daily lives of St Augustine's Spanish settlers. The city's Spanish colonial architecture and landscape have been re-created, and historical interpreters in 18th-century attire tell about the former occupants of the homes while cooking, sewing, woodworking, rebuilding a stone hearth, repairing outbuildings, or doing other chores. Ticket includes admission to all eight exhibit sites. **Open:** Daily 9am–5pm. **$$**

#### Woodworker's Shop
Under a thatched-roof structure, the carpenter repairs furniture and makes small items using hand- and foot-powered tools.

#### Gómez House
This was the home of a footsoldier and his wife, who lived in this sparsely furnished one-room cypress A-frame with their three children. The family supplemented its meager income by operating a store and part-time tavern on the premises. Some of the types of items they would have sold, such as wine, blankets, and fabrics, rosin (used heated for caulking), beans, jars of olives, and tobacco, can be seen here. The sleeping loft upstairs is where the children slept in cold weather, on straw-filled mattresses.

In the yard outdoors is a square coquina well (the family's water source) and a vegetable garden that would be typical of one from the era.

#### Gallegos House
Built in 1720, this was the home of Martín Martínez Gallegos and his wife, Victoria, who lived here with three children and Juan Garcia, a retired infantryman. The Gallegos family was more affluent than the Gómez family. Martín was an officer—an artillery sergeant stationed at the Castillo. Their two-room tabby (oyster-shell concrete) home has a built-in interior masonry stove, though most cooking was still done outside

over a wood fire. A thatch-roofed pole shed over this outdoor fire protected the cooking space from the elements. An outdoor wooden trough served as a sink, washing machine, and bathtub, with whelk shells for dippers. Note the swinging rat shelf, which was used to store food over the table. (Its motion was intended to scare rats away.)

#### Blacksmith Shop
Near the Gallegos House is the blacksmith shop, where a craftsman turns out hand-wrought hardware using 18th-century methods. He tells about his work, his life (he lives above the shop), and the everyday expressions rooted in blacksmithing, such as "strike while the iron is hot."

#### Gonzáles House
The rectangular Gonzáles House, home of cavalryman Bernardo Gonzáles, is larger than those that belonged to many of his neighbors. The architecture is typical of the first Spanish Period, with a flat roof constructed of hand-hewn boards laid across hand-hewn rafters. The house is used for spinning and weaving demonstrations using a 1797 loom. Natural yarn colors were created from berries, carrots, onion skins, marigolds, indigo, and even crushed insects. The vegetable garden is supplemented by plants used for dyes.

#### Geronimo de Hita y Salazar House
This tabby house belonged to a soldier with a large family. Here a woodworker demonstrates how typical items—furniture, kitchen implements, and religious artifacts—were made in the 18th century, using a manual lathe to turn the wood. Outside, a reconstructed coquina hearth is used for cooking.

#### De Mesa–Sanchéz House
Two historical periods are represented within this house. Two rooms date to the residence of shore guard Antonio de Mesa in the early 18th century, while a second story was added in the 19th century. Furnishings reflect the comfortable lifestyle of Charles and Mary Jane Loring, who lived here during the American Territorial Period (1821–45). The house is made of coquina, which has been plastered over and painted white.

#### José Peso de Burgo and Francisco Pellicer House
This wooden structure is a reconstruction of a two-family house dating from the British Period (1763–1783). Peso de Burgo, a Corsican, was a merchant and shopkeeper; Francisco Pellicer, a Minorcan carpenter. The families had separate kitchens. Today a shop occupies the house, selling books and other gift items relating to the period.

### OTHER MUSEUMS AND HISTORIC SITES

#### Mission of Nombre De Dios
San Marco Ave and Old Mission Rd; tel 904/824-2809. Believed to be the site of the first Indian mission in the United States, founded in 1565. A 208-foot stainless-steel cross (which is lit up at night) marks the site of the founding of St Augustine. The mission is a popular destination of

religious pilgrimages. Also on the grounds is a charming old Mission-style chapel, Our Lady of La Leche (1915). **Open:** Daily 7am–6pm. **Free**

### Castillo de San Marcos National Monument

Castillo Dr and Avenida Menendez; tel 904/829-6506. This massive stone fortress overlooking Matanzas Bay was completed by the Spanish in 1695 to defend against British advances on St Augustine. Constructed of a native shell stone called coquina, the symmetrical fort was designed with diamond-shaped ramparts at each corner for maximum firepower, a double-drawbridge entrance over a 40-foot moat, and walls 33 feet high and 14 feet thick at the base. The Castillo was never captured in battle and its walls did not crumble when pounded by enemy artillery. Today the old storerooms house exhibits documenting the history of the fort. Visitors can tour the vaulted powder magazine room, a dank prison cell, the chapel, and guard rooms, as well as the upper-level gun deck. Free guided tours daily. **Open:** Daily 8:45am–4:45pm. **$**

### Zorayda Castle

83 King St; tel 904/824-3097. A replica of one wing of the Alhambra, Spain's most famous Moorish castle. The interior reflects the lifestyle of Moorish kings. Self-guided tours. **Open:** Daily 9am–5pm. **$$**

### Oldest House

14 St Francis St; tel 904/824-2872. Also known as the Gonzáles-Alvarez House, the area's oldest colonial home evolved from a two-room coquina dwelling built between 1702 and 1727. Rooms are furnished to reflect periods of Spanish, British, and American ownership, and artifacts from each are displayed. Admission also entitles you to explore the adjacent Museum of Florida's Army and the exhibits in the Manucy Museum of St Augustine History. Tours depart on the hour and half-hour. **Open:** Daily 9am–5pm. **$$**

### Oldest Store Museum

4 Artillery Lane; tel 904/829-9729. The C F Hamblen General Store was St Augustine's one-stop shopping center from 1835 to 1960, and the museum on its premises today depicts the emporium at the turn of the century. Among the more than 100,000 items on display are a piston-operated vacuum cleaner, patent medicines, gramophones, an 1899 typewriter, and an 1885 steam tractor. Gift shop. **Open:** Mon–Sat 9am–5pm, Sun noon–5pm. **$$**

### Oldest Wooden Schoolhouse

14 St George St; tel 904/824-0192 or 800/428-0222. This red cedar and cypress structure, held together by wooden pegs and handmade nails, is more than two centuries old; its hand-wrought beams are still intact. The house served as a private residence and schoolhouse before the Civil War. **Open:** Daily 9am–5pm. **$**

### Authentic Old Jail

167 San Marco Ave; tel 904/829-3800. Exhibits at this beautifully restored Victorian prison include photographs of all the county's sheriffs from 1845 to the present, documentation of a 1908 hanging, and a collection of weapons and restraining devices. Guided tours available. **Open:** Daily 8:30am–5pm. **$$**

### Government House Museum

48 King St; tel 904/825-5033. Built on the site of a 16th-century Spanish colonial governor's office, the museum offers visitors an overview of St Augustine's history from native settlement to the Flagler era using state-of-the-art audio and visual media. Displays highlight the struggles of the first Spanish settlement, the construction of the Castillo de San Marcos, and the various inhabitants who have lived here throughout the centuries. **Open:** Daily 10am–4pm. **$**

### Florida Heritage Museum

167 San Marco Ave; tel 904/829-3800. This new museum documents state and local history in exhibits focusing on the colorful life of Henry Flagler and his Florida and East Coast Railroad and Hotel Company, which played a key role in the development of Florida tourism; the Civil War; and the Seminole Wars. Visitors can also see a replica of a Spanish galleon, and displays of actual gold, silver, and jewelry recovered from galleons sunk off Florida's coast. **Open:** Daily 8:30am–5pm. **$$**

### Lightner Museum

75 King St; tel 904/824-2874. The vast collection of Victoriana housed in the former Alcazar Hotel (1888) includes 18th- and 19th-century European porcelains, Victorian cut glass, Tiffany lamps, antique music boxes, and more. The Victorian Science and Industry room displays shells, minerals, and Native American artifacts in beautiful turn-of-the-century cases. Demonstration of Victorian mechanical musical instruments daily at 11am and 2pm. **Open:** Daily 9am–5pm. **$$**

### Museum of Weapons and Early American History

81-C King St; tel 904/829-3727. An eclectic assortment of historic artifacts and weapons from 1500 to 1900 is displayed in this private museum, located between Sevilla and Cordova Sts. Exhibits include Native American war clubs, spears, and arrowheads; 19th-century firearms; and items from the Civil War, including Confederate weapons, money, and buttons. Adjoining gift shop. **Open:** Daily 9:30am–5pm. **$$**

### Potter's Wax Museum

17 King St; tel 804/829-9056. More than 170 wax figures, each carefully researched and authentically costumed, are displayed. Portrayed are key players in local Florida history, as well as international figures. A 12-minute film is shown continuously throughout the day, and a workshop in front allows visitors to watch a wax sculptor at work. **Open:** Daily 9am–5pm. **$$**

### Ripley's Believe It or Not! Museum

19 San Marco Ave; tel 904/824-1606 or toll free 800/584-2956. Housed in a converted 1887 Moorish revival residence are hundreds of examples of the "oddities" collect-

ed by Robert Ripley in the course of his travels around the world. Videos and films at various points. **Open:** Daily 9am–10pm. **$$$**

### OTHER ATTRACTIONS

### Fountain of Youth

11 Magnolia Ave; tel 904/829-3168. A 14-acre archeological park purported to be the Native American village visited by Ponce de León upon his arrival in the New World in 1513. The legendary fountain itself flows from an underground stream located in the springhouse, which contains a coquina-stone cross believed to date from the Spanish explorer's visit. Tableaux depict a Timucuan village and the arrival of Ponce de León. All guests receive a sample of water from the spring. Guided tours begin with a planetarium show about 16th-century celestial navigation. **Open:** Daily 9am–sunset. **$$**

### Cross and Sword

St Augustine Amphitheatre, FL A1A; tel 904/471-1965. Written by historical dramatist Paul Green, the official state play of Florida recounts the founding of America's oldest city in 1565 and its turbulent early history. It features spectacular battles, elaborate choreography, and a symphonic musical score, all presented on a large outdoor stage. **Open:** July–Aug, Wed–Sun at 8:30pm. **$$$**

### St Augustine Alligator Farm

999 Anastasia Blvd (FL A1A); tel 904/824-3337. Houses the world's most complete collection of crocodilians, a category that includes alligators, crocodiles, caimans, and gavials. Major attractions include "The Land of Crocodiles," with specimens of all 22 species of crocodilians, and Gomek, the largest captive crocodile in the western hemisphere (1,700 pounds and almost 18 feet long). Other creatures on the farm include geckos, snakes, tortoises, and tropical birds. Petting zoo. **Open:** Daily 9am–5pm. **$$$**

# St Marks

About 300 people inhabit this town on the curve of Florida's Gulf Coast. It boasts San Marcos de Apalache, a 17th-century Spanish fort at the junction of the St Marks and Wakulla Rivers, and a Civil War fort used by Confederate and Union armies.

### ATTRACTIONS 🏛

### St Marks National Wildlife Refuge

Tel 904/925-6121. Bordering Ochlockonee Bay and the Gulf of Mexico, this wildlife refuge encompasses more than 70,000 acres of varied terrain. Stop first at the visitor center (open Mon–Fri 8:15am–4:15pm, Sat–Sun 10am–5pm) for an orientation, and to view the bird, waterfowl, and wildlife habitat displays. **Open:** Daily sunrise–sunset. **$$**

### San Marcos De Apalachee State Historic Site

Canal St; tel 904/925-6216. This site was visited by Spanish explorer Panfilo de Narvaez in 1528 and then by Hernando de Soto in 1539 after he followed de Narvaez's overland route. Ruins of a stone fort used by the Spanish, British, and Civil War Confederates can be toured. The visitor center has historic exhibits and artifacts excavated nearby. Picnic facilities, nature trails. **Open:** Thurs–Mon 9am–5pm. **Free**

### Edward Ball Wakulla Springs State Park

1 Spring Dr, Wakulla Springs; tel 904/922-3632. One of the world's largest and deepest freshwater springs. Visitors can take a river cruise to view indigenous wildlife of the area; glass-bottom boat tours include views of mastodon bones, limestone formations, and "Henry the Pole-vaulting Fish." Swimming, hiking, nature trails. **Open:** Daily 8am–sunset. **$$**

# St Pete Beach

Dozens of motels, eateries, and souvenir shops line the Gulf beachfront in this town of 9,500. Pass-A-Grille historic district is minutes south of town. **Information:** St Pete Beach Area Chamber of Commerce, 6990 Gulf Blvd, St Pete Beach, 33706 (tel 813/360-6957).

### PUBLIC TRANSPORTATION

**BATS City Transit Buses** Operate along St Pete Beach. Fare $1. For information call 813/360-0811.

### HOTELS 🏨

**≣≣≣ Holiday Inn St Pete Beach**
5300 Gulf Blvd, 33706; tel 813/360-6911 or toll free 800/HOLIDAY; fax 813/360-6172. Exit 4 off I-275. **Rooms:** 148 rms and stes. CI 3pm/CO 11am. Nonsmoking rms avail. **Amenities:** 🛏 ⚬ A/C, cable TV, bathrobes. Some units w/terraces. **Services:** ✕ ⬛ ⌂ Babysitting. **Facilities:** 🖼 🏋 🔲130 ₺ 2 restaurants, 3 bars (1 w/entertainment), 1 beach (ocean), games rm, washer/dryer. **Rates:** Peak (Feb–Apr) $139 S or D; $220 ste. Extra person $6. Children under age 18 stay free. Lower rates off-season. Parking: Outdoor, free. AE, DC, DISC, MC, V.

**≣≣≣ Radisson Sandpiper Beach Resort**
6000 Gulf Blvd, 33706; tel 813/360-5551 or toll free 800/333-3333; fax 813/360-0417. Exit 4 off I-275. Located on the beach, this satisfactory full-service facility caters to many families. A good bet. **Rooms:** 159 rms and stes. CI 4pm/CO noon. Nonsmoking rms avail. Many units with ocean views; some with microwaves and an extra TV. **Amenities:** 🛏 ⚬ 🗆 A/C, cable TV, refrig, bathrobes. Some units w/terraces. **Services:** ✕ ⬛ ⌂ Car-rental desk, children's program, babysitting. **Facilities:** 🖼 🏋 🔲800 ₺ 2 restaurants, 2 bars, 1 beach (ocean), games rm, racquetball, washer/dryer. **Rates:** $135–$177 S or D; $198–$612 ste. Extra person $15. Children under age 17 stay free. Parking: Indoor/outdoor, free. AE, DC, DISC, MC, V.

≣≣≣ **St Pete Beach Holiday Inn Hotel & Suites**
5250 Gulf Blvd, 33706; tel 813/360-1811 or toll free 800/ 448-0901; fax 813/360-6919. Pinellas Bayway exit off I-275. A one-time beach leader, it still offers a wide variety of facilities for couples and families. **Rooms:** 169 rms and stes. CI 3pm/CO 11am. Nonsmoking rms avail. **Amenities:** 🛆 🗚 A/C, cable TV w/movies, refrig, voice mail, in-rm safe. All units w/terraces, some w/whirlpools. **Services:** ✗ ▣ ⌂ ⇩ Babysitting. **Facilities:** 🛆 ⚠ ⚓ ▶ 🏐 🔲 ⚓ 2 restaurants, 3 bars (2 w/entertainment), 1 beach (ocean), volleyball, games rm, snorkeling, playground, washer/dryer. Revolving roof lounge provides romantic views of the Gulf. **Rates:** Peak (Feb–Apr) $100–$160 S or D; $250 ste. Children under age 18 stay free. Lower rates off-season. Parking: Outdoor, free. AE, DC, DISC, MC, V.

## MOTELS

≣≣ **Colonial Gateway Inn**
6300 Gulf Blvd, 33706; tel 813/367-3711 or toll free 800/ 237-8918; fax 813/367-7068. Exit 4 off I-275. Take Pinellas Bayway W 2½ miles to Gulf Blvd. Low-rise property with lovely gardens and beach. **Rooms:** 200 rms and effic. CI 2pm/CO 11am. Nonsmoking rms avail. **Amenities:** 🛆 🖏 A/C, cable TV w/movies. **Services:** ✗ ⌂ ⇩ ⇨ Tours available to area attractions. **Facilities:** 🛆 🔲 1 restaurant (bkfst and dinner only), 2 bars (1 w/entertainment), 1 beach (ocean), games rm. Beach bar. **Rates:** Peak (Feb–Apr) $95–$121 S or D; $105–$121 effic. Extra person $6. Children under age 12 stay free. Lower rates off-season. Parking: Outdoor, free. AE, CB, DC, DISC, ER, MC, V.

≣≣ **Days Inn Island Beach Resort**
6200 Gulf Blvd, 33706; tel 813/367-1902 or toll free 800/ 544-4222; fax 813/367-4422. 2 mi N of Pinellas Bayway. Well-kept establishment with private beach; offers a variety of activities. **Rooms:** 102 rms and effic. CI 4pm/CO 11am. Nonsmoking rms avail. **Amenities:** 🛆 🖏 A/C, cable TV, refrig. Some units w/terraces. **Services:** ⌂ ⇩ Babysitting. **Facilities:** 🛆 ⚠ ⚓ 2 bars (1 w/entertainment), 1 beach (ocean), volleyball, games rm. Sports bar with wide-screen TV and complimentary hors d'oeuvres. Beach bar with nightly live entertainment. **Rates:** Peak (Feb–Apr) $128–$148 S or D; $128 effic. Extra person $20. Children under age 16 stay free. Lower rates off-season. Parking: Outdoor, free. AE, CB, DC, DISC, JCB, MC, V.

≣≣ **Dolphin Beach Resort**
4900 Gulf Blvd, 33706; tel 813/360-7011 or toll free 800/ 237-8916; fax 813/367-5909. Exit 4 off I-275 S. Beachfront resort catering to both families and couples. **Rooms:** 173 rms and effic. CI 4pm/CO 11am. **Amenities:** 🛆 A/C, satel TV. Some units w/terraces. **Services:** ✗ 🚐 ⌂ ⇩ Car-rental desk, babysitting. Tours arranged by the knowledgeable staff depart from the lobby. **Facilities:** 🛆 🔲 ⚓ 1 restaurant, 2 bars (1 w/entertainment), 1 beach (ocean), games rm, washer/

dryer. **Rates:** Peak (Feb–Apr) $98–$118 S or D; $110–$130 effic. Min stay special events. Lower rates off-season. Parking: Outdoor, free. AE, CB, DC, MC, V.

≣≣ **Howard Johnson Lodge**
6100 Gulf Blvd, 33706; tel 813/360-7041 or toll free 800/ 231-1419; fax 813/360-8941. 2 mi N of Pinellas Bayway. This five-story beachfront property is popular among families. **Rooms:** 135 rms, stes, and effic. CI 3pm/CO noon. Nonsmoking rms avail. **Amenities:** 🛆 🖏 🗚 A/C, cable TV, refrig, in-rm safe. Some units w/terraces, some w/whirlpools. **Facilities:** 🛆 ⚓ 1 restaurant, 1 beach (ocean), games rm, washer/dryer. **Rates:** $94–$105 S or D; $185–$350 ste; $104–$218 effic. Extra person $10. Children under age 18 stay free. Lower rates off-season. Parking: Outdoor, free. AE, CB, DC, DISC, JCB, MC, V.

≣ **Pass-A-Grille Beach Motel**
709 Gulf Way, 33706; tel 813/367-4726; fax 813/367-4726. Bayway exit off I-275. Located across from the beach. A good candidate for the budget-conscious. **Rooms:** 25 effic. CI 3pm/CO 11am. Nonsmoking rms avail. Basic, comfortable furnishings. **Amenities:** 🛆 🗚 A/C, cable TV, refrig. 1 unit w/whirlpool. **Facilities:** 1 beach (ocean), washer/dryer. **Rates:** Peak (late Dec–mid-Apr) $60–$80 effic. Extra person $5. Lower rates off-season. Parking: Outdoor, free. MC, V.

## RESORTS

≣≣≣≣ **The Don CeSar Beach Resort & Spa**
3400 Gulf Blvd, 33706; tel 813/360-1881 or toll free 800/ 282-1116; fax 813/367-6952. Exit 4 off I-275. One of Florida's golden oldies, this striking faux-Moorish structure done up in pink has been well maintained, retaining much of its sparkle and glitter. It was a playground for Al Capone and F Scott and Zelda Fitzgerald during the Roaring Twenties, but today the clientele is a mix of families and professionals. The endless beach, shared with private homes and condos, is one of the resort's major attractions. There's even a resident ghost named Thomas Rowe. **Rooms:** 275 rms and stes. CI 4pm/CO noon. Nonsmoking rms avail. Aside from a few duds facing the courtyard (room 272, with its cubbyhole closet, should be avoided), the lodgings are adequate, with few glimmerings of decorating flair evident. **Amenities:** 🛆 🖏 🗚 A/C, cable TV w/movies, dataport, voice mail, bathrobes. All units w/minibars, some w/terraces. **Services:** ⎃ ▣ ⱽᴾ ⌂ ⇩ Masseur, children's program, babysitting. Young, gung-ho staff. A psychic reader sometimes holds court around the pool. **Facilities:** 🛆 ⚠ ⚓ ▶ 🏐 🔲 ▢ ⚓ 4 restaurants, 3 bars (w/entertainment), 1 beach (ocean), volleyball, board surfing, games rm, spa, sauna, steam rm, whirlpool, beauty salon, day-care ctr, washer/dryer. An efficient, well-equipped business center, new fitness center, and child-care center. The classic King Charles dining room on the fifth floor is now reserved for weekend brunch. **Rates:** Peak (Feb–Apr) $265–$320 S or D; $330–$675 ste. Extra

person $15. Children under age 18 stay free. Min stay special events. Lower rates off-season. Parking: Outdoor, free. AE, CB, DC, DISC, MC, V.

### ≣ ≣ ≣ Tradewinds Resort
5500 Gulf Blvd, 33706; tel 813/367-6461 or toll free 800/237-0707; fax 813/562-1222. Bayway exit off I-275. 18 acres. Clearly the size leader on the beach, this offers an excellent selection of accommodations. Lacking the style and class of the Don CeSar, it's more the Disney-like choice on the beach scene. With so many rooms and buildings spread along the shore, it's easy to get lost in the tropical setting. **Rooms:** 577 rms, stes, and effic. CI 4pm/CO noon. Nonsmoking rms avail. Some rooms with views of the lagoon or ocean. **Amenities:** A/C, cable TV w/movies, refrig, in-rm safe. Some units w/minibars, some w/terraces. **Services:** Car-rental desk, social director, masseur, children's program, babysitting. Large staff is attentive and smartly dressed. **Facilities:** 4 restaurants, 3 bars (w/entertainment), 1 beach (ocean), volleyball, board surfing, games rm, lawn games, racquetball, snorkeling, spa, sauna, whirlpool, beauty salon, playground, washer/dryer. Paddleboats and gondolas take guests along the canals that wind through the property. **Rates:** Peak (Feb–Apr) $179–$217 S or D; $259 ste; $197 effic. Extra person $15. Children under age 12 stay free. Lower rates off-season. Parking: Outdoor, free. AE, CB, DC, DISC, EC, ER, JCB, MC, V.

## RESTAURANTS

### Crabby Bill's Seafood Restaurant
5100 Gulf Blvd; tel 813/360-8858. 38th St N exit off I-275. **Seafood.** Very casual beach house–style restaurant with terrific views of the Gulf. Known for its many types of crabs and crab dishes: steamed blue crabs, garlic crabs, soft-shell crabs, stone crab claws, crab cakes. Also available are clams, mussels, oysters, shrimp, mahimahi, and catfish. **FYI:** Reservations not accepted. Children's menu. Additional locations: 401 Gulf Blvd, Indian Rocks Beach (tel 595-4825); 6445 4th St N, St Petersburg (tel 528-6552). **Open:** Mon–Thurs 11:30am–10pm, Fri–Sat 11:30am–11pm, Sun noon–10pm. **Prices:** Main courses $5–$22. AE, MC, V.

### Hurricane
807 Gulf Way; tel 813/360-9558. **New American.** Informal, three-level indoor/outdoor restaurant specializing in Florida black grouper, which is prepared many ways. Also available are crab legs, shrimp, swordfish, barbecued ribs, and steaks. **FYI:** Reservations not accepted. Jazz. Children's menu. **Open:** Daily 8am–2am. **Prices:** Main courses $6–$18. MC, V.

### Leverock's Seafood House
10 Corey Ave; tel 813/367-4588. **Seafood.** A fun, tidy, tropical eatery overlooking Boca Ciega Bay. Fresh seafood dishes served in a cheerful setting for affordable prices attract large crowds, particularly families. **FYI:** Reservations

not accepted. Children's menu. **Open:** Daily 11:30am–10pm. **Prices:** Main courses $8–$22. AE, DC, DISC, MC, V.

### Silas Dent's
5501 Gulf Blvd; tel 813/360-6961. Across from the Tradewinds Resort. **Seafood/Steak.** Seafood linguine, fried catfish, surf-and-turf, and filet mignon are served in a rustic early Florida atmosphere. **FYI:** Reservations recommended. Dancing/reggae/rock. Children's menu. **Open:** Sun–Thurs 5–10pm, Fri–Sat 5–11pm. **Prices:** Main courses $8–$22. AE, CB, DISC, MC, V.

### Woody's Waterfront
7308 Sunset Way; tel 813/360-9165. **New American.** A popular beachgoers' hangout decorated in 1960s style, with colorful surfboards on display. Serving hot dogs, chicken wings, and some more substantial fare like grouper and other fresh fish. **FYI:** Reservations not accepted. Guitar. **Open:** Mon–Sat 11am–2am, Sun noon–1am. **Prices:** Main courses $4–$7. No CC.

# St Petersburg

See also Indian Rocks Beach, Indian Shores, Isle of Capri, Madeira Beach, St Pete Beach, Treasure Island

The Salvador Dali Museum, Museum of Fine Arts, and Florida International Museum (in a former downtown department store) grace this city of 240,000 fronting Tampa Bay. Manicured parks lead to a large pier with an aquarium, restaurants, and shops, while yachts bob near the sumptuously restored Vinoy Hotel. **Information:** St Petersburg Area Chamber of Commerce, 100 2nd Ave N #150, PO Box 1371, St Petersburg, 33731 (tel 813/821-4069).

### PUBLIC TRANSPORTATION
**Pinellas Suncoast Transit Authority/PSTA Buses** Operate throughout St Petersburg. Hours vary depending on route. Fare $1. For information call 813/530-9911.

**Treasure Island Transit System Buses** Operate along Treasure Island strip. Fare $1. For information call 813/360-0811.

## HOTELS

### ≣ ≣ Days Inn Marina Beach Resort
6800 34th St S, 33711; tel 813/867-1151 or toll free 800/227-8045; fax 813/864-4494. Exit 3 off I-275. A well-tended hotel with enticing views of Tampa Bay. Close to area attractions. **Rooms:** 157 rms, stes, and effic. CI 2pm/CO 11am. Nonsmoking rms avail. **Amenities:** A/C, cable TV, in-rm safe. Some units w/terraces. **Services:** Babysitting. **Facilities:** 2 restaurants, 2 bars (w/entertainment), 1 beach (ocean), games rm, playground, washer/dryer. Private marina; on-site sailing school. **Rates:**

Peak (Feb–Apr) $79–$117 S or D; $109–$259 ste; $99 effic. Extra person $10. Children under age 18 stay free. Lower rates off-season. Parking: Outdoor, free. AE, MC, V.

### ☰☰☰ The Heritage Holiday Inn

234 3rd Ave N, 33701; tel 813/822-4814 or toll free 800/HOLIDAY. Exit 10 off I-275. A historic hotel. The lobby is filled with antique furnishings and has hardwood floors, oriental rugs, and a fireplace. Arriving guests are greeted with classical music. **Rooms:** 71 rms and stes. CI 3pm/CO noon. Nonsmoking rms avail. Nicely appointed rooms have 1920s furnishings. **Amenities:** 🛱 ⚲ A/C, cable TV. Some units w/minibars. **Services:** ✕ 🖾 ⤷ **Facilities:** 🔓 🛏 ⅙ 1 restaurant, 1 bar, whirlpool. The bar was once a fixture in Gen Andrew Jackson's home. **Rates:** Peak (Feb–Apr) $102 S or D; $125 ste. Extra person $10. Children under age 18 stay free. Min stay special events. Lower rates off-season. Parking: Outdoor, free. AE, CB, DC, DISC, JCB, MC, V.

### ☰☰ Holiday Inn Stadium

4601 34th St S, 33711; tel 813/867-3131 or toll free 800/HOLIDAY; fax 813/867-2025. Exit 4 off I-275. With its central location, this makes a fine jumping-off point for touring area attractions. **Rooms:** 134 rms. CI 2pm/CO noon. Nonsmoking rms avail. **Amenities:** 🛱 ⚲ A/C, cable TV w/movies. **Services:** 🖾 ⤷ **Facilities:** 🔓 ⅙ 1 bar (w/entertainment), games rm, washer/dryer. Extra-large pool. **Rates:** Peak (Feb–Apr) $89 S or D. Extra person $10. Children under age 18 stay free. Lower rates off-season. Parking: Outdoor, free. AE, CB, DC, DISC, JCB, MC, V.

### ☰ Howard Johnson Hotel

3600 34th St S, 33711; tel 813/867-6070 or toll free 800/221-4335; fax 813/867-6591. Exit 6 off I-275. A basic hotel, now looking worn and tired. Exterior renovations badly needed, but the rooms are spacious. **Rooms:** 170 rms and stes. CI 3pm/CO noon. Nonsmoking rms avail. **Amenities:** 🛱 ⚲ A/C, cable TV. **Services:** 🖾 ⤷ 🔨 Babysitting. Nonrefundable $10 pet fee. **Facilities:** 🔓 🖼 🎱 ⅙ 1 bar (w/entertainment), games rm. Room key provides free admission to nearby fitness center. Poolside bar. **Rates (CP):** Peak (Feb–Apr) $58–$68 S or D; $80 ste. Extra person $6. Children under age 18 stay free. Lower rates off-season. Parking: Outdoor, free. AE, CB, DC, DISC, MC, V.

### ☰☰☰☰ Renaissance Vinoy Resort

501 5th Ave NE, 33701; tel 813/894-1000 or toll free 800/HOTELS 1; fax 813/822-2785. At Beach Dr NE. A landmark placed on the National Register, featuring a magnificently restored ballroom and palatial public areas. If you can't stay at this grand hotel, at least stop in the restaurant for a drink. **Rooms:** 360 rms and stes. CI 3pm/CO noon. Nonsmoking rms avail. Smallish standard rooms have well-equipped baths and designer decor. **Amenities:** 🛱 ⚲ 🍴 A/C, cable TV w/movies, dataport, bathrobes. All units w/minibars, some w/terraces, some w/whirlpools. Coffee and morning paper delivered to room. **Services:** 🍽 📠 🆅🅿 🚗 🖾 ⤷ Car-rental

desk, masseur, babysitting. **Facilities:** 🔓 🚲 ⛰ ⤶🅿18 🏊3 🖼11 🛶 🚗700 🖵 ⅙ 5 restaurants, 5 bars (1 w/entertainment), basketball, lawn games, spa, sauna, steam rm, whirlpool, beauty salon, washer/dryer. On-site marina. **Rates:** Peak (Jan–Apr) $239 S or D; $375 ste. Extra person $20. Children under age 18 stay free. Lower rates off-season. Parking: Indoor, $7–$10/day. AE, CB, DC, DISC, EC, ER, JCB, MC, V.

### ☰☰☰ St Petersburg Hilton and Towers

333 1st St S, 33701; tel 813/894-5000 or toll free 800/944-5500; fax 813/894-7655. Exit 9 off I-275. Top-flight hotel offering excellent facilities for businesspeople and others. Public areas are spacious and appealing. **Rooms:** 333 rms and stes. CI 3pm/CO noon. Nonsmoking rms avail. **Amenities:** 🛱 ⚲ A/C, satel TV w/movies, dataport. **Services:** ✕ 🚐 🖾 ⤷ 🔨 Babysitting. **Facilities:** 🔓 🛶 🚗1500 ⅙ 2 restaurants, 1 bar, basketball, whirlpool. Tennis and golf are nearby. Restaurant has cathedral ceiling and large windows providing expansive pool views. **Rates:** Peak (Jan 15–Apr) $104–$124 S; $114–$134 D; $239 ste. Extra person $10. Children under age 18 stay free. Lower rates off-season. Parking: Outdoor, free. AE, CB, DC, DISC, EC, ER, JCB, MC, V.

### ☰☰ Suncoast Executive Inn Athletic Center

3000 34th St S, 33711; tel 813/867-1111 or toll free 800/458-8671; fax 813/867-7068. Exit 6 off I-275. This three-story hotel, a good choice for tennis enthusiasts, offers easy access to downtown and the beaches. **Rooms:** 120 rms and stes. CI 3pm/CO 11am. Nonsmoking rms avail. **Amenities:** 🛱 A/C, cable TV. Some units w/terraces. **Services:** ⤷ 🔨 Babysitting. **Facilities:** 🔓 🖼10 🖵 ⅙ Beauty salon, day-care ctr, washer/dryer. **Rates:** $65 S or D; $85 ste. Extra person $5. Children under age 18 stay free. Lower rates off-season. Parking: Outdoor, free. AE, DISC, MC, V.

## RESTAURANTS 🍴

### Apropos

300 2nd Ave NE; tel 813/823-8934. **New American/Eclectic.** A small but popular restaurant overlooking the marina. Wine tastings every Thursday evening. Live jazz on the deck on Friday nights. **FYI:** Reservations recommended. Jazz. **Open:** Tues–Wed 7:30am–3pm, Thurs–Sun 7:30am–midnight. **Prices:** Main courses $8–$16. AE, DC, DISC, MC, V. ⛴ 🏞 ⅙

### ♣ Basta's Cantina D'Italia Ristorante

1625 4th St S; tel 813/894-7880. **Northern Italian.** An elegant, old-world restaurant with tuxedoed waiters and an elaborate menu featuring more than 300 dishes. Specialties include seafood Porto Fino, veal saltimbocca, shrimp scampi, and rack of lamb. **FYI:** Reservations recommended. Dress code. Beer and wine only. **Open:** Daily 5–11pm. **Prices:** Main courses $13–$25. AE, DC, DISC, MC, V. ♥ 🆅🅿 ⅙

## ⭐ The Garden

217 Central Ave; tel 813/896-3800. 2 blocks from downtown waterfront. **Mediterranean.** Diners at the outdoor tables share their food with the occasional squirrel while leaves drift down from above. Menu features favorites like Tunisian couscous (with lamb, carrots, cabbage, potatoes, eggplant, and raisins), grilled shrimp Pernod, and a wide selection of tapas. **FYI:** Reservations recommended. Jazz. **Open:** Daily 11:30am–2am. **Prices:** Main courses $6–$13. AE, CB, DC, DISC, ER, MC, V. 🍺 ▢ ♿

## Mulligan's Sunset Grille

9524 Blind Pass Rd; tel 813/367-6680. 5th Ave exit N off I-275, ½ block S of Blind Pass Bridge. **Seafood/Steak.** An attractive waterfront eatery with nautical decor. From the deck, watch the Florida sun set over the picturesque marina nearby. Maine lobster and local seafood dishes are specialties. **FYI:** Reservations not accepted. Guitar/singer. Children's menu. **Open:** Sun–Thurs 11am–midnight, Fri–Sat 11am–2am. **Prices:** Main courses $9–$33. AE, DISC, MC, V. ⛰ ♿

## ⭐ Ted Peter's Famous Smoked Fish

1350 Pasadena Ave S; tel 813/381-7931. 22nd Ave S exit off I-275. **Burgers/Seafood.** A family-owned and tourist-friendly operation offering smoked fish dinners at covered outdoor picnic tables. Takeout is sold by the pound. **FYI:** Reservations not accepted. Beer only. No smoking. **Open:** Wed–Mon 11:30am–7:30pm. **Prices:** Main courses $4–$14. No CC. 🍺 ▣ 👪 ♿

## ⭐ The Waterfront Steak House

8800 Bay Pines Blvd N; tel 813/345-5335. Exit 13 off I-275. **Seafood/Steak.** Enjoy wonderful views from the booths of this oceanfront restaurant. The varied menu is popular with seniors, especially at lunch. **FYI:** Reservations not accepted. Children's menu. Additional locations: 565 150th Ave, Madeira Beach (tel 393-0459); 7000 US 19 N, Pinellas Park (tel 526-9188). **Open:** Daily 11:30am–10pm. **Prices:** Main courses $6–$18. AE, DC, DISC, MC, V. ▣ ⛰ ▢ ♿

## ATTRACTIONS 🏛

### St Petersburg Historical and Flight One Museum

335 2nd Ave NE; tel 813/894-1052. This museum chronicles local and state history, with exhibits ranging from the city's founding to the world's first scheduled commercial flight, which departed from St Petersburg in 1914. **Open:** Mon–Sat 10am–5pm, Sun 1–5pm. $$

### Salvador Dali Museum

1000 3rd St S; tel 813/823-3767. Contains the world's largest collection of works by the renowned Spanish surrealist, including 95 oil paintings, over 100 watercolors and drawings, and 1,300 graphics, plus posters, photos, sculptures, objets d'art, and a 2,500-volume library. Museum store offers reproductions, jewelry, books, and gift items. **Open:** Mon–Sat 9:30am–5:30pm, Sun–Mon noon–5:30pm. $$$

### Museum of Fine Arts

255 Beach Dr NE; tel 813/896-2667. Resembling a Mediterranean waterfront villa, this museum houses a permanent collection of European, American, pre-Columbian, and Far Eastern art, with works by such artists as Fragonard, Monet, Renoir, Cezanne, and Gauguin. Also displayed are period rooms, a gallery of Steuben crystal, and rotating exhibits. Guided tours are available. **Open:** Tues–Sat 10am–5pm, Sun 1–5pm; third Thurs of each month 10am–9pm. $$

### Great Explorations

1120 4th St S; tel 813/821-8992. Offers a wide variety of entertaining hands-on exhibits that are geared toward children and adults. Kids can explore a long, dark tunnel; shoot a game of laser pinball; and paint a picture with sunlight, among other activities. **Open:** Mon–Sat 10am–5pm, Sun noon–5pm. $$

### Sunken Gardens

1825 4th St N; tel 813/896-3187. A five-acre tropical garden park containing a vast array of plants, flowers, and trees, as well as an aviary with almost 500 rare birds. There are performing bird shows throughout the day. **Open:** Daily 9am–5pm. $$$$

### The Pier

800 2nd Ave NE; tel 813/821-6164. The center of sightseeing, entertainment, and shopping in St Petersburg, this festive waterfront complex extends a quarter-mile into Tampa Bay. In addition to panoramic views of the bay, the marina, and the city's skyline, it offers five levels of shops and restaurants, plus an aquarium, nightclub, observation deck, catwalks for fishing, boat rides and docks, a small beach, miniature golf, and water-sports rentals. A free trolley service runs between the Pier entrance and nearby parking lots. Adjacent to the Pier is scenic Straub Park, 36 acres of waterfront running along Beach Drive. **Open:** Mon–Thurs 10am–9pm, Fri–Sat 10am–10pm, Sun 11am–7pm. **Free**

### Fort De Soto Park

FL 679; tel 813/866-2484. One of the oldest sections of St Petersburg, this is the largest and most diverse park in the area. A public park for over 25 years, it also offers fishing piers, shaded picnic sites, a bird and animal sanctuary, nature trails, a paved recreational trail, and 235 campsites. **Open:** Daily, sunrise–sunset. **Free**

### Sunshine Skyway Bridge

Tel 813/893-1938. Florida's first suspension bridge connects Pinellas and Manatee Counties and the city of St Petersburg with the Bradenton/Sarasota area. It rises 183 feet above the bay and is 4.1 miles long. **Open:** Daily 24 hours. $

### Boyd Hill Nature Park

1101 Country Club Way S; tel 813/893-7326. Located at the south end of Lake Maggiore, this 216-acre park has scenic trails and boardwalks lined with subtropical flora. Visitors can observe birds, young reptiles, and other native species as they walk along the paths. There is also a library and nature center, aquariums, and a beehive, as well as a picnic area and playground. **Open:** Daily 9am–5pm. **$**

### Lady Anderson Cruises

3400 Pasadena Ave S; tel 813/367-7804 or toll free 800/533-2288. Cruises are operated at lunch and dinner times aboard this three-deck boat, with buffet meal service and dance music, as well as cocktail service. Boarding is half-hour before departure. Lunch cruise 11:30am–2pm; dinner cruise 7–10pm. **Open:** Oct–May. **$$$$**

### ThunderDome

1 Stadium Dr; tel 813/825-3100. Opened in 1990, this $110-million stadium features a translucent roof that is the first cable-supported dome of its kind in the United States and one of the largest of its type in the world. The Tampa Bay Lightning hockey team plays home games here October–April. Guided tours available on non-event days. **Open:** Box office, Mon–Fri 10am–5pm.

### Al Lang Stadium

180 2nd Ave SE; tel 813/822-3384. The winter home of the St Louis Cardinals and (at least temporarily) the Baltimore Orioles. Both teams hold their spring training here, with exhibition games held in March. Following the major league exhibition season, the St Petersburg Cardinals, a Class A minor-league team, play their home games here (Apr–Sept). **$$**

# Sanford

A stone monument in Sanford's central park commemorates the town's beginnings as Fort Mellon in 1837. Today the Seminole County seat, 20 miles north of Orlando on the St Johns River, has commercial and residential districts on the National Register plus a zoo and riverboat tours. **Information:** Greater Sanford Chamber of Commerce, 400 E 1st St, Sanford, 32771 (tel 407/322-2212).

## HOTEL 🏨

### 🖿🖿🖿 Marina Hotel

530 N Palmetto Ave, 32771; tel 407/323-6500 or toll free 800/290-1910; fax 407/322-7076. Exit 52 off I-4. A two-story offering on Lake Monroe. **Rooms:** 100 rms. CI 4pm/CO noon. Nonsmoking rms avail. Rooms with lake, marina, or pool views all were recently refurbished. **Amenities:** 🛏 🕭 📲 🍽 A/C, satel TV w/movies. **Services:** ✗ 🖾 ↩ 🕸 Babysitting. Powerboats, jetskis, and fishing available with concessionaires next door. **Facilities:** 🔓 🗍50 🕁 1 restaurant (bkfst and lunch only), 1 bar. **Rates:** Peak (Feb–May 6) $55–$65 S or D. Children under age 8 stay free. Lower rates off-season. Parking: Outdoor, free. AE, DC, DISC, MC, V.

## MOTEL

### 🖿 Days Inn

4650 W FL 46, 32771; tel 407/323-6500 or toll free 800/325-2525; fax 407/323-2962. Exit 51 off I-4. Economy lodging with easy interstate access midway between Daytona and Walt Disney World. **Rooms:** 120 rms. CI 2pm/CO noon. Nonsmoking rms avail. **Amenities:** 🛏 A/C, TV. **Services:** ↩ 🕸 **Facilities:** 🔓 🕁 Washer/dryer. **Rates:** Peak (Feb–Mar) $37–$85 S or D. Children under age 12 stay free. Lower rates off-season. Parking: Outdoor, free. AE, MC, V.

# Sanibel Island

See also Captiva Island, Pine Island

A beautiful, shell-rich barrier island off southwestern Florida, connected by toll bridge to the Fort Myers area. It's home to J M "Ding" Darling National Wildlife Refuge and Sanibel Lighthouse. An October jazz festival draws hundreds to the nearby Dunes Golf & Tennis Club. **Information:** Sanibel–Captiva Islands Chamber of Commerce, 1159 Causeway Rd, Sanibel, 33957 (tel 941/472-1080).

## HOTELS 🏨

### 🖿🖿🖿 Holiday Inn Beach Resort

1231 Middle Gulf Dr, 33957; tel 941/472-4123 or toll free 800/443-0909; fax 941/472-0930. South end of island. Fine shorefront property with lovely tropical lobby and grounds. **Rooms:** 98 rms, stes, and effic. CI 3pm/CO 11am. Nonsmoking rms avail. Recently renovated rooms with a tropical motif. **Amenities:** 🛏 🕭 A/C, dataport, in-rm safe. **Services:** ✗ ↩ Children's program. **Facilities:** 🔓 ᷆ 🖾 🗍50 🕁 2 restaurants, 2 bars, 1 beach (ocean), washer/dryer. Children under 12 eat free with an adult. **Rates:** Peak (Dec 15–Apr) $119–$220 S or D; $149–$220 ste; $139–$220 effic. Children under age 18 stay free. Lower rates off-season. Parking: Outdoor, free. AE, CB, DC, DISC, MC, V.

### 🖿🖿 Pointe Santo de Sanibel

2445 W Gulf Dr, 33957; tel 941/472-9100 or toll free 800/824-5442; fax 941/472-0487. East of Tarpon Bay Rd. A seaside condominium hotel, set on a white sand beach with tall palms and lush greenery. **Rooms:** 22 effic. CI 3pm/CO 10am. All units have ocean views and tropical Florida decor. **Amenities:** 🛏 🕭 📲 A/C, satel TV w/movies, refrig, VCR, in-rm safe. All units w/terraces. **Services:** ↩ Social director, children's program, babysitting. Maid service for added charge. Free video library. **Facilities:** 🔓 🖾2 1 beach (ocean), volleyball, whirlpool, washer/dryer. Outdoor barbecue and dining under tiki huts. Often-crowded public beach nearby. **Rates:** Peak (Dec 15–Apr 15) $155–$360 effic. Min stay. Lower rates off-season. Parking: Outdoor, free. AE, DISC, MC, V.

### ≣≣ Song of the Sea
863 E Gulf Dr, 33957; tel 941/472-2220 or toll free 800/231-1045; fax 941/481-4947. E of Causeway Rd. A small, intimate establishment, with self-contained units. Architecture is a nice mix of Country French and Mission styles. **Rooms:** 30 effic. CI 3pm/CO 11am. Nonsmoking rms avail. All rooms have full kitchens and views of the Gulf. **Amenities:** ⏚ ⏛ ⏜ ⏝ A/C, cable TV, refrig, VCR, in-rm safe. All units w/terraces. Free bottle of wine upon arrival. Down pillows and comforters. **Services:** ⏞ ⏟ ⏠ Social director, children's program, babysitting. **Facilities:** ⏡ ⏢ ⏣ ⏤ 1 beach (ocean), whirlpool, washer/dryer. Shares facilities with nearby Sanibel Inn and Sundial Beach Resort. **Rates (CP):** Peak (Dec 21–Apr 20) $199–$312 effic. Extra person $15. Children under age 13 stay free. Min stay special events. Lower rates off-season. Parking: Outdoor, free. AE, CB, DC, DISC, MC, V.

### ≣≣≣ West Wind Inn
3345 W Gulf Dr, 33957; tel 941/472-1541 or toll free 800/824-0476, 800/282-2831 in FL; fax 941/472-8134. W of Tarpon Bay Rd. An enticing Gulf-front hotel with a relaxed atmosphere, private pool, and lush courtyard. **Rooms:** 104 rms and effic. CI 2pm/CO 11am. Nonsmoking rms avail. Rooms are decorated with exceptionally good taste. Two- and three-bedroom apartments available. **Amenities:** ⏚ ⏛ ⏜ A/C, cable TV, refrig, in-rm safe. All units w/terraces. **Services:** ✗ ⏞ ⏟ Attentive service throughout, even on the beach. **Facilities:** ⏡ ⏢ ⏣ ⏤² ⏥ ⁵⁰ ⏦ 1 restaurant, 2 bars (1 w/entertainment), 1 beach (ocean), volleyball, washer/dryer. Shell-cleaning hut for beachcombers. **Rates:** Peak (Dec 20–Apr) $183 S or D; $207–$573 effic. Extra person $19. Lower rates off-season. Parking: Outdoor, free. AE, DISC, MC, V.

## MOTELS

### ≣ Kona Kai
1539 Periwinkle Way, 33957; tel 941/472-1001; fax 941/472-1001. Exit 22 off I-75. Small motel located in a tropical garden setting. **Rooms:** 12 rms and effic. CI 3pm/CO 10am. Nonsmoking rms avail. **Amenities:** ⏚ ⏜ A/C, cable TV, refrig. **Services:** ⏟ Babysitting. **Facilities:** ⏡ ⏤ Washer/dryer. **Rates:** Peak (Feb–Apr) $118 S or D; $128 effic. Extra person $7. Children under age 12 stay free. Lower rates off-season. Parking: Outdoor, free. AE, DISC, MC, V.

### ≣≣ Sanibel's Seaside Inn
541 E Gulf Dr, 33957; tel 941/472-1400 or toll free 800/831-7384; fax 941/481-4947. Exit 22 off I-75. This old-timer (formerly the Gallery Motel) has been restyled to maintain its old Florida charm and outfitted with modern conveniences. **Rooms:** 32 rms and effic. CI 2pm/CO 11am. **Amenities:** ⏚ ⏛ ⏜ A/C, cable TV, refrig, VCR. All units w/terraces. **Services:** ⏟ Babysitting. **Facilities:** ⏡ ⏢ ⏤ 1 beach (ocean), washer/dryer. **Rates (CP):** Peak (Dec 22–Apr 20) $179–$259 S or D;

$205–$289 effic. Extra person $25. Children under age 13 stay free. Min stay special events. Lower rates off-season. Parking: Outdoor, free. AE, CB, DC, DISC, MC, V.

## RESORTS

### ≣≣≣ Casa Ybel Resort
2255 W Gulf Dr, 33957; tel 941/472-3145 or toll free 800/276-ISLE; fax 941/472-2109. W Gulf at Casa Ybel Rd. 30 acres. In top form, this resort on the beach occupies more than a dozen three-story buildings housing handsome condo-style accommodations. Lush, painstakingly maintained landscaping. **Rooms:** 114 effic. CI 3pm/CO 10am. **Amenities:** ⏚ ⏛ ⏜ A/C, cable TV, refrig, VCR. All units w/terraces. **Services:** ✗ ⏞ ⏟ ⏠ Social director, masseur, children's program, babysitting. **Facilities:** ⏡ ⏢ ⏣ ⏤⁶ ⏥ ⁵⁰ 1 restaurant (see "Restaurants" below), 3 bars, 1 beach (ocean), basketball, volleyball, whirlpool, playground, washer/dryer. **Rates:** Peak (Feb 15–Apr 15) $350–$395 effic. Min stay. Lower rates off-season. Parking: Indoor, free. Minimum stay for two-bedroom units. AE, DC, DISC, MC, V.

### ≣≣≣ The Sanibel Inn
937 Gulf Dr, 33957; tel 941/472-3181 or toll free 800/237-1491; fax 941/481-4947. 14 mi SW of Fort Myers, exit 21 off I-75. 8 acres. Enjoying a resurgence of popularity—the result of ambitious renovation—this friendly family place is neatly packaged on naturally landscaped grounds and has a fine beach. **Rooms:** 96 rms and effic. CI 3pm/CO 11am. Nonsmoking rms avail. Larger two-bedroom units have double screened-in furnished porches and two full baths. All units have microwaves. **Amenities:** ⏚ ⏛ ⏜ ⏝ A/C, cable TV w/movies, refrig, dataport, VCR. All units w/terraces. **Services:** ⏟ ⏠ Social director, masseur, children's program. **Facilities:** ⏡ ⏢ ⏣ ⁴⁵ ⏦ 2 restaurants, 2 bars, 1 beach (ocean), volleyball, lawn games. **Rates:** Peak (Dec 20–Apr 20) $184–$275 S or D; $205–$312 effic. Extra person $15. Children under age 14 stay free. Min stay special events. Lower rates off-season. Parking: Outdoor, free. AE, DC, DISC, MC, V.

### ≣≣≣ Sundial Beach Resort
1451 Middle Gulf Dr, 33957; tel 941/472-4151 or toll free 800/237-4184; fax 941/481-4947. 10 mi SW of Fort Myers via causeway connecting mainland at Runta Rassa. 20 acres. Sanibel's most complete resort, beautifully landscaped and geared for families. The public areas are spacious and elegantly appointed. **Rooms:** 271 effic. CI 3pm/CO 11am. Nonsmoking rms avail. Units are all privately owned and decorated, with one or two bedrooms. **Amenities:** ⏚ ⏛ ⏜ A/C, cable TV w/movies, refrig, in-rm safe. All units w/terraces. All units have full kitchens. **Services:** ✗ ⏞ ⏟ ⏠ Social director, masseur, babysitting. Fine kids' program is focused on the environment and features an on-property ecology center with marine touch tank. **Facilities:** ⏡ ⏢ ⏣ ⏥ ²⁵⁰ ⏧ ⏦ 4 restaurants (see "Restaurants" below), 2 bars (1 w/entertainment), 1 beach (ocean), games rm,

whirlpool, washer/dryer. Inviting pool and beach areas. **Rates:** Peak (Dec 20–Apr 20) $176–$399 effic. Extra person $25. Children under age 13 stay free. Lower rates off-season. Parking: Indoor/outdoor, free. AE, DC, DISC, MC, V.

## RESTAURANTS 🍽

### ♣ Greenhouse Grill
In Islander Center, 2407 Periwinkle Way; tel 941/472-0844. W end of Periwinkle Way. Bright contemporary setting with wine cruvinet and bottle selections featuring boutique wineries from around the world. Highly inventive changing menu includes goat cheese–crusted rack of lamb with Gilroy garlic and extraordinary key lime pie, and dishes using local fish and imported wild game. Owners moved from former Captiva and Thistle Lodge locations to current location. Smoking at counter only. **FYI:** Reservations recommended. Children's menu. Beer and wine only. **Open:** Peak (Dec–Apr) breakfast Mon–Fri 10:30am–3pm, Sat–Sun 8am–3pm; lunch daily 11am–3pm; dinner daily 5–10pm. Closed Sept. **Prices:** Main courses $17–$28. DISC, MC, V. 📷 ⚹

### Harbor House
1244 Periwinkle Way; tel 941/472-1242. **Seafood/Steak.** The oldest restaurant on the island lives up to its name—its nautical theme is carried through in every detail, right down to the lighthouse candle at each table. A selection of well-priced seafood and steaks make this a good value. Try the key lime pie, which is made from fresh limes. **FYI:** Reservations not accepted. Children's menu. Beer and wine only. **Open:** Peak (Jan–Apr) lunch Mon–Fri 11:15am–2:15pm; dinner daily 5–9:30pm. **Prices:** Main courses $9–$20. AE, MC, V. 🍴

### Jean-Paul's French Corner
708 Tarpon Bay Rd; tel 941/472-1493. Next door to post office. **French.** Fine dining at an attractive French cafe. Selections such as roast duckling in fruit sauce, salmon in dill sauce, and the daily fresh seafood special are available. **FYI:** Reservations recommended. Dress code. Beer and wine only. **Open:** Mon–Sat 6–10pm. Closed May–Oct. **Prices:** Main courses $19–$26. MC, V. ♥

### Ⓢ Lighthouse Cafe
In Seahorse Shops, 362 Periwinkle Way; tel 941/472-0303. **American/Seafood.** This appropriately named place is a beacon for those in search of good food at great prices. (Who can pass up eggs Benedict for $5.25?) Especially popular at breakfast. **FYI:** Reservations recommended. Children's menu. Beer and wine only. **Open:** Peak (Dec 15–Apr 15) breakfast daily 7am–3pm; lunch daily 11am–3pm; dinner daily 5–9pm. Closed Sept. **Prices:** Main courses $7–$14. MC, V. 📷 ⚹

### ♣ The Mad Hatter
6460 Sanibel Captiva Rd; tel 941/472-0033. **New American/Seafood.** Casual yet elegant dining room, serving up magnificent sunset views and the freshest local seafood. Yellowfin tuna is a favorite on the ever-changing menu. Attentive staff

and relaxed, friendly atmosphere. **FYI:** Reservations recommended. Beer and wine only. No smoking. **Open:** Peak (Jan–Mar) lunch Wed–Sun 11:30am–2pm; dinner daily 5–9:30pm. Closed Sept 1–15. **Prices:** Main courses $18–$27. AE, DC, MC, V. ♥ 📷 ⚹

### Thistle Lodge Waterfront Restaurant
In Casa Ybel Resort, 2255 W Gulf Dr, Sanibel; tel 941/472-9200. **New American.** A frilly Victorian mansion, recreated to recall a 19th-century island inn, holds a multi-room restaurant with tropically whimsical motif. The lunch menu concentrates on burgers, salads, and seafood or pasta entrees. Key-lime marinated pork chop, steak au poivre, crab cakes, and other seafood specialties dominate the dinner offerings. **FYI:** Reservations recommended. Children's menu. Dress code. **Open:** Daily 11:30am–3pm. **Prices:** Main courses $17–$30. AE, MC, V. ♥ 🍴 📷 🍴 VP ⚹

### ★ Timbers Restaurant and Fish Market
703 Tarpon Bay Rd; tel 941/472-3128. Across from the post office. **Seafood/Steak.** Fresh fish specials are the forte of this popular restaurant. (Expect a lengthy wait in season.) Adjacent sports bar (the Sanibel Grill) serves food during extended hours. **FYI:** Reservations not accepted. Children's menu. **Open:** Daily 4:30–10pm. **Prices:** Main courses $14–$20. AE, CB, DC, DISC, MC, V. 🍴 ⚹

### Windows on the Water
In Sundial Beach Resort, 1451 Middle Gulf Dr; tel 941/472-4151. **Regional American.** An airy, casual restaurant overlooking the sea and an active pool area. Enjoy a glass of wine with smoked salmon, caesar salad, or shrimp cocktail. Bronzed grouper is one of the most popular entrees. **FYI:** Reservations recommended. Children's menu. No smoking. **Open:** Breakfast Mon–Sat 7:30–10:30am, Sun 7:30–10am; lunch daily 11:30am–2pm; dinner daily 5:30–9:30pm; brunch Sun 11am–2pm. **Prices:** Main courses $17–$22. AE, DC, DISC, MC, V. ♥ 📷 ⚹

## ATTRACTIONS 🏛

### Sanibel/Captiva Conservation Foundation
3333 Sanibel-Captiva Rd; tel 941/472-2329. A library, exhibits, guest lecturers, and a variety of brochures help explain the island's unusual ecosystem. Native plants, birdhouses, books, and nature-oriented gifts for sale. Guided and self-guided tours let visitors observe wildlife, a native butterfly "head start" program, and native vegetation. The 247-acre wetlands tract features a four-mile nature trail along the Sanibel River. **Open:** Peak (Dec–Apr) Mon–Sat 8:30am–4pm. Reduced hours off-season. $

### Sealife Learning Center
Wing Surf and Sport Center, 2353 Periwinkle Way; tel 941/472-8680. The center features a 450-gallon touch tank, 230-gallon shark tank, 18 other aquariums, and other sea-animal displays to introduce nature enthusiasts to sea life in the Gulf of Mexico. Hourly guided program includes slide show and

discussion. A 3½-hour van tour explores the flora and fauna of secluded beach areas of the island. **Open:** Peak (Sept–May) daily 9am–8pm. Reduced hours off-season. **$$**

### J N "Ding" Darling National Wildlife Refuge
1 Wildlife Dr; tel 941/472-1100. Over 6,300 protected acres of vibrant wildlife habitat. Along the five-mile-long Wildlife Drive through undisturbed mangrove swamp, visitors have the chance to observe some of the hundreds of species of birds and migratory waterfowl that populate the refuge, including roseate spoonbills, white ibis, blue herons, snowy egrets, and ospreys. Also in abundance are alligators, otters, and raccoons. Hiking and winding canoe trails provide for fascinating viewing, as does the observation tower. The visitor center offers regularly scheduled slide shows. **Open:** Sat–Thurs sunrise–sunset. **$$**

# Sarasota

See also Bradenton, Lido Beach, Longboat Key, Siesta Key, Venice

Big draws in this Gulf Coast city are the two Ringling museums and the restored mansion that once belonged to John and Mabel Ringling. Nearby 28,000-acre Myakka River State Park also brings visitors. **Information:** Sarasota Convention & Visitors Bureau, 655 N Tamiami Trail, Sarasota, 34236 (tel 941/957-1877 or toll free 800/522-9799).

## HOTELS 🏨

### ≡≡≡ Hyatt Sarasota
1000 Blvd of the Arts, 34236; tel 941/953-1234 or toll free 800/233-1234; fax 941/952-1987. The longstanding choice for businesspeople who enjoy access to the adjacent marina and beaches during their free time. **Rooms:** 297 rms and stes. CI 3pm/CO noon. Nonsmoking rms avail. Sharp guest accommodations are in top form. **Amenities:** 📺 ⓐ A/C, cable TV w/movies. Some units w/terraces. **Services:** ✕ VP 🚗 ⊠ ⌂ Car-rental desk, babysitting. **Facilities:** 🛗 🚴 🏌 550 ⓓ 2 restaurants, 2 bars (1 w/entertainment). **Rates:** Peak (Jan–Apr) $175 S; $215 D; $350–$625 ste. Extra person $25. Children under age 16 stay free. Lower rates off-season. Parking: Outdoor, free. AE, DC, DISC, MC, V.

### ≡≡≡ Ramada Inn Airport
8440 N Tamiami Trail, 34243 (Sarasota-Bradenton Airport); tel 941/355-7771 or toll free 800/272-6232, 800/272-6232 in the US, 800/854-7854 in Canada; fax 941/351-7411. N of University Pkwy on US 41. Handy for those in town for a one-day meeting or those who cannot find accommodations in the beach area. **Rooms:** 105 rms and stes. CI 3pm/CO 11am. Nonsmoking rms avail. **Amenities:** 📺 ⓐ A/C, cable TV w/movies. **Services:** ✕ 🚗 ⊠ ⌂ ⊲ **Facilities:** 🛗 350 ⓓ 1 restaurant, 1 bar (w/entertainment), washer/dryer. Comedy club operates Thursday through Sunday. **Rates (CP):** Peak

(Mar–May) $85 S; $95 D; $125 ste. Extra person $5. Children under age 18 stay free. Lower rates off-season. Parking: Outdoor, free. AE, CB, DC, DISC, EC, ER, JCB, MC, V.

### ≡≡ Wellesley Inn
1803 N Tamiami Trail, 34234; tel 941/366-5128 or toll free 800/444-8888; fax 941/953-4322. 1 mile N of Fruitville Rd. Convenient location and comfortable rooms for families and business travelers. **Rooms:**. CI 2pm/CO 11am. Nonsmoking rms avail. **Amenities:** 📺 ⓐ A/C, satel TV. **Services:** 🚗 ⊠ ⌂ Five-day weather forecast posted at front desk. **Facilities:** 🛗 20 ⓓ **Rates (CP):** Peak (Jan–Apr) $90–$100 S or D; $119 ste. Extra person $6–$10. Children under age 17 stay free. Min stay special events. Lower rates off-season. Parking: Outdoor, free. AE, DC, DISC, MC, V.

## MOTELS

### ≡≡ Comfort Inn
4800 N Tamiami Trail, 34234; tel 941/355-7091 or toll free 800/228-5150; fax 941/359-1639. ¼ mile S of University Pkwy. A comfortable spot for budget-minded travelers who want clean, pleasant surroundings. **Rooms:** 87 rms, stes, and effic. CI 2pm/CO 11am. Nonsmoking rms avail. **Amenities:** 📺 ⓐ A/C, cable TV. Some units w/whirlpools. **Services:** ⊠ ⌂ ⊲ Babysitting. **Facilities:** 🛗 ⓓ Whirlpool, washer/dryer. **Rates (CP):** Peak (Jan–Apr) $80 S; $90 D; $140 ste; $110 effic. Extra person $5. Children under age 18 stay free. Lower rates off-season. Parking: Outdoor, free. AE, CB, DC, DISC, JCB, MC, V.

### ≡≡ Hampton Inn
5000 N Tamiami Trail, 34234; tel 941/351-7734 or toll free 800/336-9335; fax 941/351-8820. ¼ mi S of University Pkwy. Good for those seeking a dependable, short-stay option. **Rooms:** 97 rms. CI 2pm/CO 11am. Nonsmoking rms avail. **Amenities:** 📺 ⓐ A/C, satel TV w/movies, dataport, voice mail. Rooms furnished with dehumidifiers. **Services:** 🚗 ⊠ ⌂ Car-rental desk. **Facilities:** 🛗 🏌 30 ⓓ Washer/dryer. **Rates (CP):** Peak (Jan–Apr) $99 S or D. Children under age 18 stay free. Lower rates off-season. Parking: Outdoor, free. AE, CB, DC, DISC, EC, ER, JCB, MC, V.

## RESTAURANTS 🍴

### Bijou Cafe
1287 1st St; tel 941/366-8111. 2 blocks E of US 41 N; across the street from the Opera House. **New American/Continental.** A charming, stylish little cafe with a wonderful menu and wine list. Daily offerings may include roast duckling, veal, and New Orleans crab cakes. **FYI:** Reservations recommended. **Open:** Peak (Jan–May) lunch Mon–Fri 11:30am–2pm; dinner Sun–Thurs 5–9:30pm, Fri–Sat 5–10:30pm. **Prices:** Main courses $13–$23. AE, CB, DC, MC, V. ♥

### Buttery Cafe
470 John Ringling Blvd, St Armands Key; tel 941/388-1523. **American.** An ideal spot for breakfast, lunch, or a snack, this

informal eatery also offers light dinner dishes such as petite sirloin or prime rib, mesquite-grilled breast of chicken, lime grouper, or lemon pepper catfish. Breakfast (pancakes, waffles, omelettes) and sandwiches served all day. **FYI:** Reservations not accepted. Beer and wine only. **Open:** Tues–Sat 24 hrs, Sun–Mon 6:30am–11pm. **Prices:** Main courses $9–$13. AE, DISC, MC, V. 🕘 🔲 &

### Cafe l'Europe
431 St Armands Circle (St Armands Key); tel 941/365-7380. **Continental/French.** A cozy French cafe with exposed brick, dark wood, and brass fixtures. The menu ranges across Europe: from Wiener schnitzel to veal piccata, roast pheasant breast to veal Frangelico. **FYI:** Reservations recommended. Jazz. Children's menu. **Open:** Lunch Mon–Fri 11:30am–2pm; dinner Mon–Thurs 5:30–10:30pm, Fri–Sat 5:30–11:30pm. **Prices:** Main courses $11–$25. AE, DC, DISC, MC, V. 🔲 &

### Caragiulos
69 S Palm Ave; tel 941/951-0866. Between Ringling Blvd and Main St. **Italian/Pizza.** A small cafe near the theater district offering pizzas and pastas along with soups, salads, and sandwiches. **FYI:** Reservations not accepted. Guitar. Beer and wine only. **Open:** Mon–Thurs 11am–10pm, Fri 11am–11pm, Sat noon–11pm, Sun 4–9pm. **Prices:** Main courses $8–$13. AE, CB, DC, DISC, MC, V. 🍴 🚢 🏖 🔲 &

### ⭐ Charley's Crab
420 St Armands Circle (St Armands Key); tel 941/388-3964. **Seafood.** After a stroll around the circle, stop into this tavern-style restaurant for pasta or fresh fish from all over—including New Zealand mussels. Curbside piano draws a crowd. **FYI:** Reservations recommended. Piano. Children's menu. **Open:** Lunch Mon–Sat 11:30am–4:45pm, Sun noon–4:45pm; dinner Sun–Thurs 5–10pm, Fri–Sat 5–10:30pm. **Prices:** Main courses $10–$22. AE, CB, DC, MC, V. 🔲 &

### Coasters Seafood Bistro
1500 Stickney Point Rd; tel 941/923-4848. Just E of Stickney Point Bridge. **Regional American.** Both the floor-to-ceiling windows and the outside deck offer lovely views of the Intracoastal Waterway. Specialties include mahimahi with pineapple sweet-and-sour glaze. **FYI:** Reservations accepted. Children's menu. **Open:** Lunch daily 11:30am–3:30pm; dinner daily 4–10pm. **Prices:** Main courses $10–$17. AE, DISC, MC, V. 🏞 📵 &

### ⭐ The Columbia
411 St Armands Circle (St Armands Key); tel 941/388-3987. **Spanish.** The newest branch of this popular Spanish-Cuban chain couldn't be in a more appealing location. The menu includes meat, chicken, and seafood dishes, including three types of spicy paellas. A favorite starter is the "Original 1905 Salad," prepared tableside. Lunch specials are a great value. **FYI:** Reservations recommended. Band. Children's menu. Additional location: 800 2nd Ave NE, St Petersburg (tel 813/

822-8000). **Open:** Mon–Sat 11am–11pm, Sun noon–10pm. **Prices:** Main courses $15–$18. AE, DC, DISC, MC, V. 🏞 🔲 &

### Hemingway's
325 John Ringling Blvd, St Armands Circle; tel 941/388-3948. **New American/Continental.** This family-style restaurant may appeal to a less discerning crowd. Seafood and meat dishes are supplemented by soups and salads on the standard menu. **FYI:** Reservations accepted. Children's menu. **Open:** Sun–Thurs 11:30am–10pm, Fri–Sat 11:30am–11pm. **Prices:** Main courses $10–$25. AE, CB, DC, DISC, MC, V. 🚢 🏖 🔲 &

### ⑤ Mrs Appleton's Family Buffet
In Palm Plaza, 4458 Bee Ridge Rd; tel 941/378-1177. Exit 38 off I-75. **Buffet.** Mrs. Appleton can satisfy almost any craving with her massive smorgasbord. This cafeteria-style dining room is quite a find for hungry families. **FYI:** Reservations not accepted. Children's menu. No liquor license. **Open:** Breakfast Sat–Sun 8–10:30am; lunch daily 11am–4pm; dinner daily 4pm–8:30. **Prices:** Prix fixe $7. CB, DC, MC, V. 🏖 &

### Nick's on the Water
230 Sarasota Quay; tel 941/954-3839. **Italian/Seafood.** A comfortable waterside restaurant serving dishes such as pizza, pasta, steak pizzaiola, and the chef's special veal medallions. Terrace diners can watch boats come and go from the nearby marina. **FYI:** Reservations accepted. **Open:** Sun–Thurs 11:30am–10pm, Fri–Sat 11:30am–11pm. **Prices:** Main courses $9–$17. AE, MC, V. 🚢 🏞 🔲 🆅🅿 &

### Old Hickory
5100 N Tamiami Trail; tel 941/355-8757. At Mecca St near Ringling Museum. **Barbecue.** A comfortable, casual restaurant and lounge. Enjoy Old Hickory's famous homemade barbecue sauce on beef, pork, baby-back ribs, or chicken. All items are hickory-smoked. **FYI:** Reservations not accepted. **Open:** Mon–Sat 11:30am–10:30pm. **Prices:** Main courses $6–$13. MC, V. 🔲

### Patrick's
In Kress Plaza, 1400 Main St; tel 941/952-1170. **New American.** A casual sports bar and restaurant with a black-and-white tile floor and a veritable jungle of plants. Seafood, poultry, pasta, and burgers dominate the dinner menu; sandwiches and salads are offered at lunch. **FYI:** Reservations not accepted. **Open:** Sun–Thurs 11am–midnight, Fri–Sat 11am–1am. **Prices:** Main courses $5–$17. AE, MC, V. 🆅🅿 &

### Ristorante Bellini
1551 Main St; tel 941/365-7380. Between Orange and Lemon Aves. **Northern Italian.** A comfortable, romantic bistro with a menu featuring chicken cacciatore and a variety of pasta dishes. Highlights also include scaloppine Bellini (veal topped with asparagus and mozzarella) and sautéed snapper. **FYI:** Reservations recommended. Beer and wine

only. **Open:** Lunch Mon–Fri 11:30am–2pm; dinner Mon–Thurs 5:30–10:30pm, Fri–Sat 5:30–11:30pm. **Prices:** Main courses $11–$25. AE, DC, DISC, MC, V. 🍷 ✉ ♿

### Shells
7253 S Tamiami Trail; tel 941/924-2568. 2 mi S of Downtown Sarasota. **Seafood/Steak.** A local favorite with a cheerful staff. Choose either one of the many seafood selections or the vegetable stir-fry. **FYI:** Reservations not accepted. Children's menu. **Open:** Sun–Thurs 4–10pm, Fri–Sat 4–11pm. **Prices:** Main courses $5–$22. AE, DISC, MC, V. ♿

### ★ Yoder's
3434 Bahia Vista St; tel 941/955-7771. 3 mi E of downtown Sarasota. **Regional American/Amish.** A restaurant offering home-style atmosphere along with its home-cooked food. Full breakfasts are available for $2.95, and burgers and sandwiches are available at lunch. Mom's meat loaf with gravy and the homemade pies are dinnertime favorites. **FYI:** Reservations not accepted. Children's menu. No liquor license. No smoking. **Open:** Mon–Sat 11am–8pm. **Prices:** Main courses $5–$10. No CC. 📽 ♿

## REFRESHMENT STOP 🥤

### Joffrey's Coffee & Tea Co
26 N Blvd of the Presidents, St Armands Key; tel 941/388-5282. **Coffeehouse.** This bookstore/cafe offers a wide range of brewed coffee, beans to go, and delicious desserts. Additional location: 1345 Main St, Sarasota (tel 953-JAVA). **Open:** Mon–Sat 9am–10:30pm, Sun 9:30am–9:30pm. MC, V. ♿

## ATTRACTIONS 📷

### Ringling Museum Complex
5401 Bay Shore Rd; tel 941/359-5700 or 941/351-1660 (recorded info). This 66-acre site overlooking Sarasota Bay is the former estate of circus entrepreneur John Ringling. Attractions include the John and Mable Ringling Museum of Art, Florida's official state art museum and site of a major exhibit of baroque art; the 30-room Ringling Mansion Ca'd'zan ("House of John"), the winter residence that was modeled after a Venetian palace; the Circus Museum, devoted to circus memorabilia; and the Asolo Theater. The grounds also contain restaurants and shops. **Open:** Daily 10am–5:30pm. $$$

### Mote Marine Aquarium
1600 Thompson Pkwy; tel 941/388-4441. This facility, located in Ken Thompson Park, focuses on local marine life. Displays include a living mangrove swamp and seagrass environment, a 135,000-gallon shark tank, loggerhead turtles and their eggs, dolphins, manatees, and an extensive shell collection. Also, "research exhibits" on red tide, aquaculture enhancement, cancer in sharks, and effects of pesticide and petroleum pollution on the coast. **Open:** Daily 10am–5pm. $$$

### Marie Selby Botanical Gardens
811 S Palm Ave; tel 941/366-5730. A nine-acre museum of living plants that is home to more than 20,000 exotic plants, including over 6,000 orchids. Also featured are a waterfall garden, cactus garden, fernery, hibiscus garden, palm grove, tropical food garden, and bamboo pavilion. **Open:** Daily 10am–5pm. $$$

### Bellm's Cars & Music of Yesterday
5500 N Tamiami Trail; tel 941/355-6228. This museum displays over 50 classic and antique autos, from Rolls-Royces to Pierce Arrows. There are also over 1,200 antique music machines, from miniature music boxes to a 26-foot Belgian organ. **Open:** Daily 9:30am–5:30pm. $$$

### Myakka River State Park
13207 FL 72; tel 941/361-6511. The Myakka River has been designated a National Wild and Scenic River within Sarasota County. The park, located off FL 72, covers more than 28,000 acres of dry prairie, pine flatwoods, and numerous small wetlands. Fishing, canoe rentals, hiking, camping, nature trails. **Open:** Daily sunrise–sunset. $$

# Seaside

See Fort Walton Beach

# Sebring

Seat of Highlands County in south-central Florida's gentle hills, this city of 9,000 is known for its 24-hour auto endurance race. Four miles east of town is Highlands Hammock State Park, offering boardwalks and horse trails through some of its 3,800 acres. **Information:** Greater Sebring Chamber of Commerce, 309 S Circle, Sebring, 33870 (tel 941/385-8448).

## HOTEL 📷

### ≣≣ Holiday Inn
6525 US 27 N, 33870; tel 941/385-4500 or toll free 800/HOLIDAY; fax 941/382-4793. US 27 exit off I-4. Basic lodging on the highway. **Rooms:** 148 rms and stes. CI 4pm/CO noon. Nonsmoking rms avail. **Amenities:** 🛁 A/C, cable TV w/movies. **Services:** ✕ 🖨 ⊷ Masseur. **Facilities:** 🔃 ⛱ 🏊 ♿ 1 restaurant, 1 bar (w/entertainment), washer/dryer. **Rates:** Peak (Nov–Apr) $84–$155 S or D; $125–$300 ste. Extra person $5. Children under age 18 stay free. Lower rates off-season. Parking: Outdoor, free. AE, CB, DC, DISC, JCB, MC, V.

## ATTRACTION 📷

### Highlands Hammock State Park
Tel 941/386-6094. This is one of Florida's original state parks, which were built by the New Deal–era Civilian Conser-

vation Corps. Its 3,800 tranquil acres encompass a hardwood hammock and a cypress swamp. Hiking, nature trails, bike trails, horseback riding, camping. Ranger-led tours available Nov–Apr. $$

# Siesta Key

Two small bridges connect the southwest Florida mainland with this modern resort island just south of Sarasota. Fishing enthusiasts angle in Big Sarasota Pass at the island's north end and Midnight Pass at the south. **Information:** Siesta Key Chamber of Commerce, 5100 Ocean Blvd #B, Siesta Key, 34242 (tel 941/349-3800).

## HOTEL

### Crescent View Beach Club
6512 Midnight Pass Rd, 34242; tel 941/349-2000 or toll free 800/344-7171; fax 941/349-9748. ¼ mi S of Stickney Point Rd. A condominium-style complex, with tropical decor throughout. **Rooms:** 26 effic. CI 3pm/CO 11am. Nonsmoking rms avail. **Amenities:** A/C, cable TV w/movies, refrig. Some units w/terraces. All rooms have ceiling fans and washers and dryers. **Services:** Babysitting. **Facilities:** 1 beach (ocean), whirlpool, washer/dryer. **Rates:** Peak (Feb–Apr) $185–$285 effic. Lower rates off-season. Parking: Outdoor, free. AE, CB, DC, DISC, MC, V.

## MOTELS

### Best Western Siesta Beach Resort
5311 Ocean Blvd, 34242; tel 941/349-3211 or toll free 800/223-5786; fax 941/349-7915. Exit 38 off I-75; 2 mi N of Stickney Point Rd. Comfortable, unpretentious atmosphere, good for families. Handy to local attractions. **Rooms:** 53 rms, stes, and effic. CI 3pm/CO 11am. Nonsmoking rms avail. **Amenities:** A/C, cable TV. **Services:** Complimentary morning coffee. Free passes for the Siesta Key trolley. **Facilities:** Whirlpool, washer/dryer. **Rates:** Peak (Feb–Mar) $99–$135 S or D; $165–$250 ste; $135–$195 effic. Extra person $8. Children under age 18 stay free. Lower rates off-season. Parking: Outdoor, free. AE, CB, DC, DISC, ER, JCB, MC, V.

### Gulf Sun Motel
6722 Midnight Pass Rd, 34242; tel 941/349-2442; fax 941/349-7141. 1 mi S of Stickney Point Rd. For budget-minded families with young children. Beach access. **Rooms:** 17 rms and effic. CI 2pm/CO 10am. Nonsmoking rms avail. **Amenities:** A/C, cable TV, refrig. Gas grills, beach umbrellas, and kiddie toys are available to guests. **Services:** **Facilities:** Washer/dryer. **Rates:** Peak (Jan–Apr) $90 S or D; $125 effic. Extra person $10. Children under age 2 stay free. Min stay peak. Lower rates off-season. Parking: Outdoor, free. MC, V.

## RESTAURANT

### Turtle's
8875 Midnight Pass Rd; tel 941/346-2207. 5 mi S of Sarasota. **Seafood/Steak.** Dine along the water's edge at this marina-side restaurant. The menu features grouper in potato crust, sautéed Dungeness crab cakes, and rack of lamb. Prix fixe dinner is for two people and comes with a bottle of wine. **FYI:** Reservations recommended. Singer. Children's menu. **Open:** Daily 11:30am–11:30pm. **Prices:** Main courses $11–$18; prix fixe $50. AE, DISC, MC, V.

# Silver Springs

Located in central Florida and named for the world's largest artesian spring (which is actually a network of 150 underground spouts of crystalline water). Silver Springs Wildlife Park offers naturalist tours in glass-bottom boats; Wild Waters amusement park offers man-made water play.

## MOTELS

### Holiday Inn
5751 E Silver Springs Blvd, PO Box 156, 32688; tel 352/236-2575 or toll free 800/HOLIDAY; fax 352/236-2575 ext 163. Located at the entrance to Silver Springs; suited for families. **Rooms:** 103 rms and stes. CI 2pm/CO noon. Nonsmoking rms avail. **Amenities:** A/C, cable TV w/movies, in-rm safe. **Services:** **Facilities:** 1 restaurant, 1 bar. **Rates:** Peak (Feb–Apr/June–Aug) $49–$65 S or D; $79–$99 ste. Extra person $6. Children under age 18 stay free. Lower rates off-season. Parking: Outdoor, free. AE, CB, DC, DISC, JCB, MC, V.

### Howard Johnson Lodge
5565 E Silver Springs Blvd, PO Box 475, 34489; tel 352/236-2616 or toll free 800/I GO HOJO; fax 352/236-1941. Exit 69 off I-75. Its two two-story buildings lie opposite Wild Waters water park and within walking distance of Silver Springs. **Rooms:** 44 rms. CI 11am/CO noon. Nonsmoking rms avail. **Amenities:** A/C, cable TV. **Services:** **Facilities:** Italian restaurant next door offers discounts to guests and delivers to rooms. **Rates:** $70 S or D. Extra person $8. Children under age 18 stay free. Parking: Outdoor, free. AE, DC, DISC, JCB, MC, V.

## ATTRACTION

### Silver Springs
Tel 352/236-1212 or 800/234-7458. Located just off I-75. Venerated by Native Americans since ancient times, the springs have produced half a billion gallons of water daily for the past 100,000 years. Glass-bottom boats ply the waters of this 350-acre site, making 4 tours that highlight the area's 7 major springs. In addition, the Jungle Cruise passes through a waterway lined with habitats containing 25 species of exotic animals from across the globe, while the Lost River Voyage

traverses untouched areas. A stop is made on this tour for a presentation at the wildlife outpost, where injured animals are nursed back to health. Safari trams wind through jungle habitats where visitors can see roaming zebras, deer, monkeys, and even the occasional tapir or sloth. With petting zoo and animal shows. A recent addition is the Touch of Garlits antique and race car museum. **Open:** Daily 9am–5:30pm. $$$$

# Singer Island

See Palm Beach, Riviera Beach

# Spring Hill

## ATTRACTION 📷

**Weeki Wachee Spring**
6131 Commercial Way; tel 352/596-2062 or 800/678-9335. "The City of Mermaids" has been drawing visitors to its underwater performances since 1947, when a former US Navy frogman taught underwater breathing techniques to a few young women, dressed them in mermaid outfits, and began staging shows 16 feet below the surface of the clear waters of Weeki Wachee ("winding waters") Spring. Guests watch the show through thick plate glass windows. Shows take place several times daily on two underwater "stages." Shows on dry land include the Birds of Prey show, with free-flying eagles, falcons, hawks, and owls, and the Exotic Bird Show, with trained parrots, macaws, and other birds. There is also a petting zoo.

The **Wilderness River Cruise** is a boat tour down a waterway filled with native foliage and wildlife. One highlight is Pelican Preserve, a refuge that treats and releases injured birds.

Adjacent is **Buccaneer Bay** (separate admission), the only Florida water park that uses water from a natural spring. Features include water slides, Lazy River tube ride, beach volleyball, and a children's area. **Open:** Daily 9:30am–5:30pm. $$$$

# Stuart

Founded in the 1880s, this southeastern city of 13,000 is renowned for freshwater and deep-sea fishing. The Martin County seat offers a restored downtown, boating on Lake Okeechobee or the Loxahatchee River, and Gilbert's Bar House of Refuge Museum (built in 1875 to house shipwrecked sailors). **Information:** Stuart–Martin County Chamber of Commerce, 1650 S Kanner Hwy, Stuart, 34994 (tel 561/287-1088).

## MOTELS 🏨

### ▦▦ **Holiday Inn Downtown**
1209 S Federal Hwy, PO Box 566, 34995; tel 561/287-6200 or toll free 800/HOLIDAY; fax 561/287-6200 ext 100. Exit 63 off I-95. Although located on a busy commercial road, guests have access to the beach through the nearby Holiday Inn Surfside. Caribbean island theme; Custom House lobby is decked with potted palms and overhead fans. **Rooms:** 119 rms and stes. CI open/CO noon. Nonsmoking rms avail. **Amenities:** 📺 🕐 A/C, cable TV w/movies. All units w/terraces. **Services:** ✕ 🖨 🔁 Babysitting. **Facilities:** 🛗 🏋 🔲 1 restaurant, 1 bar (w/entertainment), sauna, washer/dryer. **Rates:** Peak (Dec–Apr) $91 S or D; $180 ste. Extra person $8. Children under age 18 stay free. Lower rates off-season. Parking: Outdoor, free. AE, DC, DISC, MC, V.

### ▦▦ **Howard Johnson Lodge**
950 S Federal Hwy, 34994; tel 561/287-3171 or toll free 800/I GO HOJO; fax 561/220-3594. ½ mi S of jct FL 76 on US 1. This centrally located, two-story motel is fine for families not requiring beach frontage. **Rooms:** 80 rms. CI 11/CO noon. Nonsmoking rms avail. **Amenities:** 📺 🕐 A/C, cable TV w/movies. All units w/terraces. **Services:** ✕ 🖨 🔁 **Facilities:** 🛗 🏋 🔲 🕭 1 restaurant, 1 bar (w/entertainment), whirlpool. Attractive landscaped pool area with lounge chairs. **Rates (CP):** Peak (Jan–May) $85 S or D. Extra person $8. Children under age 18 stay free. Min stay special events. Lower rates off-season. Parking: Outdoor, free. AE, CB, DC, DISC, MC, V.

## RESORT

### ▦▦▦ **Indian River Plantation Beach Resort**
555 NE Ocean Blvd, 34996; tel 561/225-3700 or toll free 800/444-3389; fax 561/225-0003. Exit 61 or 67 off I-95. 250 acres. Occupying a former pineapple plantation, this resort is by far the largest of its kind on Hutchinson Island. It offers lush surroundings and a white lattice-and-wicker lobby filled with plants. The numerous activities available to both adults and children make this an excellent choice for families. **Rooms:** 306 rms, stes, and effic. CI 3pm/CO 11am. Nonsmoking rms avail. Larger accommodations offer complete kitchen facilities. Standard units have two-poster beds and trendy color combinations. **Amenities:** 📺 🕐 📟 🍴 A/C, cable TV, dataport, bathrobes. Some units w/terraces. **Services:** 🍽 🔑 VP 🚐 🖨 🔁 🛎 Car-rental desk, social director, children's program, babysitting. **Facilities:** 🛗 🚴 ⛰ ⛳18 🎾 🏊 🏋 🔲 🕭 5 restaurants, 4 bars (2 w/entertainment), 2 beaches (ocean, bay), volleyball, board surfing, games rm, racquetball, snorkeling, sauna, whirlpool, playground, washer/dryer. **Rates:** Peak (Dec–Apr) $160 S or D; $230 ste; $170 effic. Extra person $20. Children under age 17 stay free. Lower rates off-season. AP and MAP rates avail. Parking: Indoor/outdoor, free. AE, CB, DISC, MC, V.

## RESTAURANTS 🍴

### ★ Ashley Restaurant
61 SW Osceola St; tel 561/221-9476. **Regional American/ French.** Delightful art deco styling, inventive cuisine. Popular menu selections include duck à l'orange and steak pizzaiola. **FYI:** Reservations not accepted. Guitar/singer. **Open:** Lunch daily 11:30am–2:30pm; dinner daily 5–10pm. **Prices:** Main courses $7–$18. AE, DISC, MC, V. 🅿 ♿

### China Star
1501 S Federal Hwy; tel 561/283-8378. 1 mile S of Colorado Ave. **Chinese.** Decor featuring Asian murals and handsome lacquered furniture set the tone in this cool, pleasant eatery. Extensive menu. **FYI:** Reservations recommended. Beer and wine only. **Open:** Daily 11am–10pm. **Prices:** Main courses $7–$13. AE, DISC, MC, V. ♿

### ⑤ ★ Flagler Grill
47 SW Flagler Ave; tel 561/221-9517. **Eclectic.** A casual eatery where crayons are provided for doodling on the paper tablecloths. Patrons can watch their meals being prepared in the open kitchen. The menu features delicacies such as Caribbean lobster with a light curry sauce and tropical salsa and saffron-mushroom tagliatelle with smoked salmon, caviar, and mussels. Wine list has over 150 selections. **FYI:** Reservations recommended. Beer and wine only. No smoking. **Open:** Daily 5:30–9:30pm. **Prices:** Main courses $16–$21. AE, DISC, MC, V. ♥ ♿

### ★ Nature's Way Cafe
In the Post Office Arcade, 25 Osceola St; tel 561/220-7306. **Deli/Health/Spa.** A casual yet lively place attracting a hip, health-conscious crowd. You can create your own salad or choose one of the tropical fruit salads on the menu. Young, energetic staff. **FYI:** Reservations not accepted. No liquor license. No smoking. **Open:** Mon–Fri 10am–4pm, Sat 11am–3pm. **Prices:** Lunch main courses $4–$9. No CC. ♿

## REFRESHMENT STOP 🥤

### ★ Osceola Bakery
38 W Osceola St; tel 561/287-BAKE. **Deli.** A fun, casual place filled with enticing aromas. Wide variety of delectable desserts and pastries. **Open:** Mon–Fri 8am–5pm, Sat 9am–4pm. No CC. ♿

## ATTRACTIONS 🏛

### Elliott Museum
825 NE Ocean Blvd; tel 561/225-1961. Built in honor of the inventor Sterling Elliott, this museum packed with early Americana illustrates life from the Revolutionary War to the Civil War. An apothecary, a barbershop, a blacksmith forge, and a clock and watch shop are among the life-size dioramas on view. The highlight of the museum is the display of some of Elliott's many inventions, including the first envelope-addressing machine, a mechanical knot-tier, and a quadricycle. **Open:** Daily 11am–5pm. **$$**

### Gilbert's Bar House of Refuge
301 SE MacArthur Blvd; tel 561/225-1875. Dating from 1875, the oldest structure in this area was originally a refuge center for shipwrecked sailors. Convincingly restored, today it functions as a historical museum, with displays of marine artifacts, life-boat equipment, ships' logs, and other interesting objects. **Open:** Tues–Sun 11am–4:15pm. **$**

# Sugar Loaf Key

Several large bays carve into this second-to-last island before Key West, sheltering marine life and fishermen alike. Less developed than other islands in the chain, its northwestern edge faces the Florida Keys National Marine Sanctuary.

## MOTEL 🏨

### ▤ Sugarloaf Lodge
Overseas Hwy MM 17, PO Box 148, 33044; tel 305/745-3211; fax 305/745-3389. More motel than lodge, with a few extras. **Rooms:** 55 rms and effic. CI 1pm/CO 11am. Inexpensively furnished rooms with 1960s look. **Amenities:** 🛏 A/C, cable TV. Some units w/terraces. **Services:** ✕ 🛎 🖐 Babysitting. **Facilities:** ⚠ 🔲 1 restaurant (see "Restaurants" below), 1 bar (w/entertainment), 1 beach (ocean), snorkeling, washer/dryer. Dolphin Sanctuary and dolphin show three times daily. Three-thousand-foot airstrip available. Small beach is grassy and weedy. **Rates:** Peak (Dec 19–Apr) $55–$85 S; $60–$95 D; $70–$100 effic. Extra person $10. Children under age 12 stay free. Min stay special events. Lower rates off-season. Parking: Outdoor, free. AE, CB, DC, DISC, MC, V.

## RESTAURANTS 🍴

### ★ Mangrove Mama's
Overseas Hwy MM 20; tel 305/745-3030. **Eclectic.** This family-owned restaurant offers local seafood, steaks, and ribs in a relaxed setting. Menu specialties include coconut shrimp and chicken-and-scallop Caribbean. **FYI:** Reservations recommended. Reggae. Children's menu. **Open:** Daily 11:30am–10pm. **Prices:** Main courses $15–$22. CB, DC, DISC, MC, V. ⚓

### The Restaurant at Sugarloaf Lodge
In Sugarloaf Lodge, Overseas Hwy MM 17; tel 305/745-3741. **American.** Particular care has been taken to preserve the atmosphere of the Keys in the 1960s: coral-and-aquamarine prints, tropical plants, and charming local artwork fill the dining room. Before dinner, enjoy the sunsets and the antics of the dolphins at the recently constructed tiki bar. **FYI:** Reservations accepted. Country music/dancing/jazz. **Open:** Daily 7:30am–10pm. **Prices:** Main courses $14–$28. AE, DC, DISC, MC, V. 🏔 🅿

# Summerland Key

## RESTAURANT 🍴

### Monte's Restaurant & Fish Market
Overseas Hwy MM 25; tel 305/745-3731. **Seafood.** A former fisherman owns and runs this open-air eatery and fresh-fish market where, depending on the day's catch, the menu might offer tuna, lobster, and/or stone crabs. **FYI:** Reservations not accepted. Beer and wine only. **Open:** Mon–Sat 9:30am–10pm, Sun 11am–9pm. **Prices:** Main courses $7–$14. No CC. 🥪

# Sunny Isles

This Dade County community is one of the ritzy northern suburbs of Miami Beach. **Information:** Sunny Isles Beach Chamber of Commerce, 17100 Collins Ave #217, Sunny Isles, 33160 (tel 305/947-5826).

## HOTELS 🏨

### ≣≣≣ Hotel Riu Pan American Ocean Resort
17875 Collins Ave, 33160; tel 305/932-1100 or toll free 800/327-5678; fax 305/935-2769. Curved stucco walls and fountain at entry lead to this three-story oceanfront hotel. Caters to older crowd without children. **Rooms:** 146 rms and stes. CI 4pm/CO noon. Nonsmoking rms avail. Good-quality accommodations employ pastel color schemes and have dark rattan furniture. Most rooms have ocean view. **Amenities:** 🛏 🍴 A/C, cable TV w/movies, refrig, in-rm safe. All units w/minibars, some w/terraces. **Services:** ✗ 🔑 VP 🧺 🛎 Car-rental desk. Afternoon tea served at 3:30pm. Manager's cocktail party Mondays. **Facilities:** 🔦 🍸2 🍽 💻 🛋 1 restaurant, 2 bars (1 w/entertainment), 1 beach (ocean), washer/dryer. **Rates:** Peak (Dec 22–Apr) $159–$199 S or D; $205 ste. Extra person $15. Children under age 17 stay free. Lower rates off-season. Parking: Outdoor, free. AE, CB, DC, DISC, MC, V.

### ≣≣ Suez Oceanfront Resort
18215 Collins Ave, 33160; tel 305/932-0661 or toll free 800/327-5278, 800/327-5278, 800/432-3661 in FL; fax 305/937-0058. Off FL 826 E. Built in the 1950s glamour days, this facility is definitely more impressive inside than outside. Courtyard with fountains and pool are set on manicured grounds. **Rooms:** 196 rms, stes, and effic. CI 3pm/CO noon. Nonsmoking rms avail. **Amenities:** 🛏 🍴 🍷 A/C, cable TV w/movies, refrig. Some units w/terraces. **Services:** ✗ 🔑 🧺 🛎 Twice-daily maid svce, social director. **Facilities:** 🔦 🏊 🍽 1 restaurant, 1 bar (w/entertainment), 1 beach (ocean), lifeguard, volleyball, snorkeling, sauna, steam rm, whirlpool, playground, washer/dryer. Fenced-in area good for children at play. **Rates:** Peak (Dec 15–Apr 15) $65–$93 S or D; $175 ste; $80 effic. Extra person $15. Children under age 16 stay free. Lower rates off-season. AP rates avail. MAP rates avail. Parking: Outdoor, free. AE, DC, DISC, MC, V.

## MOTELS

### ≣≣ Desert Inn
17201 Collins Ave, 33160; tel 305/947-0621 or toll free 800/327-6361; fax 305/944-7050. At 163rd St. A complex of motel rooms and condominiums that are privately owned and decorated with some individuality. Shops and restaurants across the street. **Rooms:** 100 rms and effic. CI 2pm/CO noon. Nonsmoking rms avail. Many units have Murphy beds. **Amenities:** 🛏 A/C, cable TV, refrig. Some units w/terraces. **Services:** 🛎 Babysitting. **Facilities:** 🔦 🍸1 1 restaurant, 1 bar (w/entertainment), 1 beach (ocean), lifeguard. **Rates:** Peak (Feb–Apr) $75–$95 S or D; $85–$95 effic. Extra person $10. Children under age 13 stay free. Lower rates off-season. MAP rates avail. Parking: Outdoor, free. AE, MC, V.

### ≣≣ Driftwood Resort Motel
17121 Collins Ave, 33160 (Sunny Isles Beach); tel 305/944-5141 or toll free 800/327-1263; fax 305/945-0763. A traditional motel with clean, basic rooms. **Rooms:** 114 effic. CI 11am/CO 11am. **Amenities:** 🛏 A/C, cable TV, refrig. Some units w/terraces. **Services:** 🔌 🚗 🛎 Babysitting. **Facilities:** 🔦 🛳150 1 restaurant, 2 bars (1 w/entertainment), 1 beach (ocean), lifeguard, lawn games, playground, washer/dryer. Pool bar with picnic tables. **Rates:** Peak (Dec 20–Apr 19) $52–$78 effic. Children under age 18 stay free. Min stay special events. Lower rates off-season. Parking: Outdoor, free. AE, CB, DC, DISC, MC, V.

### ≣≣ Ocean Roc
19505 Collins Ave, 33160; tel 305/931-7600 or toll free 800/327-0553; fax 305/866-5881. Basic accommodations are satisfactory but lack warmth or style. Painting and general repairs are needed. **Rooms:** 95 rms and effic. CI noon/CO noon. **Amenities:** 🛏 A/C, TV w/movies. Some units w/terraces. **Services:** ✗ **Facilities:** 🔦 1 restaurant, 1 beach (ocean), washer/dryer. **Rates:** Peak (Dec 24–Mar) $40–$60 S or D; $66 effic. Extra person $6. Children under age 18 stay free. Lower rates off-season. Parking: Outdoor, free. AE, CB, DC, MC, V.

## RESORT

### ≣≣≣ Radisson Aventura Beach Resort
192nd St, North Miami Beach, 33160; tel 305/932-2233 or toll free 800/333-3333, 800/327-6363, 800/432-3664 in FL; fax 305/935-5009. Exit 18 off I-95 at Collins Ave. 10 acres. A large hotel catering to older couples who have been coming here since the days when this was the Marco Polo Resort. The enormous marbled lobby is almost always filled with activity. Fun-and-games atmosphere. **Rooms:** 320 rms, stes, and effic. CI 3pm/CO noon. Nonsmoking rms avail. Rooms are spacious, and are decorated with understated tropical prints. **Amenities:** 🛏 🍴 🎁 🍷 A/C, cable TV

w/movies, refrig. Some units w/terraces. Minibar available upon request. **Services:** ✗ ☞ VP 🚐 🗺 ♫ Social director, babysitting. Staff can be disorganized at times. **Facilities:** 🏋 🚲 ⛺ 🏠 🎿 🏓 [600] 💻 ♿ 2 restaurants, 2 bars (1 w/entertainment), 1 beach (ocean), lifeguard, games rm, beauty salon, washer/dryer. Dinner theater is very popular. Arcade of shops. **Rates:** Peak (Dec 21–Apr 15) $139–$179 S or D; $199–$229 ste; $149–$189 effic. Extra person $10. Children under age 17 stay free. Lower rates off-season. Parking: Outdoor, free. AE, DC, DISC, MC, V.

## ATTRACTION 🏛

### Spanish Monastery Cloisters
16711 W Dixie Hwy; tel 305/945-1462. First erected in 1141 in Segovia, Spain, the monastery was purchased by newspaper magnate William Randolph Hearst and shipped overseas in crates where it remained in a New York warehouse until after Hearst's death. In 1954 Miami developers had it reassembled on its present site as a tourist attraction. It is now an Episcopal church. Lush formal garden. **Open:** Mon–Sat 10am–4pm, Sun noon–4pm. **$$**

# Surfside

This tiny municipality of 4,300 is on the same island as Miami Beach but about five miles north. Directly on the ocean, it's a stone's throw across Collins Avenue to exclusive Bal Harbor. Beach play and shopping are the pastimes here.

## HOTELS 🏨

### ▤▤ Coronado Hotel
9501 Collins Ave, 33154; tel 305/866-1625; fax 305/861-1881. There's a quiet, relaxed atmosphere in this two-story budget hotel sandwiched between high-rises. Has managed to retain its original charm. **Rooms:** 41 rms and effic. CI 3pm/CO 11am. Nonsmoking rms avail. Pastel-colored rooms. **Amenities:** 🏋 A/C, cable TV, refrig. Some units w/terraces. **Services:** ✗ 🚐 ♫ Car-rental desk. **Facilities:** 🏋 [75] 1 restaurant (dinner only), 1 beach (ocean). **Rates (CP):** Peak (Dec–Mar) $79–$125 S or D; $93 effic. Extra person $8. Children under age 18 stay free. Min stay special events. Lower rates off-season. Parking: Indoor, free. AE, DC, MC, V.

### ▤▤ The Palms
9449 Collins Ave, 33154; tel 305/865-3551 or toll free 800/327-6644 in the US, 800/843-6974 in Canada; fax 305/861-6596. Basic rooms on the ocean. Friendly staff persevering through continuing renovations to public areas and rooms. Many guests here are retired vacationers. **Rooms:** 170 rms. CI 3pm/CO noon. Nonsmoking rms avail. **Amenities:** 🏋 A/C, cable TV w/movies, refrig, in-rm safe. Some units w/terraces. **Services:** ✗ ♫ **Facilities:** 🏋 ♿ 1 restaurant, 1 bar, 1 beach (ocean), lifeguard, whirlpool, washer/dryer.

**Rates (AP):** Peak (mid-Dec–mid-Apr) $120–$150 S or D. Extra person $12. Children under age 18 stay free. Lower rates off-season. Parking: Outdoor, free. AE, DC, MC, V.

# Tallahassee

See also Spring Hill

Florida's land-locked capital, chosen in 1824 by then-Gov Andrew Jackson as a compromise site midway between Pensacola and St Augustine. Home to over 200,000 people, plus Florida State University and Florida A&M University. Lots of museums, moss-draped live oaks, and antebellum ambience. **Information:** Tallahassee Area Convention & Visitors Bureau, 200 W College Ave, PO Box 1369, Tallahassee, 32302 (tel 904/413-9200).

## HOTELS 🏨

### ▤▤▤ Holiday Inn Capitol Plaza Hotel
101 S Adams St, 32301; tel 904/224-5000 or toll free 800/325-3535; fax 904/224-1168. In the commercial district, near the capitol, this property caters largely to government, business, and other non-leisure clientele. **Rooms:** 244 rms and stes. Executive level. CI 3pm/CO noon. Nonsmoking rms avail. **Amenities:** 🏋 ♨ A/C, cable TV w/movies. Some units w/minibars. **Services:** ✗ 🗺 ♫ Babysitting. **Facilities:** 🏋 [350] ♿ 1 restaurant, 1 bar. Access to nearby health club. **Rates:** Peak (Feb–Apr) $110–$160 S or D; $265 ste. Children under age 12 stay free. Min stay special events. Lower rates off-season. Parking: Indoor, free. AE, DC, DISC, MC, V.

### ▤▤ Holiday Inn University Center
316 W Tennessee St, 32301; tel 904/222-8000 or toll free 800/HOLIDAY; fax 904/681-8578. 4 blocks from the capitol. Octagonal tower patronized by business travelers and others. **Rooms:** 174 rms. CI 3pm/CO 11am. **Amenities:** 🏋 ♨ A/C, cable TV w/movies, voice mail, in-rm safe. **Services:** ✗ 🗺 ♫ 🍽 **Facilities:** 🏋 [300] ♿ 1 restaurant, 2 bars. Upscale restaurant with good views. **Rates:** $99–$129 S or D. Children under age 18 stay free. Parking: Outdoor, free. AE, CB, DC, DISC, MC, V.

### ▤ Killearn Country Club and Inn
100 Tyron Circle, 32308; tel 904/893-2186 or toll free 800/668-8815; fax 904/688-7637. Exit 30 off I-10. This golf and tennis facility set in an area of luxury homes is host to several golf tournaments. **Rooms:** 35 rms and stes. CI 2pm/CO noon. Nonsmoking rms avail. Guest rooms are modest. **Amenities:** 🏋 ♨ 🎿 🍽 A/C, cable TV w/movies. Some units w/terraces. **Services:** 🗺 ♫ Masseur, babysitting. **Facilities:** 🏋 ▶27 🎿 ♣4 ⛳4 🏓 [350] 2 restaurants (lunch and dinner only), 1 bar, sauna, steam rm. **Rates (CP):** $78 S or D; $110 ste. Children under age 13 stay free. Parking: Outdoor, free. AE, CB, DC, DISC, MC, V.

### ☰☰☰ Radisson Hotel

415 N Monroe St, 32301; tel 904/224-6000 or toll free 800/333-3333; fax 904/224-6000 ext 4118. Located just beyond the shadow of the capitol building, this is one of the best choices in the downtown sector. A warm residential ambience radiates from both public areas and guest rooms. **Rooms:** 116 rms and stes. CI 3pm/CO noon. Nonsmoking rms avail. **Amenities:** 🛆 ⓪ A/C, cable TV w/movies. Some units w/whirlpools. **Services:** ✕ VP 🚐 ⊿ ⌂ Babysitting. **Facilities:** 🖳 350 ⅇ 1 restaurant, 1 bar (w/entertainment), sauna. The young and friendly staff makes a special effort to please guests. **Rates:** Peak (Feb–Apr) $100 S or D; $140 ste. Extra person $10. Children under age 18 stay free. Min stay special events. Lower rates off-season. Parking: Outdoor, free. AE, CB, DC, DISC, MC, V.

### ☰☰ Ramada Inn Tallahassee

2900 N Monroe St, 32303; tel 904/386-1027 or toll free 800/2-RAMADA; fax 904/422-1025. Exit 29 off I-10. A business-class hotel in contemporary style. **Rooms:** 198 rms and stes. CI 2pm/CO noon. Nonsmoking rms avail. **Amenities:** 🛆 ⓪ 🖵 ⓠ A/C, cable TV w/movies, refrig, voice mail. **Services:** ✕ 🚐 ⊿ ⌂ Babysitting. **Facilities:** 🖗 🖳 500 ▭ ⅇ 2 restaurants, 2 bars (1 w/entertainment). Lounge offers weekend comedy shows. **Rates:** Peak (Feb–May/Sept–Nov) $80–$85 S; $85–$90 D; $125–$200 ste. Extra person $8. Children under age 18 stay free. Lower rates off-season. Parking: Outdoor, free. AE, CB, DC, DISC, MC, V.

## MOTELS

### ☰ Best Western Pride Inn

2016 Apalachee Pkwy, 32301; tel 904/656-6312 or toll free 800/827-7390; fax 904/942-4312. 2 mi W of downtown near Governor's Square Mall. A small two-story property best suited for undemanding motorists. **Rooms:** 78 rms. CI 2pm/CO 11am. Nonsmoking rms avail. **Amenities:** 🛆 A/C, cable TV w/movies. **Services:** ⊿ ⌂ ⇦ **Facilities:** 🖗 100 Guest privileges at nearby YMCA. **Rates (CP):** $41–$50 S; $46–$55 D. Extra person $5. Children under age 15 stay free. Min stay special events. Parking: Outdoor, free. AE, CB, DC, DISC, EC, MC, V.

### ☰☰☰ Cabot Lodge East

1653 Raymond Diehl Rd, 32308; tel 904/386-7500 or toll free 800/255-6343; fax 904/386-1136. Exit 30 off I-10. Modeled after a New England country inn, geared toward the business traveler. **Rooms:** 135 rms and stes. Executive level. CI 1pm/CO 11am. Nonsmoking rms avail. Rooms are large, with plenty of seating and a sizable desk. **Amenities:** 🛆 ⓪ A/C, cable TV w/movies, dataport, voice mail. **Services:** ✕ ⊿ ⌂ Complimentary cocktail hour. **Facilities:** 🖗 38 ⅇ Washer/dryer. Lending library. Guest privileges at nearby health club. **Rates (CP):** $68 S; $78 D; $175 ste. Extra person $10. Children under age 13 stay free. Min stay special events. Parking: Outdoor, free. AE, CB, DC, DISC, MC, V.

### ☰☰ Cabot Lodge North

2735 N Monroe St, 32303; tel 904/386-8880 or toll free 800/223-1964; fax 904/386-4254. This New England–style inn caters to business clientele. **Rooms:** 160 rms. CI 2pm/CO noon. Nonsmoking rms avail. **Amenities:** 🛆 ⓪ A/C, cable TV w/movies. **Services:** ⊿ ⌂ Evening cocktails and popcorn. **Facilities:** 🖗 🖳 12 ⅇ **Rates (CP):** $59–$65 S; $65–$71 D. Extra person $6. Children under age 18 stay free. Parking: Outdoor, free. AE, DC, DISC, MC, V.

### ☰☰ Hampton Inn

3210 N Monroe St, 32303; tel 904/562-4300 or toll free 800/222-3210; fax 904/562-6735. Exit 29 off I-10. Basic, no-frills rooms. **Rooms:** 93 rms and stes. CI 3pm/CO noon. Nonsmoking rms avail. **Amenities:** 🛆 ⓪ A/C, cable TV w/movies. 1 unit w/whirlpool. **Services:** ⊿ ⌂ **Facilities:** 🖗 ⅇ Fee for use of health club located across busy four-lane highway. **Rates (CP):** $55–$75 S; $60–$75 D; $100 ste. Extra person $5. Children under age 19 stay free. Parking: Outdoor, free. AE, CB, DC, DISC, MC, V.

### ☰☰ Quality Inn & Suites

2020 Apalachee Pkwy, 32301; tel 904/877-4437 or toll free 800/553-4787; fax 904/878-9964. Near Governor's Square Mall. Capitol-area low-rise. **Rooms:** 94 rms and stes. CI 2pm/CO noon. Nonsmoking rms avail. **Amenities:** 🛆 🖵 A/C, cable TV w/movies. **Services:** ⊿ ⌂ **Facilities:** 🖗 60 ⅇ Complimentary use of nearby YMCA. **Rates (CP):** $62–$72 S; $67–$72 D; $124–$134 ste. Extra person $5. Children under age 19 stay free. Min stay special events. Parking: Outdoor, free. AE, CB, DC, DISC, MC, V.

## INN

### ☰☰☰ Governors Inn

209 S Adams St, 32301; tel 904/681-6855 or toll free 800/342-7717, 800/342-7717 in FL; fax 904/222-3105. 1 block N of Capitol Complex. Elegant, award-winning hotel opened in 1984 by the son of Florida Gov Lawton Chiles. The building, at one time a livery stable, retains part of its original architecture, including the handsome wood beams. **Rooms:** 40 rms and stes. CI 3pm/CO noon. Nonsmoking rms avail. Furnished with four-poster beds, black oak writing desks, maple armoires, and antique accoutrements. Sumptuous suites. **Amenities:** 🛆 ⓪ A/C, cable TV, bathrobes. Some units w/terraces, some w/fireplaces, 1 w/whirlpool. **Services:** ✕ VP 🚐 ⊿ ⌂ Twice-daily maid svce, babysitting, wine/sherry served. Same-day laundry service. **Facilities:** 85 Guest lounge. Breakfast and evening cocktails served in beautiful, pine-paneled Florida Room. **Rates (CP):** $119 S; $139 D. Min stay special events. Higher rates for special events/hols. Parking: Outdoor, free. AE, CB, DC, DISC, MC, V.

## RESTAURANTS 🍴

### ★ Andrew's 2nd Act

228 S Adams St; tel 904/222-3444. 1 block W of Monroe St. **Continental.** The sub-street level location gives this eatery a

dark, intimate atmosphere. Chef Greg Brown's French-inspired menu offers New York strip steak, grouper cardinale, and lamb encroûte. **FYI:** Reservations recommended. **Open:** Mon–Thurs 11:30am–11:30pm, Fri–Sat 6–11pm, Sun 6–9:30pm. **Prices:** Main courses $17–$20; prix fixe $20. AE, CB, DC, MC, V. 🌑 VP

### Anthony's
In Betton Place, 1950 Thomasville Rd; tel 904/224-1447. **Italian.** A dark, casual restaurant adorned with plants and antiques. The northern Italian–inspired menu includes shrimp scampi, fresh salmon, and New York strip steak. **FYI:** Reservations accepted. **Open:** Mon–Sat 5:30–10pm, Sun 5–9pm. **Prices:** Main courses $10–$16. AE, MC, V. ⑤

### ⑤ Food Glorious Food
In Betton Place, 1950-C Thomasville Rd; tel 904/224-9974. **International.** Small black-and-white-tiled cafe with open kitchen and a constantly changing menu. Salads, pastas, sandwiches, muffins, and cakes are always fresh and interesting. **FYI:** Reservations not accepted. Beer and wine only. No smoking. **Open:** Mon–Sat 11am–8pm. **Prices:** Main courses $6–$13. AE, MC, V.

### ★ Lucy Ho's Bamboo Garden
2814 Apalachee Pkwy; tel 904/878-3366. Off US 27 N. **Japanese.** Fans of Asian food will love Lucy Ho's, once they get past the dated and decaying exterior of this long-time Tallahassee institution. Diners may try the Chinese lunch buffet, or order from the sushi bar or the extensive menu filled with Chinese and Japanese favorites. **FYI:** Reservations recommended. Karaoke. Children's menu. Additional location: Lucy Ho's Oriental Court, 1700-5 Halstead Blvd (tel 893-4128). **Open:** Mon–Thurs 11:30am–10pm, Fri 11:30am–11pm, Sat 5:30–11pm, Sun noon–10pm. **Prices:** Main courses $6–$11. AE, DC, DISC, MC, V. 🎦

### The Melting Pot
1832 N Monroe St; tel 904/386-7440. **International/Fondue.** A dark, plainly decorated eatery offering an array of unusual fondues, which can be enjoyed with chicken, steak, seafood, and vegetables. **FYI:** Reservations recommended. Beer and wine only. **Open:** Sun–Thurs 6–10:30pm, Fri–Sat 6–11:30pm. **Prices:** Main courses $8–$18. AE, DISC, MC, V.

### Silver Slipper
531 Scotty's Lane; tel 904/386-9366. **New American.** You and your sweetheart can dine in easy splendor under the sparkling chandelier in the main room, or you can opt for one of the private dining rooms. Inventive seafood dishes and steaks are among the menu selections. **FYI:** Reservations accepted. Children's menu. **Open:** Mon–Sat 5–11pm. **Prices:** Main courses $11–$25. AE, CB, DC, DISC, MC, V. 🌑 ☑ ⑤

## ATTRACTIONS 🏛

### New Capitol Building
Duval St; tel 904/488-6167 (tour info) or 681-9200. Built in 1977 to replace the Old Capitol, the 22-story skyscraper offers a spectacular view from the top-floor observatory. The chambers of the House and Senate have public viewing galleries; the legislature convenes from early February to early April. Guided tours are given Mon–Fri at 9, 10, and 11am, and 1, 2, and 3pm; Sat–Sun, hourly 9am–4pm. **Open:** Mon–Fri 8am–5pm. **Free**

### Old Capitol Building
Monroe St and Apalachee Pkwy; tel 904/487-1902. Restored to its original beauty, the strikingly white former capitol building with playful red and white awnings and a majestic dome now serves as a museum. An eight-room exhibit details Florida's fascinating political history. Visitors can also view turn-of-the-century furnishings, cotton gins, and other interesting artifacts. **Open:** Mon–Fri 9am–4:30pm, Sat 10am–4:30pm, Sun noon–4:30pm. **Free**

### The Columns
100 N Duval St; tel 904/224-8116. This three-story, white-columned brick mansion is the city's oldest surviving building, dating from the 1830s. It has been restored and furnished with antiques, and now serves as the office of the Chamber of Commerce. **Open:** Mon–Fri 9am–5pm. **Free**

### Governor's Mansion
700 N Adams St; tel 904/488-4661. The Florida governor's residence is an impressive Georgian-style mansion, with a portico patterned after the Hermitage, Andrew Jackson's columned antebellum home. The lawns are enhanced by giant magnolia trees. Visitors can tour five of the rooms, which are furnished with antiques and adorned by paintings on loan from the John and Mabel Ringling Museum of Art. **Open:** Call for schedule. **Free**

### Brokaw–McDougall House
329 N Meridian; tel 904/488-3901. This magnificent house, built in 1856, possesses elements of both Italianate and classical revival architecture; landscaping conforms to the original design. **Open:** Mon–Fri 8am–5pm. **Free**

### Tallahassee Museum of History and Natural Science
3945 Museum Dr; tel 904/576-1636 or 575-8684. This museum features native Florida animals, including the endangered Florida panther and red wolf, in a natural woodland setting; a re-creation of an 1880s farm; science and history displays; the restored plantation home of Princess Murat; and a restored one-room schoolhouse, gristmill, old church, and railroad caboose. Special programs demonstrate butter-churning, syrup-making, blacksmithing, sheep-shearing, spinning, weaving, and quilt-making. **Open:** Mon–Sat 9am–5pm, Sun 12:30–5pm. **$$$**

### Museum of Florida History
R A Gray Building, 500 S Bronough St; tel 904/488-1484 or 488-1673. Florida's history from the paleolithic era to the present. Visitors can see ancient Native American artifacts, a mastodon skeleton 12 feet high, treasures from sunken

Spanish galleons, war relics, and a reconstructed steamboat. Guided tours, gift shop. **Open:** Mon–Fri 9am–4:30pm, Sat 10am–4:30pm, Sun noon–4:30pm. **Free**

## Black Archives Research Center and Museum
Florida A&M University; tel 904/599-3020. This illuminating center displays one of the most extensive collections of African American historical artifacts in the United States. On view are items ranging from leg irons from slavery times to letters and memorabilia of such figures as Booker T Washington, Martin Luther King Jr, Mary McLeod Bethune, and Zora Neale Hurston. There's also a 500-piece Ethiopian cross collection. **Open:** Mon–Fri 9am–4pm. **Free**

## Foster Tanner Fine Arts Gallery
Florida A&M University; tel 904/599-3161. Focuses on works by African American artists, with a variety of paintings, sculptures, and more. Exhibits change monthly. **Open:** Mon–Fri 9am–5pm. **Free**

## LeMoyne Art Foundation
125 N Gadsden St; tel 904/222-8800. Housed in a restored 1852 antebellum home, the collection features displays by local artists, traveling exhibits, sculpture, pottery, and photography. Gardens with old-fashioned gazebo. Free admission on Sundays. **Open:** Tues–Sat 10am–5pm, Sun 1–5pm. **$**

## Florida State University Museum of Fine Arts
250 Fine Arts Building, at Copeland and W Tennessee Sts; tel 904/644-6836. The permanent collection features 16th-century Dutch paintings, 20th-century American paintings, Japanese prints, pre-Columbian artifacts, and much more. Touring exhibits. **Open:** Mon–Fri 9am–5pm, Sat–Sun 1–4pm. **Free**

## Knott House Museum
301 E Park Ave; tel 904/922-2459. Anchoring the Park Avenue Historic District, this museum is a capsule of state history. Built in 1843 by a free black builder, the mansion was the site of the emancipation of the North Florida slaves in 1865. It was also the laboratory for Florida's first black physician, and the home of Supreme Court justices and key state political figures. Today it is best known as "the House that Rhymes," for the whimsical rhymes written by its last mistress, Luella Pugh Knott, and attached with satin ribbons to her Victorian furnishings. **Open:** Sept–July, Wed–Fri 1–4pm, Sat 10am–4pm. **$**

## Maclay State Gardens
3540 Thomasville Rd (US 319); tel 904/487-4115. The former winter retreat of New York financier Alfred B Maclay, an amateur gardener who, along with his wife, planted these spectacular gardens of azaleas, camellias, pansies, and dogwood and redbud trees. Over 200 varieties of flowers in all. The surrounding park has nature trails and picnicking, along with canoe rentals, boating, picnicking, swimming, and fishing. **Open:** Park, daily 8am–sunset; gardens, daily 9am–5pm; Maclay House, Jan–Apr, daily 9am–5pm. **$$**

## First Presbyterian Church
110 N Adams St; tel 904/222-4504. Tallahassee's oldest church (1838). Townspeople took refuge beneath the church steeple during the Seminole raids of 1838. Slaves were welcome to worship here as independent members. Visitors may request keys to the sanctuary at the church office during business hours. **Open:** Mon–Thurs 8:30am–5pm, Fri 8:30am–1pm. **Free**

## Old City Cemetery and Episcopal Cemetery
Park Ave and Bronough St; tel 904/545-5842. These adjacent cemeteries contain the graves of Prince Achille Murat, Napoleon's nephew, and Princess Catherine Murat, his wife and George Washington's grandniece. Also buried here are two governors and numerous Confederate and Union soldiers who died at the Battle of Natural Bridge during the Civil War. A number of slaves and the first African Americans to graduate from Florida A&M University are also among those buried here.

## Natural Bridge Battlefield State Historic Site
Natural Bridge Rd; tel 904/922-6007. This park and monument 15 miles southeast of Tallahassee commemorate the site of a battle in the closing days of the Civil War won by a small group of Confederate soldiers against a much larger contingent of Union troops. Although the Confederate victory prevented the Florida capital from falling to the Union, the war ended several weeks later. **Open:** Daily 8am–sunset. **Free**

## Lake Jackson Mounds State Archeological Site
3600 Indian Mounds Rd; tel 904/922-6007. Artifacts such as copper breastplates and ritual figures suggest that this was the site of an important Native American ceremonial center. Visitors can see two earthen temple mounds and a burial mound. **Open:** Daily 8am–sunset. **Free**

## River Bluff Picnic Site
Tel 904/922-6007. Located off FL 20 about 20 mi W of Tallahassee. Visitors can enjoy fishing, boating, and picnicking amid thick pine forest, deep ravines, and rolling hills. Abundant wildlife along the nature trail. **Open:** Daily 8am–sunset. **Free**

## De Soto Archeological and Historical Site
1022 DeSoto Park Dr; tel 904/922-6007. An archeologist searching for Spanish mission ruins in 1986 discovered the de Soto encampment site. Every winter, the de Soto Winter Encampment Festival brings art exhibits, craft demonstrations, and living history interpretations of 1539 Spanish and Apalachee tribe culture. (The festival is the only de Soto event open to the public at present.) **Open:** Call for schedule. **Free**

## San Luis Archaeological and Historic Site
2020 W Mission Rd; tel 904/487-3711. This 60-acre site located on a hilltop west of downtown Tallahassee was once an important Apalachee settlement and Spanish mission town. Visitors can observe the periodic excavations; exhibits along the trails explain the San Luis story. **Open:** Mon–Fri 9am–4:30pm, Sat 10am–4:30pm, Sun noon–4:30pm. **Free**

### Apalachicola National Forest

Crawford Field; tel 904/926-3561 or 643-2283. Located on US 319, with the closest entrance approximately 20 mi S of Tallahassee. The largest of Florida's three national forests consists of a varied woodland with lakes and streams encompassing about 600,000 acres. The Sopchoppy and Ochlockonee Rivers are popular with canoeists, and several of the lakes have campgrounds. A section of the Florida National Scenic Trail passes through the forest.

# Tampa

See also St Petersburg

A bustling cruise port midway down Florida's Gulf Coast, Tampa's lures include pro football and hockey, Busch Gardens, ritzy Harbour Island shops, a large Vietnamese community, and spring's rollicking Gasparilla Festival. Ybor City, once the heart of Cuban cigar-making, is a bohemian outpost today. **Information:** Tampa/Hillsborough Convention & Visitors Association, 111 E Madison St #1010, PO Box 519, Tampa, 33602 (tel 813/223-1111 or toll free 800/826-8358).

## PUBLIC TRANSPORTATION

**Hillsborough Area Regional Transit/HARTline** Operates local and express buses between downtown Tampa and surrounding suburbs. Local fare $1, express fare $1.50; exact change required. The Tampa Trolley links downtown with Ybor City; fare 25¢. For more information call 813/254-HART.

**The People Mover** Motorized tram on elevated tracks connecting downtown Tampa with Harbour Island. Operates Mon–Sat 7am–midnight, Sun 8am–midnight. Departs from third level of Fort Brooke Parking Garage, on Whiting St between Franklin Ave and Florida St. Fare 25¢.

## HOTELS 🏨

### ⊨⊨ Best Western Resort at Busch Gardens

820 E Busch Blvd, 33612; tel 813/933-4011 or toll free 800/288-4011; fax 813/932-1784. Exit 33 off I-275. Offers something of a retreat from the amusement park atmosphere nearby. **Rooms:** 255 rms and stes. CI 4pm/CO noon. Nonsmoking rms avail. **Amenities:** 🛏 A/C, cable TV w/movies. Some units w/terraces. **Services:** ✕ 🚐 ⚎ ⚎ Car-rental desk. **Facilities:** 🔧 ⚎ ⚎ ⚎ 350 ⚎ 1 restaurant, 1 bar, games rm, sauna, steam rm, washer/dryer. **Rates:** Peak (Jan–Apr) $79–$99 S; $89–$99 D; $159–$179 ste. Children under age 18 stay free. Lower rates off-season. Parking: Outdoor, free. AE, CB, DC, DISC, MC, V.

### ⊨⊨⊨ Camberley Plaza Sabal Park

10221 Princess Palm Ave, 33610; tel 813/623-6363 or toll free 800/555-8000; fax 813/621-7224. Exit 52 off I-75. Situated in an office park; will appeal mainly to business travelers. Stylish design. **Rooms:** 265 rms and stes. CI 3pm/CO noon. Nonsmoking rms avail. Smart, sophisticated decor.

**Amenities:** 🛏 ⚎ ⚎ A/C, cable TV w/movies. Some units w/terraces, some w/whirlpools. **Services:** ✕ 🚐 VP 🚐 ⚎ ⚎ Car-rental desk, babysitting. **Facilities:** 🔧 ⚎ ⚎ 500 ⚎ 1 restaurant, 1 bar (w/entertainment), whirlpool, beauty salon. **Rates:** $140 S; $150 D; $160 ste. Extra person $10. Children under age 19 stay free. Parking: Outdoor, free. AE, DC, DISC, MC, V.

### ⊨⊨ Courtyard by Marriott

3805 W Cypress St, 33607; tel 813/874-0555 or toll free 800/321-2211; fax 813/870-0685. Exit 23B off I-275. At US 92. Solid hotel providing reliable service and a comfortable stay. **Rooms:** 145 rms and stes. CI 3pm/CO noon. Nonsmoking rms avail. **Amenities:** 🛏 ⚎ ⚎ A/C, cable TV w/movies. Free in-room coffee. **Services:** 🚐 ⚎ ⚎ Babysitting. **Facilities:** 🔧 ⚎ ⚎ 35 ⚎ 1 restaurant, 1 bar, sauna, whirlpool, washer/dryer. **Rates:** $109 S; $119 D; $125 ste. Extra person $10. Children under age 18 stay free. Parking: Outdoor, free. AE, DC, DISC, MC, V.

### ⊨⊨⊨ Crowne Plaza Hotel Tampa Westshore

700 N Westshore Blvd, 33609; tel 813/289-8200 or toll free 800/2-CROWNE; fax 813/289-9166. Westshore Blvd exit off I-275. Well located for Westshore business and shopping, with recently renovated guest rooms. **Rooms:** 272 rms and stes. CI 3pm/CO noon. Nonsmoking rms avail. **Amenities:** 🛏 ⚎ ⚎ ⚎ A/C, cable TV w/movies, dataport, voice mail, bathrobes. **Services:** ✕ 🚐 VP 🚐 ⚎ ⚎ Car-rental desk, babysitting. **Facilities:** 🔧 ⚎ ⚎ 650 ⚎ 1 restaurant, 1 bar, spa, sauna, whirlpool. **Rates:** Peak (Jan–Apr 7) $149–$164 S or D; $275–$325 ste. Extra person $10. Children under age 18 stay free. Lower rates off-season. Parking: Indoor, free. Parking: Outdoor, free. AE, CB, DC, DISC, MC, V.

### ⊨⊨ Days Inn Rocky Point

7627 Courtney Campbell Causeway, 33607 (Tampa Int'l Airport); tel 813/281-0000 or toll free 800/237-2555; fax 813/281-1067. Exit 20 off I-275. 2 mi W of Tampa Int'l Airport. Clustered with other hotels near the causeway in a high-rent district. **Rooms:** 144 rms and stes. CI 2pm/CO noon. Nonsmoking rms avail. **Amenities:** 🛏 A/C, cable TV w/movies, in-rm safe. **Services:** 🚐 ⚎ ⚎ Free shuttle to area restaurants and shopping. **Facilities:** 🔧 ⚠ ⚎ 2 ⚎ 300 1 restaurant, 1 bar (w/entertainment), 1 beach (bay), games rm, playground, washer/dryer. Game room with wide-screen TV, two pool tables, jukebox, and video games. **Rates:** Peak (Nov–Apr) $75–$105 S or D; $150 ste. Extra person $5. Children under age 12 stay free. Lower rates off-season. Parking: Outdoor, free. AE, CB, DC, DISC, EC, MC, V.

### ⊨⊨ DoubleTree Guest Suites Busch Gardens

11310 N 30th St, 33612; tel 813/971-7690 or toll free 800/222-8733; fax 813/972-5525. Exit 33 off I-275. A quiet spot in an otherwise bustling area. The lobby, with wicker furnishings and floral patterns, opens to a lush courtyard pool with abutting waterfall. **Rooms:** 129 stes. CI 3pm/CO noon. Nonsmoking rms avail. **Amenities:** 🛏 ⚎ ⚎ A/C, cable TV w/movies, refrig, dataport, voice mail. All suites with wet bar and microwave. **Services:** ☒ ⤴ Babysitting. Complimentary beverages served 5:30–7:30pm daily. Free shuttle to area attractions. **Facilities:** �🎿 🛏 ⅙ 1 bar (w/entertainment), whirlpool, washer/dryer. **Rates (BB):** Peak (Jan–Apr) $109–$129 ste. Extra person $10. Children under age 13 stay free. Min stay special events. Lower rates off-season. Parking: Outdoor, free. AE, CB, DC, DISC, EC, JCB, MC, V.

### ≡ ≡ ≡ DoubleTree Guest Suites Westshore
4400 W Cypress St, 33607; tel 813/873-8675; fax 813/879-7196. Exit 22 off I-275. A well-respected all-suites hotel situated in the dense off-airport hub of hotels, near a shopping mall. Mediterranean touches inside and out. Atrium lobby. **Rooms:** 260 stes. CI 3pm/CO noon. Nonsmoking rms avail. Living rooms separated by french doors. Fine upholstery. **Amenities:** 🎿 🛏 🖥 A/C, cable TV w/movies, refrig, voice mail. All units w/terraces. **Services:** ☒ 🚐 ☒ ⤴ Babysitting. **Facilities:** 🎿 🛏 🛏 ⅙ 1 restaurant, 1 bar, sauna, steam rm, whirlpool, washer/dryer. **Rates (BB):** Peak (Dec–Apr) $145 ste. Extra person $10. Children under age 12 stay free. Lower rates off-season. Parking: Outdoor, free. AE, CB, DC, DISC, JCB, MC, V.

### ≡ ≡ ≡ Embassy Suites Hotel
555 N Westshore Blvd, 33609 (Tampa Int'l Airport); tel 813/875-1555 or toll free 800/362-2779; fax 813/287-3664. 2.5 mi S of the airport. Westshore Blvd exit off I-275. Sophisticated appeal, designed for the business traveler. Lobby with vaulted ceiling. **Rooms:** 221 stes. CI 3pm/CO noon. Nonsmoking rms avail. **Amenities:** 🎿 🛏 🖥 🍴 A/C, cable TV w/movies, refrig. All units w/minibars, some w/terraces. **Services:** ☒ VP 🚐 ☒ ⤴ ⊲ Babysitting. Shuttle service within a three-mile radius. **Facilities:** 🎿 🛏 🛏 ⅙ 1 restaurant, 1 bar, sauna, whirlpool, washer/dryer. **Rates (BB):** Peak (Dec–Mar) $119–$139 ste. Extra person $10. Children under age 18 stay free. Lower rates off-season. Parking: Indoor/outdoor, free. AE, DC, DISC, MC, V.

### ≡ ≡ ≡ Guest Quarters Suite Hotel on Tampa Bay
3050 N Rocky Point Dr W, 33607; tel 813/888-8800; fax 813/888-8743. Exit 20 off I-75. A sleek establishment offering varied fitness facilities, located just off the causeway to Clearwater. **Rooms:** 203 stes. CI 3pm/CO noon. Nonsmoking rms avail. **Amenities:** 🎿 🛏 🖥 🍴 A/C, cable TV w/movies, refrig. All units w/minibars, some w/terraces. **Services:** ☒ 🔑 🚐 ☒ ⤴ Car-rental desk, children's program, babysitting. **Facilities:** 🎿 🛏 🛏 ⬚ ⅙ 1 restaurant, 1 bar, spa, sauna, whirlpool, washer/dryer. **Rates (CP):** Peak (Jan–Apr) $155 ste. Extra person $20. Children under age 18 stay free. Lower rates off-season. Parking: Outdoor, free. AE, CB, DC, DISC, MC, V.

### ≡ ≡ ≡ Holiday Inn Ashley Plaza
111 W Fortune St, 33602 (Downtown); tel 813/223-1351 or toll free 800/ASK-VALU; fax 813/221-2000. Exit 25 off I-275. Handy to convention center functions, downtown

businesses, and adjacent Tampa Bay Performing Arts Center. Only major downtown hotel with free parking. **Rooms:** 312 rms and stes. Executive level. CI 3pm/CO 11am. Nonsmoking rms avail. **Amenities:** 🎿 🛏 A/C, cable TV w/movies, dataport. Executive-floor rooms have coffeemakers. **Services:** ☒ 🔑 🚐 ☒ ⤴ Car-rental desk. **Facilities:** 🎿 🛏 🛏 ⅙ 2 restaurants, 1 bar (w/entertainment), whirlpool, washer/dryer. **Rates (BB): Rates (CP):** Peak (Jan–Apr) $100 S or D; $164 ste. Extra person $10. Children under age 18 stay free. Min stay special events. Lower rates off-season. Parking: Outdoor, free. AE, CB, DC, DISC, ER, JCB, MC, V.

### ≡ ≡ Holiday Inn Busch Gardens
2701 E Fowler Ave, 33612; tel 813/971-4710 or toll free 800/99-BUSCH; fax 813/977-0155. Exit 34 off I-275. This complex of two-story buildings does a brisk business for both salespeople and tourists visiting nearby Busch Gardens. Parents will appreciate the courtyard with pool. **Rooms:** 396 rms and stes. CI 3pm/CO noon. Nonsmoking rms avail. **Amenities:** 🎿 🛏 A/C, cable TV w/movies. Some units w/minibars, some w/whirlpools. **Services:** ☒ 🔑 ☒ ⤴ ⊲ Car-rental desk, babysitting. **Facilities:** 🎿 🛏 ⅙ 1 restaurant, 2 bars, washer/dryer. **Rates:** Peak (Jan–Apr) $80–$90 S or D; $160–$260 ste. Children under age 18 stay free. Lower rates off-season. Parking: Outdoor, free. AE, DC, DISC, JCB, MC, V.

### ≡ ≡ Holiday Inn Express Stadium/Airport Area
4732 N Dale Mabry Hwy, 33614; tel 813/877-6061 or toll free 800/898-4484; fax 813/876-1531. Exit 23A off I-275. Great location for football games at Tampa Stadium or baseball games at the New York Yankees' Legend Field. **Rooms:** 205 rms. CI 3pm/CO noon. Nonsmoking rms avail. **Amenities:** 🎿 🛏 A/C, cable TV w/movies, dataport. Some units w/whirlpools. **Services:** 🚐 ☒ ⤴ ⊲ Twice-daily maid svce, babysitting. **Facilities:** 🎿 🛏 🛏 ⅙ 1 restaurant (lunch and dinner only), 1 bar, games rm, spa, washer/dryer. **Rates (CP):** Peak (Jan–Apr) $79 S; $89 D. Extra person $10. Children under age 19 stay free. Lower rates off-season. Parking: Outdoor, free. AE, CB, DC, DISC, MC, V.

### ≡ ≡ ≡ Hyatt Regency Tampa
2 Tampa City Center, 33602 (Downtown); tel 813/225-1234 or toll free 800/233-1234; fax 813/273-0234. At Tampa and Jackson Sts. The local glossy high-rise, this slick and inviting mainstay offers all the features of a major convention and business hotel. **Rooms:** 518 rms and stes. Executive level. CI 3pm/CO noon. Nonsmoking rms avail. **Amenities:** 🎿 🛏 🍴 A/C, cable TV w/movies. Some units w/whirlpools. **Services:** ☒ 🔑 VP 🚐 ☒ ⤴ Car-rental desk, babysitting. **Facilities:** 🎿 🛏 🛏 ⬚ ⅙ 2 restaurants (see "Restaurants" below), 1 bar (w/entertainment), sauna, whirlpool, washer/dryer. **Rates:** $169 S; $194 D; $265 ste. Extra person $25. Children under age 18 stay free. Parking: Indoor/outdoor, $7/day. AE, CB, DC, DISC, MC, V.

### ≡≡≡≡ Hyatt Regency Westshore

6200 Courtney Campbell Causeway, 33607 (Tampa Int'l Airport); tel 813/874-1234 or toll free 800/233-1234; fax 813/281-9168. Airport exit off I-275. 35 acres. One of the city's best hotels, a world-class operation with a top-notch staff and facilities to support its rates. With lush landscaping and palm-lined entry. **Rooms:** 397 rms and stes; 48 cottages/villas. Executive level. CI 3pm/CO noon. Nonsmoking rms avail. Rooms done in sophisticated designs. Marble baths. Corner rooms have particularly nice views. **Amenities:** 🛏 🕹 A/C, cable TV w/movies, in-rm safe. All units w/minibars, some w/terraces. **Services:** ✕ 🆅🅿 🚐 ⛵ ↻ Car-rental desk, masseur, babysitting. **Facilities:** 🛢 🏊 🍽 🛎 🖥 👤 ⅙ 3 restaurants (see "Restaurants" below), 3 bars (2 w/entertainment), sauna, whirlpool. Boardwalk from hotel to Oystercatchers Restaurant passes through wild Florida mangroves. **Rates:** Peak (Jan–Mar) $179 S; $204 D; $300–$515 ste; $189 cottage/villa. Extra person $25. Children under age 18 stay free. Min stay special events. Lower rates off-season. Parking: Indoor/outdoor, free. AE, CB, DC, DISC, MC, V.

### ≡≡ La Quinta Airport

4730 W Spruce St, 33607; tel 813/287-0440 or toll free 800/531-5900; fax 813/286-7399. Exit 21 off I-275. Super-clean establishment designed with Spanish-style accents. Recent renovations to grounds and public areas. **Rooms:** 122 rms and stes. CI 2pm/CO noon. Nonsmoking rms avail. **Amenities:** 🛏 🕹 A/C, cable TV w/movies. Free local calls. **Services:** 🚐 🏊 ↻ 🐾 **Facilities:** 🛢 🏊 ⅙ 1 restaurant. Family restaurant is open 24 hours. **Rates (CP):** Peak (Jan–Apr) $74–$81 S; $82–$89 D; $109–$117 ste. Extra person $7. Children under age 18 stay free. Lower rates off-season. Parking: Outdoor, free. AE, CB, DC, DISC, MC, V.

### ≡≡ Quality Hotel Riverside

200 N Ashley Dr, 33602 (Downtown); tel 813/223-2222; fax 813/273-0839. Exit 25 off I-275. **Rooms:** 286 rms and stes. CI 3pm/CO noon. Nonsmoking rms avail. **Amenities:** 🛏 🕹 A/C, cable TV. Some units w/minibars, some w/terraces. **Services:** ✕ 🚐 🏊 ↻ Babysitting. **Facilities:** 🛢 🛎 🖥 ⅙ 1 bar (w/entertainment), games rm, sauna. **Rates (CP):** $60–$80 S or D; $130 ste. Extra person $10. Children under age 18 stay free. Parking: Indoor, $4.50/day. AE, DC, DISC, MC, V.

### ≡≡ Quality Suites Busch Gardens

3001 University Center Dr, 33612; tel 813/971-8930 or toll free 800/786-7446; fax 813/971-8935. At 30th. Often fully booked because of its convenient location and pleasing amenities. The lobby is draped with memorabilia from the many sports teams that have stayed here. **Rooms:** 150 stes. CI 3pm/CO noon. Nonsmoking rms avail. **Amenities:** 🛏 🕹 🖥 🍴 A/C, cable TV w/movies, refrig, dataport, VCR, CD/tape player, voice mail. All units w/terraces. All rooms with microwaves. **Services:** 🏊 ↻ Babysitting. Complimentary evening cocktails. The front desk rents videos and also dispenses snacks and frozen dinners. **Facilities:** 🛢 🖥 ⅙

Whirlpool, washer/dryer. **Rates (BB):** Peak (Feb–Mar) $89–$159 ste. Extra person $5. Children under age 18 stay free. Lower rates off-season. Parking: Outdoor, free. AE, CB, DC, DISC, MC, V.

### ≡≡≡ Radisson Bay Harbor Inn

7700 Courtney Campbell Causeway, 33607 (Tampa Int'l Airport); tel 813/281-8900 or toll free 800/333-3333; fax 813/281-0189. Airport exit off I-275. Close to the airport and overlooking the bay, this fine hotel receives many business travelers and conventioneers drawn by its beachfront location, a tough find in Tampa. **Rooms:** 257 rms and stes. CI 3pm/CO noon. Nonsmoking rms avail. **Amenities:** 🛏 🕹 A/C, cable TV w/movies. Some units w/minibars, all w/terraces. **Services:** ✕ 🆅🅿 🚐 🏊 ↻ Twice-daily maid svce, babysitting. **Facilities:** 🛢 🚲 🖥 🛎 🖥 ⅙ 1 restaurant, 1 bar (w/entertainment), 1 beach (ocean), games rm, beauty salon, washer/dryer. **Rates:** Peak (Jan–Apr) $125–$140 S or D; $150–$400 ste. Extra person $10. Children under age 18 stay free. Lower rates off-season. Parking: Outdoor, free. AE, CB, DC, DISC, MC, V.

### ≡≡ Residence Inn by Marriott

3075 N Rocky Point Dr, 33607; tel 813/281-5677 or toll free 800/331-3131. Exit 20 off I-75. Small village of homey apartments in a quiet bayside location. **Rooms:** 176 effic. CI 3pm/CO noon. Nonsmoking rms avail. Fully equipped kitchens. **Amenities:** 🛏 🕹 🖥 A/C, cable TV. Some units w/terraces, some w/fireplaces. **Services:** 🚐 🏊 ↻ Babysitting. Complimentary morning newspaper. Free shuttle service serving surrounding area. Staff will shop for groceries. **Facilities:** 🛢 🖥 ⅙ Whirlpool, washer/dryer. **Rates (CP):** $125–$175 effic. Extra person $10. Children under age 18 stay free. Parking: Outdoor, free. AE, CB, DC, DISC, MC, V.

### ≡≡ Sailport Resort

2506 Rocky Point Dr, 33607; tel 813/281-9599 or toll free 800/255-9599, 800/321-9599 in Canada; fax 813/281-9510. Off Courtney Campbell Causeway from I-275. This on-the-bay all-suites resort, with its fully equipped units, is perfect for lengthy stays or family vacations. Beautiful bay views and nearby area attractions bring repeat business. **Rooms:** 212 stes. CI 3pm/CO 11am. Nonsmoking rms avail. **Amenities:** 🛏 🕹 🖥 A/C, cable TV, refrig, voice mail. All units w/terraces. **Services:** 🏊 ↻ Babysitting. **Facilities:** 🛢 🖥 🖥 ⅙ Washer/dryer. Fishing pier; barbecue grills. **Rates (CP):** Peak (Jan–Apr) $99 ste. Extra person $5. Children under age 12 stay free. Lower rates off-season. Parking: Indoor/outdoor, free. AE, CB, DC, MC, V.

### ≡≡≡ Sheraton Grand Hotel

4860 W Kennedy Blvd, 33607; tel 813/286-4400 or toll free 800/325-3535; fax 813/286-4053. Exit 21 off I-275. This smoked-glass hotel is a favorite address for businesspeople, and it's close to shops and restaurants. Subdued and attractive lobby. **Rooms:** 124 rms and stes. CI 3pm/CO noon. Nonsmoking rms avail. **Amenities:** 🛏 🕹 🖥 🍴 A/C, cable TV w/movies. **Services:** ✗ ⌨ VP 🚐 ⛱ ♬ Babysitting. **Facilities:** 🏋 💇 500 ♿ 2 restaurants (*see* "Restaurants" below), 2 bars, beauty salon. **Rates:** Peak (Jan–Apr) $149 S; $164 D; $295–$580 ste. Extra person $10. Children under age 18 stay free. Lower rates off-season. Parking: Indoor, free. AE, DC, DISC, MC, V.

### ≋≋≋ Sheraton Inn Tampa & Conference Center
7401 E Hillsborough Ave, 33610; tel 813/626-0999 or toll free 800/325-3535; fax 813/622-7893. Exit 6 off I-4. Standard Sheraton made up of both low- and mid-rise buildings. Value pricing for tourists. **Rooms:** 276 rms and stes. CI 3pm/CO noon. Nonsmoking rms avail. Rooms in tower have been updated more recently than others. **Amenities:** 🛁 🍴 A/C, cable TV w/movies. Some units w/terraces. **Services:** ✗ 🚐 ⛱ ♬ 🐾 Babysitting. **Facilities:** 🏋 💇 1200 ♿ 2 restaurants, 2 bars, whirlpool. **Rates:** Peak (Jan–Mar) $129 S or D; $400 ste. Extra person $10. Children under age 19 stay free. Lower rates off-season. Parking: Outdoor, free. AE, CB, DC, DISC, MC, V.

### ≋≋≋ Tampa Airport Hilton at Metro Center
2225 N Lois Ave, 33607; tel 813/877-6688 or toll free 800/445-8667; fax 813/879-3264. Exit 22 off I-275. Lofty two-story lobby makes a fine entrance to this business hotel close to the airport. Better suited to commercial needs than to tourists', although weekend rates may be attractive to families. **Rooms:** 238 rms and stes. CI 3pm/CO noon. Nonsmoking rms avail. **Amenities:** 🛁 🍴 A/C, cable TV w/movies. Some units w/terraces. **Services:** ✗ 🚐 ⛱ ♬ Babysitting. **Facilities:** 🏋 📺 💇 700 ♿ 1 restaurant, 1 bar, whirlpool. **Rates:** Peak (Jan–Apr) $89–$179 S or D; $189–$329 ste. Extra person $10. Children under age 18 stay free. Lower rates off-season. Parking: Outdoor, free. AE, CB, DC, DISC, MC, V.

### ≋≋≋ Tampa Airport Marriott
Tampa International Airport, 33607; tel 813/879-5151 or toll free 800/228-9290, 800/228-9290; fax 813/870-0355. Airport exit off I-275. This well-run Marriott connected to the airport terminal is designed to handle its large capacity and is outfitted with ample staff. Spacious public areas. **Rooms:** 296 rms and stes. CI 3pm/CO 1pm. Nonsmoking rms avail. **Amenities:** 🛁 🍴 A/C, cable TV w/movies, voice mail. All units w/terraces. **Services:** ✗ ⌨ VP 🚐 ⛱ ♬ Babysitting. **Facilities:** 🏋 💇 500 🖥 ♿ 2 restaurants (*see* "Restaurants" below), 2 bars. Revolving rooftop restaurant. **Rates:** Peak (Nov–Apr) $139 S; $154 D; $250–$400 ste. Children under age 18 stay free. Lower rates off-season. Parking: Indoor/outdoor, free. AE, CB, DC, DISC, ER, MC, V.

### ≋≋≋ Tampa Marriott Westshore
1001 N Westshore Blvd, 33607; tel 813/287-2555 or toll free 800/228-9290; fax 813/289-5464. Exit 21 off I-75. This major operation in the center of the Westshore hotel cluster is well received by business travelers. **Rooms:** 309 rms and

stes. Executive level. CI 4pm/CO 1pm. Nonsmoking rms avail. **Amenities:** 🛁 🍴 A/C, satel TV w/movies, dataport, voice mail. Some units w/terraces. **Services:** ✗ ⌨ 🚐 ⛱ ♬ Car-rental desk, babysitting. **Facilities:** 🏋 💇 500 ♿ 2 restaurants, 2 bars (1 w/entertainment), games rm, spa, sauna, whirlpool, washer/dryer. **Rates:** Peak (Jan–June) $139–$159 S or D; $200 ste. Extra person $15. Children under age 18 stay free. Min stay special events. Lower rates off-season. Parking: Outdoor, free. AE, CB, DC, DISC, MC, V.

### ≋≋≋≋ Wyndham Harbour Island Hotel
725 S Harbour Island Blvd, 33602; tel 813/229-5000 or toll free 800/822-4200, 800/822-4200 in the US, 800/631-4200 in Canada; fax 813/229-5322. Exit Ashley St off I-275. Cross the bridge to Harbour Island; hotel is adjacent to Tampa Convention Center. A rather elaborate hotel with a dignified, stately look and style. **Rooms:** 300 rms and stes. CI 3pm/CO noon. Nonsmoking rms avail. Classic guest rooms decorated in posh style; all have views of the water. **Amenities:** 🛁 🍴 📺 ♫ A/C, cable TV w/movies. All units w/minibars. **Services:** ✗ ⌨ VP 🚐 ⛱ ♬ Car-rental desk, babysitting. **Facilities:** 🏋 650 ♿ 1 restaurant, 1 bar. 50 boat slips. **Rates:** Peak (Dec–Mar) $139–$179 S; $159–$199 D; $300–$700 ste. Extra person $20. Children under age 18 stay free. Min stay special events. Lower rates off-season. Parking: Indoor/outdoor, $6/day. AE, CB, DC, DISC, EC, JCB, MC, V.

## MOTELS

### ≋≋ Comfort Inn
2106 E Busch Blvd, 33612; tel 813/931-3313 or toll free 800/221-2222; fax 813/933-8140. Offering the basics, this is a favored site for tourists due to its proximity to Busch Gardens. **Rooms:** 50 rms. CI 2pm/CO 11am. Nonsmoking rms avail. **Amenities:** 🛁 A/C, cable TV w/movies. **Services:** ♬ **Facilities:** 🏋 ♿ Whirlpool. **Rates:** $59 S or D. Extra person $5. Children under age 18 stay free. Parking: Outdoor, free. AE, DC, DISC, MC, V.

### ≋ John Henry's Econo Lodge
1701 E Busch Blvd, 33612; tel 813/933-7681 or toll free 800/783-7681; fax 813/935-3301. 1 mi W of Busch Gardens, exit 33 off I-275 N. Serves its purpose as a place to rest your head. Popular only for its proximity to Busch Gardens. **Rooms:** 238 rms. CI 11am/CO 11am. Nonsmoking rms avail. **Amenities:** 🛁 A/C, cable TV. **Services:** ♬ 🐾 **Facilities:** 🏋 100 1 restaurant, 1 bar, washer/dryer. **Rates:** Peak (Feb–Aug) $55 S or D. Extra person $5. Children under age 18 stay free. Lower rates off-season. Parking: Outdoor, free. AE, CB, DC, DISC, MC, V.

## RESORT

### ≋≋≋≋ Saddlebrook
5700 Saddlebrook Resort, Wesley Chapel, 33543; tel 813/973-1111 or toll free 800/729-8383; fax 813/973-4504. Exit 58 off I-75. 480 acres. This sprawling complex dotting the

fairways offers an array of dining and entertainment choices to complement its many sports facilities. **Rooms:** 790 rms and effic. CI 3pm/CO noon. Nonsmoking rms avail. Rooms may be combined to form suites, which include cooking facilities. **Amenities:** 🎛 ⬭ ⬭ A/C, cable TV w/movies, dataport. Some units w/minibars, all w/terraces. **Services:** ✕ ⬭ VP ⬭ ⬭ ⬭ Social director, masseur, children's program, babysitting. **Facilities:** 🎛 ⬭ ⬭ ▶36 ⬭ ⬭40 ⬭5 ⬭ 1000 ⬭ ⬭ 4 restaurants, 3 bars (1 w/entertainment), basketball, volleyball, lawn games, spa, sauna, steam rm, whirlpool, beauty salon, washer/dryer. The tennis complex is one of the largest in Florida. **Rates:** Peak (Jan 15–Apr) $215 S or D; $240 effic. Extra person $20. Children under age 13 stay free. Min stay special events. Lower rates off-season. Parking: Outdoor, free. AE, DC, DISC, MC, V.

## RESTAURANTS 🍽

### 🍷 Armani's
In the Hyatt Regency Westshore, 6200 Courtney Campbell Causeway (Tampa Int'l Airport); tel 813/281-9165. Exit 20 B off I-275. **Northern Italian.** The views are breathtaking from this lovely, stylish room, located on the top floor of the world-class Hyatt Regency Westshore. Seafood and northern Italian dishes are highlights, as is the vast antipasto bar. **FYI:** Reservations recommended. Piano. Jacket required. **Open:** Mon–Thurs 6–10pm, Fri–Sat 6–11pm. **Prices:** Main courses $15–$27. AE, CB, DC, DISC, MC, V. ⬭ VP ⬭

### 🍷 Bern's Steak House
1208 S Howard Ave; tel 813/251-2421. **Steak.** This stalwart one-of-a-kind Tampa institution features seven rooms and a separate dessert lounge. Wonderful, aged steaks come with onion soup, salad, baked potato, garlic toast, and onion rings. Encyclopedic wine list. **FYI:** Reservations accepted. No smoking. **Open:** Daily 5–11pm. **Prices:** Lunch main courses $1–$3. No CC. VP ⬭

### Cafe Winberie
In Olde Hyde Park Village, 1610 W Swann Ave at Dakota St; tel 813/253-6500. **New American.** Rotisserie chicken salad and other good-for-you items are the highlight at this fun, casual eatery. **FYI:** Reservations not accepted. Children's menu. **Open:** Mon–Thurs 11am–11pm, Fri–Sat 11am–midnight, Sun 10:30am–10:30pm. **Prices:** Main courses $5–$13. AE, CB, DC, DISC, MC, V. ⬭ ⬭

### ★ CardeVila's at La Teresita
3248 West Columbia Dr; tel 813/875-2007. 1 mi NE of Tampa stadium, off Columbus. **Cuban.** Abundant portions of classic Cuban food served up in a noisy but fun atmosphere. Adjacent La Teresita Cafe (open 24 hours on weekends) offers inexpensive Cuban sandwiches, strong *café cubano*, and lots of local color. **FYI:** Reservations recommended. Children's menu. Additional locations: 8218 Hanley Road, Temple Terrace (tel 888-8988); 7101 66th St N, Pinellas Park (tel

546-5785). **Open:** Sun–Thurs 8am–10pm, Fri–Sat 8am–11pm. **Prices:** Main courses $4–$14. AE, CB, DC, DISC, MC, V. ⬭⬭

### The Castaway
7720 Courtney Campbell Causeway (Tampa Int'l Airport); tel 813/281-0770. **Seafood.** Popular with the locals, this dimly lit eatery has a casual atmosphere, fresh seafood, and a superb view of the ocean. **FYI:** Reservations accepted. Children's menu. **Open:** Lunch Mon–Sat 11am–4pm; dinner Sun–Thurs 5–10:30pm, Fri–Sat 5–11:30pm; brunch Sun 9:30am–3pm. **Prices:** Main courses $16–$30. AE, CB, DC, DISC, ER, MC, V. ⬭ ⬭ VP ⬭

### City Center Cafe
In Hyatt Regency Tampa, 2 City Center; tel 813/225-1234. At Tampa and Jackson St. **Italian.** During the day, this cafe features a buffet and casual lunch menu. At night, lights go down and the kitchen gears up for an imaginative array of appetizers, pastas, and entrees prepared with an Italian accent. **FYI:** Reservations recommended. Children's menu. **Open:** Breakfast daily 6am–3pm; dinner daily 5–11pm. **Prices:** Main courses $10–$17. AE, CB, DC, DISC, ER, MC, V. ⬭ VP ⬭

### CK's
In the Tampa Airport Marriott, Tampa International Airport; tel 813/879-5178. **Continental/Steak.** Tampa's only revolving restaurant has terrific views as well as appetizing steaks, veal, lamb, salmon, and caesar salad. **FYI:** Reservations accepted. Children's menu. **Open:** Dinner Sun–Thurs 5–10pm, Fri–Sat 5–11pm; brunch Sun 10:30am–2:30pm. **Prices:** Main courses $17–$23. AE, MC, V. ⬭ ⬭ VP ⬭

### ★ The Colonnade
3401 Bayshore Blvd; tel 813/839-7558. **Seafood/Steak.** This restaurant has been satisfying customers with its fabulous food for over 60 years. Order the fresh grouper sandwich or choose one of their many platter specials, and top it off with a slice of coconut cream or key lime pie. **FYI:** Reservations not accepted. Children's menu. **Open:** Sun–Thurs 11am–10pm, Fri–Sat 11am–11pm. **Prices:** Main courses $10–$26. AE, CB, DC, DISC, MC, V. ⬭⬭⬭

### Crabby Tom's Old Time Oyster Bar and Seafood
3120 W Hillsborough Ave; tel 813/870-1652. **Seafood.** The name isn't the only amazing mouthful at this seafood palace. Enjoy a variety of tasty ocean treats at red-tableclothed picnic tables. **FYI:** Reservations not accepted. Children's menu. Beer and wine only. **Open:** Peak (Nov–May) Mon–Sat 5:30pm–close. **Prices:** Main courses $19–$30; prix fixe $55–$85. AE, MC, V.

### Crawdaddy's
2500 Rocky Point Dr; tel 813/281-0407. **Regional American/Seafood.** Enjoy down-home cooking and beautiful bay views at this romantic, antique-filled Victorian dining room.

FYI: Reservations accepted. Children's menu. **Open:** Sun–Thurs 5–11pm, Fri–Sat 5pm–midnight. **Prices:** Main courses $13–$22. AE, DC, DISC, MC, V. ◉ ▲ ♥ VP ♿

**⑤ Donatello**
232 N Dale Mabry Hwy; tel 813/875-6660. **Northern Italian.** Soft lights, lovely decor, and an attentive tuxedoed staff make this a place for romance. Try the Maine lobster over linguine, the veal chop, or a well-prepared Italian dish. **FYI:** Reservations recommended. Piano. **Open:** Lunch Mon–Fri 11:30am–2:30pm; dinner daily 6–11pm. **Prices:** Main courses $16–$40. Lunch main courses $7–$11. AE, CB, DC, DISC, ER, MC, V. ◉ VP ♿

**Lauro Ristorante Italiano**
3915 Henderson Blvd; tel 813/281-2100. 2 blocks W of Dale Mabry Hwy. **Northern Italian.** Classic decor, soft music. Specialties include fresh mozzarella and grilled vegetable linguine with lobster and Dover sole. **FYI:** Reservations recommended. **Open:** Lunch Mon–Fri 11:30am–2pm; dinner Mon–Sat 6–11pm. **Prices:** Main courses $12–$20; prix fixe $25–$50. AE, CB, DC, DISC, MC, V. VP ♿

**Le Bordeaux**
1502 S Howard Ave; tel 813/254-4387. 1 block north of Bayshore Ave. **French.** The daily menu—scribbled on chalkboards scattered around the restaurant—features a rotating selection of duck, fish, pork, and chicken dishes prepared Provençal-style. Salmon en croûte, pot au feu, and homemade patés and pastries are popular options. **FYI:** Reservations recommended. Dancing/jazz. **Open:** Mon–Fri 5:30–10pm, Sat–Sun 5–11pm. **Prices:** Main courses $8–$19. AE, CB, DC, MC, V. VP

**⑤ Mel's Hot Dogs**
4136 E Busch Blvd; tel 813/985-8000. **American.** Great family fun and value. Choose from a variety of franks, or try a beef burger or the fried chicken basket. **FYI:** Reservations not accepted. Children's menu. Beer and wine only. **Open:** Sun 11am–9pm, Mon–Sat 10am–10pm. **Prices:** Main courses $3–$7. No CC. ♿

**★ Mise en Place**
422 W Kennedy Blvd; tel 813/254-5373. **New American.** A casual, contemporary bistro serving hearty fare with a healthy twist. Entrees might include roast duck with wild strawberry sauce or grilled swordfish with melon and mint salsa. **FYI:** Reservations not accepted. **Open:** Lunch Mon–Sat 11:30am–2:30pm; dinner Tues–Thurs 5:30–10pm, Fri–Sat 5:30–11pm. **Prices:** Main courses $11–$18. AE, CB, DC, DISC, MC, V. ▦ ♿

**★ Oystercatchers**
In the Hyatt Regency Westshore, 6200 Courtney Campbell Causeway (Tampa Int'l Airport); tel 813/281-9116. **Seafood.** Dine while overlooking Tampa Bay from the deck or from indoor bay-window booths. Menu includes catch of the day, steaks, beef, and nightly specials. **FYI:** Reservations recommended. Reggae. Dress code. **Open:** Lunch Mon–Fri

11:30am–2:30pm, Sun 10:30am–3pm; dinner Sun–Thurs 6–10:30pm, Fri–Sat 6–11pm. **Prices:** Main courses $9–$27. AE, CB, DC, DISC, MC, V. ⛴ ▲ VP ♿

**Rumpelmayer's Restaurant**
In Ambassador Square Shopping Center, 4812 E Busch Blvd; tel 813/989-9563. 8 blocks E of Busch Gardens at 48th St. **German.** Walk through the doors of this whimsical eatery and straight into the heart of Europe. Flemish shrimp, chicken cordon bleu, and a variety of German dishes highlight the menu. More than 60 imported beers are available. **FYI:** Reservations recommended. Karaoke/singer. Children's menu. Beer and wine only. **Open:** Sun–Sat 11am–11pm. **Prices:** Main courses $9–$18; prix fixe $40. AE, CB, DC, MC, V. ♥

**★ Saltwaters Bar and Grille**
In Hyatt Regency Tampa, 2 City Center; tel 813/225-1234. **American/Pasta.** The mix-and-match pasta and sauce luncheon menu is a major hit with the business crowd. **FYI:** Reservations accepted. Jazz. **Open:** Daily 11:30am–12:30am. **Prices:** Main courses $4–$8. AE, DC, DISC, MC, V. VP ♿

**Selena's**
In Olde Hyde Park, 1623 Snow Ave; tel 813/251-2116. **Creole/Italian.** Patrons can dine either in the casual, comfortable Antique Room, or in the more formal Queen Anne Room, with its lace and linen. The Creole-inspired menu offers new twists on pasta, shrimp scampi, and chicken parmagiana. A low-fat menu is available. **FYI:** Reservations recommended. Children's menu. **Open:** Sun–Mon 11am–9pm, Tues–Wed 11am–10pm, Thurs 11am–11pm, Fri–Sat 11am–midnight. **Prices:** Main courses $7–$16. AE, DC, MC, V. ⛴ ♿

**Shells**
202 S Dale Mabry Hwy; tel 813/875-3467. **Seafood.** A basic and affordable eatery particularly suitable for families. While seafood is the primary offering, some beef and chicken dishes are offered as well. **FYI:** Reservations not accepted. Children's menu. Additional location: 11010 N 30th St (tel 977-8450). **Open:** Sun–Thurs 5–10pm, Fri–Sat 5–11pm. **Prices:** Main courses $5–$23. AE, DISC, MC, V. ♿

**♣ Shula's Steak House**
In Sheraton Grand Hotel, 4860 W Kennedy Blvd; tel 813/286-4366. At Westshore Blvd. **Seafood/Steak.** Superb service and steaks set in a football-theme environment. Not just for Miami Dolphins fans; the steaks score by themselves. **FYI:** Reservations recommended. Children's menu. **Open:** Lunch Mon–Fri 11:30am–2:30pm; dinner Sun–Thurs 5:30–10:30pm, Fri–Sat 5:30–11pm. **Prices:** Main courses $16–$58. AE, CB, DC, DISC, MC, V. VP ♿

**The Wine Exchange**
In Olde Hyde Park Village, 1611 W Swann Ave; tel 813/254-9463. **International.** The menu at this lively bistro is big on seafood and vegetarian dishes. Soups (made fresh daily) are also a popular option, especially at lunch. **FYI:** Reserva-

tions not accepted. Beer and wine only. No smoking. **Open:** Sun–Thurs 11:30am–10:15pm, Fri–Sat 11:30am–11:15pm. **Prices:** Main courses $8–$14. AE, MC, V. &

## REFRESHMENT STOP

### Joffrey's Coffee & Tea Co
In Old Hyde Park, 1628 W Snow Circle; tel 813/251-3315. **Coffeehouse.** Brick floors, track lighting, and glass-topped tables help to create a cool, contemporary feel. Wide assortment of appetizing desserts and pastries. This is a great post-shopping stop for coffee, tea, or cappuccino; you can even purchase coffee by the pound to take home with you. Additional locations: 13168-A N Dale Mabry (tel 264-1649); 1616 7th Ave (tel 248-5282). **Open:** Mon–Thurs 7:30–11pm, Fri 7:30am–midnight, Sat 8am–midnight, Sun 9am–11pm. AE, MC, V. &

## ATTRACTIONS

### Henry B Plant Museum
401 W Kennedy Blvd; tel 813/254-1891. This landmark was modeled after the Alhambra Palace in Spain. It was built as the 511-room Tampa Bay Hotel in 1891, at the outrageous cost (for those days) of $2 million. The facility showcases original furnishings and art pieces (chosen by Plant for the hotel) in historic room settings. In December the museum is festively decorated during the Victorian Christmas Stroll. **Open:** Tues–Sat 10am–4pm, Sun noon–4pm. $

### Busch Gardens
3000 E Busch Blvd; tel 813/987-5082. This 300-acre theme park has grown to become the most popular attraction on Florida's west coast. The park contains one of the largest collections of free-roaming wild animals in the United States, as well as dozens of rides, live entertainment, restaurants, and shops. It's divided into eight sections, among them **Timbuktu,** featuring African artisans at work, a shopping bazaar, dolphin shows, and a 1,200-seat German-style dining hall with music and dancing; **Serengeti Plain,** home to hippos, buffalo, impala, gazelles, giraffes, rhinos, elephants, and ostriches; **Nairobi,** with a baby-animal nursery and petting zoo; and **Morocco,** a walled city featuring crafts demonstrations, a sultan's tent with snake charmers, and an ice show. Crown Colony, the newest area of the park, is home to a team of Clydesdale horses and is the location of Questor, a flight simulator–based ride.

The park also offers the Anheuser-Busch brewery tour to observe the beer-making process and get a chance to sample the famous brews. Air-conditioned monorail, open-air skyride, and train all circle the park. **Open:** Daily 9am–sunset; extended seasonal hours. $$$$

### Adventure Island
4545 Bougainvillea Ave; tel 813/987-5660. Adjacent to Busch Gardens, this separate 23-acre outdoor water theme park has pools, water slides, an arcade, and picnic areas. **Open:** Apr–Oct, daily 10am–sunset. $$$$

### Lowry Park Zoo
7530 North Blvd; tel 813/932-0245. This 24-acre zoo houses animals in settings that closely resemble their natural habitats. Highlights include an aviary in a subtropical forest setting; a wildlife center showcasing Florida's native animals and plants. The manatee center has two large viewing tanks and facilities for the treatment and rehabilitation of injured manatees. There's also a children's petting zoo. **Open:** Daily 9:30am–5pm. $$$

### Fun Forest at Lowry Park
7520 North Blvd; tel 813/935-5503. An old-fashioned theme park offering a dozen traditional kiddie rides, including a Ferris wheel, a merry-go-round, and bumper cars. **Open:** Daily 11am–6pm. $$$

### Museum of Science and Industry (MOSI)
4801 E Fowler Ave; tel 813/985-5531. Located a mile north of Busch Gardens, MOSI has permanent and changing exhibits that focus on industry, technology, and the physical and natural sciences. It includes a ham radio station, communications gallery, power plant model, and weather station. Other attractions are the *Challenger* Center, a memorial to the seven *Challenger* astronauts, which features a simulated space shuttle mission; and the Back Woods, a 40-acre wooded area that contains nature trails, a planetarium, an interactive butterfly garden, and a fossil garden. **Open:** Sun–Thurs 9am–4:30pm, Fri–Sat 9am–9pm. $$$

### Tampa Museum of Art
600 N Ashley Dr; tel 813/274-8130. This visual arts complex offers seven galleries with changing exhibits ranging from Greek and Roman antiquities to American expressionist painting and contemporary photography. Tours Wed, Sat, and Sun at 1pm. **Open:** Mon–Tues and Thurs–Sat 10am–5pm, Wed 10am–9pm, Sun 1–5pm. $$

### Museum of African-American Art
1308 N Marion St; tel 813/272-2466. This museum is the first of its kind in Florida. It houses the Barnett-Aden Collection, valued at $7.5 million and considered by many to be the country's foremost collection of African American art. More than 80 artists are represented in the collection, which includes 32 pieces of sculpture and 106 paintings. **Open:** Tues–Sat 10am–4:30pm, Sun 1–4:30pm. $

### Florida Center for Contemporary Art
1513 E 8th Ave; tel 813/974-2849. A gallery for alternative visual arts within a growing creative community in Ybor City, emphasizing Florida artists. Many exhibitors at this nonprofit space offer their works for sale. **Open:** Wed–Sat 11am–5pm. Call ahead to confirm hours. **Free**

### University of South Florida Contemporary Art Museum
4202 E Fowler Ave; tel 813/974-2849. This 10,000-square-foot facility spotlights contemporary artworks from around the world. Highlights include valuable collections of pre-

Columbian and African artifacts, as well as contemporary prints from the southeastern United States. **Open:** Mon–Fri 10am–5pm, Sat 1–4pm. **Free**

### Ybor City State Museum
1818 9th Ave; tel 813/247-6323. Exhibits housed in the former Ferlita Bakery (1896–1973) depict the political, social, and cultural influences that shaped this section of Tampa, with a particular emphasis on the once-flourishing cigar industry. The museum includes a collection of cigar memorabilia and works by local artisans. Adjacent to the park is Preservation Park, the site of three renovated cigar workers' cottages with original furnishings from the turn of the century. Cottage tours are offered twice daily, in the morning and afternoon. **Open:** Tues–Sat 9am–noon and 1–5pm. **$**

### Seminole Indian Village
5221 N Orient Rd; tel 813/620-3077. Located on Tampa's Seminole Reservation, this museum traces the history of the Seminoles in the area. Visitors can watch skilled Seminole craftspeople as they practice beadwork, wood carving, basket-making, and patchwork sewing. More lively demonstrations include alligator-wrestling and snake-handling. The grounds also serve as a natural habitat for Florida black bears, panthers, otters, bobcats, and deer. There is a gift shop with handmade crafts. Tours available every hour on the half-hour, with last tour at 3:30pm. **Open:** Mon–Sat 9am–5pm, Sun noon–5pm. **$$**

### Children's Museum of Tampa
7550 North Blvd; tel 813/935-8441. Geared for children 2–10, this museum's interactive exhibits are designed to increase curiosity and imagination. Activities range from grocery shopping to blowing giant bubbles to papermaking. Safety Village is Tampa in miniature, a place for kids to learn the rules of safety, with miniature traffic lights, buildings, and paved streets. **Open:** Mon–Thurs 9am–4:30pm, Sat 10am–5pm, Sun 1–5pm. **$**

### Gondola Getaway Cruises
Waterwalk Dock; tel 813/855-8518. See the skyscrapers and other downtown highlights as you float across the waters of Tampa Bay and the lower Hillsborough River in an authentic 70-year-old Venetian gondola. Each 30-foot gondola is capable of carrying up to 4 passengers. Ice bucket and glasses can be supplied for passengers bringing wine. Cruises offered Mon–Sat 6pm–midnight, Sun noon–9pm; other times by appointment. Reservations accepted 9am–7pm. **$$$$**

### Starlite Princess
Tampa Garrison Seaport, 401 2nd St E, Indian Rocks Beach; tel 813/595-1212. A variety of cruises are offered aboard this authentic paddlewheeler: luncheon/sightseeing (lunch optional), ecological/sightseeing, "Melodies in Motion" lunch/dance, and dinner-and-dance. (No Monday cruises available.) **Open:** Call for cruise schedule. Reservations required. **$$$**

### Tampa Stadium
4201 N Dale Mabry Hwy; tel 813/872-7977. Home base for the Tampa Bay Buccaneers football team and the Tampa Bay Rowdies soccer team, this 74,296-capacity stadium also hosts a wide variety of sporting events, shows, and concerts. Call in advance for information on games and events or reserve through Ticketmaster outlets.

### Hillsborough River State Park
15402 US 301 N, Thonotosassa; tel 813/987-6771. The Hillsborough River runs through this 3,000-acre park, located off US 301, with a string of rapids and a swinging bridge spanning its banks. A small museum contains memorabilia from Fort Foster, built in 1847 during the Second Seminole War. Self-guided tours of a reconstruction of the fort. Swimming (Mem Day–Labor Day), fishing, canoe rentals, hiking, camping, bicycle rentals, nature trail. **Open:** Daily 8am–sunset. **$$**

# Tarpon Springs

Tourists swarm the sponge docks and downtown antique shops in this quaint Gulf Coast community. St Nicholas Greek Orthodox Cathedral and plentiful Greek restaurants attest to its Mediterranean heritage. A broad hiking and biking trail cuts through town. **Information:** Tarpon Springs Chamber of Commerce, 210 S Pinellas Ave #120, Tarpon Springs, 34689 (tel 813/937-6109).

## HOTEL 🏨

### ▋▋ Best Western Tahitian Resort
2337 US 19, 34691; or toll free 800/528-1234; fax 813/937-3806. A well-maintained facility with fresh decor and a small but capable staff. Set on modestly landscaped grounds. **Rooms:** 140 rms and effic. CI 3pm/CO 11am. Nonsmoking rms avail. **Amenities:** 🛁 ⚲ A/C, cable TV w/movies. **Services:** ✕ ⟲ ⇆ **Facilities:** 🛝 ♿ 1 restaurant, 1 bar (w/entertainment), washer/dryer. **Rates:** Peak (Feb–Apr) $61–$76 S; $66–$81 D; $66 effic. Extra person $5. Children under age 13 stay free. Lower rates off-season. Parking: Outdoor, free. AE, CB, DC, DISC, MC, V.

## ATTRACTION 🏛

### Konger Coral Sea Aquarium
850 Dodecanese Blvd; tel 813/938-5378. This aquarium features a wide collection of fish indigenous to the Gulf of Mexico and the Caribbean Sea, including lemon sharks, angelfish, puffers, and stingrays. Feeding shows every 90 minutes beginning at 10:30am. **Open:** Daily 10am–5pm. **$$**

# Titusville

Gateway to Kennedy Space Center on Merritt Island, where shuttles launch over the Atlantic. Related venues include the

US Astronaut Hall of Fame. **Information:** Titusville Area Chamber of Commerce, 2000 S Washington Ave, Titusville, 32780 (tel 407/267-3036).

## HOTELS 🏨

### ⊨⊨ Holiday Inn Titusville

4951 S Washington Ave, 32780; tel 407/269-2121 or toll free 800/HOLIDAY; fax 407/267-4739. Exit 79 off I-95. The hotel closest to the Kennedy Space Center, it overlooks the launch site as well as the Intracoastal Waterway. **Rooms:** 117 rms. CI 3pm/CO noon. Nonsmoking rms avail. Standard guest rooms are in fresh condition. **Amenities:** 🕐 ⚓ A/C, cable TV w/movies, dataport. **Services:** ✕ 🖽 🍴 🏧 **Facilities:** 🛝 🔟 1 restaurant, 1 bar, games rm, washer/dryer. **Rates:** Peak (Jan–Apr 13) $69 S or D. Extra person $6. Lower rates off-season. Parking: Outdoor, free. AE, CB, DC, DISC, EC, ER, JCB, MC, V.

### ⊨⊨ Ramada Inn Kennedy Space Center

3500 Cheney Hwy, 32780; tel 407/269-5510 or toll free 800/292-1192; fax 407/269-3796. Exit 79 off I-95. A roadside plain Jane composed of one- and two-story buildings surrounding a sunny pool deck. **Rooms:** 124 rms and effic. CI 1pm/CO noon. Nonsmoking rms avail. Modern, appealing overall room decor. **Amenities:** 🕐 ⚓ A/C, cable TV w/movies. **Services:** ✕ 🖽 🍴 Car-rental desk. **Facilities:** 🛝 📷2 ♨ ⚴ 1 restaurant, 1 bar, basketball, games rm, sauna, whirlpool, playground, washer/dryer. **Rates:** Peak (Jan 19–Apr 14) $66–$89 S; $69–$89 D; $89 effic. Extra person $6. Children under age 17 stay free. Lower rates off-season. Parking: Outdoor, free. AE, DC, DISC, MC, V.

## MOTEL

### ⊨⊨ Comfort Inn Kennedy Space Center

3810 S Washington Ave, 32780; tel 407/267-9111 or toll free 800/525-2765; fax 407/267-0750. 7 mi NW of Kennedy Space Center, exit 79 off I-95. Well-kept two-story property has guest rooms that open to the pool and courtyard. **Rooms:** 102 rms. CI 2pm/CO 11am. Nonsmoking rms avail. **Amenities:** 🕐 A/C. Some units with microwaves and refrigerators. **Services:** ✕ 🖽 🍴 **Facilities:** 🛝 ♨ 🔟 Games rm, playground, washer/dryer. **Rates (CP):** Peak (Dec 20–Apr 15) $55–$75 S or D. Extra person $7. Children under age 19 stay free. Lower rates off-season. Parking: Outdoor, free. AE, CB, DC, DISC, EC, ER, JCB, MC, V.

## ATTRACTIONS 🏛

### US Astronaut Hall of Fame

6225 Vectorspace Blvd; tel 407/269-6100. Exhibits honoring the first 20 Americans in space include Wally Schirra's *Sigma 7* capsule, Gus Grissom's *Mercury* space suit, rare film footage, and many other artifacts and mementos. A 20-minute film called *Shuttle to Tomorrow* is screened aboard a full-scale space shuttle mock-up, and visitors may climb into a re-created *Mercury* capsule for a short tour narrated by John Glenn. Also here is US Space Camp, where children from across the country spend five days learning how math and science are applied in astronaut training (advance reservation required). **Open:** Daily 9am–5pm. **$$$**

### Valiant Air Command Museum

6600 Tico Rd; tel 407/268-1941. Rotating exhibits of usually 10–12 restored and flyable aircraft from the World War II era and afterward. A C-47 transport plane is open for inspection, and kids can jump into a cockpit trainer to get a feel for the controls. Exhibits include rebuilt airplane engines and a large memorabilia room with artifacts from both world wars. Guided tours are available on request. The museum also hosts an annual airshow in March or April. **Open:** Daily 10am–6pm. **$$$**

# Treasure Island

Immediately north of St Pete Beach on the Gulf Coast, this tourist and retiree town offers organized fun such as Memorial Day weekend's "Taste of Treasure Island," Fourth of July's "Pirate Days," and several pro volleyball tournaments. **Information:** Treasure Island Chamber of Commerce, 152-108th Ave, Treasure Island, 33706 (tel 813/367-4529).

## HOTELS 🏨

### ⊨⊨ Bilmar Beach Resort Hotel

10650 Gulf Blvd, 33706; tel 813/360-5531 or toll free 800/826-9724; fax 813/360-2915. 5th Ave N exit off I-275. A delightful beach complex with some commanding views of the Gulf. **Rooms:** 172 rms, stes, and effic. CI 2pm/CO 11am. Nonsmoking rms avail. **Amenities:** 🕐 ⚓ 🖥 ♀ A/C, cable TV, refrig, in-rm safe. Some units w/terraces. **Services:** ✕ 🖽 🍴 Babysitting. **Facilities:** 🛝 200 ⚴ 2 restaurants, 2 bars (w/entertainment), 1 beach (ocean), whirlpool. Dixieland jazz offered Wednesday and Sunday evenings. **Rates:** Peak (Feb 8–Apr 17) $113–$128 S or D; $194–$208 ste; $113–$128 effic. Extra person $10. Children under age 18 stay free. Min stay special events. Lower rates off-season. Parking: Outdoor, free. AE, CB, DC, MC, V.

### ⊨⊨ Sand Pebble Resort

12300 Gulf Blvd, 33706; tel 813/360-1845; fax 813/367-9309. At 123rd Ave. An all-condominium vacation resort, with marvelous sunset views from the beach below. **Rooms:** 49 effic. CI 4pm/CO 10am. Fully equipped units, many updated in Key West style. **Amenities:** 🕐 ⚓ 🖥 ♀ A/C, cable TV, refrig. Some units w/terraces. **Services:** 🍴 Social director, children's program, babysitting. **Facilities:** 🛝 ⚴ 1 beach (ocean), volleyball, games rm, whirlpool, washer/dryer. **Rates:** Peak (Mar–mid-Apr) $70–$220 effic. Extra person $8. Children under age 12 stay free. Min stay. Lower rates off-season. Parking: Outdoor, free. AE, DISC, ER, MC, V.

## MOTEL

### ≣≣ Ramada Inn Treasure Island

12000 Gulf Blvd, 33706; tel 813/360-7051 or toll free 800/228-2828; fax 813/367-6641. Exit 11 off I-275. Beachfront location in a quiet neighborhood. Some great views and lots of sun. **Rooms:** 121 rms and effic. CI 3pm/CO noon. Nonsmoking rms avail. **Amenities:** 🔒 🕭 A/C, cable TV w/movies, VCR, in-rm safe. Some units w/whirlpools. **Services:** ✗ 🖺 🖵 Babysitting. Children under 12 eat free. **Facilities:** 🖼 🕭 1 restaurant, 2 bars (w/entertainment), 1 beach (ocean), volleyball, games rm, spa, whirlpool, playground, washer/dryer. Poolside bar. **Rates:** Peak (Feb–Apr) $110–$130 S or D; $120 effic. Extra person $10. Children under age 18 stay free. Lower rates off-season. Parking: Outdoor, free. AE, CB, DC, DISC, EC, ER, MC, V.

# Venice

Canals recall the Italian namesake of this Gulf Coast community south of Sarasota. It's a charming study in contrast: winter home to the Ringling circus and its Clown College plus opera, symphony, and theater. Also billed as shark's tooth capital of the world. **Information:** Venice Area Chamber of Commerce, 257 Tamiami Trail N, Venice, 34285 (tel 941/488-2236).

## HOTELS 🏨

### ≣≣≣ Best Western Sandbar Beach Resort

811 The Esplanade N, 34285; tel 941/488-2251 or toll free 800/822-4853; fax 941/485-2894. Exit 35 off I-75. Recent upgrades have made this property a very pleasant place to stay. Boasts a private beach. **Rooms:** 44 rms, stes, and effic. CI 2pm/CO 11am. Nonsmoking rms avail. **Amenities:** 🔒 🕭 🖥 A/C, cable TV, dataport. All units w/terraces. **Services:** ✗ 🖺 🖵 Car-rental desk, children's program. **Facilities:** 🖼 ⚠ 1 restaurant, 1 beach (ocean), volleyball, washer/dryer. **Rates:** Peak (Dec 23–Apr 23) $135–$275 S or D; $135–$275 ste; $135–$275 effic. Children under age 18 stay free. Lower rates off-season. Parking: Outdoor, free. AE, CB, DC, DISC, MC, V.

### ≣≣ Best Western Venice Resort

455 US 41 Bypass, 34292; tel 941/485-5411 or toll free 800/237-3712; fax 941/484-6193. 10 mi S of Sarasota exit 35 off I-75 W on Venice Ave to US 41 N ¼ mi on left. About a mile from the water, this two-story lodging receives a mix of guests, from golfers to American families and European tourists. **Rooms:** 162 rms and stes. CI 3pm/CO 11am. Nonsmoking rms avail. **Amenities:** 🔒 A/C, cable TV. **Services:** 🖺 🖵 🖘 Car-rental desk. **Facilities:** 🖼 300 1 restaurant (bkfst and dinner only), 1 bar (w/entertainment), whirlpool, playground, washer/dryer. Dinner theater operates mid-summer and October to May. **Rates:** Peak (Feb 15–

Apr 15) $86–$98 S or D; $150–$175 ste. Extra person $6. Children under age 18 stay free. Lower rates off-season. Parking: Outdoor, free. AE, CB, DC, DISC, JCB, MC, V.

## RESTAURANT 🍴

### The Crow's Nest Marina Restaurant

1968 Tarpon Center Dr; tel 941/484-9551. **Seafood/Steak.** The menu changes daily according to the availability of fresh seafood. Try the Grouper Key Largo, which is sautéed with shrimp, scallops, crab, mushrooms, and hollandaise sauce. Ten different wines offered by the glass daily. **FYI:** Reservations accepted. Children's menu. Dress code. **Open:** Peak (Jan–Mar) lunch Mon–Sun 11am–3pm; dinner Mon–Sun 5–10pm. **Prices:** Main courses $12–$20. AE, DISC, MC, V. 📷

## ATTRACTION 💼

### Oscar Scherer State Park

1843 S Tamiami Trail, Osprey; tel 941/483-5956. This park encompasses about 1,400 acres of scrub and pine flatwoods and includes a freshwater lake. Swimming, fishing, canoe rentals, hiking, camping, nature trails. **$$**

# Vero Beach

A historic railroad station and a modern airport share this central Atlantic coast community. A wealthy Florida town since its founding in 1925, it offers sophisticated theater, art and shopping, golf, tennis, and water sports.

## HOTELS 🏨

### ≣≣≣ DoubleTree Guest Suites

3500 Ocean Dr, 32963; tel 561/231-5666 or toll free 800/841-5666; fax 561/234-4866. US 60 off I-95. One of the area's best facilities, offering an all-suites arrangement in a four-story contemporary building with Mediterranean accents. **Rooms:** 55 stes. CI 3pm/CO noon. Nonsmoking rms avail. Spacious rooms proffer handsome furnishings and an efficient layout. **Amenities:** 🔒 🕭 🖥 🍴 A/C, cable TV w/movies, refrig, dataport. All units w/terraces. **Services:** ✗ 🖛 🖺 🖵 Car-rental desk, babysitting. **Facilities:** 🖼 50 🕭 2 restaurants, 1 bar, 1 beach (ocean), whirlpool, washer/dryer. **Rates:** Peak (Dec–Apr) $205–$295 ste. Extra person $10. Children under age 18 stay free. Lower rates off-season. Parking: Outdoor, free. AE, DC, DISC, MC, V.

### ≣≣ Holiday Inn West Countryside

8797 20th St, 32966; tel 561/567-8321 or toll free 800/HOLIDAY; fax 561/569-8558. Exit 68 off I-95. Standard low-rise family hotel. **Rooms:** 117 rms. CI 2pm/CO noon. Nonsmoking rms avail. **Amenities:** 🔒 🕭 A/C, cable TV w/movies, dataport. **Services:** ✗ 🖺 🖵 🖘 **Facilities:** 🖼 200 1 restaurant, 1 bar (w/entertainment), volleyball, washer/

dryer. **Rates:** Peak (Jan–Apr) $70 S; $78 D. Extra person $8. Children under age 19 stay free. Lower rates off-season. Parking: Outdoor, free. AE, CB, DC, DISC, MC, V.

### ≣≣ Riviera Inn

1605 S Ocean Dr, 32963; tel 561/234-4112; fax 561/234-4112 ext 118. US 60 off I-95. Attractive accommodations with oversized rooms. **Rooms:** 17 rms and effic. CI 2pm/CO 11am. **Amenities:** 🎁 🍸 A/C, cable TV w/movies. Some units w/terraces. **Services:** ⬅ **Facilities:** 🛢 🔲 1 restaurant. **Rates:** Peak (Feb–Apr) $69 S or D; $89 effic. Extra person $10. Children under age 12 stay free. Lower rates off-season. Parking: Outdoor, free. AE, MC, V.

## MOTELS

### ≣ Islander Motel

3101 Ocean Dr, 32963; tel 561/231-4431 or toll free 800/952-5886; fax 561/231-4431 ext 31. US 60 off I-95. Well located in downtown Vero Beach, this small, modest, aqua-colored motel is fine for undemanding couples. **Rooms:** 16 rms and effic. CI 2pm/CO 11am. **Amenities:** 🎁 🍸 A/C, cable TV w/movies. Some units w/terraces. Some rooms have refrigerators. **Services:** ✕ ⬅ **Facilities:** 🛢 Washer/dryer. Small, walk-up cafe. Barbecue area. **Rates:** Peak (Jan–mid-Apr) $89 S or D; $99 effic. Extra person $7. Children under age 12 stay free. Min stay peak and special events. Lower rates off-season. Parking: Outdoor, free. AE, MC, V.

### ≣≣ Vero Beach Inn

4700 N FL A1A, 32963; tel 561/231-1600 or toll free 800/227-8615; fax 561/231-9547. Exit 68 off I-95. This white-columned, four-story brick structure set on the beach is a short drive from most local shops, restaurants, and attractions. **Rooms:** 104 rms and stes. CI 2pm/CO 11am. Non-smoking rms avail. Comfortable rooms. **Amenities:** 🎁 🍸 📺 A/C, cable TV w/movies, dataport, in-rm safe. All units w/terraces. **Services:** ✕ 🚐 🖼 ⬅ ⏪ **Facilities:** 🛢 🔲 🍸 1 restaurant, 1 bar, washer/dryer. Pool is partly enclosed by the hotel and partly outside. Restaurant has ocean and pool views. A lively tiki bar operates every day in season and on weekends out of season. **Rates:** Peak (Feb–Apr) $79 S; $85 D; $130 ste. Extra person $12. Children under age 18 stay free. Lower rates off-season. Parking: Outdoor, free. AE, CB, DISC, MC, V.

## RESTAURANTS 🍽

### ♛ The Black Pearl

1409 FL A1A; tel 561/234-4426. 1 mi S of 17th St Causeway. **Regional American/French.** A casually elegant establishment with pink-and-green decor reminiscent of the famed Polo Lounge in Beverly Hills. The daily menu is centered around seafood dishes—six to eight different ones are usually available. The British owners also own the nearby Pearl's Caribbean Bistro, a scaled-down, more festive spot. **FYI:**

Reservations recommended. Children's menu. Beer and wine only. **Open:** Daily 6–10pm. **Prices:** Main courses $15–$30. AE, DISC, MC, V. ♥ 🎬 ♿

### ✹ Charley Brown's

1410 S FL A1A; tel 561/231-6310. ¼ mi S of 17th St Bridge. **American.** A comfortable eatery with an animated atmosphere that's fun for the whole family. Great steaks, chicken, and seafood entrees. **FYI:** Reservations accepted. Children's menu. **Open:** Mon–Thurs 5–9:30pm, Fri–Sat 5–10pm. **Prices:** Main courses $10–$19. AE, DISC, MC, V. 🎬 ♿

### ♛ ✹ Ocean Grill

1050 Sexton Plaza; tel 561/231-5409. At the end of US 60. **American.** An elegant restaurant with shining hardwood floors, lovely antiques, and superb views of the water. Prime rib, chicken Oscar, and filet mignon are just a few of the house specialties. **FYI:** Reservations accepted. Children's menu. Dress code. **Open:** Lunch Mon–Fri 11:30am–2:30pm; dinner daily 5:45–10pm. **Prices:** Main courses $15–$25. AE, DC, DISC, MC, V. 🏞 ♿

## ATTRACTIONS 🏛

### McClarty Center Museum

13180 N FL A1A; tel 561/589-2147. Dealing primarily with the sinking of a Spanish fleet off the coast here in 1715, this museum is built on the site where survivors came ashore. On view are replicas and some original pieces of the salvaged treasure. Dioramas, talking displays, 28-minute video. **Open:** Daily 10am–4:30pm. **$**

### Center for the Arts in Vero Beach

3001 Riverside Park Dr; tel 561/231-0707. The Holmes Gallery features major national and international exhibitions, ranging from American photography to Greco-Roman antiquities; the Florida Gallery is devoted to works by Florida artists. A sculpture garden is devoted to large-scale works. "Center Cinema" screens foreign and independent American films every Thursday at 3pm and 8pm. Guided tours available Wed–Sun 1:30–3:30pm. Gift shop. **Open:** Fri–Wed 10am–4:30pm, Thurs 10am–8pm. **$**

### Dodgertown

4101 26th St; tel 561/569-4900. The winter home of the LA Dodgers, this 450-acre sports and recreation complex includes two golf courses and a country club where baseball players can sometimes be sighted. Spring training games are played here at Holman Stadium, as are regular home games of the minor-league Vero Beach Dodgers. **Open:** Daily 8am–11pm. **$$$**

# Walt Disney World

**See Lake Buena Vista. See also Altamonte Springs, Davenport, Haines City, Kissimmee, Maitland, Winter Park**

# Wesley Chapel

See Tampa

# West Palm Beach

See also Riviera Beach

Conservative elegance characterizes this oceanside city north of Miami. Home to the outstanding Norton Museum of Art plus Ballet Florida, Dreher Park Zoo, and private polo clubs. May's five-day SunFest showcases music and art. **Information:** Tourism Development Council, 1555 Palm Beach Lake Blvd #204, West Palm Beach, 33401 (tel 561/471-3995 or toll free 800/833-5733).

## HOTELS 📠

### ⬛▤ Courtyard by Marriott

600 Northpointe Pkwy, 33407; tel 561/640-9000 or toll free 800/321-2211; fax 561/471-0122. Suitable for both business travelers and families on holiday. Convenient to area restaurants. **Rooms:** 149 rms and stes. CI 4pm/CO noon. Nonsmoking rms avail. **Amenities:** 📺 ⛲ ☕ A/C, cable TV w/movies. Some units w/terraces. **Services:** 🚗 ⟳ Babysitting. **Facilities:** ⛳ 🏋 ⌐50⌐ 1 restaurant, 1 bar, whirlpool, washer/dryer. **Rates:** Peak (Dec 15–Apr 15) $95–$105 S or D; $110–$120 ste. Children under age 17 stay free. Lower rates off-season. Parking: Outdoor, free. AE, DC, DISC, MC, V.

### ⬛▤ Hampton Inn Airport

1505 Belvedere Rd, 33406; tel 561/471-8700 or toll free 800/888-0175; fax 561/689-7385. Well-run middle-grade establishment with a friendly staff. **Rooms:** 136 rms. CI 3pm/CO noon. Nonsmoking rms avail. **Amenities:** 📺 ⛲ A/C, cable TV w/movies. **Services:** 🚗 ⟳ **Facilities:** ⛳ ⌐20⌐ ⛶ **Rates (CP):** Peak (Dec–May) $79–$99 S or D. Children under age 18 stay free. Lower rates off-season. Parking: Outdoor, free. AE, CB, DC, DISC, EC, ER, JCB, MC, V.

### ⬛▤▤ Holiday Inn Airport

1301 Belvedere Rd, 33405; tel 561/659-3880 or toll free 800/HOLIDAY; fax 561/655-8886. Belvedere Rd exit off I-95. This V-shaped high-rise of concrete and glass sits on a wider base that contains public areas nestled around an L-shaped pool. Attracts mainly business travelers. **Rooms:** 199 rms and stes. CI 2pm/CO 11am. Nonsmoking rms avail. **Amenities:** 📺 ⛲ A/C, cable TV w/movies. Some units w/terraces. **Services:** ✕ 🚗 ⟳ **Facilities:** ⛳ 🏋 ⌐270⌐ ⛶ 1 restaurant, 1 bar, sauna. **Rates (CP):** Peak (Jan–Apr) $90 S or D; $185 ste. Children under age 18 stay free. Lower rates off-season. Parking: Outdoor, free. AE, CB, DC, DISC, MC, V.

### ⬛▤▤▤ The Omni West Palm Beach Hotel

1601 Belvedere Rd, 33405; tel 561/689-6400 or toll free 800/THE-OMNI; fax 561/683-7150. Belvedere Rd exit off I-95. Often busy airport hotel. **Rooms:** 220 rms and stes. CI 4pm/CO 1pm. Nonsmoking rms avail. **Amenities:** 📺 ⛲ A/C, cable TV w/movies. Some units w/minibars, some w/terraces. **Services:** ✕ 🚗 ⟳ Car-rental desk, babysitting. **Facilities:** 🏋 ⌐400⌐ 1 restaurant, 1 bar (w/entertainment), sauna. **Rates:** Peak (Jan–Apr) $139 S; $149 D; $160 ste. Extra person $10. Children under age 18 stay free. Min stay special events. Lower rates off-season. Parking: Outdoor, free. AE, DISC, MC, V.

### ▤▤▤ Palm Beach Airport Hilton

150 Australian Ave, 33406; tel 561/684-9400; fax 561/683-5010. Southern Blvd exit off I-95. Offers a bit more pizzazz than the nearby competition. Pleasant, small lake in back is an unusual feature for an airport hotel. Smart-looking lobby is sometimes understaffed. **Rooms:** 247 rms and stes. CI 3pm/CO noon. Nonsmoking rms avail. **Amenities:** 📺 ⛲ A/C, cable TV. **Services:** ✕ VP 🚗 ⟳ **Facilities:** ⛳ ⌐500⌐ ⛶ 1 restaurant, 1 bar (w/entertainment), games rm. **Rates (CP):** Peak (Dec–Apr) $109–$139 S or D; $475–$575 ste. Extra person $10. Children under age 18 stay free. Lower rates off-season. Parking: Outdoor, free. AE, CB, DC, DISC, JCB, MC, V.

### ▤▤▤ Radisson Suite Inn Palm Beach Airport

1808 S Australian Ave, 33409; tel 561/689-6888 or toll free 800/333-3333; fax 561/683-5783. Exit 51 off I-95. A popular rendezvous for business travelers who drop in for both long and short stays and who appreciate the extra space in their private quarters. **Rooms:** 174 stes. CI 3pm/CO noon. Nonsmoking rms avail. **Amenities:** 📺 ⛲ 🖥 A/C, cable TV w/movies, refrig, VCR, CD/tape player, in-rm safe. All units w/minibars. **Services:** ✕ 🚗 ⟳ Babysitting. **Facilities:** ⛳ 🏋 ⌐100⌐ ⛶ 1 restaurant, 1 bar, spa, sauna, steam rm, whirlpool, washer/dryer. **Rates:** Peak (Jan–Mar) $149 ste. Extra person $10. Children under age 18 stay free. Lower rates off-season. Parking: Outdoor, free. AE, CB, DC, DISC, ER, JCB, MC, V.

### ▤▤▤ Sheraton West Palm Beach Hotel

630 Clearwater Park Rd WPB, 33407 (Palm Beach Int'l Airport); tel 561/833-1234 or toll free 800/272-6232; fax 561/833-1255. Exit 52A off I-95. Go under Australian Ave overpass; make left into parking lot. The colorful 10-story building houses a Key West–style dining room and a dance club. **Rooms:** 349 rms and stes. Executive level. CI 3pm/CO noon. Nonsmoking rms avail. Pleasant, though unstylish, rooms may have city views or views of the lake. **Amenities:** 📺 ⛲ 🖥 A/C, cable TV w/movies, dataport, voice mail. Some units w/terraces. **Services:** ✕ VP 🚗 ⟳ ⟳ Babysitting. **Facilities:** ⛳ 🎱 🏋 ⌐800⌐ ⛶ 2 restaurants, 2 bars (w/entertainment), whirlpool. **Rates:** Peak (Dec 31–Apr 14) $95–$145 S or D; $225–$425 ste. Extra person $15. Children under age 17 stay free. Lower rates off-season. Parking: Outdoor, free. AE, CB, DISC, MC, V.

## MOTELS

### &#x2261;&#x2261; Comfort Inn

1901 Palm Beach Lakes Blvd, 33409; tel 561/689-6100 or toll free 800/228-5150; fax 561/686-6177. Exit 53 off I-95. Just 10 minutes from beaches and easily accessible from I-95, this polished mid-priced offering has some lofty two-story suites in addition to its standardized guest rooms. **Rooms:** 157 rms and stes. CI 2pm/CO noon. Nonsmoking rms avail. **Amenities:** 🛅 🕭 🖲 A/C, cable TV w/movies, refrig. Some units w/terraces. **Services:** ✕ 🛎 **Rates:** Peak (Dec–Apr) $60 S; $80 D; $90 ste. Extra person $10. Children under age 18 stay free. Lower rates off-season. Parking: Outdoor, free. AE, MC, V.

### &#x2261;&#x2261;&#x2261; Wellesley Inn

1910 Palm Beach Lakes Blvd, 33409; tel 561/689-8540 or toll free 800/444-8888; fax 561/687-8090. Exit 53 off I-95. Solid budget accommodations. Restaurants are nearby. **Rooms:** 106 rms and stes. CI 2pm/CO 11am. Nonsmoking rms avail. **Amenities:** 🛅 🕭 🖲 A/C, cable TV w/movies, refrig, in-rm safe. **Services:** ✕ 🖼 🛎 🍽 Babysitting. **Facilities:** 🔲 **Rates (CP):** Peak (Dec–Apr) $89–$99 S or D; $109–$149 ste. Extra person $7. Children under age 18 stay free. Min stay special events. Lower rates off-season. Parking: Outdoor, free. AE, DC, MC, V.

## RESORT

### &#x2261;&#x2261;&#x2261; Palm Beach Polo and Country Club

13198 Forest Hill Blvd, 33414; tel 561/798-7000; fax 561/798-7330. Forest Hill Blvd off I-95. 2,200 acres. Located in a gated, self-contained enclave, it offers much for the golfer, tennis player, and polo pony. This high-brow establishment is best suited to thoroughbreds and not Mr Eds. **Rooms:** 60 stes and effic. CI 3pm/CO noon. Nonsmoking rms avail. Varied accommodations range from small units to multi-bedroom villas with individual decor. **Amenities:** 🛅 🕭 🖲 A/C, cable TV w/movies, refrig, in-rm safe. All units w/terraces. **Services:** ✕ 🖼 🛎 Social director, masseur, children's program, babysitting. **Facilities:** 🔲 🚲 ⛳₄₅ 🎿 🖼 🎾₉ 🏊₁₅ 🏓 🎱₅₀₀ 🖥 3 restaurants, 5 bars (2 w/entertainment), games rm, lawn games, sauna, steam rm, whirlpool, playground, washer/dryer. **Rates:** Peak (Dec 21–Apr 15) $195 ste; $290–$515 effic. Children under age 12 stay free. Min stay peak. Lower rates off-season. Parking: Outdoor, free. AE, MC, V.

## RESTAURANTS 🍴

### ★ Aleyda's

1890 S Military Trail; tel 561/642-2500. At Forest Hill Rd. **Tex-Mex.** Tex-Mex food presented in an authentic Mexican setting. Festive and affordable. **FYI:** Reservations recommended. Children's menu. Additional location: 1890 Okeechobee Blvd (tel 688-9033). **Open:** Dinner Mon–Thurs 5–10pm, Fri–Sat 5–11pm, Sun 5–10pm. **Prices:** Main courses $8–$16. AE, DISC, MC, V. 🖼 &#x267F;

### ★ Bimini Bay Cafe

104 Clematis St; tel 561/833-9554. Between Datura and Clamitis Sts. **American.** Enjoy a cool breeze and a cool drink as you dine on the outdoor patio of this casual eatery. Inside there's a jungle of hanging plants. Specialties include lobster bisque served with a small chicken caesar salad; buffalo shrimp; and Maryland lump crab cakes. **FYI:** Reservations accepted. Children's menu. **Open:** Daily 11am–midnight. **Prices:** Main courses $7–$20. AE, DISC, MC, V. 🖼 &#x267F;

### Bohemian Garden

5450 Lake Worth Rd, Green Acres; tel 561/968-4111. 3 mi E of FL Tpk. **Continental.** A popular, rather elegant, old-world-style restaurant with burgundy and pink linens adorning glass-topped tables. Menu offerings range from duck and frogs' legs to veal and Bohemian specialties. The early-bird specials are a great value. **FYI:** Reservations recommended. Children's menu. **Open:** Tues–Sat 4:30–10pm, Sun 4–9pm. **Prices:** Main courses $7–$18. AE, CB, DC, DISC, MC, V. 🔲 &#x267F;

### Morton's of Chicago

In Phillips Point Building, 777 S Flagler Dr; tel 561/835-9664. **Seafood/Steak.** An upscale restaurant with romantic ambience. Extensive wine list. **FYI:** Reservations recommended. Dress code. **Open:** Mon–Sat 5pm–2am, Sun 5–10pm. **Prices:** Main courses $17–$30. AE, DISC, MC, V. ❤ 🆅🅿 &#x267F;

### ★ Orchids of Siam

3027 Forest Hill Blvd; tel 561/969-2444. At Congress Rd. **Continental/Thai.** An unassuming dining room serving traditional Thai specialties as well as Thai-inspired twists on such dishes as seafood pasta, Norwegian salmon, and veal marsala. **FYI:** Reservations accepted. **Open:** Lunch Mon–Fri 11:30am–2:30pm; dinner Mon–Thurs 4:30–10pm, Fri–Sat 4:30–11pm, Sun 4:30–10pm. **Prices:** Main courses $8–$16. AE, DISC, MC, V. 🖼 🔲 &#x267F;

### Proctor's

2511 S Dixie Hwy; tel 561/832-6686. 1 block N of Belvedere Rd. **American.** The accent is more on food than decor in this family-oriented fish house. The seafood dishes are very popular, as is the roast beef with gravy and the T-bone steaks. The early afternoon specials, featured from 2–5pm, are absolute bargains. **FYI:** Reservations not accepted. Beer and wine only. **Open:** Mon–Sat 11am–8:30pm. **Prices:** Main courses $8–$11. AE, MC, V. No CC. &#x267F;

### ★ Randy's Bageland

In The Village Shopping Center, 911 Village Blvd; tel 561/640-0203. **Jewish/Kosher.** A very casual eatery offering fresh bagels, pastries, deli sandwiches, and kosher dishes. **FYI:** Reservations not accepted. No liquor license. **Open:** Mon–Thurs 7am–7:30pm, Fri–Sun 7am–8pm. **Prices:** Main courses $5–$10. MC, V. 🖼 &#x267F;

**Sagami**

In Village Commons Shopping Center, 871 Village Blvd; tel 561/683-4600. Between Community Dr and Palm Beach Lakes Blvd. **Japanese.** An intimate, tidy, traditional Japanese cafe and sushi bar serving familiar pan-Asian dishes like spare ribs, shrimp tempura, and ginger pork. **FYI:** Reservations accepted. Beer and wine only. **Open:** Lunch Mon–Fri noon–2:30; dinner Sun–Thurs 5–10:30pm, Fri–Sat 5–11pm. **Prices:** Main courses $11–$20. MC, V. ⅊

## ATTRACTIONS 🏛

**South Florida Science Museum**

4801 Dreher Trail N; tel 561/832-1988. The more than 40 exhibits deal mainly with the physical sciences and include Gravity Well, Fly's Eye, Electric Fleas, Plasma Ball, Echo Tube, Garden of Smells, and Spectroscopy. The Aldrin Planetarium has shows daily and laser shows Friday nights. The Gibson Observatory is open for stargazing Fridays from sunset to 10pm, weather permitting. **Open:** Sat–Thurs 10am–5pm, Fri 10am–10pm. $$

**Norton Museum of Art**

1451 S Olive Ave; tel 561/832-5194. Collections include 19th- and 20th-century European paintings and sculpture by Gauguin, Klee, and Picasso, among others; as well as highly regarded 20th-century American works. Also exhibited is a stunning collection of Chinese art that includes sculptured Buddhas from circa 700 AD. **Open:** Tues–Sat 10am–5pm, Sun 1–5pm. $$

**Dreher Park Zoo**

1301 Summit Blvd; tel 561/533-0887. More than 500 animals, representing over 100 different species, inhabit this 22-acre zoo, including the endangered Florida panther. Special features include the ARK (Animals Reaching Kids) Encounter Area, Reptile House, a boardwalk nature trail, and the Baker Lake Boat Tour. Also here is the nation's first outdoor exhibit of Goeldi's monkeys. **Open:** Daily 9am–5pm. $$

**Lion Country Safari**

Southernmost Blvd W; tel 561/793-1084. A 500-acre, cageless, drive-through wildlife preserve inhabited by 1,300 animals from around the world. The preserve serves as a breeding ground for endangered species. Adjacent amusement park; picnic and camping facilities. **Open:** Daily 9:30am–5:30pm. $$$$

# Windley Key

## MOTEL 🏨

**🏨🏨 Howard Johnson's Resort at Holiday Isle**

84001 Overseas Hwy MM 84, 33036; tel 305/664-2711 or toll free 800/327-7070; fax 305/664-2703. Standardized accommodations offered in a low-rise property, with an L-shaped pool surrounded by lawn. **Rooms:** 140 rms, stes, and

effic. CI 3:30pm/CO 11am. Nonsmoking rms avail. **Amenities:** 🛏 A/C, cable TV w/movies, in-rm safe. All units w/terraces. **Services:** 🛎 **Facilities:** 🛝 ⛰ 🛟 ⚓ ⛵ 🚤 [135] ⅊ 5 restaurants, 2 bars (w/entertainment), 1 beach (ocean), snorkeling, playground, washer/dryer. **Rates:** Peak (Dec–Apr) $135–$185 S or D; $275–$415 ste; $140–$220 effic. Extra person $10–$15. Children under age 18 stay free. Min stay wknds and special events. Lower rates off-season. Parking: Outdoor, free. AE, CB, DC, DISC, MC, V.

# Winter Haven

On the shores of Lake Eloise in central Florida, its biggest draw is Cypress Gardens. Water-ski shows, lush foliage, and a November chrysanthemum festival have been attracting tourists since the 1940s. **Information:** Winter Haven Area Chamber of Commerce, 401 Ave B NW, PO Box 1420, Winter Haven, 33882 (tel 941/293-2138).

## HOTELS 🏨

**🏨🏨 Best Western Admiral's Inn**

5665 Cypress Gardens Blvd, 33884; tel 941/324-5950 or toll free 800/247-2799; fax 941/324-2376. Popular among visitors to Cypress Gardens for its great location, just a five-minute walk from the front gate. Many groups and families here. **Rooms:** 160 rms and stes. CI 3pm/CO 11am. Nonsmoking rms avail. **Amenities:** 🛏 ⅊ A/C, cable TV w/movies. Some units w/terraces. **Services:** 🛌 🛎 ⛟ Babysitting. **Facilities:** 🛝 [600] ⅊ 1 restaurant (bkfst and dinner only), 1 bar, games rm, beauty salon. Olympic-sized pool. Lounge offers karaoke singing. **Rates:** Peak (Jan–Apr) $63–$68 S or D; $139–$159 ste. Extra person $6. Children under age 12 stay free. Lower rates off-season. Parking: Outdoor, free. AE, CB, DC, DISC, MC, V.

**🏨🏨 Holiday Inn Winter Haven/Cypress Gardens**

1150 3rd St SW, 33880; tel 941/294-4451 or toll free 800/465-4329; fax 941/293-9829. A spring-training hotel for the Cleveland Indians, with nearby access to Cypress Gardens and Bok Tower Gardens. Much of the action arrives with the start of the Grapefruit League season, when the team arrives with loyal fans in tow. **Rooms:** 225 rms and stes. CI 3pm/CO noon. Nonsmoking rms avail. **Amenities:** 🛏 ⅊ A/C, cable TV. **Services:** ✗ 🛌 🛎 ⛟ **Facilities:** 🛝 [200] 1 restaurant (bkfst and dinner only), 1 bar, washer/dryer. **Rates:** Peak (Feb–Apr) $90–$98 S or D; $205 ste. Extra person $8. Children under age 19 stay free. Lower rates off-season. Parking: Outdoor, free. AE, CB, DC, DISC, MC, V.

**🏨🏨 Howard Johnson Lodge**

1300 3rd St SW, 33380; tel 941/294-7321 or toll free 800/654-2000; fax 941/299-1673. Casual family atmosphere. Friendly staff. **Rooms:** 98 rms. CI 3pm/CO noon. Nonsmoking rms avail. **Amenities:** 🛏 A/C, cable TV w/movies. **Services:** 🛌 🛎 ⛟ **Facilities:** 🛝 [50] ⅊ 1 restaurant (bkfst

and lunch only), 1 bar, lawn games, playground, washer/
dryer. Miniature-golf course. **Rates:** Peak (Feb–Apr) $85–
$89 S or D. Extra person $5. Children under age 12 stay free.
Lower rates off-season. Parking: Outdoor, free. AE, CB, DC,
DISC, MC, V.

## MOTEL

### 🗮🗮 Days Inn
200 Cypress Gardens Blvd, 33880; tel 941/299-1151 or toll
free 800/329-7466; fax 941/297-8019. 3 mi W of Cypress
Gardens. Stay here and walk to the Chain of Lakes Stadium,
the winter home of baseball's Cleveland Indians. Also close to
shopping. **Rooms:** 106 rms. CI 2pm/CO noon. Nonsmoking
rms avail. **Amenities:** 🛅 A/C, cable TV. **Services:** 🖾 🍽 🕬
**Facilities:** 🛗 🏊1 🏊90 🕭 Volleyball, games rm, playground,
washer/dryer. **Rates (CP):** Peak (Jan–Apr) $60–$69 S or D.
Extra person $5. Children under age 18 stay free. Lower
rates off-season. Parking: Outdoor, free. AE, CB, DC, DISC,
MC, V.

## ATTRACTION 🖼

### Cypress Gardens
2641 S Lake Summit Drive (off US 27); tel 941/324-2111 or
toll free 800/237-4826 or 282-2123. At its founding in 1936,
Cypress Gardens occupied 16 acres of land on the shores of
Lake Eloise, with cypress-wood-block pathways and thousands of tropical and subtropical plants. Today it has grown
to more than 200 acres, with ponds and lagoons, waterfalls,
Italian fountains, sculptures, topiary, and lush, manicured
lawns, all against the backdrop of ancient, moss-shrouded
cypress trees and ever-changing floral displays.

Three shows are scheduled several times each day: the
Greatest American Ski Team performs waterski acrobatics,
Feathered Follies features a variety of performing birds, and
Variété International showcases specialty acts from all over
the world. Exhibits include Wings of Wonder, a butterfly
aviary in a Victorian-style glass conservatory; Kodak's Island
in the Sky, an observation platform 153 feet in the air;
Carousel Cove, with kiddie rides and arcades; and Cypress
Junction, an elaborately landscaped model railroad. Museums, lake cruises; restaurants, shops. **Open:** Daily 9:30am–
5:30pm, with extended hours during special seasons. $$$$

# Winter Park

Just north of Orlando, this long-time wintering ground of the
wealthy is home to Rollins College, Mead Botanical Gardens,
and a fantastic Tiffany glass collection at Morse Museum.
Exclusive shops dot Park Avenue. **Information:** Winter Park
Chamber of Commerce, 150 N New York Ave, PO Box 280,
Winter Park, 32790 (tel 407/644-8281).

## HOTELS 🏨

### 🗮🗮 Best Western Mount Vernon Inn
110 S Orlando Ave, 32789; tel 407/647-1166 or toll free
800/992-3379; fax 407/647-8011. At Morse Rd. Recently
remodeled, this Best Western is nicely appointed and sparkling clean. Friendly staff can offer information on area
attractions. **Rooms:** 147 rms. CI 3pm/CO 11am. Nonsmoking rms avail. Attractive Early American furnishings.
**Amenities:** 🛅 ⚗ A/C, cable TV w/movies, refrig, dataport.
Some units w/terraces. Deluxe rooms have larger TVs.
**Services:** ✕ 🖾 🍽 **Facilities:** 🛗 🏊125 🕭 1 restaurant (bkfst and
lunch only), 1 bar (w/entertainment). **Rates:** $72–$82 S;
$78–$88 D. Extra person $6. Children under age 18 stay
free. Parking: Outdoor, free. AE, CB, DC, DISC, MC, V.

### 🗮🗮🗮 The Langford Resort Hotel
300 E New England Ave, 32789; tel 407/644-3400; fax 407/
628-1952. One block E of Park Ave. Friendly, family-run
establishment was, in pre-Disney days, one of central Florida's most popular resorts, entertaining many celebrity guests.
Still attractive, it offers extensive facilities at very reasonable
rates. Set on a lovely street lined with oaks draped with
Spanish moss, just a block from Park Avenue, Winter Park's
ritzy shopping street. **Rooms:** 215 rms, stes, and effic. CI
2pm/CO 11am. Nonsmoking rms avail. East Wing rooms
feature rattan and bamboo furnishings. Suites are theme
decorated. **Amenities:** 🛅 A/C, cable TV w/movies. All units
w/terraces. **Services:** ✕ 🍽 🚗 🖾 🍽 🕬 Car-rental desk,
masseur, babysitting. **Facilities:** 🛗 🏊450 1 restaurant, 1 bar
(w/entertainment), games rm, spa, sauna, steam rm, beauty
salon, washer/dryer. **Rates:** $65–$100 S; $75–$105 D; $200
ste; $85–$115 effic. Extra person $10. Children under age
18 stay free. Min stay special events. Parking: Outdoor, free.
AE, CB, DC, MC, V.

## MOTEL

### 🗮 Days Inn
901 N Orlando Ave, 33789; tel 407/644-0032 or toll free
800/DAYS INN. Lee Rd exit off I-4. Not one of this chain's
best efforts. Adequate, but needs more work to give it
broader appeal. **Rooms:** 105 rms. CI 3pm/CO 11am. Nonsmoking rms avail. Rooms are small and rather spartan.
**Amenities:** 🛅 A/C, cable TV w/movies. **Services:** 🚗 🖾 🍽
🕬 **Facilities:** 🛗 🏊25 🕭 1 restaurant (bkfst and dinner only),
washer/dryer. **Rates:** Peak (June–Aug) $70–$80 S or D.
Children under age 18 stay free. Lower rates off-season.
Parking: Outdoor, free. AE, DC, DISC, MC, V.

## RESTAURANTS 🍴

### ⓢ ★ Boston's Fish House
6860 Aloma Ave; tel 407/678-2107. Between Forsyth Rd and
Palmetto Rd. **Seafood.** This small, nondescript eatery packs
them in with fresh seafood flown in daily from Massachusetts.
Ipswich clams and chowders are excellent choices. **FYI:**

Reservations not accepted. Children's menu. Beer and wine only. **Open:** Tues–Thurs 11am–8:30pm, Fri–Sat 11am–9:30pm, Sun 11am–8:30pm. **Prices:** Main courses $8–$12. No CC. &

### Cafe de France
526 S Park Ave; tel 407/647-1869. Fairbanks Ave exit off I-4, E to Park Ave. **French.** This sidewalk cafe at the southern foot of Winter Park's trendy shopping district is a perfect place to slow down, enjoy a glass of wine, and relax. Also popular for authentic French cuisine that doesn't take itself too seriously: rack of lamb, venison, and lots of fresh Florida seafood. Accompanying sauces may be chosen from a separate list of selections. **FYI:** Reservations recommended. Beer and wine only. **Open:** Lunch Tues–Sat 11:30am–2:30pm; dinner Tues–Sat 6–10pm. **Prices:** Main courses $16–$24. AE, CB, DC, DISC, MC, V. ⬥

### Le Cordon Bleu
537 W Fairbanks Ave; tel 407/647-7575. At Pennsylvania Ave. **Continental/French.** An elegant bistro originally established as Harper's Tavern in 1927, now known locally for its French cuisine. Ask for the house specialty: Filet Chez Nous, an herb-seasoned filet of beef. Entertainment is provided several evenings each week in the adjoining Harper's Tavern, which is still a part of the main structure. **FYI:** Reservations recommended. Dancing/rock. Children's menu. **Open:** Lunch Mon–Fri 11:30am–2:30pm; dinner Mon–Sat 5:30–11pm. **Prices:** Main courses $18–$30. AE, CB, DC, DISC, MC, V.

### Maison des Crepes
In Hidden Gardens, 348 N Park Ave; tel 407/647-4469. **Continental/French.** A charming, casual cafe. The crepes are made fresh on the premises. Seafood chowder is a popular starter and there are three fresh fish entrees daily. **FYI:** Reservations recommended. Children's menu. Beer and wine only. **Open:** Lunch Mon–Fri 11:30am–3pm, Sat 11:30am–4pm; dinner Tues–Thurs 5:30–10pm, Fri–Sat 5:30–10:30pm. **Prices:** Main courses $12–$25. AE, CB, DC, DISC, MC, V. ⬥ ⬥

### Outback Steakhouse
In Winter Park Corners Shopping Center, 1927 Aloma Ave; tel 407/679-1050. **Steak.** An Australian-style steak house serving some of the best beef this side of the International Date Line. Specialties include the "Bloomin' Onion" and prime rib. **FYI:** Reservations not accepted. Children's menu. Additional locations: 1301 Florida Mall Ave, Orlando (tel 240-6857); 5891 Red Bug Lake Rd, Altamonte Springs (tel 699-0900). **Open:** Sun–Thurs 4–10:30pm, Fri–Sat 4–11pm. **Prices:** Main courses $11–$18. AE, DISC, MC, V. &

### ★ Park Plaza Gardens
319 S Park Ave; tel 407/645-2475. At New England Ave. **Regional American.** An enclosed, air-conditioned garden with skylights, live plants, and attractive brickwork makes this a pleasant place to be in rain, shine, or suffocating summer heat. Recommended menu choices include rack of lamb and West Indian salmon with a horseradish crust. Limited menu selection available in the bar 11am–11pm daily. **FYI:** Reservations recommended. **Open:** Lunch Mon–Sat 11am–2pm; dinner daily 6–10pm. **Prices:** Main courses $19–$28. AE, CB, DC, DISC, MC, V.

## ATTRACTION 🖼

### Charles Hosmer Morse Museum of American Art
445 Park Ave N; tel 407/645-5311. This museum's holdings include the most comprehensive collection of the works of Louis Comfort Tiffany in the world, including his famous chapel exhibited at the Chicago Columbian Exposition of 1893. On permanent display are works from Tiffany's personal collection. Other prominent American artists of the Arts and Crafts period are represented as well, in collections focusing on the fine and decorative arts of the late 19th and early 20th centuries. **Open:** Tues–Sat 9:30am–4pm, Sun 1–4pm. $

# Index

*Listings are arranged alphabetically, followed by a code indicating the type of establishment, and then by city and page number. The codes for type of establishment are defined as follows: (H) = Hotel, (M) = Motel, (I) = Inn, (L) = Lodge, (RE) = Resort, (R) = Restaurant, (RS) = Refreshment Stop, (A) = Attraction.*

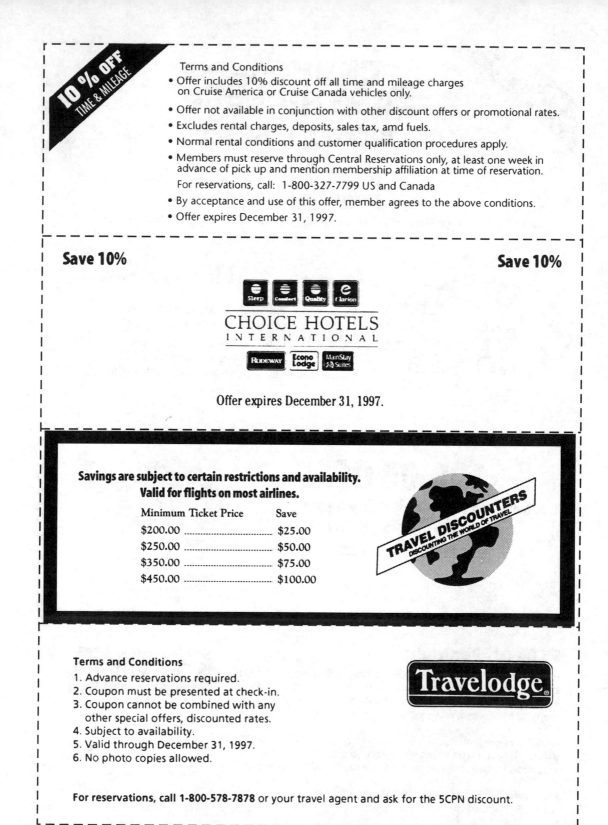

**10% OFF** TIME & MILEAGE

Terms and Conditions

- Offer includes 10% discount off all time and mileage charges on Cruise America or Cruise Canada vehicles only.
- Offer not available in conjunction with other discount offers or promotional rates.
- Excludes rental charges, deposits, sales tax, amd fuels.
- Normal rental conditions and customer qualification procedures apply.
- Members must reserve through Central Reservations only, at least one week in advance of pick up and mention membership affiliation at time of reservation.

  For reservations, call: 1-800-327-7799 US and Canada

- By acceptance and use of this offer, member agrees to the above conditions.
- Offer expires December 31, 1997.

---

**Save 10%**                                                                 **Save 10%**

Sleep   Comfort   Quality   Clarion

**CHOICE HOTELS**
I N T E R N A T I O N A L

RODEWAY   Econo Lodge   MainStay Suites

Offer expires December 31, 1997.

---

**Savings are subject to certain restrictions and availability.**
**Valid for flights on most airlines.**

| Minimum Ticket Price | Save |
|---|---|
| $200.00 | $25.00 |
| $250.00 | $50.00 |
| $350.00 | $75.00 |
| $450.00 | $100.00 |

**TRAVEL DISCOUNTERS** DISCOUNTING THE WORLD OF TRAVEL

---

**Terms and Conditions**

1. Advance reservations required.
2. Coupon must be presented at check-in.
3. Coupon cannot be combined with any other special offers, discounted rates.
4. Subject to availability.
5. Valid through December 31, 1997.
6. No photo copies allowed.

**Travelodge**

**For reservations, call 1-800-578-7878** or your travel agent and ask for the 5CPN discount.

All reservations must be made by calling our toll free reservation system, Superline. Any reservation requiring a guarantee must be guaranteed with the corporate V.I.P. identification number and the individual traveler's major credit card. If a guaranteed reservation is made and subsequently neither used nor cancelled, the corporate traveler will be billed for the one night's room charge plus tax.

## Redeemable at participating Dollar® locations only.

This coupon entitles you to a one class upgrade from a compact or economy car to the next higher car group at no extra charge. Simply make a reservation for a compact or economy class car, then present this coupon to any Dollar rental agent when you arrive. You'll receive an upgrade to the next car class at no additional charge. Upgrade subject to vehicle availability. Renter must meet Dollar age, driver and credit requirements. This coupon must be surrendered at time of rental and may not be used in conjunction with any other offer and has no cash value. **EXPIRES 12/15/97.**

For worldwide reservations, call your travel agent or
**800-800-4000**

**D●LLAR**
RENT A CAR
**DOLLAR MAKES SENSE.**

# Mention code "afbg2" when you place your first order and receive 15% OFF

*Offer expires December 31, 1997*

PO Box 5485-AF2,  Santa Barbara, CA  93150

*Magellan's*

**10% OFF**

**DAYS INN**
Follow the Sun

- Available at participating properties.
- This coupon cannot be combined with any other special discount offer.
- Limit one coupon per room, per stay. Expires December 31, 1997.
- Not valid during blackout periods or special events.
- Void where prohibited.
- No reproductions accepted.
1-800-DAYS INN

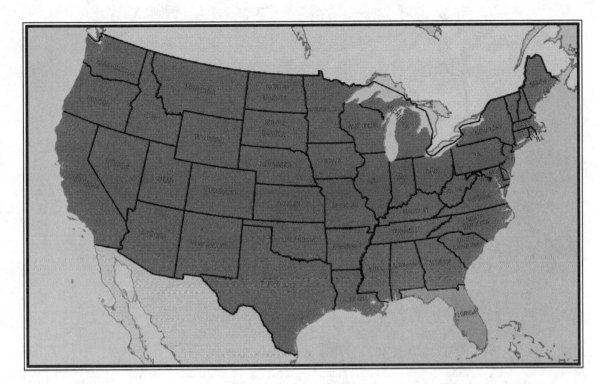

## CONTENTS

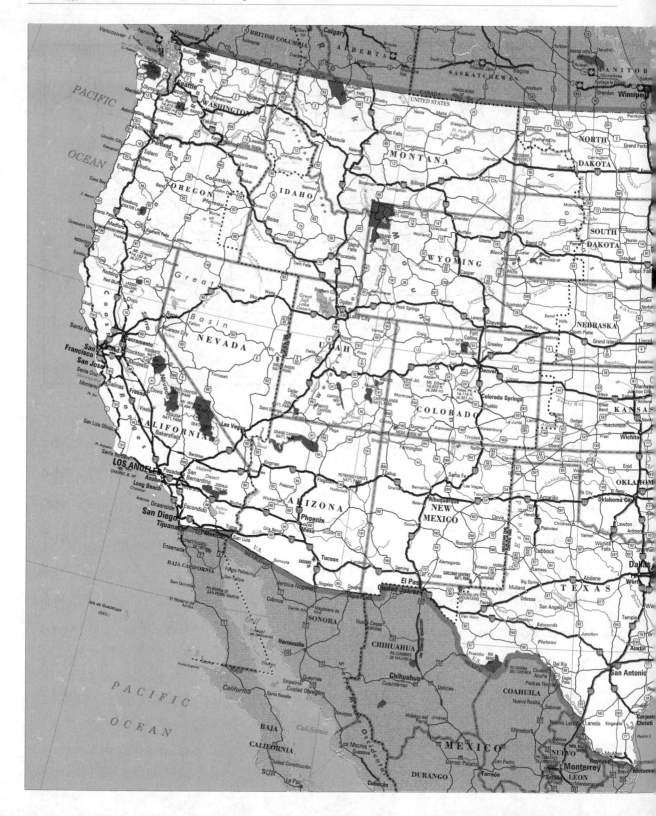

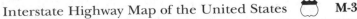
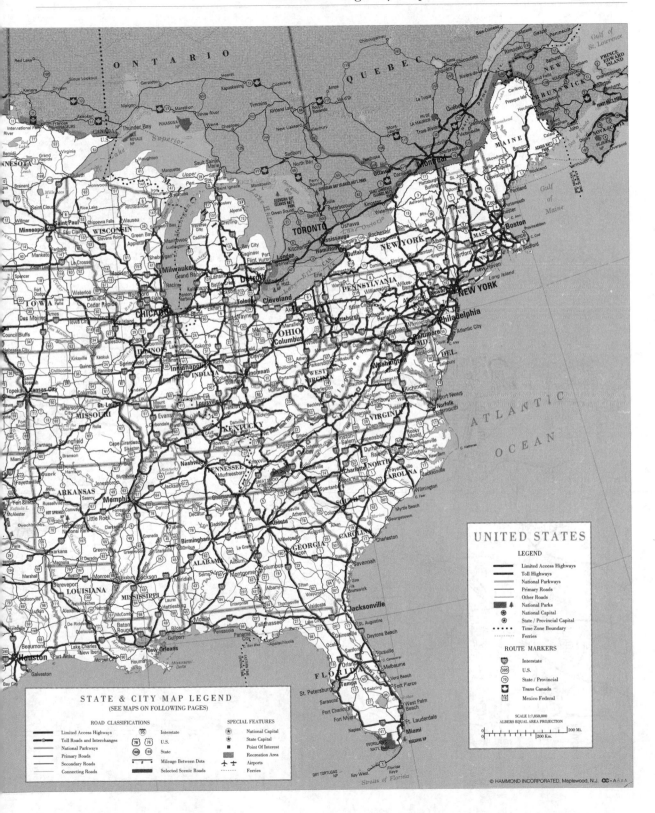

UNITED STATES

LEGEND

—— Limited Access Highways
—— Toll Highways
—— National Parkways
—— Primary Roads
—— Other Roads
■ ▲ National Parks
⊛ National Capital
⊛ State / Provincial Capital
• • • • Time Zone Boundary
- - - - Ferries

ROUTE MARKERS

Interstate
U.S.
State / Provincial
Trans Canada
Mexico Federal

SCALE 1:7,850,000
ALBERS EQUAL AREA PROJECTION

0 _____ 200 Mi.
0 _____ 200 Km.

STATE & CITY MAP LEGEND
(SEE MAPS ON FOLLOWING PAGES)

ROAD CLASSIFICATIONS

—— Limited Access Highways
—— Toll Roads and Interchanges
—— National Parkways
—— Primary Roads
—— Secondary Roads
—— Connecting Roads

95 Interstate
76 76 U.S.
148 148 State
• • • • Mileage Between Dots
—— Selected Scenic Roads

SPECIAL FEATURES

★ National Capital
★ State Capital
■ Point Of Interest
Recreation Area
✈ Airports
- - - - Ferries

© HAMMOND INCORPORATED, Maplewood, N.J. CC-A ▲▲▲

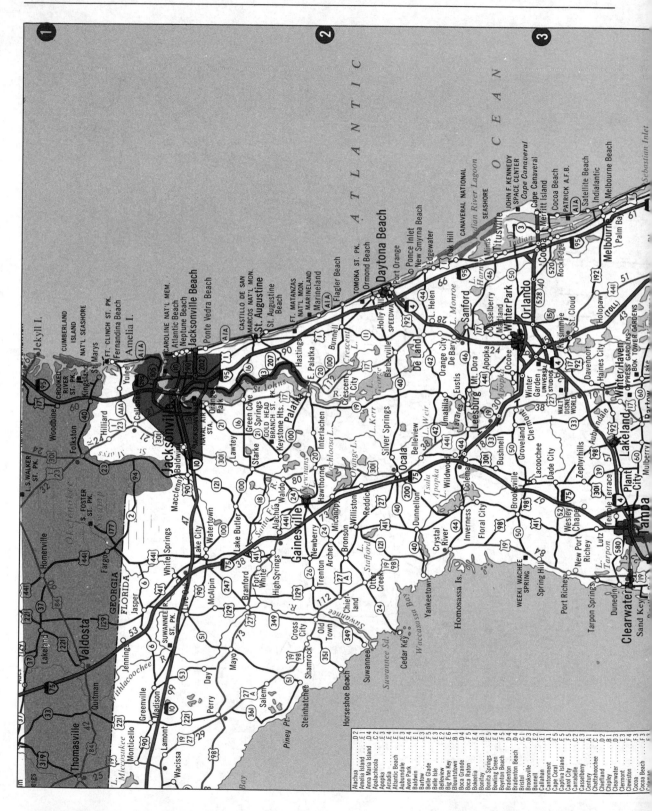

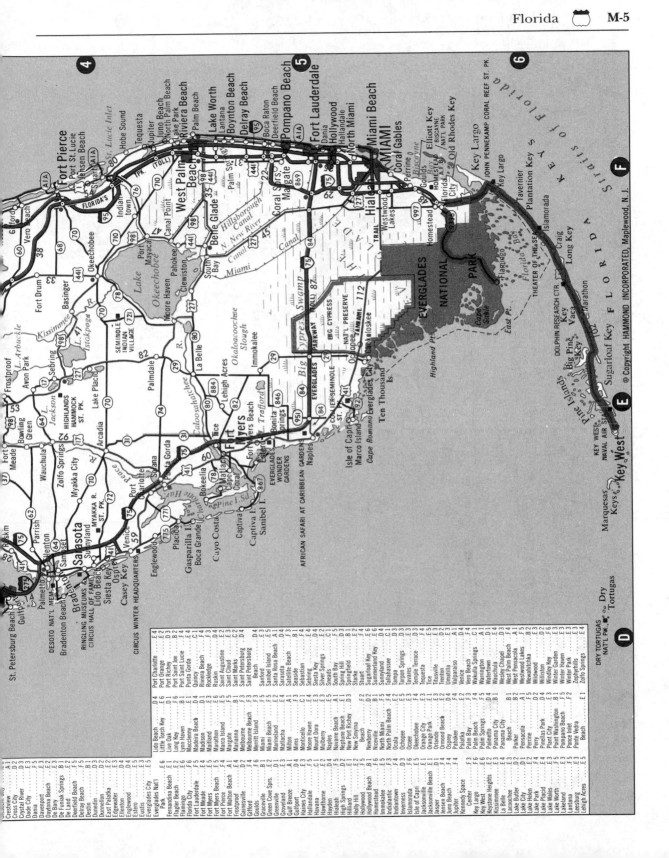

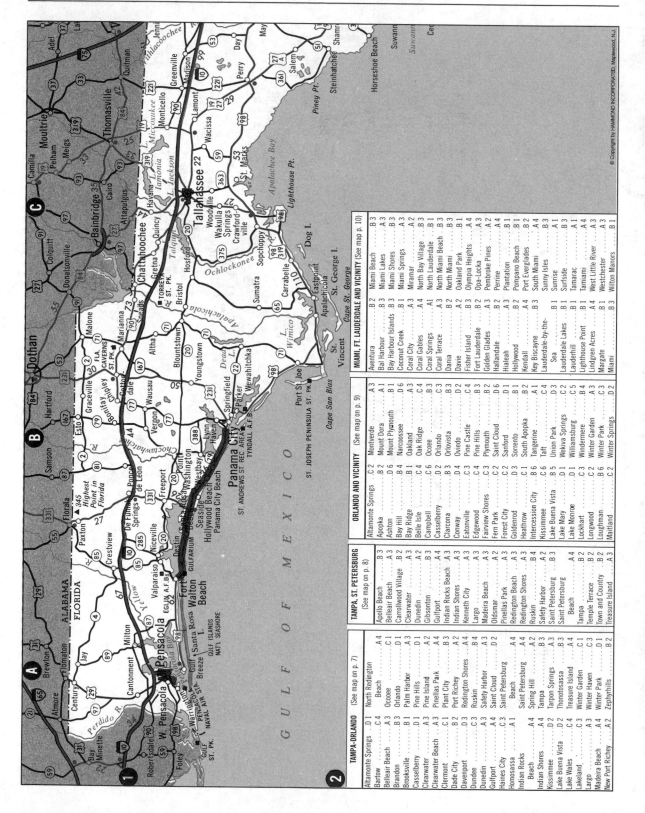

**MIAMI, FT. LAUDERDALE AND VICINITY (See map p. 10)**

| | | | | |
|---|---|---|---|---|
| Aventura | A 3 | Miami Beach | B 3 |
| Bal Harbour | B 2 | Miami Lakes | B 3 |
| Bay Harbour Islands | B 3 | Miami Shores | B 3 |
| Coconut Creek | D 6 | Miami Springs | A 3 |
| Coral City | A 3 | Miramar | A 2 |
| Coral Gables | C 4 | North Bay Village | B 3 |
| Coral Springs | A 1 | North Lauderdale | B 1 |
| Coral Terrace | B 3 | North Miami Beach | B 3 |
| Dania | B 2 | North Miami | B 1 |
| Davie | A 2 | Oakland Park | A 4 |
| Fisher Island | B 3 | Olympia Heights | A 3 |
| Fort Lauderdale | B 2 | Opa-Locka | A 2 |
| Golden Glades | B 2 | Pembroke Pines | A 4 |
| Hallandale | B 2 | Perrine | A 4 |
| Hialeah | A 3 | Plantation | B 1 |
| Hollywood | B 2 | Pompano Beach | A 4 |
| Kendall | B 3 | Port Everglades | B 2 |
| Key Biscayne | B 3 | South Miami | A 4 |
| Lauderdale-by-the- | | Sunny Isles | B 3 |
| Sea | B 1 | Sunrise | A 1 |
| Lauderdale Lakes | B 1 | Surfside | A 1 |
| Lauderhill | B 1 | Tamarac | A 4 |
| Lighthouse Point | B 4 | Tamiami | A 1 |
| Lindgren Acres | A 4 | West Little River | A 3 |
| Margate | B 1 | Westchester | A 3 |
| Miami | B 3 | Wilton Manors | B 1 |

**ORLANDO AND VICINITY** (See map on p. 9)

| | | | | |
|---|---|---|---|---|
| Altamonte Springs | A 3 | Montverde | C 2 |
| Apopka | B 2 | Mount Dora | A 1 |
| Ashton | D 6 | Mount Plymouth | B 1 |
| Bay Hill | B 4 | Narcoossee | D 6 |
| Bay Ridge | B 1 | Oakland | A 3 |
| Belle Isle | C 4 | Oak Ridge | C 4 |
| Campbell | C 6 | Ocoee | B 3 |
| Casselberry | D 2 | Orlando | D 2 |
| Clarcona | B 3 | Orlovista | B 3 |
| Conway | D 4 | Oviedo | D 1 |
| Eatonville | C 3 | Pine Castle | C 4 |
| Edgewood | C 4 | Pine Hills | B 3 |
| Fairview Shores | C 3 | Plymouth | B 2 |
| Fern Park | C 2 | Saint Cloud | D 6 |
| Forest City | C 2 | Sanford | D 1 |
| Goldenrod | D 3 | Sorrento | B 1 |
| Heathrow | C 1 | South Apopka | B 2 |
| Intercession City | B 6 | Taft | C 4 |
| Kissimmee | C 6 | Tangerine | A 1 |
| Lake Buena Vista | B 5 | Union Park | C 4 |
| Lake Mary | D 1 | Wekiva Springs | C 2 |
| Lake Monroe | D 1 | Williamsburg | C 5 |
| Lockhart | C 3 | Windermere | B 4 |
| Longwood | C 2 | Winter Garden | A 3 |
| Loughman | B 6 | Winter Park | C 3 |
| Maitland | C 2 | Winter Springs | D 2 |

**TAMPA, ST. PETERSBURG**
(See map on p. 8)

| | | | | |
|---|---|---|---|---|
| Apollo Beach | B 3 | | |
| Belleair Beach | A 3 | | |
| Carrollwood Village | B 2 | | |
| Clearwater | A 3 | | |
| Dunedin | A 2 | | |
| Gibsonton | B 3 | | |
| Gulfport | A 4 | | |
| Indian Rocks Beach | A 3 | | |
| Indian Shores | A 3 | | |
| Kenneth City | A 3 | | |
| Largo | A 3 | | |
| Madeira Beach | A 3 | | |
| Oldsmar | A 2 | | |
| Pinellas Park | A 3 | | |
| Redington Beach | A 3 | | |
| Redington Shores | A 3 | | |
| Ruskin | B 4 | | |
| Safety Harbor | A 2 | | |
| Saint Petersburg | B 3 | | |
| Saint Petersburg | | | |
| Beach | A 4 | | |
| Tampa | B 2 | | |
| Temple Terrace | B 2 | | |
| Town and Country | B 2 | | |
| Treasure Island | A 3 | | |

**TAMPA-ORLANDO**

| | | | | |
|---|---|---|---|---|
| Altamonte Springs | D 1 | North Redington | |
| Bartow | C 4 | Beach | A 4 |
| Belleair Beach | A 3 | Ocoee | C 1 |
| Brandon | B 3 | Orlando | D 1 |
| Brooksville | B 1 | Palm Harbor | A 3 |
| Casselberry | D 1 | Pine Hills | D 1 |
| Clearwater | A 3 | Pine Island | B 3 |
| Clearwater Beach | A 2 | Pinellas Park | A 4 |
| Clermont | C 1 | Plant City | B 3 |
| Dade City | B 2 | Port Richey | D 3 |
| Davenport | D 3 | Redington Shores | A 4 |
| Dundee | C 3 | Ruskin | B 4 |
| Dunedin | A 3 | Safety Harbor | A 3 |
| Gulfport | A 4 | Saint Cloud | D 2 |
| Haines City | C 3 | Saint Petersburg | A 4 |
| Homosassa | A 1 | Beach | A 4 |
| Indian Rocks | | Saint Petersburg | A 4 |
| Beach | A 4 | Spring Hill | A 2 |
| Indian Shores | A 3 | Tampa | B 3 |
| Kissimmee | D 2 | Tarpon Springs | A 3 |
| Lake Buena Vista | D 2 | Thonotosassa | B 3 |
| Lake Wales | C 4 | Treasure Island | A 4 |
| Lakeland | C 3 | Winter Garden | C 1 |
| Largo | A 3 | Winter Haven | C 3 |
| Madeira Beach | A 4 | Winter Park | D 1 |
| New Port Richey | A 2 | Zephyrhills | B 2 |

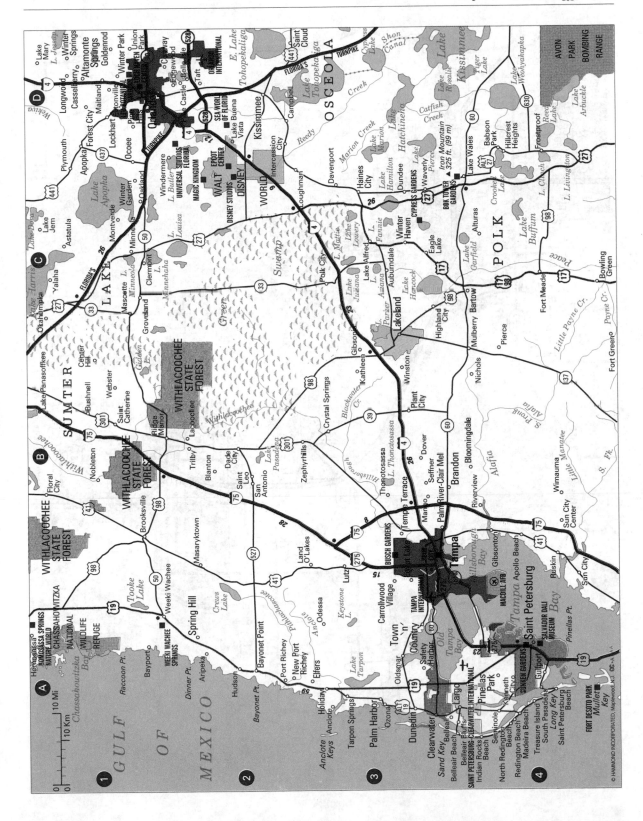

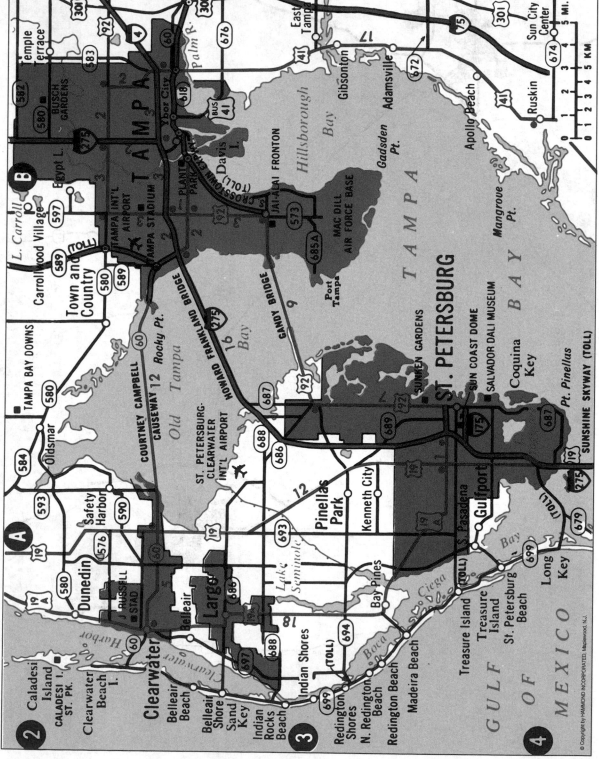

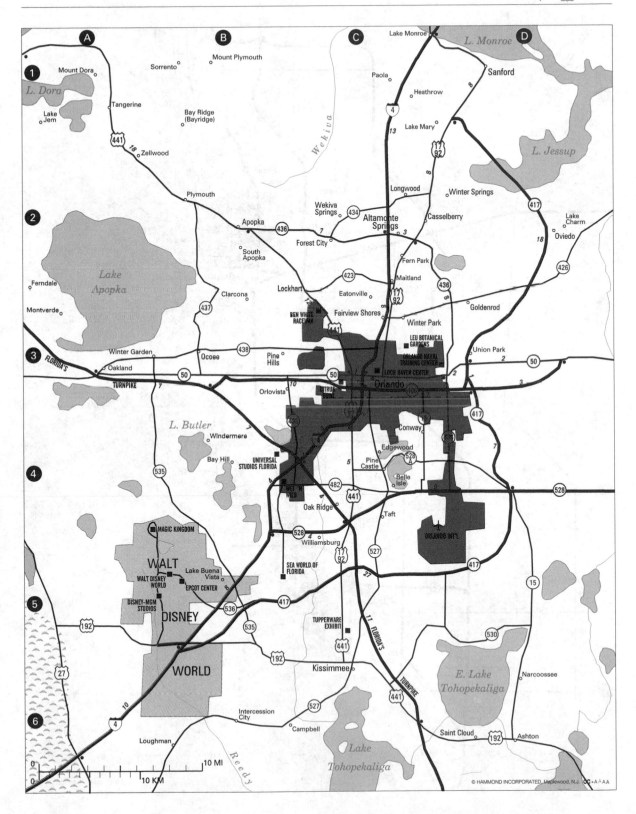

© HAMMOND INCORPORATED, Maplewood, N.J.

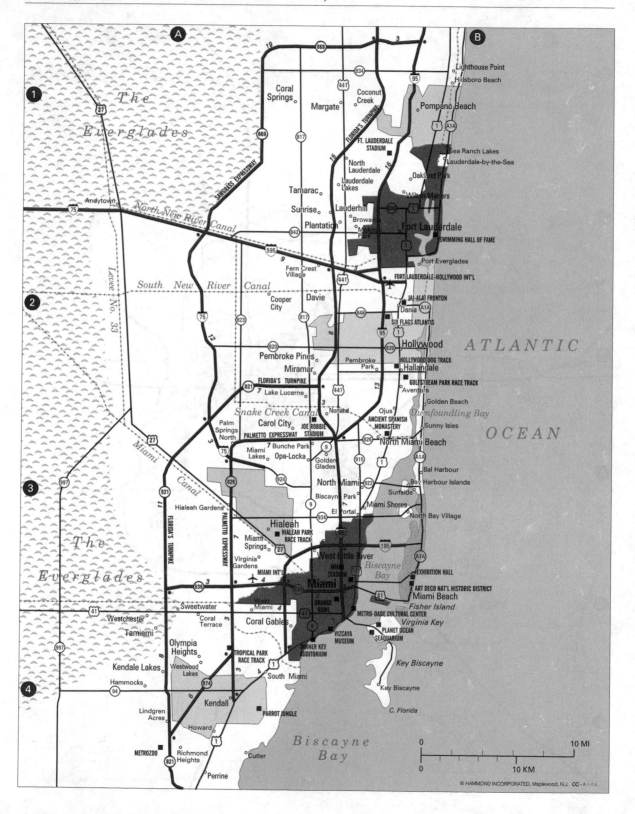

© HAMMOND INCORPORATED, Maplewood, N.J. CC · A·R·A·A

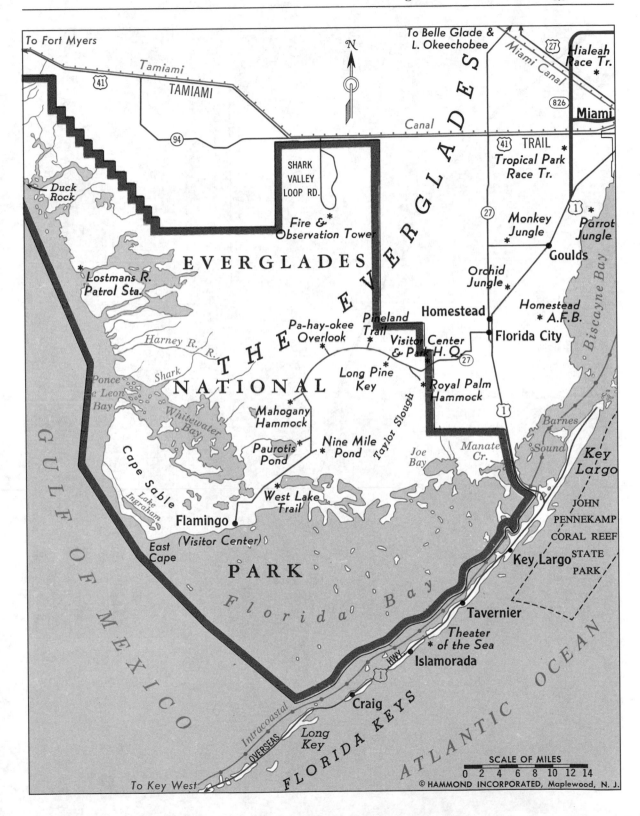

To Fort Myers

*Tamiami*
**TAMIAMI**
41
94

*Duck Rock*

SHARK VALLEY LOOP RD.

*Fire & Observation Tower* *

**EVERGLADES**

*Lostmans R. Patrol Sta.* *

**THE EVERGLADES**

To Belle Glade & L. Okeechobee

*Miami Canal*
27

*Hialeah Race Tr.* *

826

**Miami**

*Canal*

41 TRAIL
*Tropical Park Race Tr.* *

27

*Monkey Jungle* *

1

*Parrot Jungle* *

*Orchid Jungle* *

**Goulds**

*Biscayne Bay*

*Harney R. R.*

*Shark*

**NATIONAL**

*Pa-hay-okee Overlook* *

*Pineland Trail* *

*Visitor Center & Park H.Q.* *

**Homestead**

*Homestead A.F.B.* *

**Florida City**

27

*Ponce de Leon Bay*

*Long Pine Key*

*Taylor Slough*

*Royal Palm Hammock* *

1

*Whitewater Bay*

*Mahogany Hammock* *

*Paurotis Pond* *

*Nine Mile Pond* *

*Joe Bay*

*Manatee Cr.*

*Barnes Sound*

**Key Largo**

*Cape Sable*
*Lake Ingraham*

*West Lake Trail* *

JOHN PENNEKAMP CORAL REEF STATE PARK

**Flamingo**
*(Visitor Center)*

*East Cape*

**PARK**

*Florida Bay*

**Key Largo**

**Tavernier**

*Theater of the Sea* *

**G U L F   O F   M E X I C O**

HWY
1

**Islamorada**

**Craig**

*Long Key*

*Intracoastal*

OVERSEAS

**F L O R I D A   K E Y S**

**A T L A N T I C   O C E A N**

To Key West

SCALE OF MILES
0  2  4  6  8  10 12 14

© HAMMOND INCORPORATED, Maplewood, N. J.

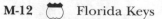

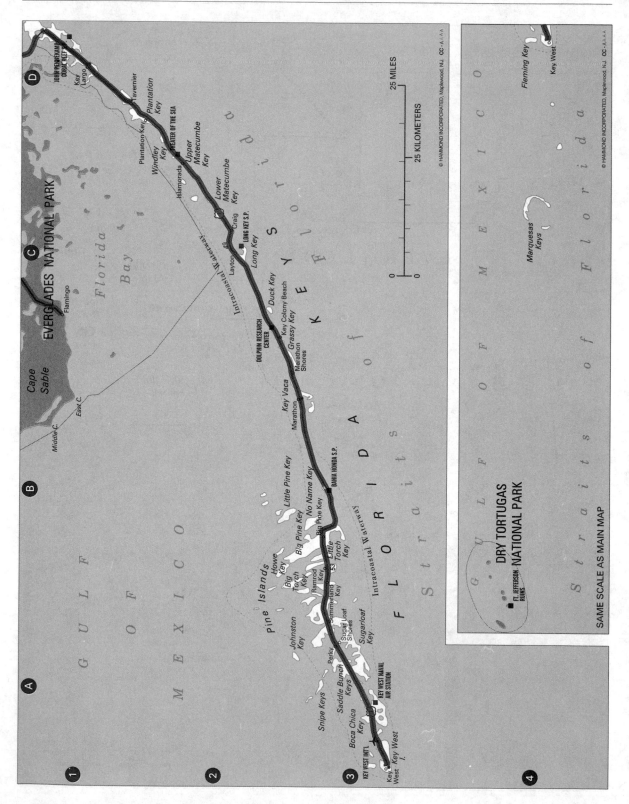

EVERGLADES NATIONAL PARK

Cape Sable

Flamingo

Middle C.

East C.

Florida Bay

G U L F   O F   M E X I C O

JOHN PENNEKAMP CORAL REEF

Key Largo

Tavernier

Plantation Key

Plantation Key

Windley Key

THEATER OF THE SEA

Islamorada

Upper Matecumbe Key

Lower Matecumbe Key

Craig

Layton

LONG KEY S.P.

Long Key

Intracoastal Waterway

Duck Key

Key Colony Beach

Grassy Key

DOLPHIN RESEARCH CENTER

Marathon Shores

Key Vaca

Marathon

K   E   Y

F   L   O   R

Little Pine Key

No Name Key

Big Pine Key

BAHIA HONDA S.P.

Howe Key

Big Torch Key

Little Torch Key

Ramrod Key

Summerland Key

Sugar Loaf Shores

Sugarloaf Key

Johnston Key

Perky

Saddle Bunch Keys

Snipe Keys

Boca Chica Key

KEY WEST NAVAL AIR STATION

KEY WEST INT'L

Key West

West Key West I.

Pine Islands

Intracoastal Waterway

F   L   O   R   I   D   A   of

S   t   r   a   i   t   s

© HAMMOND INCORPORATED, Maplewood, N.J.   CC-A-AA

0   25 MILES

0   25 KILOMETERS

DRY TORTUGAS NATIONAL PARK

FT. JEFFERSON RUINS

G   U   L   F   O   F   M   E   X   I   C   O

Marquesas Keys

S   t   r   a   i   t   s   o   f   F   l   o   r   i   d   a

SAME SCALE AS MAIN MAP

© HAMMOND INCORPORATED, Maplewood, N.J.   CC-A-AA

Fleming Key

Key West

A   B   C   D

1   2   3   4